T0330120

Agriculture and the Rural Economy in Pakistan

 This book is published by the University of Pennsylvania Press (UPP) on behalf of the International Food Policy Research Institute (IFPRI) as part of a joint-publication series. Books in the series present research on food security and economic development with the aim of reducing poverty and eliminating hunger and malnutrition in developing nations. They are the product of peer-reviewed IFPRI research and are selected by mutual agreement between the parties for publication under the joint IFPRI-UPP imprint.

Agriculture and the Rural Economy in Pakistan

Issues, Outlooks, and Policy Priorities

Edited by David J. Spielman, Sohail J. Malik, Paul Dorosh, and Nuzhat Ahmad

Published for the International Food Policy Research Institute

PENN

University of Pennsylvania Press
Philadelphia

Published by
University of Pennsylvania Press
Philadelphia, Pennsylvania 19104-4112
www.upenn.edu/pennpress

Library of Congress Cataloging-in-Publication Data is available.

Printed in the United States of America on acid-free paper.
10 9 8 7 6 5 4 3 2 1

Contents

Tables and Figures and Box

Tables

Figures

Foreword

Even before the Green Revolution began in the mid-1960s, Pakistan was one of several developing countries that helped demonstrate the critical importance of agriculture, providing the international community with empirical evidence that agricultural sector growth can drive broader economic development. The agricultural surpluses, rural incomes, and industrial inputs produced by millions of farm households residing in Pakistan's irrigated plains helped fuel the country's growth and development well into the early years of this millennium.

Now, however, Pakistan's agricultural sector has become increasingly vulnerable to volatile weather patterns, long-term climate change, and extensive degradation of the country's natural resources. Economic signals also suggest that persistent poverty and inequality will continue to chip away at economic growth. These signals are most apparent in Pakistan's rural economy, where the needs of the poor remain unmet.

This book documents many of the challenges associated with Pakistan's elusive quest for broad-based and inclusive economic growth. It is a collaborative work that illustrates the depth and breadth of IFPRI's productive relationships with scholars and organizations working on food, agriculture, and rural development issues in Pakistan.

The contributors provide a systematic review and in-depth treatment of a range of basic issues that have received too little attention recently, including the need for policy change in support of competitive agricultural input markets, effective management of the Indus Basin Irrigation System, and commodity price management. The book also examines the role of human and social capital—particularly the needs and aspirations of rural women and youth—and priorities for improving policies and performance in the areas of rural health, education, water, sanitation, and governance.

Most significantly, by linking micro-level empirical analyses with macro-level scenario analyses, the book puts forward several policy options that deserve attention from decision makers at all levels. Making these policy options the basis for future investment strategies offers a significant opportunity for Pakistan's agricultural sector and its wider rural economy to make a sizable contribution to the country's ongoing efforts to foster inclusive economic growth and development.

Shenggen Fan
Director General, International Food Policy Research Institute

Acknowledgments

This book would not have been possible without contributions and support from numerous people, many of whom have provided support under the auspices of the Pakistan Strategy Support Program (PSSP). We express our gratitude to Ahsan Iqbal, federal minister for planning, development, and reform, deputy chairman of the Planning Commission, and chair of the PSSP's National Advisory Committee (NAC), as well as Nadeem ul-Haq, former deputy chairman of the Planning Commission and former chair of the NAC.

We also thank Aamer Irshad, Abid Suleri, and other NAC colleagues for their continuous support, as well as Greg Gottlieb, Catherine Moore, Nancy Estes, Scott Hocklander, Michael Wyzan, and Nazim Ali at the United States Agency for International Development, whose generous support made this book and the PSSP possible. We also acknowledge support from the CGIAR Research Program on Policies, Institutions, and Markets.

We extend our appreciation to Derek Byerlee, Madhur Gautam, Cem Mete, Safdar Parvez, and Sofia Shakil, all of whom provided insights, comments, and critiques on earlier versions of the book or its various chapters; and Iftikhar Ahmed, Syed Ghazanfar Abbas, M. Azeem Khan, Umar Farooq, and the staff of the Pakistan Agricultural Research Council for their continual support.

We acknowledge the guidance provided by the Publications Review Committee (PRC) at the International Food Policy Research Institute (IFPRI), particularly Gershon Feder, the chair of the PRC; Corinne Garber, the PRC secretary; members of the committee; and the three anonymous reviewers who offered comments, criticisms, and suggestions.

We also thank IFPRI colleagues who provided technical input. Mekamu Kedir provided technical assistance with the spatial analysis contained in this book, while Hamza Haider, Shehryar Rashid, Asjad Tariq, Saqib Shahzad, and Omar Majeed provided research assistance with much of the household data and statistics used in the book. In addition, we thank Fatima Zaidi for her extensive support on both the research and editorial fronts.

We extend our appreciation to Saira Malik, Najeeb Khan, Arshad Khurshid, and Ehtesham-ul Haq for their contributions to managing the PSSP; John Whitehead and Andrea Pedolsky for support throughout the editorial and production process; Ramela Carrion and Lorena Danessi for their administrative support; and Imran Malik and the team at Innovative Development Strategies (Pvt.) Ltd.

We thank Mehrab Malek who served not only as a coauthor on several chapters in the book, but also as a research assistant, reviewer, fact checker, copyeditor, and production manager during the book's preparation. His conscientious attention to detail was essential to the book's publication. Of course, any remaining errors and omissions in the book are the responsibilities of the coauthors and the coeditors.

We are extremely grateful to policy makers, academics, researchers, students, and civil society representatives who continuously engaged with PSSP and provided their valuable input at the various workshops, conferences, and seminars held across Pakistan during the past five years, particularly those at the PSSP Fourth Annual Conference held in 2015. It is our hope that this book, produced with contributions from all of those mentioned above and from our coauthors, will prove useful not only to our colleagues in government and academia, but also to students, researchers, development practitioners, and rural communities whose work is essential to accelerating growth, development, and poverty reduction in Pakistan.

Chapter 1

FOOD, AGRICULTURE, AND RURAL DEVELOPMENT IN PAKISTAN

David J. Spielman, Sohail J. Malik, Paul Dorosh, and Nuzhat Ahmad

Introduction

At the same time that policy makers, media, and the international community focus their attention on Pakistan's ongoing security challenges, the potential of the agricultural sector and rural economy to improve the well-being of Pakistan's population is being neglected. Pakistan's agricultural sector and rural economy have a central role to play in national development, food security, and poverty reduction. Since independence in 1947, the country's rich natural resource base, its hardworking farmers, and its rural communities have done much to drive national economic growth and development. Aided by public investments in irrigation, roads, agricultural technology, and market development, agriculture was at the heart of Pakistan's economic growth trajectory through the country's first four decades.

But the subsequent decline in evidence-based policy making on agricultural-sector issues has changed the prospects for the rural economy's role in Pakistan's development. As a result, growth in the rural economy has lost momentum, leaving Pakistan's rural population to face continuing high levels of poverty, and food insecurity, as well as limited access to the public services and markets required for a modern economy. Today, the country's rural poor make up 76 percent of the poor population, but only 9 percent of the overall population (GoP various years, *Pakistan Economic Survey*). Addressing their needs will require renewed attention both to agriculture and to investments in rural development more broadly. This book aims to revitalize interest in Pakistan's agricultural sector and the rural economy. And, more specifically, it seeks to identify public policy solutions that can accelerate agricultural growth, expand the rural economy, and improve the welfare and livelihoods of the rural poor.

The agricultural sector—comprising the subsectors of crops, livestock and poultry, fisheries, and forestry—has traditionally served as the backbone of Pakistan's economy. Until the early 1960s, agriculture generated approximately 40 percent of Pakistan's gross domestic product (GDP) (GoP various years, *Pakistan Economic Survey*). Since then, growth in the industrial and service sectors has outpaced positive, but often only moderate, growth in the agricultural sector. As a result, since 2010 the share of agriculture in GDP has dropped to approximately 20 percent, while the combined share of the industrial and services sectors has risen to more than 80 percent, led primarily by growth in the services sector (Figure 1.1). This means that agriculture is no longer a major channel for promoting overall economic growth and development, though as we will show in this book, it remains a major instrument for rural and overall poverty reduction.

Despite the slow but steady structural transformation of Pakistan's economy since the 1960s, the agricultural sector is still a key component of the national economy. First, agriculture remains central to the livelihoods of almost half the country's population and is essential to the future of rural areas. Agriculture is the main sector of employment for approximately 24 million people—who make up approximately 47 percent of the country's labor force. Second, agriculture provides Pakistan's rapidly growing population with the basic food staples and sources of micronutrients. Third, agriculture is essential for many parts of the industrial and services sectors, providing both an important market for industrial products (for example, farm machinery and inorganic fertilizer) and critical inputs to those products. Textile manufacturing, for example, which accounted for about 30 percent of the total industrial GDP in 2013/2014, is highly dependent on domestic cotton production. Foreign exchange earnings are similarly dependent on agriculture: cotton, rice, and leather accounted for nearly 11 percent of Pakistan's export earnings in 2013/2014, while cotton textiles and ready-made garments accounted for another 27 percent (GoP 2014).

Beyond these direct contributions, the rural economy encompasses much more than agricultural production. Pakistan's rural nonfarm economy plays a significant role in generating output and employment through a wide and diversified range of enterprises. Various estimates from the early to mid-2000s indicate that nonfarm incomes contributed between 40 and 57 percent to total rural household income, and even households engaged specifically in farming derived between 36 percent and 51 percent of their household income from nonfarm rural sources (Farooq 2014; World Bank 2007; Dorosh et al. 2003). These nonfarm income sources include a variety of enterprises, ranging from small village shops selling everyday consumables to equipment repair shops, transportation services, small-scale rural processors, and other enterprises; other sources include jobs in local schools, clinics, and government

FIGURE 1.1 Shares of sectors in national GDP at factor cost, FY1960–FY2014

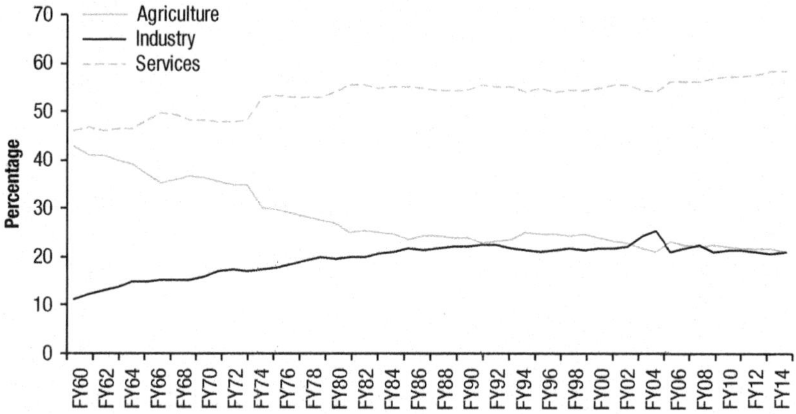

Source: Authors, based on data from GoP (various years), *Pakistan Economic Survey*.

offices and services. Estimates from the same period suggest that there were roughly 3.8 to 5 million nonfarm rural enterprises in Pakistan (Farooq 2014; World Bank 2007). Pakistan's experience has been consistent with the wealth of theoretical and empirical evidence on agriculture's central role in economic development via intersectoral linkages that support industrialization (Vogel 1994; Adelman 1984; Singer 1979; Johnston and Mellor 1961) and via rural nonfarm activities (Haggblade, Hazell, and Reardon 2010; Start 2001; Lanjouw and Lanjouw 2001; Fan, Hazell, and Thorat 1999).

Given these linkages to the broader economy, as well as the large share of the population supported directly by agriculture, the agricultural sector and the rural nonfarm economy clearly have a crucial role to play in promoting growth and reducing poverty in Pakistan (Dorosh, Niazi, and Niazi 2003). Thus, the slow growth of agriculture in recent years is particularly problematic. The annual agricultural growth rate has averaged just 2.8 percent over the four years 2010–2014, nearly a full percentage point lower than the average of 3.7 percent per year during the previous decade of 2000–2010, and approximately 2 percentage points lower than the period between 1990 and 2000 when the growth rate averaged 4.6 percent per year (Table 1.1). On a per capita basis, agricultural GDP grew at 1.3 percent per year during 2000–2010, well below the 2.5 percent growth rate attained during the 1990s. And in comparison to the rest of the economy, growth rates of the agricultural sector have been lagging: the services and industrial sectors grew significantly faster

TABLE 1.1 Value added to Pakistan's economy and growth rate by sector, 1990–2014

	2014 value added			Growth rate (%)		
	PKR (billion)	Share of GDP (percent)	Share of Ag GDP (percent)	1990–2000	2000–2010	2010–2014
Agriculture	2,152	21.05	100.00	4.59	3.71	2.76
Major Crops	550	5.38	25.55	2.99	2.82	3.73
Other Crops	251	2.45	11.65	4.27	1.10	−0.85
Cotton Ginning	61	0.59	2.81			0.97
Livestock	1,203	11.77	55.91	6.24	4.61	3.48
Forestry	44	0.43	2.04	0.10	−5.89	2.08
Fishing	44	0.43	2.03	3.28	6.31	−1.78
Industry	2,129	20.82	98.92	3.27	4.28	3.23
Services	5,945	58.14	276.23	3.69	4.99	4.42
Total	10,227	100.00	n.a.	3.81	4.54	3.81
Agricultural GDP per capita (PKR/year)	11,559.8	n.a.	n.a.	2.46	1.32	0.71
Cropped area (million ha)	19.0	n.a.	n.a.	0.92	0.86	−0.60
Crop GDP/ha (PKR thousands/year)	42.2	n.a.	n.a.	2.54	1.30	2.79

Source: Authors, based on data from the GoP (various years), *Pakistan Economic Survey.*

Note: Growth rates are calculated as logarithmic estimates of annual growth based on data from 1990 to 2014. n.a. = not applicable; PKR = Pakistani rupees; ha = hectares.

than agriculture during 2000–2010, at 5.0 percent and 4.3 percent per year, respectively, compared with 3.7 percent for the agricultural sector.

The book examines the performance of both agriculture and the rural economy in the face of the frequent macroeconomic crises and weather-related shocks that have occurred in recent decades. It also appraises the causes and consequences of Pakistan's substandard social indicators among its rural population. While it does not provide a comprehensive treatment of every policy dimension under the broad topic of agriculture and rural development, it presents new evidence on a range of essential issues. These include not only availability of agricultural inputs (water, seeds, fertilizer) and agricultural markets, but also the provision of public services (education, water and sanitation, electricity, health), women's empowerment, aspirations of the large youth population, and the impact of decentralization (brought about by the 18th Amendment)—all of which play a vital role in shaping rural development.

To set the stage for the book's wider analysis, this introduction proceeds as follows. First, it reviews the historical evolution of public policy on food security, agriculture, and the rural economy in Pakistan. Second, it describes the current state of affairs with respect to agricultural growth, rural development, and poverty reduction. Third, it outlines the main messages emerging from the research and analysis presented in the remainder of the book, highlighting the major issues on which evidence-based insights can assist decision makers in Pakistan in their pursuit of beneficial policy outcomes. Fourth, it describes the types of data and analysis used in the book. A final section provides a brief summary of the book's chapters.

A Historical Perspective

To understand the state of the agricultural sector and rural development today, we need to take a historical perspective. Many factors have contributed to Pakistan's erratic economic and social progress in recent decades, and lagging agricultural performance is only one among several. But because agriculture is so central to Pakistan's economy, society, and politics, a narrative of Pakistan is incomplete without devoting careful attention to agriculture and the rural economy. To this end, we briefly examine the history of policy engagement with agriculture and rural development in Pakistan and its impacts on the rural economy since independence (Table 1.2).

During the two decades that followed independence in 1947, Pakistan was largely fed by the bounty of Punjab Province, which is home to the rich alluvial soils and vast irrigation system in the Indus River basin. Unfortunately, the cleaving of Punjab across two separate countries diminished the depth and breadth of agricultural markets served by farmers on Pakistan's side of the new border (Murgai, Ali, and Byerlee 2001; Krishna 1963). The effects of this reduced market were exacerbated by the neglect of agricultural development by public policy makers, who followed much of the developing world in turning their attention to industrialization. However, as Pakistan became a net importer of food grains in the early 1950s, about half a million tons annually, attitudes in the government changed. In particular, a severe drought in 1952 forced Pakistan to import one million tons of wheat to meet basic food staple requirements, reminding policy makers of the insecurity of the young country's food supply. Policy makers acknowledged the fundamental importance of agriculture and the rural sector to Pakistan's future with the introduction in 1953 of the Village Agricultural and Industrial Development Program (commonly referred to as Village AID)—a social protection program created to provide rural employment opportunities on short-duration projects (Green 1957).

TABLE 1.2 Major events and policies relating to food security, agriculture, and rural development in Pakistan's history, 1947 to present

Year	Event/policy
1947	Pakistan gains independence.
1953	Village Aid Program, Pakistan's first rural social protection program, is established.
1955–1960	First Five-Year Plan is produced.
1958	Water and Power Development Authority is created.
1959–1960	Land reforms are pursued through various ordinances and regulations.
1960	India and Pakistan sign the Indus Waters Treaty.
1959–1970	Basic Democracies system, including district and union councils, is established.
1963	Rural Works Program is introduced.
1964	Pakistan and the International Maize and Wheat Improvement Center (CIMMYT) begin collaboration on high-yielding wheat.
1965–1985	Pakistan Perspective Plan introduces 20-year vision to national development strategy.
1966	Pakistan and the International Rice Research Institute (IRRI) begin collaboration on high-yielding rice.
1970–1990	Green Revolution is put into practice in growing wheat and rice.
1971	East Pakistan secedes to become Bangladesh.
1972	New land reforms are undertaken; Peoples Work Program and Integrated Rural Development Program are introduced.
1980	National Agricultural Policy is introduced; economic liberalization measures are pursued in the agricultural sector.
1981	Agricultural Prices Commission (APC) and Pakistan Agricultural Research Council (PARC) are established.
1987	National Agricultural Commission, recommending a new strategy for agricultural development, is established.
1991	National Agricultural Policy is introduced; Pakistan Water Apportionment Accord is signed.
2004	Agricultural Perspective and Policy is drafted but not formally adopted.
2008	Prime Minister's Task Force on Food Security is established following global food price shock.
2010	18th Amendment of the national constitution devolves responsibilities for agriculture and other key sectors from the federal to provincial governments.
2010	Massive floods take place in the Indus River basin.
2011	New Framework for Economic Growth is introduced.
2014	Agriculture and Food Security Policy is drafted.

Source: Authors' compilation.

Pakistan's policies for the agricultural sector and rural development, beginning with a series of five-year development plans, have focused on aggregate production, land distribution, and governance, with varying degrees of commitment and impact across the years. During the course of the First Five-Year Plan (1955–1960), the Government of Pakistan set bold targets to increase both cereal and cash crop production. Few of these targets were met, despite allocations of 24 percent of the national development budget per year for agriculture and water. Nevertheless, the period did see several major changes in the institutional landscape of Pakistan's agricultural sector, and in the government apparatus designed to promote its growth and development. In 1958 policy makers took aim at harnessing Pakistan's vast natural endowment of water resources in the Indus River basin with the establishment of the Water and Power Development Authority (WAPDA). WAPDA was created to coordinate activities in the water and power sectors that had previously been managed by provincial departments of electricity and irrigation. WAPDA assumed oversight over efforts to manage the Indus River basin for both irrigation and power generation purposes, and over schemes designed to reclaim waterlogged, sodic, and saline lands for use in agriculture.

The Food and Agriculture Commission was created in 1959 to assess the causes of and solutions to poor performance in the country's agricultural sector. This step led to the creation of the Agriculture Development Corporation, which sought to improve the implementation and coordination of policies pertaining to agricultural development. These initiatives were consistent with strategies pursued in many other developing countries at the time, but their impact was likely mixed at best.

Similarly, beginning in 1959, Pakistan pursued efforts to address equity issues related to land tenure. Prior to partition in 1947, Hindus and Sikhs had owned vast stretches of agricultural land in Punjab, Sindh, and the present-day Khyber Pakhtunkhwa (KPK). The British had allocated this land, particularly in settlements along the canals in Punjab, to powerful elites and members of the upper castes in exchange for state patronage. After partition, and what was the largest mass migration in human history, millions of Muslim refugees left India for Pakistan and settled in the 2.7 million hectares of cultivable land made vacant following the migration of approximately five million Hindus and Sikhs to the newly divided east Punjab just across the border (Kapur 2010). Some of the incoming migrants undoubtedly benefitted from this resettlement. However, this process was extremely skewed and essentially mirrored the hierarchical colonial social patterns, leaving millions landless while concentrating ownership in a few hands. This inequity eventually pressured the government into introducing land reforms in 1959. Policy makers put in place several key ordinances and regulations that were designed to address the skewed land tenure patterns. These policy shifts sought to protect the small-scale sharecroppers from the exploitative hold of the large and often absent landlords through legislation to ensure that the landlords shared not only in the revenue but also in the cost of inputs, while limits were also placed on the maximum size of landholding. On the formal records, approximately 2.5 million acres, or 5 percent of the country's total farm area, were brought under land reforms that sought to abolish large landholdings and reallocate land from landlords to tenants (Gazdar 2009; Nabi, Hamid, and Zahid 1986). The impact of these land reforms was marginal at best and did little to bring about more effective reforms in subsequent decades.

Land reforms occurred at roughly the same time as Pakistan rolled out its Basic Democracies system (1959–1970). This system was designed to build grassroots democratic institutions throughout the country that would engage and involve communities in development planning and implementation. The Basic Democracies and their associated district and union councils (referred to frequently throughout the book) were expected to play a central role in fostering agricultural productivity growth and wider rural development. The system, while only somewhat effective in engaging the rural population in governance, encouraged other, later experiments in decentralized governance.

During the Second Five-Year Plan (1960–1965), Pakistan began to reap some modest gains from land reforms and efforts to manage its water resources and to reverse degradation of the land. These gains were partly due to the historic Indus Waters Treaty that was signed with India in 1960, which opened the way for the construction of the Tarbela Dam and other major irrigation investments. On the social side, the poorly performing Village Aid Program was replaced by the Rural Works Program (1963–1972), which, alongside Basic Democracies, aimed to sustain the country's commitment to social protection and accelerate rural growth.

Food staple output and yield growth increased substantially during the Second Five-Year Plan, supported by the first large-scale investments in improved cultivars, plant protection chemicals, mechanization, and tube wells. These investments were accompanied by input subsidies designed to promote the adoption of the new technologies among farmers. Area cultivated and production increased substantially: Pakistan realized a 10 percent rise in net area sown, a massive surge in double cropping, and increases in production on the order of 5 percent per year for major and minor food staple crops and

4 percent per year for the agricultural sector overall (World Bank 2007; Ali and Byerlee 2002; Murgai, Ali, and Byerlee 2001).

The 20-year Pakistan Perspective Plan, issued in 1965, laid out a longer-term vision for Pakistan's economy and society. However, urgent, short-term considerations, including war, drought, and escalating food prices, forced themselves onto center stage in the late 1960s. Despite these setbacks, the Green Revolution began to bring major improvements in agricultural yields, in large part through the rapid introduction of new high-yielding, semidwarf wheat varieties that were highly responsive to inorganic fertilizer and irrigation. These varieties were bred through a research collaboration between Pakistan's national agricultural research system and the International Maize and Wheat Improvement Center (CIMMYT) in Mexico (CIMMYT 1989). A similar research collaboration between Pakistan's research system and the International Rice Research Institute (IRRI) in the Philippines led to the introduction of high-yielding rice varieties (IRRI 2013). Concerted efforts were made by Pakistan's research and extension system to distribute these improved varieties, complementary inputs, and the knowledge required to rapidly intensify cultivation (Hazell 2010; Evenson and Gollin 2003; Lipton, with Longhurst 1989). Policies at the federal and provincial levels that promoted modern inputs and technology, stabilized commodity markets with procurement pricing, and increased public investment in other critical inputs—irrigation, infrastructure, and agricultural science—also led to growth in agricultural productivity.

By 1970 the Green Revolution had swept across Pakistan's irrigated farmlands. Intensification of rice and wheat production was concentrated primarily in the Punjab, where 52 percent of the area under wheat cultivation came to be sown with modern varieties, and comparable rates were achieved with modern rice varieties. Nationally, the agricultural sector grew by an average of 6.4 percent per year between 1966 and 1970, with the production of major crops increasing by 9 percent per year (GoP, various years, *Pakistan Economic Survey*). While the gains in productivity from the Green Revolution are among the most notable achievements in the agricultural sector, serious concerns have arisen about the narrow crop focus of the Green Revolution, its contribution to accelerating natural resource degradation, and its heterogeneous impacts across regional lines (Ali and Byerlee 2002; Byerlee and Husain 1992).

Following the rapid growth in production induced by the Green Revolution and despite the introduction of new development programs, agricultural-sector growth slowed during the 1970s. Pakistan effectively did away with its five-year plans for most of the decade as it lurched from crisis to crisis—war, political instability, and martial law—while contending with exogenous shocks including the 1973 oil crisis and three major droughts. In the agricultural sector, a new round of land reforms was introduced in 1972, as were several other initiatives focused on strengthening the rural economy. These included the People's Works Program, which was a revision of the previous social protection initiatives, and the Integrated Rural Development Program, which was designed to simultaneously increase smallholder productivity, expand rural industrialization and employment, and improve access to public services such as healthcare and education. Yet the agricultural sector grew during this period at a rate of only slightly less than 2 percent, while growth rates for the production of major crops fell to less than 1 percent, a decline only partly offset by growth in the production of minor crops and livestock.

In 1977 a third attempt was made at land reform under the direction of the Pakistan Peoples Party (PPP). However, this civil government was removed from power shortly after the land reforms were introduced, resulting in limited changes in land tenure patterns. With a military government then in place, Pakistan resumed the use of five-year plans and placed agriculture high on the agenda of its Fifth Five-Year Plan (1978–1983). Recognizing that aggregate production goals—crop yields and outputs, measured in tons and percentages—were insufficient to address rural development, the new five-year plan introduced two new measures of food security: nutrition and diversification. Drawing partly on the results of the 1976–1977 Micro-Nutrient Survey, which found that 60 percent of children under five years old were malnourished in Pakistan (GoP 2011a), the new plan gave careful consideration to the role of fruits, vegetables, and oilseeds for both consumption and export purposes. Unfortunately, the ambitious plan target of a 6 percent growth rate in the agricultural sector was paired with a relatively small actual allocation from the federal development budget.

In 1980 Pakistan's first explicit policy statement on agriculture—the National Agriculture Policy—established food self-sufficiency as a national priority. The policy affirmed the importance of modern inputs, irrigation, extension services, and mechanization to Pakistan's agricultural sector. It also emphasized the need for improvements in the institutional landscape designed to implement and coordinate agricultural and rural development policies in the country. The National Agricultural Policy was followed closely by the establishment of the National Agricultural Prices Commission, which provided the government with a critical mechanism with which to manage weather- and market-induced risk and uncertainty in agricultural markets through various forms of price interventions.

The National Agricultural Policy and the National Agricultural Prices Commission—aided by several years of favorable weather—contributed to a number of important achievements during the decade that followed. The policy, as part of a wider agenda of economic liberalization, led to the withdrawal of distortionary government interventions in most commodity markets in Pakistan during the 1980s. This included the removal of price subsidies on inputs and the implementation of price supports for import-substituting crops. It also led to a shift from rules that required compulsory use of nitrogenous fertilizers to voluntary use. These changes made some headway toward addressing what was increasingly recognized as the elite capture of subsidies and price interventions by large-scale farmers at the expense of small-scale farmers. However, distortions remained in the wheat market, where policies of price supports persisted, at significant cost to the government, and in the fertilizer market, most notably through subsidies provided to producers in the form of interventions in gas pricing.

In a related development, the Pakistan Water Apportionment Accord of 1991 made significant headway in setting down long-term rules to govern water allocations from the Indus River basin across Punjab, Sindh, KPK, and Balochistan. The 1991 accord represents an important political compromise across the provinces in support of agriculture, although it also raised issues with respect to the trade-offs between the use of water for irrigation versus for energy, the relative productivity of water across provinces, and the absence of infrastructure in KPK and Balochistan to make effective use of their respective allocations (Briscoe et al. 2005).

Efforts to further improve the trajectory of Pakistan's agricultural sector were tackled by successive commissions and panels, which in turn informed a series of new policy initiatives, although many of these were not implemented. Most notable is the National Agricultural Commission of 1987, which recommended a renewed focus on social equity, national self-reliance in food, a stronger export orientation in agriculture, the introduction of more sustainable agricultural practices, and higher productivity, to be achieved with particular emphasis on small-scale farmers, rainfed areas, and institutional reform. While the resulting National Agricultural Policy of 1991 reiterated these aims in its action plan, neither a budget allocation nor an implementation strategy followed the document. The 2004 Agricultural Perspective and Policy, which was never formally adopted by the Government of Pakistan, likewise lacked funding and an implementation strategy, as did the Vision 2030, which the government announced in 2007. The New Framework for Economic Growth, announced in 2011, continued the trend toward neglect of the agricultural sector, relegating agriculture to the backburner of Pakistan's economic growth and development agenda.

In coming years, major changes in the agricultural sector can be expected as a result of a recent constitutional amendment supporting decentralization. Adopted in 2010, the 18th Amendment devolves policy making and a range of other functions related to agricultural matters from the federal government to the provinces (NSPP 2012). It has already led to the demise of the Ministry of Food, Agriculture, and Livestock at the federal level, the establishment of the Ministry of National Food Security and Research (MNFSR), and a fair amount of confusion over the allocation of organizations and functions between the federal and provincial governments. The long-term results for policy design, coordination, and implementation remain to be seen, although both the provinces and the federal government are working to craft strategies to address matters of agriculture and food security that have been reorganized as a result of the 18th Amendment. It is still too early to fully comprehend the impacts and necessary responses to the amendment, and these issues are examined in detail throughout the book.

In retrospect, while the record on implementation has been mixed, there has been no shortage of public policy designed to develop Pakistan's agricultural sector. During the 1970s and 1980s, Pakistan demonstrated that a combination of strategic development policies and appropriate agricultural technologies could drive growth and development. Several notable successes contributed to rapid growth of agriculture and the rural economy, including the Indus Waters Treaty and the Green Revolution. But the historical record also suggests that over the past two decades, policy reforms have struggled to strengthen Pakistan's agricultural sector and rural economy.

Development, Growth, and Poverty Reduction

Agricultural productivity growth has driven Pakistan's economic growth and development in the past, particularly when public policy has been supportive of the agricultural sector and the wider rural economy. Chapter 2 expands on this point. However, the past two decades have seen a slowdown in both sector growth and improvements in the social indicators of rural development, and this section explores those outcomes.

Pakistan's economy grew by 6.3 percent per year during the 1980s, boosted substantially by agricultural-sector growth of about 4.0 percent per year.

FIGURE 1.2 GDP, agricultural GDP, and share of labor in agricultural GDP, FY1980–FY2014

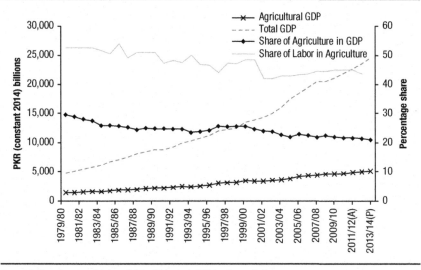

Source: Authors, based on data from GoP (various years), *Pakistan Economic Survey.*
Notes: PKR = Pakistani rupees; A = actual; P = provisional.

Moreover, during the 1980s, per capita income rose by 2.8 percent per year. In the 1990s, growth decelerated but was irregular, punctuated by occasional booms and busts. Real GDP growth between 1990 and 2000 slowed to 3.9 percent per year, increasing only slightly between 2000 and 2012 to 4.1 percent per year (Figure 1.2, Table 1.3). Per capita income growth followed a similar pattern, decreasing from 2.8 percent to 1.3 percent per year in the 1990s before rising to 2.2 percent per year during the period 2000–2012. In 2012 GDP per capita (measured in constant [2005] US dollars) averaged US$773, which was about 47 percent higher than the US$525 per capita GDP attained in 1990 (Table 1.3).

The agricultural-sector growth rate during the 1990s remained relatively unchanged from the 1980s, at 4.4 percent. But while the economy showed a slight recovery in the 2000–2012 period, growth in the agricultural sector slowed to just 2.6 percent per year (Table 1.3).

This economic roller coaster has done little to improve overall economic welfare in the country. There is evidence that the poverty headcount ratio fell from 66.5 percent in 1987 to 48.1 percent in 1997, and further to 35.9 percent in 2002, although rural poverty consistently remained higher than urban poverty (World Bank 2014; Figure 1.3). Alternative figures presented in this book suggest otherwise, indicating how controversial poverty estimates are in Pakistan. Recent figures on poverty reduction point to *increases* in poverty

TABLE 1.3 Selected economic variables, 1980–2012

Indicator	Year				Annual growth rate (%)		
	1980	1990	2000	2012	1980–1990	1990–2000	2000–2012
Population (millions)	80.0	111.1	143.8	179.2	3.3	2.6	1.8
GDP (constant 2005, million US$)	31,707	58,314	85,822	138,472	6.3	3.9	4.1
GDP per capita (constant 2005, US$)	396.4	524.9	596.7	772.9	2.8	1.3	2.2
GDP (constant 2005, billion PKR)	2,241	4,121	6,065	9,785	6.3	3.9	4.1
Agriculture GDP (constant 2005, billion PKR)	657	973	1,501	2,045	4.0	4.4	2.6
Share of agriculture (% of GDP)	29.3	23.6	24.8	20.9	−2.1	0.5	−1.4
Share of industry (% of GDP)	15.0	17.2	17.6	20.3	1.4	0.2	1.2
Share of manufacturing (% of GDP)	8.5	10.1	10.1	12.8	1.8	−0.1	2.0
Share of services (% of GDP)	47.2	48.7	51.3	56.1	0.3	0.5	0.7
Gross domestic savings (% of GDP)	6.9	11.1	16.0	7.0	4.9	3.7	−6.7
Gross capital formation (% of GDP)	18.5	18.9	17.2	14.9	0.2	−0.9	−1.2
Exports of goods and services (% of GDP)	12.5	15.5	13.4	12.3	2.2	−1.4	−0.7
Imports of goods and services (% of GDP)	24.1	23.4	14.7	20.3	−0.3	−4.5	2.7
Official exchange rate (PKR/US$)	9.9	21.7	53.6	93.4	8.2	9.5	4.7
Consumer price index	16.48	32.26	77.83	221.91	7.0	9.2	9.1

Source: Authors, based on data from World Bank (2014).

Note: Sectoral shares of GDP are calculated by the authors based on constant GDP data from World Bank (2014). For example, agriculture's share in GDP is calculated by taking constant (2005) agricultural GDP/constant (2005) GDP.

during the 2000s, along with high levels of food insecurity and malnutrition, issues that are explored in greater detail in Chapter 3. But only in recent years has the Government of Pakistan begun to realize that progress has not been made on the increases in employment and income at levels that will be required to reduce poverty significantly (see, for example, GoP, various years, *Pakistan Economic Survey*).

Moreover, public expenditures on agriculture as a ratio of Poverty Reduction Strategy Programs have generally been declining over time with significant year-on-year fluctuations (Figure 1.4). On average, between 2007/2008 and 2012/2013, the ratio of agricultural expenditures to total poverty expenditures is 5.8 percent and agricultural expenditures to total subsidies is 9.5 percent (GoP, various years, *Pakistan Economic Survey*).

There are several possible explanations for the slowdown in economic growth compared to the 1980s, including a decline in overall investment, a lack of growth in the nonfarm rural economy, and persistent inequality in the

FIGURE 1.3 Real gross national income per capita and poverty in Pakistan, 1980–2013

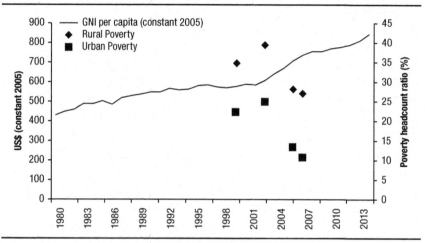

Source: Authors, based on data from World Bank (2014); Cheema (2005).

Note: The poverty headcount ratio is the proportion of people living below the adult equivalent of a US$1.25/day expenditure level based on purchasing power parity exchange rates. The rural poverty and urban poverty rates reported here are measured at their respective poverty lines. Alternative rural poverty estimates are discussed in detail in Chapter 3. GNI = gross national income

FIGURE 1.4 Share of agriculture expenditure in total poverty expenditure, 2007/2008–2012/2013

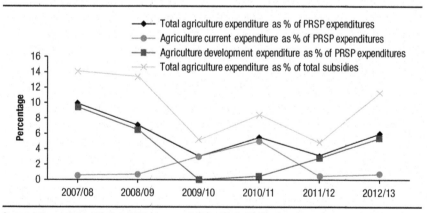

Source: Authors, based on data from GoP (various years), *Federal Budget Publications*.

Note: PRSP = Poverty Reduction Strategy Paper.

agricultural sector. At the national level, overall investment decreased from 18.9 percent of GDP in 1990 to 14.9 percent in 2012. Gross domestic savings declined even more sharply, falling from 11.1 percent of GDP in 1990 to 7.0 percent of GDP in 2012. Only an increase in foreign savings (as indicated by the widening gap between foreign revenues, that is, exports plus remittances, less imports) has prevented an even sharper decline in investment in Pakistan (Figure 1.5).

The slowdown may also hinge on the rate at which the rural nonfarm economy is expanding to provide opportunities for the diversification of rural labor into higher-productivity activities. This implies diversification of rural labor out of wheat and cotton production and other on-farm activities, or diversification out of agriculture entirely and into rural enterprises. There are few in-depth studies of Pakistan's nonfarm rural economy, but rural investment climate and labor force surveys suggest that improvements in rural enterprise financing, infrastructure (particularly electricity), and control of corruption are essential to accelerate the growth of Pakistan's rural nonfarm sector (World Bank 2007). These issues are examined throughout the book.

Yet another cause of the slowdown may be persistent inequality in land ownership and the increasing prevalence of highly fragmented, suboptimal farm sizes (discussed in Chapter 2). Land reform efforts notwithstanding, the distribution of landholdings remains highly unequal in Pakistan, with the proportion of farms of less than 5 acres increasing over time. The share of farms smaller than 5 acres increased from 19 percent of all farms in 1960 to 65 percent in 2010. In addition, the average size of these smallholdings has fallen from 2.2 acres to 1.9 acres, a size that is likely to be economically unviable. At the other end of the spectrum, farms larger than 25 acres account for only 3.8 percent of farms but for 34 percent of total area in 2010. Fragmentation and the decline in average farm size has major implications for poverty levels; most rural households that have access to less than 5 acres of land are categorized as "poor," according to the 2010–2011 Household Integrated Economic Survey (HIES) (GoP 2011b).

The links between land fragmentation, productivity, population growth, and poverty have been a focus of policy making and research for decades in Pakistan. Chapter 2 discusses the structure of land ownership, growing fragmentation, and the impediments to effective land markets. While Binswanger (1994) cautions that the influence of fragmentation on productivity can be overstated, there is sufficient evidence from the extensive body of past work to indicate that inequality of landownership and the political economy factors

FIGURE 1.5 Exports, imports, and exports plus remittances in Pakistan, 1980/1981–2012/2013

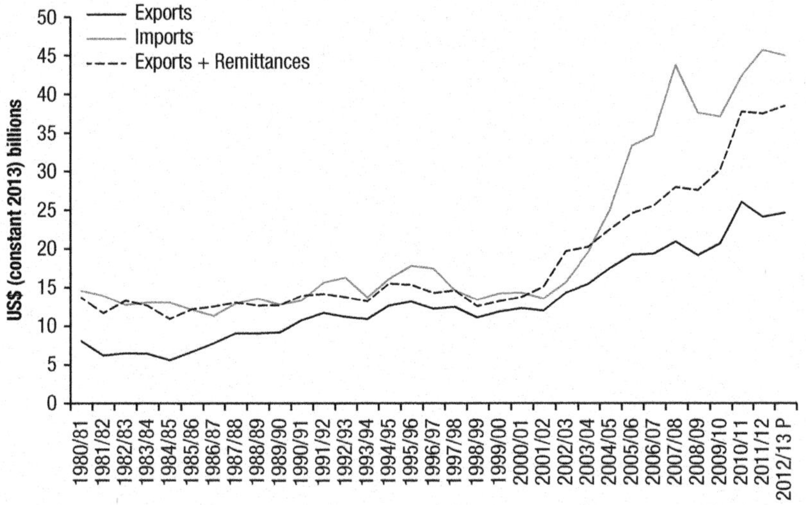

Source: Authors, based on GoP (various years), *Pakistan Economic Survey.*
Note: P = provisional.

that sustain this inequality remain an impediment to Pakistan's development (Qureshi and Qureshi 2004; GoP 1988; Heston and Kumar 1983).

Other indicators generally paint a picture of modest economic and social progress in Pakistan over the past two decades (Table 1.4), despite important changes. Notably, using the pre-2001 administrative definitions of urban areas, the proportion of the population living in urban areas has grown from 28.1 percent in 1980 to 36.5 percent in 2012. A broader definition of urbanization—a measure of population density and travel time to major urban centers—shows a near doubling of the urbanization figures, to about two-thirds of the population, growth that has been facilitated by the increase in paved roads. Nevertheless, poverty remains concentrated in Pakistan's rural areas. Several chapters of this book discuss the impact of the growing urban sector on rural development. Food insecurity and malnutrition, discussed in more detail in Chapter 3, remain serious problems, as is access to public services, discussed in Chapter 8.

The limitations of progress are evident when we measure it against the achievements of Pakistan's South Asian neighbors, many of which do not enjoy the same rich natural endowments of fertile land and abundant water resources. Most revealing is the comparison of the growth in per capita

TABLE 1.4 Selected economic and social indicators, 1980–2012

Indicator	Year				Annualized growth rate (%)		
	1980	1990	2000	2012	1980–1990	1990–2000	2000–2012
Infrastructure							
Paved roads (thousand kilometers)	—	169.2	248.3	262.6[a]	—	3.9	0.5
Urban population (millions)	22.4	34.0	47.7	65.5	4.2	3.4	2.9
Urbanization rate (% of population)	28.1	30.6	33.1	36.5	0.9	0.8	0.9
Life expectancy at birth							
Females	58.5	61.9	64.7	67.3	0.6	0.4	0.4
Males	57.7	60.5	63.1	65.6	0.5	0.4	0.3
Total	58.1	61.2	63.9	66.4	0.5	0.4	0.4
Adult literacy rate[b]	25.7	42.7	49.9	54.9	3.0	2.2	2.4
Poverty headcount ratio at US$1.25/day (PPP)[c]	66.5	48.1	35.9	21.0	−2.9	−5.7	−12.5
Poverty headcount ratio at US$2/day (PPP)[c]	89.2	83.3	73.9	60.2	−0.6	−2.4	−5.0
Personal remittances received (current US$) (millions)	2,048	2,006	1,075	14,007	−0.2	−5.5	26.3
Personal remittances received (% GDP)	8.6	5.0	1.5	6.2	−4.8	−10.6	14.1

Source: Authors, based on data from World Bank (2014).

Note: — = Data not available. PPP = purchasing power parity exchange rates.

[a] Paved road data are from 2011, the latest year of available data.

[b] Literacy rates are for 1981, 1998, 2005, and 2009.

[c] Poverty rates are for 1987, 1997, 2002, and 2008.

incomes (Table 1.5). Between 2000 and 2010, per capita GDP growth in Pakistan was only 2.3 percent per year, while India, Bangladesh, and Sri Lanka achieved annual per capita GDP growth rates of 6.0, 4.4, and 4.4 percent, respectively.

Pakistan also performs poorly on social indicators when it is compared with its neighbors. The World Bank (2014) estimates that approximately 20 percent of Pakistan's population was undernourished in 2010–2012, compared with 17–18 percent of the populations in Bangladesh, India, and Nepal. The starkest difference in indicators is observed for the mortality rate of children under five years of age, which is closely associated with access to water, sanitation, and healthcare. In Pakistan in 2013, 69 children per 1,000 live births die before the age of five, as compared with 41 children in India, 33 children in Bangladesh, and only 8 children in Sri Lanka. Pakistan fares better than its South Asian neighbors only in terms of the percentage of

TABLE 1.5 Selected social and economic indicators for Pakistan and South Asia

Indicator	Pakistan	India	Bangladesh	Nepal	Sri Lanka
Population (millions)	179.2	1,236.7	154.7	27.5	20.3
Population growth rate (2000–2010, %)	1.9	1.5	1.3	1.5	0.8
GDP per capita (2012, in constant 2005 US$)	772.9	1,123.2	597.0	398.8	1,884.2
GDP per capita growth rate (2000–2010, %)	2.3	6.0	4.4	2.4	4.4
Agriculture, value added (2012, as % of GDP)	24.4	17.5	17.7	37.0	11.1
Agricultural GDP growth rate (2000–2010, %)	3.5	5.0	2.5	2.8	0.6
Poverty headcount ratio at US$1.25 a day (2012, in PPP terms)[a]	21.0	32.7	43.3	24.8	4.1
Global Hunger Index value (2013)	19.3	21.3	19.4	17.3	15.6
Undernourished population (2010–2012, %)	19.9	17.5	16.8	18	24
Underweight children under five years old (2008–2012, %)	30.9	40.2	36.8	29.1	21.6
Under-five mortality rate (2013, per 1,000 live births)	69	41	33	32	8

Source: Authors, based on data from World Bank (2014); von Grebmer et al. (2013).

Note: The Global Hunger Index (GHI) is a multidimensional indicator of hunger that combines three component measures into one index. The first component is undernourishment, which measures the proportion of undernourished people (insufficient caloric intake) as a percentage of the total population. Underweight children measures the proportion of children under the age of five who have low weight for their age, reflecting wasting (low weight for height), stunted growth (low height for age), or both. The final component is under-five mortality rate. Beginning 2014, the GHI explicitly includes stunting and wasting as individual components.

[a] 2008 data for Pakistan; 2010 data for remaining countries. Alternative estimates of poverty in Pakistan are explored in depth in Chapter 3.

underweight children under five years old: the rate for Pakistan (31 percent) is lower than that for Bangladesh (37 percent) and India (40 percent), though it is still higher than that for Sri Lanka (22 percent).

These data strongly suggest that Pakistan's agricultural sector has not been contributing to growth and development, notably with respect to poverty reduction, as it did prior to the 1990s. Nevertheless, there are some positive examples of the sector's potential for progress—even in the absence of policy support—that are worth highlighting here. At a macroeconomic level, evidence suggests that the transmission of volatility of growth in agricultural GDP to the wider economy has dampened as the economy has diversified into industry and services (World Bank 2007). At the farm level, there are also success stories in which small-scale farmers have reaped significant gains from the production and marketing of higher-value agricultural products for both domestic and foreign markets. Three examples stand out.

First is the success of hybrid maize. Prior to the 1990s, low-yielding maize varieties were cultivated in limited areas in the barani (rainfed) agroecological zones of KPK and northern Punjab, and in other parts of Punjab, primarily for private-sector interests in the corn oil business. During the 1990s, higher-yielding hybrid maize was introduced in new areas of central Punjab, giving life to the livestock and poultry feed industries, and supplying corn for human consumption in affluent urban areas. Yet the rapid growth of both maize area and yield occurred with little support from the public sector and no government intervention in its pricing. Maize also brought additional benefits such as a lower environmental footprint than the sugarcane crop that it replaces in central Punjab, while also improving farmers' access to competitive markets and market prices that were generally elusive because of long-standing oligopsonies in the milling of sugarcane (Riaz 2006).

Second is the success of high-value agriculture, specifically improved practices in vegetable cultivation and value-addition in citrus cultivation. The introduction of plastic-tunnel farming, combined with more intensive husbandry and marketing practices, has allowed farmers in many parts of Punjab to secure higher returns on cucumber, tomato, and sweet pepper production. Small-scale processors of citrus who grade, sort, wax, and pack citrus products—specifically, the kinnow variety that is grown in orchards dotting the Sargodha and Bhalwal areas of Punjab—have generated similar returns to farmers, exporting to markets in Central Asia, the Middle East, and the Far East (Riaz 2006).

Third is the rapid growth of small-scale commercial dairy farming. This success is exemplified by the Idara-e-Kissan Halla Dairy Cooperative, which brings together approximately 80,000 members, the majority of whom are female. The cooperative provides veterinary services for its members, helps to increase livestock productivity, ensures product quality, and markets dairy products for Pakistan's growing consumer market. Incentive, compatibility, and accountability are the main factors responsible for this success. The cooperative employs its own veterinary specialists, and its members provide oversight of the service delivery (Riaz 2008).

These success stories—just a few of the many inspiring narratives that typify Pakistan's farmers and rural entrepreneurs—highlight the potential of Pakistan's agricultural sector and the productive and innovative capabilities of its people. They also suggest that as was the case with maize, some successes are possible in the absence of effective government policy or government interventions in the market. That said, an enabling policy environment could encourage more successes that engage a wider and deeper share of the agricultural sector and rural economy. With policies that explicitly focus on that enabling environment, agriculture can potentially make a greater contribution to economic growth and poverty reduction in Pakistan.

Main Messages: Managing and Building on Agricultural Growth

While these success stories are cause for optimism, the central question is whether Pakistan's agricultural sector and rural economy can once again play a significant role in the economy, particularly with respect to poverty reduction. The analyses conducted for this book point to the potential and possibility, but they also highlight the limits imposed by a changing economy.

First and foremost, Pakistan's agricultural sector is changing in terms of both structure and composition. While agriculture is still the foundation of Pakistan's economy, its share of total output, and thus its capacity to drive growth and development, is diminishing. Although a declining share of agriculture in both employment and in GDP is a normal pattern of economic development, historically the fastest growing countries have also achieved steady growth in agricultural GDP at the same time. In these countries, because nonagricultural growth occurred at a faster rate than agricultural growth, the share of agriculture in GDP fell even while agricultural incomes rose. Moreover, given the large share of agriculture in total GDP, it will be extremely difficult for Pakistan to achieve high overall growth without substantial agricultural growth and the resulting positive growth linkage effects on nonagricultural sectors. A slow pace of agricultural growth could lead to other problems as well: without continued growth in agricultural and rural nonfarm incomes, an excessively rapid rural-to-urban migration could result in large-scale urban unemployment, urban congestion, and political instability. The challenge for Pakistan's development strategy is how to take advantage of opportunities to continuously increase agricultural productivity and incomes, thereby facilitating a smooth spatial and structural transformation of the overall economy.

Second, agriculture is beset by increasingly acute trade-offs—between productivity growth and resource degradation, between water and energy, and between urban consumers' demands for diverse foods and poorly diversified farms. A shift to a higher, more equitable, and more sustainable growth trajectory for Pakistan's economy requires careful consideration of these trade-offs. Achieving such a growth trajectory is feasible if policy choices build on a foundation of balanced growth and development in the agricultural sector and the rural economy. The country's agroclimatic diversity and natural resource endowments continue to favor this trajectory, but it can be achieved only through intensive efforts to manage land, soil, water, and energy more judiciously.

Third, markets can play a critical role in providing farmers with access to the land, inputs, science, and price incentives required to accelerate productivity growth, provided that policies and regulations governing markets for seed, fertilizer, land, and commodities such as wheat are strengthened to provide more appropriate signals. Even greater potential for balanced growth and development can be realized if more policy attention is paid to land tenure issues and rural enterprise development to encourage growth in the rural economy.

Fourth, agricultural-productivity growth and increased rural economic activity will not, in themselves, be sufficient to eliminate rural poverty in Pakistan. Declining real rural wages, consumption patterns skewed toward cheaper, less nutritious calorie sources, and weak social protection mechanisms to insulate vulnerable households from shocks all contribute to rural Pakistan's persistently high malnutrition levels, especially among children. Greater attention needs to be given to the provision of rural public services, especially with respect to safety nets, healthcare, education, community development, and women's empowerment.

Finally, bold policy measures emerging from devolution under the 18th Amendment to the constitution can play a central role in strengthening the provision of the public goods and services that are critical to shifting Pakistan's economy to this higher, more equitable, and more sustainable growth trajectory. The challenge, however, will be to ensure on a continuing basis greater political and community buy-in and effective implementation—both pacing and sequencing—of the myriad reforms, regulations, and investments that need to follow from the 18th Amendment.

The Critical Importance of Data and Analysis

Because this book is a nuanced exploration of poverty and agriculture in Pakistan—and because works like this are relatively rare in the literature on Pakistan—we believe that it offers a unique contribution not only in terms of subject matter but also in the analytical perspectives we take on the issues discussed. As such, it is important to point out the unique manner in which the book combines a range of data, data sources, and methods to illustrate the key messages set forth above.

First, the book draws on a range of analytical tools and methods to capture the multifaceted nature of the agricultural sector and rural poverty. It makes use of analytical tools of geography (Chapters 2 and 12) and microeconomics (Chapters 3, 8, and 9) to characterize and highlight the impacts of public policies and investments on Pakistan's agricultural sector and rural population in terms of productivity, poverty, gender inequality, and access to public services. The book extends its microeconomic analysis into a discussion of the social and behavioral dimensions of rural development, such as the role of aspirations in motivating Pakistan's youthful rural population (Chapter 11). The book also extends its reach with political economy analyses that deconstruct the evolution and impact of policies in specific elements of the economy, such as the seed industry (Chapter 5) and the wider governance landscape (Chapter 9). Finally, the book employs a diverse set of economic modeling approaches, ranging from microsimulations to computable general equilibrium in order to quantify alternative scenarios associated with prospective reforms to policies on water and irrigation (Chapter 4), fertilizer (Chapter 6), markets and trade (Chapter 7), and the overall economy (Chapter 12).

Second, the book draws on a diversity of data sources. Frequently referenced sources include publications and datasets from the Government of Pakistan—namely, successive years and rounds of the Pakistan Economic Survey, the Pakistan Agriculture Census, and the Pakistan Household Integrated Economic Survey.[1] In addition to these sources, several chapters draw on data from the first survey rounds of the Pakistan Rural Household Panel Survey (RHPS) that was conducted in 2012 (Nazli and Haider 2012) (Annex A). The survey represents the first rounds in the recent longer-term longitudinal survey of income-poverty dynamics, which expands on previous efforts undertaken in Pakistan during the late 1980s and early 1990s.

The RHPS provides a unique panel dataset that expands the opportunities to analyze rural welfare across multiple dimensions. Unlike many other surveys conducted in Pakistan, the RHPS collects comprehensive information on agricultural production, including detailed information on inputs, outputs, and expenditures at the crop and plot level. These data allow for in-depth study of farming systems, rural factor markets, nonfarm linkages, and farm household behavior at a micro level. The RHPS also collects

---

1   Since 1998/1999 the name has been changed from the Household Income and Expenditure Survey to the Household Integrated Economic Survey. The Federal Bureau of Statistics was renamed the Pakistan Bureau of Statistics in 2013. In this book, we use the acronym *HIES* to refer to both the previous Household Income and Expenditure Surveys and the renamed Household Integrated Economic Survey.

gender-disaggregated data from multiple sources within the household, including, but not limited to, the female spouse of the household head. Topics covered include educational attainment, health status, mobility, employment, and social connectivity, all of which allow for the study of gender roles in farm households, markets, and rural communities. Finally, the RHPS is designed to measure poverty as a multifaceted issue by including not only consumption and expenditure variables but also measures of insecurity, powerlessness, exclusion, and aspirations. Similarly, the RHPS collects data on conflict, governance, and political participation that allow for in-depth analysis of the economic and social consequences of the current political and security situation.

Throughout the book, the RHPS is referred to by year and round and cited as "IFPRI/IDS (various years)." Where relevant, reference to the 2012 RHPS includes mention of the specific survey round from which the data were drawn. Note, however, that the RHPS is not a nationally representative household survey, so caution is always advised in interpreting both data and analysis presented in the book.

Layout of the Book

This book proceeds as follows. The first section introduces the topics of food security, rural development, and agriculture in Pakistan, placing them in the context of the country's history. Chapter 2 introduces Pakistan's agricultural sector, addressing its agroclimatic diversity, the composition and growth of the agricultural sector, drivers of the growth of agricultural productivity, and the persistent challenges posed by land tenure patterns and landholding fragmentation. The analysis helps to explain how the patterns and trends in public investments, technological change, and market expansion influence national and local trajectories in growth, development, and poverty reduction. Chapter 3 turns to the human dimensions of rural development in Pakistan with an in-depth analysis of consumption, nutrition, and poverty trends. The analysis highlights not only the lack of substantive progress on poverty reduction but also the fundamental issue of whether poverty and poverty trends are being measured accurately and are informing policy decisions effectively. The critical role of food security in defining and shaping the outcomes of poverty is also highlighted.

The second section focuses on the role of major agricultural inputs and markets in agricultural production. Chapter 4 provides an in-depth look at water in Pakistan, particularly the supply and management of scarce groundwater and surface water resources in the Indus Basin Irrigation System

(IBIS)—the world's largest contiguous irrigation system and the lifeline of Pakistan's agricultural sector. IBIS faces major challenges: insufficient investment in infrastructure and management; controversial water allocation across provinces, communities, and farms; competition over water use for agriculture, industry, urban consumption, and energy; diminishing water supply in many regions; and fluctuations in water supply resulting from short-term variability of rainfall and long-term climate change. These issues demand that particular attention be given to both (1) the effect of overutilization of finite groundwater resources on agricultural productivity, and (2) the costs and benefits of major infrastructure investments, such as the Diamer-Bhasha Dam. Findings provide a complex but insightful picture of the economic trade-offs of alternative policies and investments designed to improve the efficiency and management of Pakistan's groundwater and surface water resources.

Chapter 5 analyzes Pakistan's seed system—an important topic given that seed is the very embodiment of technological change in agriculture. The legislative and institutional framework governing seed provision, cultivar improvement, and biotechnology in Pakistan is limiting the continuous flow of good-quality planting material and new technological options to farmers, with significant implications for efforts to enhance on-farm productivity. As several new policy initiatives slowly wind their way through government, more attention is needed to strengthen not only the wider policy framework but also the rules, regulations, and organizational capacities required to improve farmers' access to quality seed and to encourage appropriate roles for both the public and the private sectors in Pakistan's seed system.

Chapter 6 addresses a closely related topic, the architecture and performance of Pakistan's fertilizer industry. Valued at an estimated PKR (Pakistani rupees) 336 billion in 2011/2012 (US$3.76 billion), the industry has been operating at about 75 percent of capacity in recent years, while enjoying subsidies on both production and distribution that total approximately PKR 64 billion (US$0.72 billion).[2] Estimates of the impact of several alternative policy scenarios, including reductions in fertilizer production subsidies that are allocated through the pricing of natural gas, suggest that there is need for a far-reaching reform agenda that includes withdrawal of subsidies and increased reliance on market signals to encourage higher-capacity utilization, competition, and more balanced fertilizer application by farmers.

---

2   The exchange rate for fiscal year 2012 was US$1 = PKR 89.34, calculated based on International Monetary Fund data (IMF 2014).

From natural resources and input markets, Chapter 7 moves to markets and trade, particularly with respect to wheat, Pakistan's primary food staple. The Government of Pakistan has long played a role in Pakistan's agricultural commodity markets, to ensure affordable prices of food staples to consumers, encourage domestic production, and limit the impacts of price volatility on the poor. While the economic reforms mentioned earlier have eliminated many of Pakistan's more traditional market intervention mechanisms, the government continues to use exchange rate, trade, and agricultural pricing policies to manage agricultural price incentives. Estimates of the impact of nominal and effective rates of protection—inclusive of the effects of input fertilizer and irrigation subsidies—on agricultural price incentives demonstrate that most major crops continue to face implicit, though somewhat decreasing, taxation that still favors the industrial sector over agriculture. The discussion focuses on pricing policies for wheat, the major staple crop, and on alternatives to reduce the costs of wheat price stabilization.

The third section expands beyond agriculture to explore dimensions of human capital formation, public goods provision, and governance in the wider rural economy, all of which play a critical role in the well-being of the rural population. Chapter 8 first takes up the topic with an exploration of five key elements of rural service provision: health and nutrition, education, electricity, water, and sanitation. An examination of provision of these five services in rural Pakistan highlights the tremendous need for improvement, particularly with respect to the governance and implementation. Chapter 9 explores these issues further with a discussion of the likely influence on the rural economy of the 18th Amendment, devolution, and greater local governance. In its recent history, Pakistan has experienced several rounds of decentralization and devolution (and bouts of recentralization) that, with widely varying degrees of success, have dispersed central government responsibilities and transferred authority, accountability, and decision making on financial and administrative matters to provincial and local governments. The 18th Amendment, promulgated in 2010, represents the most far-reaching decentralization initiative in Pakistan's history. The chapter examines the processes that followed from the 18th Amendment and assesses how reforms have affected subnational autonomy, capacity, and accountability; shifted government expenditures; and changed the perception of public services.

In this analysis of economic and social well-being, particular attention must be given to the issue of gender inequality in Pakistan, as we do in Chapter 10. On all counts, Pakistan performs poorly with respect to gender equality, women's empowerment, and any number of other gender-related indicators. But few studies of Pakistan actually measure the multiple dimensions along which women are marginalized or disenfranchised, particularly in the country's expansive rural areas. The chapter examines women's control and influence over individual and household decisions—which is synthesized into an Index for Women's Empowerment in Agriculture—and reveals some surprising insights and sets a baseline for measuring progress achieved through economic and social policy initiatives designed to address the long-standing neglect of women in Pakistan.

Adding to the richness of these analyses, Chapter 11 frames the economic behavior of Pakistan's rural population in terms of aspirations, that is, the goals that people set and attempt to achieve. Aspirations are important to gain an understanding of the opportunities that exist to break the poverty cycle—opportunities that are often closely associated with poverty-reduction strategies, policies, and investments. Aspirations are also important to gain an understanding of an individual's willingness to take advantage of these opportunities, which is itself a function of the underlying social and psychological dimensions of human economic behavior. Given that one of the largest demographic groups in Pakistan is rural youth, an insight into individual aspirations reveals much about the future of the rural economy. The analysis focuses not only on the challenging question of measurement but also on absolute and relative aspiration levels in rural Pakistan, the cognitive processes and external factors that shape individual aspirations, the policies and institutions that might raise aspirations, and the potential benefits of higher aspiration levels. Findings point to specific subpopulations in Pakistan that are particularly vulnerable to aspiration-induced poverty traps, and they associate aspirations with a range of productivity-enhancing agricultural practices, as well as nonfarm rural enterprise activity. The analysis suggests some leverage points through which policy could increase aspirations and encourage greater human, social, and economic development in rural Pakistan.

The fourth section investigates wider perspectives on the economy to gain a better understanding of the long-term future impacts of policy on agriculture and the rural sector. To accomplish this, Chapter 12 uses a data-intensive economy-wide modeling approach to shed light on how Pakistan's economy functions and to simulate the effects of alternative policies and investments on incomes and poverty. The analysis reveals the weak contribution of Pakistan's rural nonfarm economy to the country's ongoing structural change process, which has been a significant factor in the rural economy's poor performance in recent years. The analysis then examines the structure of the rural nonfarm economy and presents simulations that explore the implications of growth in both the agricultural and rural nonfarm sectors for the rural poor. The results suggest that while growth in agriculture is still the most effective means of improving the welfare of Pakistan's poorest rural households, the pro-poor contribution of the rural nonfarm economy—especially through rural agro-processing—cannot be overlooked.

Chapter 13 concludes the book with reflections on the prospects for improving food security, reducing poverty, and fostering economic growth in Pakistan. The chapter reiterates the common argument that underlies the chapters in the book: given the social and economic structure of Pakistan, a vibrant agricultural sector is essential for improving the welfare of the rural poor and for realizing overall growth and poverty reduction. Drawing on the evidence presented in the preceding chapters, the chapter proposes a bold policy reform agenda that follows from this.

This book covers a vast amount of analytical territory because a broad understanding of agriculture's many components is necessary to reverse the trend toward slowing growth and continuing high levels of food insecurity and poverty. Much work remains to be done in Pakistan to meet the pressing needs of the country's agricultural sector and its rural population. The task of designing legislation, regulations, and ordinances requires excruciating attention to detail. The work required to implement a reform agenda is even more challenging—it is a long and arduous process to move a good idea into proposal preparation for the Planning Commission, or to ensure that funds are disbursed for public projects transparently and effectively. Work is also needed to build an effective partnership with private-sector and civil-society actors that strengthens and sustains their contribution to agriculture's growth and wider economic development. Nevertheless, with careful attention to monitoring and evaluation of the intended and unintended consequences of policy change, Pakistan faces great scope for change. And by seizing opportunities presented by major structural changes such as the 18th Amendment to the constitution, Pakistan has a chance to reexamine and rationalize roles and responsibilities pertaining to agriculture and food security at the ministerial, secretariat, and governmental levels. We believe that this book provides new insights into how economic growth, poverty reduction, and welfare improvement in Pakistan can be achieved through pragmatic and evidence-based policies and investments in food security, rural development, and agriculture.

References

Adelman, I. 1984. "Beyond Export-Led Growth." *World Development* 12 (9): 937–949.

Ali, M., and M. Ashraf. 2007. *Strategic Direction for Agriculture Research in Pakistan.* Islamabad/ Manila: Pakistan Agricultural Research Council/Asian Development Bank.

Ali, M., and D. Byerlee. 2002. "Productivity Growth and Resource Degradation in Pakistan's Punjab: A Decomposition Analysis." *Economic Development and Cultural Change* 50 (4): 839–863.

Anderson, J. R. 1999. "Institutional Reforms for Getting an Agricultural Knowledge System to Play Its Role in Economic Growth." *Pakistan Development Review* 38 (4): 333–350.

Binswanger, H. P. 1994. "Agricultural and Rural Development: Painful Lessons." *Agrekon* 33 (4): 158–166.

Briscoe, J., U. Qamar, M. Contijoch, P. Amir, and D. Blackmore. 2005. *Pakistan's Water Economy: Running Dry.* Washington, DC/Islamabad: World Bank.

Byerlee, D., and T. Husain. 1992. *Farming Systems of Pakistan: Diagnosing Priorities for Agricultural Research.* Lahore: Vanguard Books.

CERP (Center for Economic Research in Pakistan). 2013. *Data Resources.* http://cerp.org.pk/ dataresources/. Accessed April 2015.

Cheema, I. A. 2005. *A Profile of Poverty in Pakistan.* Islamabad: Centre for Research on Poverty Reduction and Income Distribution, Planning Commission, Ministry of Planning, Government of Pakistan.

CIMMYT (International Maize and Wheat Improvement Center). 1989. *Wheat Research and Development in Pakistan.* Mexico, DF: CIMMYT.

Dorosh, P. A., M. K. Niazi, and H. Nazli. 2003. "Distributional Impacts of Agricultural Growth in Pakistan: A Multiplier Analysis." *Pakistan Development Review* 42 (3): 249–275.

Evenson, R. E., and D. Gollin. 2003. "Assessing the Impact of the Green Revolution, 1960 to 2000." *Science* 300 (5620): 758–762.

Fan, S., P. Hazell, and S. Thorat. 1999. *Linkages between Government Spending, Growth and Poverty in Rural India.* IFPRI Research Report 110. Washington, DC: International Food Policy Research Institute.

Farooq, S. 2014. *The Rural Non-farm Economy, Livelihood Strategies and Household Welfare in Rural Pakistan.* Technical Paper for the Second Asian Development Bank Asian Think Tank Development Forum. http://www.adb-asianthinktanks.org/sites/all/libraries/researchpapers/ TheRuralNonfarmEconomyLivelihoodStrategiesHouseholdWelfareinRuralPakistanfarooq .pdf. Accessed July 2015.

Gazdar, H. 2009. *The Fourth Round, and Why They Fight On: An Essay on the History of Land and Reform in Pakistan*. Karachi: Collective for Social Science Research.

GoP (Government of Pakistan). Various years. *Federal Budget Publications: Federal Budget Details of Demands for Grants and Appropriations 2015–16 (Current and Development Expenditures)*. Islamabad: Ministry of Finance.

———. Various years. *Pakistan Economic Survey*. Islamabad: Ministry of Finance, Government of Pakistan.

———. 1988. *Report of the National Commission on Agriculture*. Islamabad: Ministry of Food and Agriculture.

———. 1991. *National Agricultural Policy*. Islamabad: Ministry of Food, Agriculture and Cooperatives.

———. 2000. *Agricultural Census*. Islamabad: Agricultural Census Wing, Pakistan Bureau of Statistics.

———. 2004. *Agricultural Perspective and Policy*. Islamabad: Ministry of Food, Agriculture and Livestock. January.

———. 2007. *Pakistan in the 21st Century: Vision 2030*. Islamabad: Planning Commission, Government of Pakistan.

———. 2009. *Census of Manufacturing Industries 2005–06*. Islamabad: Statistics Division, Government of Pakistan.

———. 2010. *Agricultural Census*. Islamabad: Agricultural Census Wing, Pakistan Bureau of Statistics. http://www.pbs.gov.pk/content/agricultural-census-wing.

———. 2011a. *National Nutrition Survey 2011*. Islamabad: Planning Commission, Government of Pakistan.

———. 2011b. *Household Integrated Economic Survey 2010–11*. Islamabad: Pakistan Bureau of Statistics.

———. 2014. "Pakistan: Agriculture and Food Security Policy (Draft)." Islamabad: Ministry of National Food Security and Research, Government of Pakistan.

Green, J. W. 1957. "Rural Community Development in Pakistan: The Village AID Program." *Community Development Review* 6 (September).

Haggblade, S., P. Hazell, and T. Reardon. 2010. "The Rural Non-farm Economy: Prospects for Growth and Poverty Reduction." *World Development* 38 (10): 1429–1441.

Hazell, P. B. R. 2010. "The Asian Green Revolution." In *Proven Successes in Agricultural Development: A Technical Compendium to Millions Fed,* edited by D. J. Spielman, and R. Pandya-Lorch. Washington, DC: IFPRI

Heston, A., and D. Kumar. 1983. "The Persistence of Land Fragmentation in Peasant Agriculture: An Analysis of South Asian Cases." *Explorations in Economic History* 20: 199–220.

IFPRI/IDS (International Food Policy Research Institute/Innovative Development Strategies). 2012. Pakistan Rural Household Panel Survey 2012 dataset. Washington, DC/Islamabad, Pakistan: IFPRI/IDS. Round 1: http://dx.doi.org/10.7910/DVN/28558. Round 1.5: http://dx.doi.org/10.7910/DVN/T9GGYA. Accessed July 22, 2016.

IMF (International Monetary Fund). 2014. International Financial Statistics database. http://elibrary-data.imf.org/DataExplorer.aspx. Accessed October 2014.

IRRI (International Rice Research Institute). 2013. "Pakistan." http://irri.org/our-work/locations/pakistan. Accessed September 2014.

Johnston, B., and J. Mellor. 1961. "The Role of Agriculture in Economic Development." *American Economic Review* 51 (4): 566–593.

Kapur, D. 2010. *Diaspora Development and Democracy: The Domestic Impact of International Migration from India.* Princeton, NJ: Princeton University Press.

Krishna, R. 1963. "Farm Supply Response in India-Pakistan: A Case Study of the Punjab Region." *The Economic Journal* 73 (291): 477–487.

Lanjouw, J. O., and P. Lanjouw. 2001. "The Rural Non-farm Sector: Issues and Evidence from Developing Countries." *Agricultural Economics* 26: 1–23.

Lewis, W. A. 1954. "Economic Development with Unlimited Supplies of Labor." *Manchester School of Economic and Social Studies* 22 (2): 139–191.

Lipton, M., with R. Longhurst. 1989. *New Seeds and Poor People.* London: Unwin Hymen.

LUMS (Lahore University of Management Sciences). 2015. List of Datasets dataset. http://dru.lums.edu.pk/dslist.php. Accessed April 2015.

Murgai, R., M. Ali, and D. Byerlee. 2001. "Productivity Growth and Sustainability in Post-Green Revolution Agriculture: The Case of the Indian and Pakistan Punjabs." *The World Bank Research Observer* 16 (2): 199–218.

Nabi, I., N. Hamid, and S. Zahid. 1986. *The Agrarian Economy of Pakistan: Issues and Policies.* Karachi: Oxford University Press.

Nazli, H., and S. H. Haider. 2012. *Pakistan Rural Household Panel Survey 2012 (Round 1)— Methodology and Community Characteristics.* PSSP Working Paper 007. Washington, DC: International Food Policy Research Institute.

NSPP (Senior Management Wing, National Management College, National School of Public Policy). 2012. *Strategic Appraisal of 18th Amendment: Federal/Provincial Roles and Impact on Service Delivery.* Lahore: NSPP.

PARC (Pakistan Agricultural Research Council). 2010. "Country Study on the National Agricultural Research System (NARS) in Pakistan—An Analysis of System Diversity." Mimeo. Islamabad: PARC.

PBS (Pakistan Bureau of Statistics). 2015a. "Household Integrated Economic Survey (HIES) 2011–12." http://www.pbs.gov.pk/content/household-integrated-economic-survey-hies-2011–12. Accessed April 2015.

———. 2015b. "Pakistan Social and Living Standards Measurement (2004–2015)." http://www.pbs.gov.pk/content/pakistan-social-and-living-standards-measurement. Accessed April 2015.

PIDE (Pakistan Institute of Development Economics). 2013. Data Bank. http://www.pide.org.pk/index.php/facilities/data-bank. Accessed May 31, 2016.

Qureshi, M. G., and S. K. Qureshi. 2004. "Impact of Changing Profile of Rural Land Market in Pakistan on Resource Allocation and Equity." *Pakistan Development Review* 43 (4): 471–492.

Qureshi, S. 2001. *An Overview of Government's Poverty Alleviation Policies and Programmes.* MIMAP Technical Paper Series 12. Islamabad: Pakistan Institute of Development Economics.

Ranis, G., and J. C. Fei. 1961. "A Theory of Development." *American Economic Review* 51: 533–558.

Riaz, K. 2006. *Analyzing Success Stories in Pakistan Agriculture: Case Studies of Milk Processing, Tunnel Farming for Vegetables, and Citrus Marketing and Export Sectors.* Washington, DC: World Bank.

———. 2008. "A Case Study of Milk Processing Sector: The Idara-e-Kissan Cooperative." *Lahore Journal of Economics* 13 (1): 81–128.

Salam, A. 2012. *Review of Input and Output Policies for Cereals Production in Pakistan.* IFPRI Discussion Paper 01223. Washington, DC: International Food Policy Research Institute.

Singer, H. 1979. "Policy Implications of the Lima Target." *Industry and Development* 3: 17–23.

Start, D. 2001. "The Rise and Fall of the Rural Non-farm Economy: Poverty Impacts and Policy Options." *Development Policy Review* 19 (4): 491–505.

Vogel, S. J. 1994. "Structural Changes in Agriculture: Production Linkages and Agricultural Demand–Led Industrialization." *Oxford Economic Papers* 46 (1): 136–156.

von Grebmer, K., D. Headey, T. Olofinbiyi, D. Wiesmann, H. Fritschel, S. Yin, Y. Yohannes, C. Foley, C. von Oppeln, B. Iseli, and C. Bénéé. 2013. *Global Hunger Index 2013*. Washington, DC: International Food Policy Research Institute.

World Bank. 2004. *Rural Factor Markets Policy Reforms for Growth and Equity.* Report 30381-PK. Washington, DC: World Bank.

———. 2007. *Pakistan: Promoting Rural Growth and Poverty Reduction.* Report 39303-PK. Washington, DC: World Bank.

———. 2014. World Development Indicators Database. Washington, DC: The World Bank.

Annex A: Pakistan Rural Household Panel Survey

The demographic and socioeconomic data available in Pakistan have largely been generated by censuses and household surveys. Table A1.1 provides a list of prominent household-level datasets in Pakistan. Most of these surveys are cross-sectional, in the form of district level or provincial aggregates and therefore do not provide an opportunity to study socioeconomic dynamics and trends over time. Such analyses are possible primarily through longitudinal surveys, which are costly both in terms of time and money. There is no publicly available panel dataset that provides up-to-date gender-disaggregated, individual-level data for rural Pakistan.

Tracking the same individuals over time through a panel enables researchers to account for time-invariant household- and individual-level characteristics, thereby providing an opportunity for causal analysis. The original Pakistan Rural Household Survey (PRHS) is the only known panel survey ever conducted on rural households in Pakistan. The survey was conducted by the International Food Policy Research Institute (IFPRI) from 1986 to 1991 and collected several rounds of panel data from 800 rural households, with extension of the survey subsequently conducted by the Pakistan Institute of Development Economics (PIDE) and the World Bank. More than a dozen PhD dissertations and more than 100 MSc and MPhil dissertations have been completed using this dataset. The PRHS is a rich resource for researchers, academics, and policy makers who are interested in empirical analyses on a wide range of research questions related to development issues in Pakistan.

In an effort to recapture the value of such surveys, a new panel survey—the Pakistan Rural Household Panel Survey (RHPS)—was conducted by IFPRI and Innovative Development Strategies (Pvt.) Ltd. (IDS), under the auspices of the Pakistan Strategy Support Program (PSSP) in 2012. The aim of the survey was to collect information on poverty dynamics and microlevel constraints on income generation and economic growth for rural households in Pakistan. The survey covers topics that are standard to most household income and expenditure surveys in developing countries, while extending its coverage to health and nutrition; agricultural production; natural resource management; gender and labor issues; and topics related to security, governance, and access to public services. The RHPS builds on several other panel surveys conducted in Pakistan. See Nazli and Haider (2012) for complete details.

The first RHPS round (referred to in subsequent chapters as "RHPS Round 1") was conducted in March 2012 in Punjab, Sindh, and KPK provinces. The sample universe of RHPS Round 1 included all households in rural

Punjab, Sindh, and KPK, although certain districts in KPK were not included for security reasons. Similarly, Balochistan and the Federally Administered Tribal Areas were dropped from the sampling frame for security reasons, while Gilgit-Baltistan—Pakistan's northernmost territory—was similarly excluded for logistical reasons. This round covered 2,090 households from 76 villages in 19 districts, 12 of which are in Punjab, 5 in Sindh, and 2 in KPK. A sample of households that participated in the earlier (1986–1991) PRHS were also traced to provide a basis for long-term assessment of family circumstances and poverty dynamics.

To ensure that the sampling frame captured Pakistan's rural population as adequately as possible, the RHPS uses data on enumeration blocks provided by the 1988 Population Census, as well as population projections to the year 2030, to identify revenue villages (*mouzas*) for possible inclusion in the sample. All enumeration blocks classified as "urban" in the 1998 population census were removed from consideration. In an effort to reduce the possible sampling of *mouzas* that were originally rural in 1998 but had become largely urban by 2011, all enumeration blocks where the projected population in 2011 exceeded 25,000 were also removed from consideration.

Next, the RHPS used a multistage, stratified sampling technique to capture variation in Pakistan's rural population. In the first stage, probability proportionate to size was used to select districts. This method ensures that districts with more rural households have a greater chance of being selected. The proportion of rural households in each province determined the number of districts chosen from the province. Across the three provinces, 19 districts were selected (12 from Punjab, 5 from Sindh, and 2 from KPK). In each district, 4 *mouzas* were selected, resulting in a total of 76 *mouzas*: 48 from Punjab, 20 from Sindh, and 8 from KPK. The equal probability systematic selection method was used so that *mouzas* with smaller populations had the same probability of being selected as highly populated *mouzas*. One enumeration block was randomly selected from each *mouza,* and a complete household listing was conducted to randomly select 28 households from each block. In the end, 2,124 households were randomly selected, and, with 34 refusals to participate, the final sample totaled 2,090 households.

In November 2012, a follow-up survey round (hereinafter referred to as "RHPS Round 1.5") was conducted on a subsample of households from the original 2,090 households. The subsample consisted of 981 households (47 percent of the original sample) that cultivated land at any point during the year prior to the survey. These households that were specifically engaged in production were surveyed with a questionnaire on agricultural production for each crop and for each individual plot under cultivation during the kharif 2011 and rabi 2011/2012 seasons. While the RHPS Round 1.5 sample is not representative of households engaged in agricultural production in Pakistan because it is extracted from a larger representative sample of rural households, it does capture a constructive level and degree of variation with which to conduct several analyses that are presented in subsequent chapters.

Subsequent rounds of the RHPS were conducted to build the panel further. Specifically, RHPS Round 2 was conducted from April to July 2013, followed by Round 3 from May to August 2014. Despite some attrition among respondents, the sample sizes for these rounds remained representative of the population of interest, with 2,002 and 1,876 households, respectively. In addition to the primary respondents for the household survey, a total of 3,254 women were interviewed for a module on "women's position and opinion" in RHPS Round 3. Respondents included not only the female household head or spouse of the head but also the eldest female and the youngest female over 15 years of age in the household.

In an effort to ensure broad access and use of the RHPS data among researchers and other interested stakeholders, IFPRI and IDS are making the data for successive rounds available in the public domain. At present RHPS Rounds 1 and 1.5 data from 2012 have been made available via IFPRI on the Harvard Dataverse, a global data sharing platform (see IFPRI/IDS 2012). Additional rounds will become available in due course.

TABLE A1.1 Prominent household-level datasets, Pakistan

	Survey	Organization	Years
1.	Labor Force Survey (LFS) **Note:** Started in 1963; revised in 1990; 1995; 2001/02; 2005.	Government of Pakistan; Federal Bureau of Statistics	2005–06 2006–07 2007–08 2008–09 2009–10 2010–11 2012–13
2.	Time Use Survey (TUS)	Government of Pakistan; Federal Bureau of Statistics	2007
3.	Household Integrated Economic Survey (HIES) **Note:** Started in 1963; revised in 1990; 1998/99	Government of Pakistan; Federal Bureau of Statistics	1990–91 1992–93 1993–94 1996–97
4.	Pakistan Integrated Household Survey (PIHS)	Government of Pakistan; Federal Bureau of Statistics; World Bank	1991 1995–96 1996–97
5.	Pakistan Integrated Household Survey(PIHS)–HIES **Note:** HIES integrated with PIHS in 1998/99 and 2001/02.	Government of Pakistan; Federal Bureau of Statistics	1998–99 2001–02
6.	Pakistan Socioeconomic Survey (PSES)	Pakistan Institute of Development Economics	1998–99
7.	Pakistan Social and Living Standards Measurement Survey–Household Integrated Economic Survey (PSLM-HIES) **Note:** HIES-PIHS was renamed PSLM-HIES in 2004	Government of Pakistan; Federal Bureau of Statistics	2004–05 2005–06 2007–08 2010–11 2011–12
8.	Pakistan Social and Living Standards Measurement Survey (PSLM)–Core Welfare Indicators Questionnaire	Government of Pakistan; Federal Bureau of Statistics	2004–05

Primary modules	Unit of analysis	Sample size (n)	Level
Household composition and demographics, activity of all household members (10 years and over), Underemployment, Paid employment, Occupational injuries and diseases, Unemployment	Household	32,744 32,778 36,272 36,400 36,400 36,464 35,488	National
Household information and demographics, Time-use pattern	Household	19,600	National
Household composition and demographics, Employment, Household expenditures (monthly/yearly; durable/nondurable), Assets, Transfers, Income, Land utilization, Crops harvested, Livestock, Labor, Revenues and expenses (mining, hotels and restaurants, transport, trade, construction); *submodules for agricultural and nonagricultural establishments*	Household	6,393 14,594 14,668 15,453	National
Household composition and demographics, Employment and income, Education, Expenditure, Health and child survival, Immunization, Consumption, Farming and livestock, Transfer and remittance, Migration, Marriage history, Housing, Household access to facilities, Facilities, Community and price survey instrument	Household	4,794 12,381 12,622	National
Household information, Occupation, Education, Household expenditure, Income, Transfers, Financial assets and liabilities, Land utilization and crop harvesting, Livestock/poultry/forestry, Immunization, Pregnancy history, Family planning, Pre- and postnatal care; *submodules for agricultural and nonagricultural establishments*	Household	16,341 15,807	National
Household composition, Labor force and employment, Income and expenditure, Birth history of women ages 15–49 years, Nutritional and immunization status of children and pregnant and lactating women, Health and healthcare status, Housing conditions, Assets; *submodules for agricultural and nonagricultural establishments*	Household	3,564	National
Household composition and demographics, Employment, Household expenditures (monthly/yearly; durable/nondurable), Assets, Transfers, Income, Land utilization, Crops harvested, Livestock, Labor, Revenues and expenses (mining, hotels and restaurants, transport, trade, construction), Immunization, Maternal history, Family planning, Women in decision making, Pre- and postnatal care; *submodules for agricultural and nonagricultural establishments*		14,708	National
Household information, Employment, Education, Health, Assets, Diarrhea, Immunization, Pregnancy and maternal history, Pre- and postnatal care, Housing, Consumption expenditure, Household borrowing, Facilities and services		77,000	District

(continued)

TABLE A1.1 Prominent household-level datasets, Pakistan *(continued)*

	Survey	Organization	Years
9.	Pakistan Panel Survey (PPS)	International Food Policy Research Institute	1986–91 *(12–15 rounds over July 1986– September 1991)*
10.	Pakistan Rural Household Survey (PRHS)	Pakistan Institute of Development Economics; World Bank	2001 2004 *(continuation of PPS)*
11.	Pakistan Panel Household Survey (PPHS)	Pakistan Institute of Development Economics; World Bank	2010 *(Round 3 of PRHS)*
12.	National Nutrition Survey	Pakistan Institute of Development Economics	2001–02
13.	Pakistan Demographic Survey (PDS)	Government of Pakistan; Federal Bureau of Statistics	2003
14.	Pakistan Reproductive Health and Family Planning Survey (PRHFPS)	National Institute of Population Studies	2000
15.	Child Labor Survey (CLS)	Government of Pakistan; Federal Bureau of Statistics; International Labor Organization (ILO)	1995–96 1997–98
16.	Pakistan Fertility and Family Planning Survey (PFFPS)	National Institute of Population Studies	1996–97
17.	Status of Women Reproductive Health and Family Planning Survey (SWRHFPS)	National Institute of Population Studies	2003
18.	Pakistan Demographic and Health Survey (PDHS)	United States Agency for International Development (USAID; National Institute of Population Studies (NIPS)	1990–91 2006–07 2012–13

Source: PBS (2015a, 2015b); PIDE (2013); LUMS (2015); CERP (2013).

Note: The sample sizes stated in the table may vary between different data sources.

[a] Rural areas of four districts; Balochistan excluded; [b] Rural areas of 16 districts in round 1 and 10 districts in round 2; National (Round 1); [c] Rural and urban areas of 16 districts; National.

Primary modules	Unit of analysis	Sample size (n)	Level
Household composition, Land ownership and tenure arrangements, Crop production and distribution, Farm and nonfarm expenditures, Labor use, Assets, Credit, Livestock/poultry, Fertility, Health and nutrition, Income and transfers, Anthropometrics	Household	800	See note[a]
Household composition, Education, Agriculture, Nonfarm enterprise, Employment, Migration, Credit	Household	2,721 1,907	See note[b]
Household composition, Education, Agriculture, Nonfarm enterprise, Employment, Migration, Consumption, Health, Shocks and coping strategies, Security, Subjective welfare, Assets, Business and enterprise, Transfers	Household	4,142	See note[c]
Household demographic and socioeconomic information, Sanitation, Knowledge and practice on iodine deficiency disorders (IDD) and iodized salt consumption, Nutrition and health information (mother and preschool children), Clinical examination and anthropometric measurements (mother and preschool children)	Household	10,656	National
Household composition and detailed demographics	Household	30,947	National
Household composition, Household conditions, Female questionnaire: Reproduction, Adolescents, Healthcare during last pregnancy, Delivery postnatal care and breastfeeding, Current health status, Contraception, Fertility preference, Socioeconomic factors	Household	6,857	National
Household composition and demographic information, Household activities, Current activities of persons (15 and over), Current activity of each child (5–14 years), Perception of parents/guardians, Children questionnaire (5–14 years), Household income and expenditure, Housing conditions	Household	10,460 18,960	National
Household composition, Housing conditions; Female questionnaire: Education, Reproduction, Contraception, Pregnancy and breast-feeding, Marriage, Fertility preferences, Socioeconomic factors	Household	7,325	National
Household composition, Education, Housing conditions, Female questionnaire: Reproduction, Women's status, Reproductive health, Contraception, Fertility preferences	Household	9,401	National
Household composition, Facilities, Household characteristics, Fertility levels, Reproduction, Marriage, Fertility preferences, Awareness and use of family-planning methods, Child feeding practices, Childhood mortality, Maternal and child health, Nutritional status, awareness and attitudes regarding HIV/AIDS, Knowledge about tuberculosis/hepatitis, Domestic violence	Household	8,019 102,060 13,944	National

Chapter 2

AGRICULTURE, LAND, AND PRODUCTIVITY IN PAKISTAN

Sohail J. Malik, Shujat Ali, Khalid Riaz, Edward Whitney,
Mehrab Malek, and Ahmad Waqas

Introduction

Much of Pakistan's comparative advantage in agriculture resides in its rich natural resource endowment. Pakistan is home to the high mountains of the Karakoram and Hindu Kush ranges of the Himalaya Mountains, and entire civilizations have been fed by their melting glacial waters and rich alluvial soils for millennia. Pakistan boasts the world's largest gravity-fed irrigation system—a network of rivers, barrages, and canals that make up the Indus Basin Irrigation System (IBIS)—as well as the world's largest earthen dam at Tarbela, which provides nearly a quarter of the country's electrical power.

But agriculture in Pakistan also faces growing water scarcity and degradation of its natural resource base. The country ranges across vast stretches of arid and semiarid lands, where water constraints mean that agriculture is largely driven by the low-input, low-yield production of crops and livestock. Approximately 92 percent of the country's land area is located in semiarid to arid agroclimatic zones (Pinckney 1989). Major portions of the country are constrained by decreasing soil fertility, soil salinization, waterlogging, erosion, and a host of other challenges. The low potential for expanding agricultural production into these natural resource–constrained areas implies that agricultural production in the short to medium term will have to come from intensification on existing agricultural land.

There is huge potential for intensifying agricultural production in Pakistan through technical change and improvements in the ways in which inputs are used. Much can be gained just by efforts to close the large gaps between the potential (controlled-experimental) yields, the achievable (progressive-farmer) yields, and the national yield averages (for example, PARC 2011). Unfortunately, yield gap reductions and annual output targets for a few major crops have been the mainstay of agricultural policy analysis in Pakistan, ultimately painting an overly simplified picture of the potential in Pakistan's agricultural sector. Rarely do these analyses take into account the high variability in Pakistan in terms of agroclimatic conditions, soil quality, water resource availability, landholding sizes and tenure status, input and output market development, and access to public services and infrastructure. This variability—and the potential for growth and development that this variation offers Pakistan's wider economy—is generally masked in the aggregate statistics on agriculture production in Pakistan, and insufficient consideration of these factors lies at the heart of some of the more worrisome trends presented in this chapter.

Thus, this chapter looks beyond the aggregate statistics to provide a more nuanced understanding of the agricultural sector's diversity, its contribution to Pakistan's economic growth and development, and the underlying constraints to accelerating its growth. The chapter proceeds as follows. The first section describes Pakistan's agroclimatic diversity. The second section looks at the agricultural sector, its subsectors, and trends in agricultural-sector growth. The third section examines the total factor productivity trends and analyzes crop-specific growth trends to gain an understanding of why agricultural growth has been less than optimal. The fourth section draws attention to the centrality of land tenureship and landholding size in the discussion of agricultural-sector growth. The last section presents concluding remarks.

Pakistan's Agroclimatic Diversity: A Changing Landscape

Spatial and temporal variations in temperature, moisture, soil quality, slope, and other factors shape both land use and agricultural livelihood strategies in Pakistan. While several agroclimatic classification systems exist for Pakistan, the most widely cited classification is based on nine zones, developed by Pinckney (1989).[1] These zones capture the closely related dimensions of (1) geographic and climatic conditions, including access to surface water or groundwater irrigation, (2) the farming systems and practices employed by farmers who work the land, and (3) the cultivation of crops associated with the two main agricultural seasons. These seasons are the monsoon-fed

---

1   In keeping with Pinckney's (1989) analysis, we use the term *agroclimatic zone* throughout this chapter. Note, however, that agroecological zones, as opposed to agroclimatic zones, are defined on the basis of soil and landform characteristics in addition to climatic characteristics. Together, these characteristics holistically determine land suitability and potential production and environmental impact, and, by definition, they allow for the coexistence of several agroclimatic divisions within the same agroecological zone (FAO 1996).

kharif season, which occurs from April to November and supports cotton, rice, maize, sorghum, and sugarcane cultivation, and the drier, cooler rabi season, which occurs from November to April and sustains wheat, barley, and oilseeds production. For the purposes of this book, the main agroclimatic zones are defined as Barani Punjab, Mixed Punjab, Low-Intensity Punjab, Rice/Wheat Punjab, and Cotton/Wheat Punjab; Cotton/Wheat Sindh and Rice/Other Sindh; Southern KPK and Foothills/Plains KPK; and Balochistan (see Annex A, Table A2.1 for a mapping of districts to agroecological zones).[2]

The relative sizes of these zones in terms of the land area and cultivated acreage, the distribution of rural population, and the level of urban agglomerations illustrates the wide diversity found in Pakistan. Three of the agroclimatic zones in Punjab encompass the most urbanized areas, with rural populations ranging from only 3.1 percent to 19.8 percent. Two-thirds of the country's cultivated area is also situated in three of the five agroclimatic zones of Punjab. Further, Sindh and Punjab together account for 87 percent of cropped area (Table 2.1; Figure 2.1). Cotton/Wheat Punjab is the largest zone, followed by Rice/Wheat Punjab and Mixed Punjab. These are followed by Low-Intensity Punjab, Cotton/Wheat Sindh, and Foothills/Plains KPK.

The wide variation in the acreage and output under each of the five major crops (wheat, rice, maize, cotton, and sugarcane) and a category that aggregates all the other cereals for the year 2010/2011 in each of these agroclimatic zones is highlighted in Table 2.2.[3] These data help define the structure of the acreage and output of these crops in Pakistan.

Perhaps not surprisingly, the Cotton/Wheat Punjab agroclimatic zone is the largest producer of wheat and cotton in terms of both acreage and output (Table 2.2). Rice/Wheat Punjab dominates rice production, accounting for nearly half of total rice acreage and nearly 45 percent of output. Barani Punjab is the leading producer of other cereals. Mixed Punjab produces nearly 30 percent of all sugarcane, grown on nearly the same percentage of acreage. KPK Plains/Foothills accounts for 40 percent of all maize acreage and

---

2   This classification is based on areas that are more suitable for rice cultivation and those that are better suited to cotton growth. The cotton- or rice-specific zones include Rice/Wheat Punjab, Cotton/Wheat Punjab, Cotton/Wheat Sindh, and Rice/Other Sindh. Mixed Punjab zone contains a balanced allocation between rice and cotton. Barani areas include the rainfed regions of Punjab and are classified as a separate zone. Low-Intensity Punjab is termed as such due to the nature of irrigation facilities in the area and the resultant low cropping intensity. Southern KPK, Plains KPK, and Balochistan constitute independent zones, as they contribute only a minuscule percentage of the aggregate wheat production (Pinckney 1989; Arif and Ahmad 2001).

3   The existing literature on Pakistan lists four major crops (GoP 1988); as we show later in this chapter, in recent years, maize has emerged as the fifth major crop.

TABLE 2.1 Area, acreage under cultivation, rural population, and urban agglomeration rank of agroclimatic zones, 2010

Zone	Total area (km²)	Area in zone (% of total)	Area under cultivation (million ha)	Area cultivated (% of area cultivated)	Rural population (% of total)	Urban agglomeration index rank
Barani Punjab	23,205	3.02	609	3.8	19.8	3
Rice/Wheat Punjab	28,945	3.76	3,013	18.8	3.1	1
Mixed Punjab	34,866	4.53	2,213	13.8	7.9	2
Cotton/Wheat Punjab	66,758	8.68	4,342	27.1	50.1	4
Low-Intensity Punjab	52,890	6.87	1,694	10.6	53.5	5
Cotton/Wheat Sindh	79,356	10.31	1,284	8.0	75.0	8
Rice/Other Sindh	61,589	8.01	931	5.8	64.2	6
KPK	77,038	10.01	1,351	8.4	71.6	7
Balochistan	344,712	44.81	611	3.8	93.3	9

Source: Authors, based on data from GoP (2010a, 2010b).

Notes: KPK = Khyber Pakhtunkhwa; km = kilometers; ha = hectares.

FIGURE 2.1 Agroclimatic zones' share of total cultivated area, 2010/2011

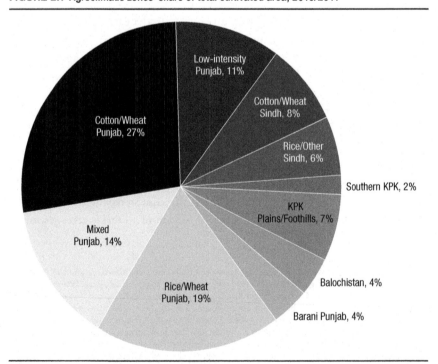

Source: Authors, based on data from GoP (2010a, 2010b).

Note: KPK = Khyber Pakhtunkhwa.

TABLE 2.2 Share of acreage and output of leading crops by agroclimatic zone (%), 2010/2011

Agroclimatic zone	Wheat		Rice		Maize		Cotton		Other cereals		Sugarcane	
	Acreage	Output	Acreage	Output	Acreage	Output	Acreage	Output	Acreage	Output	Acreage	Output
Barani Punjab	5.2	2.8	0.1	0	8.4	3.4	0	0	22.8	24.2	0	0
Rice/Wheat Punjab	18.7	18.5	49.1	44.2	5.8	7.8	0.7	0.3	13.5	13.9	11.6	9.7
Mixed Punjab	14.1	15.2	12.8	9.6	17.6	28.1	7.6	4.7	6.6	6.7	29.6	28.7
Cotton/Wheat Punjab	23.1	25.8	10	12.4	21.6	38.9	62.2	54.8	8.7	8.8	18	20.6
Low-Intensity Punjab	13.7	13.1	2.4	3.1	0.7	0.3	11.3	8.6	15.4	9.9	7.3	7.2
Total Punjab	*74.8*	*75.4*	*74.4*	*69.3*	*54.1*	*78.5*	*81.8*	*68.4*	*67*	*63.5*	*66.5*	*66.2*
Cotton/Wheat Sindh	7.8	11	5.2	9.2	0.2	0.0	13.9	24.4	2.8	3.1	9.7	10.3
Rice/Other Sindh	5.2	6.3	10.3	17	0.1	0.0	3.1	6.5	5	4.4	14.3	15.7
Total Sindh	*13.0*	*17.3*	*15.5*	*26.2*	*0.3*	*0.0*	*17.0*	*30.9*	*7.8*	*7.5*	*24.0*	*26.0*
Southern KPK	2.3	1.1	0.4	0.4	4.5	1.6	0.0	0.0	6.7	6.7	2.4	2
KPK Plains/Foothills	5.9	3.4	1.6	1.3	40.5	19.6	0.0	0.0	5.1	6.1	6.9	5.6
Total KPK	*8.2*	*4.5*	*2*	*1.7*	*45*	*21.2*	*0*	*0.0*	*11.8*	*12.8*	*9.3*	*7.6*
Total Balochistan	*3.9*	*2.9*	*8.2*	*2.8*	*0.6*	*0.2*	*1.2*	*0.6*	*13.3*	*16.2*	*0.1*	*0.1*
Total Overall (%)	100	100	100	100	100	100	100	100	100	100	100	100
Total Overall (quantity)[a]	8,793	24,833	2,333	4,696	940	3,485	2,686	1,947	302	221	944	52,853

Source: Authors, based on data from GoP (2013).

Note: KPK = Khyber Pakhtunkhwa.

[a] "Total quantity" units are thousands of acres for acreage, and thousands of metric tons for output.

TABLE 2.3 Variability of crop yields in selected cereal crops by agroclimatic zone, 2010/2011

Agroclimatic zone	Wheat (kg/ha)	Rice (kg/ha)	Maize (kg/ha)
Barani Punjab	1,500	1,574	1,483
Rice/Wheat Punjab	2,802	1,814	4,976
Mixed Punjab	3,033	1,516	5,921
Cotton/Wheat Punjab	3,153	2,491	6,671
Low-Intensity Punjab	2,684	2,544	1,713
Cotton/Wheat Sindh	3,978	3,556	667
Rice/Other Sindh	3,400	3,330	571
Southern KPK	1,275	1,760	1,354
KPK Plains/Foothills	1,634	1,685	1,795
Balochistan	2,140	683	1,075
Coefficient of Variation (%)	31.39	38.16	77.35
Mean	2,584	2,088	2,721
SD	811.2	796.8	2104.7

Source: Authors, based on data from GoP (2013).

Note: KPK = Khyber Pakhtunkhwa.

yet contributes only 20 percent of total maize output, while Cotton/Wheat Punjab produces 39 percent of all maize output with only 20 percent of total maize acreage.

There is considerable variation in crop yields by agroclimatic zone (Table 2.3). For example, wheat yields were highest in Cotton/Wheat Sindh and Rice/Other Sindh, despite the fact that these are not the largest zones for these crops. Maize yields were highest in Cotton/Wheat Punjab, Mixed Punjab, and Rice/Wheat Punjab, close to or above 5,000 kilograms/hectare (kg/ha), while the rest of the zones averaged far lower, at approximately 1,500 kg/ha. Maize yields increased by 3.7 percent annually between 1981 and 2012, albeit with wide variation across zones. The three zones with the highest growth rates witnessed maize yield growth rates above 5 percent during this period, with the largest share of the growth occurring in the last 12 years. The largest growth of maize yields also occurred in the Punjab zones (Annex B, Table B2.2).

Between 2000 and 2012, annual growth rates of output in these zones were influenced by changes in both the mix of crops produced and their yields. For Cotton/Wheat Punjab, annual growth of output—estimated at 4 percent per year—was driven primarily by maize production, which increased by 17.3 percent, followed by sugarcane (8.1 percent) and rice (5.7 percent). In

TABLE 2.4 Cultivated area by water source and irrigation type, 2010

Cultivated area, by irrigation type	Punjab	Sindh	KPK	Balochistan	Pakistan
Total cultivated area (thousand acres)	27,034.0	7,643.5	4,453.1	3,491.9	42,622.5
Rainfed (%)	17.6	6.6	41.8	37.0	19.7
Irrigated (%)	82.4	93.1	57.4	62.2	80.0
Area with irrigation facilities					
Canal irrigation (%)	18.9	86.2	52.0	30.1	36.1
Canal and tube well (%)	58.2	10.3	4.9	3.5	40.7
Tube well only (%)	22.0	1.7	11.8	35.4	17.8
Other (%)	0.2	0.2	16.4	5.6	1.8
Not irrigated (%)	0.6	0.5	13.7	18.2	2.7

Source: Authors, based on data from GoP (2010a).
Note: KPK = Khyber Pakhtunkhwa.

Low-Intensity Punjab, where annual output growth also reached 4 percent during the same period, sugarcane production was the primary driver of growth (7.3 percent). Both Barani Punjab and Rice/Other Sindh experienced growth in wheat output (4.7 percent and 9.8 percent, respectively). For Rice/Wheat Punjab, maize and cotton production grew annually by 19.7 percent and 11.1 percent, respectively, during this period. In KPK Plains/Foothills, the decline in rice production (−3.8 percent) was offset by a 4.1 percent annual growth in wheat production (Annex Table B2.2).

Because of differences in climate, soil type, and water supply, a broad range of production potentials and farming systems are found in Pakistan. While some areas within Pakistan are endowed with greater agroclimatic potential, agriculture is located primarily in the irrigated areas of the Indus River basin, highlighting the importance of irrigation for the agricultural sector (Chapter 4 discusses water and irrigation issues). The extent to which geography and agroclimatic potential are shaping agricultural production patterns and trends in Pakistan is explored throughout this chapter.

Productivity across this agroclimatic diversity is inextricably linked to water, particularly that supplied by Pakistan's investments in large-scale surface irrigation in the Indus River basin, the largest contiguous irrigation network in the world (Briscoe and Qamar 2005). The storage reservoirs, barrages, and canals irrigate approximately 18 million hectares of agricultural land in Pakistan (Archer et al. 2010). Of this, approximately 36 percent of the area is irrigated with canal water, 40 percent with a mix of canal water and tube well irrigation, and 18 percent with solely tube well water (GoP 2010a; Table 2.4).

Since independence in 1947, cultivated area has increased by approximately 50 percent, primarily due to increases in water supply at the farm level (Qureshi 2004).

However, the system is increasingly beset by inefficiencies associated with conveyance losses because of poor lining of the canal system, flooding during the monsoon season, waterlogging, salinity, silting, and insufficient storage capacity in the reservoir and canal system that limit the ability to moderate the oscillation between floods and droughts (Qureshi et al. 2010, 2008; Kamal 2009; Briscoe and Qamar 2005; Bhutta and Smedema 2007). These issues have received extensive attention from administrators, hydrologists, and engineers since independence, but long-term solutions (discussed in Chapter 4) continue to challenge policy making in Pakistan.

Finally, the line between Pakistan's rural areas—inclusive of its agro-climatic diversity and the rural economy it sustains—and its urban and peri-urban environments is increasingly blurred. Changes in population densities, access to transportation, and infrastructure are playing a significant role in redefining the rural farm and nonfarm economy in Pakistan. Rural areas are now better connected to urban agglomerations, and a significant share of rural households have become peri-urban (Arif and Hamid 2009; Arif 2003). This change has been facilitated by an increase in the extent of paved roads by 55 percent between 1990 and 2011, largely carried out in the 1990s. These roads present a major opportunity to develop linkages via improved transportation infrastructure and greater urbanization to facilitate rural access to labor markets, and improved access to product markets, thus allowing rural households to more easily buy and sell goods. Past investments in rural electrification and overall energy expansion have presented similar opportunities, and new investments are expected to lead to higher economic growth, for example via the growth in the number of businesses or farms that use electricity, have access to information, and gain flexibility in labor hours.

Consider the following: First, the share of the urban population in Pakistan has increased significantly because of the establishment of new cities and improvement in road infrastructure between cities. Lahore, Faisalabad, and Gujranwala grew into more networked cities and agglomerated corridors within Punjab. According to our agglomeration index analysis,[4] only 6 percent

---

4   Urban populations are defined as those living within one hour of a city of at least 500,000 people (major city) with a population density of 150 people per square kilometer; peri-urban populations are those living within one to three hours of a major city with a population density of 150 people per square kilometer; rural populations are those that are more than three hours from a major city.

TABLE 2.5 Population and percentage urban by province, 1965–2010

Province	1965 Total population (thousands)	1965 Urban population (%)	1994 Total population (thousands)	1994 Urban population (%)	2010 Total population (thousands)	2010 Urban population (%)
Islamabad	554.8	—	1,241.3	96.9	1,734.9	97.9
Punjab	34,120.6	10.4	76,465.5	30.7	107,007.5	39.1
Sindh	13,847.6	5.9	31,066.7	35.1	43,528.0	38.6
Khyber Pakhtunkhwa	8,332.5	—	18,688.7	16.7	26,172.0	25.8
Balochistan	2,825.7	—	6,618.4	10.9	9,556.8	12.7
FATA	1,470.2	—	3,307.5	6.7	4,647.4	7.4
AJK	991.4	—	2,226.6	—	3,120.8	0.3
Disputed area	4,344.0	—	9,753.5	0.0	13,679.0	0.6
Gilgit Baltistan	1,147.1	—	2,610.9	—	3,697.9	—
Pakistan	67,633.9	6.4	151,979.0	26.1	213,144.3	32.3

Source: Authors, based on data from GoP (2010b).

Note: — = data not available; FATA = Federally Administered Tribal Areas; AJK = Azad Jammu and Kashmir.

of the total population of Pakistan was urban in 1965, compared to 32 percent in 2010 (Table 2.5).[5] In Punjab approximately 10 percent of the population was urban in 1965, compared to 39 percent in 2010. In Sindh, 6 percent of the population was urban in 1965, compared to 39 percent in 2010.

Second, between 1965 and 1994, the share of the population living more than 10 hours from a city of at least 500,000 population (considered a major city for economic agglomeration analysis in Pakistan)[6] decreased from 13.5 percent to 1.2 percent. Similarly, only 24 percent of the population was within three hours' travel time to a major city in 1965, compared to more than 70 percent of the population in 1994. Accessibility within one hour of a major city increased from 20.3 percent in 1994 to 31.4 percent in 2010 (Figure 2.2).

Efficient transportation networks within and between major cities of Pakistan help to link rural goods to peri-urban activities and manufacturing services, and facilitate national and international trade in urban areas. According to the Government of Pakistan (2010b), total road length increased by 13 percent between 1996 and 2011. A large focus of the investment (almost 70 percent) was on primary paved roads. In addition, unpaved roads were

5   For this analysis, 1961 census data is paired with 1965 road and rail infrastructure data, 1998 census data is paired with 1994 infrastructure data, and population projections are paired with 2010 infrastructure data.

6   For more details on the methodology, see Kedir, Schmidt, and Waqas (2015).

FIGURE 2.2 Access times to a city of at least 500,000 population by province, 2010

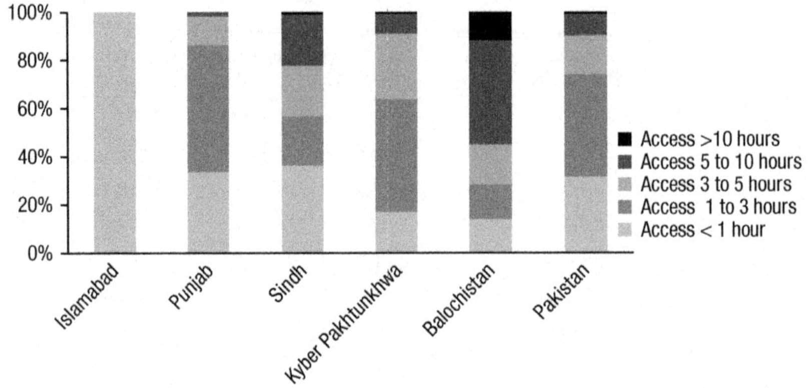

Source: Kedir, Schmidt, and Waqas (forthcoming).

converted to paved roads in order to improve degraded transportation systems in key areas.

Pakistan's Agricultural Sector

Concurrent with these trends in urbanization, Pakistan's economy has undergone a steady process of structural transformation. In the decade that followed independence in 1947, agriculture accounted for over 60 percent of the country's gross domestic product (GDP) (GoP 1988). By 2014 that share had declined to about 21 percent, but significant variability in the annual growth rates of agriculture—characterized by short-lived booms (episodes of growth above 5 percent per year) followed by busts—tend to affect the wider economy. Although the correlation between this variability and the variability in economic growth has been declining in recent years (Ahmed and Gautam 2013), its persistence demonstrates how Pakistan's fortunes are still closely tied to agriculture. Add to this the fact that nearly 47 percent of the country's labor force is still directly associated with agriculture (GoP 2014), and it should be clear why agricultural growth still merits attention from economists, development practitioners, and others working on issues of food security, employment generation, and poverty reduction (Husain 2005; Malik 2005). An appreciation of the diversity and complexity of agriculture in Pakistan is key to translating this attention into actionable programs for investment and development.

FIGURE 2.3 Shares of agricultural subsectors in agricultural GDP, 1990/1991–2012/2013

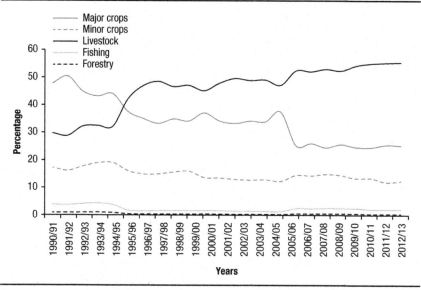

Source: Authors, based on data from GOP (2014).
Note: All shares measured at constant factor cost.

The agricultural sector is conventionally defined in Pakistan to include major crops (wheat, cotton, rice, and sugarcane), minor crops, livestock, forestry, and fisheries. Until the early 1990s, the combined (major and minor) crop subsectors contributed over two-thirds of the agricultural GDP, while livestock contributed approximately 30 percent.[7] By 2013/2014 the share of livestock's contribution to agricultural GDP had increased to 56 percent, while that of the combined crop subsectors had declined to 38 percent, with major crops accounting for 26 percent and minor crops for 12 percent (Figure 2.3). The GDP of all subsectors grew at slower rates during 2000–2009 as compared to those observed during the 1990s. In particular, the production of the major crops—accounting for over 53 percent of the country's total crop area—grew marginally more slowly, averaging 2.8 percent during 2000–2009 compared to 3.0 percent during 1990–1999. Only in the period 2000–2013 did the production of major crops increase slightly, with an

---

7 All GDP comparisons presented here are based on real values with the base year of 2005/2006. See GoP (2014).

TABLE 2.6 Average production for crops and livestock, 2010–2013, and growth rates, 1990–2013

Agricultural subsector	Average production (thousands of MT)	Annual growth rate (%)		
	2010–2013	1990–1999	2000–2009	2010–2013
Major Crops	n.a.	3.0	2.8	3.7
Wheat	24,075.2	2.5	1.5	1.4
Rice	5,860.6	4.2	3.4	−6.8
Cotton	2,172.8	0.3	0.6	0.3
Sugarcane	56,707.0	5.0	0.9	8.9
Minor Crops	n.a.	4.3	1.1	−0.9
Maize	3,881.8	3.9	9.0	9.0
Bajra	313.5	0.5	7.4	2.0
Jowar	140.5	−1.5	−3.1	−7.2
Barley	68.6	0.5	−4.0	−2.4
Gram	507.8	2.4	3.1	7.0[a]
Mung	95.9	5.3	5.8	−7.9
Mash	10.9	-4.9	−6.0	0.0
Masoor	11.8	2.6	−9.5	0.6
Potato	3,341.1	9.0	5.2	2.6
Onion	1,777.5	5.3	0.4	−0.2[a]
Livestock	n.a.	6.2	4.6	3.5
Milk[b]	38,102.3	6.0	3.6	3.2
Beef	1,741.0	3.1	5.5	3.4
Mutton	622.8	0.2	−1.0	2.2
All agriculture	n.a.	4.6	3.7	2.8

Source: Authors, based on data from GoP (2013).

Notes: MT = metric tons. n.a. = not applicable. Bajra is pearl millet, masoor is red lentils, and jowar is sorghum.

[a] Growth rates given are for the period 2010–12 only due to data availability.

[b] Milk is measured in thousands of metric tons of calculated human consumption.

annual growth rate of 3.7 percent, although this occurred concurrently with an average decline of 0.9 percent in the growth rate of minor crops (Table 2.6).

Despite several data-related anomalies in these trends—the unexplained surges in livestock's contribution to agricultural GDP in 1995 and 2005 (see Malik 2005)—the long-term trends indicate that the sources of agricultural-sector growth have changed in recent years. In particular, livestock production has expanded dramatically relative to that of major crops (Annex B,

TABLE 2.7 Growth of area cultivated and yield of selected crops, 1990–2014

	Area cultivated 2014 (thousands of ha)	Share of area in total (%)	Area cultivated growth rate			Yield 2014 (MT/ha)	Yield growth rate		
			(FY90– FY00)	(FY00– FY10)	(FY10– FY14)		(FY90– FY00)	(FY00– FY10)	(FY10– FY14)
Major Crops									
Wheat	9,039	47.6	0.65	1.02	−0.48	2.80	2.51	1.11	1.71
Rice	2,789	14.7	1.82	2.25	−0.90	2.44	3.06	1.91	2.05
Cotton	2,806	14.8	1.34	0.20	−1.34	0.77	−1.97	1.71	2.44
Sugarcane	1,173	6.2	2.36	0.25	5.86	56.67	1.49	1.25	1.68
Minor Crops									
Maize	1,117	5.9	1.24	0.81	4.50	4.05	2.36	9.13	3.51
Other food grains	744	3.9	−1.55	−0.08	−3.14	0.65	1.15	0.42	0.84
Gram	975	5.1	0.16	1.75	−2.38	0.49	3.45	1.43	3.25
Tobacco	50	0.3	1.82	0.67	−2.43	2.16	1.33	1.33	1.00
Others (not specified above)	280	1.5	1.67	−3.02	−14.77	0.76	−3.92	0.47	4.56
Total	18,973	100.0	0.92	0.86	−0.60	5.61	2.62	1.23	1.82

Source: Authors, based on data from GoP (2013).

Note: MT = metric tons. ha = hectares. Growth rates are calculated as logarithmic estimates of annual growth based on data from 1990 to 2014.

Table B2.1). These trends have emerged despite the fact that government policy has focused primarily on the four major crops—wheat, rice, cotton, and sugarcane—which together made up only 26 percent of total agricultural GDP in 2014.

Several trends in the crop subsector are worth highlighting. First, while the shares in GDP of the various crops have declined over time, production levels have kept pace with population growth. Based on official data not reported here, the value of production on a per capita basis has remained more or less steady for most crops, with wheat production per capita showing a modest upward trend in recent years. This is due largely to the fact that the declining growth rates in production for most crops over time have been matched by a decreasing rate of population growth.

Second, while wheat remains the central commodity of Pakistan's agricultural sector, the rate of growth in wheat output is declining. Since 1996–1997, wheat has consistently been the largest contributor to agricultural GDP among all crops. Production has increased from approximately 16 million tons per year in the 1990s to 20 million tons in 2000–2009, and to 24 million tons in 2010–2013. However, the growth rate of output declined from 2.5 percent

FIGURE 2.4 Yield per hectare of major crops and maize, 1990/1991–2012/2013

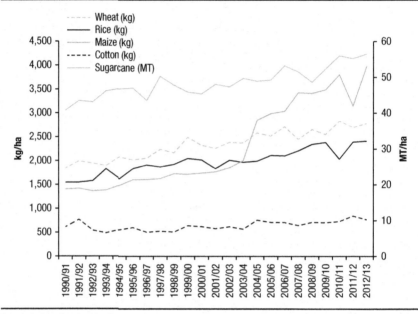

Source: Authors, based on data from GoP (2013).
Note: kg = kilograms; ha = hectares; MT = metric tons.

per year in the 1990s to 1.5 percent in 2000–2009, and to 1.4 percent in 2010–2013. During this period, the growth rate of wheat yields has also stagnated. Other major crops showed similar production and yield trends (Table 2.7; Figure 2.4).

Third, despite the demonstrated potential of several minor crops—particularly high-value fruit and vegetables for domestic and export markets (Riaz 2009)—the contribution of minor crops to agricultural GDP declined during 2000–2010 an average of 1.3 percent per year and continued to decline at 0.9 percent per year during 2010–2014. Meanwhile the area of vegetables, orchards, and other crops under cultivation has remained almost constant since 1990, as has the area of the major crops such as wheat and cotton (Table 2.8). The major exception to this trend has been maize—primarily a feed crop—for which production increased rapidly between 1990 and 2013, almost tripling in quantity and growing at an average rate of 9 percent per year.

These rather straightforward observations raise several questions. Is there room for complacency around production and yield growth for wheat and

TABLE 2.8 Cropped areas (thousands of ha) and percentage shares of total cropped area by farm size, 1990–2010

Crop	All farms			Under 0.5 ha			2 to under 5 ha			20 ha and above		
	1990	2000	2010	1990	2000	2010	1990	2000	2010	1990	2000	2010
Total cropped area	21,340	23,422	27,482	297	212	888	6,981	7,659	9,304	3,455	3,103	3,071
Grains (%)	58	59	63	69	73	69	61	61	62	53	50	56
Wheat (%)	38	40	42	41	43	45	39	41	42	35	36	38
Cotton (%)	13	14	14	7	6	10	12	13	14	15	14	13
Wheat + Cotton (%)	51	54	56	48	49	55	51	54	56	50	50	51
Pulses (%)	5	5	5	1	1	2	3	4	5	8	11	7
Sugarcane (%)	3	4	4	1	1	2	4	4	4	3	4	6
Oilseed (%)	2	2	2	0	1	1	2	2	2	3	2	3
Fodder (%)	13	11	9	14	14	12	14	12	10	9	7	5
Vegetables (%)	2	2	2	3	2	2	2	2	2	3	4	4
Orchards (%)	2	2	2	2	1	1	1	1	1	4	4	4
Other crops (%)	1	1	1	1	1	1	1	1	1	1	1	1

Source: Authors, based on data from GoP (1990, 2000, 2010a).
Note: ha = hectares.

the other major crops? Does the relatively low rate of diversification into high-value crops and more-traditional minor crops such as pulses and legumes constrain agricultural-sector growth, the development of the rural economy, and poverty reduction efforts? And are there lessons to be learned from the successes in maize production or in selected market niches such as high-value fruits and vegetables? These questions are examined in detail below and considered from a variety or perspectives throughout the book.

Total Factor Productivity and Overall Agricultural Growth

Estimates of total factor productivity (TFP) growth for the agricultural sector can provide useful insights into what is driving the trends discussed above, even though such estimates tend to be aggregate values and mask enormous variations, as this discussion will demonstrate. TFP growth provides a broad indication of agricultural-productivity growth by estimating the portion of agricultural output that is not explained by the quantities of inputs used in production. In effect TFP growth measures changes in the efficiency and intensity of input use: where output growth exceeds total input growth, TFP is increasing. Importantly, TFP helps to determine if agricultural-sector growth is driven by the increasingly intensive use of inputs—resulting from interventions in input costs and investments in agricultural infrastructure— or by productivity improvement that comes from combining the factors of production (labor, land, and capital) in more economically or technically efficient ways, for example through applications of science, improvements in the quality of human capital, or changes in institutions and incentives.

Studies of agricultural total factor productivity measurement have looked at the issue of TFP in Pakistan from several vantage points and used various types of data and methods (see Touseef and Riaz 2013). Each approach has its strengths and limitations (see Annex C), making it important to interpret changes in TFP in light of the levels of aggregation, coverage, and methodological approaches employed. Table 2.9 summarizes the key features of previous studies on agricultural productivity growth in Pakistan. Most studies found positive TFP growth rates for agriculture in Pakistan, although studies vary in terms of geographic coverage (all Pakistan versus provincial analysis), subsectors (crops only versus crops and livestock), and methodology. Except for Ahmed (2001) and Kiani (2008a, 2008b, 2008c), studies employed a descriptive approach involving either the Törnqvist-Theil index or arithmetic index.

We compute TFP growth of the entire agricultural sector, including both crop and livestock sectors, using the Törnqvist-Theil (T-T) index for the period 1960/1961–2012/2013, extending the earlier analysis by Ali and Byerlee (2002). Data are drawn from published statistics in the Economic Surveys of the Ministry of Finance, the Agricultural Statistics of Pakistan of the Ministry of Food Security and Agricultural Research (GoP 2014, 2013), and unpublished data collected by the Agriculture Policy Institute of the Ministry of National Food Security and Research. The extent of coverage here is dictated by the availability of data from the latter source. The coverage of crop sector output includes wheat, rice, cotton, sugarcane, maize, gram, mung beans, green lentils, red lentils, millet, sorghum, potatoes, and onions. Coverage of livestock sector output includes beef, mutton, and milk. Standard inputs such as labor, capital, and land as well as intermediate inputs such as fertilizer and pesticides are included.

Figure 2.5 and Figure 2.6 present our estimates of TFP growth rates for Pakistan's agricultural sector as a whole by period. The analysis by period indicates that the highest rate of TFP growth was achieved during 1966–1970, which is the period during which improved rice and wheat cultivars were

TABLE 2.9 Studies on total factor productivity in Pakistan's agricultural sector

Study	Period of analysis	Geographic coverage/ sector of analysis	Estimation methodology and nature of data	Average annual TFP growth rate (%)
Wizarat (1981)	1953–79	Pakistan/crop sector	Arithmetic index/annual time series	1.10
Rosegrant and Evenson (1993)	1957–85	Pakistan/crop sector	Törnqvist-Theil index/ annual time series	1.07
	1957–65			1.65
	1965–75			1.86
	1975–85			−0.36
Khan (1994)	1980–93	Pakistan/crop sector	Arithmetic index/annual time series	2.10
Khan (1997)	1960–96	Pakistan/crop sector	Törnqvist-Theil index/ annual time series	0.92
Ali (2004)	1960–96	Pakistan/crop and livestock sectors	Arithmetic index/(Weights 1960/61)	2.17
			(Weights 1980/81)	0.40
			Törnqvist-Theil index/ annual time series	2.30
Saboor et al. (2006)	1960–2002	Pakistan/crop and livestock sectors	Arithmetic index/annual time series	4.6
Ahmed et al. (2008)	1965–2005	Pakistan/crop sector	Growth accounting/annual time series	0.28
Ali and Byerlee (2002)	1966–94	Punjab/crop and livestock sectors	Törnqvist-Theil index/ cross-sectional	1.26
Ahmed (2001)	1991–99	Punjab/crop sector	Cobb–Douglas Production frontier/cross sectional	1.97
Kiani (2008a)	1970–2004	Punjab/crop sector	Malmquist index/annual time series	−1.38[a]
Kiani (2008b)	1970–2004	Sindh/crop sector	Törnqvist-Theil index/ annual time series	1.8
Kiani (2008c)	1970–2004	Balochistan/crop sector	Törnqvist-Theil index/ annual time series	1.5
Touseef and Riaz (2013)	1960–2006	Balochistan, KPK, Punjab, Sindh/crops, forestry, livestock, and fisheries sectors	Malmquist index/annual time series	0.99

Source: Authors, based on Touseef and Riaz (2013) and Ahmad, Chaudry, and Ilyas (2008).

Note: KPK = Khyber Pakhtunkhwa; TFP = total factor productivity.

[a] Only provincial average reported. District-level TFP growth rates are detailed in Kiani (2008a).

FIGURE 2.5 Growth rates of agricultural production and TFP, 1961–1965 to 2011–2013

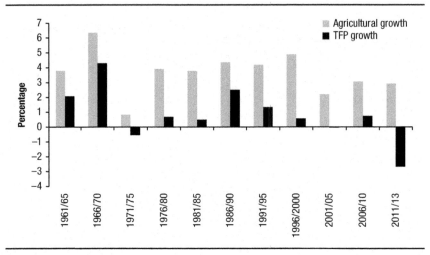

Source: Authors, based on data from GoP (2013).
Note: TFP = total factor productivity.

FIGURE 2.6 Growth of agricultural inputs and outputs and TFP, 1960/1961–2012/2013

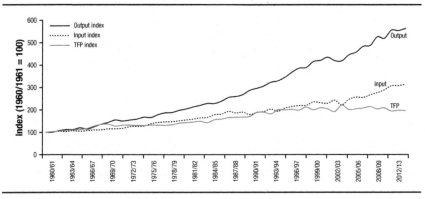

Source: Authors, based on data from GoP (2013).
Note: TFP = total factor productivity.

introduced in irrigated agricultural zones as part of the Green Revolution. Immediately thereafter, the TFP growth rate decreased, and after experiencing a low growth rate throughout the late 1970s and early 1980s, it increased again to 2.5 percent in 1986–1990. This was the last time of rapid growth in aggregate TFP to date. Moreover, beginning from about 2002–2003 and continuing to 2011–2013, these estimates suggest that agricultural-sector growth has been driven largely by increases in input use, while TFP growth has declined.

But because aggregate TFP growth estimates are of only limited use to gain an understanding of what is driving agricultural-sector trends discussed earlier, a province-level analysis may be more informative. Touseef and Riaz (2013) provide this, despite the difficulty in compiling, from official statistics, provincial input and output data beyond major and minor crops. The TFP indexes estimates by Touseef and Riaz (2013) show that there were considerable variations in patterns of TFP change among the provinces during the period 1960–2006 (Table 2.10). The estimates indicate that TFP growth was negative in the two main agricultural provinces, Punjab and Sindh, with average TFP declines estimated at −0.50 and −0.18 percent per year, respectively. They further indicate that TFP growth in Balochistan and KPK was positive during the same period, at 0.60 and 0.16 percent per year, respectively.

Several common themes emerge from the findings of the studies discussed here. First, agricultural productivity growth in Pakistan has been largely driven by increases in input use rather than technical change. For example, for the Punjab crop sector, Kiani (2008a) reported a −1.38 percent average rate of TFP change during 1970–2004. Ali and Byerlee (2002) estimate that TFP declined 1.04 percent during the Green Revolution period, 1966–1974, although they did find positive TFP growth for the entire study period (1966–2003). These findings are consistent with our results and those of Touseef and Riaz (2013), presented above. Second, the absence of sustained TFP growth and the trend toward input intensification is closely linked to resource degradation. Concerns over increasing resource-use inefficiency and resource degradation were raised by Ali and Byerlee (2002) and Murgai, Ali, and Byerlee (2001), and these trends seem to continue more than a decade later.

Finally, spatial TFP patterns exhibit sensitivity to degree of intensification. For example, Ahmed (2001) found that the highest rates of TFP growth were observed in the mung bean–wheat zone, followed by the barani (rainfed) zone, where constraints on irrigation limited the possibilities for intensification. On the other hand, the lowest TFP growth was observed in the intensively irrigated rice-wheat zone, and more generally, in areas with higher cropping intensities. These findings are consistent with those of Murgai (1999) and Pagiola (1995), who studied the Indian Punjab and Bangladesh, respectively.

In short, agriculture in Pakistan may be experiencing resource-degrading growth that is driven by intensive input use, with limited growth because of technological change. But can we say more about this growth pattern? If technological change has not been a key driver of agricultural growth, can

TABLE 2.10 Growth in agricultural TFP by province, 1960–2006

Province	Malmquist TFP index	Efficiency change	Technical change	Pure efficiency change	Scale change
Punjab	0.771	1.000	0.771	1.000	1.000
Sindh	0.917	1.000	0.917	1.000	1.000
KPK	1.075	1.000	1.075	1.000	1.000
Balochistan	1.275	1.000	1.275	1.000	1.000
Average	0.989	1.000	0.989	1.000	1.000

Source: Touseef and Riaz (2013).

Note: KPK = Khyber Pakhtunkhwa, formerly North-West Frontier Province; TFP = total factor productivity.

we decompose the trends to account not only for technological change and input use but also for crop-specific changes in areas under cultivation? To do this, we draw on work by Saeed (1976) and a more contemporary approach to decomposition analysis provided by Taffesse (2009) to examine the respective role of changes in yields and area allocated to crop production.[8]

Results of our decomposition analysis draw attention to two key trends (Table 2.11). First, for wheat production, the effect of changes in area dominates over the effect of changes in yield in nearly all zones. Second, for maize production, the effect of changes in yield dominate over the effect of changes in area. Traditionally maize has been the main staple crop in the KPK zone and certain parts of the Barani zone. Yet maize has grown much more rapidly in the nontraditional maize zones. The effect of yields on maize production are highest in nontraditional maize zones such as the Cotton/Wheat Sindh, Mixed Punjab, and Rice/Wheat Punjab zones, where acreage was shifted away from sugarcane and other crops toward maize.

Land Tenure, Agricultural Growth, and Productivity

Agricultural-sector growth, technological change, and productivity are closely tied to issues associated with land: land is central to almost all economic and social dimensions of rural livelihoods in Pakistan (Qureshi, Qureshi, and Salam 2004; Renkow 1993; Nabi, Hamid, and Zahid 1986). A variety of land policy and tenure laws have been created since British rule in Pakistan, but

---

8 Specifically, we decompose growth as
$$dQ_i \cong A_i dy_i + y_i dA_i$$
where, for crop i, Q represents total output, A represents total acreage allocated, and y represents yield.

TABLE 2.11 Decomposition of growth of production of major cereals by agroclimatic zone, 1981/1982–2011/2012 (%)

| | | Production of: | | | | | |
| | | Wheat | | Rice | | Maize | |
Agroclimatic zone	Period	Area effect	Yield effect	Area effect	Yield effect	Area effect	Yield effect
Barani Punjab	1981/1982–2011/2012	88.89	11.11	n.a.	n.a.	59.83	40.17
	1981/1982–1989/1990	84.27	15.73	n.a.	n.a.	78.27	21.73
	1990/1991–1999/2000	92.08	7.92	n.a.	n.a.	33.24	66.76
	2000/2001–2011/2012	87.69	12.31	n.a.	n.a.	68.47	31.53
Rice/wheat Punjab	1981/1982–2011/2012	86.80	13.20	45.27	54.73	55.68	44.32
	1981/1982–1989/1990	94.16	5.84	7.05	92.95	63.95	36.05
	1990/1991–1999/2000	76.78	23.22	72.00	28.00	-3.13	103.13
	2000/2001–2011/2012	93.14	6.86	32.84	67.16	52.60	47.40
Mixed Punjab	1981/1982–2011/2012	88.52	11.48	20.75	79.25	63.53	36.47
	1981/1982–1989/1990	104.35	-4.35	51.18	48.82	50.99	49.01
	1990/1991–1999/2000	96.60	3.40	13.78	86.22	67.86	32.14
	2000/2001–2011/2012	71.52	28.48	11.00	89.00	72.78	27.22
Cotton/wheat Punjab	1981/1982–2011/2012	102.18	-2.18	25.55	74.45	30.25	69.75
	1981/1982–1989/1990	121.25	-21.25	27.37	72.63	56.71	43.29
	1990/1991–1999/2000	86.05	13.95	59.64	40.36	20.55	79.45
	2000/2001–2011/2012	89.91	10.09	10.86	89.14	30.25	69.75
Low-intensity Punjab	1981/1982–2011/2012	88.06	11.94	23.73	76.27	10.69	89.31
	1981/1982–1989/1990	94.96	5.04	19.64	80.36	36.45	63.55
	1990/1991–1999/2000	86.07	13.93	46.06	53.94	15.58	84.42
	2000/2001–2011/2012	78.96	21.04	18.30	81.70	-1.14	101.14
Cotton/wheat Sindh	1981/1982–2011/2012	88.96	11.04	48.76	51.24	0.70	99.30
	1981/1982–1989/1990	99.38	0.62	45.73	54.27	0.70	99.30
	1990/1991–1999/2000	95.62	4.38	64.78	35.22	-0.10	100.10
	2000/2001–2011/2012	71.37	28.63	18.51	81.49	-1.05	101.05
Rice/other Sindh	1981/1982–2011/2012	71.24	28.76	35.36	64.64	1.72	98.28
	1981/1982–1989/1990	77.69	22.31	23.64	76.36	-9.92	109.92
	1990/1991–1999/2000	85.88	14.12	53.26	46.74	-23.55	123.55
	2000/2001–2011/2012	60.77	39.23	20.19	79.81	33.30	66.70
Southern KPK	1981/1982–2011/2012	51.59	48.41	22.92	77.08	-3.94	103.94
	1981/1982–1989/1990	43.85	56.15	-5.51	105.51	-13.20	113.20
	1990/1991–1999/2000	13.32	86.68	23.74	76.26	8.36	91.64
	2000/2001–2011/2012	70.55	29.45	30.04	69.96	-11.46	111.46
KPK plains/foothills	1981/1982–2011/2012	77.15	22.85	59.39	40.61	67.66	32.34
	1981/1982–1989/1990	61.27	38.73	29.66	70.34	24.83	75.17
	1990/1991–1999/2000	75.01	24.99	63.71	36.29	102.51	-2.51
	2000/2001–2011/2012	103.26	-3.26	70.86	29.14	64.13	35.87
Balochistan	1981/1982–2011/2012	8.75	91.25	24.20	75.80	-1.18	96.63
	1981/1982–1989/1990	-11.87	111.87	14.11	85.89	0.70	99.30
	1990/1991–1999/2000	-18.20	118.20	24.20	75.80	-4.71	104.71
	2000/2001–2011/2012	88.96	11.04	43.88	56.12	55.97	44.03

Source: Authors, based on data from GoP (2013).

Note: n.a. = not applicable; KPK = Khyber Pakhtunkhwa.

current policies still reflect their colonial antecedents. Importantly, the sale and purchase of land is governed by the law of *haq shufa*, which dictates that the first right of purchase goes to family or neighbors (Qureshi 2004). The persistent land tenure issues in parts of Pakistan, combined with relatively thin markets for land sales, necessarily affect the willingness of a farmer to invest in productivity-enhancing inputs, services, and infrastructure. This willingness is determined by a range of factors, including the ability to gain access to land through ownership, use rights, or rental markets; access to markets for inputs, equipment, and credit; access to public services and infrastructure such as extension and irrigation; and the transaction costs associated with securing access to all of these essentials. Policy makers and researchers alike have given much attention to the relationships between land, productivity, and poverty for several decades in Pakistan (for example, Jacoby and Mansuri 2009; Qureshi et al. 2004; Renkow 1993). They have been informed by a rich literature on these issues (for example, Jin and Deininger 2009; Deininger, Jin, and Nagarajan 2008; Binswanger, Deininger, and Feder 1995; Binswanger 1994). This section presents a brief overview of land and land tenure in Pakistan, and the challenges they present for agricultural-sector growth and development.

During the period immediately before the consolidation of British rule in 1858, rural elites acquired large tracts of agricultural land in Punjab and surrounding areas. After British rule was consolidated, officials recognized the elites' proprietary land rights in order to gain political support and cooperation (Naqvi, Khan, and Chaudhry 1987). In addition, the British granted large areas of land (*jagirs*) to individuals who helped conquer areas of what are today Punjab and Sindh. Thus, the existence of landlords with large tracts of land became widespread and set the pattern for Pakistan.

During British rule, two land tenure systems developed: a landlord-tenancy (*zamindari*) system and a peasant-proprietor system (Qureshi and Qureshi 2004).[9] Whereas the landlord-tenancy system was characterized by absentee landlords and verbal or customary tenancy arrangements, the peasant-proprietorship provided peasants with ownership rights and allowed farmers to cultivate land as they saw fit. The landlord-tenancy system was tied to colonial rule, and two subsystems developed: revenue-free land estates granted by the government to *jagirdars* (those who assisted the British in

---

9   Other systems also existed in the region, for example the *mahalwary* system, which was more common in eastern Punjab (today the state of Punjab in India), which required peasants to pay land revenues directly to the British.

consolidating their administrative control) and estates in which landowners (*zamindars*) were required to pay a land tax to the government. Under the *jagirdari* system, tenant farmers were classified in two categories: occupancy tenants who had permanent, heritable, and transferable rights to cultivate *jagir* land; and tenants-at-will, or *haris,* who held no legal rights. Under the *zamindari* system, a majority of the land held by landowners was rented or parceled out and cultivated by sharecroppers and tenants, on whom the tax burden fell (Nabi, Hamid, and Zahid 1986; Qureshi and Qureshi 2004).

Contracts between tenant and landlord were typically verbal and usually short-term. Tenants were shifted among different plots on the land so that a single individual was not listed on a particular plot for more than one year, and were often required to provide free labor to the landlord in addition to a significant share of their plot's output. This led to bonded labor arrangements in which workers were tied to an employer at very low wages or to repay debts at very high interest rates. These arrangements still exist today in some parts of Pakistan: a study in 2000 found that the majority of the 1.7 million landless agricultural workers in Sindh were in a debt bondage arrangement (Agrodev 2000; Qureshi 2004).

Pakistan's efforts to address land issues began in 1950 with the introduction of successive national and provincial acts and orders designed to effect a more equitable redistribution of tenure rights (see Chapter 1). Pakistan implemented three major land reforms—in 1959, 1972, and 1977. Provisions included prescribed terms for the manner in which production inputs and outputs were shared between landlords and tenants, legal occupancy rights for tenants, curtailment of the conditions under which tenants could be evicted, and ceilings on individual landholdings; other tenure reforms were also introduced (Gazdar 2009; Naqvi, Khan, and Chaudhry 1987; Nabi, Hamid, and Zahid 1986).[10] The 1959 and 1972 land reforms attempted to redistribute land from large landowners—who accounted for about 8 percent of total cultivated area in Pakistan—to tenants, smallholders, and the landless. However, much of the redistributed land was of poor quality and was never allocated to its intended beneficiaries, resulting in relatively little change in landholding concentration or tenure. The 1977 land reforms were never implemented. In effect, land reforms have had little success in changing the status quo in Pakistan and almost no impact on production or productivity (Gazdar 2009;

---

10 See Jacoby and Mansuri (2008, 2006) for a more comprehensive discussion of land tenure policy and the effects of tenancy arrangements on production.

TABLE 2.12 Number and area of farms by ownership type, 2000–2010

Ownership	2000	2010
Number of farms (thousands)	6,620.1	8,264.5
Owned	77.6%	81.6%
Tenant	14.0%	11.1%
Owner cum tenant	8.4%	7.3%
Total area (thousand of acres)	50,425.2	52,910.1
Area cultivated by owners	73.3%	74.5%
Area solely tenant farmed	12.2%	11.1%
Area owner cum tenant	14.5%	14.3%
Average size of cultivated area (acres)	6.2	5.2

Source: Authors, based on data from GoP (2000, 2010a).

Naqvi, Khan, and Chaudhry 1989; Nabi, Hamid, and Zahid 1986). Since these reforms, only minor amendments to land laws have occurred, and high levels of land concentration remain common throughout most of Pakistan, owing partly to the political power of large landowners (Qureshi 2004; Husain 1999; Nabi, Hamid, and Zahid 1986; Heston and Kumar 1983).

As a result, land ownership in Pakistan remains characterized by owner-cultivators, sharecropping arrangements, or some combination of the two. In 2010, 82 percent of farms, making up 75 percent of the country's farm area, were operated by owner-cultivators, while 11 percent of farms, making up 11 percent of the area, were operated under tenancy arrangements, with the remaining farms and area under a combination of the two (Table 2.12). While studies suggest that owner cultivation has increased at the expense of sharecropping since the 1950s (Cheema and Naseer 2010; Nasim, Dinar, and Helfand 2014), the ability of large landowners to protect their landholdings through various legal mechanisms makes it difficult to assess the true extent of its persistence (Ali 2015). For example, a land sale transaction on inherited land with a nonfamily member can be impeded by the right of first refusal. Sales of small plots can be hindered by high transaction costs, even if all parties are willing to accept the terms of the sale. Historically, there has been a lack of explicit land titles, and informal and customary rights have been in force, contributing to high transaction costs. While land rights are individually allocated today, due to these historical factors, land markets in Pakistan remain thin, and land fragmentation is high (Qureshi and Qureshi 2004; Heston and Kumar 1983).

Access to rural credit is an issue closely related to land markets in Pakistan. Credit markets allow farmers to combine factors of production and enhance farm-level productivity, but only where those markets function effectively, and particularly where they serve the needs of small-scale owner-cultivators. There is rich body of literature that examines credit constraints in rural Pakistan and their effects on productivity growth, poverty reduction, and the wider rural economy (see Zubeiri 1989; Malik, Mushtaq, and Gill 1991; Qureshi, Nabi, and Faruqee 1996; Malik 1999; Malik and Nazli 1999; Amjad and Hasnu 2007). All the studies point to the challenges posed by credit constraints or the institutional architecture of both formal and informal credit sources: the Zarai Taraqiati Bank (ZTBL), the primary source of formal agricultural credit; and the commission agents; input dealers; professional moneylenders; and landlords who extend informal loans in cash or kind. Further exploration of Pakistan's credit markets is needed.

All of this points to the persistent policy challenge for Pakistan: how to improve the allocation of land to more productive uses. Here, Pakistan faces the difficult reality that land rarely changes hands outside of inheritance, limiting the scope for alternatives to owner cultivation or sharecropping. Small farmers face the dual challenges of entrenched large landholders on the one hand, and increasing fragmentation of smallholder landholdings on the other hand. Much evidence suggests that transaction costs associated with the sale and purchase of land are a key constraint to individual efforts to consolidate land into economically viable units, an obstacle that is possibly exacerbated by speculative prices that exceed the discounted value of potential agricultural earnings from land (Qureshi et al. 2004; Ahmed and Gautam 2013). In 2000, for example, only 0.2 percent of agricultural land was sold, according to data from the Pakistan Rural Household Survey (2001–02) (PIDE 2001).[11]

Predictably, the persistence of high transaction costs in land sales, thin rental markets, and land inheritance requirements has been accompanied by increased fragmentation of landholdings, with growing concerns that average farm sizes are quickly falling below the minimum sustainable operational level. According to Agricultural Census data, between 1960 and 2010, the proportion of farms under 5 acres increased from 19 percent to 65 percent, while the proportion of farms between 5 and 25 acres decreased from 68 percent to 32 percent (Figure 2.7; Table 2.13). By 2010, only 3.8 percent of farms were larger than 25 acres, while farms of larger than 25 acres make up 34 percent of all farm area in Pakistan. This suggests that growth in the

---

11 The small percentage of sales of land is also confirmed by data from IFPRI/IDS (2012).

FIGURE 2.7 Distribution of private farms by size and total number of farms, 1960–2010

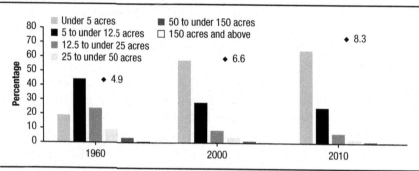

Source: Authors, based on data from GoP (2000, 2010a).
Note: The total number of farms, in millions, is denoted by diamond-shaped markers.

number of farms under 5 acres has resulted from the fragmentation of farms in the 5 to 12.5 acre and the 12.5 to 25 acre categories—farms that were otherwise considered to be an important and economically viable source of agricultural output growth in Pakistan. Meanwhile, the number of farms larger than 50 acres has remained relatively constant throughout this period, and increased slightly from 2000 to 2010, suggesting that fragmentation has not occurred among large landholders.

Between 1990 and 2010, the average size of farms in the now predominant category of farms under 5 acres declined from 2.2 acres to 1.9 acres, with a more significant decline seen in KPK, from 1.9 acres to 1.5 acres (Table 2.14). This decrease in size further suggests that the land fragmentation process is intensifying within already fragmented landholdings. These trends are further exacerbated by growing inequality associated with land tenure. Nearly 92 percent of all rural households in Pakistan fall in the category of "landless or less than 5 acres of land operated," with nearly 95 percent of households in this category classified as poor, according to data from the 2010/2011 HIES (GoP 2011) (Table 2.15).

In sum, while farmers with larger landholdings have been able to protect the size of their holdings from fragmentation, their neighbors with medium- and small-size landholdings, because of their poor economic status, are forced to subdivide and fragment their landholdings by following inheritance laws. This means that over generations, their farms become smaller and smaller and the plots become farther apart, making it impossible for farmers to farm efficiently. The farm families with larger farms do not subdivide as quickly as those with the medium- and small-size farms. As medium and

TABLE 2.13 Percentage of farms and farm area by farm size, 1960–2010

Farm size in acres (hectares)	Share of farms (%)							Farm area (%)						
	1960	1972	1980	1990	2000	2010		1960	1972	1980	1990	2000	2010
<5 (<2)	19.0	28.2	34.1	47.5	57.6	64.7		3.0	5.2	7.1	11.3	15.5	19.2
5–12.5 (2–5)	44.3	39.9	39.4	33.4	28.1	24.8		23.6	25.2	27.3	27.5	27.9	28.8
12.5–25 (5–10)	23.8	21.1	17.3	12.2	8.8	6.8		27.0	26.6	24.7	21.5	19.1	17.7
25–50 (10–20)	9.0	7.7	6.5	4.7	3.9	2.6		19.0	18.8	17.8	15.8	16.3	12.7
50–150 (20–61)	3.3	2.7	2.4	1.8	1.2	1.0		16.0	15.1	14.7	13.9	9.6	10.5
>150 (>61)	0.5	0.4	0.3	0.3	0.2	0.2		11.5	9.1	8.5	10.1	11.6	11.1
Total	100	100	100	100	100	100		100	100	100	100	100	100

Source: Authors, based on data from GoP (1960, 1972, 1980, 1990, 2000, and 2010a).

TABLE 2.14 Percentage of farms and farm area by province, 1990 and 2010

Source and province	All farms			Under 5.0 acres		
	Number of farms (%)	Farm area (%)	Average size (acres)	Number of farms (%)	Farm area (%)	Average size (acres)
Census 1990						
Punjab	58	61	9.2	56	57	2.2
Sindh	16	19	10.7	11	14	2.9
KPK	21	13	5.5	31	26	1.9
Balochistan	5	6	11.8	2	2	1.7
Pakistan	100	100	8.8	100	99	2.2
Pakistan (total numbers and acres)	5,070,960	44,410,269		2,404,103	5,270,622	
Census 2010						
Punjab	64	55	5.6	63	64	1.9
Sindh	13	19	8.8	12	15	2.4
KPK	19	11	2.9	23	18	1.5
Balochistan	2	15	9.7	2	3	2.4
Pakistan	100	100	6.4	100	100	1.9
Pakistan (total numbers and acres)	8,064,479	52,910,408		5,350,946	10,184,052	

Source: Authors, based on data from GoP (1990, 2010a).

Note: Totals may not add to 100 due to rounding. KPK = Khyber Pakhtunkhwa.

TABLE 2.15 Distribution of rural households by household status, land cultivated, and poverty status, 2010

Household status	Rural households		Poor rural households	
	Number	% of total	Number	% of total
Farm households	524,829	2.6	281,684	3.5
Nonfarm households	12,896,993	64.1	5,218,954	64.8
Farm/nonfarm households	6,705,084	33.3	2,559,312	31.8
Total	20,126,906	100.0	8,059,950	100.0
Land cultivated				
Landless and less than 5 acres	18,481,146	91.8	7,631,516	94.7
5 to 12.5 acres	1,208,359	6.0	359,142	4.5
12.5 to 25 acres	335,979	1.7	64,783	0.8
25 to 50 acres	64,237	0.3	2,852	0.0
50 acres plus	37,184	0.2	1,658	0.0
Overall	20,126,906	100.0	8,059,950	100.0

Source: Authors, based on data from GoP (2011).

small farms become smaller and smaller, those sizes and the scarcity of other resources make it difficult for them to be economically sustainable, let alone to increase productivity.

Conclusions

Somewhat paradoxically, this chapter has illustrated how Pakistan's agriculture is changing while, at the same time, remaining in somewhat of a state of stasis. The country's agroclimatic diversity and endowment of natural resources remain its greatest asset, but it is fast becoming a nation plagued by acute water scarcities (see Chapter 4). Agricultural production and productivity continue to grow, albeit slowly, but increasingly growth is on the back of unsustainable input intensification patterns rather than technological change. Growth in rural infrastructure, transportation networks, and urban agglomerations are reducing the time, effort, and cost of linking production to consumption, yet agricultural diversification into commodities that serve urban demand remains limited.

Public policy clearly has a role to play in addressing these paradoxes. But shifts in attention given to agricultural policy since independence are closely tied to the observed fluctuations in Pakistan's agricultural growth rates. For example, the growth in TFP during 1966–1970 is clearly attributable to the initial gains made by the Green Revolution—technical change driven by technology transfers and investments in research and extension, and supported by a range of policy incentives designed to encourage productivity growth. The next upswing during 1986–1990 occurred at a time when agriculture received renewed attention on the national development agenda after having been marginalized in the late 1970s and early 1980s. This growth was likely associated with the convening of the National Agriculture Commission, the publication of the Agricultural Commission Report, and subsequent policies designed to encourage agricultural productivity growth, many of which are discussed in detail in other chapters (GoP 1988). The subsequent slowdown in TFP growth, to just 0.56 percent during 1996–2000, may similarly be associated with a decline in the attention paid to agricultural policy, as may be the case since 2001—when TFP growth has averaged just 0.35 percent per year and was a negative 2.67 percent in 2011–2013. This is partly explained by the declining official budgetary allocations to agriculture in the Public Sector Development Program and a lack of support for new reform initiatives designed to encourage a greater role for the private sector in Pakistan's agriculture.

The verdicts are fairly clear: agriculture has not performed to its full potential and functions in a low productivity trap. Scope for technological change exists, but the gains associated with the Green Revolution have long disappeared, indicating the need to redouble efforts to introduce farmers to new productivity-enhancing technologies and practices. Scope for diversification also exists, but current policies do not explicitly encourage a move out of low-value food staples and into higher-value crops and livestock where agroclimatic conditions and market infrastructure are otherwise conducive. Furthermore, the continued fragmentation of cropped area from the economically viable medium-size farms into smaller and economically unviable farms continues unabated, with little chance of addressing the weak institutions and high transaction costs found in local land markets or the political power issues that allow large landowners to protect their landholdings.

There have been many strategies and policies designed to address these constraints in recent decades, from the land reforms introduced in 1950 to the detailed recommendations of the National Commission on Agriculture in 1987. All were emblems of the government's commitment to agricultural development and productivity growth. Unfortunately, policy makers continue to emphasize aggregates—output targets for the major crops only—that obfuscate the importance of Pakistan's socioeconomic and agroclimatic diversity. Furthermore, their strategies have fallen short when it comes to translating good intentions into action by federal and provincial governments to develop subsector-specific priorities, integrate these priorities into overall national economic policy, and recognize the need for commensurate financial resource allocations. To identify policies appropriate to a particular subsector and allocate the necessary resources to them requires good data and sound policy analysis that turns such data into implementable policy steps. Additionally, better monitoring and evaluation of such data are necessary for fine-tuning, replicating, and improving public policies, investments, and programs to encourage agricultural-sector growth, productivity improvement, and poverty reduction in Pakistan.

References

Agrodev. 2000. *Sindh Rural Development Project: Final Report Prepared for Planning and Development*. The Government of Sindh and the Asian Development Bank, Agrodev Canada, Inc.

Ahmad, K., M. A. Chaudry, and M. Ilyas. 2008. "Trends in Total Factor Productivity in Pakistan Agricultural Sector." *Pakistan Economic and Social Review* 46 (2): 117–132.

Ahmed, M. 2001. "Agriculture Productivity Growth Differential in Punjab: A District Level Analysis." *The Pakistan Development Review* 40 (1).

Ahmed, S. A., and M. Gautam. 2013. *Agriculture and Water Policy: Toward Sustainable Inclusive Growth.* Washington, DC: World Bank. https://openknowledge.worldbank.org/handle/10986/17864 License: CC BY 3.0 IGO.

Ali, M. 2015. *Development, Poverty, and Power in Pakistan: The Impact of State and Donor Interventions on Farmers.* New York: Routledge.

Ali, M., and D. Byerlee. 2002. "Productivity Growth and Resource Degradation in Pakistan's Punjab: A Decomposition Analysis." *Economic Development and Cultural Change* 50 (4).

Amjad, S., and S. Hasnu. 2007. "Smallholders' Access to Rural Credit: Evidence from Pakistan." *The Lahore Journal of Economics* 12 (2): 1–25.

Archer, D. R., N. Forsythe, H. J. Fowler, and S. M. Shah. 2010. "Sustainability of Water Resources Management in the Indus Basin under Changing Climatic and Socioeconomic Conditions." *Hydrology and Earth System Sciences* 14: 1669–1680.

Arif, G. M. 2003. "Urbanization in Pakistan: Trends, Growth and Evaluation of the 1998 Census." In UNFPA, *Population of Pakistan: An Analysis of 1998 Population and Housing Census,* edited by A. R. Kemal, M. Irfan, and N. Mahmood. Islamabad: Pakistan Institute of Development Economics.

Arif, G. M., and M. Ahmed. 2001. *Poverty across the Agro-Ecological Zones in Rural Pakistan.* Islamabad: Pakistan Institute of Development Economics.

Arif, G. M., and S. Hamid. 2009. "Urbanization, City Growth and Quality of Life in Pakistan." *European Journal of Social Sciences* 10 (2).

Bhutta, M. N., and L. K. Smedema. 2007. "One Hundred Years of Waterlogging and Salinity Control in the Indus Valley, Pakistan: A Historical Review." *Irrigation and Drainage* 56: 581–590.

Binswanger, H. 1994. "Agricultural and Rural Development: Painful Lessons." *Agrekon: Agricultural Economics Research, Policy and Practice in Southern Africa* 33, Issue 4.

Binswanger, H., K. Deininger, and G. Feder. 1995. "Power, Distortions, Revolt and Reform in Agricultural Land Relations." In *Handbook of Development Economics* 3B: 2659–2772.

Briscoe, J., and U. Qamar. 2005. *Pakistan's Water Economy: Running Dry.* Washington, DC: World Bank.

Capalbo, S. M., and J. M. Antle. 1988. *Agricultural Productivity: Measurement and Explanation.* Washington, DC: Resources for the Future.

Chambers, R. G. 1988. *Applied Production Analysis: A Dual Approach*. Cambridge: Cambridge University Press.

Cheema, A., and F. Naseer. 2010. "Poverty, Mobility and Institutions in Rural Sargodha: Evidence for Social Protection Reforms." Report submitted to the Planning and Development Department (P & DD) of Government of Punjab.

Deininger, K., S. Jin, H. K. Nagarajan. 2008. "Efficiency and Equity Impacts of Rural Land Rental Restrictions: Evidence from India." *European Economic Review* 52 (5): 892–918.

FAO (Food and Agriculture Organization of the United Nations). 1996. *Agro-ecological Zoning: Guidelines*. http://www.fao.org/docrep/w2962e/w2962e-03.htm. Accessed May 15, 2015.

Faruqee, R. 1995. *Government's Role in Pakistan Agriculture: Major Reforms Are Needed*. Policy Research Working Paper 1468. Washington, DC.: World Bank.

GoP (Government of Pakistan). 1960. *Agricultural Census*. Islamabad: Agricultural Census Wing, Pakistan Bureau of Statistics.

———. 1972. *Agricultural Census*. Islamabad: Agricultural Census Wing, Pakistan Bureau of Statistics.

———. 1980. *Agricultural Census*. Islamabad: Agricultural Census Wing, Pakistan Bureau of Statistics.

———. 1988. *Report of the National Commission on Agriculture*. Islamabad: Ministry of Food and Agriculture, Government of Pakistan.

———. 1990. *Agricultural Census*. Islamabad: Agricultural Census Wing, Pakistan Bureau of Statistics.

———. 2000. *Agricultural Census*. Islamabad: Agricultural Census Wing, Pakistan Bureau of Statistics.

———. 2010a. *Agricultural Census*. Islamabad: Agricultural Census Wing, Pakistan Bureau of Statistics. http://www.pbs.gov.pk/content/agricultural-census-wing.

———. 2010b. *Pakistan Economic Survey 2009–10*. Islamabad: Ministry of Finance. http://www.finance.gov.pk/survey_0910.html.

———. 2011. *Household Integrated Economic Survey (HIES)*. Pakistan Bureau of Statistics, Islamabad.

———. 2013. *Agricultural Statistics of Pakistan 2011–12*. Islamabad: Ministry of National Food Security and Research.

———. 2014. *Pakistan Economic Survey 2013–14*. Islamabad: Ministry of Finance,.

Gazdar, H. 2009. *The Fourth Round, and Why They Fight On: An Essay on the History of Land and Reform in Pakistan*. Karachi: Collective for Social Science Research.

Heston, A., and D. Kumar. 1983. "The Persistence of Land Fragmentation in Peasant Agriculture: An Analysis of South Asian Cases." *Explorations in Economic History* 20: 199–220.

Husain, I. 1999. *Pakistan: The Economy of an Elitist State.* Karachi: Oxford University Press.

———. 2005. *Current Issues in Pakistan's Economy.* Karachi: State Bank of Pakistan.

IFPRI/IDS (International Food Policy Research Institute/Innovative Development Strategies [Pvt.] Ltd.). 2012. Pakistan Rural Household Panel Survey 2012 Rounds 1 and 1.5 dataset. Washington, DC/Islamabad: IFPRI/IDS.

Jacoby, H. G., and G. Mansuri. 2006. *Incomplete Contracts and Investment: A Study of Land Tenancy in Pakistan.* Policy Research Working Paper Series 3826. Washington, DC: World Bank.

———. 2008. "Land Tenancy and Non-contractible Investment in Rural Pakistan." *Review of Economic Studies* 75 (3): 763–788.

———. 2009. "Incentives, Supervision, and Sharecropper Productivity." *Development Economics* 88 (2): 232–241.

Jin, S., and K. Deininger. 2009. "Land Rental Markets in the Process of Rural Structural Transformation: Productivity and Equity Impacts from China." *Comparative Economics* 37 (1): 629–646.

Kamal, S. 2009. *Pakistan's Water Challenges: Entitlement, Access, Efficiency and Equity in Kugelman:* Running on Empty: Pakistan's Water Crisis. Washington, DC: Woodrow Wilson International Center for Scholars.

Kedir, M., E. Schmidt, and A. Waqas. Forthcoming. *Pakistan's Changing Demography: Urbanization and Peri-urban Transformation over Time.* PSSP Working Paper. Islamabad: PSSP.

Kiani, A. K. 2008a. "An Empirical Analysis of TFP Gains in the Agricultural Crop Sector of Punjab: A Multi Criteria Approach." *European Journal of Scientific Research* 24 (3): 339–347.

Kiani, A. K. 2008b. "TFP and MIRR in the Agricultural Crop Sub-Sector of Sindh." *European Journal of Social Sciences* 7 (1): 43–57.

Kiani, A. K. 2008c. "TFP and MIRR Using Almon Distributed Lag Model: A Case Study of Balochistan (1970–2004)." *European Journal of Scientific Research* 23 (1): 49–60.

Malik, S. J. 1999. *Poverty and Rural Credit: The Case of Pakistan.* Islamabad: Pakistan Institute of Development Economics.

———. 2005. *Agriculture Growth and Rural Poverty: A Review of the Evidence.* The Asian Development Bank Working Paper Series. Working Paper 2. Islamabad: Asian Development Bank, Pakistan Resident Mission.

Malik, S. J., M. Mushtaq, and M. A. Gill. 1991. "The Role of Institutional Credit in the Agricultural Development of Pakistan." *The Pakistan Development Review* 30 (4): 1039–1048.

Malik, S. J., and H. Nazli. 1999. "Rural Poverty and Credit Use: Evidence from Pakistan." *The Pakistan Development Review* 38 (4): 699–716.

Murgai, R. 1999. *The Green Revolution and Productivity Paradox: Evidence from the Indian Punjab.* World Bank Policy Research Working Paper 2234. Washington, DC: World Bank.

Murgai, R., M. Ali, and D. Byerlee. 2001. "Productivity Growth and Sustainability in Post–Green Revolution Agriculture: The Case of the Indian and Pakistan Punjabs." *World Bank Research Observer* 16 (2): 199–218.

Nabi, I., N. Hamid, and S. Zahid. 1986. *The Agrarian Economy of Pakistan: Issues and Policies.* Karachi: Oxford University Press.

Naqvi, S. N. H., M. H. Khan, and M. G. Chaudhry. 1987. *Land Reforms in Pakistan: A Historical Perspective.* Islamabad: Pakistan Institute of Development Economics.

———. 1989. *Structural Change in Pakistan's Agriculture.* Islamabad: Pakistan Institute of Development Economics.

Nasim, S., A. Dinar, and S. Helfand. 2014. *Allocative Inefficiency and Tenure Arrangement in Irrigated Agriculture in Pakistan.* PSSP working paper 015. Islamabad: International Food Policy Research Institute.

Pagiola, S. 1995. *Environmental and Natural Resource Degradation in Intensive Agriculture in Bangladesh.* Environment Economic series 15, Washington DC: World Bank.

PARC (Pakistan Agricultural Research Council). 2011. *PARC Annual Report 2010–11.* Islamabad: PARC.

PIDE (Pakistan Institute of Development Economics). 2001. *Pakistan Rural Household Survey, Round 1 2001–02.* Islamabad: Pakistan Institute of Development Economics; World Bank.

Pinckney, T. 1989. *The Demand for Public Storage of Wheat in Pakistan.* IFPRI Research Report 85. Washington, DC: IFPRI.

Qureshi, M. G., and S. K. Qureshi. 2004. "Impact of Changing Profile of Rural Land Market in Pakistan on Resource Allocation and Equity." *The Pakistan Development Review* 43 (4): 471–492.

Qureshi, M. G., S. K. Qureshi, and A. Salam. 2004. "Impact of Changing Profile of Rural Land Market in Pakistan on Resource Allocation and Equity." *Pakistan Development Review* 43 (4): 471–492.

Qureshi, S. 2004. *Rural Land Markets in Pakistan: Institutions and Constraints.* Background paper for Pakistan Rural Factor Markets Study, World Bank Report 30381-PK. Washington, DC: World Bank.

Qureshi, S., P. G. McCornick, M. Qadir, and Z. Aslam. 2008. "Managing Salinity and Waterlogging in the Indus Basin of Pakistan." *Agricultural Water Management* 95 (1): 1–10.

Qureshi, S., P. G. McCornick, A. Sarwar, and B. R. Sharma. 2010. "Challenges and Prospects of Sustainable Groundwater Management in the Indus Basin, Pakistan." *Water Resource Management* 24: 1551–1569.

Qureshi, S., I. Nabi, and R. Faruqee. 1996. *Rural Finance for Growth and Poverty Alleviation.* Policy Research Paper 1593. Washington DC: World Bank.

Renkow, M. 1993. "Land Prices, Land Rents, and Technological Change: Evidence from Pakistan." *World Development* 21 (5): 791–803.

Riaz, K. 2009. "Revealed Comparative Advantage Analysis of Pakistan's Agricultural Exports." *Applied Economics* 19 (2): 103–127.

Saeed, Z. 1976. "Growth of Crop Output in Pakistan—An Analysis by Component Elements." *Pakistan Development Review* 3: 319–329.

Taffesse, A. S. 2009. *Cereal Production in Ethiopia: Recent Trends and Sources of Growth.* Washington, DC: IFPRI.

Thirtle, C., and P. Bottomley. 1992. "Total Factor Productivity in U.K. Agriculture, 1967–90." *Journal of Agricultural Economics* 43 (3): 381–400.

Touseef, H., and K. Riaz. 2013. "Agricultural TFP Growth: A Provincial Level Analysis." *Journal of Social Sciences* (GC University, Faisalabad) 15 (2).

Wen, G. J. 1993. "Total Factor Productivity Change in China's Farming Sector: 1952–1989." *Economic Development and Cultural Change* 42 (1): 1–41.

Zubeiri, Habib A. 1989. "Production Function, Institutional Credit and Agricultural Development in Pakistan." *The Pakistan Development Review* 28 (1): 43–56.

Annex A: Classification of Districts into Agroclimatic (Crop) Zones

TABLE A2.1 Classification of districts into agroclimatic zones

Zone	Districts
Barani Punjab	Attock, Rawalpindi, Islamabad, Jhelum, Chakwal
Mixed Punjab	Sargodha, Khushab, Faisalabad, Toba Tek Singh, Jhang, Okara
Low-intensity Punjab	Mianwali, Bhakkar, M. Garh, Layyah, D.G. Khan, Rajanpur
Cotton/wheat Punjab	Sahiwal, Pakpattan, Multan, Lodhran, Khanewal, Vehari, Bahawalpur, Rahimyar, Khan, Bahawalnagar
Rice/wheat Punjab	Gujrat, M.B. Din, Sialkot, Narowal, Gujranwala, Hafizabad, Sheikhupura, NanKana Sahib, Lahore, Kasur
Cotton/wheat Sindh	Khairpur, Ghotki, Sukkur, N. Feroze, Nawabshah, Sanghar, Thar parkar, Mirpur khas, Umarkot
Rice/other Sindh	Jacobabad, Kashmore, Shikarpur, Larkana, K.S.Kot, Dadu, Jamshoro, Hyderabad, Matiari, Tando Allahyar, T.M. Khan, Badin, Thatta, Karachi
Southern KPK	Peshawar, Kohat, Hangu, Karak, D.I. Khan, Tank, Bannu, Lakki Marwat, Mohmand Agency, Northern Waziristan, Southern Waziristan, F.R. Peshawar, F.R. Kohat, F.R. Bannu, F.R. D.I. Khan
Plains/foothills KPK	Charsadda, Nowshera, Mardan, Swabi, Mansehra, Battagram, Abbottabad, Haripur, Kohistan, Malakand, Swat, Bunir, Shangla, Dir Lower, Dir Upper, Chitral, Khyber, Kurram, Orakzai, Bajour
Balochistan	All districts

Source: Authors, adapted from Pinckney (1989).
Note: KPK = Khyber Pakhtunkhwa

Annex B: Agricultural Production Shares and Growth Rates

TABLE B2.1 Average share of crops and livestock in value of agricultural production and growth of share (%), 1990–2013

Crop	Average share in value			Growth in share
	1990–1999	2000–2009	2010–2013	1990–2013
Wheat	18.8	18.1	17.5	−6.9
Rice	6.4	5.8	5.9	−7.8
Cotton	10.2	11.1	13.9	36.3
Sugarcane	6.5	4.9	5.7	−12.3
Maize	1.7	1.5	2.0	17.6
Bajra	0.3	0.2	0.1	−66.7
Jowar	0.3	0.1	0.1	−66.7
Barley	0.1	0.1	0	−100.0
Gram	3.3	4.0	1.9	−42.4
Mung	0.2	0.1	0.1	−50.0
Mash	0.1	0	0	−100.0
Masoor	0.1	0	0	−100.0
Potato	0.6	1.3	1.1	83.3
Onion	0.5	1.3	0.9	80.0
Milk	35.2	39.3	38.0	8.0
Beef	6.5	5.9	7.5	15.4
Mutton	9.2	6.2	5.3	−42.4

Source: Authors, based on data from GoP (2014).

Note: Values are computed by multiplying the total production in the year by the average wholesale price in that year.

TABLE B2.2 Annual growth in acreage and production by crop and agroclimatic zone (%), 1981/1982–2011/2012

Agroclimatic zone	Period	Wheat		Rice	
		Acreage	Production	Acreage	Production
Barani Punjab	1981/1982–2011/2012	−0.54	0.26	0.05	2.00
	1981/1982–1989/1990	−1.10	2.56	−4.41	−4.90
	1990/1991–1999/2000	0.13	0.06	4.14	5.54
	2000/2001–2011/2012	0.12	4.72	0.14	1.49
Rice/wheat Punjab	1981/1982–2011/2012	0.90	3.31	1.14	2.17
	1981/1982–1989/1990	0.36	4.16	1.82	−0.08
	1990/1991–1999/2000	1.12	4.81	2.05	5.64
	2000/2001–2011/2012	1.04	2.14	−0.24	0.80
Mixed Punjab	1981/1982–2011/2012	0.19	2.48	2.08	2.55
	1981/1982–1989/1990	0.83	4.56	2.25	1.94
	1990/1991–1999/2000	0.08	3.58	1.79	3.13
	2000/2001–2011/2012	−0.43	0.13	2.31	2.83
Cotton/wheat Punjab	1981/1982–2011/2012	0.81	2.07	2.61	4.85
	1981/1982–1989/1990	1.77	1.10	1.26	0.00
	1990/1991–1999/2000	1.06	5.87	7.12	10.35
	2000/2001–2011/2012	−0.51	0.30	0.88	5.68
Low intensity Punjab	1981/1982–2011/2012	1.40	3.33	1.17	3.11
	1981/1982–1989/1990	2.23	4.82	1.84	0.33
	1990/1991–1999/2000	1.05	4.57	1.63	5.47
	2000/2001–2011/2012	0.88	1.57	0.75	3.32
Cotton/wheat Sindh	1981/1982–2011/2012	−0.45	1.46	−2.18	−0.59
	1981/1982–1989/1990	0.09	0.60	−2.40	−6.13
	1990/1991–1999/2000	0.59	2.73	−0.63	5.32
	2000/2001–2011/2012	0.87	2.30	−2.10	−0.50
Rice/other Sindh	1981/1982–2011/2012	0.94	2.94	0.84	2.29
	1981/1982–1989/1990	0.41	−0.23	0.12	1.30
	1990/1991–1999/2000	1.30	3.03	0.80	3.25
	2000/2001–2011/2012	4.34	9.78	3.61	4.15
Southern KPK	1981/1982–2011/2012	−1.94	−2.19	0.59	2.11
	1981/1982–1989/1990	−0.27	−0.63	0.50	4.88
	1990/1991–1999/2000	−1.53	−3.63	−1.36	−1.04
	2000/2001–2011/2012	−2.57	−0.03	3.37	3.32
KPK Plains/foothills	1981/1982–2011/2012	1.14	2.19	−1.34	−0.97
	1981/1982–1989/1990	2.91	4.78	−1.47	−0.18
	1990/1991–1999/2000	0.27	0.65	1.08	1.23
	2000/2001–2011/2012	0.16	4.05	−3.33	−3.82
Balochistan	1981/1982–2011/2012	1.91	3.19	2.08	2.03
	1981/1982–1989/1990	3.58	6.57	2.00	−0.02
	1990/1991–1999/2000	0.82	−1.70	3.17	3.94
	2000/2001–2011/2012	1.51	2.67	1.51	2.10
National	1981/1982–2011/2012	0.58	2.35	0.82	1.86
	1981/1982–1989/1990	1.05	2.72	0.72	−0.70
	1990/1991–1999/2000	0.68	3.77	1.76	4.69
	2000/2001–2011/2012	0.37	1.64	0.56	1.97

Source: Authors, based on data from GoP (2013).
Note: KPK = Khyber Pakhtunkhwa

Maize		Cotton		Sugarcane		All crops
Acreage	Production	Acreage	Production	Acreage	Production	Acreage
1.05	3.06	−3.40	−1.02	−2.21	−0.73	−1.59
1.45	2.86	−4.41	−3.67	−7.41	−6.58	−0.52
3.48	5.22	0.00	1.84	2.26	4.59	0.39
−0.89	1.78	0.21	4.52	0.00	0.09	−3.59
1.57	6.91	−2.32	0.66	0.03	0.85	0.79
1.35	1.64	−6.24	0.60	−0.16	0.07	0.65
−3.24	−1.38	−6.42	−4.31	1.50	1.36	1.35
6.96	19.65	5.52	11.07	0.15	1.39	0.43
1.03	6.16	−0.20	2.79	0.75	1.71	0.24
1.07	1.84	−0.37	9.54	−1.50	−1.63	0.47
1.87	6.64	−4.06	−5.73	4.03	4.94	0.45
0.79	9.88	2.84	5.43	−0.37	1.04	−0.22
3.29	8.63	1.61	4.51	−0.91	0.98	1.07
−1.33	−0.77	3.79	11.82	−6.89	−7.34	1.86
6.19	11.23	0.57	−0.18	−0.64	0.39	1.10
6.71	17.32	0.26	2.47	4.15	8.09	0.12
0.35	1.11	3.15	5.79	1.75	3.99	1.46
3.74	3.70	3.38	10.45	−3.93	−3.78	1.64
−3.03	−1.64	6.02	6.75	4.81	6.23	2.16
1.04	2.16	0.14	0.16	3.88	7.33	0.62
−9.55	−9.82	−2.75	1.29	0.42	1.61	−1.87
−1.55	−2.67	−1.18	−3.61	3.62	4.78	−0.73
−8.50	−7.52	2.11	8.12	−0.15	3.72	−0.35
−15.94	−16.98	−5.99	−0.08	−2.41	−1.87	−2.63
−3.91	−1.35	−3.53	1.72	0.17	0.88	0.35
2.44	0.92	−2.63	−4.24	4.51	6.41	0.68
−6.96	−6.45	−1.31	5.57	−1.50	0.71	0.20
−3.61	3.07	−3.37	6.88	−1.47	0.02	2.57
−1.40	−2.25	−7.59	−5.03	−3.06	−2.67	−2.18
−0.93	−3.00	−9.50	−6.79	−8.10	−7.34	−1.10
−1.12	−1.45	−9.34	−7.44	−2.54	−2.51	−1.76
−1.17	−1.75	1.32	4.08	−0.01	0.29	−2.33
1.10	2.67	−8.22	−6.37	2.85	3.17	1.00
3.78	5.89	−100.00	−100.00	8.65	9.69	3.12
0.99	1.40	0.00	0.00	1.26	2.19	0.61
−0.99	0.16	0.00	0.00	−0.01	−0.32	−0.47
2.69	3.48	17.23	18.95	−2.21	−0.68	1.81
7.50	8.59	−4.41	0.00	−10.07	−5.46	3.18
−5.71	−3.97	58.49	60.86	4.81	6.28	1.04
6.74	7.22	7.55	6.60	0.67	−0.21	1.61
1.21	4.97	0.80	3.70	0.21	1.37	0.39
1.94	2.84	1.79	7.68	−1.12	−0.32	0.88
1.30	3.38	1.14	1.56	1.34	2.56	0.77
0.91	7.95	−0.28	1.98	0.40	2.07	−0.12

Annex C: Estimating Total Factor Productivity

TFP studies can be broadly divided into the following categories: (1) highly aggregated national-level studies, often having a limited coverage of agricultural products, and at times restricted to only crop agriculture; (2) studies that use a descriptive approach to productivity measurement and employ index numbers such as the Törnqvist-Theil index; and (3) studies that use a normative approach involving the estimation of frontier production functions or data envelopment analysis, both of which use an external norm (such as a best-practice frontier formed by observations from other regions) as the reference for measuring productivity. The aggregative national studies generally fail to capture important regional productivity differentials, particularly if their coverage of inputs or outputs is limited. This, in turn, can limit the relevance of TFP growth analysis to the wider analysis of agricultural policy.

There are two techniques that are commonly applied to computing total factor productivity using a descriptive approach: the arithmetic index and the Törnqvist-Theil index. The arithmetic index is the ratio of a total output index to a total input index, considered the simplest measure of TFP for the agricultural sector. The input index is a linear aggregation of inputs, weighted by input shares in total input cost, and assumes that production functions are linear and homogeneous and that labor markets are competitive (Wen 1993).

More widely used is the Törnqvist-Theil (T-T) approximation of the Divisia index. Based on Chambers (1988), Capalbo and Antle (1988), and Thirtle and Bottomley (1992), the T-T formulation can be written as:

$$\ln(TFP_t / TFP_{t-1}) = 1/2 \sum (R_{it} + R_{it-1}) \ln(Y_{it} / Y_{it-1})$$
$$-1/2 \sum (S_{jt} + S_{jt-1}) \ln(X_{jt} / X_{jt-1})$$

where R_{it} is the share of output i in total revenue, Y_{it} is output i, S_{jt} is the share of input j in total input cost, and X_{jt} is input j, all in period t. In this specification, revenue shares for the output index and cost shares for the input index are updated for every time period. We use this approach in the analysis set forth in this chapter.

Chapter 3

CONSUMPTION, NUTRITION, AND POVERTY

Sohail J. Malik, Hina Nazli, Edward Whitney,
Asma Shahzad, and Amina Mehmood

Introduction

While the slow pace of overall economic growth in Pakistan—particularly in the agricultural sector and the wider rural economy—was discussed in Chapter 2, the picture is incomplete without a closer examination of poverty, nutrition, and food security, both throughout the country and in its rural areas. Traditional measures of poverty focus on income, taking a "money-metric approach," but a more complete understanding of poverty dynamics requires data on other aspects of human well-being. Among the most important is access to sufficient, nutritious food; for the poor in Pakistan, who spend more than half of their incomes on food, food prices can have a major impact, not only on health and education expenditures but on health and long-term nutritional outcomes as well. Poverty measures thus benefit from a strong understanding of food consumption patterns, costs, and security.

The official estimates of poverty incidence, set forth in the Ministry of Finance Economic Survey 2013–2014 (GoP 2014), and earlier in the Planning Commission of Pakistan's *Millennium Development Goals Report 2013*, place the figure at just 12 percent in 2010/2011, down from 34.5 percent in 2001/2002 (GoP 2013b). Yet official estimates of child malnutrition from the 2011 National Nutrition Survey (NNS) place the prevalence of underweight, stunting, and wasting at 32, 44, and 15 percent, respectively—figures that are relatively unchanged from similar estimates produced a decade earlier (NNS 2011). Various estimates of both poverty and malnutrition also show significantly higher incidences in rural Pakistan than in urban Pakistan.

At first glance, the evidence suggests that progress in poverty reduction has not been accompanied by improvements in health and nutrition in Pakistan. While this is not necessarily surprising—the pathway from economic growth to nutritional improvement is often circuitous—the issue at hand may be even more complex. The analysis of poverty dynamics in Pakistan requires more attention—greater disaggregation, higher resolution, and finer detail—to fully understand the forces at play. Disaggregation of poverty figures between provinces and agroecological zones, between urban and rural populations, and over short and long time frames is critical to fully understand the prevalence and nature of poverty in Pakistan.

The discourse around policy making for poverty reduction in Pakistan is increasingly highlighting the importance of a range of related issues, from poverty measurement to micronutrient malnutrition to the linkages between agriculture, health, and nutrition. This suggests that there is growing demand for more and better analyses that further the understanding of poverty dynamics in Pakistan and, ultimately, inform policy making in support of inclusive growth strategies and social protection programs.

This chapter attempts to deepen the analysis of poverty dynamics in Pakistan. It does so by drawing on and comparing several key sources of data and analyses that are useful in estimating poverty in Pakistan across different dimensions. First and foremost, the chapter draws on household survey data from various sources. These surveys, referred to throughout the chapter, provide important information on household demographics and the consumption, nutrition, and health status of individuals in those households.

The main source of household data derives from successive rounds of the Pakistan Household Income and Expenditure Survey (HIES) that has been conducted by the Pakistan Bureau of Statistics in both the rural and urban areas of all provinces since 1963.[1] The HIES collects information on household characteristics, consumption patterns, household income by source, and social indicators. With this data, we can estimate, across various sectors of society, both income distribution and income and nonincome measures of poverty. The chapter also draws on analysis from the official series of nutrition and health surveys conducted by government agencies and partner institutions between 1977 and 2011, as well as independent surveys conducted by various universities, research institutes, and others between 2001 and 2010. Finally, the chapter also uses data from the Pakistan Rural Household Panel Survey (RHPS) Round 1 (IFPRI/IDS 2012) and Round 2 (IFPRI/IDS 2013; see Chapter 1 for details).

The chapter proceeds as follows. The second section explores household consumption patterns to gain an initial understanding of how food

---

1 Since 1998/1999 the name has been changed to the Household Integrated Economic Surveys. The Federal Bureau of Statistics was renamed as the Pakistan Bureau of Statistics in 2013. In this chapter we use the acronym *HIES* to refer to both the previous Household Income and Expenditure Surveys and the renamed Household Integrated Economic Surveys.

consumption and household welfare are measured in Pakistan, and how changes in prices and public policy can affect welfare. The third section explores the impact of these consumption patterns on nutrition, specifically the nutritional status of children in Pakistan. The fourth section examines poverty estimates for Pakistan and offers several novel insights on both poverty levels and trends that help explain the apparent disconnect between official poverty figures and the persistence of malnutrition. The fifth section offers concluding thoughts on policy options required to address poverty, malnutrition, and food security in Pakistan.

Consumption and Expenditure Patterns

Consumption patterns are central to understanding poverty because they provide an accurate picture not only of a household's income but also its savings and dissavings, the public transfers and private remittances it receives, and the shocks it must weather in bad times. Because estimates of the value of consumption and poverty levels over time hinge on consumer price indexes (CPIs), these consumption measures have far-reaching policy impacts. For example, a CPI that underestimates the true increase in consumer prices will exaggerate the true economic performance of an economy. This in turn affects not only decision making on broad monetary and fiscal policies but also the design of programs that are focused on productivity growth or poverty reduction. Thus, a nuanced understanding of the construction of Pakistan's CPI and how accurately it reflects consumption patterns—especially food consumption patterns—is essential to determining how price and policy changes affect poverty in the country.

Average monthly consumption expenditures, calculated from successive rounds of the HIES, show that, between 2001/2002 and 2010/2011, urban households spent a significantly larger amount on consumption than rural households, with urban consumption exceeding rural consumption by 40 to 55 percent. While the gap in rural-urban expenditure has not widened sharply, the consistently large differences may indicate several factors at play: the baskets of goods and services consumed in each sector may be different, the prices facing consumers in each sector may be different, the baskets and prices may have changed over time and at different rates across sectors, or some combination of all of these factors may be in play. Given these potential differences, policy makers need to be aware of how well the CPI reflects the aggregate movements in prices that affect poverty, because the CPI is a key input to the official measurement of poverty and, in turn, poverty alleviation policy.

TABLE 3.1 Shares of expenditure categories in total expenditure in two surveys, 2007/2008

Expenditure category	FBS 2007/2008 (%)	HIES 2007/2008 (%)		
		Pakistan	Urban areas	Rural areas
Food and nonalcoholic beverages	34.83	43.61	36.82	50.60
Restaurants and hotels	1.23	0.97	1.27	0.67
Alcoholic beverages and tobacco	1.41	1.12	0.82	1.44
Clothing and footwear	7.57	6.62	5.87	7.38
Furnished household equipment and house	4.21	2.80	3.24	2.36
Housing, water, electricity, gas, other	29.41	23.61	28.86	18.20
Health	2.19	3.69	3.12	4.27
Transportation	7.20	8.26	8.34	8.19
Communication	3.22	2.21	2.66	1.75
Recreation and culture	2.02	2.15	2.86	1.42
Education	3.94	2.33	3.32	1.30
Miscellaneous goods and services	2.76	2.63	2.82	2.43
Total	100.00	100.00	100.00	100.00

Source: Authors, based on data from GoP (2008b, 2008c).

Note: FBS = *Family Budget Survey*; HIES = *Household Integrated Economic Survey*.

To better understand its impact, we first consider whether the CPI understates the share of food in the consumer's consumption basket. Comparing HIES 2007/2008 (GoP 2008c) data with the Family Budget Survey 2007/2008 (GoP 2008b) data, which forms the basis of the CPI, we find that the latter understates the share of food and nonalcoholic beverages by about 9 percentage points (Table 3.1). Similarly, food accounts for nearly 49 percent in total expenditure in HIES 2010/2011 (GoP 2011); that is, a share that is 14 percentage points higher than that in the FBS 2007/2008. Data from RHPS Round 1 (IFPRI/IDS 2012) further validate the HIES finding: according to this survey, rural households allocate nearly 57 percent of their expenditures to food. The HIES 2007/2008 data also indicate that the share of food in total expenditure in rural areas is 13.8 percentage points higher than that in urban areas (GoP 2008c).

Importantly, the CPI also fails to capture significant differences in the prices of several key food items between urban and rural areas (Table 3.2). Most of the items that are produced in rural areas, such as cereals, pulses, meat, and milk, are relatively more expensive in urban areas, while processed items such as edible oil/ghee and sugar are more expensive in rural areas. Yet as Malik et al. (2014a) indicate, the prices used to compute the CPI are urban

TABLE 3.2 Unit costs of selected food items in urban and rural areas of Pakistan, 2010/2011

Food item category	Detailed food item	Urban (PKR)	Rural (PKR)	Urban/rural difference (%)
Cereals	Wheat and wheat flour	29.8	28.5	4.6
	Rice and rice flour	63.7	58.8	8.3
Pulses	Gram (black and white)	80.2	79.8	0.5
	Lentils (masoor)	132.0	133	−0.8
Milk and milk products	Milk	49.4	44.6	10.8
	Yogurt	59.0	49.8	18.5
Oil and ghee	Hydrogenated vegetable oil (banaspati ghee)	149.6	150.2	−0.4
	Other cooking oil	150.6	153.5	−1.9
Meat	Beef	234.7	222.5	5.5
	Mutton	409.4	394.7	3.7
Vegetables	Potatoes	26.8	27.5	−2.5
	Onion	32.8	34.4	−4.7
Fruits	Banana	32.1	30.8	4.2
Sweeteners	Sugar	74.3	76.5	−2.9

Source: Authors, based on data from GoP (2011).

Note: PKR = Pakistani rupees.

based, collected from 40 urban centers and no rural locations. While computation of the official CPI is based on a systematic and standard international method, the survey used to collect information on the basket of goods and services and commodity prices focuses only on urban areas and is based on a survey design that is not publicly available for scrutiny (Malik et al. 2014a). It is not surprising that the sizeable differences between rural and urban sectors in terms of economic, social, and demographic attributes, and specifically prices, are not reflected; this has led to an underestimation of the share of food expenditures in the CPI. Given the much higher food expenditure shares and the size of the rural sector, the expenditure patterns of the "average Pakistani consumer" can be reasonably expected to be substantially different from those of the "average urban consumer," which the CPI represents (State Bank of Pakistan 2002; Jamal 2012; Malik et al. 2014a). The data presented in Table 3.2 confirm that this is the case.

Because food accounts for a large share of total expenditures of Pakistani households, food price inflation has a significant effect on the purchasing power of the population and on the incidence of poverty. However, the effects of movements in the prices that consumers face are not captured if the CPI

FIGURE 3.1 Food price inflation and overall inflation, 2006/2007–2010/2011

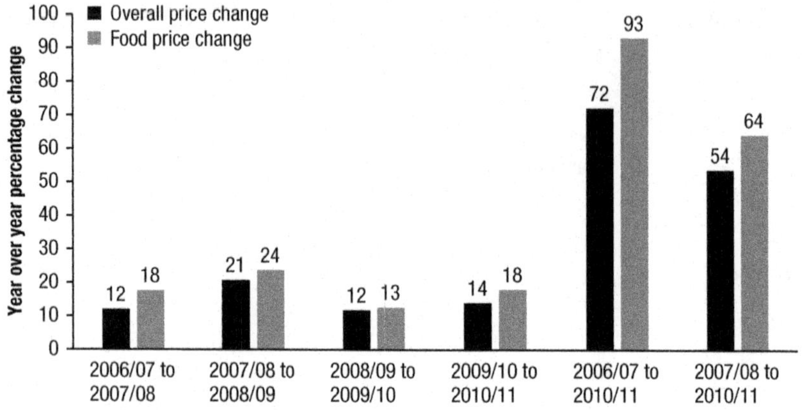

Source: Authors, based on data from GoP (2013a).

estimate does not adequately reflect the share of food expenditures, their constituent items, or changes over time. There is thus strong reason to review the CPI methodology to assess how well it reflects both the real consumption baskets of people and the price trends over time.[2]

The data indicate that food prices have been increasing, with a 93 percent rise between 2006/2007 and 2010/2011 (Figure 3.1). This trend has persisted to the present: a month-to-month comparison reported in the 2014 Pakistan Economic Survey indicates that the prices of wheat, lentils, and milk went up by 21 percent, 15 percent, and 6 percent, respectively, between March 2013 and March 2014 (GoP 2014). These price increases have adversely affected purchasing power. For example, real wages in three of Pakistan's main cities, measured in terms of the wheat flour equivalent of one day's wages, have noticeably declined (Figure 3.2).

Rural–Urban Variations

In an effort to further disentangle rural–urban differences in consumption expenditures, we examine consumption data from HIES 2010/2011 (GoP 2011) in greater detail. Tabling the limitations of a solely money-metric estimation of poverty to a later point in this chapter, we classify households in

---

2   On February 11–12, 2015, the Pakistan Bureau of Statistics held a conference on Change of Base of Price Indexes in Islamabad at which many of these aspects were discussed, and a consensus was established on addressing these shortcomings.

FIGURE 3.2 Kilograms of flour purchased by one day's wages in three cities, 2006–2012

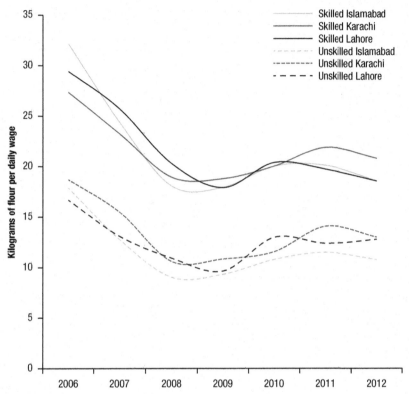

Source: Authors' calculations based on GoP (2013a).

the HIES data that are in the lowest two expenditure quintiles as "poor," and those that are in the higher three quintiles as "non-poor." We control for variations in household size by using the standard adult equivalence scale for Pakistan to transform the number of persons in a household to adult equivalents (GoP 2003).

Food is the major expenditure category in the typical household budget in Pakistan. According to data from HIES 2010/2011 (GoP 2011), food accounts for 53 percent of total expenditure: 46 percent in urban areas and 57 percent in rural areas. Understandably, the poor allocate a higher proportion, about 57 percent of their expenditures, to food, while the non-poor allocate 51 percent. Translated into an equivalent in US dollar terms, poor households spend less than 50 cents per day per adult equivalent, of which about 30 cents is spent on food and 20 cents on nonfood. This amount is

TABLE 3.3 Budget shares of food items by poverty status for urban, rural, and all households, 2010/2011

Food item	Pakistan			Urban			Rural		
	Overall	Non-poor	Poor	Overall	Non-poor	Poor	Overall	Non-poor	Poor
Percentage of food expenditure									
Wheat	17.5	14.6	21.9	15.1	11.8	20.1	18.8	16.1	22.8
Rice	3.8	3.7	3.9	3.8	3.6	4.1	3.8	3.8	3.9
Other cereals	0.4	0.4	0.4	0.3	0.4	0.3	0.4	0.4	0.4
Pulses	3.0	3.0	3.1	3.0	2.8	3.2	3.0	3.0	3.1
Fruits, vegetables	13.0	13.1	12.8	13.2	13.4	12.9	12.8	12.9	12.7
Dairy	24.3	26.7	20.7	24.5	26.6	21.2	24.2	26.8	20.4
Meats	9.7	11.4	7.1	12.2	14.7	8.4	8.4	9.7	6.4
Oils	10.9	10.1	12.1	10.5	9.5	12.0	11.1	10.4	12.1
Sugars	9.0	8.9	9.2	8.6	8.5	8.8	9.2	9.1	9.3
Other	7.0	6.9	7.1	7.8	7.9	7.7	6.6	6.4	6.8
Total	100	100	100	100	100	100	100	100	100
Total monthly per adult equivalent food expenditure									
Mean (PKR)	1,624	1,972	1,102	1,754	2,147	1,165	1,556	1,880	1,069
Food share (%)	53.1	50.9	56.5	45.8	42.1	51.3	56.9	55.5	59.2

Source: Authors' estimates based on GoP (2011).
Note: PKR = Pakistani rupees.

substantially less than half the US$1.25 per day per adult equivalent that is used to define income level of the poor.

A breakdown of budget allocations to specific food items reveals more about poverty in rural and urban Pakistan. On average, households spent nearly two-thirds of their food budget on four items in 2010/2011: wheat (18 percent), dairy (24 percent), oils (11 percent), and sugars (9 percent) (Table 3.3). Poor households spent 22 percent of food expenditures on wheat—20 percent in urban areas and 23 percent in rural areas. Non-poor households spent 15 percent of food expenditures on wheat—12 percent in urban areas and 16 percent in rural areas. The non-poor spent three times as much on dairy products as did the poor. Most of the dairy products are consumed in the form of milk (mostly for tea) and ghee (clarified butter used for cooking).

These shares of food item expenditure illustrate considerable differences in both caloric intake and the range of foods from which the intake is derived, both of which are important aspects of poverty and welfare measurement.

TABLE 3.4 Calorie shares of food items by poverty status across urban, rural, and all households, 2010/2011

Category	Pakistan			Urban			Rural		
	Overall	Non-Poor	Poor	Overall	Non-Poor	Poor	Overall	Non-Poor	Poor
Percentage of calories									
Wheat	46.5	43.0	51.8	42.5	38.0	49.3	48.6	45.7	53.0
Rice	5.7	5.6	5.7	6.0	5.9	6.1	5.5	5.5	5.5
Other cereals	0.6	0.7	0.5	0.4	0.5	0.3	0.7	0.7	0.6
Pulses	2.3	2.4	2.1	2.5	2.6	2.4	2.2	2.3	2.0
Fruits, vegetables	4.5	4.7	4.1	5.0	5.4	4.5	4.2	4.4	4.0
Dairy	13.1	15.1	10.1	13.5	15.8	10.0	12.9	14.8	10.1
Meats	2.5	3.1	1.6	3.5	4.4	2.1	2.0	2.5	1.4
Oils	13.9	14.1	13.6	15.4	15.8	14.8	13.1	13.2	12.9
Sugars	4.4	4.6	4.0	4.9	5.2	4.3	4.1	4.3	3.8
Other	0.9	1.0	0.6	1.3	1.6	0.9	0.6	0.7	0.5
Total	100	100	100	100	100	100	100	100	100
Total calories per adult equivalent per day									
Mean	2260.1	2535.6	1847.0	2086.7	2291.9	1779.1	2350.6	2662.7	1882.5

Source: Authors' estimates based on GoP (2011).

Poverty limits the diversity in consumption to a narrower range of foods. Table 3.3 indicates that poor households rely on wheat, oils, and sugars to a greater extent than do non-poor households.

Using the HIES 2010/2011 data (GoP 2011), we calculate that the average calorie consumption per adult equivalent per day is 2,260 calories, which is slightly less than the recommended allowance of 2,350 calories per day (Table 3.4). The poor fall far below the national average in calorie consumption. The average calorie intake for the poor is only 1,847 calories per day— 1,883 for the rural poor and 1,779 for the urban poor.

Wheat not only accounts for the largest proportion of food expenditures, but Table 3.4 shows that it also supplies the bulk of calories consumed. For the poor, more than half of all calories are derived from wheat consumption, with the rural poor relying on wheat significantly more than the urban poor. Variation in the source of calories also exists across and within provinces.

Using the average food expenditures and calories intakes (per adult equivalent per day), we compute the average cost of 100 calories of food. And given the importance of wheat in the average diet and household budget, we also

TABLE 3.5 Consumption of calories and the cost of calories by poverty status of households, 2010/2011

Poverty status of households	Population (%)	Total calories	Food expenditure (PKR)	Cost to obtain 100 calories (PKR)	Calories from wheat	Expenditure on wheat (PKR)	Wheat cost to obtain 100 calories (PKR)
Rural poor	31.2	1,883	35.63	1.89	1,007	8.15	0.81
Rural non-poor	35.6	2,663	62.67	2.35	1,208	7.73	0.64
Urban poor	15.8	1,779	38.83	2.18	881	9.20	1.04
Urban non-poor	17.5	2,292	71.56	3.12	872	7.25	0.83
National	100.0	2,260	54.12	2.39	1,041	7.28	0.70

Source: Authors' estimates based on GoP (2011).

Note: Total calories, Food expenditure, Calories from wheat, and Expenditure on wheat are daily per adult equivalent. PKR = Pakistani rupees.

compute the cost of 100 calories derived from wheat. Our calculations indicate that a household must spend an average of PKR 2.39 to obtain 100 calories (Table 3.5). However, 100 calories from wheat costs only PKR 0.70. Understandably, given the wider range and possibly better quality of their food intake, non-poor households spend more than poor households to obtain 100 calories in both urban and rural areas. Interestingly, the cost of calories from wheat is higher for poor households than for non-poor households— possibly a consequence of the markets where smaller-quantity bags and unpackaged quantities are sold at higher prices.

Because of the centrality of wheat in consumption patterns in Pakistan, Table 3.6 presents the budget share, average consumption, and expenditure and price elasticities of wheat. On average, an adult consumes nearly 9 kilograms of wheat in a month (304 grams of wheat every day). Wheat consumption and the percentage expenditure are higher in rural areas than in urban areas. Non-poor households in rural areas consume more wheat than poor households in rural areas, whereas little difference is observed between poor and non-poor households in urban areas. Poor households spend more than one-fifth of their food expenditure on wheat. The expenditure and price elasticities reported in this table—figures that are consistent with Haq, Nazli, and Meilke (2008) and Haq, Nazli, and Meilke (2011)—indicate that an increase in income (expenditure) by 10 percent increases the demand for wheat by more than 7.7 percent. Poor households have higher expenditure and price elasticities than non-poor households, while urban poor households have higher expenditure elasticity (0.92) as compared to rural poor households

TABLE 3.6 Budget share and elasticity of wheat consumption by poverty status and rural and urban location, 2010/2011

Poverty status	Consumption (kg/adult equivalent/ day)	Budget share on wheat (%)	Expenditure elasticity	Own-price uncompensated elasticity[a]	Own-price compensated elasticity[a]	Wheat-rice elasticity
Rural areas	0.334	18.8	0.79	−0.32	−0.21	0.01
Poor	0.301	22.8	0.84	−0.35	−0.17	−0.01
Non-poor	0.356	16.1	0.75	−0.35	−0.23	0.02
Urban areas	0.244	15.1	0.74	−0.31	−0.12	0.01
Poor	0.248	20.1	0.92	−0.36	−0.16	−0.00
Non-poor	0.242	11.8	0.67	−0.20	−0.11	−0.00
Pakistan	0.304	17.5	0.77	−0.32	−0.18	0.01
Poor	0.277	21.9	0.81	−0.21	−0.16	−0.01
Non-poor	0.310	14.6	0.76	−0.39	−0.17	0.02

Source: Authors' estimates based on GoP (2011).

Note: kg = kilogram.

[a] Own-price uncompensated elasticities denote any change in the quantity demanded of a commodity when its price changes. This change in demand results in a change in the consumption level. Own-price compensated elasticities maintain original consumption levels by making possible substitution between two commodities if the price of one commodity changes.

(0.84). However, an increase in the price of wheat has only a small effect on the demand for wheat, because the price elasticity of demand for wheat is generally low across all categories.

A useful way of illustrating the sensitivity of consumption to changes in food prices—and thus the vulnerability of the poor to price shocks—is to examine Pakistan's experience during the recent food price crisis (for international experience, see Harttgen and Klasen 2012; De Hoyos, Rafael, and Medvedev 2009; Ivanic and Martin 2008; World Bank 2010; Headey and Fan 2010; for Pakistan's experience, see Haq, Nazli, and Meilke 2008; Friedman, Hong, and Hou 2011). This crisis was manifested in the 42 percent increase in the world food price index between 2006 and 2013/2014 and by sharp price spikes during the period 2006–2008. Although the crisis was largely driven by cereal price increases on the order of 60 percent between 2006 and 2013, the prices of meats, dairy products, oils, and sugars also increased during the period by 31, 59, 47, and 4 percent, respectively (FAO, IFAD, and WFP 2014).

In Pakistan prices of most food items increased by more than 100 percent during the period 2000/2001–2008/2009. For example, the price of wheat increased by 162 percent, rice by 207 percent, milk by 101 percent, ghee by

147 percent, and onions by 140 percent (GoP 2013a). Estimates of compensating variation by Haq, Nazli, and Meilke (2008) and Friedman, Hong, and Hou (2011) provide a measure of the extent of the decline in the welfare of households attributable to these food price increases in Pakistan. Haq, Nazli, and Meilke (2008) found that after the food price crisis of 2008, PKR 44.3 per adult equivalent per month in urban areas and PKR 40.3 per adult equivalent per month in rural areas were required to maintain consumption at 2004/2005 levels. Similarly, Friedman, Hong, and Hou (2011) suggest that average households would need an additional amount equivalent to 38 percent of their pre-crisis expenditures to maintain pre-crisis consumption levels, and estimated that average household caloric provision fell by almost 8 percent between 2006 and the first half of 2008. Moreover, Friedman, Hong, and Hou (2011) found that urban households were relatively worse off than rural households during the crisis and declines in the welfare of households widened the inequality between the poor and non-poor. Our estimates indicate that the demand for wheat changes little when prices rise—as they did during the 2007/2008 food price crisis—meaning that households must allocate a larger share of their budgets to the purchase of wheat, often at the expense of other foods that are required to maintain a balanced diet.

In summary, the cost of meeting either national averages of calories or recommended daily allowances of calories remains a struggle for the poor. Levels of calorie consumption for a large proportion of Pakistan's population indicate, as discussed above, the possibility of a high prevalence of malnutrition—which is measured in the simplest of terms as an inability to meet minimum dietary energy requirements.

This conclusion is in line with the increasing awareness that food consumption levels are well below the minimum defined food basket for most households due to high food price inflation during 2010/2011 (GoP 2013a). Gazdar and Mallah (2013) conclude that given the high poverty and unemployment levels in the country, the increase in the cost of vital food items in recent years has adversely affected the poorer sectors of the population. Food price inflation, together with other shocks affecting the household, forces families to cut down on the consumption of nonstaple items and reduce the food intake, which further increases both vulnerability and malnutrition. But the question of how to use these conclusions to move poverty reduction strategies in Pakistan toward viable solutions—effective programs for social protection, nutrition, and health, for example—remains an important part of the ongoing discussion in both government and civil society.

Nutrition and the Nutritional Status of Children

Although discussions about poverty and food security often revolve around standard measures of caloric intake and costs per calorie, it is important to examine the nutritional consequences of limited dietary diversity in Pakistan and the extensive reliance on wheat as a source of nourishment. A growing body of research suggests that persistent malnutrition in Pakistan is characterized by significant but hidden micronutrient deficiencies that arise from limited diversity in the diet (Malik and Malik 1993; Alderman and Garcia 1993; Ibrahim 1999; Qureshi, Nazli, and Soomro 2001; Arif et al. 2012; Di Cesare et al. 2015). The consequences of micronutrient malnutrition—limited cognitive development early in life and low economic productivity later in life—are well established (FAO, IFAD, and WFP 2014; von Grebmer et al. 2014). But recognition of the important linkages between health and nutrition, on the one hand, and agriculture and the rural economy, on the other hand, have only recently emerged in the public discourse on poverty in Pakistan (see, for example, Gazdar and Mallah 2013). There is now some recognition in official circles in Pakistan that food consumption levels are below the minimum defined food basket for most households, and that the food basket itself might need closer scrutiny to identify the sources of micronutrient malnutrition and strategies to address it (GoP 2013a).

Clearly, the relationships between household budgets and food prices discussed earlier fall short in explaining the trade-offs that households make among food options, that is, substitution between good-quality and inferior-quality food. A decline in real incomes as a result of high food prices may force households to substitute cheaper or inferior food for more nutritious options. Of concern is the fact that for poor households that may already be consuming inferior or cheaper foods, substitution may take place between food and essential nonfood items that may be related to, for example, health and education. Restricting expenditures on health and education may affect labor productivity in the short term and school attendance and performance in the long term (Behrman 1993; Chapter 8 on public service provision).

Recent research demonstrates the impact of food price increases on the intake of micronutrients such as calcium, zinc, and iron (Ecker and Qaim 2011; Harttgen and Klasen 2012; Zaki et al. 2014). A closer look at the HIES 2010/2011 (GoP 2011) data sheds light on the issue of micronutrient malnutrition and dietary diversity. HIES 2010/2011 data contain a considerable amount of detail on the types of fruits and vegetables that poor and non-poor households consume. Poor households primarily spend their money on onions and potatoes and few other fruits and vegetables. Non-poor households, on the other hand, spend more on fruits and vegetables other than onions and potatoes. Differences are also found in the types of meat consumed by poor and non-poor households, with poor households spending more on beef and non-poor households spending more on mutton and chicken. While these figures suggest that the poor have limited diversity in their diets, the overall picture suggests that all Pakistani households, irrespective of their location of residence or poverty status, have similar narrow diets comprising primarily cereals, dairy products, oils, and sugars, and lower amounts of green leafy vegetables and fruits.

Data from the NNS 2010/2011 (NNS 2011) provide insight into the consequences of limited micronutrient consumption and dietary diversity. The data indicate that nearly half of women of childbearing age are suffering from anemia, 43 percent from vitamin A deficiency, 48 percent from zinc deficiency, and 69 percent from vitamin D deficiency. The micronutrient malnutrition of women is also reflected in children. The NNS (2011) data show that a large number of children under five years of age in Pakistan also suffer from vitamin A deficiency (54 percent), zinc deficiency (39 percent), and iron deficiency (62 percent). In addition, the prevalence of protein-energy malnutrition (PEM) is not only high but has also increased over time.[3] In 2011 estimates indicated that nearly 44 percent of children were stunted, 15 percent were wasted, and 32 percent were underweight. These estimates in 2001 were 32.5 percent stunted, 11.2 percent wasted, and 42.3 percent underweight.

All of the national nutritional surveys—from the first Micro Nutrient Survey of Pakistan of 1977 to the most recent NNS conducted in 2011—show extremely high rates of child malnutrition in Pakistan (Table 3.7). There is considerable variation in levels of malnutrition across these surveys, making them difficult to compare and even more difficult to track over time. However, what is consistent across these surveys is data that suggest high levels of malnutrition.

This high incidence of malnutrition is confirmed by a number of studies conducted among preschool children in Pakistan (Malik and Malik 1993; Alderman and Garcia 1993; Ibrahim 1999; Qureshi et al. 2001; Arif et al. 2012). The association between child malnutrition and various socioeconomic

---

3   The anthropometric indicators that reflect the protein-energy malnutrition, measured by heights and weights of children at different ages, are considered to be robust measures of children's nutritional status. The PEM is defined by measurements that fall below minus two standard deviations of the normal weight for age (underweight), height for age (stunting), and weight for height (wasting).

TABLE 3.7 Levels of malnutrition found by surveys (%), 1977–2013

Data source	Underweight	Stunted	Wasted
Micro Nutrient Survey 1977	53.3	43.3	8.6
National Nutrition Survey 1985–1987	47.9	41.8	10.8
Pakistan Demographic and Health Survey 1990	40.4	50.2	9.2
National Nutrition Survey 2001	31.5	41.6	14.3
Pakistan Socio-Economic Survey 2001	51.4	52.7	—
Pakistan Rural Household Survey 2001	56.6	64.4	18.4
Pakistan Panel Household Survey 2010	39.8	64.5	17.2
National Nutrition Survey 2011	31.5	43.7	15.1
Rural Panel Household Survey 2013	39.7	45.9	23.1

Source: Authors, based on data from NNS (2011); NIPS (1992); PIDE (2001, 2002, 2010); IFPRI/IDS (2013).
Note: — = not available.

TABLE 3.8 Indicators of malnutrition by province in rural Pakistan (%), RHPS 2013

	Underweight (WAZ)	Stunting (HAZ)	Wasting (WHZ)
All Pakistan	39.7	45.9	23.1
Punjab	35.4	40.9	22.0
Sindh	51.6	59.1	28.1
Khyber Pakhtunkhwa	30.9	37.5	15.9

Source: Authors' estimates, based on the RHPS (IFPRI/IDS 2013).
Note: RHPS = Rural Health Panel Survey; WAZ = weight-for-age; HAZ = height-for-age; WHZ = weight-for-height.

and demographic indicators is also well documented in Pakistan (Qureshi, Nazli, and Soomro 2001; Arif et al. 2012; Bhutta et al. 2013; Di Cesare et al. 2015). While the scope, coverage, and methodologies differ across these studies, their results consistently show a high proportion of malnourished children as indicated by stunting, wasting, and underweight. In an effort to add to this body of work with more up-to-date data specifically on rural Pakistan, we present in Table 3.8 estimates of nutritional status and corresponding determinants based on the RHPS (IFPRI/IDS 2013) to estimate the z-score values for three common indicators, namely, underweight (weight-for-age [WAZ]), stunting (height-for-age [HAZ]), and wasting (weight-for-height [WHZ]). Annex A describes the data and methodology used in this analysis.

Results indicate that overall 39.7 percent of rural children were underweight, 45.9 percent were stunted, and 23.1 percent were wasted in the sampled population in 2013. Of particular note is the high rates of wasting relative to the studies summarized in Table 3.7. On a provincial basis, Sindh showed the highest levels of stunting, wasting, and underweight, and Punjab and Khyber Pakhtunkhwa (KPK) showed levels that were lower than the national average.

Results also indicate a close association between various socioeconomic, demographic, community, and location variables and the nutritional status of children under five years of age. We use a logistic regression model to estimate the determinants of a z-score ranging from −2 to −6, noting that according to standards set by the World Health Organization (WHO), if a z-score for weight-for-age (WAZ), height-for-age (HAZ), or weight-for-height (WHZ) is less than −2, then the child is considered malnourished (WHO 2008). Estimation results given in Table 3.9 indicate the probability of a child being malnourished based on the three measures (WAZ, HAZ, and WHZ); an odds ratio of greater than 1 indicates that the probability of being malnourished is positively correlated with the explanatory variable, and an odds ratio of less than 1 indicates that the probability of being malnourished is negatively correlated.

Results indicate that the nutritional status of children is significantly and negatively correlated with the mother's education, the presence of a toilet facility, and the presence of a healthcare provider within the community. The probability of being stunted increases with a child's age. This may be due to the fact that younger children are protected because of breastfeeding; after weaning, children may not get adequate food for their age. The incidence of wasting declines with age,[4] implying a declining mortality rate with age.[5] Better hygiene, indicated by the presence of a flush toilet in the house, reduces the risk of exposure to infectious diseases and therefore reduces the incidence of stunting. The presence of a Lady Health Visitor (LHV) and access to healthcare services significantly reduces the incidence of underweight and wasting; however, no effect on stunting has been observed. This indicates that the presence of LHVs improves the short-term nutritional status of children but does not play a significant role for the long-term growth of children. This is consistent with the fact that the LHV's role in Pakistan is confined primarily to child birthing. These workers are responsible for providing maternal and child health services, including basic curative care and essential drugs

---

4 Wasting is generally considered to be a strong indicator of mortality among children under five years of age.

5 These results are consistent with Qureshi, Nazli, and Soomro (2001), whereas Arif et al. (2012) found a nonlinear relationship between age and stunting. However, the definition of poverty status in terms of households in consumption levels in the lowest two quintiles versus those in the upper three quintiles does not accurately define poverty.

TABLE 3.9 Determinants of malnutrition among children under age five, rural Pakistan

Variables	Underweight (WAZ)	Stunting (HAZ)	Wasting (WHZ)
Age of child (months)	1.004 (0.003)	1.011*** (0.003)	0.990*** (0.004)
Sex (male = 1)	1.011 (0.117)	1.124 (0.127)	0.791** (0.103)
Mother age at childbirth (years)	0.995 (0.009)	1.000 (0.009)	1.007 (0.011)
Mother literacy (Literate = 1)	0.671*** (0.098)	0.745** (0.103)	0.818 (0.135)
Number of siblings	1.010 (0.032)	0.997 (0.030)	0.990 (0.035)
Family type (Nuclear = 1)	0.946 (0.117)	0.896 (0.108)	1.082 (0.152)
Household type (Farm = 1)	0.957 (0.114)	0.911 (0.106)	0.938 (0.126)
Toilet facility (Yes = 1)	0.930 (0.125)	0.697*** (0.091)	1.031 (0.158)
Presence of a Lady Health Visitor (Yes = 1)	0.719*** (0.096)	1.066 (0.138)	0.778** (0.118)
Distance from Basic Health Unit (km)	0.980** (0.010)	1.000 (0.009)	0.968** (0.012)
Sindh	1.887*** (0.282)	1.702*** (0.253)	1.361** (0.229)
Khyber Pakhtunkhwa	0.971 (0.193)	0.873 (0.164)	0.768 (0.184)
Constant	0.831 (0.308)	0.798 (0.289)	0.475** (0.197)
	1,352	1,352	1,352

Source: Authors' estimates based on the RHPS (IFPRI/IDS 2013).

Note: Standard errors reported in parentheses. Asterisks denote statistical significance at the * 10 percent, ** 5 percent, and *** 1 percent levels. WAZ = weight-for-age; HAZ = height-for-age; WHZ = weight-for-height; km = kilometers.

for the treatment of minor ailments such as diarrhea, malaria, acute respiratory tract infection, and intestinal worms. They can play a significant role in controlling long-term malnutrition as well by creating nutritional awareness among mothers.

Poverty can be an important determinant of the incidence of malnutrition. However, for analytic purposes, since poverty and malnutrition are determined by the same variables, inclusion of poverty as explanatory variable may cause the problem of endogeneity (Arif et al. 2012). In fact malnutrition indicators are often used as a proxy for poverty (Reinhard and Wijayaratne 2002; Setboonsarng 2005; Heltberg 2009; Klaver 2010).

Poverty Indicators

Considerable debate has taken place in Pakistan over the level of the poverty line and resulting estimates of poverty in recent years. In part, this is due to alternative methodologies for the determination of a poverty line derived from a minimum calorie consumption level. In addition, the data problems discussed above involving the calculation of appropriate CPIs have added more uncertainty to calculations of poverty lines and poverty levels over time. (See Annex B for a discussion of methodology and alternative estimates of poverty levels and trends.)

Given these uncertainties in money-metric measures of poverty, we present several other indicators of welfare, along with the official estimates of poverty. As shown below, while there are some differences in the timing and magnitude of variations in these other indicators, a broadly consistent picture emerges of relatively small changes in the welfare of the poor since the early 1990s, in contrast to the sharp downward trend in official poverty estimates.

Table 3.10 presents the official estimates of poverty in Pakistan. According to these estimates, poverty fell sharply between 2001/2002 and 2010/2011, from 34.5 percent to 12.4 percent.[6] The estimates also show a dramatic 24 percentage point decline in the rural poverty headcount ratio during the same period—a decline that is much greater than the corresponding decline in the urban poverty headcount ratio. Despite the greater decline, the rural poverty headcount ratio in 2010/2011 remains higher than the urban poverty headcount ratio.

However, survey data on food budget shares over the same period suggest that the welfare of households in Pakistan has changed relatively little.[7] As Figure 3.3 shows, food budget shares of rural and urban households remained steady, consistent with the absence of a change in real incomes of these groups. (Food expenditures are, in general, income inelastic, that is, a 1 percent gain in income results in less than a 1 percent increase in quantities consumed. Thus, the budget share of food is expected to decline when incomes rise.)[8]

Various indicators of malnutrition also suggest that income levels of the poor may not have risen (and poverty rates may not have fallen) in this period

---

6   The estimates for 2010/2011 were first reported in the Government of Pakistan's Millennium Development Goals progress report (GoP 2013b) and were officially released in the 2014 *Pakistan Economic Survey* (GoP 2014).

7   For details see the official survey reports on various issues of HIES, which are available at the Government of Pakistan website (GoP 2015).

8   This phenomenon is known as Engel's Law (Engel 1857) and is widely cited in consumption and poverty analysis. See, for example, Timmer, Falcon, and Pearson (1983).

TABLE 3.10 Poverty indicators based on the official poverty line, 1992/1993–2010/2011

Year	Poverty headcount ratio (%)			Poverty gap			Severity of poverty		
	Urban	Rural	Pakistan	Urban	Rural	Pakistan	Urban	Rural	Pakistan
1992/1993	20.0	27.6	25.5	3.4	4.6	4.3	0.9	1.2	1.1
1993/1994	15.9	33.5	28.2	2.7	6.3	5.2	0.7	1.8	1.4
1996/1997	15.8	30.2	25.8	2.4	5.3	4.4	0.6	1.4	1.1
1998/1999	20.9	34.7	30.6	4.3	7.6	6.4	1.3	2.4	2.0
2001/2002	22.7	39.3	34.5	4.6	8.0	7.0	1.4	2.4	2.1
2004/2005	14.9	28.1	23.9	2.9	5.6	4.8	0.8	1.8	1.5
2005/2006	13.1	27.0	22.3	2.1	5.0	4.0	0.5	1.4	1.1
2007/2008	10.0	20.6	17.2	—	—	—	—	—	—
2010/2011	7.1	15.1	12.4	—	—	—	—	—	—

Source: Cheema (2005); GoP (2008a, 2014).

Note: — = not available. No official estimates were released for the excluded years prior to 2010/2011.

FIGURE 3.3 Food budget share of total expenditure of rural and urban households, 2001/2002–2012/2013

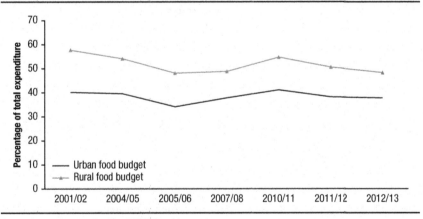

Source: Authors, based on data from HIES (GoP various years).

(Figure 3.4). Both the percentage of children underweight (measured by weight-for-age) and stunted (height-for-age) showed substantial improvement between 1990 and 2001, which was a period of strong agricultural growth and total national income (including remittances) growth. Surprisingly, wasting (weight-for-height), an indicator of acute (short-term) malnutrition, actually increased. Between 2001 and 2011, however, all three indicators of malnutrition either remained the same or increased slightly.

FIGURE 3.4 Indicators of malnourishment in Pakistan, 1990–2011

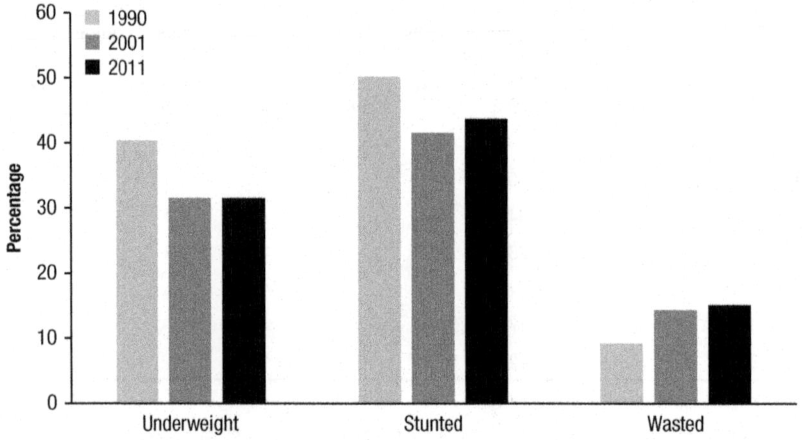

Source: Authors, based on data from NNS (2011); NIPS (1992); PIDE (2001, 2002, 2010).

Putting aside the issues of sensitivity of poverty estimates to methodology and specification, we examine the concentration of poor households across agroclimatic zones (Table 3.11).[9] We assume a poverty line here that is consistent with the expenditure to obtain to 2,350 calories per day per adult equivalent, based on the consumption of the lowest 66 percent of the population. Our analysis indicates that a large proportion of the rural poor are in the cotton/wheat areas. Table 3.11 shows that 19.6 percent of the poor are located in Cotton/Wheat Punjab and another 11.7 percent in Cotton/ Wheat Sindh. Together, these two zones account for 31 percent of Pakistan's rural poor but only 28 percent of the total rural population (17.6 percent in Cotton/Wheat Punjab and 10.0 percent in Cotton/Wheat Sindh). The second column in Table 3.11 shows the poverty headcount ratio within each zone. Overall rural poverty is 47.5 percent, which is higher than overall poverty as defined above; this result is consistent with the persistent higher poverty rates for rural Pakistan, also highlighted above. Poverty headcount ratios are highest in Low-Intensity Punjab (63.0 percent), Rice/Other Sindh (58.3 percent), Cotton/Wheat Sindh (55.6 percent), and Cotton/Wheat Punjab (53.0 percent).

To further explore the intensity of poverty by agroclimatic zone, we calculate an index that is based on the ratio of the following two ratios: the

---

9   Based on the cropping patterns, Pinckney (1989) classifies districts of Pakistan into agroclimatic zones. These zones are described in Chapter 2.

TABLE 3.11 Indicators of the concentration of rural poor by agroclimatic zones, 2011

Agroclimatic zone	Percentage of rural population	Percentage of poor within zone	Percentage of rural poor	Index: Intensity of poor	Percentage of farm income in total income
Rice/wheat Punjab	14.6	35.7	10.9	0.75	44.5
Mixed Punjab	11.9	39.1	9.8	0.82	46.9
Cotton/wheat Punjab	17.6	53.0	19.6	1.11	54.0
Low-intensity Punjab	8.9	63.0	11.8	1.32	48.6
Barani Punjab	5.6	33.7	3.9	0.71	14.5
Cotton/wheat Sindh	10.0	55.6	11.7	1.17	41.1
Rice/other Sindh	8.2	58.3	10.1	1.23	50.6
Khyber Pakhtunkhwa	17.4	45.4	16.6	0.96	17.4
Balochistan	5.9	44.8	5.6	0.94	22.4
Total (%)	100	47.5	100.0	1.00	39.8
Total (number)	86,963,986		34,832,395		

Source: Authors' estimates based on GoP (2011).

Note: For the index, an index value of 1 implies that the zone has a share of the poor equal to its share of the rural population, a value greater than 1 shows that the zone has a share of poor higher than its share of the rural population, and a value less than 1 shows a share of poor smaller than its share of the rural population.

proportion of the poor in that zone out of total rural poor and the proportion of the population in each zone relative to total rural population.[10] The index values (Table 3.11) show that Low-Intensity Punjab has the highest proportion of poor relative to its share of population, followed by Rice/Other Sindh, Cotton/Wheat Sindh, and Cotton/Wheat Punjab. Other zones have a lower concentration of poverty, that is, a smaller share of poor households relative to the zone's share of the rural population. Barani Punjab has 71 percent of its share of poor compared to its share of the rural population. Relatively low poverty in the barani areas of northern Punjab is attributed to a number of socioeconomic characteristics, including the lowest dependency ratio; the highest levels of literacy, particularly female literacy; and the lowest number of unpaid family workers. These factors reflect the health of the region's economy. The rural areas in this region are well integrated with prosperous urban centers that have strong linkages to the services sector, and the region's labor force is employed primarily in the armed forces and the government sector. A high incidence of domestic and overseas migration means that remittances

10 An index value of 1 implies that the region has a share of the poor equal to its share of the rural population, a value greater than 1 shows that the zone has a share of poor higher than its share of the rural population, and a value less than 1 shows a share of poor smaller than its share of the rural population.

contribute a significant proportion to total household income in the barani areas of Punjab. In contrast, in the zones where the incidence of poverty is higher, households' dependence on farm income is much higher. For example, farm income accounts for 54 percent of the total income generated in Cotton/Wheat Punjab, 50.6 percent in Rice/Other Sindh, and 48.6 percent in Low-Intensity Punjab.

Social Protection Policies

In an effort to reduce poverty and increase resilience to shocks among the poor, the Government of Pakistan has identified priority areas for intervention in its social protection strategy, which was developed in 2007. This Social Protection Strategy to Reach the Poor and Vulnerable aims to (1) support chronically poor households and protect them from destitution, food insecurity, exploitation, and social exclusion; (2) protect poor and vulnerable households from the impacts of adverse shocks to their consumption and well-being that, if not mitigated, would push them into poverty or, if already poor, into deeper poverty; and (3) promote investment in human and physical assets, including their health, nutrition, and education, by poor households that would give them the capability to maintain their resilience in the medium term and interrupt the intergenerational cycle of poverty. The strategy emphasizes the need to expand the coverage of cash transfers through a combination of unconditional programs, conditional programs aimed at increasing school enrollments and reducing malnutrition, and other interventions that would combine cash transfers with skills-development interventions aimed at "graduating" the poor out of poverty (GoP 2015a).

Yet the formal safety net system in Pakistan that is required to implement this vision of social protection is, at present, insufficient in size and scope to cope with the challenge (World Bank 2013). Prior to 2008, Pakistan's formal safety net system was much smaller and was composed of two main cash transfer programs: Zakat, or the formal collection and distribution of taxes for charitable use mandated by Islam and administered by the Ministry of Religious Affairs, and the Food Support Program, administered by the Bait-ul-al under the Ministry of Social Welfare and Special Education (Ahmad and Farooq 2010). Both programs were weakly targeted to the poor: only 46 percent of total Bait-ul-Mal expenditures (and 43 percent of total Zakat expenditures) reached the poorest 40 percent of the population (World Bank 2007). At present the main vehicle for social protection—the Benazir Income Support Program, launched in 2008—has grown rapidly, from 1.7 million households served in 2008/2009 to 4.7 million in late 2014. Further attention to sustainability, targeting, graduation, monitoring, and evaluation are required to expand the reach and impact of the program (World Bank 2013).

Conclusions

The foregoing analysis highlights several issues that deserve attention as Pakistan continues its struggle against persistent poverty and malnutrition. Food insecurity is high and relatively unchanging, while calorie intake remains low, consumption patterns are skewed toward cheaper sources of calories, and malnutrition levels remain high, especially among children. Low levels of calorie consumption, overall and by the poor in particular, and, equally important, limited dietary diversity warrant immediate attention. To address these problems, public policy and poverty programs need to take a broader view of poverty, beyond the money-metric approach.

Better design and implementation of public poverty reduction programs are critically needed to address the country's persistent challenge of malnutrition and poverty. Programs need to take a multidimensional approach to the issue by addressing not only the most basic food security concerns—access to calories—but also by improving healthcare services, increasing awareness about sanitation and hygiene, engaging communities in healthcare provision, and empowering women to tackle child and infant malnutrition. There is clearly a need for addressing these issues throughout the country, in its rural areas, and especially in Sindh.

Additional investments in healthcare, education, and poverty reduction programs are also vitally important (Chapters 8 and 10 examine these programs further). For example, there are potential gains to be made from expanding the LHV's role beyond providing assistance with childbirth alone to purveying nutritional information that would shift preferences away from fats and sugars and toward more calorie-efficient and micronutrient-dense foods. Other national programs are also worth supporting with higher levels of investment. The Zero Hunger Program, which was launched in 2012, has made progress in addressing the issue of food insecurity. The Pakistan Integrated Nutrition Strategy, launched in 2013, aims to address the underlying causes of malnutrition such as lack of food diversity, and the Water, Sanitation, and Hygiene (WASH) program and various school feeding programs approach these issues from other angles. The Scaling-Up Nutrition program, initiated in 2013, aims to identify the hurdles in access to food and address the issue of malnutrition in Pakistan. In addition to these programs, the federal and provincial governments have opportunities to mainstream poverty and malnutrition concerns into the integrated programs for economic growth and development that are currently being pursued.

But experience shows there is a need for a stronger monitoring and evaluation system to improve program implementation and effectiveness. There is opportunity to strengthen the statistical framework for better policy research and implementation. Our analyses of the CPI calculations demonstrate the need for scrutiny and improvement of the statistical basis that underlies the analysis of consumption and nutrition. Specifically, the Family Budget Survey that forms the basis of the CPI estimation needs to be updated and restructured in order to make it representative of rural-urban distinctions. Similarly, the methodology behind the CPI calculations needs to be revised and updated to reflect the actual (higher) weights of the food expenditures as well as the evolving consumption patterns and prices of the rural sector. Since the Family Budget Surveys are conducted every five years, whereas prices and consumption patterns change frequently, it is important to test for and continuously remove the potential biases that may arise in calculating the CPI. This can be done through smaller, more periodic sample surveys.

In sum, consumption, nutrition, and poverty must remain central to the wider discussion of growth and development in Pakistan's overall economy, in the agricultural sector, and in the rural economy. There is scope to refine both the measurement of poverty in Pakistan—to capture a broader understanding of its causes and consequences—and to strengthen public policies and programs designed to reduce poverty and malnutrition. The national discourse around policy making for poverty reduction in Pakistan is headed in the right direction insofar as poverty measurement, micronutrient malnutrition, and agriculture-health-nutrition linkages are all on the agenda. This discourse signals the need for higher-quality analysis of poverty dynamics in Pakistan to provide the evidence base needed for informed policy making on inclusive growth strategies and social protection.

References

Ahmad, M., and U. Farooq. 2010. "The State of Food Security in Pakistan: Future Challenges and Coping Strategies." *Pakistan Development Review* 49 (4) Part 2: 903–923.

Alderman, H., and M. Garcia. 1993. *Poverty, Household Food Security, Nutrition in Pakistan.* IFPRI Research Report 96. Washington, DC: International Food Policy Research Institute.

Arif, G. M., S. Nazir, M. N. Satti, and S. Farooq. 2012. *Child Malnutrition in Pakistan: Trends and Determinants.* PSDPS 3. Islamabad: Pakistan Institute of Development Economics.

Arndt, C., and K. R. Simler. 2010. "Estimating Utility-Consistent Poverty Lines with Applications to Egypt and Mozambique." *Economic Development and Cultural Change* 58 (3): 449–474.

Arndt, C., and F. Tarp, eds. 2015. *Lowering the Barriers to Entry to Measuring Poverty and Wellbeing.* Oxford: Oxford University Press.

Behrman, J. R. 1993. "The Economic Rationale for Investing in Nutrition in Developing Countries." *World Development* 21 (11): 1749–1771.

Bhutta, Z. A., H. Gazdar, and L. Haddad. 2013. "Seeing the Unseen: Breaking the Logjam of Undernutrition in Pakistan." *IDS Bulletin* 44 (3).

Cheema, I. A. 2005. *A Profile of Poverty in Pakistan.* Islamabad: Centre for Research on Poverty Reduction and Income Distribution Planning Commission.

De Hoyos, E. R., and D. Medvedev. 2009. *Poverty Effects of Higher Food Prices: A Global Perspective.* Policy Research Working Paper 4887. Washington, DC: World Bank.

Deaton, A., and M. Grosh. 2000. "Chapter 17. Consumption." In *Designing Household Survey Questionnaires for Developing Countries: Lessons from Ten Years of LSMS Experience,* edited by M. Grosh and P. Glewwe. Washington, DC: World Bank.

Deaton, A., and S. Zaidi. 2002. *Guidelines for Constructing Consumption Aggregates for Welfare Analysis.* Living Standards Measurement Study Working Paper 135. Washington, DC: World Bank.

Di Cesare, M., Z. Bhatti, S. B. Soofi, L. Fortunato, M. Ezzati, and Z. A. Bhutta. 2015. "Geographical and Socioeconomic Inequalities in Women and Children's Nutritional Status in Pakistan in 2011: An Analysis of Data from a Nationally Representative Survey." *Lancet Global Health* 3 (4): e229–239.

Ecker, O., and M. Qaim. 2011. "Analyzing Nutritional Impacts of Policies: An Empirical Study for Malawi." *World Development* 39 (3): 412–428.

Engel, E. 1857. "Die Productions- und Consumtionsverhaltnisse des Konigreichs Sachsen." *Zeitschrift des Statistischen Bureaus des Koniglich-Sachsischen* 8 (9): 1–54.

FAO, IFAD, and WFP (Food and Agriculture Organization of the United Nations, International Fund for Agricultural Development, and World Food Programme). 2014. *The State of Food Insecurity in the World 2014: Strengthening the Enabling Environment for Food Security and Nutrition.* Rome: FAO.

Friedman, J., S. Y. Hong, and X. Hou. 2011. *The Impact of the Food Price Crisis on Consumption and Availability in Pakistan: Evidence from Repeated Cross-Sectional and Panel Data.* HNP Discussion Paper. Washington, DC: World Bank.

Gazdar, H., and H. B. Mallah. 2013. "Inflation and Food Security in Pakistan: Impact and Coping Strategies." *IDS Bulletin* 44 (3).

GoP (Government of Pakistan). 2001a. *Food Consumption Table for Pakistan*. Islamabad: Ministry of Planning and Development, Government of Pakistan; UNICEF; Peshawar: Department of Agricultural Chemistry, NWFP Agriculture University.

———. 2001b. *Household Integrated Economic Survey 2001–02*. Islamabad: Federal Bureau of Statistics, Government of Pakistan.

———. 2003. *Accelerating Economic Growth and Reducing Poverty: The Road Ahead*. Poverty Reduction Strategy Paper. Islamabad: Ministry of Finance, Government of Pakistan.

———. 2005. *Household Integrated Economic Survey 2004–05*. Islamabad: Federal Bureau of Statistics, Government of Pakistan.

———. 2006. *Household Integrated Economic Survey 2005–06*. Islamabad: Federal Bureau of Statistics, Government of Pakistan.

———. 2008a. *Pakistan Economic Survey 2007–08*. Islamabad: Ministry of Finance, Government of Pakistan.

———. 2008b. *Family Budget Survey 2007–08*. Islamabad: Federal Bureau of Statistics, Government of Pakistan.

———. 2008c. *Household Integrated Economic Survey 2007–08*. Islamabad: Federal Bureau of Statistics, Government of Pakistan.

———. 2011. *Household Integrated Economic Survey 2010–11*. Islamabad: Federal Bureau of Statistics, Government of Pakistan.

———. 2013a. *Pakistan Economic Survey 2012–13*. Islamabad: Ministry of Finance, Government of Pakistan.

———. 2013b. *Pakistan Millennium Development Goals Report 2013*. Islamabad: Ministry of Planning, Development and Reform, Government of Pakistan.

———. 2014. *Pakistan Economic Survey 2013–14*. Islamabad: Ministry of Finance, Government of Pakistan.

———. 2015a. Benazir Income Support Programme. http://www.bisp.gov.pk/. Accessed July 2015.

———. 2015b. *Pakistan Social and Living Standards Measurement*. Islamabad: Federal Bureau of Statistics. http://www.pbs.gov.pk/content/pakistan-social-and-living-standards-measurement. Accessed April 2, 2016.

Haq, Z., H. Nazli, and K. Meilke. 2008. "Implications of High Food Prices for Poverty in Pakistan." *Agricultural Economics* 39: 477–484.

Haq, Z., H. Nazli, K. Meilke, M. Ishaq, A. Khattak, A. H. Hashmi, and F. U. Rehman. 2011. "Food Demand Patterns in Pakistani Punjab." *Sarhad Journal of Agriculture* 27 (2): 305–311.

Harttgen, K., and S. Klasen. 2012. *Analyzing Nutritional Impacts of Price and Income Related Shocks in Malawi and Uganda*. WP 2012–014. Addis Ababa, Ethiopia: United Nations Development Programme.

Headey, D., and S. Fan. 2010. *Reflections on the Global Food Crisis: How Did It Happen? How Has It Hurt? And How Can We Prevent the Next One?* IFPRI Research Monograph 165. Washington, DC: International Food Policy Research Institute.

Heltberg, R. 2009. "Malnutrition, Poverty, and Economic Growth." *Health Economics* 18, Supplement 1: S77–S88.

Ibrahim, S. 1999. "Anthropometric Patterns and Correlates of Growth Attainments in Under-Five Pakistani Children." *Pakistan Development Review* 38 (2): 131–152.

IFPRI/IDS (International Food Policy Research Institute/Innovative Development Strategies). 2012. Pakistan Rural Household Panel Survey 2012 Round 1 dataset. Washington, DC: IFPRI; Islamabad: IDS.

———. 2013. Pakistan Rural Household Panel Survey 2013 Round 2 dataset. Washington, DC: IFPRI; Islamabad: IDS.

Ivanic, M., and W. Martin. 2008. "Implications of Higher Global Food Prices for Poverty in Low-Income Countries." *Agricultural Economics* 39 (1): 405–416.

Jamal, H. 2012. *Pakistan Poverty Statistics: Estimates for 2011*. Research Report 84. Karachi: Social Policy Development Center.

Klaver, W. 2010. *Underweight or Stunting as an Indicator of the MDG on Poverty and Hunger*. ASC Working Paper 92/2010. Leiden, Netherlands: African Studies Centre.

Malik, N., and S. J. Malik. 1993. *Reporting on the World Nutrition Situation: The Case of Pakistan*. Second Report of World Nutrition Situation. Vol. 2. Geneva: UN/ACC/SCN.

Malik, S. J., H. Nazli, A. Mehmood, and A. Shahzad. 2014a. *Issues in the Measurement of Consumer Price Index in Pakistan*. PSSP Working Paper 20. Islamabad: Pakistan Strategy Support Program of International Food Policy Research Institute.

Malik, S. J., H. Nazli, and E. Whitney. 2014b. *The Official Estimates of Poverty in Pakistan—What Is Wrong and Why?—Illustrations Using the Government of Pakistan's Household Integrated Economic Survey 2010–11*. PSSP Working Paper 26. Islamabad: Pakistan Strategy Support Program of International Food Policy Research Institute.

NIPS (National Institute of Population Studies). 1992. *Pakistan Demographic and Health Survey 1990–91*. Islamabad: National Institute of Population Studies.

NNS (National Nutrition Survey). 2011. *National Nutrition Survey of Pakistan*. Islamabad: Government of Pakistan; Karachi: Aga Khan University.

PIDE (Pakistan Institute of Development Economics). 2001. *Pakistan Rural Household Survey, Round 1 2001–02*. Islamabad: Pakistan Institute of Development Economics; World Bank.

———. 2002. *Pakistan Socioeconomic Survey 2001–02*. Islamabad: Pakistan Institute of Development Economics.

———. 2010. *Pakistan Panel Household Survey*. Islamabad: Pakistan Institute of Development Economics; World Bank.

Pinckney, T. C. 1989. *The Demand for Public Storage of Wheat in Pakistan*. Research Report 77. Washington, DC: International Food Policy Research Institute.

Qureshi, S., H. Nazli, and G. Y. Soomro. 2001. *Nutritional Status in Pakistan*. MIMAP Technical Paper Series 8. Islamabad: Pakistan Institute of Development Economics.

Ravallion, M. 1998. *Poverty Lines in Theory and Practice*. LSMS Working Paper 133. Washington, DC: World Bank.

Ravallion, M., and B. Bidani. 1994. "How Robust Is a Poverty Profile?" *World Bank Economic Review* 8: 75–102.

Reinhard, I., and K. B. S. Wijayaratne. 2002. *The Use of Stunting and Wasting as Indicators for Food Insecurity and Poverty*. Working Paper 27. PIMU Open Forum. Trincomalee, Sri Lanka: Integrated Food Security Program.

Setboonsarng, S. 2005. *Child Malnutrition as a Poverty Indicator: An Evaluation in the Context of Different Development: Interventions in Indonesia*. ADB Institute Discussion Paper 21. Tokyo: Asian Development Bank. http://www.adb.org/sites/default/files/publication/156773/adbi-dp21.pdf.

State Bank of Pakistan. 2002. *Annual Report 2001–02*. Karachi: State Bank of Pakistan.

Timmer, P. C., W. P. Falcon, and S. R. Pearson. 1983. *Food Policy Analysis*. Baltimore: The Johns Hopkins University Press. For the World Bank.

von Grebmer, K., A. Saltzman, E. Birol, D. Wiesmann, N. Prasai, S. Yin, Y. Yohannes, P. Menon, J. Thompson, and A. Sonntag. 2014. *2014 Global Hunger Index: The Challenge of Hidden Hunger*. Bonn: Welthungerhilfe; Washington, DC: International Food Policy Research Institute; and Dublin: Concern Worldwide.

WHO (World Health Organization). 2008. *Measuring a Child's Growth. Training Course on Child Growth Assessment*. WHO Child Growth Standards. Geneva: Department of Nutrition for Health and Development, World Health Organization.

World Bank. 2007. *Social Protection in Pakistan: Managing Household Risks and Vulnerability*. Washington, DC: World Bank.

———. 2010. *Food Price Increases in South Asia: National Responses and Regional Dimensions.* Washington, DC: World Bank, South Asia Region, Sustainable Development Department, Agriculture and Rural Development Unit.

———. 2013. *Pakistan Towards an Integrated National Safety Net System; Assisting Poor and Vulnerable Households: An Analysis of Pakistan's Main Cash Transfer Program.* Washington, DC: World Bank, Human Development Sector, South Asia Region. https://openknowledge .worldbank.org/bitstream/handle/10986/13254/664210ESW0P1180C0disclosed 020110130.pdf?sequence=1. Accessed July 2015.

Zaki, S. A., J. Chaaban, L. Nasreddine, and A. Chalak. 2014. "The Impact of Food Price Increases on Nutrient Intake in Lebanon." *Agricultural and Food Economics* 2 (3): 1–15.

Annex A: Estimation of Malnutrition among Children, Using Data from the Rural Household Panel Survey

As part of the RHPS, a team of trained interviewers, monitored by supervisors, administered the questionnaire to the mothers of children under five years of age and conducted the anthropometric measurement of the children. The WHO guidelines for nutritional assessment were used for taking the anthropometric measurements. Children less than two years old were weighed using a tared weighing method (WHO 2008). In this method, first the mother/helper is weighed alone; then the mother/helper and child are weighed together and the mother's weight is subtracted to determine the child's weight. The weight of children between two and five years old was measured on regular weighing scales. Height or length was measured with a wooden height board. The interviewers were asked to measure the length for children less than two years in the recumbent position using special measurement boards. The heights for children more than two years old were measured with the child standing up.

Data were prepared following WHO guidelines. All observations with weights less than 0.9 kilograms and more than 58 kilograms were dropped. Likewise, all observations with heights less than 38 centimeters and more than 150 centimeters were dropped. A total of 336 observations for weight and height were dropped. The software WHO Anthro was used to estimate the z-score values for three common indicators, namely, stunting (height-for-age), underweight (weight-for-age), and wasting (weight-for-height). In order to examine the status of child malnutrition, a comparison with a reference child of the same age and sex was made. The growth reference of the United States

National Center for Health Statistics is commonly used as basis for this comparison. A z-score is calculated using the median value and standard deviation (SD) of the reference population. The percentage of children whose z-score falls below a defined cutoff point—that is, −2SD from the median of the international reference population—defines the malnourished children.

The analysis presented here uses the data from the second round of the RHPS conducted in April–May 2013. A total of 1,753 children under five years of age were included in the sample; 51 percent were boys, and 49 percent were girls. Of these, 58 percent of the children resided in Punjab, 29 percent in Sindh, and 13 percent in KPK. After cleaning, 1,403 valid cases were left for analysis.

Using these data, we estimated the standard anthropometric measures by estimating z-scores.

$$z\text{-}score = \frac{observed\ value - median\ value\ of\ reference\ population}{standard\ deviation\ value\ of\ reference\ population}$$

Annex B: Alternative Poverty Line Methodologies and Poverty Estimates

This annex describes three alternative methodologies for estimating the poverty line in Pakistan, and summarizes the resulting poverty estimates. The first methodology, referred to as "Official Methodology," is taken directly from the *Poverty Reduction Strategy Paper* produced by the Government of Pakistan in 2003 (GoP 2003). This methodology employs a single regression of calorie consumption on total household expenditures using data for all of Pakistan for each year having a national household survey. The poverty line in the baseline year is derived from the fitted regression curve as the level of expenditure that corresponds to a threshold level of 2,350 calories per day per adult equivalent household member. Poverty lines for subsequent years are calculated using changes in the national CPI. The second methodology, the "Official Methodology (Regional Estimates)" is based on separate regressions of calorie consumption on total household expenditures for rural and urban households in each of the four major provinces of Pakistan. The third methodology, referred to as the "Arndt-Simler (2010) methodology," employs the poverty estimation toolkit presented in Arndt and Simler (2010), then adjusts the consumption basket used to calculate poverty lines to ensure consistency across space and over time, as described below.

FIGURE B3.1 CPI, CPI for food, and poverty line expenditure, 2000/2001–2010/2011

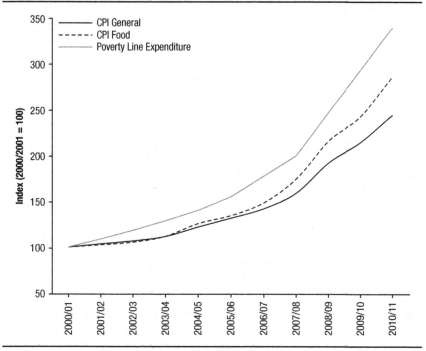

Source: Authors' calculations based on HIES datasets (GoP various years) and GoP (2013a).
Note: CPI = consumer price index.

Official government estimates of poverty are based on a single poverty line for the entire nation. This poverty line represents the cost of obtaining the minimum threshold of 2,350 calories per day for each adult equivalent household member, and it represents a national average of individual item quantities and the prices of those items for households in the bottom three quintiles of the population in terms of per capita expenditures.

However, as discussed in this chapter and in Malik et al. (2014b), the prices and consumption preferences for major calorie sources vary across provinces and across urban and rural areas. A single national poverty line masks this variation in prices and consumption preferences, thus providing an inaccurate portrayal of poverty across the country.

We highlight this issue by comparing trends in the estimates of poverty line expenditures computed for each year directly from the successive HIES datasets (Malik, Nazli, and Whitney 2014b) and the national CPI. As shown in Figure B3.1, poverty lines calculated from new regressions using the values of household expenditures for each survey year (and therefore price data from each HIES rather than price data used in the CPI) are consistently higher than those derived using percentage changes in the national CPI. (The CPI for food rose from 100 in 2001/2002 to 280 in 2010/2011, while the poverty line index increased to 348 over the same period, a difference of nearly 70 percentage points.) To the extent that these official poverty lines are too high, the poverty rates will be overstated.

In principle, estimating separate poverty lines for each spatial domain enables the calculation of even more accurate poverty numbers by capturing regional price differences as well as differences in consumption patterns of the poor. Thus, for our Official Methodology (Regional Estimates), we estimate poverty lines separately by spatial domain by regressing logged adult equivalent household expenditures on calories consumed per day per adult equivalent.[11]

In contrast to the official government methodology, the Arndt-Simler (2010) methodology yields poverty lines that represent consistent levels of utility across spatial domains and across time. Similar to the estimates from the Official Methodology (Regional Estimates), the data source for these estimates is the Government of Pakistan's HIES data for five available survey years. As described in Arndt and Tarp (2015), the toolkit includes the following specifications. First, using household demographics, we calculate a weighted average of calorie requirements for each household in a spatial domain using 2,150 calories as the minimum daily threshold for an adult equivalent household member. Second, we calculate consumption aggregates in the same way as the Official Methodology (Regional Estimates), with the exception that we include the use value of assets and we omit items for which only total value is reported (for example, ready-made meals and some miscellaneous "other" items, which together represent a small portion of total consumption).

The consumption basket and prices used in calculating poverty lines are a product of an iterative process developed by Ravallion (1998) that yields the consumption basket and prices for the household at the poverty line. For each spatial domain and for each survey year, the steps in the iterative process used to produce the Arndt-Simler (2010) methodology are described as follows:

---

11 The household expenditures aggregate is constructed using the food expenditures and nonfood expenditures recorded in the consumption modules of the HIES. In addition to purchases, we include consumption from gifts, transfers, in-kind payments, and own production. We estimate housing costs using a hedonic regression approach and omit the use value of assets.

1. Calculate average quantities, prices, and budget shares for all food commodities for individuals in the bottom 60 percent of the per capita expenditure distribution.

2. Using the average budget shares and the average prices faced by the bottom 60 percent of the per capita expenditure distribution, define the poverty line as the level of expenditures needed to reach 2,350 daily calories per adult equivalent.

3. Recalculate quantities, prices, and budget shares for all food commodities for poor households using the new poverty line defined in the previous step.

4. Using the budget shares and prices from the previous step, define a new poverty line as the level of expenditures needed to reach 2,350 daily calories per adult equivalent.

5. Repeat steps 3 and 4 until the series of estimated poverty lines converge.[12]

Using this procedure, the final poverty line should be consistent with the average budget shares of the individuals falling at or below the poverty line.[13] However, additional steps are necessary in order to produce poverty lines that are utility consistent across spatial domains and time. Arndt and Simler (2010) provide a method to ensure that the composition of consumption baskets satisfies revealed preference constraints and thus provides utility consistent estimates of poverty across spatial domains and time.[14]

Results

National estimates of poverty incidence using the three methodologies are presented in Annex Table B3.1 and Annex Figure B3.2. Both sets of survey-based estimates indicate that, contrary to the official money-metric estimates, the incidence of poverty in Pakistan has not decreased between 2001/2002 and 2010/2011. These findings are consistent with the evidence presented earlier

---

12 This approach is based on the Cost of Basic Needs (CBN) method, developed by Ravallion (1998) and Ravallion and Bidani (1994) and explained in greater detail in Ravallion (1999), Deaton and Zaidi (2002), and Deaton and Grosh (2000).

13 See Ravallion (1998) for a discussion of possible instances where convergence does not take place.

14 See Arndt and Simler (2010) for a detailed description of the entropy approach used to impose revealed preference conditions across consumption baskets.

TABLE B3.1 Estimates of the poverty headcount ratio by three methodologies (%), 2001/2002–2010/2011

Source of estimate	Coverage	2001/2002	2004/2005	2005/2006	2007/2008	2010/2011
1. Official methodology (poverty lines extrapolated CPI)	National	34.5	23.9	22.3	17.2	12.4
	Urban	22.7	14.9	13.1	10.0	7.1
	Rural	39.3	28.1	27.0	20.6	15.1
2. Official methodology (poverty lines estimated)	National	38.6	39.7	42.4	43.7	45.6
	Urban	31.8	30.5	35.6	36.7	39.7
	Rural	41.4	44.0	45.9	47.1	48.6
3. Arndt-Simler (2010) methodology	National	21.7	18.4	20.5	20.4	22.9
	Urban	15.9	13.3	11.6	13.7	14.4
	Rural	24.0	20.7	24.9	23.6	27.2

Source: Official methodology (poverty lines extrapolated CPI): Cheema (2005) and GoP (2008a, 2014); Official methodology (poverty lines estimated) and Arndt-Simler (2010) methodology: authors' estimates based on GOP (2001, 2005, 2006, 2008, 2011).

Note: CPI = consumer price index.

in the chapter of rising food prices and declining real wages as reflected in the declining purchasing power of a day's wages to buy wheat flour.

A comparison of the three estimates of the poverty headcount ratios confirms the sensitivity of the estimates to the methodology used and the large underestimation of official poverty estimates compared to the two alternatives. The official estimates, based on the household consumption patterns prevailing in 1998/1999, do not capture changes in consumption patterns over time. In particular, the substantial increases in the prices of food and fuel after 2007 resulted in higher shares of these items in consumption baskets of the poor after that, which raised the cost of the minimum consumption basket, thereby resulting in higher estimates of the poverty line. Adjusting the poverty line using the CPI, which suffers from urban bias both in consumption weights and prices of the consumption basket, does not fully capture the real increase in prices, especially for the poor. As a result, the official poverty estimates show a decline in poverty in rural and urban areas.

In contrast with the official estimates, both alternative sets of estimates presented here show that poverty incidence increased during the period of food and fuel price increases. The direct estimates (method 2 in Table B3.1) are higher than estimates using the Arndt and Simler (2010) methodology (method 3 in Table B3.1), reflecting differences in the regression model and adjustments for changes in consumption baskets across households. Because there is a large percentage of rural households with per capita expenditures

FIGURE B3.2 Estimates of poverty incidence using three methodologies, 2001/2002–2010/2011

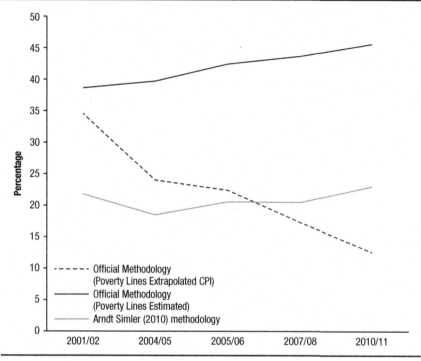

Source: Official Methodology (Poverty Lines Extrapolated CPI): Cheema (2005) and GOP (2008a, 2014); Official Methodology (Poverty Lines Estimated) and Arndt-Simler (2010) methodology: authors' estimates based on GOP (2001b, 2005, 2006, 2008c, 2011).

Note: CPI = consumer price index.

FIGURE B3.3 Estimate of poverty lines (logged) and CDF of logged expenditures, 2010/2011

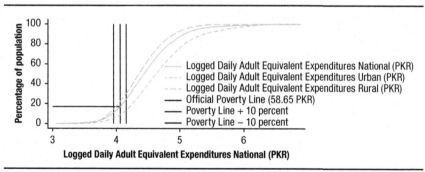

Source: Official Methodology (Poverty Lines Extrapolated CPI): Cheema (2005) and GoP (2008a, 2014); Official Methodology (Poverty Lines Estimated) and Arndt-Simler (2010) methodology: authors' estimates based on GOP (2001, 2005, 2006, 2008, 2011).

Note: Intersection of poverty line with CDF curve indicates corresponding (read horizontally across) y-axis value of poverty headcount. CPI = consumer price index; CDF = cumulative distribution function; PKR = Pakistani rupees.

near the poverty line, a small change in the poverty line results in a large change in estimates of the incidence of poverty (Figure B3.3). For example, a 10 percent increase in the poverty line lowers the poverty rate from 17.3 percent to 10.6 percent of the population. A 10 percent decrease in the poverty line increases the poverty rate to 24.5 percent of the population.

The estimate using the Arndt and Simler (2010) methodology finds rural poverty to be 13.3 percentage points higher than urban poverty, as compared to the 10.0 percentage point difference in the rural and urban poverty estimates based on the official methodology. Note, though, that in all three estimates presented, rural poverty is always higher than urban poverty.

Chapter 4

IRRIGATION AND WATER MANAGEMENT IN THE INDUS BASIN: INFRASTRUCTURE AND MANAGEMENT STRATEGIES TO IMPROVE AGRICULTURAL PRODUCTIVITY

Stephen Davies, Arthur Gueneau, Dawit Mekonnen,
Claudia Ringler, and Sherman Robinson

Introduction

Pakistan's large and complex agricultural sector is heavily dependent on irrigation and the hydrological dynamics of the Indus Basin Irrigation System (IBIS), supported by a massive configuration of infrastructure involving both surface water and groundwater irrigation. This system faces a number of major challenges: a rapidly increasing demand for water for industry and urban use without commensurate or adequate infrastructure investment; diminishing water availability in many regions; poor and often controversial allocations of water across provinces; inadequately coordinated management of surface and groundwater; large fluctuations in annual rainfall; and the effects of long-term changes in climate. A recent review of the water resources in Pakistan identifies five key areas of need for policy makers to focus on: (1) construction of new and major infrastructure, and rehabilitation and modernization of existing infrastructure; (2) improvement of efficiency of the water system through better canal management, on-farm water management, and judicious use of scarce groundwater; (3) revision of water charges to better reflect the economic costs of providing irrigation water; (4) lack of awareness of impacts of climate change as construction projects are undertaken; and (5) investment in capacity building and knowledge management (FoDP-WSTF 2012). These issues and options are additionally reviewed well in several recent publications, including Laghari, Vanham, and Rauch (2012), Chaudhry (2010), Qureshi (2011), and Briscoe and Qamar (2006).

This chapter provides an economic assessment of investment, policy, and improved management options that encourage higher-valued and sustainable use of water resources in Pakistan. The presentation follows Laghari, Vanham, and Rauch (2012), who argue that solutions to water resources issues can be split into supply-side options (reservoir management; wastewater infrastructure; desalination and recycling of wastewater; and land use planning, soil conservation, and flood management) and demand-side options (joint management of surface and groundwater, rehabilitation and modernization of existing infrastructure, increased water productivity for agriculture, crop planning and diversification, economic instruments, and changing food demand patterns and limiting post-harvest losses).

The chapter focuses mainly on the economic dimensions of five major solutions they propose, which are either directly related to agriculture or can be achieved by changes within water resources institutions. It combines an analysis of the determinants of on-farm productivity and technical efficiency with an economy-wide model, examining the following solutions in depth: (1) reservoir management, (2) coordinated management of surface and groundwater, (3) rehabilitation and modernization of existing infrastructure, (4) increased water productivity for agriculture, and (5) economic instruments.

The analyses permit us to look at the proposed solutions from more varied economic perspectives than have been provided in the literature so far. Specifically, to help direct investment and policies to areas where they will have the highest impacts, the analysis provides estimates of the relative benefits of each solution. Moreover, it allows us to consider how these alternative solutions affect water supply and show how cropping patterns might change in favor of greater cotton cultivation at the expense of wheat production, thereby affecting a key food security priority in the country.

The second section begins by providing an overview of key issues in Pakistan's water resources sector. The third section assesses the benefits of large-scale storage to the IBIS by simulating the effects of the proposed Diamer-Bhasha Dam. These results are provided under four climate change scenarios to show effects on the overall economy and on water use by crops. (Annex C discusses the implications for income distribution.) The fourth section then uses our model to explore alternative investments and policies that can improve performance of the IBIS. Specifically, it looks at the effects of reducing losses in distribution from lining watercourses, the effects of better-timed deliveries in the surface water system, which produces the same responsiveness to demand that groundwater provides, and the effects of allowing water trading in excess of the provisions of the 1991 Water Accord. These are compared singly and in combination with the Diamer-Bhasha Dam benefits. The sections also look at the effects on gross domestic product (GDP) and on water use by crops. The fifth section examines the conjunctive use of groundwater versus surface water in an analysis based on data from Round 1.5

of the Rural Household Panel Survey (RHPS), conducted in 2012 (IFPRI/ IDS 2012; see Chapter 1). The sixth section reflects on these findings and provides concluding remarks.

Overview of Key Issues in the Water Resources Sector

The water resources sector in Pakistan has a long history of development, with political objectives often being a central part of the storyline. The first canals were developed by the British Raj in the second half of the 19th century to reward political supporters and allies from the Punjab, provide a stable environment against possible Russian intrusion from Central Asia, and create a breadbasket as protection from the recurring famines in eastern India (GoP 1960; Lieftinck 1968; Chaudhry 2010; Bisht 2013). Thus began the development of the largest contiguous irrigated system in the world.

However, in 1947 the hydrology of the vast Indus River basin was ignored in boundary decisions that carved out the independent nations of Pakistan and India. The headwaters of the Indus River were left in India, while the main productive lands went to Pakistan, leaving the country with a permanent sense of being lower riparian (Bisht 2013). This tension led to an extended negotiation between India and Pakistan, facilitated by the World Bank, that resulted in the Indus Water Treaty in 1960. According to provisions of the treaty, water was diverted to India from three eastern rivers (the Ravi, Sutlej, and Beas Rivers) in return for the development of a series of dams to permit Pakistan to capture water that would otherwise have flowed unused into the Arabian Sea (although those flows would also support a larger delta than currently exists). Additionally, link canals were built to move 20 million acre-feet (MAF) from the western to the eastern rivers, which had ceded water to India (Chaudhry 2010; FoDP-WSTF 2012). While three significant dams were built, little storage has been added since the 1970s. Indeed, there is only 30 days' worth of storage in Pakistan, versus about 1,000 days on the Colorado River in the United States and a similar amount in the Murray Darling Basin in Australia (FoDP-WSTF 2012).

Water allocation issues were no less contentious within Pakistan. The Water Accord of 1991, which resulted from a highly sensitive political compromise, allocates Indus basin waters across the four provinces in Pakistan and mandates that current dams be managed with a priority for irrigation, even though hydropower has been a progressively greater contributor of value from large storage dams (Amir 2005; Davies 2012). Moreover, the Water Accord allocates a higher amount of surface water per irrigated acre to Sindh than in the other provinces, which was in line with historical diversions (Lashari et al. 2013). Additionally, some of the higher flows to the Sindh are to keep seawater out of the delta and help preserve wetlands. Balochistan and Khyber Pakhtunkhwa (KPK) cannot use their current allocations under the accord due to a lack of infrastructure, although they were given access to water in anticipation of the completion of certain projects that had been started.

Since the 1960s, increases in irrigation and the expansion of irrigated areas have played a major role in Pakistan's agricultural and economic growth. The total irrigated area nearly doubled between 1960 and 2010, from 10.4 to 20.6 million hectares, because of expanded surface water diversions of about 20 MAF and the growth in water extracted by tube wells by 36.1 MAF over these 50 years (Lieftinck Report 1968; Chaudhry 2010). In 2010, according to the Agricultural Census, 36 percent of irrigated land was watered solely with canal water, and 41 percent with canal and tube well water, while 18 percent was irrigated solely with tube well water (GoP 2010). Other forms of irrigation, such as wells, canals with wells, and tanks, accounted for the remaining 5 percent. About 60 percent of irrigated water available at farm gate comes from canal water; the remaining 40 percent is supplied by groundwater (World Bank 2004), while in drought years the proportion can rise to 50 percent (Chaudhry 2010).

The number of tube wells in the IBIS, and particularly in the Punjab, has grown dramatically since the Salinity Control and Reclamation Programs (SCARPs) began in the 1960s to improve drainage. Using groundwater as a supplement to the surface water *warabandi* system produces several benefits.[1] In addition to providing a buffer during droughts, it also permits farmers to better match supply and demand for water. In some cases, farms are entirely dependent on groundwater, as surface water is either insufficient or nonexistent. This is most prevalent in the tail ends of watercourses (or secondary canals) or outside the command areas of the IBIS. However, there is growing understanding that the current reliance on groundwater is unsustainable, and thus for long-term food security, surface water resources will need to be used more judiciously.

---

1   "The *warabandi* is a rotational water distribution method whereby water is allocated to each farmer typically once a week—hence the frequency of irrigation is at most once per week. . . . The duration of irrigation is determined pro-rata with area. Hence for example in the Punjab a farmer will typically receive 19 minutes of water per acre of land" (Anwar and Aslam 2015).

Examining the overall water balance in the IBIS can be useful.[2] Annual precipitation within Pakistan and in the Indus River basin averages 166 MAF, of which about 82 MAF, or almost 50 percent, goes directly into use by vegetation (green water). The remainder goes into the surface water system, either directly as rainfall or later through snowmelt or glacial runoff. The 82 MAF of precipitation represents about 55 percent of the 150 MAF of water required by crops; 30 percent of the remaining water requirement comes from surface water, and 15 percent from groundwater. Groundwater supports crop water requirements with less applied water, because 53 percent of deliveries are used productively as opposed to 45 percent from surface water.

An average of about two-thirds (102 MAF) of the total water flow in the Indus basin is diverted to canals. Of this diverted water, the 45 percent noted above goes for productive uses, and the remainder goes to Indus treaty allocations to India (8.4 MAF) or groundwater recharge (36.1 MAF) (Chaudhry 2010). The flows into the Arabian Sea are about 40 MAF on average but vary substantially from year to year, as the following discussion will show. These flows to the delta near Karachi need to be at least 8.6 MAF per year to maintain environmental sustainability and to prevent incursion of seawater into the Indus basin delta. Alternatively, an annual minimum flow of 3.6 MAF with an added 25 MAF every five years is needed to meet the requirements for a healthy Indus delta (FoDP-WSTF 2012).

Figures 4.1 and 4.2 show water flows in the Indus, by year and within a given year, and indicate some of the challenges to managing and using those flows productively. Figure 4.1 shows canal diversions and flows to the Arabian Sea from 1975/1976 to 2010/2011. Four elements are included in the figure: the diversions to the canals in kharif and rabi, and the surplus flows to the sea in each season. The figure shows that the variations in total flows can be large, ranging from 80 MAF in drought years to over 180 MAF during years when snowmelt and precipitation are at their highest. The diversions to canals, seen in the bottom two portions of each bar, are limited in kharif by the capacity of canals to handle the available water flowing through the Indus. The diversions in rabi are lower, so the canal capacity is greater than the volume of water available during this part of the year.

The most variable flow is the surplus to estuaries during kharif (the monsoon season). These can range from virtually nothing to very large flows when the volume from snowmelt and rainfall is high, and these flows cannot be stored or diverted for use in irrigation. For example, in the early years of the

---

2   These estimates are drawn from Laghari, Vanham, and Rauch (2012) and Chaudhry (2010).

FIGURE 4.1 Diversion of Indus River flow to canals and surplus flow by season, 1975/1976–2010/2011

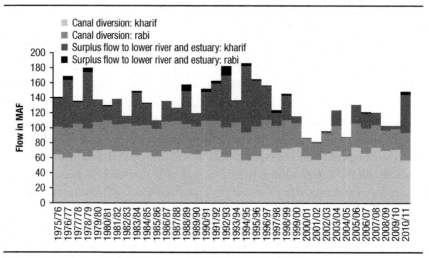

Source: Authors, based on data from GoP (various years), *Pakistan Statistical Yearbook.*
Note: MAF = million acre-feet.

2000–2009 decade, total water flows into the Indus basin dropped sharply because of drought, reducing availability of water at the tail end of the system. The kharif season canal diversions were 3.8 MAF (6 percent) lower during the drought period than the long-term average. The rabi shortfalls were much larger, at 11.8 MAF. Surplus flows fell drastically, by 95 percent in the kharif season and 99 percent in rabi. But in 1995/1996 and 2010/2011, monsoons and snowmelt came when storage was already full or came in high concentrations in a short period such that the water could not be retained and large flows had to be released into the sea.[3]

Figure 4.2 shows the flows into and out of the Tarbela Dam, which is the largest storage facility in the system. Over three years, from 2008 to 2010, inflows to the reservoir were low from October through April, while outflows exceeded inflows by small volumes. As a result, storage dropped during these months, which make up the rabi season. The main demand for water is for irrigation of wheat during these months, especially from January to April, and this crop thus faces a lack of water. The crop water requirements in kharif are estimated to be 46 MAF versus 30 MAF in rabi, a 50 percent higher demand in the summer season (Ahmad 2005; FoDP-WSTF 2012). However, because nearly 80 percent of

---

3   A heavy monsoon in 2010 caused some of the worst floods ever recorded in Pakistan, devastating crops and livelihoods (Dorosh, Malik, and Krausova 2011).

FIGURE 4.2 Average reservoir inflows, outflows, and storage levels in Tarbela Dam, 2008–2010

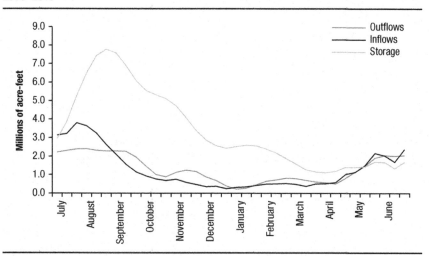

Source: Davies (2012).

precipitation and inflows into the IBIS occur from April through September, the relative growth in crop production and water demand could alter the use of water during kharif and change the amount available for use later in the year.

Beginning in April, the outflows rise, but inflows rise more rapidly, so the volume stored in the reservoir rises, slowly from April to June and then rapidly in July and August as the snowmelt and monsoon rains reach their peaks. The reservoir is full by the end of August. Outflows grow in proportion to the kharif season's needs, which are at their highest during the summer, but the high inflows from snowmelt and monsoons also require management of releases beyond the immediate need for irrigation. Of course, with climate change, if the monsoon occurs later in the year, the reservoir's ability to manage the excess water is limited, and floods can be more damaging.

Figures 4.1 and 4.2 show that the monsoon rainfall and snowmelt are concentrated in the period from June to August, but use could be spread across the entire year, so there is a need for storage. The main storage infrastructure developed to date consists of dams on the Indus and Jhelum Rivers, which were built shortly after the Indus Water Treaty. Little volume has been added to these dams since the original construction, but much loss in capacity has occurred from sedimentation. Archer et al. (2010) estimate that storage has decreased 28 percent in Tarbela and 20 percent in Mangla, although with the raising of the height of the Mangla Dam, there is now greater capacity in that reservoir. In addition to sedimentation, some estimates of the effects of climate change suggest that smaller water flows are occurring in the spring and summer, even with higher total rainfall, because of a shifting season and lower flows from snowmelt (Laghari, Vanham, and Rauch 2012). For example, Immerzeel, Beek, and Bierkens (2010) suggest that upstream water supply will decline in the Indus by 8.4 percent starting in 2046. This suggests the need to examine the impacts of greater reservoir capacity more closely.

Economic Effects of Expanded Storage: Diamer-Bhasha Dam and Climate Change

This section examines the value of adding reservoir capacity to the IBIS using a whole-economy simulation model (the CGE-W). It presents that model and its baseline solution and looks at the economic benefits of adding storage using the multipurpose Diamer-Bhasha Dam project (described in detail below) as an example. The section highlights GDP benefits under various climate change outcomes, along with water allocation and household income effects. The income effects are presented in Annex C.

The Computable General Equilibrium–Water (CGE-W) Model for Pakistan. The whole-economy model used in this analysis links an economic model with several water modules, drawing on the strengths of both approaches. The suite of models is called, collectively, the computable general equilibrium–water (CGE-W) simulation model for Pakistan. The CGE-W modeling framework and its underlying philosophy are described in Robinson and Gueneau (2014). The model provides a flexible and robust framework for linking and integrating separate economic and water models.

In our simulation, we run the CGE-W model dynamically from 2008 to 2050. In the model, water shortages affect only the agricultural sector and hydropower. Shortages are treated as shocks to total factor productivity in the production functions for crops, proportional to the shock in actual yields. Hydropower output varies with the water level in the reservoirs, and adds to the supply of energy for the general economy. Each year, the CGE model is run in a two-step procedure. It is first solved with average historical water stress to determine farmer decisions on cropping patterns based on expected water availability and economic trends. Then the actual inflows (provided by an external hydrology model, given climate information) are distributed to different canal commands, and water allocation and stress modules allocate available water to different crops based on the impact of water stress on yields and crop values. Finally, the CGE model is solved a second time given the optimal yields derived from the calculated shortages, assuming that the allocation of land to crops is fixed and the model solves for the final values of all economic variables. (Appendix A gives details of each component of this framework.)

The Baseline Simulation. To examine the effects of new storage, a baseline solution is generated using a number of exogenously varied growth rates, which then permits variations from the addition of Bhasha Dam and changes from several climate change scenarios to be explored. Figure 4.3 describes the national GDP and provincial agricultural production growth trends for the baseline scenario, highlighting the two provinces of Pakistan that consume the most water (Punjab and Sindh), while an aggregated representation is included for the rest of the country. In 2008, the baseline year, 63 percent of production comes from Punjab, 20 percent from Sindh, and 17 percent from the rest of Pakistan. Most of the production in Punjab and Sindh is irrigated by the Indus River basin, while agriculture is mostly rainfed in the rest of Pakistan. For the baseline scenario, we specify an economic growth rate of about 3 percent per year.[4] The amount of agricultural land does not increase, but its productivity grows, so less land is needed per unit of output over time. Under these assumptions, Sindh's agricultural production increases with its GDP because of improved yields, while Punjab's production increases in line with GDP until 2035 but slows thereafter due to pressures of rising industrial and domestic water demand on already stressed water supplies. Agricultural commodity prices increase in real terms by an average of about 30 percent when the last years of the simulation are reached.

The Diamer-Bhasha Dam. The Diamer-Bhasha Dam (often called the Bhasha Dam), on which construction officially started in 2011, is a large dam project situated in Gilgit-Baltistan on the Indus River, upstream of the Tarbela Dam. It will be 272 meters high and is projected to hold 8.1 MAF of water, including 6.4 MAF of live storage that can be delivered out of the reservoir. The associated hydropower station will have a total installed capacity of 4.5 gigawatts. As of 2011, the project's cost was estimated at US$13.6 billion, with completion expected in 12 years.

Although efforts to assess the costs and benefits of the Bhasha Dam have been controversial, there are clearly some significant advantages to this project. According to the Water and Power Development Authority (WAPDA),

---

4   The calibration of the growth rate is essentially done by specifying exogenous rates of total factor productivity growth. Labor force growth is also exogenous and includes some productivity increases in addition to the added supply, while growth of the capital stock is endogenous, determined by aggregate annual savings and investment.

FIGURE 4.3 Baseline projections of CGE-W of GDP and agricultural production by province, 2008–2050

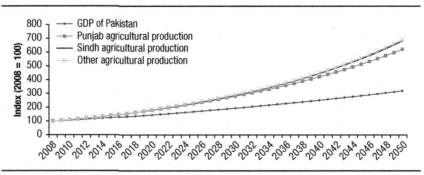

Source: Authors, results from the CGE-W model.
Note: CGE-W = computable general equilibrium-water; GDP = gross domestic product.

which is in charge of building and operating the dam, the live storage is valued at US$0.63 billion annually for irrigation purposes and at US$2.2 billion for hydroelectricity generation, paying back construction costs in eight years.

Using the CGE-W framework, we reestimate GDP benefits and other dimensions while doing the following: (1) explicitly modeling the impact of the new capacity on irrigation water supply and hydropower, (2) accounting for both direct and indirect effects of improved agricultural production and increased energy production on the economy, and (3) considering climate change impacts on crop production and hydropower.

Figure 4.4 presents the GDP results for three different scenarios. In the first scenario, represented with a gray line with hash marks and labeled "Average with Bhasha," every year experiences the same weather as the average year (which means no dry or wet spells), assuming—for convenience in this modeling exercise—that the Diamer-Bhasha Dam came online in 2009.[5] In the first year of operation, GDP rises by 0.3 percent, mostly due to hydropower benefits. Agricultural benefits, on the other hand, remain flat until 2020, as water stress is not significant in the earlier years. These benefits rise to 0.55 percentage points above the baseline GDP by 2050.[6] Overall, the

---

5 Specifically, the model uses historical data and creates future scenarios from those data using 2008 as the base year and 2009 as the first year in the simulation.

6 The results for scenarios run without hydropower benefits are not shown here.

FIGURE 4.4 Estimated change from baseline GDP with historical inflows and Bhasha Dam, 2008–2050

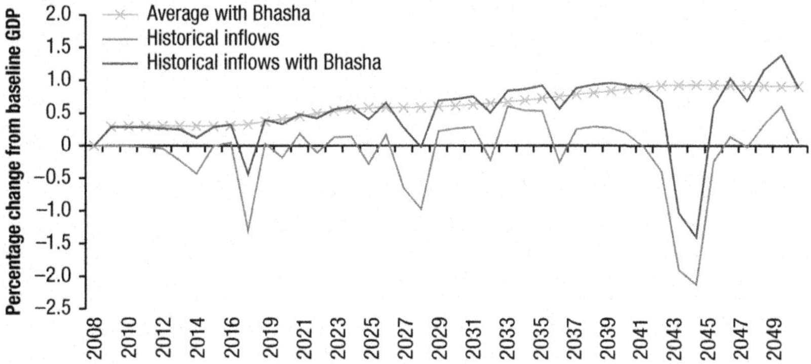

Source: Authors, based on results from the CGE-W model.
Note: CGE-W = computable general equilibrium-water; GDP = gross domestic product.

benefits go up to 0.9 percent above the baseline GDP by 2050.[7] Total agricultural production goes up by 2.6 percent in Punjab and 0.6 percent in Sindh. Punjab gets higher benefits from the dam in 2050, as under our baseline scenario it is the most water-stressed province. Conceptually, the dam helps Punjab alleviate increased water stress due to population and economic growth, while Sindh is somewhat protected by the 1991 Water Accords.

In the second scenario (shown by the dark gray line labeled "Historical inflows"), we introduce annual variability. To do so, we reproduce the time series of flows of the major rivers for the years 1966/1967–2007/2008. Droughts can create up to a 4 percent loss in GDP (in 2043 and 2044),[8] while a relatively wet year may increase GDP by about 1 percent (in 2033). Drought impacts can be seen even at the beginning of the period. Nonagricultural water demand is growing along with the economy, so a drought or a wet year in later years will have more impact on GDP than one in earlier years.

In the third scenario (the solid line labeled "Historical inflows with Bhasha"), the addition of the Diamer-Bhasha Dam improves GDP by approximately the same amount as in the first scenario under average weather. The

---

7   We do not take into account the cost of building the dam in this analysis. Conceptually, the dam appears on the Indus on the first day of the 2009 water year, which runs from April to March. The model as implemented here measures benefits but does not consider costs. Moreover, we do not consider dam silting, which is likely to reduce storage over time.

8   Because we are mapping to historical years, the 2043/2044 drought corresponds to the historical 2001/2002 drought in Pakistan. The GDP shock we calculate here is in line with estimates from the State Bank of Pakistan (2002).

main difference is that it provides some insurance against droughts. For example, in 2014 the drought impact on agricultural production is reduced by three-quarters because of the addition of the Diamer-Bhasha Dam. During a drought, the dam can save as much as 2 percentage points of GDP because it protects agricultural production, and in wet years, it can add an extra 0.5 percentage point.

   A Note on Price Behavior. In order to see the context of the simulations in this section and the next one, which also uses results from the CGE-W, and to gain an understanding of key assumptions behind the future scenarios, we look at prices. Price levels observed for selected years, relative to a baseline of 1.0 in 2008, provide a good initial window into those assumptions. Table 4.1 provides real prices in the historical simulation, which models historical water flows being repeated in the future but without Bhasha Dam being present, for 2029 and 2050. The first column gives the comparison in prices for commodities in 2029. The upper panel contains crops most affected by changes in water availability and that see only moderate price increases halfway through the projections. In this group, cotton, sugarcane, and horticultural crops see the highest price increases in 2029, as they are commodities with higher growth in demand from rising incomes.

   The bottom part of the table, which covers commodities and sectors with fewer land or water constraints, shows that price increases in services, manufactures, and textiles tend to be smaller, despite anticipated growth in those sectors. In contrast, the crop-related products, including livestock and processed food, see fairly high price increases because of rising prices of raw materials and feed inputs, but also because of rising demand.

   The picture changes substantially in 2050 as all prices for agricultural products (except livestock) rise, and some are 50 percent higher than 2008 prices in real terms. The staple products rise the fastest in the final 20 years of the projection, with wheat, sugarcane, and horticultural crops climbing between 30 and 40 percentage points. The highest water users among the agricultural products, cotton and rice, see the largest price gains, with basmati rice doubling and cotton rising by 60 percentage points. This scenario clearly shows the growing effect of a growing population and limited resources in agriculture, and the relative ease of expanding nonagricultural sectors, thereby keeping those prices lower as textiles, manufacturing, and services see little real price increases over the years.

   Because real prices are rising, growth in demand must be exceeding supply. The two major factors are population on the demand side and productivity on the supply side. The overall growth in population was assumed initially to be

TABLE 4.1 Historical simulations of real price changes of crops and other commodities, 2029 and 2050

	Price Level (2008 = 1)	
Crops	2029	2050
Water-sensitive crops		
Wheat	1.04	1.40
IRRI rice	1.01	1.43
Basmati rice	0.94	2.15
Cotton	1.13	1.73
Sugarcane	1.09	1.44
Horticultural crops	1.35	1.69
Other commodities/sectors		
Livestock	1.43	1.39
Processed food	1.37	1.44
Textiles	1.06	1.15
Manufactures	1.17	1.11
Services	1.03	0.94

Source: Authors, based on results from the CGE-W model.

Note: CGE-W = computable general equilibrium-water.

1.5 percent per year, and it declined over the simulations to zero in the last five years, thus implying a reduction in population growth rates. However, even with a declining annual rate of growth, population grows by 41 percent across the 42 years in the simulation, so the total population in 2050 reaches 233 million. (This is close to the low estimate of the United Nations. With a medium UN projection of 271 million and a high projection of 311 million people, our projections may underestimate demand growth and thus real price increases.)

The average total factor productivity growth was about 0.6 percent per year, or slightly less than 27 percent over the 42 years in the simulations. These rates did not vary significantly across sectors, so price differences are not due to productivity changes. Additionally, factor-specific technical change is assumed for the land, labor, and capital inputs, and runs from 0.5 percent to 1 percent per year for agricultural labor productivity. It is much higher, up to a maximum of 4 percent per year, for skilled labor and land. These assumptions relax the constraint on land otherwise imposed in all simulations. In general, these gains raise the productivity of land, so growth in output per unit of land increases substantially for most crops. In contrast, the actual growth in yields over the past 40 years has been less than 1.0 percent over the period 1969/1970–2010/2011 for most crops, and was highest in maize, at 3.2 percent. The actual cotton and wheat growth rates are half the simulated values of 2.2 percent and 2.1 percent, respectively. If we had used the actual yield increases, prices would rise more because of lower productivity growth, so it may well be that real prices could be higher due to both productivity and population reasons.

The pattern of imports and exports in the historical simulations, with and without Bhasha Dam, give further support to the perspectives above. Consistent with a higher demand for all goods and services, total imports rise by 5.1 percent per year in the historical simulations, with manufactured goods, business services, petroleum, mining, and chemical products being the largest imports in 2008 and 2050. A reduced supply of water to the wheat crop, discussed below, leads to higher wheat imports, with a 7 percent growth rate per year. This is likely because of rising water use in kharif, especially late in the season, from cotton, sugarcane, and basmati rice crops, and the lack of storage to provide water for the rabi season. Also, exports show a shift toward textiles, where that sector ends up with nearly 60 percent of total exports versus 45 percent in 2008. (The percentage for 2008 may be low, however, because of the worldwide financial crisis in that year. The reported textiles exports were 53 percent in 2013 and 55 percent of all exports in 2014 [GoP 2015]). This is also consistent with the rise in water use shown earlier for cotton. Cotton lint exports, however, decline, as the raw cotton lint is used for higher value-added processing into cloth.

Economic Dimensions of New Storage in the Face of Climate Change. Table 4.2 shows the effects of climate change on Pakistan's GDP and agricultural production under four climate change scenarios, which are presented as deviations from the historical baseline scenarios with and without Bhasha, which are given in Figure 4.4. Inflows are affected by changes in runoff in the Himalayas, along with variations in minor river inflows, runoff in Pakistan, and rainfall, while crop water requirements are adjusted to reflect changes in plant evapotranspiration and other transfers of water to the atmosphere.

All climate change scenarios produce similar negative impacts on Pakistan's water system, which are driven mostly by temperature change and increases in evapotranspiration. Climate impacts on irrigated agriculture cost Pakistan an average of between 0.5 and 1.2 percentage points of GDP annually by 2050, with a 0.7 percent to 1.3 percent annual decrease in agricultural production compared to the historical baseline and with Punjab and Sindh bearing roughly equal impacts. The Diamer-Bhasha Dam mitigates the impact on agricultural production until the 2030s in the MIROC A1B

TABLE 4.2 Average annual changes in GDP and agricultural production from climate change, with and without Bhasha Dam, 2010s to 2040s

Scenarios*	Average annual GDP change (%)			
	2010s	2020s	2030s	2040s
MIROC A1B	−0.10	−0.30	−0.44	−1.22
MIROC A1B with Bhasha	0.48	0.44	0.33	0.24
MIROC B1	−0.68	−0.21	−0.37	−0.65
MIROC B1 with Bhasha	0.49	0.49	0.40	0.48
CSIRO A1B	−0.05	−0.19	−0.35	−1.11
CSIRO A1B with Bhasha	0.50	0.49	0.40	0.37
CSIRO B1	−0.03	−0.11	−0.19	−0.45
CSIRO B1 with Bhasha	0.51	0.57	0.56	0.73
	Average annual change in agricultural production (%)			
MIROC A1B	−0.22	−0.98	−1.24	−1.01
MIROC A1B with Bhasha	0.37	0.34	−0.07	−0.24
MIROC B1	−0.07	−0.79	−1.06	−1.30
MIROC B1 with Bhasha	0.40	0.50	0.12	0.17
CSIRO A1B	−0.12	−0.62	−0.97	−0.73
CSIRO A1B with Bhasha	0.42	0.62	0.16	0.09
CSIRO B1	−0.06	−0.36	−0.57	−0.95
CSIRO B1 with Bhasha	0.44	0.91	0.62	0.68

Source: Authors, based on results from the CGE-W model.

Note: *Climate change is modeled using four different AR4 (Fourth Assessment Report) general circulation models: CSIRO and MIROC, A1B and B1. CSIRO is based on a model of Australia's Commonwealth Scientific and Industrial Research Organization (CSIRO), and MIROC is based on the Model for Interdisciplinary Research on Climate (MIROC), produced by the University of Tokyo's Center for Climate System Research (following the methodology of Jones and Thornton [2013]). The two CSIRO scenarios have smaller but more evenly distributed precipitation increases. The two MIROC scenarios have higher increases in precipitation but more variability.

scenario and until the 2050s in the other scenarios, as shown in Table 4.2. Moreover, because of hydropower benefits, the overall GDP of Pakistan remains higher with Diamer-Bhasha Dam in 2050 than it would be without climate change and without the dam.

Economic Valuation of Added Storage and Hydropower from the Diamer-Bhasha Dam. Standard measures used to evaluate large engineering projects include benefit-cost ratios (BCR) and internal rates of return (IRR). The analysis requires a comprehensive measure of the benefits of the project, including both direct and indirect benefits, the latter of which are usually hard to measure (Cestti and Malik 2012). The CGE-W helps to solve this problem by including a complete view of the country's economic conditions, which facilitates construction of counterfactuals that include all benefits.

Using the CGE-W system of models, we can compute the BCR and IRR of the Diamer-Bhasha Dam based on the change in GDP between scenarios with and without the dam. Under the baseline scenario (without weather variability or climate change), the BCR of Bhasha Dam is 2.8 percent and the IRR is 10.3 percent, while under historical weather variability, the BCR is 3.2 percent and the IRR is 11.1 percent.[9] The IRR and benefit-cost ratios of Diamer-Bhasha Dam also increase with climate change, with BCRs of 3.3 to 3.9 and IRR values from 11.3 percent to 13.9 percent.

Water Allocation Effects from Bhasha Dam and Climate Change Simulations. To provide more-detailed measures of performance than seen in the GDP variation, we examine the effects on water allocation to crops and provinces of different climate change scenarios. In all these climate change scenarios, Bhasha Dam is included and the effects are taken into account. We also examine income distribution effects, which are generally similar in direction though slightly different in magnitudes, under various scenarios in Annex C.

Figure 4.5 shows the total water allocated to crops as estimated by four simulations. The first is the historical simulation, which reflects the same scenario, without Bhasha, as shown in Figure 4.4. Figure 4.5 also shows simulations of water applied to crops with the addition of Bhasha Dam and for two climate change scenarios, MIROC A1B and CSIRO B1, both with Bhasha Dam included. These three simulations are used to capture differences in the models used and also to represent the upper and lower bounds from the GDP outcomes seen earlier.

All four simulations shown in Figure 4.5 experience approximately the same historical shocks, but the three that include Bhasha Dam shift upward relative to the historical simulation. They all have variable trends at or above 80 MAF until the last 15 years, when, after 2032, water supply to crops can decline to close to 75 MAF, depending on the scenario. The addition of Bhasha Dam adds 3–4 MAF relative to the historical simulation after the first 15 years, and the two climate change simulations, which include Bhasha, shift water supply further upward. The CSIRO B1 simulation rises about 1 MAF above Bhasha Dam alone during the last decade, while the MIROC A1B adds 1 MAF more of water supply above CSIRO B1. Thus, the construction of Bhasha Dam in the presence of climate change could raise available water for

---

9   We use a discount rate of 5 percent per year in the benefit-cost analysis.

FIGURE 4.5 Four simulations of total water supplied to crops, 2008–2050

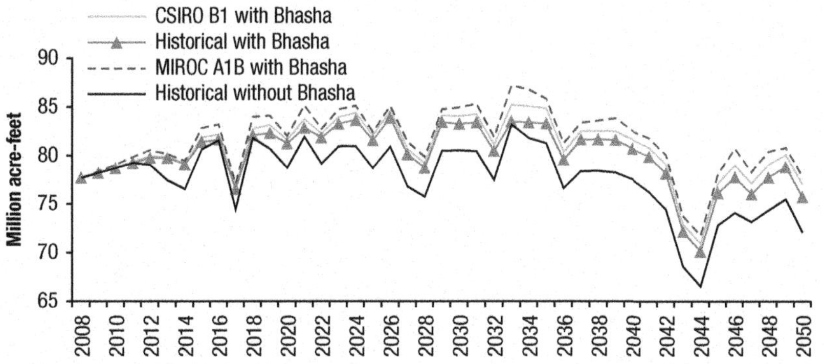

Source: Authors, based on results from the CGE-W model.
Note: CGE-W = computable general equilibrium-water.

agricultural purposes by nearly 5 MAF under the assumptions of each simulation, as described in the note to Table 4.2.

These changes can also be examined from the perspective of each province. For example, in MIROC A1B, which adds the most water to crops, Sindh, KPK, and the irrigated portion of Balochistan receive larger allocations: nearly 10, 24, and 32 percent more water applied to crops, respectively. The loss in water supply to crops seen in the later years of Figure 4.5 therefore comes from the Punjab, which loses 9.7 MAF, or nearly 15 percent of its allocation.

With changing overall water supply and other factors, such as population, income, and productivity, growing over time, water applied to crops changes during the historical simulation, as shown in Figure 4.6. The most dramatic change is a doubling of water applied to cotton. Water applied to wheat drops from 18 MAF to about 10 MAF, a reduction of nearly half. Water applied to fodder also declines, as does water applied to rice, but the latter recovers somewhat. Thus, the simulation shows that water availability in the presence of other forecasted changes is expected to cause significant shifts in water use by crop. These shifts will have indirect effects on several commodities. Textiles will have a much larger domestic source of a key input, cotton, but it is likely that the growth in demand for textiles is increasing the profitability of cotton production, so the cotton crop expands its water use dramatically. It might also be expected that livestock would decline because key sources of feed, fodder and wheat straw, decrease. However, as constructed in this model, livestock can use feed from a wide variety of crops, including cotton, so animals have access to adequate sources of feed. In fact, as shown in Table 4.1, livestock

FIGURE 4.6 Historical simulation of water supply by crop, without Bhasha, 2008–2050

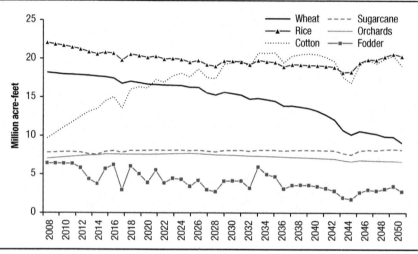

Source: Authors, based on results from the CGE-W model.
Note: CGE-W = computable general equilibrium-water.

prices actually decline somewhat, even though demand will clearly grow with higher incomes.

To illustrate the effects of climate change and new storage in the Bhasha Dam on particular crops, Figure 4.7 and 4.8 show how water application increases across the three scenarios for cotton and wheat, which are the two crops that see the largest effects. Cotton gains 1.5 MAF in all scenarios with Bhasha Dam added, in addition to the already high growth found in the historical scenario, and the fluctuations over time are similar across all simulations. In Figure 4.6, without Bhasha Dam, wheat experiences large drops in water supplies, but with Bhasha Dam included, all three simulations lead to a 1.2 MAF increase in applied water to that crop by 2050 (Figure 4.8).

In contrast, the fluctuations over time in the application of water to wheat vary. With just Bhasha Dam added, the amount of additional water grows slowly until the last decade of the simulation and then accelerates because of a combination of higher prices for staple products as demand rises, a roughly 3 percent increase in evaporation, and the availability of water storage, which makes water more readily available outside the rainy kharif season. In the two climate change simulations, however, more water is available for wheat because the major outcome of these scenarios is a shift to later in the year, for both inflows to the IBIS and rainfall. The October to December period, part of which falls in the historically drier rabi season, nevertheless sees an increase in inflows of 2 percent and

FIGURE 4.7 Changes from historical simulation of water supplied to cotton from climate change and Bhasha, 2008–2050

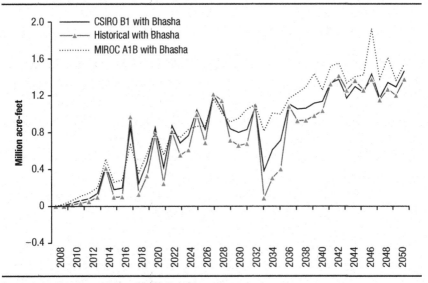

Source: Authors, based on results from the CGE-W model.

Note: This figure shows deviations from the historical simulation, which is without Bhasha Dam or climate change. CGE-W = computable general equilibrium-water.

FIGURE 4.8 Changes from historical simulation of water supplied to wheat from climate change and Bhasha, 2008–2050

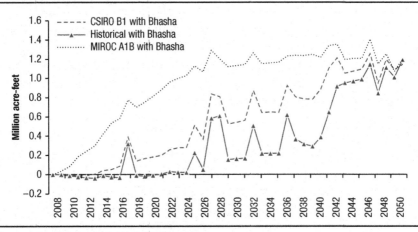

Source: Authors, based on results from the CGE-W model.

Note: This figure shows deviations from the historical simulation, which is without Bhasha Dam or climate change. CGE-W = computable general equilibrium-water.

of rainfall of 4 percent relative to the baseline. Additionally, the overall increase from adding Bhasha Dam and the climate change scenarios shown in Figure 4.5 adds water over and above the seasonal shift.

Strategies to Increase Agricultural Productivity and Modernize Existing Irrigation Infrastructure

The previous section examines the economic effects of added storage of water with the addition of the Bhasha Dam. This section uses the CGE-W model to look at additional strategies to solve pressing water issues, including effects of measures suggested by Laghari, Vanham, and Rauch, "rehabilitation and modernization of existing infrastructure," "increasing water productivity in agriculture," and "economic instruments" (Laghari, Vanham, and Rauch 2012). We use both the CGE-W model and the stochastic frontier model that is described in the section below to gain insights into these areas. The CGE-W model is used particularly to investigate the following possible solutions to selected issues: watercourse efficiency, improved timing of water delivery, and permitting of water trading across provinces. This section focuses on GDP and water allocation, and Annex C discusses income distribution effects.

Watercourse Efficiency. This simulation examines the effects of improving efficiency in watercourses, which amounts to reducing losses in distribution. It does so by raising water distribution efficiency to 70 percent (compared to an average of 55 percent used in the baseline CGE-W model), which can come from watercourse and canal lining, or from better allocation via water user associations. This is a good example of the benefits of "rehabilitation and modernization of existing infrastructure." Indeed, the Punjab government has been undertaking major projects on watercourse lining for many years. Since 1981 the province has improved 14,252 watercourses, with the assistance of the World Bank, under the National Program for Improvement of Watercourses in Pakistan (Punjab Component), and it is planning to line 7,000 additional watercourses in the Punjab Irrigated Agriculture Productivity Improvement Project (PIPIP) (DG Agriculture 2011). This improvement in infrastructure leads to a greater availability of surface water, so our simulation increases the proportion of water that reaches the field. We call this simulation "watercourse efficiency" (WCE) to refer to the simulations that raise water distribution efficiency.

Improved Timing of Water Delivery. Improved timing of water delivery is a central focus in the econometric analysis, discussed in the following section "Economic Benefits from the Use of Groundwater and Surface Water in

Irrigation" and in Annex B, which identifies significant productivity gains from using groundwater at the farm level. The gains from better timing come through matching supply and demand for water more closely so that adequate water is available when crops have higher demand. Access to groundwater improves timing, but better timing also comes from the improved delivery described above, as seepage losses are reduced and the velocity of water through the watercourse is increased, thereby allowing farmers in lower reaches of the watercourse to irrigate more land in a given turn. This simulation, called TMG for "timing," captures this benefit by simulating direct gains in yields, at the level farmers get when they use sufficient, but also perfectly timed, groundwater. The econometric analysis shows an increase of 13 percent in the value of output as groundwater proportions increase, so this simulation adjusts the overall yield in various regions by this amount, depending on the proportion of surface water used, assuming that the groundwater portion is already leading to higher yields.

Permitting Water Trading across Provinces. The 1991 Water Accord creates relatively fixed allocations of water across provinces, so the third option we pursue is to examine the effect of reducing those restrictions so that trading among provinces can be pursued to create the highest economic benefit. In the simulation, called TRADE, different allocations are permitted depending on the volume of water in the Indus, and predicting these on a monthly basis in a model, taking into account both future and past dimensions, is difficult. Thus, meeting the requirements of the Water Accord is a soft rather than a hard constraint. The focus of the TRADE simulation is to see the effect of releasing the allocations specified under the Water Accord. It is an example of an "economic instruments" solution.

Figure 4.9 presents differences in each simulation compared to the historical scenario levels of overall GDP from 2008 until 2050; the simulations include the same productivity and population assumptions used for the earlier Bhasha Dam and climate change simulations. The figure presents the GDP outcomes from four individual simulations, including TMG, TRADE, and WCE as described above, with Bhasha Dam (called BDAM) added as a fourth individual simulation.[10] We also present the combined scenario that has the highest benefit, to provide an example of the benefits of multiple investments.

---

10 This is the same simulation as the one presented in Figure 4.4 as "Historical inflows with Bhasha" to look at climate change effects, but is renamed to facilitate a comparison between the four different proposed solutions.

FIGURE 4.9 Changes in GDP from historical baseline from selected improvements in IBIS water management, 2008–2050

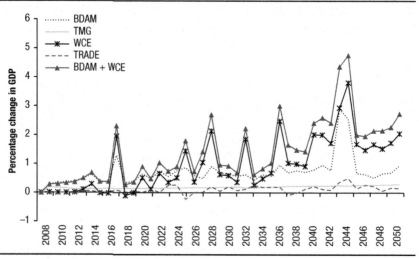

Source: Authors, based on results from CGE-W model.
Note: The simulations included are BDAM, adding Diamer-Bhasha Dam alone; TMG, better timing of water application; TRADE, relaxation of the 1991 Water Accord; and WCE, reduced seepage losses in water courses. The combined scenario with the highest impact BDAM + WCE is also included. This figure shows deviations from the historical simulation, which is without Bhasha Dam or climate change. GDP = gross domestic product. IBIS = Indus Basin Irrigation System.

Figure 4.9 shows that three improvements are most beneficial to GDP growth. The WCE simulation, which involves watercourse efficiency improvements, mainly through lining the watercourses, adds 2.0 percent to GDP over the historical simulation, and the BDAM scenario adds more than 1.0 percent by 2050. The best performer is the combined simulation of BDAM + WCE, which exceeds the historical simulation by 2.8 percent in 2050. The two other improvements considered, TRADE and TMG, add just 0.2 percent to GDP by 2050.

With scarce, and fixed, land and water resources serving the strong population growth and gains in real income, increased water supply provides growing benefits over time and helps reduce prices of key commodities relative to the baseline scenario (shown in Table 4.1). Because both BDAM and WCE add water, either through storage or reduced losses in distribution, they are the simulations that have the best performance. In the early years, BDAM benefits from growth in hydropower. However, with a fixed reservoir volume, that benefit does not continue to grow, and it ends up contributing only 1.0 percent to GDP by 2050, with half of the benefits from hydropower, while WCE contributes 2.0 percent to GDP. Because the combination of WCE and

BDAM adds water to crops in a complementary fashion, investing in both of them together gives the highest contribution to GDP.

Among the three simulations that add the most to GDP, one clear pattern in the results is the upward spikes in GDP only in years when the historical series by itself has downward shocks (these shocks are shown in Figure 4.4). These upward spikes occur because in Figure 4.9 the presentation is in terms of the difference between the historical series and a given simulation. Therefore, the existence of BDAM or WCE provides protection against the declining GDP in drought years, and that can be substantial at times. In the largest drought year, 2044, BDAM saves 2.6 percent in GDP, WCE saves 3.8 percent, and the two combined investments save 4.8 percent in GDP. The combination of BDAM + WCE appears to be above WCE alone by only 1 percent, and therefore some redundancy in water provision may be evident, as the benefits are not a simple addition of the two investments.

Stepping back for an overview, we see that among the individual runs, WCE clearly attains the highest GDP benefits. In fact, from a purely economic standpoint given the expense of constructing Bhasha Dam as in the BDAM scenario, WCE may be the best choice (and is being done via projects now). Therefore, the relative costs, and the political and institutional requirements, should be assessed closely to determine whether investing in large dams is beneficial, or whether capturing economic gains of infrastructure investment could best be done through enhancements in watercourse efficiency.[11]

Water Allocation Effects of Solutions to Modernize Infrastructure and Enhance Water Agricultural Productivity. The preceding section examined the GDP effects for the four policies/investments: BDAM, TMG, TRADE, and WCE. It also looked at variations in the amount of water applied to key crops in the historical simulation. This section presents changes in the amount of water applied across the four scenarios, first by province and then as comparisons with the historical scenario for the two crops most affected, wheat and cotton. These policies/investments relate to modernizing infrastructure, increasing water productivity in agriculture, and economic instruments—three approaches suggested in Laghari, Vanham, and Rauch (2012).

---

11 The scenarios reported here are considered separately and interact only moderately. For example, timing benefits are not modified if watercourse efficiency is improved, although lined watercourses actually improve timing through increased velocity. BDAM affects the whole IBIS and surely interacts with other elements. Also, the model does not account for groundwater perfectly, so WCE ignores changes in groundwater recharge, and its value may be overestimated.

Figure 4.10 shows the changing water allocations to crops in the Punjab and Sindh for the simulations examined (BDAM, TMG, TRADE, and WCE). While these simulations do not show changes as large as the earlier climate change simulations, some of them do produce significant effects.

In the Punjab, the WCE simulation, showing a significant effect like that on GDP, raises the amount of water by over 15 percent; BDAM adds about 6 percent. WCE also has the greatest effect on the water applied to crops in the Sindh, increasing water supply by 4.8 percent. The likely explanation for WCE's greater effect relative to BDAM is that the large surface water system that exists in each province benefits from reduced losses in distribution and the fact that losses are reduced throughout the year, whereas BDAM tends to have a more concentrated seasonal effect. Compared to its contribution to GDP, TRADE has fairly significant effects on the amount of water applied to crops in both provinces, as it assists in moving supply to higher-valued uses: water is first directed to high-value uses in the Punjab before flowing downstream to the Sindh. Because TMG affects only yields, not water distribution, it has little impact.

In addition to looking at the impacts on water use by province, we examine how water consumption of key crops changes relative to the historical outcomes presented in Figure 4.6. That figure shows that water use is highest for rice and cotton, and the water used for cotton nearly doubles, from 10 MAF to 20 MAF, where it remains for the last 20 years of the simulation. Water use for wheat drops significantly from 18 MAF to about 10 MAF, a reduction by nearly half. Water use for fodder also declines, as does water applied to rice, but the latter recovers somewhat.

Figures 4.11 and 4.12 show how, compared to the amounts shown in Figure 4.6, water applied to cotton and wheat changes with various policies and investments. Figure 4.11 shows that compared to the historical simulation, cotton receives the most added water in the WCE individual simulation and the BDAM + WCE simulation. The WCE simulation provides increasing water throughout the years, rising to 6.2 MAF over the historical simulation. BDAM adds 2.0 MAF, and together WCE + BDAM add 7.7 MAF. The two simulations in general protect cotton production against the decline in overall allocations in the historical simulations (hence the spikes as in the GDP analysis in Figure 4.9), and WCE is particularly effective in that regard. The other alternatives do not play that role much at all. While the TRADE simulation has a small effect on water allocation, it does so opposite of WCE and BDAM, as it has the greatest contribution in allocating surpluses as opposed to maintaining water in times of drought.

Finally, water allocation to wheat, in Figure 4.12, in aggregate receives

FIGURE 4.10 Percentage change from historical baseline in crop water supply, Sindh and Punjab Provinces

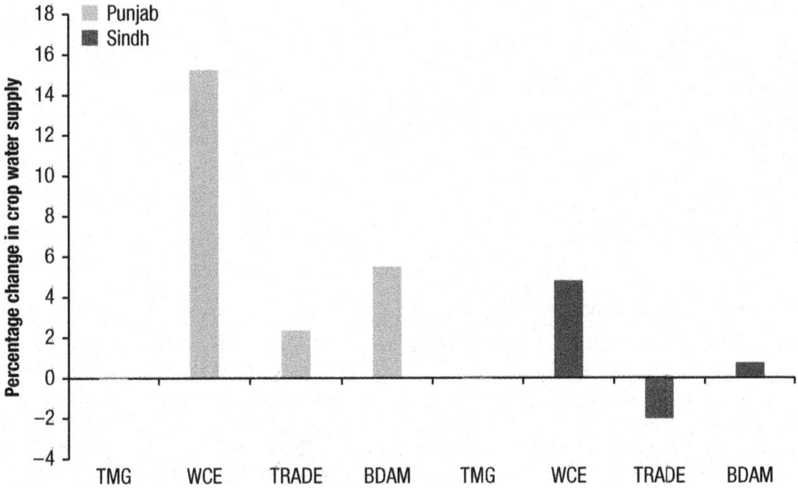

Source: Authors, based on results from CGE-W model.

Note: The simulations included are BDAM, Diamer-Bhasha Dam; TMG, better timing of water application; TRADE, relaxation of the 1991 Water Accord; and WCE, reduced seepage losses in watercourses. The changes are evaluated in the last year of the simulation, 2050.

significantly decreased allocations, and does not get much additional allocation in any simulations during most years. Prior to the last few years, the amounts are not large, rarely more than 200,000 acre-feet. However, as with cotton in the GDP analysis, the WCE and BDAM scenarios, individually and in combination, protect water for wheat in times of drought. The WCE value found in Figure 4.12 in 2044 is about 1.26 MAF, nearly twice that of BDAM. Together, the BDAM and WCE simulations retain 1.44 MAF of water in wheat production. These large spikes, as noted, are really protection afforded to wheat production in a major drought year, spikes that are at their highest when the drought is at its worst. That is, together, BDAM and WCE provide the most additional allocation of water to wheat in 2044, and TMG provides the least.

The section below finds further support for the WCE's value, as the econometric results demonstrate that a *khal panchayat* (water users' association) on a watercourse raises efficiency, as farmers with those institutions are 20 and 21 percent more efficient in kharif and rabi, respectively, than farmers without such institutions. However, many of the *khal panchayats* in Pakistan came about through an on-farm water management project that requires establishment of these institutions as a precondition for infrastructural improvements

FIGURE 4.11 Change from historical simulation of water supplied to cotton from selected improvements in IBIS water management, 2008–2050

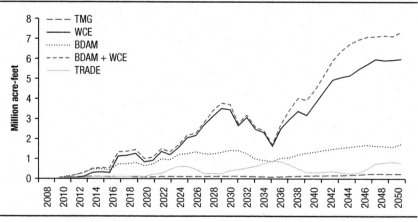

Source: Authors, based on results from CGE-W model.

Note: IBIS = Indus Basin Irrigation System. The simulations included BDAM, Diamer-Bhasha Dam; TMG, better timing of water application; TRADE, relaxation of the 1991 Water Accord; WCE, reduced seepage losses in watercourses; and BDAM + WCE, a combined scenario.

FIGURE 4.12 Changes from baseline simulation of water supply to wheat from selected improvements in IBIS water management, 2008–2050

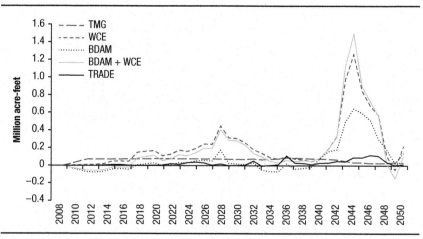

Source: Authors, based on results from CGE-W model.

Note: IBIS = Indus Basin Irrigation System. The simulations included BDAM, Diamer-Bhasha Dam; TMG, better timing of water application; TRADE, relaxation of the 1991 Water Accord; WCE, reduced seepage losses in watercourses; and BDAM + WCE, a combined scenario.

such as canal lining (Mekonnen, Channa, and Ringler 2014; DG Agriculture 2011). Thus, the efficiency-enhancing effects of *khal panchayats* come from a functioning farmers' institution that maintains the watercourse over time, but these effects may also be a proxy for watercourse-lining development. There is thus consistency in the value of watercourse lining from both research approaches. However, the econometric work also suggests that the use of groundwater raises efficiency, which was interpreted as increasing yields from better timing (TMG) in the CGE-W analyses. This did not have the same effect in the whole-economy models as in the microeconomic analysis.

Economic Benefits from the Use of Groundwater and Surface Water in Irrigation

The rise of public sector SCARP tube well programs, designed to improve drainage after the expanded IBIS irrigation system led to increased water tables, is well documented in many water reviews (Basharat 2012; FoDP-WSTF 2012). One effect of this program was a vast increase in private wells, and overabstraction of groundwater became a serious problem in parts of the country, as about 40 percent of irrigation water is supplied by groundwater. However, farmers demonstrated a willingness to pay for electricity and to rent water, thereby showing the value of on-demand water availability, but sometimes implying a lack of other options (Davies 2012; Shah et al. 2009).

Issues also arise with the interaction of groundwater and surface water. Farmers at the head, or beginning, of a watercourse often use more water than optimal, leading to shortages downstream and more salinity in the tail, or the end, of the watercourse and thereby forcing farmers at the tail to depend more on groundwater. If the surface water system could be managed to match the accessibility of groundwater, and incentives could be in place to use water at optimal levels, significant systemwide benefits could result. This section gives a sense of the value of groundwater, and of the costs and benefits of location on a watercourse.

First, we analyze data from the RHPS Round 1.5, which indicates that groundwater use in Pakistan is prevalent, particularly in Punjab and KPK Provinces (IFPRI/IDS 2012). Nine out of 10 farmers in Punjab and 7 out of 10 farmers in KPK use groundwater for irrigation purposes (Table 4.3). Groundwater use is not significant in Sindh because the province faces salinity problems (Lashari et al. 2013), but 2 out of 10 farmers in Sindh still use groundwater for agricultural production. The majority of farmers who use groundwater in Sindh and KPK do not have access to surface water, while

TABLE 4.3 Households' use of groundwater and surface water by province, in kharif 2011 and rabi 2011/2012

Households' type of water use	Punjab	Sindh	KPK	Total
Canal water in kharif 2011 and rabi 2011/2012 (%)	0.685	0.820	0.431	0.718
Groundwater in kharif 2011 and rabi 2011/2012 (%)	0.890	0.190	0.706	0.629
Groundwater in kharif 2011 and rabi 2011/2012 (%)	0.315	0.174	0.569	0.280
Canal water in kharif 2011 and rabi 2011/2012 (%)	0.110	0.803	0.294	0.368
Both canal and groundwater in kharif 2011 and rabi 2011/2012 (%)	0.575	0.016	0.137	0.350
Observations	499	305	51	855

Source: Authors, based on data from RHPS (IFPRI/IDS 2012).
Note: KPK = Khyber Pakhtunkhwa.

58 percent of farmers in Punjab use groundwater in conjunction with canal water. Our survey shows that KPK relies heavily on groundwater, with 57 percent of farmers using only groundwater for irrigation. In contrast, more than 80 percent of farmers in Sindh use only canal water. Thus, policy instruments to either encourage or discourage groundwater use should take into consideration differences in the reliance of farmers on water resources across provinces.

Water productivity in agriculture is often tied to the types of irrigation methods practiced by farmers, and research on ways to encourage high-efficiency irrigation techniques is of great interest. Improvements in irrigation methods are the focus of major projects such as the new PIPIP, assisted by the World Bank, which started in 2011/2012 and intends to put 120,000 acres under drip irrigation (DG Agriculture 2011). The RHPS Round 1.5 shows that these newer methods are rarely used, as flood irrigation is predominant for both surface water and groundwater users, accounting for 82 percent of users in Punjab, 77 percent in Sindh, and 60 percent in KPK (Table 4.4). Furrows are used by many farmers, mainly in KPK, but the bed and furrow irrigation method is rarely used. The predominance of flood irrigation is surprising given the costs of groundwater, which would seem to encourage more water conservation, and that predominance limits efforts to improve agricultural water productivity.

Moreover, our survey data also give insights into the extent of exchanges of groundwater. On about 57 percent of plots, households indicated that they purchased groundwater from someone else on the watercourse, but simultaneously less than 2 percent of households said that they sold groundwater (Table 4.5). These responses could perhaps indicate the presence of a few

TABLE 4.4 Types of irrigation methods for surface water and groundwater by province, 2011/2012

Type	Punjab		Sindh		Khyber Pakhtunkhwa		Total	
	Number of plots	(%)	Number of plots	(%)	Number of plots	(%)	Number of plots	(%)
Flood	1016	81.80	456	77.29	91	60.26	1563	78.82
Furrow	202	16.26	70	11.86	47	31.13	319	16.09
Bed and furrow	24	1.93	64	10.85	13	8.61	101	5.09
Total	1242	100.00	590	100.00	151	100.00	1983	100.00

Source: Authors, based on data from RHPS (IFPRI/IDS 2012).
Note: Plot is the unit of observation in this table.

TABLE 4.5 Depth of wells and households' groundwater exchanges by province, 2011/2012

	Punjab	Sindh	KPK	Total
Depth of well (feet)	128.3 (91.99)	211.4 (133.3)	112.7 (64.83)	131.7 (94.99)
Households that sold groundwater to someone on the watercourse (%)	0.0132 (0.114)	0 (0)	0.0495 (0.218)	0.0154 (0.123)
Households that used groundwater that they purchased from a seller on the watercourse (%)	0.552 (0.498)	0.571 (0.498)	0.752 (0.434)	0.569 (0.495)
Observations	1,066	70	101	1,237

Source: Authors, based on data from RHPS (IFPRI/IDS 2012).
Note: Standard deviations are in parentheses. KPK = Khyber Pakhtunkhwa.

large tube well owners who sold groundwater to a number of other neighboring farmers. The responses could also mean information is being withheld, for a variety of reasons. Nonetheless, this kind of water marketing, although at a local level, is extensive, and is a type of economic instrument that should be promoted, perhaps through legislation that officially encourages this activity.

Econometric Analysis of the Impacts of Groundwater and Surface Water Use. To further investigate the relationship between groundwater and surface water, we estimate a frontier production function for irrigated agriculture in Pakistan and examine factors that determine the level of technical efficiency. This section emphasizes the conjunctive use and related issues; important insights from this analysis are examined in the following section.

The production function relates the value of output per unit of land, logarithmically transformed, to a set of production inputs: fertilizer, capital, pesticide, labor, volume of irrigation water (surface and groundwater are

considered separately), and interactions of variables.[12] Additionally, there is
an error term that is composed of statistical noise and production inefficiency,
which permits an examination of the technical inefficiency of production by
measuring the percentage of output lost due to inefficiency. In essence, this
measurement describes how far a given observation is from the frontier, or the
maximum production that can be obtained. The variables that influence the
extent of inefficiency are included in the estimation to show what causes inefficiency, where the estimation is for kharif and rabi seasons separately.

We use the RHPS data described earlier to examine the nature of water
use for the analysis of technical efficiency (IFPRI/IDS 2012). Given the large
number of crops grown by households, we focus on the two major crops in rabi
(wheat and berseem) and five crops in kharif (rice, cotton, sugarcane, sorghum,
and millet), and control for these differences in the estimation. These crops
account for more than 90 percent of harvested land in their respective seasons.
For the purposes of this chapter, the two important variables included in the
production function (*not* in the technical efficiency analysis) are groundwater and surface water use, which are specified as total inches used from each
irrigation source in each season. The only significant variable (and only at
10 percent) was the total inches of groundwater used in rabi, and it was negative. Thus, based on these results, it appears that water use is not a key problem.

However, this effect varies across levels, and is positive and significant at
reasonable levels. To show this outcome, Figure 4.13 depicts the elasticity of
the value of output per acre for different levels of groundwater use in the sample. The results indicate that the responsiveness of output to groundwater is
negative when groundwater use is greater than 2.7 inches (which is high compared to the average of 2 inches used in the sample), but it is positive at lower
levels of use. A related analysis shows that the value of output per acre drops
for those households that exclusively rely on groundwater and hence are most
likely to overdraw the resource. Part of the reason seems to be that higher
levels of groundwater use is associated with higher levels of groundwater
depth, where groundwater tends to be more saline and thus affects the value
of output.

Evaluation of Conjunctive Use Effects on Technical Efficiency. The stochastic frontier model jointly estimates a production function and an inefficiency effects model to capture the determinants of technical inefficiency of
production. The inefficiency effects model permits an assessment of factors

---

12 The econometric results are provided in Annex B, which gives the full results from the stochas-
    tic frontier production function and the estimates of technical inefficiency.

FIGURE 4.13 Elasticity of values of output per acre in kharif with increasing groundwater use

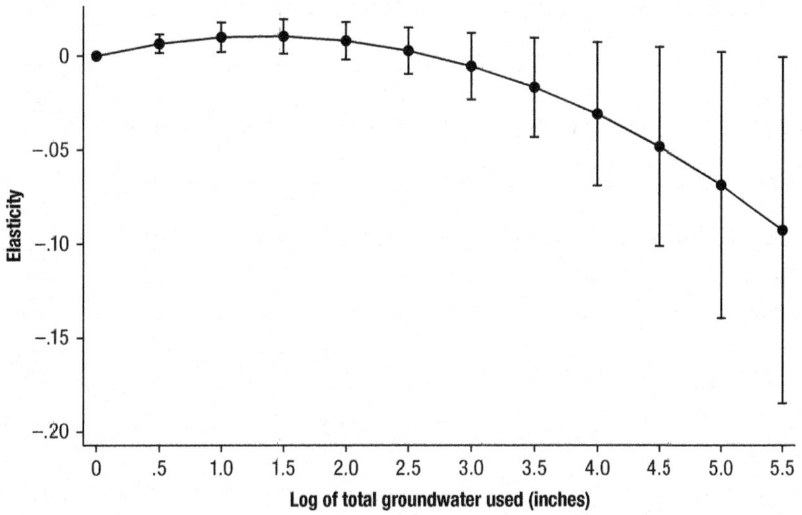

Source: Authors' calculations.
Note: Values are presented with 95 percent confidence interval.

that affect efficiency levels, after differences in the use of inputs are accounted for in the production function. Based on this analysis, the mean technical efficiency score for irrigated agriculture in Pakistan in rabi is about 75 percent. Thus, there is a potential to increase output per acre by one-third (because of the calculation [100 – 75] / 75) through improved management of existing use of inputs. In the kharif season, the mean technical efficiency score is about 47 percent, implying an even greater potential gain from efficiency improvements than in rabi.

The technical efficiency of irrigated agriculture also varies significantly across the three provinces by season. During kharif, Sindh is more efficient than KPK and Punjab. Punjab is more productive, in the sense that it has a higher output per acre, but once the level of input use is taken into consideration, Sindh appears to be more efficient than Punjab or KPK in kharif (see the upper panel of Table B4.2 in Annex B). In rabi, the efficiency differential among the three provinces is not statistically different from zero.

The marginal effects on technical inefficiency for variables that are statistically significant in at least one season are presented in Table 4.6. The table shows the extent to which the variables have effects on the reduction of inefficiency, and the direction of that effect. Most of the terms are related to water

TABLE 4.6 Marginal effects of inefficiency-explaining variables on the mean of technical inefficiency by season

Explanatory variables	Kharif		Rabi	
	Mean	Standard deviation	Mean	Standard deviation
Ratio of groundwater to total irrigation water	−0.319	(0.154)	0.190	(0.105)
Rainfall was available on the plot	−0.275	(0.133)	0.0306	(0.0169)
Sindh[a]	−0.889	(0.430)	−0.0886	(0.0488)
Located at the head of the watercourse[b]	−0.182	(0.0880)	0.0673	(0.0371)
Located at the tail of the watercourse[b]	0.116	(0.0559)	0.100	(0.0552)
Household did not sell any crops in season	−0.0637	(0.0308)	0.0986	(0.0544)
Rented-in plots[c]	0.0514	(0.0249)	−0.0165	(0.00911)
Sharecropped-in plots[c]	0.258	(0.125)	0.0688	(0.0379)
Slightly sloped land[d]	−0.265	(0.128)	−0.0270	(0.0149)
Sandy soil[e]	0.169	(0.0818)	0.152	(0.0838)
Sandy loam soil[e]	0.00901	(0.00435)	0.124	(0.0682)
Average length of an irrigation turn (minutes)	0.124	(0.0598)	−0.0827	(0.0456)
Distance of plot from homestead	0.0328	(0.0159)	0.00343	(0.00189)
Flood irrigation used	0.217	(0.105)	−0.117	(0.0643)
Khal panchayat exist on the watercourse	−0.198	(0.0956)	−0.208	(0.115)
Log of age of household head	0.0928	(0.0448)	0.0644	(0.0355)
Plots experience waterlogging	0.269	(0.130)	−0.0697	(0.0385)
Producing sorghum only in kharif[f]	0.519	(0.251)	n.a.	n.a.
Producing cotton only in kharif[f]	0.553	(0.267)	n.a.	n.a.
Producing cotton and sorghum in kharif[f]	0.497	(0.240)	n.a.	n.a.
Producing only wheat[g]			−0.115	(0.121)
Observations	583		618	

Source: Authors' calculation using data from the RHPS (IFPRI/IDS 2012).

Note: *Khal panchayat* = water users' association. Marginal effects on mean inefficiency score are reported for variables that are statistically significant in at least one season as shown in the lower panel of Table B4.2. A negative sign indicates that the variable reduces inefficiency if its value rises. n.a. = not available.

[a] The base group is Punjab.

[b] The base group is households located at the middle of the watercourse.

[c] The base group of tenancy is privately owned plots.

[d] Base group is moderately sloped land.

[e] The base group is clay soil.

[f] The base group is producing only rice in kharif.

[g] The base group is producing both wheat and berseem in rabi.

issues in one form or another. First, the relative reliance on groundwater as a source of irrigation water has different impacts in rabi and kharif seasons. Farmers with a higher reliance on groundwater manage to get a higher output per acre in kharif, but not in rabi. This outcome may arise from the greater shortage of water in kharif relative to crop water requirements (though more water is available in kharif than in rabi, main kharif crops that consume more water such as rice and sugarcane may imply water shortages relative to crop water requirements in the season), so a farmer accessing more groundwater can better match supply and demand in that season. As Table 4.6 implies, increasing the ratio of groundwater use to 0.3, from its current level of 0.2, leads to a 3.2 percent reduction in technical inefficiency in kharif, thus increasing technical efficiency in that season from 47 percent to 50 percent, after controlling for the inches of groundwater and surface water used in the underlying production function estimation.

If all irrigation water comes from groundwater, assuming the marginal effect remains the same, technical inefficiency would drop by almost one-fourth, from 53 percent to 40 percent, or an increase in efficiency from 47 to 60 percent, a 13 percentage point efficiency gain. As a result, the value of output per acre could increase by about 13 percent. In practice, this means that surface water needs to be made as responsive as groundwater because current utilization of groundwater is felt to be at a maximum, or even excessive (Qureshi 2011). Also, this computation ignores some complications from increased use of groundwater, such as changes in quality, energy use, overabstraction and other environmental concerns that arise as more groundwater is brought into use. Despite its simplicity, however, it shows, at least regarding the current share of groundwater use, the possible benefit of improving accessibility and reliability of surface water to approach that of groundwater. The alternative of just using more groundwater is not an option in the IBIS, because there is already evidence of groundwater reaching the maximum level of abstraction.

The analysis also sheds light on conjunctive-use issues related to location on the watercourse. Farmers located in the middle of a watercourse are more efficient than tail-enders, in both kharif and rabi seasons. As shown in Table 4.6, this translates into a 12 percent efficiency differential between tail-enders and those located in the middle of the watercourse. The efficiency comparison between head-enders and those located in the middle varies by season. In kharif, where there are more limited water resources relative to crop water requirements, head-enders are 18 percent more efficient than those located in the middle, but this efficiency differential vanishes during rabi, when those in the middle are more efficient. The fact that in rabi, head-end water users lose efficiency to farmers located in the middle seems to support an oft-repeated point that in a *warabandi* system, overwatering occurs at the head of a watercourse—as happens to head-enders in rabi in this sample.

An important perspective on the evaluation of technical efficiency is whether farms have the discretion to alter the variables being examined or not. Clearly, farmers have a choice about how much groundwater to use and thus can affect the level of technical efficiency in that way. (This decision is then endogenous to the level of efficiency estimated.) In contrast, the location on the watercourse is not easily changed and might be thought of as a control variable that affects the level of inefficiency but cannot be part of a decision by farmers. However, from the perspective of groups of farmers on a watercourse, there is considerable opportunity to change performance related to locations along the watercourse.

The technical efficiency results shed light on other solutions proposed for the IBIS. One is land use planning and soil conservation, because the results show that farmers cultivating slightly sloped plots are 27 percent more technically efficient than those with moderately sloped plots in kharif. Farmers on slightly sloped land presumably have a more even distribution of water and achieve better water productivity and higher output. Also, farmers on sandy soils or sandy-loam soils are less efficient during the rabi season. Water leaves the root zone more quickly with sandy soils, so insufficient moisture is retained for crop use. Programs that enhance organic matter in the soil, and hold more water on the root zone, should aid water productivity.

There were also some puzzling outcomes. The average length of an irrigation turn has different impacts in rabi and kharif; increasing its length improves efficiency in rabi but does the opposite in kharif. This may be related to a higher water shortage in rabi, so that longer turns decrease the shortage, while it points to overwatering in kharif, a possibility with higher water velocities during that season. These outcomes are consistent with the flood irrigation results, which also have the unexpected result of increasing efficiency in rabi but leading to a decline, as expected, in kharif. This may again point to a relatively higher water shortage in rabi. Part of the issue at the head of the watercourse may be waterlogging from overuse of water, which is found to significantly reduce technical efficiency of farmers in kharif, because plots that are waterlogged are nearly 27 percent less efficient (Table 4.6). However, waterlogging in rabi is associated with better efficiency, again pointing to the shortage in that season. Thus, all three of these differing views on seasonal water shortages give a similar conclusion.

Finally, groundwater aquifers can be thought of as a large reservoir, so our analyses indirectly extend to the benefits of enhancing artificial groundwater recharge Laghari, Vanham, and Rauch (2012); Qureshi (2011). There may be situations when this approach is more advantageous and cost effective than using conventional storage options.

Conclusions

This chapter focuses on the economic dimensions of five possible solutions to issues in water resources. Using a microeconomic-level analysis and an aggregate, whole-economy approach (the CGE-W model), we examine five solutions in depth: reservoir management; coordinated management of surface water and groundwater; rehabilitation and modernization of existing infrastructure; increased water productivity for agriculture; and water trading in excess of the 1991 Water Accord. The analyses permit us to look at proposed solutions to challenges in the IBIS—solutions with more economic content than those contained in the literature to date.

The chapter assesses five solutions first in regard to economic benefits from possible improvements in each area. Assessments are made either by looking at GDP or the impacts on the value of agricultural production. The analysis shows that climate change reduces GDP at an annual rate between 0.5 percent and 1.2 percent by 2050, and causes an annual 0.7 percent to 1.3 percent decrease in agricultural production. To counteract this, the chapter examines large storage additions by simulating the effects of the proposed Diamer-Bhasha Dam. Our cost-benefit analyses in this case show that the IRR and BCR of Diamer-Bhasha Dam increase with climate change, with IRR calculations from 11.3 percent to 13.9 percent and BCR of 3.3 to 3.9. Expanded reservoir capacity therefore appears to be economically viable. However, this type of infrastructure contributes less over time because of its fixed water and energy contributions.

The chapter also uses the CGE-W model to examine three additional topics: rehabilitation and modernization of existing infrastructure, increased water productivity for agriculture, and water trading. The infrastructure analysis simulates the impacts of watercourse lining, which reduces losses in distribution; such development of watercourse lining is currently a major project in Pakistan. Agricultural productivity analysis looks at the effects of yield improvements from better timing of surface water deliveries. (We include Bhasha Dam for comparison purposes.) Of the options considered, watercourse lining, a type of improved infrastructure, is clearly the best option. It yields a nearly 2 percent gain in GDP by 2050 and provides protection against drought by making more water available in those years. For example, adding lining helps retain 6 MAF of water in cotton production and nearly 1.3 MAF in wheat production in years of drought. Putting Diamer-Bhasha Dam in place adds similar protection, but with smaller effects in all cases. The combination of these two investments always produces the largest effects, although the contribution of added storage via Bhasha Dam was smaller than watercourse lining. The other two investments evaluated, water trading and improved efficiency in matching water supply and demand, produce quite small effects.

Some important conclusions came from the review of water supply changes to crops across the various scenarios. The most dramatic change is that the water applied to cotton nearly doubles, which forces a decline in water applied to wheat, from 18 MAF to about 10 MAF. In a simulation with the presence of climate change and Bhasha Dam, cotton gains 1.5 MAF in applied water in addition to the already high application growth in the historical scenario, while wheat gains 1.2 MAF in water applied to partially offset the large decline in its share of irrigation water. Cotton receives added water in all simulations, but the amount is greatest in the lining and storage simulations. Rice, in contrast, gets reduced amounts of water in most simulations.

The analysis of the value of groundwater, and its interaction with the surface water system, is based on a frontier production function, using mainly an evaluation of technical efficiency. The benefits of using groundwater are substantial. If all irrigation water came from groundwater, technical inefficiency in crop production would drop by almost one-fourth, from 53 percent to 40 percent, and the value of output per acre could increase by about 13 percent. In practice, this means that given that current groundwater utilization is at a maximum, surface water needs to be made as responsive as groundwater. (This does not, however, appear to be that important in the CGE-W analysis.) Moreover, it is useful to think of groundwater aquifers as reservoirs and compare costs and benefits of management of that resource with more traditional storage facilities.

Two conclusions have major implications for areas of further research and more in-depth analysis. Storage clearly provides valuable economic benefits, and large storage, such as Bhasha Dam, provides a measure of insurance against the adverse effects of climate change. However, given that watercourse lining achieves many of the same objectives, probably with less investment costs and noting that half of the benefits from storage come from electricity, other combinations might make sense. Thus, it is possible that a combination of complementary investments, such as run of the river hydropower projects, which generate electricity from energy in river flows and not from stored water, watercourse lining, and more aggressive management of aquifers might achieve the same levels of benefits shown in this chapter.

Finally, the modeling results, based on maximization of total economic benefit, shows an increased allocation of water to cotton, less water to wheat, and correspondingly an increase in cotton production and a decrease in wheat production. However, food security is highly dependent on wheat as the major staple crop, and it is likely that small, food-insecure producers will continue to produce that crop, but at a disadvantage with less water. Therefore, based on this research, it may be that one of the best ways to improve food security could come from raising the water productivity in cotton production, which would allow water to be stored and carried into rabi for wheat production. This strategy might have a greater impact than one that approaches food security within wheat issues alone.

References

Ahmad, M., A. Brooke, and G. P. Kutcher. 1990. *Guide to the Indus Basin Model Revised*. Washington, DC: The World Bank Environment Operations and Strategy Division.

Ahmad, S. 2005. "Water Balance and Evapo-transpiration." Background Paper No. 5. In *Pakistan's Water Economy: Running Dry—Background Papers*, by J. Briscoe and U. Qamar. Washington, DC: World Bank. http://water.worldbank.org/publications/pakistans-water-economy-running-dry-background-papers.

Aigner, D., C. A. Knox Lovell, and P. Schmidt. 1977. "Formulation and Estimation of Stochastic Frontier Production Models." *Journal of Econometrics* 6: 21–37.

Amir, P. 2005. "The Role of Large Dams in the Indus Basin." Background Paper No. 10. In *Pakistan's Water Economy: Running Dry—Background Papers*, by J. Briscoe and U. Qamar. Washington, DC: World Bank. http://water.worldbank.org/publications/pakistans-water-economy-running-dry-background-papers.

Anwar, A., and M. Aslam, eds. 2015. "Pakistan Water Dialogue: Consensus Action Plan to Increase Water-Use Efficiency and Water Capture for Agriculture." Unpublished, International Water Management Institute and USDA, Lahore.

Archer, D. R., N. Forsythe, H. J. Fowler, and S. M. Shah. 2010. "Sustainability of Water Resources Management in the Indus Basin under Changing Climatic and Socio-economic Conditions." *Hydrology and Earth System Sciences* 14: 1669–1680.

Basharat, M. 2012. "Spatial and Temporal Appraisal of Groundwater Depth and Quality in LBDC Command-Issues and Options." *Pakistani Journal of Engineering and Applied Science* 11: 14–29.

Battese, G. E., and T. J. Coelli. 1995. "A Model for Technical Inefficiency Effects in a Stochastic Frontier Production Function for Panel Data." *Empirical Economics* 20 (2): 325–332.

Bisht, M. 2013. *Water Sector in Pakistan: Policy, Politics, Management*. IDSA Monograph Series 18. New Delhi: Institute for Defence Studies and Analyses (IDSA).

Briscoe, J., and U. Qamar. 2005. *Pakistan's Water Economy: Running Dry—Background Papers*. Washington, DC: World Bank. http://water.worldbank.org/publications/pakistans-water -economy-running-dry-background-papers.

———. 2006. *Pakistan's Water Economy: Running Dry*. Karachi: Oxford University Press; Islamabad: The World Bank.

Cestti, R., and R. P. S. Malik. 2012. "Indirect Economic Impacts of Dams." In *Impacts of Large Dams: A Global Assessment,* edited by C. Tortajada, D. Altinbilek, and A. K. Biswas. Berlin, Heidelberg: Springer.

Chaudhry, S. 2010. "Pakistan: Indus Basin Water Strategy—Past, Present and Future." *The Lahore Journal of Economics* 15 SE (September 2010): 187–211.

Davies, S. 2012. *Selected Economic Dimensions of Major Infrastructure and Irrigation System Development in Pakistan*. A Background paper for the Friends of Democratic Pakistan's (FoDP) Water Sector Task Force (WSTF). Fort Collins, CO: CSU Department of Agricultural and Resource Economics.

Debowicz, D., P. Dorosh, S. Robinson, and S. H. Haider. 2012. *2007–08 Social Accounting Matrix for Pakistan*. PSSP Working Paper 1. Islamabad: Pakistan Strategy Support Program. http:// www.ifpri.org/publication/2007-08-social-accounting-matrix-pakistan.

DG Agriculture. 2011. *Punjab Irrigated-Agriculture Productivity Improvement Project (PIPIP). A PC-1 Proposal*. Lahore: Government of Punjab. http://www.ofwm.agripunjab.gov.pk/ system/files/PC-1-PIPIP.pdf.

Doorenbos, J., and A. H. Kassam. 1979. *Yield Response to Water*. Rome: Food and Agricultural Organization.

Dorosh, P., S. Malik, and M. Krausova. 2011. "Rehabilitating Agriculture and Promoting Food Security Following the 2010 Pakistan Floods." *Pakistan Development Review* 49 (3): 167–192.

Dorosh, P., M. K. Niazi, and H. Nazli. 2006. *A Social Accounting Matrix for Pakistan, 2001–02: Methodology and Results*. Washington, DC: The World Bank East Asian Bureau of Economic Research.

FoDP-WSTF (Friends of Democratic Pakistan, Water Sector Task Force). 2012. *A Productive and Water-Secure Pakistan: Infrastructure; Institutions; Strategy.* Report of the Water Sector Task Force of the Friends of Democratic Pakistan. Government of Pakistan; Asian Development Bank.

GoP (Government of Pakistan). 1960. *Indus Water Treaty 1960.* http://siteresources.worldbank .org/INTSOUTHASIA/ Resources/223497-1105737253588/IndusWatersTreaty1960.pdf.

———. 2010. *Agricultural Census.* Islamabad: Agricultural Census Wing, Pakistan Bureau of Statistics. http://www.pbs.gov.pk/content/agriculture-census-wing.

———. 2015. *Pakistan Economic Survey 2014–15.* Islamabad: Ministry of Finance. http://www .finance.gov.pk/survey_0910.html.

———. Various years. *Pakistan Statistical Yearbook.* Islamabad: Bureau of Statistics.

Hanks, R. J. 1974. "Model for Predicting Plant Yield as Influenced by Water Use." *Agronomy Journal* 66 (5): 660.

IFPRI/IDS (International Food Policy Research Institute/Innovative Development Strategies). 2012. Pakistan Rural Household Panel Survey 2012 Rounds 1 and 1.5 dataset. Washington, DC: IFPRI; Islamabad: IDS.

Immerzeel, W. W., L. P. H. van Beek, and M. F. Bierkens. 2010. "Climate Change Will Affect the Asian Water Towers." *Science* 328: 1382–1385.

Jensen, M. E. 1968. "Water Consumption by Agricultural Plants." In *Plant Water Consumption and Response.* Vol. 2, *Water Deficits and Plant Growth*, edited by T. T. Kozlowski. New York: Academic Press.

Jones, P. G., and P. K. Thornton. 2013. "Generating Downscaled Weather Data from a Suite of Climate Models for Agricultural Modelling Applications." *Agricultural Systems* 114 (January 15): 1–5.

Laghari, A. N., D. Vanham, and W. Rauch. 2012. "The Indus Basin in the Framework of Current and Future Water Resources Management." *Hydrology and Earth System Sciences* 16: 1063–1083.

Lashari, B. K., H. Ursani, M. Basharat, F. van Steenbergen, M. Ujan, Z. Khero, N. Essani Memon, S. Esin, et al. 2013. *The Promise of Conjunctive Management of Surface and Groundwater in Sindh: Shared Discussion Paper.* Jamshoro, Pakistan: Mehran University of Engineering and Technology.

Lieftinck, P. 1968. *Water and Power Resources of West Pakistan: A Study in Sectoral Planning.* 3 vols. Washington, DC: World Bank; Baltimore: The John Hopkins Press.

Löfgren, H., R. L. Harris, and S. Robinson. 2001. *A Standard Computable General Equilibrium (CGE) Model in GAMS.* Washington, DC: International Food Policy Research Institute.

Mekonnen, D., H. Channa, and C. Ringler. 2014. *The Impact of Water Users' Associations on the Productivity of Irrigated Agriculture in Pakistani Punjab.* Paper presented at the Agricultural & Applied Economics Associations 2014 annual meeting, Minneapolis, MN, July 27–29, 2014.

Qureshi, A. S. 2011. "Water Management in the Indus Basin in Pakistan: Challenges and Opportunities." *Mountain Research and Development* 31 (3): 252–260.

Raes, D., S. Geerts, E. Kipkorir, J. Wellens, and A. Sahli. 2006. "Simulation of Yield Decline as a Result of Water Stress with a Robust Soil Water Balance Model." *Agricultural Water Management* 81 (3) (March): 335–357.

Robinson, S., and A. Gueneau. 2014. *CGE-W: An Integrated Modeling Framework for Analyzing Water-Economy Links.* Washington, DC: International Food Policy Research Institute.

Shah, T. S., et al. 2009. "Is Irrigation Water Free? A Reality Check in the Indo-Gangetic Basin." *World Development* 37 (2): 422–434.

State Bank of Pakistan. 2002. *Annual Report 2001–02.* Karachi: State Bank of Pakistan.

World Bank. 2004. *Accelerated Development of Water Resources and Irrigated Agriculture.* Public expenditure review (PER). Washington, DC: World Bank Group. http://documents .worldbank.org/curated/en/2004/01/2884943/pakistan-public-expenditure-management -strategic-issues-reform-agenda-vol-2-2-accelerated-development-water-resources-irrigated -agriculture. Accessed May 2016.

———. 2007. *Pakistan: Promoting Rural Growth and Poverty Reduction.* Report 39303-PK. Washington DC: World Bank.

Yu, W., Y. Yang, A. Savitsky, D. Alford, C. Brown, J. Wescoat, D. Debowicz, and S. Robinson. 2013. *The Indus Basin of Pakistan: The Impacts of Climate Risks on Water and Agriculture.* Washington, DC: The World Bank.

Annex A: The Computable General Equilibrium–Water Model for Pakistan

In a country like Pakistan that is arid and relies heavily on irrigated agriculture (Briscoe and Qamar 2005), the water system is much more complex than can be considered by economic models that incorporate water in a simple manner. Water basin models that include some economic production track the direct effects of changes in the water system on only part of the economy and fail to encompass the direct and indirect repercussions on the broader economy, which are likely to be important in economies that are heavily dependent on water such as Pakistan. We need to integrate our knowledge of the entire economic system and its links to water systems to consider the challenges posed by climate change and potential adaptation strategies that involve a significant share of overall economic activity.

Our goal was to develop a model system that links economic and water models, drawing on the strengths of both approaches. This section presents such a model, the computable general equilibrium–water (CGE-W) simulation model applied to Pakistan. The economic model is a national CGE model adapted to link with a suite of water models that include hydrology, water demand, water basin management, and water stress, which are described in detail in Robinson and Gueneau (2014). Additionally, there is a hydropower module that calculates the electricity generated. It provides a flexible and robust framework for linking and integrating separate economic and water models.

The CGE-W Framework Applied to Pakistan

The CGE-W model of Pakistan consists of a national computable general equilibrium (CGE) simulation model that interfaces with a set of different water models: a water demand module, which translates economic values from the CGE into physical quantities of demand for water; a water basin management model (the Regional Water System Model for Pakistan [RWSM-Pak]), which optimizes water distribution over months and regions, and calculates related water shortages; and an associated water allocation model that allocates available water to crops based on the impact of water stress on crop yields and crop values (called the water allocation and stress model, or WASM). The water models all run on a monthly time increment. This set of models are linked together during each simulation. Outside of this set of interactions, a separate hydrology model calculates monthly precipitation and runoff to the river systems, given different climate scenarios, while another outside simulation, the hydropower model, calculates the electricity generated from water flows, which vary with the different climate change scenarios. All component models in this implementation of the CGE-W framework are coded in the General Algebraic Model System, which allows for integrated solution of the suite of models. Figure A4.1 presents a schematic view of how the system of simulation models operates year by year.[13]

The CGE-W model is solved dynamically (Figure A4.1). First, the CGE model is solved for a given year, assuming exogenous trends on various parameters. Solving the model yields projected outputs by sector and allocation of land to crops. The assumption behind this first run is that the expected water stress is set to the average of the previous three years, which sets harvest expectations for the allocation of land to different crops. The water demand module then calculates physical water demand for crops, industry, households, and livestock. Crop demand is calculated for each crop using evapotranspiration and effective rainfall; industrial water demand is assumed to be related to the square root of industrial GDP; livestock demand is the square root of livestock GDP; and household demand is calculated linearly to aggregate household income. RWSM-Pak uses these water demands, along with river flows provided by a hydrology model (or historical data) and climate parameters, to provide the monthly repartition of water among crops and regions given the objective function described above.

The water allocation and stress module (WASM) then allocates water among crops in an area, given the economic value of the crop. We use the FAO Ky approach (Doorenbos and Kassam 1979) to measure water stress using a multiplicative approach to include seasonality of water stress impacts (Jensen 1968; Hanks 1974; Raes et al. 2006). Because optimizing the total value of production given fixed prices leads to a tendency to specialize in high-value crops, we include a measure of risk aversion for farmers in the objective function, which preserves a diversified production structure even in case of a drought. The stress model produces a measure of yield stress for every crop—both irrigated and rainfed—in each of the twelve agroecological zones, which is then aggregated to the provincial level to match the regions in the CGE model.

Finally, the new yield shocks are calculated and applied to the CGE model, which is solved a second time for the final equilibrium, but the allocation of land to crops is assumed to be fixed because farmers cannot change their

---

13 Robinson and Gueneau (2013) describe the CGE-W framework in detail.

FIGURE A4.1 The CGE-W framework: Operation of the system of models in a given year

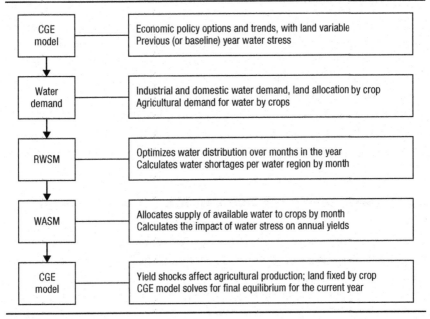

Source: Authors.

Note: CGE = Computable General Equilibrium; RWSM = Regional Water System Model; WASM = water allocation and stress module.

cropping decisions after planting. This solution yields all economic variables, including quantities and prices of outputs and inputs and all income flows. We then move to the next year, update various parameters on trends, and start the process again.

The IFPRI Standard CGE Model of Pakistan

The database for the IFPRI CGE model of Pakistan is based on a social accounting matrix (SAM) developed by Dorosh, Niazi, and Nazli (2006) and updated by Debowicz et al. (2012). The CGE model includes agricultural detail that allows for a good representation of water shocks on the economy, as well as disaggregated labor and household categories, to capture the distributional impacts of different policy choices. The SAM includes 45 sectors (or activities), 27 factors of production, and 18 household groups, allowing tracing of direct and indirect effects of potential scenarios through production and consumption linkages, including distributional effects. The model code starts from a new version of the IFPRI standard CGE model (Löfgren, Harris, and Robinson 2001).

The shock caused by water stress is defined as the ratio of crop yields for the current year compared to the baseline year yield. The baseline year data define the equilibrium of the water system in 2007/2008 under an average weather pattern. In the first run of the CGE model in each year, the external water shock anticipated by farmers is assumed to be the average of the four previous years, so farmers anticipate a short-term moving average level of water stress that allows for some adaptation. The CGE model then solves for the allocation of crops to irrigated and rainfed land based on these expectations.

The Regional Water System Model for Pakistan

RWSM-Pak is a water basin management model, but it does not include any economic measures because the economic links are handled in the CGE model. The basin management model covers only the Indus basin, which represents more than 90 percent of agricultural production in Pakistan. It is largely inspired by the original Indus Basin Model Revised (Ahmad, Brooke, and Kutcher 1990; recently updated by Yu et al. 2013). It models the nine main rivers of the Indus River basin that flow through Pakistan and provide irrigation water: from east to west, the Sutlej, the Ravi, the Chenab, the Jhelum, the Soan, the Indus, the Swat, the Kabul, and the Haro. It also models the main dams in the system: Tarbela, Mangla, Chasma, and Chotiari. The water is routed through 47 nodes of the Indus system in Pakistan. These nodes include (1) reservoirs, (2) link canals between rivers, and (3) barrages for irrigation outlets. Inflows, precipitation, runoff, and crop water-need data are generated externally by a climate model that is downscaled to Pakistan using historical data. The routing model takes into account river routing time, reservoir evaporation, and link canal capacity.

The model disaggregates the 45 main irrigation canals of the Pakistan Indus basin into 12 agroeconomic zones, based on provinces and crops grown. Four of these zones are in Sindh, five in Punjab, two in Khyber Pakhtunkhwa, and one in Balochistan. Three other zones, in Punjab, Balochistan, and Khyber Pakhtunkhwa, cover the rest of Pakistan. These zones are assumed to have a constant water stress, allowing us to isolate the effects of investments in the Indus basin. Agricultural land area, irrigation capacity, and groundwater pumping are disaggregated to this level. Groundwater pumping is allowed only in nonsaline groundwater areas (each zone is disaggregated into fresh and saline areas, if relevant), though we place a cap on maximum annual abstractions consistent with a sustainable yield for the Indus aquifer (50 MAF, according to Briscoe and Qamar [2005] and Yu et al. [2013]). RWSM-Pak assumes nonirrigation water is drawn from groundwater only. For this study, all water data are drawn from the new Indus Basin Model Revised, developed by the National Engineering Services Pakistan and the WAPDA, while crop data come from the 2010 Agricultural Census of Pakistan (GoP 2010).

The Water Accord of 1991, which reflects a highly sensitive political compromise, dictates the sharing of water between the four provinces and that dams should be managed with irrigation as a priority (Briscoe and Qamar 2005). Implementing the Water Accord in the model leads us to impose rule-based constraints on the simulated system. The objective function is constrained by these stringent rules on dam storage while maximizing the water delivered to cultivated areas. However we do not constrain individual canal releases to follow historical patterns, because this is a usage not enshrined in provincial law. Eight MAF of water are reserved as an outflow to keep the delta healthy, which is also mandated by the Water Accord.

The Hydropower Module

Benefits from the Diamer-Bhasha Dam include not only extra irrigation water but also extra electricity production. We include a hydropower module to simulate the extra electricity that would be produced by the dam. Hydropower generation depends on water flow and head (height of the dam and water level of the reservoir). Given that Pakistan explicitly gives priority to irrigation, we do not include hydropower generation in the objective function of the RWSM-Pak model. Instead, we compute hydropower electricity production after allocating water to the crops and include it as a source of energy in the CGE model.[14] Hydropower is represented as a fixed quantity of the total energy production, because we assume no other hydroelectric dam than Diamer-Bhasha is built. The additional energy production is included in GDP and valued as a benefit of the dam.

---

14 The current CGE model does not disaggregate energy sources or consider substitution possibilities across energy types. More detailed data is currently being developed for the Pakistan SAM and will be included in future models.

Annex B: Discussion of the Translog Stochastic Frontier Production Function

The model used to further investigate the relationship between groundwater and surface water is a translog stochastic frontier production function. The empirical model follows the stochastic frontier model developed by Aigner, Lovell, and Schmidt (1977) and extended by Battese and Coelli (1995). The basic formulation is

$$y_i = x_i\beta + v_i - u_i \tag{1}$$

for households $i = 1 \ldots N$, where y_i is the natural log of the value of output per unit of land for household i, x_i is a vector of the log of production inputs (fertilizer, capital, pesticide, labor, and the volume of irrigation water—both surface and groundwater estimated separately and as interactions of these variables), and v_i is a zero mean random error, assumed to be independently and identically distributed as $N(0,\sigma_v^2)$. The u_i is a nonnegative random variable associated with the technical inefficiency of production, which measures the percentage of output lost due to inefficiency and is assumed to be distributed as a truncated normal $N^+(u,\sigma_v^2)$. The technical inefficiency component of the error term, u_i, is expressed as $u_i = f(z_i\delta)$, where z_i is a vector of variables thought to explain inefficiency, such as the relative reliance of the household on groundwater compared to surface water, and other controls that can affect technical efficiency. The δ is a vector of associated coefficients to be estimated. The technical efficiency score (TE) of farm i is computed as $TE = \exp(-u_i)$. Thus, the production function component, y_i, and the inefficiency effects, u_i, are estimated together in one step. We have estimated the model for the kharif and rabi seasons separately.

As the previous paragraph indicates, there are two separate estimations included in the single model, one for the production function, and a second for technical inefficiency. The technical efficiency is discussed in depth in the main body of the chapter, with the marginal effects used for that discussion. This annex looks at the production function, which was discussed only briefly in the groundwater section in the chapter, and then presents the full regression model in Table B4.1. Because the dependent variable is the log of value of output per acre, crop mixes are expected to have significant effects, so dummy variables for possible crop combinations grown are included. The final sample size has 618 households in the rabi season and 583 households in kharif.

The production function relates the value of agricultural output per acre in Pakistan to several typical inputs. The results in Table B4.1 show that output

TABLE B4.1 Marginal effects and elasticity of value of output to agricultural inputs in kharif and rabi

Independent variable	Dependent variable: Log of value of output per acre			
	Kharif		Rabi	
	Marginal effects	Implied elasticity	Marginal effects	Implied elasticity
Log of labor days used (days/acre)	0.156***	0.076***	0.097***	0.046***
	(0.044)	(0.020)	(0.024)	(0.011)
Log of fertilizer used (kg/acre)	0.124***	0.052***	−0.002	−0.001
	(0.045)	(0.019)	(0.032)	(0.015)
Log of machinery hours used per acre	−0.010	0.007	−0.014	0.004
	(0.049)	(0.006)	(0.034)	(0.005)
Log of number of sprays used per acre	0.006	0.004	0.021	−0.002
	(0.039)	(0.003)	(0.021)	(0.002)
Total groundwater used (inches)	0.045	−0.014*	0.022	−0.004
	(0.029)	(0.009)	(0.016)	(0.005)
Total surface water used (inches)	−0.011	−0.010	0.019	−0.003
	(0.024)	(0.010)	(0.017)	(0.003)
Observations	583	583	618	618

Source: Authors' compilation using data from the RHPS (IFPRI/IDS 2012).

Note: Standard errors in parentheses. Asterisks (*, **, ***) denote significance at the 10, 5, and 1 percent levels, respectively. kg = kilograms.

is responsive to increased labor in agriculture both in kharif and rabi seasons. A 1 percent increase in farm labor days leads to a 0.08 percent increase in the value of output per acre in the kharif season and a 0.05 percent increase in rabi. The effect of additional labor is stronger in kharif, possibly because of the water-intensive nature of kharif crops, with the associated increased labor demand for more water applications, in addition to the higher labor requirements in general for crops in the season. In addition, agricultural production is responsive to increased fertilizer application rates in kharif, as a 1 percent increase in fertilizer application rates leads to a 0.05 percent increase in the value of output per acre in the season.

Table B4.2 shows the complete stochastic frontier production function model results.

TABLE B4.2 Regression results of a stochastic production function and inefficiency effects

| | Dependent variable: Log of value of output per acre | | | |
| | Kharif | | Rabi | |
Independent variable	Coefficient	Standard error	Coefficient	Standard error
Log of labor days used (days/acre)	−0.575	(0.446)	0.334	(0.204)
Log of fertilizer used (kg/acre)	0.197	(0.200)	0.152	(0.107)
Log of machinery hours used per acre	0.446	(0.393)	0.296	(0.240)
Log of number of sprays used per acre	−0.276	(0.355)	−0.354	(0.231)
Total groundwater used (inches)	0.159	(0.194)	0.208*	(0.120)
Total surface water used (inches)	0.115	(0.172)	0.102	(0.098)
Labor*fertilizer used	−0.018	(0.035)	−0.016	(0.018)
Labor*capital	−0.063	(0.070)	−0.103***	(0.034)
Labor*pesticide	0.061	(0.054)	0.076***	(0.029)
Labor*groundwater	0.043	(0.031)	−0.006	(0.016)
Labor*surface water	−0.012	(0.027)	0.006	(0.013)
Labor square	0.158*	(0.082)	0.006	(0.033)
Fertilizer*capital	−0.066*	(0.037)	−0.032	(0.024)
Fertilizer*pesticide	−0.007	(0.053)	0.001	(0.036)
Fertilizer*groundwater	−0.022	(0.021)	−0.008	(0.016)
Fertilizer*surface water	-0.027	(0.019)	−0.007	(0.013)
Fertilizer square	0.051**	(0.023)	0.001	(0.017)
Capital*pesticide	0.111*	(0.064)	−0.037	(0.040)
Capital*groundwater	−0.121***	(0.031)	−0.017	(0.027)
Capital*surface water	0.065**	(0.029)	−0.025	(0.020)
Capital square	0.178	(0.118)	0.280***	(0.067)
Pesticide*groundwater	−0.062**	(0.024)	0.021	(0.014)
Pesticide*surface water	-0.008	(0.023)	−0.011	(0.013)
Pesticide square	0.087	(0.055)	−0.018	(0.034)
Groundwater*surface water	0.015	(0.013)	−0.002	(0.008)
Groundwater square	−0.067**	(0.028)	−0.034**	(0.017)
Surface water square	−0.019	(0.028)	−0.028*	(0.017)
Sindh	−0.922***	(0.109)	−0.266***	(0.090)
KPK	−0.646***	(0.198)	−0.163	(0.110)
Constant	11.480***	(1.348)	8.701***	(0.692)
Determinants of technical inefficiency				
Ratio of groundwater to total irrigation water	−0.505**	(0.233)	0.453***	(0.173)
Rainfall was available on the plot	−0.436***	(0.102)	0.073	(0.102)

	Dependent variable: Log of value of output per acre			
	Kharif		Rabi	
Independent variable	Coefficient	Standard error	Coefficient	Standard error
Sindh	−1.408***	(0.268)	−0.211	(0.256)
KPK	−0.168	(0.362)	0.178	(0.202)
Soil and water conservation structure	0.097	(0.097)	0.060	(0.081)
Plot exposed to erosion	0.135	(0.133)	0.072	(0.094)
Canal water not used	0.121	(0.304)	−0.475	(0.299)
Located at the head of the watercourse	−0.288*	(0.158)	0.161	(0.126)
Located at the tail of the watercourse	0.183*	(0.099)	0.239**	(0.110)
Timely supply of canal water (Yes = 1, No = 0)	−0.138	(0.137)	−0.105	(0.137)
Household did not sell any crops in season	−0.101	(0.159)	0.235**	(0.105)
Rented-in plots	0.081	(0.108)	−0.039	(0.091)
Sharecropped-in plots	0.409***	(0.155)	0.164	(0.100)
Minutes to irrigate an acre using canal water	−0.050	(0.049)	−0.021	(0.054)
Flat land	−0.177	(0.164)	−0.146	(0.141)
Slightly sloping land	−0.420**	(0.180)	−0.064	(0.145)
Sandy soil	0.268	(0.202)	0.363**	(0.173)
Sand loam soil	0.014	(0.122)	0.295***	(0.109)
Loam soil	0.019	(0.120)	0.007	(0.101)
Average length of an irrigation turn (minutes)	0.196***	(0.065)	−0.197***	(0.058)
Distance of plot from homestead	0.052*	(0.029)	0.008	(0.027)
Flood irrigation used	0.343***	(0.104)	−0.278**	(0.128)
Khal panchayat exists on the watercourse	−0.313***	(0.112)	−0.497*	(0.263)
Household head attended school	0.077	(0.078)	−0.024	(0.064)
Log of age of household head	0.147*	(0.084)	0.154***	(0.057)
Plots experience waterlogging	0.426***	(0.160)	−0.166	(0.160)
Plots experience salinity	−0.021	(0.173)	−0.067	(0.157)
Producing sorghum only in kharif	0.822***	(0.256)	n.a.	n.a.
Producing cotton only in kharif	0.875***	(0.225)	n.a.	n.a.
Producing cotton and sorghum in kharif	0.787***	(0.217)	n.a.	n.a.
Producing cotton and millet in kharif	0.030	(0.231)	n.a.	n.a.
Producing sugar and sorghum in kharif	−0.103	(0.246)	n.a.	n.a.
Producing other miscellaneous combinations	0.066	(0.202)	n.a.	n.a.
Producing only berseem in rabi	n.a.	n.a.	−0.338	(0.209)
Producing only wheat	n.a.	n.a.	0.319***	(0.102)

(continued)

TABLE B4.2 *(continued)*

	Dependent variable: Log of value of output per acre			
	Kharif		Rabi	
Independent variable	Coefficient	Standard error	Coefficient	Standard error
σ_v	0.176***	(0.024)	0.218***	(0.019)
σ_u	0.639***	(0.035)	0.332***	(0.048)
Observations	583		618	

Source: Authors' estimation.

Note: The rabi crops are wheat and berseem. The kharif crops are rice, cotton, sugarcane, sorghum, and millet. n.a. = not applicable. A negative sign in the coefficients in the bottom panel implies that an increase in the variable reduces technical inefficiency, and hence improves efficiency. Asterisks (*, **, ***) denote significance at the 10, 5, and 1 percent levels, respectively. kg = kilograms; KPK = Khyber Pakhtunkhwa.

Annex C: Income Growth and Distribution in the Simulations

Income effects are presented for six household groups, which have varying levels of dependence on different sectors that affect income, to see how they are affected by climate outcomes and the presence of added storage. Table C4.1 shows the baseline household income for six groups and two forecasted years, 2029 and 2050. Four of the income groups are agriculturally related, including three different farm types (small, medium, and large), with landless agricultural workers as the fourth category. There are two nonagricultural households: nonfarm households in rural areas and urban households. The income of the six household groups from the historical simulation is given in the first column. Nearly 44 percent of total household income goes to urban households, and 23 percent goes to nonagricultural households in rural areas, leaving the farming community with about one-third of total household income. Of that, small farmers receive close to 17 percent, and medium farmers earn 10 percent. The better-off large farmers and agricultural laborers each earn less than 5 percent of the economy's household income. These proportions change only slightly between 2029 and 2050, although average household income grows about 5.2 percent per year after 2029.

The second column shows the annual percentage changes in income to different household groups from the addition of Bhasha Dam. All groups gain except for medium farmers. The small and large farm households see gains relative to the historical scenario of 0.26 percent and 0.30 percent. The nonfarm and urban households, with 0.74 percent gains in income, receive more than twice the rate of gain of farmers. Interestingly, agricultural workers see higher percentage gains in 2029 with Bhasha than do owner-operators. We

TABLE C4.1 Simulations with Bhasha Dam and climate change of annual changes in income from the historical simulation, 2029 and 2050

Household groups	Historical income	Simulation		
		Bhasha Dam	CSIRO B1 + Bhasha	MIROC A1B + Bhasha
	Billions PKR in 2029	Annual change from baseline simulation in 2029 (%)		
Small farms	4,684	0.26	0.08	0.08
Medium farms	2,592	−0.11	−0.47	−0.60
Large farms	1,106	0.30	0.22	0.23
Agricultural workers	850	0.59	0.65	0.74
Nonfarm households	6,514	0.74	0.76	0.88
Urban households	12,786	0.74	0.79	0.92
Total income	28,532			
	Billions PKR in 2050	Annual change from baseline simulation in 2050 (%)		
Small farms	13,394	0.87	0.35	0.53
Medium farms	8,084	0.70	0.34	0.36
Large farms	3,155	0.69	0.29	0.48
Agricultural workers	2,354	0.87	0.33	0.67
Nonfarm households	18,352	0.98	0.38	0.75
Urban households	35,305	0.95	0.34	0.73
Total income	80,644			

Source: Authors, based on results from the CGE-W model.

Note: The simulations included are Diamer-Bhasha Dam and two climate change scenarios. CSIRO is based on a model of Australia's Commonwealth Scientific and Industrial Research Organization (CSIRO) and MIROC on the Model for Interdisciplinary Research on Climate (MIROC), produced by the University of Tokyo's Center for Climate System Research (following the methodology of Jones and Thornton [2013]). The CSIRO scenario has smaller but more evenly distributed precipitation increases. The MIROC scenario has higher increases in precipitation on average but more variability. PKR = Pakistani rupees.

have controlled for many factors by showing changes relative to the historical model, which makes it clear that varying water availability has important effects on income growth over the longer run.

As before, the climate change scenarios examined are MIROC A1B and CSIRO B1, both with Bhasha Dam included. All farm households lose income as climate change occurs, again with the exception of agricultural workers. With more precipitation and runoff, the average level of the Bhasha reservoir is higher, and more electricity is delivered, which helps industry and services more and leads to higher incomes for nonagricultural households across all three scenarios.

In 2050 a fundamental shift occurs because of the growing demand from population and income versus productivity growth and limits on water and other resources. In this case, all income groups benefit from Bhasha Dam, approaching 1 percent gains in real income in some groups. However, in the CSIRO B1 climate change scenario, all incomes decline by about 0.5 percentage point from the Bhasha simulation alone, even with Bhasha Dam in place. In the higher water supply scenario, MIROC A1B, the decrease is not as great. While evaporation is higher in the MIROC A1B scenario and crop water requirements rise, water availability rises from precipitation and runoff in the July–December period, helping kharif crops in July and August and wheat in the latter months. Thus, incomes are not hurt as much in the MIROC A1B scenario.

Because prices rise by about 30 percent, the annual income growth rate is closer to 4.5 percent. Even if growth rates by household category are roughly the same, absolute values differ if the starting values differ: small farmers have a real income gain of PKR 8.7 trillion, while urban households gain PKR 11.8 trillion, with about the same percentage of additions to income.

Next, we explore income distribution effects related to watercourse efficiency improvements and agricultural productivity gains. The baseline values of income for the six household groups shown in the first column of Table C4.2 are similar to the earlier climate change simulations, but they change somewhat because of the use of an updated model. The next columns show percentage changes in income relative to the baseline scenario in 2029 and 2050 for the same options examined for GDP and water allocation. The highest gains to households in individual simulations are from BDAM in 2029 and TMG in 2050. The highest growth in household income in combination simulations occurs in the combinations of BDAM and TMG. In the latter case, real income gains exceed 0.50 percent for some household groups. While seemingly not large, a 0.30 percent difference in growth rates per year would lead to an 81 percent income differential over 20 years. Also, as noted in the earlier section on income distribution, when initial levels of income differ, equal percentage growth rates create a widening absolute gap.

For individual simulations, BDAM and TMG show significant gains across all household groups (except for TMG for medium farms in 2029). For the WCE simulation, however, farmers lose while other income groups gain, and this simulation adds the least to income, both in 2029 and 2050. The differences across households are smaller for these alternatives than in the climate change results because total water available does not vary. As before, agricultural workers see higher gains in both years and for all simulations compared to owner-operators.

TABLE C4.2 Alternative simulations of annual changes in income from the baseline simulation, 2029 and 2050

Household groups	Base income	Simulation					
		BDAM	TMG	WCE	BDAM + WCE	TMG + WCE	BDAM + TMG
	Billions PKR in 2029	Annual change from baseline simulation in 2029					
Small farms	4,612	0.30	0.08	−0.04	0.27	0.04	0.22
Medium farms	2,563	0.25	−0.14	−0.20	0.22	−0.13	0.35
Large farms	1,090	0.33	0.14	−0.01	0.27	0.08	0.40
Agricultural workers	834	0.40	0.29	0.13	0.37	0.22	0.54
Nonfarm households	6,326	0.45	0.36	0.12	0.41	0.27	0.62
Urban households	12,432	0.43	0.37	0.14	0.38	0.28	0.60
Total income	27,857						
	Billions PKR in 2050	Annual change from baseline simulation in 2050					
Small farms	12,942	0.19	0.23	−0.08	0.11	0.17	0.13
Medium farms	7,680	0.11	0.19	−0.22	0.03	0.07	0.31
Large farms	3,050	0.23	0.31	−0.04	0.12	0.21	0.37
Agricultural workers	2,298	0.31	0.39	0.10	0.24	0.32	0.55
Nonfarm households	17,634	0.34	0.43	0.06	0.25	0.35	0.58
Urban households	34,130	0.33	0.43	0.10	0.24	0.36	0.58
Total income	77,734						

Source: Authors, based on results from the CGE-W model.
Note: The simulations included are BDAM, Diamer-Bhasha Dam; TMG, better timing of water applications; and WCE, reduced seepage losses in watercourses. Three of these scenarios are combined: BDAM + WCE, TMG + WCE, and BDAM + TMG. CGE-W = computable general equilibrium-water

The individual simulations contribute varying amounts in 2029 and 2050. BDAM's contribution comes early because of immediate additions of hydropower and water, but it does not grow over time. As such, the rate of growth in household income is less in 2050 than in 2029. In contrast, TMG's income contributions are higher in later years as the value of better yields grows with the scarcity of resources. While WCE's contribution is low in both years, we find opposite conclusions in the microeconomic analysis.

Chapter 5

THE ARCHITECTURE OF THE PAKISTANI SEED SYSTEM: A CASE OF MARKET-REGULATION DISSONANCE

Muhammad Ahsan Rana, David J. Spielman, and Fatima Zaidi

Introduction

Applications of modern science to the improvement of cultivated crop varieties ("cultivars") have yielded tremendous gains for food security in Pakistan since the 1960s. The introduction of semidwarf rice and wheat cultivars—alongside strategic investments in the distribution of synthetic fertilizers, provision of irrigation, advice on crop management, and price support policies—encouraged rapid intensification in Pakistan's high-potential areas in a manner that is still recognized as one of the country's greatest development achievements. But since that moment in history, a constant onslaught of new threats to productivity growth—new pests and diseases, diminishing natural resources, weather shocks and climate volatility, changing demands from farmers and consumers, and new market forces—have highlighted the need for continuous innovation in cultivar improvement and seed provisioning strategies for farmers. By most accounts, innovation has fallen short of the challenge.

The breeding and provision of improved cultivars is often viewed as a "first-best" means of inducing technological change in agriculture, and historical evidence suggests that genetic improvement in major food staple crops has been a primary driver of productivity growth in developing countries (Evenson and Gollin 2003). Several factors underlie this observation. First, realization of the benefits from improved cultivars is generally neutral with respect to landholding size and scale, meaning that smallholders can often benefit from the technology in the same way that farmers with large holdings might (Lipton 1989). This has been a consistently important dimension of Pakistan's experience with improved cultivars because small and marginal farms (operating less than 5 acres of land) currently account for 64 percent of all private farms in Pakistan (GoP 2010).

Second, realization of the benefits from improved cultivars is mostly sustained from season to season through farmers' practices of saving grain from harvest for subsequent use as seed[1] and their practice of readily exchanging seed embodying desirable traits with other farmers. These nearly costless practices augmented the efforts of public research, seed multiplication programs, seed enterprises, and extension services to disseminate the semidwarf rice and wheat varieties introduced during Pakistan's Green Revolution of the 1960s and 1970s.

Since that time, however, circumstances have changed in Pakistan. On the demand side, farmers have been slow to switch to newer varieties of wheat, cotton, and rice, and their preferences have concentrated around a few top-performing varieties (Farooq and Iqbal 2000; Khan, Morgan, and Sofranko 1990; Heisey et al. 1997, 1993; Heisey 1990). Many of the adoption constraints facing Pakistan's farmers reflect what is already highlighted in the extensive literature on this topic, which relates primarily to institutional and behavioral characteristics—farmers' experience with new technologies, their risk preferences, exposure to peer effects, or other sociopsychological factors—or incomplete markets for land, labor, inputs, commodities, credit, and insurance (Jack 2011; Feder and Umali 1993; Feder, Just, and Zilberman 1985; Feder and Slade 1984). Many of the early studies on these topics were, in fact, first investigated in Pakistan (for example, Smale et al. 1998; Heisey et al. 1997, 1993; Heisey 1990).

On the supply side, Pakistan faces real challenges to its efforts to maintain and expand the system architecture required to continuously supply improved cultivars to farmers, particularly resource-poor, small-scale farmers. A modern seed industry requires long-term investments in science—plant breeding, agronomy, biological and molecular sciences—and constant revision

---

1   This is the case for many, but not all, crops. Realizing improved cultivars' benefits also depends partly on the capacity of farmers to collect and store seed in a way that minimizes the presence of pests, diseases, and foreign material in saved seed. Hybrids are an important exception. Hybrids are plants that exhibit a high level of genetic vigor (heterosis) that is associated with an increase in yield or uniformity resulting from the crossing of inbred parental lines. However, yield gains conferred by heterosis decrease substantially after the first generation is planted from hybrid seed. This compels farmers to purchase seed—rather than save harvested grain as seed—in order to continually realize yield gains conferred by heterosis. Hybrids of maize and many horticultural crops are commonly cultivated worldwide, while hybrids of sorghum, pearl millet, cotton, and rice have also been developed and marketed extensively. The reproductive biology associated with hybrids contrasts with open-pollinated varieties (OPVs), self-pollinating inbred varieties, and vegetatively propagated varieties, for which harvested grain or plant parts can be stored and used by farmers as seed in the following year.

of seed production, regulation, and distribution systems.[2] Decisions made on how to build that industry must balance a complex set of social and economic trade-offs that, in effect, are captured, on the one hand, in the struggle to ensure farmers' access to affordable seed of improved cultivars and, on the other hand, the need to incentivize investment in breeding, seed production, and marketing. These trade-offs raise a host of issues, including, for example, the appropriate roles for the public and private sectors in the seed industry; the distribution of the gains from innovation among plant breeders, entrepreneurs, seed companies, public research organizations, and farmers; and the marginal cost of rules and regulations designed to encourage innovation, ensure quality, protect human and environmental health, or otherwise steer seed industry development (Spielman et al. 2015; Byerlee and Fischer 2002). As Pakistan's seed industry continues to grow in volume, value, and coverage, these trade-offs become increasingly important. Unfortunately, too little analysis of these trade-offs has been done to date.

This chapter fills this knowledge gap with a close examination of the legislative and institutional framework governing cultivar improvement and seed provision in Pakistan. It underscores the need to give greater attention to the institutional and organizational architecture of Pakistan's seed system—to identify the appropriate roles for the public and private sectors, their political and economic interests in continuing or changing the existing system, and the available policy solutions to improve investment policies, regulatory systems, and opportunities for entrepreneurship.

The second section of this chapter identifies data sources for this study. The third section provides a brief history of the development of the seed business in Pakistan. The fourth section describes the existing legal and institutional structure to regulate seed provision, and identifies gaps that constrain the private sector's participation in seed provision. The fifth section identifies key actors in the sector, explores their respective interests in and capacity to influence potential reform, and briefly discusses important professional networks that these actors can deploy to pursue their interests. The sixth

---

2   Throughout this chapter, we refer to Pakistan's "seed industry" to describe the sector of the economy in which seed and other planting materials are produced for use by farmers. This term can be used interchangeably with other common descriptors such as "seed system," which suggests a greater focus on the public service dimensions of the industry, for example, the research and regulatory systems; "seed market," which suggests a greater focus on exchanges, for example, at the wholesale or retail levels; or "seed sector," which suggests the importance of strategic planning by government to ensure national food security. We choose the term "seed industry" merely to emphasize the growing role of private companies in the development, production, and marketing of seed.

section discusses recent efforts to reform the legal framework, which we contend have so far been unsuccessful, largely because the proposed legislation merely extends regulatory oversight over the workings of the private sector without offering anything in return. The seventh section discusses the boundary between the formal and the informal seed industry, pointing out that it is more blurred in Pakistan than is often recognized.

Data and Data Sources

This chapter draws on data from four sources: (1) the Federal Seed Certification and Registration Department (FSC&RD), (2) academic papers and industry reports, (3) key informant interviews, and (4) the first rounds (Round 1 and 1.5) of the Pakistan Rural Household Panel Survey (RHPS), conducted in 2012.

FSC&RD. Data from the FSC&RD—the seed industry's principal regulator and a department of the federal Ministry of National Food Security and Research (MNFSR)—are used to gain insight on the formal (organized) seed industry in Pakistan. This includes data on variety releases, seed provider operations, seed supply requirements, seed certification, imports, and exports, as well as rules and regulations governing the formal seed industry. Significant gaps exist in FSC&RD's data, but the data nonetheless provide enough insight on levels and trends to inform the analysis in this chapter.

Academic Literature. To augment FSC&RD data, this chapter draws on academic papers and industry reports. Unfortunately, rigorous policy analyses of Pakistan's seed sector are scarce, and the topic has not attracted much academic interest in Pakistan. Most of the recent work focuses on specific crops or technologies, such as genetically modified insect-resistant Bt cotton (for example, Rana et al. 2013; Kouser and Qaim 2013; Nazli et al. 2012; Ali and Abdulai 2010; Ali et al. 2007), rather than on the institutional and governance framework that enables or impedes this diffusion. Few studies examine the seed sector holistically beyond the usual litany of complaints (for example, Hussain 2011; Sarwar 2007). Nevertheless, these academic papers and industry reports provide useful insights into specific aspects of seed provision, especially when they are considered alongside papers and reports from other developing countries that explore how public policies and regulatory frameworks have evolved elsewhere (see Byerlee and Fischer 2002).

Informant Interviews. The third source—officials from the seed corporations, federal ministry officials, provincial agriculture departments, seed companies, and farmers—is a particularly valuable source for understanding the nuances of Pakistan's seed industry. These key informant interviews were conducted from 2012 to 2014 in a relatively open-ended manner and under a range of circumstances, including one-on-one interviews, discussions at public policy forums, telephone conversations, and other forms of interaction and correspondence.

Household Surveys. Finally, household data are drawn from Round 1.5 of the Pakistan RHPS, conducted in 2012 (IFPRI/IDS 2012; see Chapter 1 for details). Data on seed sources and quantities are specifically drawn from a subsample of 942 agricultural households across three provinces that was surveyed in November 2012 under RHPS Round 1.5.

A Historical Perspective on Pakistan's Seed Industry

Pakistan's seed industry has passed through four phases. The first phase—1947 to the late 1950s—was characterized by small-scale research and development (R&D) in the public sector and a continuation of the colonial focus on a few major crops in the rich alluvial plains of Pakistan's two agricultural provinces, Punjab and Sindh. The second phase—late 1950s to the mid-1970s—was characterized by development of an elaborate network of public-sector organizations that were designed to develop and deliver improved cultivars. The third phase—mid-1970s to mid-1990s—was a period of legal and institutional development. The fourth phase—mid-1990s to date—has seen rapid growth of the private sector and a gradual shift of functions from seed companies and other actors. A brief discussion of each phase follows.

Small-scale R&D. When Pakistan was established in 1947, the only (public or private) organization that carried out agricultural research was the Punjab Agricultural College and Research Institute, Lyallpur (later renamed Faisalabad). New cultivars were developed as public goods. Because their commercialization was not intended, no formal system of cultivar approval and registration existed at the time. New cultivars were simply handed over by breeders to the provincial agriculture departments for seed production and distribution to farmers. While seed certification was not an entirely unknown concept, the absence of an appropriate legal and institutional framework meant that formal certification operations could not be put into operation. Overall, the Lyallpur institute played a small role in seed provision, and farmers mostly depended on their own seed production (Ali and Ali 2004).

Public Institutions. Pakistan's ambitious development planning of the 1950s and 1960s warranted an increase in agricultural productivity to spur economic growth. This necessitated the establishment of elaborate arrangements for agricultural research and seed production. The government responded through two major initiatives in 1961. One was the bifurcation of the Lyallpur College and Institute into the Agricultural University at Lyallpur and the Ayub Agricultural Research Institute (AARI). The other was the establishment of the West Pakistan Agricultural Development Corporation (WPADC).[3] These three organizations grew quickly and emerged as dedicated institutional hubs for agricultural research and teaching (Agricultural University at Lyallpur), cultivar development (AARI), and seed production (WPADC). Given the nature of these activities, overlaps were inevitable. The Agricultural University at Lyallpur started academic programs in multiple disciplines, AARI upgraded and expanded the existing system of cultivar development, and WPADC established seed farms and developed a system of seed certification.

AARI and WPADC provided a convenient conduit for transmitting to farmers new cultivars and related technologies developed by the international agricultural research system. However, AARI and WPADC were constrained in what they could achieve given the resources available at the time. Capacity limitations—mainly a shortage of skilled scientific and technical expertise and a low base from which operations were scaled up—meant that they could concentrate their R&D on only a few major crops and focus only on the high-potential irrigated areas in Punjab and Sindh to the exclusion of other provinces. While AARI continued to grow in the third and the fourth phases, WPADC ceased operations in 1972, soon after West Pakistan was divided administratively into provinces. The function of seed production and marketing was assigned to provincial organizations, namely, the Punjab Agricultural Development and Supplies Corporation and the Sindh Agricultural Supplies Organization. Balochistan and the Northwest Frontier Province (NWFP, now Khyber Pakhtunkhwa) continued to rely on seed produced by Punjab- and Sindh-based organizations and on farmers' saved seeds.

Until the promulgation of Pakistan's first seed law—the West Pakistan Seeds and Fruit Plants Ordinance, 1965—AARI and WPADC operated in the absence of a legal framework that set out procedures and protocols of variety approval. The ordinance was a basic instrument that provided for the registration of growers for production of certified seeds and establishment

---

3   Punjab, Sindh, Balochistan, Northwest Frontier Province (now Khyber Pakhtunkhwa), and tribal areas were merged in 1954 into one unit called West Pakistan. The one unit was dissolved in 1970.

of nurseries. Registered growers could voluntarily apply for certification. Certified seed was to be sold to the government, while only leftover certified seed could be sold in the open market. The ordinance did not prohibit production of uncertified seed (other than the seed of fruit plants), which meant that seed producers could develop seed for the market but had to register with the government and maintain standards if they wished to have their seeds certified.

Reform. The third phase started in 1973 when the Pakistan government sought help from the World Bank to review its seed provision system and formulate recommendations for comprehensive reform (Salam 2012; Ahmad and Nagy 1999). This was the beginning of Pakistan's first large-scale seed industry project, under which wide-ranging legal and institutional reforms were undertaken to improve seed provisioning to farmers.

The most salient feature of this project was the enactment of the Seed Act in 1976, which specified procedures for variety registration and seed certification. The act also created elaborate institutional infrastructure for its implementation, including the National Seed Council, provincial seed councils, and two separate agencies (under the federal Ministry of Agriculture) for variety registration and seed certification. These agencies were merged in 1998 to constitute the FSC&RD as it stands today. The mandate of Punjab and Sindh corporations for agricultural supplies was redefined, and these were converted into the Punjab Seed Corporation and Sindh Seed Corporation. In NWFP, an Agriculture Development Authority was established, which was mandated to produce seed for local consumption. In Balochistan, no separate institutional arrangements were made, and the provincial agriculture department continued to provide seed on a limited scale.

A shift from the previous tradition during this phase was to assign a formal role—albeit marginal—to the private sector, namely, seed multiplication on farmers' fields. But this was how far the act went: it assigned all other functions in the seed development chain—cultivar development; production of breeder nucleus seed, pre-basic seed, and basic seed;[4] seed testing; and seed certification—to the public sector. It also did not provide for registration of private seed companies. Such an exclusive focus reflected a broader economic policy designed around broad-spectrum nationalization of industry in the 1970s. Several projects carried out in the 1970s to strengthen the public sector

---

4   Breeder nucleus seed is the pure seed of an improved cultivar produced by a breeder. This seed is produced in very small quantities. It is multiplied to produce pre-basic seed, which in turn is multiplied by the breeder or another seed producer to produce basic seed. Seed purity declines somewhat in each multiplication.

involved establishing seed production farms, setting up seed-testing laboratories, installing seed-processing plants, and training seed technologists.

Private-sector Growth. The fourth phase in the development of the seed industry in Pakistan began in the late 1970s when FSC&RD—consistent with the broader government policy of agricultural market and trade liberalization—proactively attempted to promote private-sector participation in the seed business. The first seed company was formally registered in 1981. Another eight seed companies, all based in Punjab, launched their businesses in the next few years (Sarwar 2007).

The pace picked up in the 1990s. In 1994 the seed business was formally categorized as an industry (Ali and Ali 2004) and was granted privileges associated with that designation. By 2000, 291 private seed companies had registered with FSC&RD (Ali and Ali 2004). Sindh, KPK, and Balochistan had their first seed companies in 1996, 1996, and 1998, respectively. Four multinational corporations (MNCs) established their Pakistan affiliates during the 1980s and 1990s, and the total number of companies engaged in seed production and marketing grew to more than 960 by 2012.

Initially, Pakistani seed companies were limited to multiplication of basic seeds that they obtained from public seed corporations. Very quickly, however, they established their own breeding programs and brought a number of new cultivars to the market. As their operations grew, they started to displace public-sector corporations from the market. Several companies also started to import and export planting material. Gradually, they became the lead providers in several crops—cotton, vegetables, oilseeds, maize, and fodder. The leadership of the Pakistani seed industry thus has quietly shifted to the private sector during the past two decades.

The Governance Framework

Cultivar improvement and seed provision activities in Pakistan are governed by the Seed Act of 1976, which is federal legislation. Under the 1973 Constitution of Pakistan, agriculture is a provincial subject. Ipso facto, only a provincial government can legislate on matters related to agriculture. So when the federal government sought to regulate seed provision in Pakistan, it had to persuade provincial governments to surrender their legislative authority to this extent to the federal government under Article 144 of the constitution. This enabled the federal government to enact the Seed Act of 1976 and provide a uniform structure for seed sector activities in all provinces. This is an important feature of the Seed Act, which affects the seed sector in several ways.

The Seed Act's specific objective is to regulate seed quality, and to do so, it establishes a set of institutions, specifies procedures for registering new cultivars and producing seed, defines breaches of the laws, and sets out penalties for committing breaches. The act creates three institutions: (1) the National Seed Council, (2) provincial seed councils, and (3) FSC&RD. Chaired by the federal minister of agriculture, the National Seed Council is required to perform a range of regulatory and advisory functions.[5] These functions include specifying seed standards, regulating the interprovincial movement of seeds, guiding the administration of seed quality standards, advising the government in general on seed policy, and ensuring and protecting investment in the seed industry. Provincial seed councils perform similar functions in the provinces. FSC&RD is responsible for registration of new cultivars and for seed certification.

The act prohibits the stocking or sale of seed of a notified cultivar (that is, a cultivar approved by the government and notified as such in the official gazette) unless it conforms to seed quality standards and bears a label including the required information. It is important to note that this stipulation is only for notified cultivars. The act also specifies procedures for seed certification, but it does not make certification mandatory for seed producers. In other words, seed producers *may* register their new cultivars with FSC&RD and *may* get seed of their registered cultivars certified, in which case they are subject to seed quality standards. By implication, they may, as well, carry out their seed provision activities without registering a cultivar and/or without certifying their seeds. The act allows seed officials to inspect seed production facilities, collect samples, and carry out necessary tests to see whether or not seed quality standards are being met. Violating any provision of the act or preventing lawful functioning by a duly-appointed person is declared an offense punishable with fairly nominal fines, imprisonment, or both.

The act does not provide for registration or regulation of private seed companies. The only role it assigns to the private sector is seed multiplication, for which FSC&RD is required to register seed growers. When official policy shifted to market and trade liberalization in the late 1970s, FSC&RD also started exploring ways and means to encourage the private sector's

---

5   Both national and provincial seed councils are composed principally of public officials. Farmer representation is limited to one farmer, nominated by the respective government, in each case.

participation in seed provision beyond seed multiplication. The legal basis for such enhanced participation could be provided by amending the Seed Act of 1976. But because agriculture is a provincial subject, the federal government wanted to consult provincial governments before comprehensively amending the Seed Act to reflect changes in the policy paradigm. As a stop-gap arrangement, the federal government's Economic Coordination Committee, in a meeting on December 31, 1979, established an Interministerial Working Group to register or deregister new seed companies (Hussain 2011). The objective was to formalize the private sector's organized participation in the seed business. In effect, however, the creation of the Working Group added a layer of complexity to private investment in the seed sector, because it required companies to establish themselves both under existing instruments of law (for example, the Companies Ordinance, 1984) and through an application for registration with the Working Group.

To facilitate the implementation of the Seed Act, the federal government framed the following three sets of rules: (1) Seed (Registration) Rules, 1987; (2) Seeds (Truth-in-Labeling) Rules, 1991; and (3) Pakistan Fruit Plants Certification Rules, 1998. While the latter two sets of rules are fairly standard provisions in any seed system, the first set of rules does raise several issues.

The Seed (Registration) Rules establish a Federal Seed Registration Committee, which is charged with evaluating candidate varieties for compliance with variety registration standards. Rule 7 of the Seed (Registration) Rules of 1987 requires a new variety to be both (1) superior to existing varieties in at least one important aspect and (2) at least satisfactory in other major characteristics. Rule 9 prohibits the production or certification of seed of any variety of a crop included in a Schedule to the Rules, unless the variety is validly registered with FSC&RD.[6]

This prohibition is unusual. Rules, being subordinate legislation carried out by the government without recourse to the parliament (or a provincial assembly), are meant to elaborate and explain, rather than add to or contradict the parent legislation. But by prohibiting production of seed of unregistered varieties, Rule 9 is effectively an unlegislated addition to the Seed Act, which is silent on the production of seed of unregistered varieties.

Read alone (which was definitely the case between 1976 and 1987), the act indicates that if a breeder wants to register his variety with FSC&RD, he *may* apply in the prescribed form, and the variety will be registered if it meets the criteria. Once the variety has been notified, he *may* seek certification of

---

6   The schedule is an extensive list and includes all major and minor crops.

its seed. But both are optional for the breeder. If he does not seek registration of his variety, he may market it at his own risk and cost. Read with the Seed (Registration) Rules, 1987, the Seed Act indicates that if a breeder does not register his variety or his application fails, seed of such variety cannot be produced.[7]

Another important component of the seed sector's legal framework is the Pakistan Biosafety Rules and National Biosafety Guidelines of 2005. Framed under the 1997 Pakistan Environmental Protection Act, these rules regulate various aspects relating to genetically modified organisms (GMOs). They prohibit the import, export, sale, purchase, or trade of GMOs and their products without a license from the federal government. They also provide for the establishment an interministerial National Biosafety Committee (NBC) and a Technical Advisory Committee (TAC) at the federal level as part of the Ministry of Climate Change.

NBC's functions include granting approvals for the import, export, trial, and commercial release of genetically modified (GM) cultivars. It reviews recommendations from the TAC charged with reviewing biosafety data and analysis of GM products submitted for commercialization. So far, the NBC has approved the commercial release only of Bt cotton, although it has allowed limited trials for a range of GM crops, including drought-tolerant wheat and herbicide-tolerant and insect-resistant maize, which were developed by both public and private entities.[8]

As the above discussion indicated, FSC&RD and NBC have emerged as two key institutions for governance of the seed sector. Both have suffered a few years of institutional uncertainty in the aftermath of the 18th Constitutional Amendment of 2010, which devolved several federal functions to the provinces. The devolution led to abolition of the federal Ministry of Agriculture and Livestock, and the Ministry of Environment. Yet, the federal

7   According to Rule 9 of the Seed (Registration) Rules of 1987, "Effect of non-registration—No variety of the crop specified in Schedule 1 shall be eligible for seed production and certification in any Province of Pakistan or part thereof unless the said variety has been registered and the necessary certificate to that effect has been obtained from the National Registration Agency." Rule 9 prohibits seed production, rather than sale or offering for sale, so technically farmer seed saving should also be problematic. Because not all farmer-saved seed varieties are registered or notified, at least theoretically, farmers will violate Rule 9 when they produce traditional seed varieties. However, this strictly legal interpretation is unlikely to apply in practice.

8   The first approval of genetically modified cotton was granted in 2010 for cotton containing genes from the soil bacterium *Bacillus thuringiensis* (Bt). The genes confer resistance to certain types of insects, namely bollworms and other insects in the order Lepidoptera. The wheat and maize were developed by the National Institute of Biotechnology and Genetic Engineering and Monsanto, respectively.

bureaucracy was able to make a successful case for re-creating the dissolved ministries into the new Ministry of National Food Security and Research (MNFSR) and the Ministry of Climate Change (Rana 2013). FSC&RD, whose responsibilities were initially expected to be delegated to provinces, was first assigned to the Ministry of Science and Technology and later, in 2011, to the MNFSR. Similarly, following a few months of administrative confusion, NBC was assigned to the new Ministry of Climate Change.

Seed Markets and Actors

Pakistan's seed system—similar to seed systems in most countries—comprises a research system, regulatory agencies, and seed producers. They interact in a market that is difficult to estimate in terms of value or volume, though Hussain (2011) approximates the total value of the Pakistani seed market at US$845 million in 2008/2009.

The Pakistani seed system comprises two segments: the formal seed system and the informal seed system. The formal seed system comprises breeding institutes, state-owned seed corporations, privately owned seed companies, regulatory organizations (that is, the seed councils and FSC&RD, as well as NBC for GM crops), agricultural input dealers, and farmers. The informal seed system comprises many of these same actors—farmers, input dealers, seed companies, and breeding institutes—implying that formal sector actors also operate as part of the informal sector to the extent that part of their seed business operates outside of formally defined market channels. Figure 5.1 graphically depicts the flow of seed and its information from one actor to the other in the seed system. The role of various actors in the formal and the informal segments is described in the following pages.

As is evident from Figure 5.1, a key component of this system is Pakistan's public agricultural research system, which is one of the larger agricultural research systems among developing countries, with an estimated 3,513 full-time-equivalent researchers (Flaherty, Sharif, and Spielman 2012). The main research entities at the federal level include the Pakistan Agricultural Research Council (PARC), Pakistan Central Cotton Committee (PCCC), and agricultural research institutes of the Pakistan Atomic Energy Commission (PAEC). At the provincial level, the Punjab government's AARI stands out as a key research entity: AARI has led the system's most productive breeding program, accounting for 39 percent of the total number of varieties released to date (Table 5.1).

FIGURE 5.1 Flow diagram of seed provision in the formal and the informal seed sectors

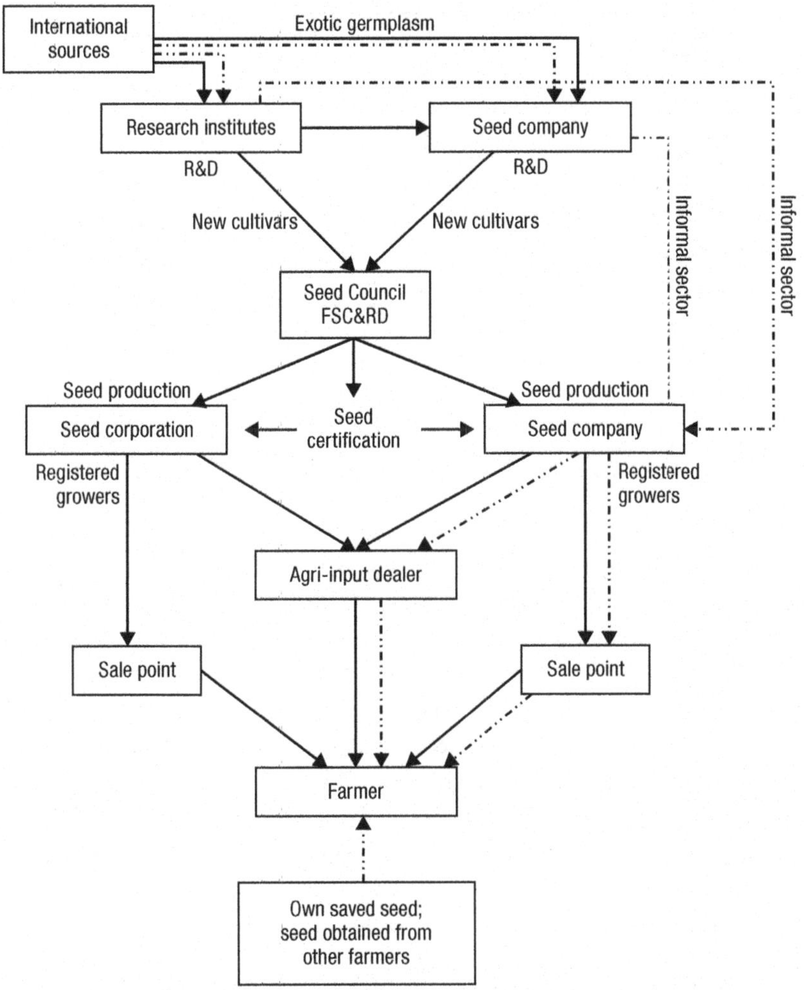

Source: Authors.
Note: Dotted lines show informal sector operations.

In addition to these federal and provincial entities, five major agricultural universities in Pakistan carry out R&D activities. The largest of these is the University of Agriculture, Faisalabad (UAF) which has about 12,000 students and employs 593 faculty members, of whom 49 percent hold a PhD (UAF 2013; Flaherty, Sharif, and Spielman 2012). The academic programs of

TABLE 5.1 Share of crop varieties released by provincial research institutions, cumulative prior to June 2013

Institute	Share of all varieties released (%)
Ayub Agricultural Research Institute (AARI)	39
Pakistan Agricultural Research Council (PARC)	2
Pakistan Atomic Energy Commission (PAEC)	8
Central Cotton Research Institute (CCRI)	9
Agricultural Research Institute (ARI)	13
Others	29
Total	100

Source: Authors, based on Federal Seed Certification and Registration Department data.

these universities conduct research across a range of disciplines and provide a trained workforce for the seed industry and other agribusinesses.

Four important observations about the research system's contribution to Pakistan's seed industry are worth noting here. First, the public sector accounts for 96 percent of all cultivars released to date (Table 5.2). The private sector has only recently started developing its own cultivars for commercial release for a small number of crops, such as transgenic Bt cotton (Rana 2013). Second, breeding activities are limited to a small set of crops. Even among these crops, cotton and wheat account for 40 percent of all cultivars released to date (Table 5.2). Such narrow R&D focus forces farmers to rely on unimproved traditional cultivars for other crops. Third, Punjab-based institutes and companies have developed almost half of all cultivars. KPK-based institutes and companies have also developed a large number of cultivars. But the relatively small number of new cultivars developed in Sindh and Balochistan shows that farmers in these provinces have to rely on breeding programs in agroecologically different Punjab and KPK.

Fourth, there is significant overlap and duplication among the federal, provincial, and university breeding programs. Perhaps the most obvious case is PCCC's Central Cotton Research Institute (CCRI) in Multan. CCRI has elaborate plant-breeding facilities, and has developed several popular cotton cultivars. Situated across the road from CCRI is AARI's premier Cotton Research Station, which pursues the same mandate and has similar facilities. Yet the two institutes exist as separate entities and rarely communicate.

Finally, the release of new crop varieties and hybrids peaked during the decades of the 1990s and 2000–2009, which was also the period when most seed companies were established (Table 5.3). Although public-sector entities

TABLE 5.2 Number of new cultivars registered with FSC&RD by province, cumulative prior to June 2013

Crop	Public sector					Private sector	Total
	Punjab	Sindh	KPK	Balochistan	Islamabad		
Wheat	59	24	40	8	3	0	134
Cotton	74	21	1	0	0	13	109
Pulses	43	4	19	1	5	0	72
Oilseed	20	5	22	0	8	5	60
Vegetables	36	1	12	8	0	0	57
Sugarcane	14	8	16	0	0	1	39
Fodder	27	0	7	1	0	2	37
Rice	16	13	6	0	0	0	35
Fruits	2	0	33	0	0	0	35
Maize	11	0	12	0	0	2	25
Barley	3	0	3	4	0	0	10
Total	305	76	171	22	16	23	613

Source: Authors, based on FSC&RD data.
Note: FSC&RD = Federal Seed Certification and Registration Department; KPK = Khyber Pakhtunkhwa. Designation of province is by the geographic location of the research institute that developed these varieties.

TABLE 5.3 Number of crop varieties and hybrids released, 1933–2013

Crop	Pre-1970	1970–1979	1980–1989	1990–1999	2000–2009	2010–2013	Total
Wheat	0	13	20	35	44	22	134
Cotton	2	9	11	28	32	27	109
Pulses	0	0	8	26	32	6	72
Oilseed	0	0	8	31	15	6	60
Vegetables	3	2	2	30	15	5	57
Sugarcane	0	0	3	15	15	6	39
Fodder and forage	0	0	10	6	14	7	37
Rice	5	3	10	8	8	1	35
Fruit	0	0	0	7	20	8	35
Maize	0	5	2	9	5	4	25
Barley	0	0	3	3	2	2	10
Total	10	32	77	198	202	94	613

Source: Authors, based on Federal Seed Certification and Registration Department data.

were still releasing new varieties and hybrids during this period, the private sector's growing participation seems to have played a key role in Pakistan's seed market development. Private-sector participation not only increased market size but also—and more importantly—generated awareness and demand among farmers for differentiated products.

Beyond research and the release of new varieties, the tasks of seed multiplication, distribution, and marketing fall to several actors in Pakistan's seed system. Among the public seed producers established in the 1970s, only the Punjab Seed Corporation remains as a significant seed producer.[9] PSC has an impressive infrastructure for the production and distribution of seed across a wide range of crops. Its infrastructure includes seed farms on 7,303 acres, processing plants with a capacity of 72,000 metric tons, ginning capacity of 22.5 bales per hour, delinting capacity of 13,500 metric tons, storage capacity of 6,700 metric tons, more than 1,200 registered growers, and a marketing network of 1,136 dealers and 19 sales points in Punjab and 70 dealers in other provinces (PSC 2008). That said, PSC faces many of the challenges associated with running a large state-owned seed enterprise: difficulties in estimating demand and managing inventories, a governance structure that struggles to balance commercial considerations with government development priorities, and farm management issues.[10]

Alongside the PSC is a vibrant private sector, although exact numbers are difficult to come by.[11] A total of 963 Pakistani seed companies have registered with FSC&RD since 1981, although 213 companies were deregistered over the years after they were found to be involved in irregularities (Salam 2012) (Table 5.4). Several of these companies were started by contract growers of a provincial seed corporation with sufficient experience in producing seed for the public sector, or by successful farmers who had been providing seed in the neighborhood and wanted to formalize the arrangement. Other companies were established by members of the value chain (for example, a ginning factory, an exporter, or an agrochemical company) that were seeking to

---

9   The ADA, in KPK, was disbanded in 2001, and operations of the Sindh Seed Corporation (SSC) were suspended in 2002. Although operations were revived in 2006, SSC plays a marginal role in seed provision at present.

10   For example, since 2006–2008, tenants on PSC's largest farm in Khanewal have illegally occupied a large part of the farm and refused to grow seed or pay rent. As a result, more than 5,000 acres are effectively lost to PSC.

11   It is common for seed companies to enter and exit the seed business. Hence, not all registered seed companies may be currently active. In 2003/2004, FSC&RD circulated a questionnaire to update its database: only 73 companies responded (Hussain and Hussain 2007), indicating how difficult it is to maintain updated figures.

TABLE 5.4 Number of seed producers registered with FSC&RD, 1981–2012

Type of company	Punjab	Sindh	KPK	GB and Islamabad	Balochistan	Total
Public sector	1	1	1	0	1	4
Private (national)	803	121	28	3	8	963
Private (multinational)	4	1	0	0	0	5
Total registered	808	123	29	3	9	972
Deregistered	182	23	5	0	3	213
Total currently registered	626	100	24	3	6	759

	Before 1991	1991–1995	1996–2000	2001–2005	2006–2010	2011–2012
Number of companies registered by period	6	56	229	257	312	103

Source: Authors, based on FSC&RD data.

Notes: GB = Gilgit Baltistan; KPK = Khyber Pakhtunkhwa; FSC&RD = Federal Seed Certification and Registration Department.

diversify their business portfolios. Another five companies are Pakistani subsidiaries of leading multinational enterprises: (1) Monsanto Pakistan Agritech, (2) ICI Pakistan, (3) Pioneer Pakistan Seed, (4) Bayer CropSciences, and (5) Syngenta Pakistan. Although none of them engage in significant R&D activities in Pakistan, they are popular suppliers of (mostly imported) hybrid seeds of maize, sunflower, fodder, canola, alfalfa, and sorghum (Hussain and Hussain 2007).

Available data suggest several important trends. First, Pakistan's seed business is concentrated in Punjab, with 82 percent of companies having their registered offices there (Rana 2013). Most of these companies are located in southern Punjab, which enables them to also serve the markets in Sindh and Balochistan. Second, the total number of companies is large and growing, although there is little evidence indicating the emergence of strategic behavior—mergers, acquisitions, joint ventures, and technical collaborations—that often accompanies seed industry growth (Table 5.4).

Third, MNCs have played a key role in introducing hybrid seed. Monsanto and Pioneer were central to introducing hybrids of maize and sorghum, while ICI introduced a canola hybrid to Pakistan. During the 1990s, Pioneer also invested in wheat, and Monsanto invested in wheat, cotton, and rice, although both have withdrawn from these markets because of their limited profitability and other issues (Rana 2010; Hussain and Hussain 2007). Fourth, seed companies have positioned themselves to influence policy decisions related to seed regulation, biotechnology, biosafety, and a range of related policy issues

in Pakistan. They have done so both individually and through several industry associations, including one formed exclusively by the MNCs (ARM 2008;
FSC&RD 2001). The most active of these associations, the Seed Association
of Pakistan, has used the platform to present seed companies' perspective on
pending seed legislation, which is discussed below.

Table 5.5 presents data on the private sector's share in the provision of certified seed of selected crops, showing that seed companies dominate the certified seed market. Private companies' market share (measured in terms of local
production plus imports) ranges from 72 percent for wheat to 100 percent for
vegetables and fodder. And for crops such as cotton, maize, and vegetables,
some of the seed sold by the private companies originates from their own registered cultivars. For example, 10 out of 17 Bt cotton varieties approved for
commercial cultivation in Pakistan were developed by (and are registered with
FSC&RD in the name of) Pakistani seed companies.[12]

In the case of cotton, recent surveys (for example, Rana et al. 2013) suggest that these private companies compete not only on genetics (that is, the
genetic superiority of the company's particular cultivar) but also on quality
of service—purity and germination of seed, timeliness of delivery, quality of
packaging, brand reputation, or other such dimensions. This is particularly
important for those companies that do not invest in breeding programs and
confine their business to the multiplication and marketing of public varieties.
Rana et al. (2013) find in their survey of cottonseed in Sindh that companies sell seeds of the same varieties of Bt cotton at substantially different rates.
This suggests that farmers are willing to pay a premium for quality, and that
brand names have started to emerge in the Pakistani seed market.

Another way to illustrate the presence of competition is to examine prices
paid by farmers for seed in the 2012 RHPS data (IFPRI/IDS 2012). As
Table 5.6 shows, cotton, maize, and rice seed prices vary significantly, both
within and across provinces, possibly reflecting the presence of competitive
pricing and product differentiation between companies, although other price
determinants such as transportation costs may also account for these differences. Wheat, on the other hand, exhibits far lower price variation, which
is again unsurprising given the difficulty companies face in differentiating
and marketing publicly developed open-pollinated varieties that can also
be easily saved and exchanged between farmers. An analysis of the determinants of seed prices for wheat, cotton, maize, and rice seed using a Heckman

---

12 The actual number of Bt cotton varieties developed by the private sector may be larger, given
    that companies often enter the market directly without recourse to FSC&RD. See Rana (2010).

TABLE 5.5 Availability and sources of certified seed, 2012/2013

Crop	Total estimated seed requirement	Total certified seed available	Certified seed domestic production			Certified seed imported by the private sector[a]	Private-sector production share of domestic production	Private-sector imports share of total certified seed available	Certified seed available as share of estimated requirement
			Total	By the public sector	By the private sector				
	MT	MT	MT	MT	MT	MT	%	%	%
Wheat	1,085,400	259,904	259,904	72,112	187,792	—	72	0	28
Rice	42,480	49,492	45,767	5,068	40,699	3,725	82	8	116[b]
Maize	31,914	14,008	3,705	245	3,460	10,303	25	74	44
Cotton	40,000	4,630	4,630	801	3,829	—	83	0	12
Potatoes	372,725	4,621	63	34	29	4,558	0	99	1
Pulses	47,496	917	916	24	892	—	97	0	2
Oilseed	10,582	1,866	582	134	448	1,284	24	69	18
Vegetables	5,070	5,418	241	4	237	5,177	4	96	107[b]
Fodder	40,138	21,279	26	12	14	21,253	0	100	53
Total	1,675,804	362,137	315,834	78,434	237,400	46,300	n.a.	n.a.	n.a.

Source: Authors, based on FSC&RD data.

Note: — = not available; MT = metric tons; n.a. = not applicable; FSC&RD = Federal Seed Certification and Registration Department.

[a] The public sector does not import seed; all seed imports are conducted by the private sector.

[b] This means that either total seed requirement for rice and vegetables is more than what FSC&RD estimates or some of the certified seed remains unused.

TABLE 5.6 Average price paid for seed by crop and province, 2012

Province	Mean price of seed (PKR/kilogram)			
	Wheat n = 414	Cotton n = 266	Maize n = 54	Rice n = 259
Punjab	37.4 (8.8)	236.2 (306.3)	276.6 (240.4)	108.1 (46.8)
Sindh	36.5 (7.9)	191.8 (126.3)	—	202.3 (271.4)
KPK	36.7 (6.7)	—	447.5 (414.4)	—

Source: Authors, based on data from IFPRI/IDS (2012).

Note: Numbers in parentheses are standard deviations. — = not available; KPK = Khyber Pakhtunkhwa; PKR = Pakistani rupees.

(1976, 1979) selection estimation model suggests the following (for details, see Annex A). First, for all three crops, price is significantly associated with variety type, although variations in this variety-price relationship exist between wheat and cotton, on the one hand, and rice, on the other hand. Second, while farmer contact with an extension agent is also correlated with price, these correlations are again crop specific. Third, other variables that might explain price variation—for example, landholding size and farmer experience, which could proxy for bargaining power in seed purchasing and pricing—are insignificant, suggesting that farmers are generally price takers in the seed markets for these major field crops.

Companies operating in Pakistan's seed market face several constraints. Limited access to breeder seed from public-sector research institutes is a continuing issue for many companies that multiply and market public varieties or use public germplasm in their breeding programs. The relatively small size of the domestic market is a likely disincentive to investment, particularly given the barriers to seed trade with India, without which doors could open to massive opportunity in an integrated regional market. The absence of intellectual property rights (IPR) protection—the combination of legislation and enforcement of both plant breeders' rights and patents for transgenic events—may also disincentivize private R&D investment.

But perhaps the most salient constraint is the inadequate legislative and institutional framework governing Pakistan's seed system. The challenges begin with FSC&RD, Pakistan's premier agency for regulating seed provision, which is responsible for (1) registration of seed companies, (2) registration of varieties, (3) seed certification, and (4) enforcement of the 1976 Seed Act. In 2013/2014, FSC&RD employed about 434 seed professionals and support staff in the Islamabad office and field outlets and had a total budget of PKR 160.4 million. In that year, the cost of maintaining these employees was 93 percent of the total expenditure (Ministry of Finance 2014), which left little for other activities such as training, facilitation of seed providers, seed market surveillance, or development of databases. FSC&RD is seriously understaffed, especially given the prevalent regulatory framework in which each variety is to be evaluated and registered before it can be sold, and seed lots are examined for certification at the production stage. It is practically impossible for the professional staff (about 30 percent of the total) at FSC&RD to expeditiously process applications for company and cultivar registration and seed certification. The result is inordinate delay in some cases and poor oversight in others. This is what the 2012–13 Year Book of MNFSR (2013) lists as the tasks that were undertaken by FSC&RD during 2012/2013: (1) registration of 61 new seed companies; (2) registration of 24 new cultivars after observing their performance during trials; (3) inspection of 524,564 acres for seed certification purposes; (4) sampling and testing of 206,273 metric tons of seeds of various crops; and (5) field testing of 20 percent of seed lots of all certified seed of cotton, wheat, and rice. It is a herculean task to meaningfully accomplish all this with a professional and support staff of only 434 people and a budget of a mere PKR 160.4 million.

The case of NBC is similar. NBC is a small organization that is tasked with the important job of evaluating GM cultivars for biosafety. Limited technical capacity, understaffing, and administrative confusion during 2011–2013 (discussed above) resulted in delayed processing of breeders' applications for biosafety approvals for cultivar trials and commercialization. Spielman et al. (2015) note that the NBC could not convene during 2011–2013; as a result, out of a total of 34 GM cultivars for which biosafety approval has so far been granted, 21 cultivars received biosafety approval one to two years *after* the PSC had granted its approval.

The end result is a slow and cumbersome cultivar registration process that renders new cultivars vulnerable to misappropriation by unscrupulous handlers at various stages of testing. This has effectively discouraged many breeders in the public and private sectors from registering their new varieties with FSC&RD. For example, 10 out of the 14 cotton varieties under large-scale cultivation in 2012 in Sindh were not registered with FSC&RD (Rana et al. 2013).

Because seed of only registered cultivars can be certified by FSC&RD, such common practice of commercial release of cultivars without FSC&RD registration translates into a consistent shortfall in supply of certified seed. Table 5.5 and Table 5.7 show that for most crops, certified seed production

TABLE 5.7 Certified seed requirements and availability for selected crops, 1996–2013

	Wheat			Rice			Maize		
	MT		Available/ Required %	MT		Available/ Required %	MT		Available/ Required %
Year	Required	Available		Required	Available		Required	Available	
1995/1996	1,005,180	78,929	8	30,265	1,848	6	18,774	1,854	10
1996/1997	973,092	73,618	8	31,515	1,378	4	18,554	1,961	11
1997/1998	1,002,552	78,544	8	32,442	2,047	6	18,652	1,498	8
1998/1999	987,588	104,213	11	33,930	2,281	7	19,244	3,028	16
1999/2000	1,015,560	106,379	10	35,216	3,845	11	19,234	2,564	13
2000/2001	981,708	159,220	16	33,272	2,106	6	18,882	2,119	11
2001/2002	966,900	134,954	14	29,599	3,541	12	18,832	2,636	14
2002/2003	964,068	120,610	13	31,153	4,678	15	18,710	4,040	22
2003/2004	985,944	135,499	14	34,448	7,547	22	18,942	5,321	28
2004/2005	1,002,960	173,557	17	35,274	9,840	28	19,456	8,867	46
2005/2006	1,013,748	166,627	16	36,700	12,157	33	20,840	9,063	43
2006/2007	1,029,384	203,837	20	36,137	10,727	30	20,338	8,647	43
2007/2008	1,025,976	188,879	18	35,216	11,474	33	21,034	9,951	47
2008/2009	1,085,520	196,029	18	41,476	22,688	55	21,042	12,380	59
2009/2010	1,095,792	284,344	26	40,363	22,253	57	18,702	9,785	33
2010/2011	1,085,400	319,023	29	42,480	28,895	68	31,914	9,041	28
2011/2012	1,085,400	259,904	24	42,480	34,528	81	31,914	12,550	39
2012/2013	1,085,400	259,904	24	42,480	49,492	116	31,914	14,008	44

Source: Authors, based on Salam (2012) and data from FSC&RD.
Note: MT = metric tons.

represents a small proportion of the country's total seed requirement. In potatoes and pulses, it is 1–2 percent; even in cotton and wheat, it is only 12 percent and 28 percent respectively (Table 5.5). The only two exceptions are vegetables and rice, where the supply of certified seed has grown in recent years because of an increase in imports of vegetable seed and the adoption of hybrid seed for rice. For other crops, such as cotton and oilseeds, the availability of certified seed has declined over the years (Rana 2014). The rest of the seed requirement is supplied from farmer-saved seed and uncertified seed sold by agricultural input dealers and seed companies.

It is noteworthy, however, that although certified seed represents only about 20 percent of the total seed market in Pakistan, quality seed may compose a much larger share. To clarify this point, a distinction should be made between quality seed and certified seed. The two are not the same thing:

rather, certified seed is a subset of quality seed. The key concept here is seed quality, rather than official sanction. Pure seed of non-notified varieties *may* also be quality seed, despite being uncertified. Similarly, seed of a notified variety not presented for certification for any reason *may* also fall in this category. A prime example of this situation is the Bt cottonseed supplied by a few reputable private companies during 2005–2010 without certification but nonetheless with in-house quality assurances.

Uncertified seed, which supplies about 80 percent of the country's total seed requirement every year, is provided by a large informal sector that comprises (1) farmer-to-farmer seed exchange on a noncommercial basis, (2) small-scale farmer-to-farmer seed sale, (3) farmer-saved seed for planting in subsequent years, and (4) medium- to large-scale sale of seed in "brown-bag exchanges" (Figure 5.1). Farmer-to-farmer exchange on a noncommercial basis and small-scale sales are not rare, but the volume of such exchange or sale is negligible as a proportion of Pakistan's total seed requirement. The third and fourth categories constitute the bulk of the informal sector.

Sometimes seed companies also sell uncertified seed—usually because the variety is unapproved but otherwise ready for market. Companies sell uncertified seeds through their own outlets, as well as through the vast network of input dealers. The undocumented character of such transactions places them in the informal, rather than the formal, category. Sometimes these seeds are sold in company packaging bearing a company label. Weak enforcement of seed laws allows companies to conduct their operations in the informal sector. Usually, however, uncertified seeds are sold through brown-bag exchanges, meaning that little indication of source or quality accompanies the seed. Farmers, input dealers, and other value chain actors (for example, cotton ginners and sugar mills) also engage in such transactions, often without official sanction and sometimes in violation of express injunctions.

Data from the 2012 RHPS provide a more nuanced sense of the role played by various seed providers in the formal and the informal market (IFPRI/IDS 2012). Table 5.8 shows that input dealers and seed companies are the main retail sources of seed for four of Pakistan's major crops. Given that these figures are fairly consistent across all four major crops, the implication is that both public seed enterprises and private seed companies rely on the private sector to distribute their varieties to farmers. Importantly, data from the 2012 RHPS also indicate that farmers' reliance on these private-sector sources is fairly consistent across landholding sizes, suggesting that the private sector services a wide range of farmer types and does not concentrate on particularly large landholders (Annex B). Input dealers are not a seed source per se; they

TABLE 5.8 Sources of purchased seeds by crop, 2012

Source	Wheat (%) n = 414	Cotton (%) n = 266	Maize (%) n = 54	Rice (%) n = 261
Punjab Seed Corporation	2	3	0	0
Agricultural extension departments	2	0	7	0
Research institutes	1	1	3	0
Private seed companies	33	28	46	24
Input dealers	38	55	27	32
Landlords	12	7	0	35
NGOs/relief agencies	2	0	11	0
Cooperative societies	0	0	0	1
Friends/relatives/neighbors	11	6	6	7

Source: Authors, based on data from IFPRI/IDS (2012).

Note: Figures may not add up to 100 percent due to rounding. NGOs = nongovernmental organizations.

are simply a convenient conduit between the farmer and the seed provider. Seed companies sometimes maintain their own sales points, but they often market certified and uncertified seeds through input dealers.

Of the nine seed sources listed in Table 5.8, the first three on the list (Punjab Seed Corporation, agricultural extension departments, and research institutes) *mostly* operate in the formal sector, whereas the rest are part of the informal sector to a varying degree. Even PSC, extension departments, and research institutes—despite being government organizations—occasionally provide uncertified seed of unregistered varieties to meet market demand. The next two sources on the list are the seed companies and input dealers; they sell certified seed under company labels as well as uncertified seed with or without company labels. The remaining four sources are part of the informal sector. Thus, seed providers in Pakistan mostly operate in a gray area between complete formality and complete informality (Figure 5.1).

Nothing illustrates the twilight zone operations of these seed providers better than the case of Bt cotton in Pakistan. Bt cottonseeds first reached farmers' fields in Sindh in 2002/2003. They were brought by enterprising farmers from abroad and planted on a small scale. Because the seeds provided effective protection against bollworms, their popularity grew. Simultaneously, several seed companies successfully crossed exotic Bt material with local cotton varieties to produce Bt varieties of their own. By 2005/2006 several companies were marketing their Bt varieties on a large scale. By 2007 Bt varieties accounted for 80 percent and 50 percent of the total area under cotton cultivation in Sindh and Punjab, respectively (Ali et al. 2007). Because the government had not approved any of the Bt varieties by then, the entire Bt cotton diffusion process in Pakistan had occurred in the informal market.

The spread of Bt cotton through the informal sector was the result of three factors: First, none of the Bt varieties were approved by the government, which did not approve seed for considerations other than quality.[13] Second, FSC&RD and provincial agriculture departments did not have the capacity to monitor or check the spread. Third, seed companies did not feel disadvantaged in the absence of the official notification that changed the status of their Bt varieties from unapproved to approved—they had discovered that the market did not care.

Not wanting to be bypassed, public-sector research institutes and seed producers also joined the fray early on. At least two research institutes—the Centre of Excellence in Molecular Biology and the National Institute for Biotechnology and Genetic Engineering—developed cotton varieties containing local transgenic events. Meanwhile, AARI and other institutes had developed Bt varieties, while their breeders were also marketing Bt cottonseeds in the informal sector. Even the PSC was openly producing and marketing Bt cottonseeds in 2008–2010, while the seeds' production and sale were still illegal in Pakistan (Rana 2010). In short, the entire ensemble of seed providers—research institutes, breeders, seed corporations, seed companies, input dealers, and farmers—had become part of the informal sector, at least in the Bt cottonseed business.

In 2010, the situation changed with official approval of nine Bt varieties. One of these belonged to the National Institute for Biotechnology and Genetic Engineering, and eight to seed companies. While official approval hardly conferred a market advantage on these varieties, it enabled providers to market seeds under their labels. This improved quality, as companies raised the quality of seed sold under their own brand names. Because all seed providers were using the same Bt gene, they had to compete on both germplasm and seed quality.

---

13 There was some confusion in those days about Monsanto's IPRs on the transformation event used in Bt varieties. Since the government did not want to appear to violate Monsanto's IPRs, it withheld approval. See Rana (2010) for details.

In due course, several of the approved varieties quickly disappeared from the market and were replaced by new varieties. The market was then populated by new cotton varieties that had not been registered with FSC&RD, transgenic cotton varieties that had yet to receive approval from NBC, and seed that was uncertified by FSC&RD (Rana et al. 2013; Spielman et al. 2015). But this did not necessarily mean that the seed was of low quality—company branding carried with it a quality signal to farmers.

Pakistan's Bt cotton experience demonstrated how imprecise the distinction between formal and informal can be, and how little value the regulatory system confers to farmers when it is not functioning properly (see also Rana 2010, 2014). It also exemplifies how an inadequate and archaic regulation constrained the operations of an active informal market. For the better part of the last decade, the development of new Bt varieties and production of seed had to stay in the shadows simply because the regulatory framework was not dynamic enough to catch up to ground reality and market demands.

Addressing the Dissonance between Markets and Regulation Frameworks

When the Seed Act was enacted in the 1970s, all important aspects of seed provision—breeding, cultivar evaluation, germplasm imports, and seed certification—occurred within the public sector. The act and its subordinate legislation addressed only notified varieties and certified seed. With the entry of the private sector into the seed system by the mid-1990s, the act was largely unable to provide guidance on aspects that were key to private investment, such as timely varietal testing and registration processes, plant breeders' rights, branding, trademarks, market surveillance, and other issues that were pillars of a competitive seed market. Several examples illustrate today's growing dissonance between the market and the legislative framework.

Under the existing procedures, a new variety is tested for at least two years for distinctness, uniformity, and stability (DUS) as well as for value in cultivation and use (VCU) at various research stations and in farmers' fields. As long as breeding was conducted only by the public sector, this system worked well. But when companies entered into breeding, they were reluctant to hand over their germplasm for testing at competitor institutes. They also found varietal evaluation procedures to be time-consuming and bureaucratic. Because approval of a variety did not bring any value to their business—it did not create intellectual property that could be protected under existing laws—several companies started releasing their varieties directly into the market without recourse to FSC&RD approval.

In response FSC&RD necessarily felt that seed companies were releasing varieties of dubious quality—unstable trait expression, poor germination rates, or susceptibility to pests and diseases. FSC&RD was also critical of the growing practice of introducing exotic (imported) germplasm without proper testing and adaptation. Clearly, the companies and FSC&RD were at odds over one important aspect: the companies thought they were operating in an overregulated environment, whereas FSC&RD thought the regulation lacked the necessary safeguards needed to maintain seed quality and protect farmers from poor seeds and traits. Albeit for different reasons, both agreed that the legal framework was inadequate.

In another example, a key FSC&RD function was to certify seed, which was performed through field inspections during the production stage. Upon successful completion of the inspection, FSC&RD issued tags, which seed distributors were required to display prominently as a mark of quality. The private sector, however, viewed the process differently, arguing that it had the necessary know-how to produce quality seed and did not require intrusive and time-consuming FSC&RD inspections. Because a brand name, rather than an official FSC&RD tag, seemed to carry more weight in the market, private companies found seed certification of little value to their business. Companies still obtained these tags from FSC&RD, but they did so to avoid unwarranted inspections rather than for any value that these might add to their business. Moreover, because seed certification was possible only for notified varieties, its relevance diminished as the number of unregistered varieties in the market grew.

Clearly, comprehensive reform was warranted to remove the growing dissonance between the law and the market. Two types of responses emerged: (1) a comprehensive reform proposal from FSC&RD to make regulation more effective and to include the private sector in its ambit, and (2) a proposal for a regulatory shift to a truth-in-labeling system for quality assurance.

Several proposals have been put forth by various stakeholders during the past two decades to amend the 1976 Seed Act. The latest is a 2014 draft bill from FSC&RD that proposes three key amendments to the act. First, the bill substantially expands the act's mandate over a wide range of actors in the seed system and extends the act's writ over registering entrants into any aspect of the seed sector with the FSC&RD. Second, the bill is more explicit in prohibiting several activities, with more appropriate punishments, including: (1)

doing seed business without registration; (2) selling, importing, stocking, bartering, or otherwise supplying seed of an unregistered variety; and (3) selling misbranded seed. Third, it imposes more-stringent biosafety requirements for the commercialization of GM varieties.[14] The bill aims to extend regulatory oversight to all aspects of seed provision in Pakistan, and it is an unsurprising response from FSC&RD to the current free-for-all environment in Pakistan's seed system, which FSC&RD finds severely inadequate for dealing with delinquency.

At the time of this writing, the bill had passed from the federal cabinet to the parliament for discussion. If approved by the parliament, the bill will place the seed business—both public and private—firmly under FSC&RD's regulatory control. For farmers the proposed amendments offer some protection against spurious seeds and false claims on product performance. For the private sector, however, the amendment's implications are less clear. On the one hand, the existence of a legal framework makes the seed business more predictable for the seed industry, forcing all players to compete on a level, well-regulated playing field rather than in an ambiguous, informal, unregulated segment of the market. On the other hand, a legal framework subjects the seed business to external oversight on minimum standards for operations and performance while also limiting its ability to introduce nominally differentiated varieties to the market—a key marketing strategy for many seed companies in recent years (Rana 2010). As such, the proposed amendment offers little incentive for private investment in Pakistan's seed market, and it seems to address few of the issues described above that relate to the wider legal and institutional framework. Therefore, the private sector may not be enthusiastic about having it approved. Similar previous efforts by FSC&RD to push through legislative reform in the face of only lukewarm support from private seed providers ended in failure. The fate of this effort will become clear in the coming months.

Meanwhile, the Government of Punjab has also considered its own legislative and institutional reform to improve seed provision in the province, leveraging its capacity to amend the Seed Act of 1976 to the extent of its territorial jurisdiction. Several drafts have been prepared since 2010/2011 that replace FSC&RD procedures with provincial ones. However, one proposal—the

---

14 Section 22(G) of the bill proposes that no application for registration of a GM variety will be accepted unless it is accompanied by (1) an affidavit that it does not contain a gene involving "terminator" technology that will produce sterile seeds, and (2) a certificate from the National Biosafety Committee that the variety will have no adverse effect on the environment or on the life and health of any human, animal, or plant.

draft Punjab Seed Act, 2011—goes beyond this in several respects. First, the draft act states quite clearly its intention of supporting "the development of a vibrant seed industry in the province" and seeks to establish a Punjab Seed Council in which private individuals hold a majority over provincial officials (GoPb 2011). The draft act also seeks to relieve most crops from varietal registration and shift them to a truth-in-labeling-based regulatory system. This will shift seed inspections to the sales point, thereby enabling a small field force to monitor seed quality throughout the province. The purpose is to mitigate the current imbalance between legal responsibility and the institutional capacity of the seed regulator without recruiting an army of inspectors to police the seed sector. However, the draft act has not made much headway, and it remains in the official files of the Punjab Agriculture Department.

Another important piece of legislation currently pending with the federal government is the draft Plant Breeders' Rights (PBR) Act. The first draft was prepared by FSC&RD in 1999, and several versions have appeared since then. One draft was presented to the cabinet in 2007. This draft is based on the 1991 International Union for the Protection of New Varieties of Plants (UPOV) model law, which aims to create IPRs for development of new plant varieties and ensure that Pakistan is compliant with its international obligations under the agreement on Trade-Related Aspects of Intellectual Property Rights. Toward this end, the draft law proposes the creation of a Plant Breeders' Registry, to be attached to the federal Ministry of Agriculture (and housed in FSC&RD). The registry will perform several functions, such as registering new plant varieties, ensuring that the seed of registered varieties is available to farmers, documenting the varieties, and cataloging them. Any seed producer may apply to the registrar for registration if the variety is novel and meets the DUS criteria. This will dispense with the VCU criteria and allow breeders to differentiate products by means other than utility. Because VCU criteria are already meaningless in practice because of routine breeder practice of artificial differentiation for the purposes of registration, the proposal will only convert the de facto into the *de jure*.

Housing of the PBR Registry has been the subject of a turf war between FSC&RD and the newly created Intellectual Property Organization (IPO) of the federal government. The former's claim was based on its historical role since 1976, and the latter's claim emanated from its being a specialized agency to create and enforce IPRs. In 2007, the cabinet decided to house the PBR Registry in IPO (DG FSC&RD 2008). This decision not only denied FSC&RD an opportunity to extend its portfolio but also required it to redefine itself as a mere seed certification agency. The draft legislation is still pending with the government. FSC&RD still has an interest in the PBR Registry as a means of extending its control over the seed system. IPO is also promoting the legislation; however, being a new entrant to the regulatory framework, IPO may require some time to develop the necessary networks to push the legislation through the cabinet and the parliament. Pakistani seed companies are generally supportive of the legislation, but they are skeptical of the government's willingness and ability to effectively enforce plant breeders' rights, and they are possibly torn between their desire to protect their germplasm through plant breeders' rights and their desire to use others' germplasm in their breeding programs. MNCs have an interest in a stronger IPR regime, but their influence has been constrained thus far by their small numbers and limited field operations in Pakistan.

The above discussion of Seed Act amendments and plant breeders' rights exemplifies how progress on legal reform is subject to conflicting interests and contested claims between and among seed system actors, and is characterized by tensions between archaic regulation and entrepreneurs in a growing market. These conflicts and tensions have created a situation where four-fifths of market operations occur in a contested space between the formal and the informal. Clearly, reform of the seed sector governance framework is long overdue. Given the demonstrated capacity of various actors to stall reform, any meaningful effort for the same must involve identification of key actors, their interests, and how they are served or affected by existing and proposed legal and institutional arrangements.

Formalizing the Informal

The key message from the above discussion is that the legal and institutional structure for cultivar improvement and seed provision in Pakistan is inadequate and internally inconsistent. Developed four decades ago to support a state-led provision of seed, it long ago exhausted its potential to foster the growth of Pakistan's seed industry. The need to reform the legal and institutional regime is clear, but there are deep divisions on how to move forward toward this end. Various actors—the seed business, scientists, and regulators—deploy their professional networks to steer the reform process in their favor. This lack of internal agreement has hampered efforts to rewrite the regulations to suit the needs of a growing and competitive market.

A key question posed by the above discussion concerns the realistic objective of seed legislation in a dynamic, growing, and loosely monitored seed system. Should the objective be to strengthen government control and oversight on seed operations, or should it be to facilitate the private sector and to cede more space to its operations? These objectives are not mutually exclusive, but they suggest different focus in each case and reflect different theoretical positions in the age-old state-versus-market debate. Because the overarching goal is to provide quality seed to the farmer, the Government of Punjab's proposed truth-in-labeling regime seems to offer a middle ground, as it seeks to regulate the market in a manner that allows farmers to make informed choices.

Several policy recommendations emerge from the discussion in this chapter. Importantly, there is a strong and urgent case for redesigning the regulatory framework. The framework should be redesigned in a manner that allows farmers to choose seed that best suits their site-specific agroclimatic conditions. This will require the state to redefine its role from an entity that certifies, approves, registers, and licenses to an entity that defines benchmarks, enables accreditation services, and ensures compliance with benchmarks. The draft Punjab Seed Act, 2011, may be a good starting point to move forward in this direction. Its proposal to establish a private-sector-led, independent regulatory authority and to deal with scheduled and other crops differently merits consideration.

Additionally, variety release procedures should be simplified and made more transparent. In the current milieu, breeders find these procedures time-consuming and unwarranted. They are also reluctant to submit their seed to institutes for evaluation because the two compete in the market with similar products. Ideally, variety registration should be voluntary—any breeder claiming to have a marketable cultivar meeting required standards should be able to enter the market directly without recourse to the regulator. But even if an approval regime must be put in place for commercially important crops, it should aim at formalizing, rather than penalizing, the informal sector.

Related to this is the need to re-evaluate the role of seed certification. Given that seed certification has become largely irrelevant—as much because of the lax implementation regime as because of farmers' preference to rely on their own judgment rather than on an officially issued tag on the seed bag—it should be replaced with a truth-in-labeling regime. This will strengthen regulation by making it reflect current seed business practices. It is practically impossible for a 434-person-strong FSC&RD to inspect seed production fields of 759 companies and countless farmers, breeders, and agri-input dealers who produce 1.6 million metric tons of seed annually. A meaningful job at field-based inspections will require maintaining an army of seed inspectors with prohibitive costs. In comparison the number of company sales points and agri-input dealers providing seed to more than two-thirds of farmers (Table 5.8) is much smaller. Enforcement of standards at these outlets will be far easier for FSC&RD than is the case presently.

Finally, the farmer needs to be positioned at the center of policy debates. Currently, farmers are almost entirely absent from the discourse. They appear to be the passive recipients of development within the seed industry. Farmers' lack of representation in important policy forums, such as the national and provincial seed councils or the proposed PBR Registry, confirms that they play a limited role in setting agendas, determining priorities, and monitoring seed quality.

Putting the farmer first will reorient policy analyses to the informal sector. Rather than investing in collecting and analyzing data on provision of certified seed, which constitutes only 20 percent of the total seed requirement, investing in gaining an understanding the dynamics of the use and provision of uncertified seed will yield more productive results. Determining how seed providers compete on seed quality in a market with an unusually large number of providers will be instructive. It will also be useful to explore ways to support farmers in saving their seed, which will continue to be an important source of seed for most crops in the coming decades.

References

Ahmad, M., and J. C. Nagy. 1999. "Private Sector Investment in Agricultural Research in Pakistan." *Pakistan Development Review* 38 (3): 269–292.

Ali, A., and A. Abdulai. 2010. "The Adoption of Genetically Modified Cotton and Poverty Reduction in Pakistan." *Journal of Agricultural Economics* 61 (1): 175–192.

Ali, I., and S. M. Ali. 2004. *A Note on the Seed Business in Pakistan*. Lahore: Lahore University of Management Sciences.

Ali, S., S. Hameed, S. Masood, and G. M. Ali. 2007. *Status of Cotton Harboring Bt Gene in Pakistan*. Islamabad: Pakistan Agricultural Research Council (PARC).

ARM (Agricultural Reform Movement). 2008. *Green Pages*. Lahore: ARM.

Byerlee, D., and K. Fischer. 2002. "Accessing Modern Science: Policy and Institutional Options for Agricultural Biotechnology in Developing Countries." *World Development* 30 (6): 931–948.

DG FSC&RD (Director General, Federal Seed Certification and Registration Department). 2008. *Note for Secretary MINFAL dated 3 May 2008—Enactment of Plant Breeders Rights Bills, 2008*. Islamabad: Federal Seed Certification and Registration Department, Ministry of Food, Agriculture and Livestock, Government of Pakistan.

Evenson, R. E., and D. Gollin. 2003. "Assessing the Impact of the Green Revolution, 1960 to 2000." *Science* 300 (5620): 758–762.

Farooq, U., and M. Iqbal. 2000. "Attaining and Maintaining Self-Sufficiency in Wheat Production: Institutional Efforts, Farmers' Limitations." *Pakistan Development Review* 39 (4): 487–514.

Feder, G., R. E. Just, and D. Zilberman. 1985. "Adoption of Agricultural Innovations in Developing Countries: A Survey." *Economic Development and Cultural Change* 33 (2): 255–298.

Feder, G., and R. Slade. 1984. "The Acquisition of Information and the Adoption of New Technology." *American Journal of Agricultural Economics* 66: 312–320.

Feder, G., and D. Umali. 1993. "The Adoption of Agricultural Innovations: A Review." *Technological Forecasting and Social Change* 43: 215–239.

Flaherty, K., M. Sharif, and D. J. Spielman. 2012. *Pakistan: Recent Developments in Agricultural Research*. Islamabad: Pakistan Agricultural Research Council.

FSC&RD (Federal Seed Certification and Registration Department). 2001. *Seed Industry Development in Pakistan*. Islamabad: FSC&RD, Government of Pakistan.

———. 2009. *Annual Progress Report*. Islamabad: Federal Seed Certification and Registration Department, Government of Pakistan.

GoP (Government of Pakistan). 2010. *Agriculture Census: All Pakistan Tables*. Islamabad: Agricultural Census Organization. http://www.pbs.gov.pk/sites/default/files/aco/publications/agricultural_census2010/Tables%20%28Pakistan%20-%20In%20Acres%29.pdf. Accessed June 19, 2014.

GoPb (Government of Punjab). 2011. Draft Punjab Seed Act, 2011. Lahore: Department of Agriculture, Government of Punjab.

Heckman, J. 1976. "The Common Structure of Statistical Models of Truncation, Sample Selection and Limited Dependent Variables and a Simple Estimator for Such Models." *Annals of Economic and Social Measurement* 5: 475–492.

———. 1979. "Sample Selection Bias as a Specification Error." *Econometrica* 47: 153–161.

Heisey, P. W., ed. 1990. *Accelerating the Transfer of Wheat Breeding Gains to Farmers: A Study of the Dynamics of Varietal Replacement in Pakistan*. CIMMYT Research Report 1. Mexico City.

Heisey, P., M. Smale, D. Byerlee, E. Souza. 1997. "Wheat Rusts and the Costs of Genetic Diversity in the Punjab of Pakistan." *American Journal of Agricultural Economics* 79: 726–737.

Heisey, P. W., K. A. Tetlay, Z. Ahmad, and M. Ahmad. 1993. "Varietal Change in Post-Green Revolution Agriculture: Empirical Evidence for Wheat in Pakistan." *Journal of Agricultural Economics* 44 (3): 428–442.

Hussain, A. 2011. "Status of Seed Industry in Pakistan." Presentation at World Bank Roundtable Discussion on Agriculture and Water, Islamabad, March 10–11.

Hussain, A., and T. Hussain. 2007. *Seed Industry of Pakistan*. Islamabad: FSC&RD, Government of Pakistan.

IFPRI/IDS (International Food Policy Research Institute/Innovative Development Strategies [Pvt.] Ltd.). 2012. Pakistan Rural Household Panel Survey 2012 Rounds 1 and 1.5 dataset. Washington, DC: IFPRI; Islamabad: IDS.

Jack, B. K. 2011. *Market Inefficiencies and the Adoption of Agricultural Technologies in Developing Countries*. White paper prepared for the Agricultural Technology Adoption Initiative. Cambridge, MA: Abdul Latif Jameel Poverty Action Lab (MIT); Berkeley, CA: Center for Effective Global Action.

Khan, A., G. Morgan, and A. J. Sofranko. 1990. "Farmers' Utilization of Information Sources: A Study of the Farmers in NWFP." *Journal of Rural Development and Administration* 22 (1): 38–58.

Kouser, S., and M. Qaim. 2013. "Valuing the Economic, Health and Environmental Benefits of Bt Cotton Adoption in Pakistan." *Agriculture Economics* 44 (3): 323–335.

Lipton, M., with R. Longhurst. 1989. *New Seeds and Poor People*. Baltimore: Johns Hopkins University Press.

Ministry of Finance. 2014. *Budget Estimates 2014–15*. Islamabad: Government of Pakistan.

MNFSR (Ministry of National Food Security and Research). 2013. *Year Book 2012–13*. Islamabad: MNFSR, Government of Pakistan.

Nazli, H., and S. H. Haider. *Pakistan Rural Household Panel Survey 2012 (Round 1): Methodology and Community Characteristics*. Pakistan Strategy Support Program Working Paper 7. Washington DC: IFPRI.

Nazli H., D. Orden, R. Sarker, and K. Meilke. 2012. *Bt Cotton Adoption and Wellbeing of Farmers in Pakistan*. Selected paper presented at the 28th Triennial Conference of the International Association of Agricultural Economists, Foz do Iguaçu, Brazil, August 18–24.

PSC (Punjab Seed Corporation). 2008. *Introduction and Overview—A Presentation to Secretary of Agriculture*. Lahore: Punjab Seed Corporation, Agriculture Department, Government of Punjab.

———. 2013. *Overview of the Punjab Seed Corporation*. Lahore: Punjab Seed Corporation, Agriculture Department, Government of Punjab.

Rana, M. A. 2010. "Formalising the Informal: The Commercialisation of Bt Cotton in Pakistan." PhD dissertation, Melbourne School of Land and Environment, The University of Melbourne, Australia.

———. 2013. *18th Constitutional Amendment: Contextualising Fiscal and Administrative Decentralisation.* Lahore: Lahore University of Management Sciences.

———. 2014. *The Seed Industry in Pakistan: Regulation, Politics and Entrepreneurship.* Pakistan Strategy Support Program Working Paper 19. Washington, DC: IFPRI.

Rana, M. A., H. Khawar, A. Tahawar, and H. S. Rana. 2013. *Exploring Dynamics of Cotton Seed Provision in Sindh: Informing Policy and Business Decisions.* Lahore: International Growth Centre.

Salam, A. 2012. *Review of Input and Output Policies for Cereal Production in Pakistan.* Pakistan Strategy Support Program Working Paper 6. Washington, DC: IFPRI.

Sarwar, B. 2007. *Formal and Informal Seed Supply System in Pakistan.* Islamabad: Federal Seed Certification and Registration Department, Ministry of Food Security and Research, Government of Pakistan.

Smale, M., J. Hartell, P. Heisey, and B. Senauer. 1998. "The Contribution of Genetic Resources and Diversity to Wheat Productivity and Stability in the Punjab of Pakistan." *American Journal of Agricultural Economics* 80: 482–493.

Spielman, D. J., D. E. Kolady, A. J. Cavalieri, and N. C. Rao. 2014. "The Seed and Agricultural Biotechnology Industries in India: An Analysis of Industry Structure, Competition, and Policy Options." *Food Policy* 45: 88–100.

Spielman, D. J., H. Nazli, X. Ma, P. Zambrano, and F. Zaidi. 2015. "Technological Opportunity, Regulatory Uncertainty, and Bt Cotton in Pakistan." *AgBioForum* 18 (1), 98–112.

UAF (University of Agriculture, Faisalabad). 2013. *University of Agriculture, Faisalabad: Profile.* www.uaf.edu.pk. Accessed November 2013.

Annex A: Seed Price and Its Determinants, 2012 Pakistan Rural Household Panel Survey (RHPS Round 1.5)

Farmers who cultivate major field crops either purchase their seed or use seed saved from the previous season.[15] Data from the 2012 RHPS sample indicate that approximately 70 percent of rice-growing households, 81 percent of cotton-growing households, and 49 percent of wheat-growing households purchased seed in the sample (IFPRI/IDS 2012). Moreover, these data indicate significant variation in the price paid for seed by the farmers, particularly in the case of rice and cotton varieties.

In this annex, we estimate determinants of this price using a two-step selection model based on Heckman (1976, 1979) using crop-specific data from 2012 RHPS (IFPRI/IDS 2012). The model specification addresses the issue of a dependent variable (seed price) that is observable only for a restricted, nonrandom sample (farmers who purchase seed) and is not observed for a separate nonrandom sample (those who do not purchase seed). The model assumes an underlying regression relationship,

$$p_i = \beta X_i + u_{mi} \tag{1}$$

where p_i denotes the price paid for seed by the *ith* farmer as a function of some vector of explanatory variables (X_i) and a normally distributed, mean-zero random disturbance (u_{mi}). The coefficient β is the parameter to be estimated. However, because the price paid for seed is not observed where farmers save (rather than purchase) seed, then the dependent variable is only observed for

$$z_i \gamma + u_{ri} > 0 \tag{2}$$

where $z_i \gamma$ is an indicator variable denoting the farmer's decision to purchase $(z_{iy} = 1)$ rather than save $(z_{iy} = 0)$ seed, and where and u_{ri} is a mean-zero random disturbance that is joint-normally distributed with u_{mi}. Estimation of this model provides consistent, asymptotically efficient estimates for all parameters.

This estimation model is employed here for wheat, rice, and cotton for which variety-specific data are available in the 2012 RHPS (Round 1.5) data.

---

15 A mixed strategy of cultivating crops with both purchased and saved seed is uncommon in the 2012 RHPS sample. Of the 679 households that cultivated wheat in the sample, only 3 households (0.4 percent) used both purchased and saved wheat seed. Of the 292 households that cultivated cotton in the sample, only 7 households (2.4 percent) used both purchased and saved cottonseed for cultivation. No households used a mixed strategy in rice cultivation (IFPRI/IDS 2012).

TABLE A5.1 Summary statistics for wheat-growing households

Variable	N	Unit	Mean	SD
Seed price	413	PKR/kg	37.37	8.06
Top wheat varieties				
Seher-06	863	1/0	0.44	0.50
Bhakhar-02	863	1/0	0.12	0.32
Abdul Sattar	863	1/0	0.10	0.31
Inquilab-91	863	1/0	0.06	0.24
Watan-93	863	1/0	0.07	0.26
Province dummies				
Punjab	863	1/0	0.63	0.48
Sindh	863	1/0	0.18	0.38
KPK	863	1/0	0.20	0.40
Plot characteristics				
Landholding size	863	acres	19.90	28.42
Farmer characteristics				
Age of farmer	863	years	47.74	13.14
Tenure status of plot				
Tenure status = owned	863	1/0	0.66	0.47
Tenure status = rented in/sharecropped/mortgaged	863	1/0	0.34	0.47
Household characteristics				
Household head attended school	863	1/0	0.57	0.50
Household member met with an extension agent in the previous year	863	1/0	0.21	0.41
Household size	863	No. of members	7.00	3.22
Total monthly expenditure	863	PKR/month	20,691.00	10,178.00

Source: Authors' calculations, using RHPS (IFPRI/IDS 2012).
Note: N = number of observations. KPK = Khyber Pakhtunkhwa; PKR/kg = Pakistani rupees per kilogram. SD = standard deviation. A unit denoted "1/0" indicates that the variable may take on the value of 1 or 0.

Note that we exclude maize from these estimations because variety-specific data are not available in the 2012 RHPS (IFPRI/IDS 2012).

Crop-specific summary statistics are given in Table A5.1, Table A5.2, and Table A5.3. The key variable that we expect to be associated with seed prices paid by farmers is crop variety, which is a proxy for genetic characteristics such as yield potential, duration, resistance to pests and diseases, and consumption qualities. To capture the relationship between variety and seed price, we include the most popular varieties for each crop as dummy variables, and,

TABLE A5.2 Summary statistics for cotton-growing households

Variable	N	Unit	Mean	SD
Seed price	263	PKR/kg	251.74	351.04
Top cotton varieties				
MNH-886	329	1/0	0.35	0.48
Ali Akbar-703	329	1/0	0.05	0.21
Ali Akbar-802	329	1/0	0.06	0.24
B-821	329	1/0	0.06	0.24
Province dummies				
Punjab	329	1/0	0.87	0.34
Sindh	329	1/0	0.13	0.34
KPK	329	1/0	0.00	0.00
Plot characteristics				
Landholding size	329	acres	27.11	30.24
Farmer characteristics				
Age of farmer	329	years	49.20	13.00
Tenure status of plot				
Tenure status = owned	329	1/0	0.62	0.49
Tenure status = rented in/sharecropped/mortgaged	329	1/0	0.38	0.49
Household characteristics				
Household head attended school	329	1/0	0.56	0.50
Household member met with an extension agent in the previous year	329	1/0	0.32	0.47
Household size	329	No. of members	7.24	3.71
Total monthly expenditure	329	PKR/month	20,808.00	12,516.00

Source: Authors' calculations, using RHPS (IFPRI/IDS 2012).

Note: N = number of observations. KPK = Khyber Pakhtunkhwa; PKR/kg = Pakistani rupees per kilogram. SD = standard deviation. A unit denoted "1/0" indicates that the variable may take on the value of 1 or 0.

because of the small number of observations available, combine all remaining varieties (which include a large number of relatively less popular or obscure varieties).[16]

An additional variable of interest is contact with an extension agent, which may capture the extent to which extension agents facilitate farmers' access to seed at some price above or below what the market may otherwise offer. For

16 For wheat, we include the top five varieties, whereas for rice and cotton, we include the top four varieties because of collinearity in price between several top varieties. Each specific variety is specified as a binary variable that equals 1 for the variety itself and 0 otherwise.

TABLE A5.3 Summary statistics for rice-growing households

Variable	N	Unit	Mean	SD
Seed price	260	PKR/kg	214.35	280.81
Top rice varieties				
Basmati Kernal	373	1/0	0.07	0.26
Basmati Super	373	1/0	0.13	0.34
KS-282	373	1/0	0.08	0.28
Irri-6	373	1/0	0.47	0.50
Province dummies				
Punjab	373	1/0	0.28	0.45
Sindh	373	1/0	0.71	0.45
KPK	373	1/0	0.01	0.07
Plot characteristics				
Landholding size	373	acres	13.93	15.74
Farmer characteristics				
Age of farmer	373	years	43.13	13.00
Tenure status of plot				
Tenure status = owned	373	1/0	0.50	0.50
Tenure status = rented in/sharecropped/mortgaged	373	1/0	0.50	0.50
Household characteristics				
Household head attended school	373	1/0	0.41	0.49
Household member met with an extension agent in the previous year	373	1/0	0.31	0.47
Household size	373	No. of members	6.25	2.81
Total monthly expenditure	373	PKR/month	17,131.00	8,302.00

Source: Authors' calculations, using RHPS (IFPRI/IDS 2012)

Note: N = number of observations. KPK = Khyber Pakhtunkhwa. PKR/kg = Pakistani rupees per kilogram. SD = standard deviation. A unit denoted "1/0" indicates that the variable may take on the value of 1 or 0.

example, if the genetic or physical qualities of the variety are correlated with the price of seed, then farmers may choose to purchase expensive seed based on a recommendation from an extension agent. Alternatively, it may be the case that access to subsidized seed, low-cost seed starter packs, or new varietal releases that are freely distributed is contingent on the recommendation of an extension agent.

Additional variables included in the estimation conducted here are fairly standard in technology adoption studies (Feder et al. 1985; Jack 2011). For example, we include age and educational status of the head of household as a proxy for experience in farming; landholding size to capture household wealth; land tenure arrangement, which is divided between direct ownership and other arrangements, namely renting in, sharecropping in, or mortgaging in the land; household size, which includes all members of the household who have lived at least three months in the house over the past year, living and sharing meals often with the household; and household income, which is captured by total monthly expenditure on food and nonfood items. Provincial controls are also included to capture province-specific differences associated with seed market performance or provincial policy regimes.

Column 1 in Table A5.4, Table A5.5, and Table A5.6 provides results from an ordinary least squares (OLS) estimation of seed price determinants with provincial fixed effects. These results are included for comparison against the Heckman selection model results in Column 3 of the same tables. But before we explore these results, we first consider the seed-purchasing decision, or the correlates of whether a farmer purchased, rather than saved, seed in the 2012 RHPS data (IFPRI/IDS 2012). Column 2 in Tables A5.4, A5.5, and A5.6 provides probit estimation results from the first-step selection equation. We report here the marginal effects, or the probability that the decision to purchase (rather than save) seed is conditioned on the variables of interest. Results indicate that the estimated coefficients of variables such as age, tenancy status, and income are statistically significant and therefore associated with the decision to purchase (rather than save) seed. This indicates a systematic difference between farmers who purchase seed and those who save seed, further suggesting the presence of sample selection bias. To address the presence of such bias, we construct and include an Inverse Mills Ratio in the second-step treatment regression and estimate its coefficient (λ).

Estimation results from the selection equation (Column 2 in each table) also indicate that a majority of the estimated coefficients for top-variety dummy variables are statistically significant and positive for all three crops. This indicates that farmers who cultivate top varieties are more likely to purchase seed when compared to all other farmers. For example, we observe that farmers who cultivate Seher-06 wheat are 17 percent more likely to purchase seed compared to farmers who cultivate any other wheat variety. Similarly, farmers who cultivate MNH-886 cotton are 8 percent more likely to purchase seed when compared to farmers cultivating other varieties. Results also indicate that farmers who own their land are less likely to purchase seed than farmers who rent, sharecrop, or mortgage their land for all three crops. Similarly, farmers with larger landholdings are less likely to purchase seed, but only in the case of wheat and not cotton or rice.

TABLE A5.4 Correlates of price paid by farmers for wheat seed: OLS and Heckman selection model estimations

Explanatory variables	OLS estimation (1) Seed price (PKR/kg)	Heckman estimation (2) Purchased (0/1)	(3) Seed price (PKR/kg)
Seher-06	0.92 (1.39)	0.17*** (0.06)	0.68 (1.63)
Bhakhar-02	1.45 (1.41)	0.31*** (0.05)	1.03 (2.04)
Abdul Sattar	3.69** (1.46)	0.25*** (0.06)	3.36* (1.87)
INQILAB 91	4.96*** (1.86)	0.23*** (0.08)	4.64** (2.19)
Watan-93	1.50 (1.64)	0.20*** (0.08)	1.20 (1.95)
Punjab	−0.73 (1.12)	−0.13** (0.05)	−0.45 (1.47)
Sindh	−0.54 (1.11)	0.33*** (0.06)	−0.94 (1.77)
Landholding	−0.01 (0.01)	−0.00** (0.00)	−0.00 (0.02)
Met with an extension agent	2.50* (1.40)	−0.06 (0.05)	2.57* (1.40)
Has household head ever attended school?	n.a.	0.02 (0.04)	n.a. n.a.
Age (years)	n.a.	−0.00** (0.00)	n.a. n.a.
Tenancy status = owned (baseline = rented/sharecropped/mortgaged)	n.a.	−0.08* (0.04)	n.a. n.a.
Household size	n.a.	−0.01 (0.01)	n.a. n.a.
Total monthly expenditure	n.a.	0.00*** 0.00	n.a. n.a.
λ	n.a.	n.a.	−1.03 (3.59)
Constant	36.04*** (1.28)	n.a. n.a.	36.94*** (3.40)
Observations	413	863	413
R-squared	0.04	n.a.	0.04

Source: Authors, based on RHPS (IFPRI/IDS 2012).

Note: OLS = ordinary least squares. PKR/kg = Pakistani rupees per kilogram. n.a. = not applicable. Robust standard errors are in parentheses. Column 2 reports marginal effects. The Purchased variable is a binary one, which is 1 if the farmer purchased the seed and 0 otherwise. Coefficient estimates are significant at the * 10 percent, ** 5 percent, and *** 1 percent levels, respectively. All estimates are rounded to the nearest .01.

TABLE A5.5 Correlates of price paid by farmers for cottonseed: OLS and Heckman selection model estimations

Explanatory variables	OLS estimation (1) Seed price (PKR/kg)	Heckman estimation (2) Purchased (0/1)	(3) Seed price (PKR/kg)
MNH-886	92.83*	0.08*	56.23*
	(51.00)	(0.04)	(33.00)
Ali Akbar-703	190.40***	0.15***	104.90
	(28.72)	(0.05)	(67.89)
Ali Akbar-802	59.09*	0.10	−41.19
	(32.49)	(0.06)	(64.69)
B-821	41.62	0.15***	−67.26
	(34.97)	(0.05)	(96.31)
FH-901	96.89*	n.a.	n.a.
	(55.47)	n.a.	n.a.
Punjab (baseline = Sindh)	25.01	n.a.	n.a.
	(25.15)	n.a.	n.a.
Landholding	−0.01	−0.00	0.19
	(0.47)	(0.00)	(0.39)
Met with an extension agent	144.00**	−0.03	182.90*
	(69.50)	(0.05)	(93.73)
Has household head ever attended school?	n.a.	−0.07	n.a.
		(0.05)	n.a.
Age (years)	n.a.	−0.00	n.a.
		(0.00)	n.a.
Tenancy status = owned (baseline = rented/sharecropped/mortgaged)	n.a.	−0.13***	n.a.
		(0.05)	n.a.
Household size	n.a.	−0.00	n.a.
		(0.01)	n.a.
Total monthly expenditure	n.a.	0.00	n.a.
		0.00	n.a.
λ	n.a.	n.a.	−332.80
			(254.60)
Constant	130.30***	n.a.	278.70***
	(18.73)	n.a.	(88.82)
Observations	263	329	263
R-squared	0.06	n.a.	0.08

Source: Authors based on RHPS (IFPRI/IDS 2012).

Note: OLS = ordinary least squares. PKR/kg = Pakistani rupees per kilogram. n.a. = not applicable. Robust standard errors are in parentheses. Column 2 reports marginal effects. The Purchased variable is a binary one, which is 1 if the farmer purchased the seed and 0 otherwise. Coefficient estimates are significant at the * 10 percent, ** 5 percent, and *** 1 percent levels, respectively. All estimates are rounded off to the nearest .01.

TABLE A5.6 Correlates of price paid by farmers for rice seed: OLS and Heckman selection model estimations

Explanatory variable	OLS estimation (1) Seed price (PKR/kg)	Heckman estimation (2) Purchased (0/1)	Heckman estimation (1) Seed price (PKR/kg)
Basmati Kernal	−192.90** (78.87)	0.24*** (0.04)	43.46 (79.99)
Basmati Super	−227.00*** (81.56)	0.08 (0.09)	−154.30** (73.37)
KS-282	−521.60*** (48.22)	−0.06 (0.17)	−497.00*** (36.01)
Irri-6	−534.20*** (43.16)	−0.32*** (0.07)	−583.90*** (42.67)
Pukhraj	−98.37 (60.45)		
Punjab (baseline = Sindh)	250.80*** (79.45)	−0.61*** (0.11)	−464.40*** (88.48)
Landholding	−0.14 (0.98)	0.00 (0.00)	1.71 (1.09)
Met with an extension agent	−132.70*** (31.79)	−0.30*** (0.06)	−274.60*** (41.40)
Has household head ever attended school?	n.a.	0.07 (0.05)	n.a. n.a.
Age (years)	n.a.	0.00 (0.00)	n.a. n.a.
Tenancy status = owned (baseline = rented/ sharecropped/mortgaged)	n.a.	−0.13** (0.05)	n.a. n.a.
Household size	n.a.	0.01 (0.01)	n.a. n.a.
Total monthly expenditure	n.a.	0.00* (0.00)	n.a. n.a.
λ	n.a.	n.a.	289.40*** (71.42)
Constant	623.20*** (43.41)	n.a. n.a.	544.70*** (33.19)
Observations	260	373	260
R-squared	0.60		0.62

Source: Authors based on RHPS (IFPRI/IDS 2012).

Note: OLS = ordinary least squares. PKR/kg = Pakistani rupees per kilogram. Robust standard errors are in parentheses. Column 2 reports marginal effects. The Purchased variable is a binary one, which is 1 if the farmer purchased the seed and 0 otherwise. Coefficient estimates are significant at the * 10 percent, ** 5 percent, and *** 1 percent levels, respectively. All estimates are rounded off to the nearest .01. For rice the Pukhraj variety was not included because it was entirely purchased in all provinces, while the small number of observations in Khyber Pakhtunkhwa had all saved seed.

Column 3 in Tables A5.4, A5.5, and A5.6 provides estimation results from the second-step equation on seed price correlates. First, we observe that the seed price paid by farmers is generally higher for the top varieties. For example, we see that among farmers who purchased wheat seed, those who purchased Abdul Sattar and Inquilab 91 varieties paid a slightly higher seed price on average compared to all other wheat varieties. Similarly, the price paid by cotton farmers who cultivated MNH-886 was PKR 56.23/kg higher than the price paid for other cotton varieties, while cotton farmers who cultivated Ali Akbar-703 paid PKR 104.90/kg more. Only in the case of rice do we observe that the seed price paid by farmers for the top varieties was generally lower than that for all other varieties. This may warrant further exploration of the rice seed market structure and dynamics.

Second, we observe that contact with an extension agent is associated with seed prices paid by farmers. For wheat farmers who met with an extension agent in the previous crop year, the price paid for seed was PKR 2.6/kg greater than the price paid by farmers who had no contact with an extension agent. Similarly, cotton farmers who met with an extension agent paid PKR 182.9 more per kg as compared to farmers who had no contact with extension. Again, the case of rice yields contrary results: on average, farmers who had contact with an extension agent paid PKR 274.6 less per kg in comparison to those farmers who had no contact with an extension agent. From a policy perspective, this suggests a relationship between lower-cost seed and access to extension in Pakistan's rice market that is worth studying further.

Third, we observe that provincial determinants of price variation are insignificant in the case of wheat but significant in the case of rice, with seed prices being lower in Punjab than in Sindh.[17] This may reflect the crop-specific nature of seed marketing channels, differences in the extent of seed market development in individual provinces, and the crop- and province-specific roles of the public and private sectors in the distribution of seed. These issues are explored in greater depth throughout the chapter.

Finally, note that the results using the Heckman selection model improve on the biased OLS estimates presented in Column 1 of the same table. A comparison of Columns 1 and 3 shows that the estimated coefficient on the top

---

17 Provincial fixed effects could not be estimated for cotton because (1) all cotton farmers in Sindh purchased seed, and (2) the variety FH-901 (the fifth most popular purchased variety of cotton in the sample) was found only in Sindh, with seed for FH-901 having been entirely purchased in Sindh. Hence, we exclude province and FH-901 dummies from the estimation model for cotton. Similarly, for rice, the second most popular variety, Pukhraj, was entirely purchased in all provinces, while the small number of observations in KPK had all saved seed.

five varieties, particularly for several rice and cotton varieties, changes significantly with use of the Heckman selection model. For example, we observe that the coefficient on the cotton variety MNH-886 drops to 56.23 from 92.83 in the seed price regression, implying that due to the selection bias in the uncorrected model, the correlation between price and MNH-886 may have been exaggerated. For wheat, however, the results remain somewhat consistent between the two models.

Annex B: Quantities of Seed Purchased by Crop, Source, and Landholding Size

TABLE B5.1 Average quantities of cottonseed (kg/acre) purchased by source and landholding size

	Cotton (n = 266)				
	Landholding size (acres)				
Source	≤5	5–12.5	12.5–25	25–50	>50
Relative	5.7	—	—	—	—
Friend/neighbor	6.4	7.8	5.0	—	—
Input dealer	7.1	6.4	6.7	6.3	—
Landlord	8.2	8.7	—	—	—
Research institute	—	5.0	—	—	—
Punjab Seed Corporation	6.8	6.3	6.4	—	7.0
Agriculture extension department	—	—	5.0	—	—
Private seed company	7.2	6.7	6.9	6.3	5.7
NGO/relief agency	—	—	—	—	—

Source: Authors, based on RHPS (IFPRI/IDS 2012).

Note: All figures have been rounded off to the nearest 0.1 of a kilogram. NGO = nongovernmental organization. kg = kilograms; — = not available.

TABLE B5.2 Average quantities of wheat seed (kg/acre) purchased by source and landholding size

	Wheat (n = 414)				
	Landholding size (acres)				
Source	≤5	5–12.5	12.5–25	25–50	>50
Relative	60.2	60.0	—	—	—
Friend/neighbor	54.9	73.7	40.0	—	—
Input dealer	57.4	54.4	51.4	50.0	—
Landlord	67.8	72.0	66.7	—	—
Research institute	—	51.7	40.0	—	—
Punjab Seed Corporation	54.2	—	60.0	—	2.0
Agriculture extension department	56.3	66.7	64.2	—	—
Private seed company	58.1	53.8	50.2	52.2	—
NGO/relief agency	58.1	—	55.0	—	—

Source: Authors, based on RHPS (IFPRI/IDS 2012).

Note: All figures have been rounded off to the nearest 0.1 of a kilogram. NGO = nongovernmental organization. kg = kilograms; — = not available.

TABLE B5.3 Average quantities of rice seed (kg/acre) purchased by source and landholding size

	Rice (n = 261)				
	Landholding size (acres)				
Source	≤5	5–12.5	12.5–25	25–50	>50
Relative	40.0	10.7	—	—	—
Friend/neighbor	8.0	6.2	—	—	—
Input dealer	5.3	5.0	4.0	—	—
Landlord	6.2	4.9	3.1	—	—
Research institute	—	—	—	—	—
Punjab Seed Corporation	6.3	3.3	—	—	—
Agriculture extension department	—	—	—	—	—
Private seed company	6.4	9.8	4.8	3.4	5.0
NGO/relief agency	—	—	—	—	—
Cooperative society	—	2.5	—	—	—

Source: Authors, based on RHPS (IFPRI/IDS 2012).

Note: All figures have been rounded off to the nearest 0.1 of a kilogram. NGO = nongovernmental organization. kg = kilograms; — = not available.

TABLE B5.4 Average quantities of maize seed (kg/acre) purchased by source and landholding size

	Maize (n = 54)				
	Landholding size (acres)				
Source	≤5	5–12.5	12.5–25	25–50	>50
Relative	—	—	—	—	—
Friend/neighbor	16.9	—	40.0	—	—
Input dealer	23.8	22.7	18.0	—	—
Landlord	—	—	—	—	—
Research institute	10.7	14.0	—	—	—
Punjab Seed Corporation	—	—	—	—	—
Agriculture extension department	26.0	—	—	—	—
Private seed company	17.8	16.9	25.0	20.5	—
NGO/relief agency	17.0	—	16.0	—	—

Source: Authors, based on RHPS (IFPRI/IDS 2012).

Note: All figures have been rounded off to the nearest 0.1 of a kilogram. NGO = nongovernmental organization. kg = kilograms; — = not available.

Chapter 6

PAKISTAN'S FERTILIZER SECTOR: STRUCTURE, POLICIES, PERFORMANCE, AND IMPACTS

Mubarik Ali, Faryal Ahmed, Hira Channa, and Stephen Davies

Introduction

Fertilizer, along with modern seed varieties and supplementary irrigation water, has been one of the three key contributors to productivity growth in food staples during the Green Revolution that began in the 1960s in Pakistan (Byerlee and Siddiq 1994). As farmers shifted from the cultivation of traditional wheat varieties to higher-yielding, more fertilizer- and water-responsive modern varieties, yields increased fourfold between 1965 and 2013. However, with rising population growth, per capita supply from domestic production increased from just 95 kilograms (kg) to 115 kg (MNFSR 2013). The corresponding increase in fertilizer nutrient use during this period—from almost nil in 1965 to 180 kg per hectare (ha) in 2013 (NFDC 2014)—was an instrumental factor in these yield gains and the corresponding improvement in food security as per capita consumption of calories per day increased from 2,210 to 2,428 in the same period (FAO 2014).

But despite many gains attributable to increased fertilizer use, public policies that promote its production and use remain controversial. Successive governments have alternated between subsidizing its production, importation, and distribution; withdrawing these subsidies in a piecemeal manner; and reverting back to them when fertilizer prices escalated. This indicates fertilizer's popularity among policy makers as a political input to be used to gain the support of the large farming population, as well as to ensure their narrow perception of food security as just the production of cereals (CCP 2010).

As a result of these policies—alongside a host of other market and institutional factors such as the lack of scale efficiencies in fertilizer processing or the lack of institutional capacity to introduce new and more efficient fertilizer products and application methods—Pakistan now faces widespread misuse of fertilizer at the farm level, rigid oligopolies in the fertilizer industry, untenable fiscal burdens for the government, and resource degradation in the agricultural sector.

Few studies analyze the policy environment in the sector, which encompasses the whole value chain of processing, marketing, trade, and application to crops. One exception is a study by the Competition Commission of Pakistan (CCP), which describes the policy and regulatory environment of the fertilizer sector in Pakistan. However, the study lacks a farm-level perspective and does not quantify the impact of the existing regulatory framework and policy interventions on various macroeconomic parameters and stakeholders. Moreover, the situation of the fertilizer sector has dramatically changed since 2008, the most recent year of data included in the CCP (2010).

This chapter explores these issues in greater depth by reviewing the state of the fertilizer industry, identifying the main policy issues, and analyzing the costs and benefits associated with alternative policy interventions. The remainder of this chapter proceeds as follows. The second section provides a brief history of the industry. The third section describes fertilizer use and its effects on yield and soil. The fourth section reviews the performance of the fertilizer market and examines the effects of subsidies and imperfect competition. The fifth section develops an equilibrium displacement model and simulates the impacts of major government policy interventions. The final section concludes with recommendations aimed at improving the performance of Pakistan's fertilizer sector and its contribution to future agricultural productivity growth.

The Development of Pakistan's Fertilizer Industry

Fertilizer was introduced in Pakistan in the 1950s, primarily through imports (Figure 6.1). Nitrogenous chemical fertilizers were introduced through imports in 1952, followed by phosphorus in 1959 and potassium compounds in 1967 (NFDC 2014).[1] But Pakistan initially assumed that it possessed large reserves of natural gas—an input to the Haber-Bosch process used to form ammonia, a key ingredient in nitrogen fertilizers such as urea—which was interpreted to yield a comparative advantage for the domestic production of fertilizer. Beginning in the late 1950s and early 1960s, the government pursued an import-substitution industrialization policy and made strategic manufacturing investments to build a domestic fertilizer industry. These investments included both joint ventures with foreign companies, such as

---

1   Fertilizer products are a combination of three primary fertilizer nutrients, which plants need in order to grow: nitrogen (N), phosphorus (P), and potassium (K). For example, urea is 46 percent nitrogen, while DAP contains 18 percent nitrogen and 46 percent phosphorus.

FIGURE 6.1 Domestic production, imports, and total available fertilizer, 1952/1953–2013/2014

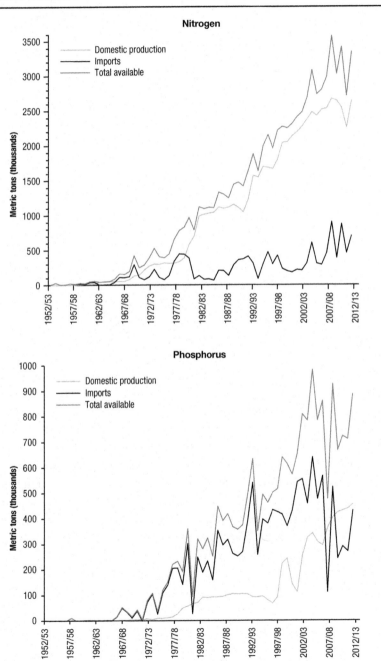

Pak-American Fertilizers (now Agritech, which was established in 1958) and Pakarab Fertilizers (established in 1973), and the establishment of domestic fertilizer plants by independent companies, like that of the Fauji Fertilizer Company (FFC; established in 1978).[2] Upon nationalization of the fertilizer industry in 1973, production for all fertilizer companies was undertaken through a parastatal, the National Fertilizer Corporation (NFC).

By the late 1960s, Pakistan's emerging domestic fertilizer industry allowed the country to simultaneously increase the national supply of fertilizer and reduce the share of fertilizer imports, which had drawn down valuable foreign exchange reserves. Of course, large quantities of certain fertilizer products produced without natural gas (for example, di-ammonium phosphate and potassium compounds) still had to be imported, but domestic production capacity for both nitrogen and phosphate fertilizers nonetheless continued to increase (Figure 6.1). By this time, as farmers began adopting high-yielding modern wheat and rice varieties in Pakistan's irrigated areas, fertilizer use was gaining momentum. The size of this industry is significant in Pakistan, as the value of fertilizer sales (at domestic retail prices) was estimated at US$3.57 billion in 2013, up from just US$554 million in 1971. Approximately 70 percent of fertilizer consumed in Pakistan is produced domestically, with domestic production supplying 75 percent of urea, 54 percent of di-ammonium phosphate (DAP), and 29 percent of potash fertilizers consumed nationally. Growth of domestic fertilizer production has been consistently higher than the growth of consumption for all nutrients since 1971, keeping import growth relatively low. For nitrogen, the production growth rate (6.15 percent) has been greater than the consumption growth rate (5.54 percent), thereby keeping the import growth at 3.40 percent between 1971 and 2014. However, less dramatic trends were observed for phosphorus and potash (the fertilizer product with potassium as the active nutrient).

Initially, fertilizer was distributed through the agriculture extension wings of the provincial agriculture departments. There was no independent marketing system for agricultural inputs until the formation of the West Pakistan Agricultural Development Corporation (WPADC) in 1961 (Hussain 2011; Hassan and Pradhan 1998). However, WAPADC was abolished in 1972, and this responsibility was transferred to the provincial governments. Later, fertilizer marketing was the responsibility of National Fertilizer Marketing Limited (NFML), a parastatal established in 1976 that became responsible for distributing all domestic production from the NFC companies, as well

---

2   Company dates of incorporation were retrieved from Agritech (2014), FFC (2014), and PFL (2014).

as all imports of fertilizer. After the privatization of all manufacturing units of NFC, NFML's role became restricted to the distribution of imported urea. Currently, domestically produced supply is marketed by private-sector processing companies through their registered dealers' networks.

The growth of fertilizer production and use in Pakistan gave rise to a series of policies designed to regulate the industry. First and foremost, from 1954 until the present, the government maintained control of the supply and allocation of natural gas to the fertilizer industry, which was formalized through successive fertilizer policies in 1989 and 2001. The later policy mainly protected the interests of fertilizer manufacturers by ensuring the supply of gas at subsidized rates, and relaxation of import duties on machinery used in fertilizer manufacturing, without addressing the interests of other stakeholders like farmers, traders, retailers, and government. Second, the Provincial Essential Commodity Act (PECA), promulgated in 1971 and amended in 1973, placed fertilizer production and marketing under the direct regulatory oversight of the federal government. At the provincial level, the Punjab Fertilizer (Control) Order of 1973 further strengthened the power of federal regulators by rendering provincial management of fertilizer subservient to PECA. Specifically, laws formulated and executed under PECA provide almost complete powers to the controller in the management of prices, imports, and even the size of daily fertilizer transactions. Other policies that have been deployed over the past 40 years include the provision of subsidies on fertilizer imports and distribution, the creation of a price environment that made the private sector unable to import urea, and the imposition of sales tax on farmers' fertilizer purchases.[3]

The introduction of these policies, alongside the growth of fertilizer production and use, also led to the establishment of several key organizations aimed at promoting fertilizer use. Fertilizer research and development (R&D) was initially undertaken by the Directorate of Soil Fertility in the Research Wing of the Agriculture Department of the Government of West Pakistan, which was converted into separate provincial Soil Fertility Research Institutes (SFRI) in 1971. Issues pertaining to economic policy—for example, those concerning production, imports, pricing, subsidies, and regulations—were addressed by the National Fertilizer Development Centre (NFDC), which was established in 1977 by the Federal Planning and Development Division.

At the farm level, the Extension Wing of the Agriculture Department of the Government of West Pakistan was responsible for conveying

---

3   For the management of prices, the controller is at the provincial agriculture department. For imports, the responsibility lies with the Commerce Ministry through NFML.

recommendations for fertilizer use to farmers, although lately the private sector has started playing a role in this activity. Credit for fertilizer purchases was made available to farmers through a variety of formal and informal sources. Initially, the primary formal source of credit was the Agricultural Development Bank of Pakistan, now known as the Zarai Taraqiati Bank Limited, established in 1961 to provide affordable financial services to rural Pakistan. Commercial banks such as Habib Bank, Askari Bank, and Punjab Bank began providing agricultural credit at market rates beginning in 1972.

The rapid expansion of Pakistan's fertilizer production capacity—alongside increases in fertilizer imports and the growth of the policy, market, and institutional infrastructure required to promote fertilizer use—led to significant yield gains in wheat and rice during the 1960s and 1970s. However, new challenges to Pakistan's agricultural sector also surfaced. First, no subsidies, or relatively smaller subsidies for nutrients other than nitrogen, led to a long-term pattern of unbalanced fertilizer use. Second, the regulators' strong control over the fertilizer industry, as set forth in PECA and later in the fertilizer policies, placed significant discretionary powers in the hands of regulators and made entry into the fertilizer industry difficult for those without strong political affiliations. Third, the public sector's extensive investment in the formation and management of Pakistan's fertilizer industry—from the pricing and allocation of natural gas to the distribution of fertilizers to farmers—created interest groups that made more market-oriented reforms difficult.

Typically, fertilizer manufacturers supply products to dealers with a recommended maximum price, which is inclusive of the dealer's profit margin. Dealers procure fertilizer stocks—usually on a cash basis, but sometimes against a bank guarantee—and sell the product through their sales agent networks at prices that are determined by the local supply and demand situation. The existence of a competitive market is, however, subject to government intervention, which is sometimes ad-hoc in nature and sometimes more structural. For example, during periods of short supply, according to interviewed dealers, the historical practice has been for the district coordination officer to call a meeting of all fertilizer dealers in the district to agree upon a price, even though deviations from this set price have become the norm. Despite the authority vested in regulators, they have almost never been able to smooth out the supply or keep prices at reasonable levels whenever shortages have occurred mainly due to mismanagement of imports controlled by NFML (Nadeem Tariq, Dawood Hercules Fertilizer Limited, personal communication, August 15, 2013).

Another issue related to fertilizer use efficiency has been the absence of research on traditional sources of nutrient such as animal and green manures. Little emphasis was given to developing standard operating procedures for composting, standards for nutrient content from these manures, and the monitoring of those standards. As a result, farmers stopped trusting these products' effectiveness, which varies dramatically compared to standard commercial fertilizer products. Testing and promotion of new products such as micronutrients, slow release fertilizers, and plant growth–promoting rhizobacteria— which not only can be cheaper and sustainable sources of soil nutrient but can also improve the efficiency of commercial fertilizers—was also ignored.

During the initial years of fertilizer introduction, provincial extension services played a major role in promoting fertilizer based on recommendations made by provincial SFRIs for every crop. However, the emphasis of these demonstrations remained focused on the expansion of fertilizer use, meaning that few products or application methods were either tested or promoted. Meanwhile, the SFRIs had little success in disseminating new general or site-specific fertilizer recommendations—such as adoption of fertilizer placement methods and proper use of fertilizer on different soil types—based on their R&D activities. These limitations in the research and extension system have exacerbated trends toward unbalanced and unsustainable use, which caused serious resource degradation (Ali and Byerlee 2002).

In recent decades, Pakistan's fertilizer industry has undergone several changes aimed at addressing several of these issues. After the gradual privatization of NFC's manufacturing units over the period 1996–2005, NFML's role was restricted to the distribution of imported urea. The government is continuing its efforts to reduce the role of NFML, and even made an abortive attempt to transfer the responsibility for distribution and imports of urea to domestic manufacturers in 2013/2014. Nonetheless, subsidies remain central to the production and distribution of fertilizer, with the Ministry of Petroleum and Natural Resources deciding on the level of the production subsidy by controlling the supply of gas to manufacturers, and the NFML deciding on the amount of fertilizer to be imported and the distribution subsidy to be applied. This lower price of gas given to nitrogen producers, relative to its opportunity cost as seen by the prices to other consumers, provides the main mechanism for a nonbudgeted subsidy to fertilizer manufacturers. Hence, the government does not directly make expenditures on this subsidy.

Total domestic installed capacity of all types of fertilizer production in Pakistan is currently estimated at 10.0 million metric tons, 69 percent of which is for urea and 31 percent for DAP and potash fertilizers. In recent

TABLE 6.1 Operating capacity of selected fertilizer manufacturers by type of fertilizer (%), 2013/2014

Firm	Urea	DAP	NPK	NP	CAN	Phosphate	Total
Fauji Fertilizers (Goth Machi)	116.6	—	—	—	—	—	116.6
Engro	80.3	—	40.0	87.5	—	—	77.8
Fatima	71.4	—	—	101.7	124.4	—	95.5
Pakarab	5.8	—	—	23.1	28.2	—	22.7
Agri Tech	31.7	—	—	—	—	—	31.7
Dawood Hercules	9.7	—	—	—	—	—	9.7
Fauji Fertilizers (Bin Qasim)	38.1	102.8	—	—	—	—	73.7
Others	—	—	—	—	—	21.0	21.0
Total	78.0	102.8	40.0	63.8	76.3	21.0	75.3

Source: Authors' calculations, based on MNFSR (2013).

Note: Operating capacity is calculated by dividing actual production (in tons) by the manufacturing plant's production capacity (in tons). The production can exceed the estimated operating capacity and thus be above 100. DAP = di-ammonium phosphate; NPK = nitrogen, phosphorus, and potassium; NP = nitrogen and phosphorus; CAN = calcium ammonium nitrate; — = a firm did not produce that type of fertilizer.

years, the industry has been operating below its full capacity, at approximately 75 percent in 2013/2014. During that year, urea production suffered the most, with operating capacity estimated at 78 percent, while DAP production ran at almost full capacity (Table 6.1). Had there been no underutilization of capacity, the production of urea would have been sufficient to meet domestic demand. However, DAP would remain short by about 50 percent even with full utilization of its installed capacity.

The production capacity and related market power in the fertilizer industry in Pakistan is concentrated in relatively few firms. The two big players, Fauji Fertilizer Company (FFC) (Gorth Machi) and Engro Corporation of Pakistan hold more than two-thirds of total installed production capacity of urea (Figure 6.2). The estimated Herfindahl-Hirschman Index of industry concentration for urea manufacturing in Pakistan was 3741 in 2013/2014, indicating that the industry was highly concentrated.[4] The CCP has come to a similar conclusion.

---

4   The Herfindahl-Hirschman Index is calculated as the sum of the squared market share of each firm in the industry (Hannah and Kay 1977). This index approaches zero when a market consists of a large number of firms of relatively equal size, and it increases both as the number of firms in the market decreases and as the disparity in size between those firms increases. Because the index takes into account the relative size and distribution of the firms in a market, it is considered a better indicator of industry concentration than the four-firm concentration ratio.

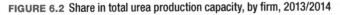

FIGURE 6.2 Share in total urea production capacity, by firm, 2013/2014

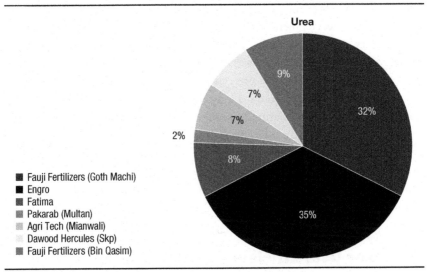

Urea

32%

9%

7%

7%

2%

8%

35%

- ■ Fauji Fertilizers (Goth Machi)
- ■ Engro
- ■ Fatima
- ▨ Pakarab (Multan)
- ▨ Agri Tech (Mianwali)
- ▨ Dawood Hercules (Skp)
- ■ Fauji Fertilizers (Bin Qasim)

Source: Authors' calculation, based on MNFSR (2013).

With respect to DAP, the situation is slightly different. The Fauji Fertilizer Bin Qasim Limited is the only domestic producer of DAP; it supplies about 54 percent of total DAP demand, while the remainder is imported by numerous smaller firms.[5] As such, there is likely greater competition in the market for DAP, and domestic DAP prices tend to be closely linked to the international price of DAP. But with this linkage comes greater exposure to international price volatility and currency risk.

There is some evidence of anticompetitive behavior in Pakistan's fertilizer industry, suggesting that firms benefiting from the government's largess described above have also invested heavily in securing and maintaining their market power. In 2012 the CCP fined FFC and the Dawood Hercules Chemical Limited for approximately PKR 6 billion for employing coalition tactics in an effort to manipulate the fertilizer market. Meanwhile, the returns on equity in Pakistan's fertilizer industry are well beyond those of international counterparts, suggesting the possibility of anticompetitive behavior that rewards investors. In Pakistan the return on equity (taken as an

---

5   Fauji Fertilizer Bin Qasim Limited is a subsidiary of FFC, which is controlled by the Fauji Foundation.

average for the years 2004–2008) for the fertilizer industry was 33 percent, compared to 9 percent in China and 16 percent in India (CCP 2010).

In sum, the development of Pakistan's fertilizer industry has been both a success story and a source of difficulty for farmers, industrialists, and policy makers alike. The success story was driven by a number of key factors: a major technological shift, initially in rice and wheat cultivation during the Green Revolution and later in cotton, sugarcane, and maize; Pakistan's perceived abundant endowment of natural gas at the time; and the willingness of policy makers and investors to build a domestic fertilizer industry from the ground up. But difficulties in sustaining this success have emerged in the form of an emerging serious shortage of gas, unbalanced fertilizer use, poor management practices, poor allocation of public resources for R&D, and noncompetitive industrial practices. The sections that follow examine these elements.

Fertilizer Use, Efficiency, and Resource Degradation

To provide a better sense of how farmers actually use fertilizer in Pakistan, this section examines fertilizer application rates, impact on yields, and the unintended consequences of fertilizer use.

Data in this section are drawn from three sources. First, data on fertilizer use across agroecological zones and provinces, at an aggregated level, were obtained from the NFDC.[6] Second, data on yield response and soil nutrient content are drawn from SFRIs, collected from laboratories present at district levels in every province.[7] Third, household data on fertilizer use, yields, and related variables are drawn from the 942 agricultural households surveyed in Round 1.5 of the Pakistan Rural Household Panel Survey (RHPS), conducted in 2012, while information on household size and education for these households is extracted from Round 1 (IFPRI/IDS 2012; see Chapter 1 for details).

---

6   All fertilizer traders in the country that are registered with the extension department are required to provide daily sales, price, and stock information to the Extension Wing of the provincial agriculture departments. The NFDC collects this information from the agriculture departments and from importers and companies directly to verify this data. Daily prices of fertilizer products are collected from the Pakistan Bureau of Statistics. We used annual values for our analysis.

7   These laboratories are engaged in research and development activities to increase agricultural production by improving plant nutrition management, together with a better use of other production factors. The Field Wings of SFRIs carry out experimentation on farmers' fields every year for various crops and cultivars to evaluate optimum nutrient requirements and provide general and site-specific fertilizer recommendations.

TABLE 6.2 Fertilizer use by province and crop region, 1990/1991–2011/2012

Crop region	1990/91 (kg/ha)	1995/96 (kg/ha)	2000/01 (kg/ha)	2005/06 (kg/ha)	2010/11 (kg/ha)	2011/12 (kg/ha)	Annual growth rate (%)
Pakistan	89.0	111.0	135.0	168.9	166.0	165.0	3.0
Punjab	90.7	114.9	107.4	150.7	158.7	157.4	2.7
Barani	19.6	22.4	23.2	30.2	58.5	36.1	2.9
Mixed crop	70.0	103.1	94.1	134.2	136.5	137.2	3.3
Wheat/cotton	137.7	175.2	148.9	209.4	213.5	210.0	2.0
Wheat/rice	70.4	90.9	83.9	134.7	160.6	157.1	3.9
Wheat/gram/mung bean	67.9	66.7	80.4	107.2	112.2	115.4	2.6
Sindh	88.0	134.7	154.9	208.8	246.5	296.5	6.0
Mixed crops	136.3	123.0	151.3	179.1	154.6	325.8	4.2
Wheat/cotton	60.4	161.6	182.6	233.6	365.1	363.9	8.9
Wheat/rice	100.4	107.1	121.8	201.5	167.6	185.0	3.0
Khyber Pakhtunkhwa	59.4	70.0	90.1	161.1	156.2	172.7	5.2
Barani	16.8	20.1	24.9	129.4	110.9	69.2	7.0
Mixed crops	72.0	88.3	108.6	169.7	166.6	199.3	5.0
Balochistan	28.7	31.9	65.0	299.5	148.2	215.2	10.1
Wheat/cotton	31.6	22.4	40.8	1496.8	65.4	109.2	6.1
Horticultural crops	26.8	43.1	100.5	325.4	256.0	352.6	13.1

Source: Authors' calculations based on NFDC (2008, 2002, 1998). The data for 2010/11 and 2011/12 were collected from NFDC headquarters in Islamabad.

Notes: All districts in a province having a common major kharif crop, like cotton, rice, or gram/mung bean are merged into separate cropping regions. For example, the wheat/cotton region implies that the region is dominated by the cotton crop in the kharif season. The district where no crop dominates in kharif is called a mixed-crop region. All districts where 85 percent of the area in a province depends on rain for irrigation are categorized as barani regions. In Balochistan, horticultural crops regions consist of districts where horticultural crops cultivation dominates. kg = kilograms; ha = hectares.

According to NFDC data, total fertilizer offtake increased over 14-fold between 1971 and 2014 in Pakistan. The three-year average of nitrogen (N) fertilizer use per ha increased from 21 kg during 1971–1974 to 133 kg during 2011–2014, while phosphate fertilizer use increased from 2 kg to 32 kg per ha in the corresponding periods. The highest increase in per-ha fertilizer use was recorded in 2009/2010, when the output-fertilizer price ratio jumped to a record level. The fertilizer application rate reached 180 kg/ha in 2013/2014. This rate is higher than that of India (141.3 kg/ha) but less than that in neighboring Indian Punjab (229 kg/ha).

In fact, fertilizer consumption in Pakistan's Punjab Province exhibited both the lowest level of nutrient use and the slowest growth rate between 1990/1991 and 2011/2012 (Table 6.2). The highest levels of nutrient use were found in Sindh, and the highest rate of growth was found in Balochistan.

Yield responses of major crops to different fertilizer nutrient levels were estimated using SFRI data collected from long-term controlled experiments conducted on farmers' fields. Experiments were conducted separately for nitrogen (N) and phosphorus (P), where the level of one specific nutrient (the one being examined) was set at five different levels while the other nutrients were fixed at recommended levels. The same layout was used every year, except that the crop variety was changed to reflect the most common variety for that year. Other management practices such as seed rate, irrigation frequency during crop season, and so forth were kept at recommended levels. To estimate the yield response of nitrogen, separate regressions were run for irrigated wheat and rice based on data for two three-year intervals (2009/2010–2011/2012 and 1997/1998–1999/2000).

The results indicate that a positive relationship exists between yield and N levels, suggesting significant increases in yield with increased N levels. However, there is a limit on that relationship, as suggested by the quadratic form that best fits the data. It turns negative at higher levels of N (because the squared term for N in the equation is negative). The N level at which yield starts declining depends on the crop and its variety, environment, and management practice. In the response function in Figure 6.3, during the latest period, the yield starts declining at about 230 kg/ha in the case of wheat and 160 kg/ha in the case of rice. This turning point is even lower in the earlier period when different crop varieties were used. The responses were relatively weak in barani areas (not reported in the figure) compared to that in irrigated areas.

The results also indicate that the most recent period had the higher intercept for nitrogen in both rice and wheat in irrigated areas, thereby indicating that changes in variety may be a primary reason for the upward shift in the yield response curve (Figure 6.3).[8]

Cropwise optimal (profit-maximizing) values of fertilizer can be calculated using the response functions estimated by the SFRI under experimental conditions, based on fertilizer and commodity prices for 2011/2012. These values can be compared with the actual levels of per ha use for different crops from the 2012 RHPS Round 1.5 data. Profit is maximized at the level where the value of the marginal product of fertilizer is equal to the marginal cost of fertilizer.

---

8   Similar trends were observed for nitrogen use in cotton and for phosphorus use in cotton, rice, and wheat. However, the earlier years were best approximated by linear functions, which was perhaps due to a narrow range of fertilizer levels used in the experiments.

FIGURE 6.3 Yield response of nitrogen fertilizer in wheat and rice, 1997/1998–1999/2000 and 2009/2010–2011/2012

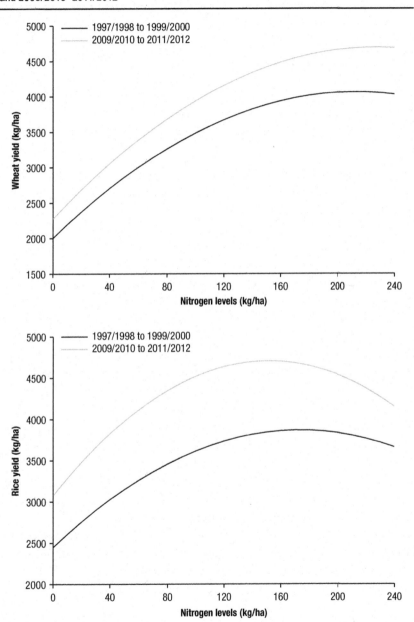

Source: Authors' calculations, based on SFRI (2013a).

Note: kg = kilograms; ha = hectares.

TABLE 6.3 Average fertilizer nutrient use by crop, 2012

Crop	N (kg/ha)	N (Optimal) (kg/ha)	Ratio N (Actual/Optimal) (%)	P (kg/ha)	P (Optimal) (kg/ha)	Ratio P (Actual/Optimal) (%)
Wheat	119.4	183.5	65	43.9	114.8	38
Rice	123.0	132.8	93	36.0	208.8	17
Cotton	123.1	209.0	59	37.3	107.2	35

Source: Authors' calculations, based on 2012 RHPS (IFPRI/IDS 2012) and SFRI (2013a).

Note: The optimal values are calculated by the authors using the nitrogen and phosphorus response equations estimated and provided by SFRI (2013a). N = nitrogen; P = phosphorus; kg = kilograms; ha = hectares.

For wheat, the optimal value of nitrogen is estimated to be 183.5 kg/ha, more than 50 percent higher than the average reported use of 119 kg/ha (Table 6.3). The difference indicates a potential of fertilizer use if all socioeconomic and institutional constraints at the farm levels are removed. However, the optimal value for wheat in barani conditions is much lower, around 108 kg/ha. This reflects the sensitivity of yield response of nutrients to timely and sufficient availability of water. For rice, the optimal value for nitrogen of 132.8 kg/ha is fairly close to the average of 123 kg/ha.

Using the RHPS Round 1.5 data, fertilizer use was analyzed under different soil and land types and by different farm categories. Overall, there was no significant difference in fertilizer nutrient applications across different soil types. Normally, lower levels of fertilizer nutrients are applied on poor land, but here the highest use was on the most fertile lands (Table 6.4). While this is contrary to the higher recommended fertilizer doses for less fertile lands, it may be because those farming on poor lands have greater cash and credit constraints.

Next, we explore the issue of fertilizer-use efficiency. Fertilizer-use efficiency (defined as fertilizer nutrient use divided by yield per hectare) has declined in Pakistan for both wheat and cotton, with more fertilizer per unit of produce being required over time (Figure 6.4). Possible explanations include increasing resource degradation, such as salinity, waterlogging, or lower levels of organic matter and other nutrient content in the soil, which we discuss further below. However in a few cases since the Green Revolution, technological changes such as the introduction of a new, more fertilizer-responsive variety or a change in soil and water management practices have helped to address this problem.[9]

---

9 An example is the introduction of a new basmati rice variety in 1996, when increasing trends in fertilizer requirements were reversed. However, the new variety led to a one-time jump in nutrient-use efficiency in rice, indicating the importance of the continuous introduction of new varieties to maintain and add to fertilizer-use efficiency.

TABLE 6.4 Average fertilizer use for farm characteristics by fertilizer type and overall, 2012

Farm characteristics	N (kg/ha)	P (kg/ha)	K (kg/ha)	Overall (kg/ha)	Farmers using fertilizer (%)
Overall fertilizer nutrient use	120.94 (1326)	38.24 (972)	0.54 (9)	159.72 (1326)	87.00
Soil type					
Sandy and sandy loam	117.56 (437)	37.12 (322)	0.37 (3)	155.05 (437)	89.73
Loam	121.48 (426)	38.56 (318)	1.01 (5)	161.06 (426)	90.25
Clay and clay loam	126.30 (463)	39.34 (334)	0.27 (1)	165.90 (463)	96.46
Land quality					
High fertility	127.44 (230)	39.42 (172)	1.14 (2)	168.00 (230)	93.12
Moderate fertility	121.66 (1069)	38.47 (788)	0.43 (7)	160.55 (1069)	91.92
Low fertility	77.70 (27)	23.83 (14)	0.00 (0)	101.54 (27)	93.10
Farm size					
Less than 12 acres	122.84 (1155)	37.37 (824)	0.56 (7)	160.77 (1155)	92.92
More than 12 acres	114.91 (171)	44.44 (150)	0.46 (2)	159.80 (171)	61.07[a]

Source: Authors' estimates, based on 2012 RHPS (IFPRI/IDS 2012).

Note: The categories are based on the definitions used in the 2012 RHPS (IFPRI/IDS 2012). Numbers in parentheses represent numbers of plots in each category. kg = kilograms; ha = hectares.

[a] This low number is because of a high number of missing values for this category.

As shown in Figure 6.4, the production of 100 kg of wheat in 1980/1981 required 4 kg of fertilizer nutrient, but by 2013/2014, the production of the same amount of wheat required 7.9 kg of fertilizer nutrient. Similar trends have been observed in cotton, although fertilizer-use efficiency in rice has remained largely unchanged over the time period.

As a result of declining marginal productivities of fertilizer and water, growth in total factor productivity (TFP) at the farm level initially slowed and later stagnated (Ali and Byerlee 2002; Ahmed and Gautam 2013). As such, Pakistan's TFP growth went from being one of the best in the world in the 1980s to being the lowest among comparable Asian nations such as Bangladesh, China, India, and Sri Lanka (Ahmed and Gautam 2013).

To determine the factors that affect fertilizer-use efficiency and estimate its optimal use under actual field conditions, we estimate a yield response

FIGURE 6.4 Fertilizer-use efficiency by crop, 1980/1981–2012/2013

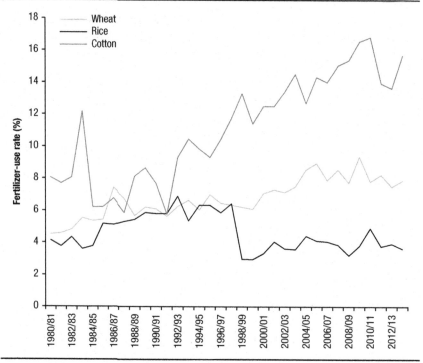

Source: Authors' calculation based on NFDC (2014); MNFSR (2013); MNFAL (2007a, 2007b).
Note: Fertilizer-use rate = fertilizer use (kg/ha)/yield (kg/ha). kg = kilograms; ha = hectares.

function for wheat from the RHPS data (see Annex A for definitions, means, and standard deviations of the variables used in the regression). To do this, a semi-log estimation was conducted in which the log of yield per ha was regressed on quantities of various inputs and their squared terms, soil fertility and salinity variables, climate-related variables, and district dummies.[10]

The results indicate the following (Table 6.5). First and most obvious is the finding that yield is significantly responsive to nitrogen use, but it is also subject to decreasing marginal returns as captured in the squared term of nitrogen use. The estimates of elasticities at average levels of input use suggest that a 1 percent increase in the use of nitrogen results in a 0.2 percent increase in wheat yield.[11]

---

10 Previous literature mostly uses a log-log functional specification (Zuberi 1989). However, in our case the semi-log form fit better.

11 The estimate is at average nitrogen use in our model, which is 115 kg/ha for wheat (including observations having no use).

TABLE 6.5 Yield response function of wheat

Variable	Log of yield (kg/ha) of wheat	Robust standard errors
Inputs		
Hired labor (hours)	0.000711***	(0.0002)
(Hired labor)²	−1.23e-06***	(0.000)
Family labor (hours)	0.000162	(0.0002)
(Family labor)²	−2.41e-07	(0.000)
Tractor usage (hours/ha)	0.0336***	(0.0126)
(Tractor usage)²	−0.00172*	(0.0010)
Total sprays (number)	0.109***	(0.0294)
(Total sprays)²	−0.0323***	(0.0074)
Nitrogen used (kg/ha)	0.00335***	(0.0011)
(Nitrogen used)²	−1.74e-05***	(0.000)
Was phosphorous applied? (Yes = 1, No = 0)	−0.0396	(0.0718)
Total seed used (kg/ha)	0.000727	(0.0021)
(Total seed used)²	1.28e-06	(0.000)
Groundwater irrigations (number)	0.00609	(0.0099)
(Groundwater irrigations)²	−0.000428	(0.0009)
Canal water irrigations (number)	0.0344***	(0.0097)
(Canal water irrigations)²	−0.00305***	(0.0011)
Resource quality		
Highly fertile soil (Yes = 1, No = 0)	0.237***	(0.0822)
Other factors		
Visit by extension agent (Yes = 1, No = 0)	−0.0308	(0.0314)
District fixed effects	Yes	
Constant	7.106***	(0.1270)
Observations	755	
R-squared	0.555	

Source: Authors' estimates, based on 2012 RHPS (IFPRI/IDS 2012).

Note: * = significant at 10%; ** = significant at 5%; *** = significant at 1%. Some insignificant results are not presented for the sake of brevity. kg = kilograms; ha = hectares.

Surprisingly, the use of phosphorus, included as a dummy variable in the model, did not have a significant impact on yield. This may be because of the large number of observations that did not report any use of phosphorus, little variation in its use across the sample, and its highly correlated use, when reported, with the use of nitrogen.

In addition to the fertilizer variable, all major inputs to wheat production were included, such as hired labor, tractor services, seed, and canal or tube well irrigation. They are generally significant with positive linear terms and declining squared terms, suggesting that there is a diminishing contribution of each input to increasing yield.

Using the elasticity estimated from our yield response function, the optimal (profit-maximizing) value of nitrogen for wheat under farmers' conditions is 125 kg/ha. This is lower than SFRI's recommended value of 183 kg/ha, which is based on experiments undertaken in controlled research environments. The actual level of nitrogen application in our sample (including zero observation) was 115 kg/ha, which is almost equal to the optimum level under the farmers' resource-quality and socioeconomic constraints.

But even at optimal use levels, there are unintended consequences of fertilizer use. The negative implications of the misuse of fertilizer on long-term sustainability of agricultural production have been pointed out by many researchers (Sankaram and Rao 2002; Bumb and Baanante 1996; Rashid et al. 2013). Failure to use fertilizer appropriately leads not only to inefficiencies at the farm level but also to wider resource degradation (Ali and Byerlee 2002; Ahmed and Gautam 2013). Both the overutilization and underutilization of fertilizer and poor management of resources have damaged not only the environment but also soil resources (Conway and Pretty 1991; Bumb and Baanante 1996; NRC 1989). Research from other parts of the world has shown that an imbalance use of urea with phosphorus and potassium results in excessive soil mining, which causes yield stagnation (Concepcion 2007). In developed countries, application of fertilizer nutrients has also been shown to lead to environmental contamination of water supplies and soils (Gruhn, Goletti, and Yudelman 2000).

Fertilizer use produces the most efficient results under the following conditions: fertilizer-responsive varieties are used; a dissolvable form of fertilizer is placed near the root zone of the plant, in the right proportion and at the appropriate time; land is precisely prepared; and other inputs like water are available and applied in a timely manner. While general and site-specific recommendations for fertilizer use along these lines are available in Pakistan, few farmers pay attention to them. The reasons for this are complex and range from exogenous constraints, such as the availability of surface irrigation or rainfall and proper technology, to more internal constraints, like the availability of credit to buy fertilizer in a timely manner, labor cost and availability, or the effort and drudgery associated with adhering precisely to recommended practices.

FIGURE 6.5 Soil nutrient levels, 2003–2009

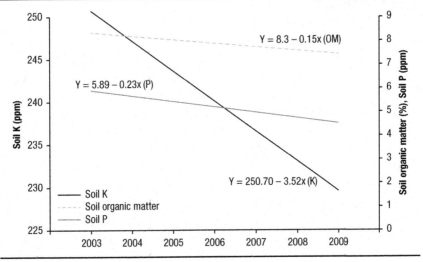

Source: SFRI (2013b).

Note: Potassium (K) is measured against the left y-axis, while the phosphorous (P) and organic matter (OM) are measured against the right y-axis. The soil K and P are measured in parts per million (ppm), and the soil organic matter measures the percentage of organic matter in soil.

Furthermore, fertilizer policies and investments in Pakistan have tended to overlook the promotion of fertilizer-efficiency-enhancing practices. For example, fertilizer subsidies have been primarily allocated to the promotion of urea despite the fact that its use is quickly reaching an optimal level, while other nutrients—namely phosphorus and potassium—are both underutilized by farmers and overlooked by the subsidy policy. Meanwhile, extension agents have had limited success in educating farmers on practices that can improve fertilizer-use efficiency, such as timeliness of application, proper application methods, and appropriate combinations of different fertilizers. The technologies to apply fertilizer in the root zone of the crop are either not accessible to farmers, or farmers are not convinced about the efficacies of these technologies.

In Pakistan, the absence of farming practices that adjust nutrient applications to land resources has resulted in mining of several essential soil micronutrients, such as phosphorus, iron, zinc, and potassium. The underutilization of micronutrients and the reduction in the application of farm manure has decreased organic matter content to threateningly low levels (Figure 6.5).

Pricing Behavior and Government Interventions in the Fertilizer Market

This section examines the relative prices of fertilizer compared to major outputs, the extent of government interventions in the fertilizer industry, and the international and regional competitiveness to infer the costs of these government interventions.

Fertilizer prices—in real terms relative to output prices—have evolved in Pakistan as follows. The grain output prices (weighted average of wheat and rice) increased more than the price of nitrogen, meaning that one unit of nitrogen purchases more grain in 2014 than in 1976. Similar decreases in real urea fertilizer prices are observed in other Asian countries like India, Bangladesh, and Indonesia, but the decline is lowest in Pakistan (Rashid et al. 2013). However, the opposite is true for phosphorus (Figure 6.6). Thus, in terms of input-output prices, farmers did not lose over time, and their profitability did not shrink because of increased nitrogen prices. But the profitability of fertilizer use did fall with the decline in fertilizer-use efficiency in Pakistan, as Figure 6.4 shows.

Against these prices, public subsidies on the production and distribution of fertilizer have also evolved. The most significant subsidy is the provision of natural gas to urea producers at prices that are lower than those charged to other industries and consumers. Approximately 16 percent of total gas consumed in the country is used by the fertilizer industry (HDIP 2013). The government subsidizes fertilizer manufacturing through a dual gas price policy, where one price exists for the fuelstock applicable to the general use of gas, and another price is for gas used in fertilizer manufacturing. The subsidy is made available to all urea producers, although issues with access to gas for smaller producers do exist.[12]

We estimate that the total value of the production subsidy on fertilizer in 2013/2014 was PKR 48 billion (Table 6.6). The subsidy to each firm depended upon the gas field from which their gas was sourced until 2010 (after which prices were constant irrespective of the gas field) and on the installation date of the plant. The largest beneficiary of the subsidy was Fauji Fertilizer, which received a subsidy of PKR 20 billion in 2013/2014. It is

---

12 The approval of new manufacturing plants from the Ministry of Industries and Production is linked to the availability of gas that could be supplied. Some firms complained about facing 35–50 days of gas shortage in a year. No schedule of gas supply was provided, which deterred companies from making operational plans. This shortage increased their fixed and operational costs (Nadeem Tariq, Dawood Hercules Fertilizer Limited, personal communication, August 15, 2013).

FIGURE 6.6 Change in output-input price ratio, 1975/1976–2013/2014

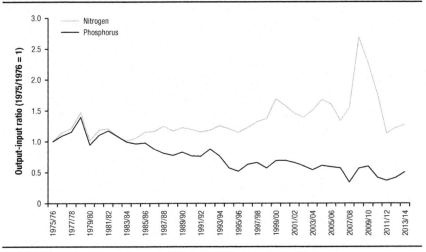

Source: Authors' estimates from NFDC (2014); MNFSR (2013); MNFAL (2007a, 2007b, 2007c).

TABLE 6.6 Subsidies of fertilizer manufacturing through natural gas pricing, 2013/2014

Natural gas network/fertilizer firm	Price (PKR/MBTU)		Gas consumption[a] (billions MBTU)	Subsidy[b] (millions PKR)
	Fuelstock	Feedstock		
Sui Southern Gas Company Limited				
Fauji Fertilizer-Bin Qasim	488.23	123.41	12,325	4,497
Sui Northern Gas Pipelines Limited				
Pakarab	488.23	123.41	3,034	1,107
Dawood Hercules	488.23	123.41	1,446	527
Pak-American	488.23	123.41	3,367	1,228
Engro Chemicals ENVEN	488.23	73.17	3,729	1,548
Mari Gas Limited				
Engro Chemicals	488.23	123.41	2,8931	10,554
Fauji Fertilizer Company	488.23	123.41	55,044	20,081
Fatima Fertilizer	488.23	73.17	20,468	8,495
Total			128,344	48,038

Source: Authors' calculations, based on NFDC (2014). The figures for 2011–2014 are collected from NFDC in Islamabad.

Note: PKR = Pakistani rupees; MBTU = millions of British thermal units. Italicized text represents the source of natural gas for each firm.

[a] The consumption of gas to each firm was reported after adjusting for the difference in pressure of each field.

[b] Subsidy figures for fertilizer are calculated as import quantity multiplied by the difference between the international and domestic prices. The international price is taken as the cost, insurance, and freight price (with US$30 in freight charges) and is inclusive of general sales tax.

important to note that this subsidy would be much higher if we also took into account the subsidy on fuelstock gas, the price for which is also lower than the international price (EIA 2014). However, many other sectors enjoy this price; this is not specific to the fertilizer sector.

In addition to domestic production subsidies, the government subsidizes the importation and distribution of fertilizers. Underutilized capacity arose because of gas shortages in 2008, which forced Pakistan to import urea alongside regular imports of DAP. NFML intervenes when the difference in domestic and international prices becomes large and domestic supply falls short of demand. The intervention is made by importing higher-priced fertilizer and selling it at a lower domestic price. Normally, this intervention is limited to imported urea, but in 2007–2009, for the first time ever, the government intervened in the DAP market through a subsidy on imported DAP.[13] As discussed earlier, in an attempt to further reduce the role of NFML, the government allowed the private sector to import urea and sell it at the domestic price in 2014, while the NFML was to cover the price difference, including transportation and handling charges. However, this decision was not implemented, and the NFML's intervention in the market is costly for the government (Table 6.7).

The government also intervenes in the fertilizer market through its tax policies. In 2001 the federal government exempted urea from the general sales tax (GST), but it withdrew the exemption in 2011, along with exemptions for other agricultural inputs. We estimate the GST revenue (offtake multiplied by price and the tax rate) from urea and DAP at approximately PKR 50 billion in 2013/2014. It appears that the government attempted to even out its loss in revenue to production subsidies with GST collections, although it is unfair to farmers because, as discussed in the next section, little money from the production subsidy is passed on to farmers while they pay 100 percent of the GST.

In 2015, after a long legal battle with the industry, the government imposed a 20 percent Gas Infrastructure Development Cess on all gas consumers, other than domestic consumers. The Gas Infrastructure Development Cess has brought the fuelstock prices closer to international prices, while the difference between fuelstock and feedstock prices will continue.[14]

---

13 The government announced a subsidy on DAP sales for 2014/2015, but it was not applied because of the lack of SOPs to implement this subsidy. However, during 2016, a subsidy of PKR 20 billion on P and K fertilizers was distributed.

14 Feedstock gas is gas used for the manufacturing of chemical products such as fertilizers and pharmaceutical products, while the fuel gas price is for gas used for other purposes.

TABLE 6.7 Subsidies on fertilizer distribution, 2004/2005–2013/2014

Year	(1) Subsidy on imported urea (billions PKR)	(2) Imports of urea (thousands of tons)	(1)/(2) Subsidy per ton of imported urea (PKR/ton)
2004/2005	1.85	307	6,026
2005/2006	4.54	825	5,503
2006/2007	2.05	281	7,295
2007/2008	2.74	181	15,138
2008/2009	17.23	905	19,039
2009/2010	12.87	1,524	8,445
2010/2011	8.41	694	12,118
2011/2012	9.55	1,075	8,884
2012/2013	10.50	833	12,605
2013/2014	4.53	1,200	3,775

Source: Authors' calculations, based on NFDC (2014). The figures for 2011–2014 are collected from NFDC in Islamabad.

Note: PKR = Pakistani rupees. Subsidy figures for urea are calculated as import quantity multiplied by the difference between the international and domestic prices. The international price is taken as the cost, insurance, and freight price (with US$30 in freight charges) and is inclusive of general sales tax.

With all the subsidies and rent-seeking behavior found in Pakistan's fertilizer industry, we might wonder whether the industry is actually competitive in the wider international market for fertilizer. One way to evaluate the industry's competitiveness is to compare international and domestic prices, both with and without these subsidies. Although the government has also provided a distribution subsidy on imported urea, and such subsidies help to stabilize the domestic market, we assume that these leave the domestic prices unchanged. (Note that the distribution subsidy per ton varies significantly across years, depending on the difference between international and domestic prices.) Therefore, direct comparison of domestic prices without the production subsidy and international prices provides an indication of competitiveness in the domestic fertilizer sector.

When viewing the domestic and international prices with the subsidy included, we find that until 2004, the domestic prices of nitrogen closely followed international trends, but despite the gas subsidy those prices remained higher than the FOB (free on board) international prices (Figure 6.7).[15] However, importing urea was not economical because the difference was negligible when shipment, loading/unloading, and in-country transportation costs were added. The domestic prices were kept higher than the FOB

---

15 FOB refers to the prices at the port of shipment, when exporting.

FIGURE 6.7 International versus domestic fertilizer prices, 1995/1996–2013/2014

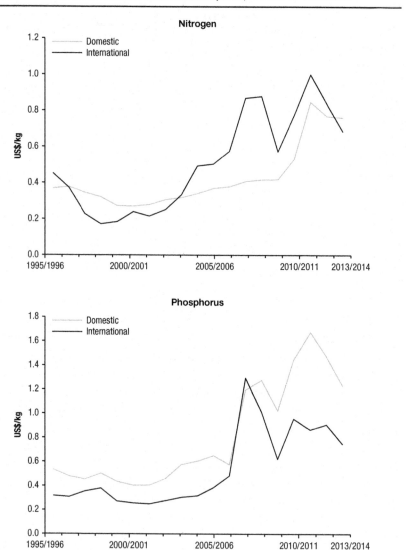

Source: Authors' estimates based on NFDC (2014).
Note: kg = kilograms.

price, perhaps to avoid smuggling. After 2004, until 2011, the domestic prices remained consistently lower than international market prices, and the difference was large enough to cover port and other handling charges, so, in principle, exports were possible. During that time, however, the government restricted fertilizer exports, but smuggling with Afghanistan would have been economical.[16] Thus, domestic manufacturing was competitive in the international market, albeit with the gas subsidy in place.[17]

The trend once again reversed during 2013/2014, when domestic prices became higher than the international prices, despite the gas subsidy on manufacturing, indicating that the sector had once again become uncompetitive with respect to the international market, despite the subsidy. However, domestic prices, for a variety of market structure and policy reasons, did not rise much, and thus the price of imported fertilizer (after covering freight, import value, and in-country distribution charges) remained higher than the domestic price. During 2015/2016, domestic prices exceeded international prices, and imported urea became economically viable, although the private sector did not pursue imports, mainly because of a lack of trust about the consistency of government policies related to import taxes/duties on urea.

What happens when we make the same comparisons without the gas subsidies? To examine this, we adjust the domestic price of urea to account for the gas subsidy by adding the per-unit subsidy to the price. Our analysis, summarized in Figure 6.8, indicates that the domestic unsubsidized price of urea was higher than the international price during 1996–2004, but lower than or equal to the international price after 2004. Our analysis suggests that the removal of the gas subsidy would have made urea producers even more uncompetitive in the international market prior to 2004 as the gap between the domestic and international prices increased. However, the domestic price from 2005 to 2011 was competitive relative to international prices, perhaps because of the presence of oligopolistic industry practices and noncompetitive imports, which led to pricing behavior that did not respond to international price changes.[18]

During 2011–2014, the trend reversed again, and domestic prices without subsidies became higher than international prices. This suggests that during those three years, the removal of the gas subsidy would have made urea

16 The incentive to smuggle urea to India does not exist because of India's higher subsidy: India's retail nitrogen prices with a subsidy remained far lower than Pakistan's throughout the period 1995–2012.

17 This price mechanism permitted the absorption of shocks in international fertilizer prices during 2007 and 2008 without creating panic in Pakistan's domestic market.

18 Our analysis shows that Pakistan is not competitive in the international market, while the CCP study concludes the reverse. The CCP's conclusion is based on eight quarters in 2008 and 2009, when international prices were high, while our conclusion is based on the period 1995–2012 (CCP 2010). In our study, the normalized prices, after adding back the subsidy on domestic prices, are lower than the international price during 2007, 2008, and 2009 as well, but over the longer run they have been higher, especially recently.

FIGURE 6.8 International versus domestic urea prices, with and without subsidy, 1995/1996–2013/2014

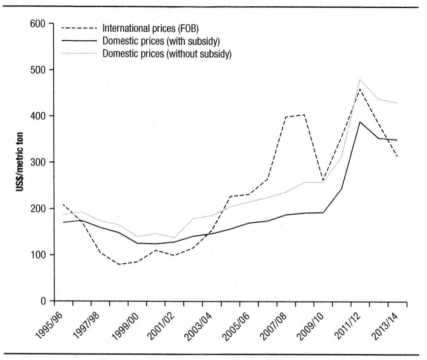

Source: Authors' estimates, based on NFDC (2014) and HDIP (2013).
Note: FOB = freight on board.

producers uncompetitive in the international market, as was the case prior to 2004. Overall, during the past 20 years, the fertilizer manufacturing sector without subsidies was competitive with the international market for only 6 years.

A comparison of fertilizer prices between India and Pakistan, keeping the subsidies intact in both countries, shows that Indian prices are far lower than Pakistani prices, suggesting a higher subsidy at the retail level in India (Figure 6.9). Indian prices after removing the subsidy in both countries, however, became basically equivalent to international market prices but slightly higher than those in Pakistan. Because nitrogen prices in Pakistan were either lower than or equal to international prices during 2004–2011, India during this period could have imported nitrogen fertilizer from Pakistan, rather than from the international market, and enjoyed the proximity advantage with Pakistan. However, Pakistan would never allow that as long as it

FIGURE 6.9 India, Pakistan, and international urea prices, 2003/2004–2013/2014

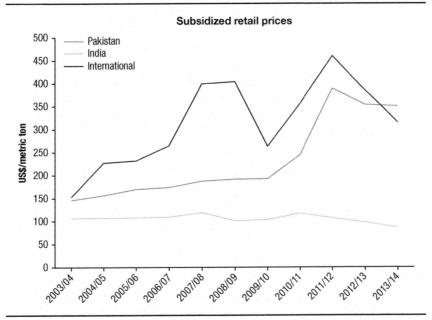

Source: Authors' estimates, based on NFDC (2014); DoP (2012); and HDIP (2013).
Note: India and Pakistan prices are subsidized retail prices.

has a shortage of domestically produced urea, because of gas shortages, which Pakistan has a chance to overcome in the long term because of its proximity to the gas-abundant region of Iran and Central Asia.

Impact of Policy Interventions

This section uses an equilibrium displacement model (EDM) to estimate the impact of exogenous policy shocks on the market for urea, DAP, and selected major crops, including cotton, rice, wheat, and other crops (sugarcane, maize, and all vegetables and fruits). It examines various policy alternatives, singly and in different combinations. These policy alternatives include (1) removing the production subsidy on natural gas, (2) increasing the supply of natural gas, (3) removing the sales tax on fertilizer, and (4) increasing investment on R&D. The analysis allows us to see changes in prices and quantities, identify winners and losers from each intervention, and thereby give policy makers information to help them make more informed decisions on fertilizer; we also give quantitative estimates of various costs and benefits.

The model uses parameters derived from demand and supply equations for the input markets (urea and DAP) and output markets (cotton, rice, wheat, and other crops).[19] (See Annex B for details.) For each crop, we assume that output supply is a function of the respective endogenously determined output price, the prices of its substitute outputs (or complements), and fertilizer prices. In addition, technology is included as an exogenous trend variable in all output supply equations. Crop demand is a function of the crop's own price, the price of its substitutes (or complements), and the income of the consumer (which is an exogenous variable).

The urea and DAP demand equations are a function of their respective prices and the quantity of production of all four crops. The urea supply equation is a function of the factory price of urea and the exogenous quantity of natural gas supplied. The DAP supply equation, similarly, is a function of its own factory price, the price and quantity of natural gas (but with smaller coefficients compared to the urea equation to reflect its reduced role in DAP production), and the price and quantity of phosphorous, which are also exogenous variables.

The marketing margins linking producer and retailer prices, both in input and output markets, are assumed to be fixed at zero, that is, changes in producers' and retailers' prices occur in the same proportions. As such, the model allows us to see the impact of changing the GST, which acts as a wedge between producer and consumer prices in both input and output markets. Improvement in input or output market efficiencies can also be potentially studied by changing this wedge.

Both input and output markets are cleared by equating domestic demand plus exports to domestic supply plus imports so that international trade balances any deficit or surplus in the domestic markets. International trade in the input and output markets is, for exports, a positive function of the domestic price of the relevant commodity and, for imports, a negative function of this price. The distinction between world price and domestic price is established by the fixed import duty/tariff/transportation cost, which is exogenously determined.[20]

These input and output markets are first reduced by substituting the demand equation in the market-clearing equation. Each equation in this

---

19 The model does not differentiate between basmati and other rice varieties because different elasticities for each variety are not available.

20 This again in effect implies that the world price has the same proportional change as domestic prices, unless we conduct a simulation changing the wedge between these prices.

linear system is then totally differentiated and manipulated so that all variables are converted into proportional changes that are functions of the choice of elasticities. (The development of this approach is given in Annexes C and D.) The equations are then used to estimate the impact of exogenous shocks on the variables of interest.

Large numbers of own-price and cross-price elasticities are needed to fully specify the relations in the model and are taken from various sources shown in Annex E.[21]

The model assumes that the elasticities for the variables used in these estimations are constant. The model also assumes no limitations on inputs such as total cropland, irrigation water, or in the case of this chapter's simulations, the quantity of natural gas.

We simulate the results in each scenario with two import elasticities of α_k at 1 and 5 to judge how ease of imports will affect the outcomes. The results of these simulations in terms of actual and percentage changes with respect to the baseline scenario of 2013/2014 are presented in Table 6.8, when α_k is equal to 1, and in Annex F, when α_k is equal to 5.

Policy Scenario 1: Removing the Subsidy on Natural Gas

To completely remove the subsidy on natural gas, the government must exogenously increase the price of fuelstock by 297 percent. The first important impact of this policy is a rise in the factory cost of urea, which shifts the supply curve back because of a higher input cost. This increases the factory price of fertilizer and reduces its domestic supply. However, a higher domestic price creates incentives for importers, so imports increase, with the amount depending upon the import elasticity (which reflects the ease of importing). In the low-elasticity scenario (with an import elasticity of 1), the equilibrium factory price of urea increases by over 10 percent, while with a high import elasticity scenario of 5, it increases by only 4 percent. The price of DAP fertilizer also increases in both scenarios, but to a lesser extent, because one unit of DAP requires less than one-half of the amount of ammonia, which is produced from natural gas, than is used in urea production. Farm gate prices of urea and DAP (including GST) increase parallel to their factory prices, as the difference between the two is only a constant wedge. The increased cost of urea and DAP processing reduces domestic supply and increases imports, and higher farm gate prices lower demand (except in the high import elasticity scenario,

---

21 When certain elasticities are not available but are important, we simulate different levels of these elasticities to understand the sensitivity of our results to particular choices of elasticities.

TABLE 6.8 Simulated changes from 2013/2014 baseline value using EDM for various policy interventions with low import elasticity ($\alpha = 1$)

Variables	Change from 2013/2014 baseline value				
	Scenario 1	Scenario 2	Scenario 3	Scenario 4	Scenario 5
Fertilizer market					
Domestic supply of urea (1,000s MT)	−696 (−14.1)	−574 (−11.6)	120 (2.4)	−576 (−11.7)	280 (5.7)
Domestic supply of DAP (1,000s MT)	−49 (−7.1)	−45 (−6.5)	13 (1.9)	−36 (−5.2)	25 (3.6)
Import supply of urea (1,000s MT)	118 (10.2)	154 (13.3)	35 (3.1)	153 (13.3)	−47 (−4.1)
Import supply of DAP (1,000s MT)	42 (4.5)	55 (5.9)	45 (4.8)	87 (9.3)	−21 (−2.3)
Demand of urea (1,000s MT)	−578 (−9.5)	−420 (−6.9)	155 (2.6)	−423 (−6.9)	233 (3.8)
Demand of DAP (1,000s MT)	−8 (−0.5)	10 (0.6)	58 (3.6)	50 (3.1)	4 (0.2)
Farmer price of urea (PKR/MT)	3729 (10.2)	4860 (13.3)	−5099 (−14)	−1369 (−3.8)	−1498 (−4.1)
Farmer price of DAP (PKR/MT)	3260 (4.5)	4309 (5.9)	−8882 (−12.2)	−5622 (−7.7)	−1653 (−2.3)
Factory price of urea[a] (PKR/MT)	3188 (10.2)	4154 (13.3)	951 (3.1)	4139 (13.3)	−1281 (−4.1)
Factory price of DAP[a] (PKR/MT)	2786 (4.5)	3683 (5.9)	2986 (4.8)	5773 (9.3)	−1412 (−2.3)
Import cost for fertilizer (billion PKR)	15 (15.2)	20 (20.2)	7 (8.7)	21 (24.5)	−6 (−6.3)
Output market					
Overall pressure on output prices (PKR/MT)	0 (−0.1)	0 (−0.4)	0 (−0.1)	0 (0)	0 (0)
Overall trade surplus (billion PKR)	−1 (−0.5)	6 (4.6)	1 (0.8)	0 (0.3)	0 (0.2)
Total crop production gain (billion PKR)	−7 (−0.3)	52 (2.2)	11 (0.5)	4 (0.2)	3 (0.1)
Fertilizer expense for farmers (billion PKR)	4 (1.2)	20 (5.9)	−37 (−10.8)	−29 (−8.5)	−3 (−1)
Production revenue (billion PKR)	−7 (−0.3)	52 (2)	11 (0.4)	4 (0.2)	3 (0.1)
Overall farmer benefit (billion PKR)	−11 (−0.5)	32 (1.4)	48 (2.1)	33 (1.5)	6 (0.3)
Gas expense (billion PKR)	38 (242.4)	40 (251.9)	0 (2.4)	40 (252)	1 (5.6)
Subsidy and others					
Fertilizer revenue (billion PKR)	−8 (−4.8)	0 (−0.1)	9 (5.8)	1 (0.8)	2 (1.3)
Overall manufacturer benefit (billion PKR)	−46 (−32.3)	−40 (−28.2)	9 (6.2)	−38 (−27.1)	1 (0.9)
Production subsidy (urea) (billion PKR)	−47 (−100)	−47 (−100)	1 (2.4)	−47 (−100)	3 (5.6)

(continued)

Variables	Change from 2013/2014 baseline value				
	Scenario 1	Scenario 2	Scenario 3	Scenario 4	Scenario 5
Retail subsidy (DAP) (billion PKR)	0 (0)	0 (0)	0 (0)	0 (0)	0 (0)
Distribution subsidy (billion PKR)	2 (16)	3 (21)	0 (3)	1 (13.3)	−1 (−6.1)
Tax revenue from fertilizer (billion PKR)	1 (1.2)	3 (5.9)	−50 (−100)	−50 (−100)	0 (−1)
All subsidies (billion PKR)	−45 (23.6)	−44 (24.6)	1 (102.5)	−46 (10.9)	2 (103.2)
Investment on R&D (billion PKR)	0 (0)	12 (0)	0 (0)	0 (0)	0 (0)
Total change in govt. revenue (billion PKR)	46 (0)	35 (0)	−51 (0)	−3 (0)	−2 (0)
Consumer crop demand (billion PKR)	−7 (−0.3)	46 (1.9)	10 (0.4)	4 (0.2)	3 (0.1)
Eventual social benefit (billion PKR)	−18 (0)	74 (0)	16 (0)	−5 (0)	8 (0)

Source: Authors' estimates.

Note: Figures in parentheses are percentage changes with respect to the baseline value of 2013/2014. DAP = diammonium phosphate; MT = metric tons; GST = general sales tax; α = trade elasticity of fertilizer; PKR = Pakistani rupees. The results for higher trade elasticity ($\alpha = 5$) are presented in Annex F. The overall social benefit does not incorporate trade loss/profit. We assumed this is already reflected in the loss/gain in crop production. In scenario 1, we remove the subsidy on natural gas; in scenario 2, we increase investment in crop research and development while removing natural gas subsidy; in scenario 3, we remove the GST; in scenario 4, we remove gas subsidy and GST simultaneously; and in scenario 5, we remove the shortage of gas.

[a] Exclusive of GST.

where imports increase more than the decrease in domestic supply, thereby offsetting some of the price rise from higher natural gas prices).

The changes in the fertilizer market trigger effects in the crop markets, which produce impacts on government, farmers, and manufacturers. The lower demand for fertilizer reduces crop output, depending on the output supply elasticity with respect to fertilizer price.[22] This leads to higher output prices. The farmers lose from the lower crop production but benefit from higher output prices and lower production cost as fertilizer demand declines. In the low import elasticity scenario, farmers' overall loss is about PKR 11 billion, or 0.5 percent of the original value of farm production. However, this loss is mitigated and turned into a profit of PKR 15 billion if imports are made flexible enough, as occurs in the simulation with high import elasticity. Although crop output still decreases and output prices increase, both are

---

22 The crop supply elasticities with respect to fertilizer prices used are from Haile, Kalkuhl, and von Braun (2014). This is an international study that reports low crop supply elasticities for Pakistan compared to older studies. One reason for high elasticities in earlier studies may be the low use of fertilizer when these elasticities were estimated. In addition, using the higher elasticities from the earlier literature blows up effects of policy interventions on crop production to what seems to be too high a level.

moderated by higher imports of fertilizers, and the farmer's losses from lower output declines from PKR 7 billion to PKR 3 billion. On the other hand, expenses on fertilizer drop by PKR 19 billion relative to the low import elasticity because of the reduction in fertilizer prices and decrease in fertilizer demand. Thus, the moderating effect of a higher import elasticity and facilitation of imports of fertilizer can be used to lower the impact on farmers from removing gas subsidies.

The government is the biggest net beneficiary, as gas subsidies decline by PKR 46 billion.[23] There is a small change in GST and distribution subsidies, so the net gain to the government is around PKR 42 billion in the high import elasticity scenario and PKR 46 billion in the low import elasticity scenario.

The decrease in crop production also affects international trade. Compared to 2013/2014, the generally higher commodity prices in Pakistan provide incentives to international traders to export more commodities or reduce imports from Pakistan. This causes Pakistan to increase imports of cotton and reduce exports of rice, wheat, and other crops, creating a trade deficit of PKR 1 billion. The trade loss is reduced when the import elasticity of fertilizer is increased.

The urea manufacturers will be the biggest losers in this scenario, as their profit declines by PKR 46 billion in the case of a low fertilizer import elasticity and PKR 58 billion in the case of a high import elasticity. The cost of gas used in fertilizer processing increases by PKR 38 billion and PKR 35 billion in the case of low and high import elasticity, respectively, while revenue from fertilizer sales decreases by PKR 8 billion and PKR 23 billion in the case of low and high import elasticity scenarios, respectively. The greater loss of manufacturers in the case of the liberal import scenario arises because more imports are brought into the country.

With the increase in output prices, consumers' demand for agricultural commodities decreases by PKR 7 billion, although the reduction is only PKR 2 billion if fertilizer imports are more liberally imported. The society as a whole loses by about PKR 5 billion in this scenario.[24]

In this simulation, we assumed that the elasticity of fertilizer supply with respect to the price of natural gas as 0.1 and 0.025 for urea and DAP,

---

23 Because the subsidy arises from an administered price of gas, the government would likely have to charge a cess, or tax, to actually recover these funds. Thus, this value should best be seen as an opportunity cost.

24 The net social gain to society was estimated as the change in the value of crop demand + government revenue + farmers' benefits + manufacturers' benefits.

respectively. As this elasticity may be argued to be low, we also simulated impacts with increased elasticities of 0.4 percent and 0.1, respectively. This further increases the manufacturers' loss, from PKR 46 billion and 58 billion in the scenarios of low and high import elasticity to PKR 70 billion and 116 billion, respectively, mainly because of the greater decline in revenues from fertilizer sales.

Policy Scenario 2: Increasing Investment in Crop Research and Development While Removing the Natural Gas Subsidy

There is little investment in agricultural R&D in Pakistan. This has reduced the flow of innovations to farmers, and, as a result, productivity-led growth has lagged behind compared to other developing countries such as China, India, Brazil, and Turkey (Ahmed and Gautam 2013). In Scenario 1, we created a "fiscal space" for the government to increase R&D investment by eliminating the production subsidy. Here, we assume that 25 percent of this savings, about PKR 12 billion, goes to R&D in the crop sector, implying a 150 percent increase in the R&D budget for agriculture of PKR 8 billion in 2011/2012 (ASTI-PARC 2012). We assume that this brings about a modest increase in crop productivity of 3 percent across the board, thereby shifting the supply curves outward.[25]

The shift in the crop supply curves induced by the R&D expenditures will create growth in the fertilizer sector, while the opposite occurred in Scenario 1. Another important difference is that unlike the earlier scenario, there is a significant time lag between the investment on R&D and returns through enhanced productivity.[26]

For the first year that the new technologies generated from R&D expenses produce a 3 percent increase in crop productivity, the shift in supply curves will increase crop production and lower the crop's prices. More fertilizer is

---

25 This productivity increase might come from a variety of sources, such as improved high-yielding varieties; development and promotion of appropriate input application techniques; improvement in the timely delivery of inputs such as fertilizer, credit, water, and information; development of new crop management models that improve productivity and also reduce postharvest losses; and so forth. We assume that the technological innovations are neutral with regard to fertilizer-use efficiency, so a general 3 percent shift in the overall supply curve occurs, rather than an increase in the fertilizer coefficient in the production function.

26 We assume here a five-year lag period between the time the investment in R&D is made and the return (including additional costs) from the investment starts flowing. The fifth-year values of additional fertilizer costs and income due to the shift in crop supply curve are reported in Scenario 2 of Table 6.8. We assumed a gradual decline in the growth in crop productivity, from 3 percent in the first year to 2.5 percent, 2.0 percent, 1.5 percent, 1.0 percent, and 0 percent in the subsequent years, and we ran the model for five years. We then discounted these benefit streams at a 15 percent rate.

required to produce the larger crop production, which will shift the fertilizer demand curve upward. The greater fertilizer demand increases both the farm and factory prices, and it induces more fertilizer manufacturing and imports. If domestic manufacturers cannot expand production capacity, importers will fill the gap (especially under the high import elasticity scenario). Although the import bill for fertilizer increases, the expanded crop supply reduces output prices and generates a higher trade surplus, which compensates for the higher import bill of fertilizer. We also generated results for four subsequent years, with 0.5 percent less productivity enhancement in each year until the value of the technology gets completely exhausted or the technology becomes completely obsolete.

The discounted benefits of the R&D investment to the farmers are PKR 59 billion in the case of a low import elasticity, and PKR 54 billion under the high import scenario. Despite assuming a modest gain of 3 percent in crop productivity after increasing the R&D investment, the gains to farmers as well as to the society are the highest of all scenarios. Despite having a similar cost (approximately PKR 12 billion), the benefits derived from this policy are more than double those from providing a subsidy on phosphate fertilizer.

Another advantage of this scenario is that, except for the manufacturers, all stakeholders including government benefit from this intervention. In fact manufacturers also benefit, through the increased fertilizer price as well as the expansion in production of fertilizer, and their losses decrease by 15 percent compared to the case when only the subsidy on gas is removed. The government benefits from the savings from eliminating subsidies, as well as increased GST from enhanced fertilizer demand. Consumers benefit from reduced output prices because of the expansion of crop production. International competitiveness increases and leads to an improvement in the trade surplus. Additional production creates new jobs and businesses in the agricultural sector.

The 25 percent investment in R&D is capable of reducing all negative impacts of removing gas subsidies, when both policy scenarios are combined together. The combined interventions reduce the urea demand by only 7 percent compared to 10 percent (in case of low import elasticity) when only gas subsidies are removed. Crop production gains become highly positive, at PKR 52 billion, instead of the decline of PKR 7 billion when the policy of a removal of the gas subsidy alone is applied. Although government savings decline by PKR 12 billion, farmers gain substantially, by PKR 32 billion, when both policies are combined, as opposed to the loss of 11 billion when the gas subsidy alone was removed. Similarly, international crop trade becomes positive with the combined policy.

Table 6.9 shows the beneficiaries of all interventions discussed above. For instance, investment in enhancing agricultural productivity, while removing the subsidy on feedstock gas, the energy source for urea manufacturing, will have positive outcomes for consumers from higher crop production, increase farmers' benefits, raise government revenues, and benefit society overall.

Policy Scenario 3: Removal of the General Sales Tax

The removal of the 17 percent GST on prices of urea and DAP will immediately reduce fertilizers' cost to farmers, while, at the same time, raising the price for manufacturers as the tax wedge is removed. With this intervention, different reactions occur in all markets, and the final outcome again depends upon the import elasticity of fertilizer.[27] In our model, the eventual decline in urea and DAP prices at the farm gate was around 14 percent and 12 percent, respectively. These lower prices also increase fertilizer demand, which pushes the factory prices of urea and DAP upward by 3 percent and 5 percent, respectively, as imports start competing with domestic manufacturers. The higher prices increase the domestic supply of urea and DAP by about 2 percent.[28] The reduction of prices at the farm gate can get close to the full value of the GST (17 percent) if import elasticity is higher. However, a higher import elasticity will reduce the impact on factory prices, and thus domestic supply further declines as imports are encouraged.

Overall, the greatest beneficiaries of the removal of the GST are farmers, as they save nearly PKR 37 billion in fertilizer cost, and their revenue from crop production also increases by about PKR 11 billion. The trade surplus in these crops increases by PKR 1 billion. Urea and DAP manufacturers gain PKR 8 billion because of higher factory prices and greater demand. However, their gains are reduced to PKR 3 billion if the high import elasticity is assumed, as some of the high fertilizer demand is captured by importers. Government revenue is affected, as the government loses tax revenues equal to PKR 50 billion. Another beneficiary of the GST removal from fertilizer sales is consumers, as their crop demand increases by 0.4 percent, or PKR 10 billion.

---

27 Here we first explain the results with a low import elasticity of 1, and then generalize to an impact of a high import elasticity of 5.

28 The model assumes that any additional input, including gas, will be freely available to produce equilibrium quantities of fertilizer (as well as crops). One may, however, obtain a small increase in fertilizer supply, as in this scenario, through enhanced efficiency even if additional gas is not available.

Policy Scenario 4: Removal of the Gas Subsidy and GST Simultaneously

Some policy makers would like to see the fertilizer sector without any tax, but also without production subsidies, so we analyze the impact of this scenario in this fourth simulation. The result is a shift of the supply curve of fertilizer upward due to a decrease in the subsidy, as well as a shift of the demand curve upward because of the removal of GST. The net results thus depend on the particular supply and demand elasticities. The removal of the GST reduces the price to farmers by 17 percent, but the cost of natural gas nearly triples, and that input is about 40 percent of the total cost for urea manufacturers. Thus, the effect of the removal of the gas subsidy is much greater than the tax reduction. In summary, under the assumed elasticities in our model, the total availability of urea decreases despite rising demand from the lower prices seen by farmers. However, in the case of DAP, the demand (increases) and farmer price (decreases) move in opposite directions. The factory prices and fertilizer supply both increase, although the response is relatively low.

The factory prices of urea and DAP increase by 13 percent and 9 percent, but their farm gate prices decrease by 4 percent and 7 percent, respectively, as farmers do not have to pay the GST. This decreases the supply of urea and DAP by 12 percent and 5 percent, respectively, mainly because of the increased manufacturing cost as the gas subsidy is removed. The import cost of fertilizer rises in the low import elasticity scenario by 24 percent to PKR 21 billion. The import cost is reduced slightly (by PKR 1 billion) by increasing the import elasticity of fertilizer. This reduction occurs because the price of fertilizer falls by a greater percentage as imports come more easily into the country, and therefore more urea fertilizer can be obtained for about the same total cost.

This change in policy leaves the government with little change in revenue, despite its loss of PKR 50 billion from the GST, because it saves PKR 47 billion from the removal of the gas subsidy.

The 7 percent decrease in the demand for urea lowers crop production and creates upward pressure on prices, which costs the economy PKR 4 billion, without much change in the trade deficit. Farmers gain PKR 33 billion from this scenario from increased output prices and lower fertilizer prices. The farmers' benefit from the policy, however, can be improved to PKR 70 billion with the higher import elasticity of fertilizer. Manufacturers are the greatest losers in this scenario, as their gas expenses increase, which is further intensified with the higher import elasticity because demand is captured by importers. The social cost of this reshuffling would be PKR 5 billion, which is turned into a social profit of PKR 20 billion when the higher import elasticity is assumed.

Policy Scenario 5: Removing the Shortage of Gas

The fertilizer industry, as of 2013/2014, was operating at around 72 percent of its installed capacity. One of the key factors affecting the future and viability of the industry will be the availability of natural gas to the sector.[29]

In this scenario, we assume that surplus gas is available, and we thus increase the amount of natural gas supplied to the fertilizer industry by 28 percent while keeping all other exogenous effects constant.[30]

The policy scenario causes a shift in the supply curve outward and decreases the prices of urea and DAP by 4 percent and 2 percent, respectively, both at the farm and factory levels, while increasing the equilibrium quantities of domestic supply by about 6 percent and 4 percent. As domestic prices decrease, imports become less competitive and are reduced by 4 percent and 2 percent, respectively (the decrease in fertilizer prices and imports is higher under the high import elasticity scenario, implying a greater increase in domestic supply as well as demand). The domestic demand of urea and DAP increases by 4 percent and 0.2 percent, respectively. The quantities of domestically produced wheat, cotton, rice, and other crops increase and put downward pressure on crop prices. Given the baseline values in 2013/2014, the value of domestic production of all crops increases by about PKR 3 billion, while the trade surplus for these crops increases insignificantly.

Farmers see a gain of nearly PKR 6 billion; half of this comes from an increase in the value of crop production (despite a decrease in prices), and the remaining half comes from lower fertilizer prices. Urea manufacturers see an increase in revenue of PKR 2 billion, but half of this is consumed by an increase in processing cost. Consumers also see a gain, of PKR 3 billion. The government subsidy on gas increases by PKR 2 billion.

Although the removal of the gas shortage benefits all stakeholders, except the government, the extent of benefits is relatively small. Moreover, removal of the gas shortage relies on the exploitation of a scarce economic resource in the country. It is estimated that, with the existing rate of use, the most extensive recoverable gas reserves available to the fertilizer sector, from the Mari

---

29 This analysis does not take into account the rapid depletion of the supply of natural gas in Pakistan and the cost to other sectors if gas is allocated from them to the fertilizer sector.

30 The model, however, only reflects use of gas that is needed by a firm to reach equilibrium demand.

TABLE 6.9 Benefits for stakeholders of policy interventions with low import elasticity ($\alpha = 1$)

Intervention	Consumers	Farmers	Manufacturers	Government	Society
Removing subsidy on feedstock gas				■	
Investing in R&D and removing gas subsidy	■			■	■
Removing GST	■				■
Removing both gas subsidy and GST	■				■
Removing gas shortage	■	■	■		■

Source: Authors.

Note: Shaded box indicates that stakeholder benefits. α = trade elasticity of fertilizer; R&D = research and development; GST = general sales tax.

field, will be exhausted in 16 years.[31] This depletion rate suggests that the government should start planning now for a gradual shift from domestic supply to imports, which is inevitable anyway, rather than promoting the speedy exploitation of a scarce resource, waiting until it is completely exhausted, and then passing through a stressful transition toward imports.

Table 6.9 shows beneficiaries of all five interventions discussed above. For instance, investment in R&D while removing the subsidy on feedstock gas will have positive outcomes for consumers from higher crop production and will increase farmers' benefits, raise government revenues, and benefit society overall.

Conclusions

Historically, Pakistan has offered a favorable setting for growth in fertilizer uptake and increased agricultural production. Beginning in the mid-1960s, the rich alluvial soils; an extensive canal irrigation system, supplemented by tube wells; and the historically rapid adoption of fertilizer-responsive wheat and rice varieties have created conditions to generate rapid increases in fertilizer demand. On the supply side, Pakistan's perceived abundance of natural gas aided in the rapid construction of a domestic fertilizer industry. That

---

31 According to data from the Ministry of Petroleum and Natural Resources, the balance of the recoverable reserve of gas from the Mari field as of December 31, 2014, was 3,382 billion cubic feet, and the utilization rate during 2014 was 211 billion cubic feet. This means the field's gas reserves will last for no more than 16 years. This is also recognized by IRG (2011) in its report on page 17.

perception has proved to be false, as evidenced by the serious shortage of gas in the country.

The general policy emphasis on building domestic production capacity and promoting urea use among farmers also occurred at the expense of a more efficient and balanced use of other nutrients, such as phosphate and potassium, resulting in a long-term trend of declining fertilizer-use efficiency and growing resource degradation. Meanwhile, policies to encourage the industry have resulted in a high concentration of capacity in the hands of a small number of manufacturers, and evidence of anticompetitive behavior is emerging (CCP 2010). Despite policies to encourage the industry and the government's effort to control price shocks through subsidies, the price of phosphorus remains highly dependent on price fluctuations in international markets due to Pakistan's high dependence on imported DAP.

Pakistan's fertilizer industry, valued at an estimated US$3.57 billion in 2013/2014, has been operating at approximately 75 percent of capacity in recent years, despite subsidies on both production and distribution. These two sources together total about PKR 53 billion in subsidies, or 14 percent of the fertilizer market value in 2013/2014. The subsidies are highly skewed toward urea, while other nutrients remain subject to international price trends.

Various policies, regulations, and organizations control the pricing, quality, promotion, manufacturing, importation, and distribution of fertilizer in Pakistan. The elaborate marketing rules provided sweeping and discretionary powers to farm-level controllers, who represent the extension wings of provincial agriculture departments. The controllers' powers included stopping or limiting sales, sealing stocks, and fixing prices. Such powers, along with the control of the gas supply and prices at the macro level, limited entry into fertilizer processing and marketing, inducing an oligopolistic cartel (CCP 2010 and our analysis).

Our analysis found that various factors positively influence fertilizer applications. These factors include the use of fertilizer-responsive crop varieties and the availability of irrigation water. Moreover, fertilizer use was not closely related to soil or land types, indicating farmers' laxity to adjust use according to their own resource base and holding size. Our survey found that smaller farms applied higher doses of fertilizer on a per-hectare basis.

The NFDC brings various stakeholders together for issue resolution and policy formulation. However, not enough attention appears to be given to policies that promote a balanced use of fertilizer and environmentally friendly products and efficient application methods. The provincial soil fertility research institutes do a good job of analyzing farmers' soil and water samples to evaluate the nutrient and productivity status of their lands and thus to advise them in adjusting nutrient application according to the needs of the specific site. However, plot-level data collected in RHPS Round 1.5 suggest that this had almost no impact, as we found that farmers did not adjust fertilizer use enough to be consistent with the SFRI recommendations such as using urea and phosphate fertilizers in a 2:1 ratio or applying more fertilizer on poor and saline soils. A more-rigorous campaign to educate farmers to adjust fertilizer use according to the natural resource endowment needs to be initiated by the provincial agriculture departments.

An EDM was developed to examine the fertilizer market and four related major agricultural product markets. The markets cleared via trade linkages to international markets and by equating supply and demand. Using the specified model, we simulated the effects of various government policies in the fertilizer and output markets, including trade, and looked at the gains to government, consumers, farmers, and manufacturers. Our results suggest that removing the gas subsidy results in a potential gain in government revenues, if a tax is used to raise the gas price (see footnote 23) but losses to manufacturers, consumers, and farmers occur. Removing the gas subsidy on urea manufacturers' key input, and the GST charged on farmers' purchases of fertilizer, simultaneously reduces farmers' expenses and increases manufacturers' expenses, but the government's potential gain is nullified. Increasing gas supply results in small benefits to consumers, manufacturers, and farmers, but government expenditure also increases because of the increased gas subsidy. Removing the GST alone results in benefits similar to those observed in increasing the gas supply, but the government loses much more revenue. Our model suggests that removing the gas subsidy and investing in agriculture R&D will result in the highest social benefit, where all major stakeholders benefit at least to some degree and the return to the society is highest. An additional advantage of R&D investment compared to other scenarios would be the highest increase in agricultural productivity and the generation of trade surplus, which will create new jobs, stimulate overall economic development, and help alleviate poverty in rural areas (Schneider and Gugerty 2011). As growth in the industrial sector is closely linked with agricultural sector growth, this will induce overall economic development in the country.

Basic changes in the philosophy and direction in fertilizer processing, marketing, and use are required to exploit the full potential of the industry without damaging the environment, and to safeguard the sustainability of agricultural resources. Our recommendations follow.

With respect to fertilizer manufacturing, policy should move away from encouraging expansion based on subsidies to promote a competitive use and modernization of existing capacity, thereby improving efficiency and preparing the industry for an era with fewer subsidies and more international competition, both in gas and fertilizer prices. Our findings also suggest that the production subsidy on gas should be removed, because doing so will not harm farmers or consumers to a great extent and the high profit in the industry will enable these firms to absorb these shocks.

However, the sector should be closely protected with antitrust laws, and approaches should be considered to distribute gas in ways that are closer to market outcomes, such as diverting more gas to efficient firms. A broad fertilizer policy should be considered to address issues of all stakeholders. A Fertilizer Board, consisting of a group of relevant stakeholders, could help monitor the performance of the sector, including pricing, import strategies, and other provisions of the policy.

Incentives for the industry need to be redesigned to reflect several dimensions in the outlook for world and domestic fertilizer and natural gas markets. We compared domestic fertilizer prices without subsidies to international fertilizer prices and found the former generally higher than the latter, suggesting that the fertilizer industry does not have much of an opportunity to sell its product in international markets. Also, a key issue is the outlook for natural gas, because domestic supplies may disappear within a decade or so. The questions are how Pakistan should prepare itself for the scenario of running its fertilizer plants with imported gas and whether importing fertilizer directly makes more sense. Given the limited reserves of natural gas, it seems unlikely that Pakistan will become an exporter, even though the CCP analysis makes some suggestions along these lines (CCP 2010). However, fertilizer trade with India may become a possibility if both countries remove subsidies on fertilizer.

With respect to fertilizer marketing, the policy focus needs to change from controlling fertilizer markets, the existing norm, to freeing the market to improve efficiency. First, laws need to be rationalized, and regulators should be allowed to operate only within some clear parameters of market failure. Second, antitrust laws need to be enforced at district levels as well, and standards for animal manure, micronutrients, plant growth–promoting rhizobacteria, and so on should be developed and strictly enforced. Farmers need to be educated about these standards so they can create demand for these products.

With respect to fertilizer promotion among farmers, our results clearly show that future policy and investment emphasis should be on improving fertilizer-use efficiency rather than promoting higher per-hectare use of fertilizer. To foster this, knowledge-based agriculture should be promoted, where farmers become aware of and trained for the use of various technological options to improve fertilizer efficiency. This support will require assessments of the capacity of agricultural extension and soil fertility labs to provide more-advanced consulting to farmers. For example, can computer-based models be developed to synchronize fertilizer use with resource quality, in order to meet plot-specific needs? These models could identify efficient fertilizer application methods such as placement, fertigation, or machinery that would be standardized for local conditions. Other ways to enhance efficiency, which can be examined for their economic value, include more efficient fertilizer materials, such as plant growth–promoting rhizobacteria, slow release fertilizer, animal manure, and micronutrients, as well as more efficient crop varieties, especially for barani areas.

Finally, issues for further research should include those of inventory management, fertilizer stocks, and the relationship of the domestic industry to the international market. Analyses of reasons that intermittent shortages of fertilizer occur would be valuable: shortages might be due to poor planning of imports or issues of allocation of public-sector supplies at the local level. Other subjects to consider include the creation of fertilizer stocks (perhaps held in the private sector but paid for by the government) to help counter sudden international shocks in fertilizer prices, or the encouragement of strategic trade negotiations to minimize fertilizer subsidies jointly with India rather than entering into a fertilizer subsidy war with India, which would not be beneficial to either country.

In summary, an opportunity exists to strengthen the fertilizer industry in Pakistan and, in turn, to strengthen the prospects for sustainable agricultural production with continued productivity growth. However, the policy and investments required to move the entire fertilizer sector—manufacturers, dealers, farmers, policy makers, and the civil service—in the right direction are challenging.

References

Agritech. 2014. "Our Company." http://www.pafl.com.pk/our-company. Accessed July 25, 2014 .

Ahmed, A. S., and M. Gautam. 2013. *Increasing Agricultural Productivity*. Pakistan Policy Note 6. Washington, DC: World Bank.

Ali, M. 1990. "The Price Response of Major Crops in Pakistan: An Application of the Simultaneous Equation Model." *The Pakistan Development Review* 29 (3/4): 305–325.

Ali, M., and D. Byerlee. 2002. "Productivity Growth and Resource Degradation in Pakistan's Punjab. A Decomposition Analysis." *Economic Development and Cultural Change* 50 (4): 839–863.

ASTI-PARC (Agricultural Science and Technology Indicators and Pakistan Agricultural Research Council). 2012. *Country Note July 2012*. Islamabad and Washington, DC.

Bumb, B., and C. Baanaate. 1996. *The Role of Fertilizer in Sustaining Food Security and Protecting the Environment in 2020*. 2020 Vision Discussion Paper 17. Washington, DC: International Food Policy Research Institute.

Byerlee, D., and A. Siddiq. 1994. "Has the Green Revolution Been Sustained? The Quantitative Impact of the Seed-Fertilizer Revolution in Pakistan Revisited." *World Development* 22 (9): 1345–1361.

CCP (Competition Commission of Pakistan). 2010. *Competition Assessment Study of the Fertilizer Sector in Pakistan*. Islamabad: Competition Commission of Pakistan, World Bank.

Concepcion, R. N. 2007. *Sustainable Fertilization Management of Croplands: The Philippines Scenario*. Bangkok: Food and Agriculture Organization. http://www.fao.org/docrep/010/ag120e/AG120E16.htm.

Conway, G. R., and J. N. Pretty. 1991. *Unwelcome Harvest: Agriculture and Pollution*. London: Earthscan Publications.

Din, M. S., and H. S. Jafry. 2007. *Pakistan Fertilizer Sector Review*. Karachi: IGI Securities.

DoF (Department of Fertilizer). 2012. *Indian Fertilizer Scenario 2012*. New Delhi: Department of Fertilizer, Ministry of Chemicals and Fertilizers, Government of India.

EIA (Energy Information Administration). 2014. "Natural Gas." http://www.eia.gov/dnav/ng/hist/rngwhhdd.htm. Accessed September 25, 2014.

FAO (Food and Agriculture Organization of the United Nations). 2014. "Food Balance/Food Balance Sheets." http://faostat3.fao.org/faostat-gateway/go/to/browse/FB/FBS/E. Accessed July 25, 2014.

FFC (Fauji Fertilizer Company Limited). 2014. "About Us." http://www.ffc.com.pk/company-profile.aspx. Accessed July 25, 2014.

Gruhn P., F. Goletti, and M. Yudelman. 2000. *Integrated Nutrient Management, Soil Fertility, and Sustainable Agriculture: Current Issues and Future Challenges*. Food, Agriculture, and the Environment Discussion Paper 32. Washington, DC: International Food Policy Research Institute.

Haile, M. G., M. Kalkuhl, and J. von Braun. 2014. "Inter- and Intra-Seasonal Crop Acreage Response to International Food Prices and Implications of Volatility." *Agricultural Economics* 45 (6): 693–710.

Hannah, L., and J. A. Kay. 1977. *Concentration in Modern Industry: Theory, Measurement and the UK Experience*. London: Macmillan.

Hassan Ul, M., and P. Pradhan. 1998. *Coordinated Services for Irrigated Agriculture in Pakistan*. Proceedings of the IWMI National Workshop, Lahore, October 29–30.

HDIP (Hydrocarbon Development Institute of Pakistan). 2013. *Pakistan Energy Yearbook 2012*. Islamabad: Hydrocarbon Development Institute of Pakistan, Ministry of Petroleum and Natural Resources, Government of Pakistan.

Hudson, D., and D. Ethridge. 2009. *The Pakistani Cotton Industry: Impacts of Policy Changes*. Lubbock: Texas Tech University.

Hussain, A. 2011. *Seed Industry in Pakistan*. Paper presented at World Bank Roundtable Discussion on Agriculture and Water, Islamabad, March 10–11.

IFPRI/IDS (International Food Policy Research Institute/Innovative Development Strategies). 2012. *Pakistan Rural Household Panel Survey*. Rounds 1 and 1.5 dataset. Washington, DC: IFPRI; Islamabad: IDS.

IRG (International Resource Group). 2011. *Pakistan Integrated Energy Model (Pak-IEM)*. Final Report, Volume II, Policy Analyses Report, ADB TA-4982 PAK. Prepared for Asian Development Bank and Ministry of Planning and Development, Government of Pakistan.

Kaneda, H. 1969. "Economic Implications of the 'Green Revolution' and the Strategy of Agricultural Development in West Pakistan." *The Pakistan Development Review* 2: 111–143.

Khan, S. A. 2014. "DAP Sales Plunge on Subsidy Issue." *Dawn*, July 12.

MNFAL (Ministry of Food, Agriculture and Livestock). 2007a. *Agricultural Statistics of Pakistan*, vol. 4 *1981–1990*. Islamabad: Ministry of Food, Agriculture and Livestock, Government of Pakistan.

———. 2007b. *Agricultural Statistics of Pakistan*, vol. 5 *1991–2000*. Islamabad: Ministry of Food, Agriculture and Livestock, Government of Pakistan.

———. 2007c. *Agricultural Statistics of Pakistan*, vol. 3 *1971–1980*. Islamabad: Ministry of Food, Agriculture and Livestock, Government of Pakistan.

MNFSR (Ministry of National Food Security and Research). 2013. *Agricultural Statistics of Pakistan 2011–2012*. Islamabad: Ministry of National Food Security and Research, Government of Pakistan.

Nazli, H., S. H. Haider, and A. Tariq. 2012. *Supply and Demand for Cereals in Pakistan, 2010–2030*. IFPRI Discussion Paper 01222. Washington, DC: International Food Policy Research Institute.

NFDC (National Fertilizer Development Centre). 1998. *Pakistan Fertilizer Related Statistics*. Islamabad: National Fertilizer Development Centre, Planning Commission, Government of Pakistan.

———. 2002. *Pakistan Fertilizer Related Statistics*. Islamabad: National Fertilizer Development Centre, Planning Commission, Government of Pakistan.

———. 2008. *Pakistan Fertilizer Related Statistics*. Islamabad: National Fertilizer Development Centre, Planning Commission, Government of Pakistan.

———. 2014. "Statistics." www.nfdc.gov.pk/stat.html. Accessed June 20, 2014.

NRC (National Research Council). 1989. *Alternative Agriculture*. Washington, DC: National Academy Press.

PFL (Pakarab Fetilizers Limited). 2014. "Company Overview." http://www.fatima-group.com/pakarabfertilizers/companyoverview.php. Accessed July 25, 2014.

PPI (Pakistan Press International). 2012. "Gas Shortage: Fertiliser Manufacturers Claim Losses of Nearly Rs5b." *The Express Tribune,* November 21.

Quddus, M. A., M. W. Siddiqi, and M. M. Riaz. 2008. "The Demand for Nitrogen, Phosphorus and Potash Fertilizer Nutrients in Pakistan." *Pakistan Economic and Social Review* 46 (2): 101–116.

Rashid, S., P. A. Dorosh, M. Malek, and S. Lemma. 2013. "Modern Input Promotion in Sub-Saharan Africa: Insights from Asian Green Revolution." *Agricultural Economics* 44: 705–721.

Sankaram, A., and P. Rao. 2002. "Perspectives of Soil Fertility Management with a Focus on Fertilizer Use for Crop Productivity." *Current Science* 82 (7): 797–807.

Schneider, K., and M. K. Gugerty. 2011 "Agricultural Productivity and Poverty Reduction: Linkages and Pathways." *The Evans School Review* 1 (1): 56–74.

SFRI (Soil Fertility Research Institute). 2013a. *Fertilizer Response Curve Studies*. Lahore: Soil Fertility Research Institute, Punjab Agriculture Department, Government of Pakistan.

———. 2013b. *Nutrient Depletion over Time*. Lahore: Soil Fertility Research Institute, Punjab Agriculture Department, Government of Pakistan.

Zuberi, H. A. 1989. "Production Function, Institutional Credit and Agricultural Development in Pakistan." *The Pakistan Development Review* 28 (1): 43–55.

Annex A: Definitions and Summary Statistics

TABLE A6.1 Definitions of variables used in the regression

Variable name	Variable definition
Dependent variable	
Yield of wheat (kg/ha)	Natural log of kilograms of wheat produced per hectare
Input variables	
Nitrogen used (kg/ha)	Total kilograms of nitrogen consumed per ha
Tractor usage (hours/ha)	Total number of hours for which tractors were used per ha
Family labor (hours)	Number of hours per ha for which family labor was used
Hired labor (hours)	Number of hours per ha for which hired labor was used
Number of pesticide sprays	Total number of pesticide sprayings on the plot
Total seed used (kg/ha)	Total kilograms of seed or seedlings used per ha
Groundwater irrigations (no)	Number of groundwater irrigations applied on the plot
Canal water irrigations (no)	Number of canal water irrigations applied on the plot
Age of the household head (years)	Age in years of household head
Average education of household (years)	Average number of education years of entire household
Indicator variables (Yes = 1, No = 0)	
Visit by extension agent	Extension agent visited the household = 1 and 0 otherwise
Seed was registered after 2005	The farmer used the seed registered after 2005 = 1 and 0 otherwise
Loss experienced during harvesting	Household experienced loss in production during harvesting of crop = 1 and 0 otherwise
Loss due to natural disaster	Household experienced loss in production due to floods, drought, frost, and so forth = 1 and 0 otherwise
Loss due to pests	Household experienced loss in production due to pests = 1 and 0 otherwise
Plot experienced salinity	Presence of salinity on plot as reported by respondent = 1 and 0 otherwise
Highly fertile soil	High quality of soil as reported by the respondent = 1 and 0 otherwise
Manure application	Whether manure was applied during the rabi 2011/2012 season = 1 and 0 otherwise

Note: kg = kilogram; ha = hectare. Each of the values was standardized by the cultivated land size in hectares.

TABLE A6.2 Summary statistics of the variables used in the regression

Variables	Mean	SD
Agricultural output		
Yield of wheat (kg/ha)	2,760.30	1,061.80
Inputs		
Canal water irrigations (no)	2.73	4.12
Groundwater irrigations (no)	4.66	5.41
Hired labor (hours/ha)	97.37	154.10
Family labor (hours/ha)	130.40	139.70
Number of pesticide sprays	1.02	1.10
Nitrogen used (kg/ha)	114.70	57.60
Age of the household head (years)	47.17	12.67
Average education of household (years)	6.43	8.47
Tractor usage (hours/ha)	8.01	4.39
Total seed used (kg/ha)	141.20	40.95
Extension, loss, seeds, and soil health (proportion answering yes)		
Was phosphorous applied?	0.83	0.38
Manure application	0.26	0.44
Plot experienced salinity	0.05	0.22
Highly fertile soil	0.96	0.20
Loss experienced during harvesting	0.06	0.24
Loss due to pests	0.04	0.19
Loss due to a natural disaster	0.20	0.40
Visit by extension agent	0.20	0.40
Seed was registered after 2005	0.61	0.50

Source: Authors' estimates, based on IFPRI/IDS (2012).

Note: SD = standard deviation. These statistics are for 755 observations that are used to estimate our yield response function.

Annex B: Initial Equations for the EDM Model

Crop market

$$Q_i^s = f(P_i^f, P_j^f, P_k, T_i)$$

$$Q_i^d = h(P_i, P_j, C_i)$$

where Q is the quantity of ith output (i = 1, 2, 3, 4, with each number representing a different crop: cotton, rice, wheat, and other crops[32]); P_i is ith domestic commodity price at the equilibrium where supply and demand curves cross each other; P_j is the price of all other commodities, where $j \neq i$; P_k is the domestic price of fertilizer k (k = u and p fertilizer, that is, urea and DAP); T is an exogenous technology variable or constant shifter in ith crop production; C_i is the income of the consumer for the ith crop; and the superscripts s and d represent domestic production, and domestic demand, respectively.

$$Q_i^d = Q_i^s + I_i$$

$$I_i = l(P_i)$$

$$P_i = P_i^f(1 + t_i)$$

$$P_i^f = P_i^w(1 + z_i)$$

where I_i is quantity import supply of ith commodity; P_i^f is the factory price of ith commodity; t_i is the general sales tax on ith crop. P_i^w is the world price of the ith crop, and z_i is the import duty/tariff/transportation cost, which establishes the difference between the world price and domestic price.

Urea market

$$Q_k^s = m(Q_g, P_g, P_k^f, Q_{po}, P_{po})$$

$$Q_k^d = r(P_k, Q_i^s)$$

where Q_k and P_k are quantity and prices of kth fertilizer, respectively; P_k^f is factory price of kth fertilizer; the superscripts and subscripts s, d, g, po are for supply, demand, world, natural gas, and phosphate, respectively.

$$Q_k^d = Q_k^s + I_k$$

$$I_k = v(P_k)$$

---

32 We do not differentiate between basmati and other rice varieties, mainly because of data constraints.

$$P_k = P_k^f (1 + t_k)$$

$$P_k^f = P_k^w (1 + z_k)$$

where Q_k^d, Q_k^s is the quantity demanded and supplied of kth fertilizer, respectively. I_k is the import of fertilizer, and t_k is the general sales tax on fertilizer. P_k^w is the world price of fertilizer, and z_k is import duty/tariff/transportation cost and represents the difference between the domestic and world price.

Annex C: Transformation of Equations

The following shows how linear equations are transformed to elasticities that yield marginal impacts. We transform the following equation for wheat:

$$Q_i^s = f(P_i^f, P_j^f, P_u, P_p, T_i)$$

In its linear form, the above equation becomes

$$Q_1^s = \zeta_1 + \zeta_2\left(P_1^f\right) + \zeta_3\left(P_2^f\right) + \zeta_4\left(P_3^f\right) + \zeta_5\left(P_4^f\right) + \zeta_6(P_u) + \zeta_7(P_p) + \zeta_8 T_1 + u_1 \ (a)$$

Where Q_1^s, the domestic production of wheat, is a function of P_1^f, the factory price of wheat—and shifters include P_2^f, P_3^f, and P_4^f, which are factory prices of rice, cotton, and other crops, respectively; P_u is the price of urea; and P_p is the price of DAP; while T is a technology adoption shifter.

Total differentiation of equation (a) yields

$$dQ_1^s = \frac{\partial Q_1^s}{\partial P_1^f} dP_1^f + \frac{\partial Q_1^s}{\partial P_2^f} dP_2^f + \frac{\partial Q_1^s}{\partial P_3^f} dP_3^f + \frac{\partial Q_1^s}{\partial P_4^f} dP_4^f + \frac{\partial Q_1^s}{\partial P_u} dP_u + \frac{\partial Q_1^s}{\partial P_p} dP_p + \frac{\partial Q_1^s}{\partial T_1} dT_1$$

Multiplying both sides by $\frac{1}{Q_1^s}$ and expanding the right-hand side by

$$\frac{P_1^f}{P_1^f}, \frac{P_2^f}{P_2^f}, \frac{P_3^f}{P_3^f}, \frac{P_4^f}{P_4^f}, \frac{P_u}{P_u}, \frac{P_p}{P_p}, \frac{T_1}{T_1},$$

respectively, yields

$$\frac{dQ_1^s}{Q_1^s} = \frac{\partial Q_1^s}{\partial P_1^f}\frac{dP_1^f}{Q_1^s}\frac{P_1^f}{P_1^f} + \frac{\partial Q_1^s}{\partial P_2^f}\frac{dP_2^f}{Q_1^s}\frac{P_2^f}{P_2^f} + \frac{\partial Q_1^s}{\partial P_3^f}\frac{dP_3^f}{Q_1^s}\frac{P_3^f}{P_3^f} + \frac{\partial Q_1^s}{\partial P_4^f}\frac{dP_4^f}{Q_1^s}\frac{P_4^f}{P_4^f} +$$

$$\frac{\partial Q_1^s}{\partial P_u}\frac{dP_u}{Q_1^s}\frac{P_u}{P_u} + \frac{\partial Q_1^s}{\partial P_p}\frac{dP_p}{Q_1^s}\frac{P_p}{P_p} + \frac{\partial Q_1^s}{\partial T_1}\frac{dT_1}{Q_1^s}\frac{T_1}{T_1}$$

This yields

$$EQ_1^s = \eta_1 EP_1^f + \sigma_{12} EP_2^f + \sigma_{13} EP_3^f + \sigma_{14} EP_4^f + \varphi_{1,1} EP_u + \varphi_{1,2} EP_p + \vartheta_1 ET_1$$

where the operator E is the proportional change in a given variable, and the various symbols denote elasticities, which are presented in Annex E.

The derivation of the tax equation is

$$P_1^f(1 + t_1) = P_1$$

$$dP_1 = P_1^f d(1 + t_1) + (1 + t_1) dP_1^f$$

Where $d(1 + t_1) = dt_1$, multiplying both sides by $\frac{1}{P_1}$ yields

$$dP_1/P_1 = (P_1^f dt_1/P_1) + ((1 + t_1) dP_1^f) / P_1$$

Substituting $P_1^f = P_1/(1 + t_1)$ and $P_1 = P_1^f(1 + t_1)$ on the right-hand side yields

$$dP_1/P_1 = (P_1 dt_1/(1 + t_1)P_1 + \left((1 + t_1) dP_1^f\right)/ P_1^f(1 + t_1)$$

Assuming initial tax rate $= 0$, $dt_1 = t_1$ and $\frac{t_1}{1+t_1} = t_1$

$$EP_U = t_u + EP_u^f$$

Annex D: Final Equations for the EDM Model

The input and output markets are first reduced by substituting the demand equation in the market-clearing equation (where demand is equal to supply and imports). Each equation in this linear system is then totally differentiated and manipulated so that all variables are converted into proportionate changes and elasticities, where the operator E applied to any variable is the proportionate change in that variable and all the other notations represent elasticities explained in Annex E. These transformed equations are entered in the General Algebraic Model System, with their respective elasticities, to estimate the impact of exogenous shocks on the endogenous variables. The final reduced and transformed equations are as follows:

$$EQ_i^s = \eta_i\left(EP_i^f\right) + \sum_{j=1}^{j \neq i, j=3} \sigma_{ij}\left(EP_j^f\right) + \sum_{k=1}^{k=2} \varphi_{ik}(EP_k) + \vartheta_i ET$$

$$EQ_i^s = \gamma_i(EP_i) + \sum_{j=1}^{j\neq i, j=3} \delta_{ij}(EP_j) + \mu_i EC_i - a_i EI_i$$

$$EI_i = \beta_i\, EP_i$$

$$EP_i^f = EP_i^w + z_i$$

$$EP_i = EP_i^f + t_i$$

$$EQ_k^s = v_k EP_k^f + \rho_k EQ_g + \xi_k EP_g + \lambda_k EQ_{po} + \varsigma_k EP_{po}$$

$$EQ_k^s = \tau_k EP_k + \sum_{i=1}^{4} \partial_{ki}(EQ_i) - b_k EI_k$$

$$EI_k = \alpha_k\, EP_k$$

$$EP_k^f = EP_k^w + z_k$$

$$EP_k = EP_k^f + t_k$$

Annex E: Values of Elasticities Used in the EDM Model

	Demand elasticity			Supply elasticity	
Descriptor	Symbol	Elasticity	Descriptor	Symbol	Elasticity
Crop market					
Own-price elasticity			*Own-price elasticity*		
Wheat	γ_1	−0.400	Wheat	η_1	0.228
Rice	γ_2	−0.537	Rice	η_2	0.407
Cotton	γ_3	−0.300	Cotton	η_3	0.715
Other crops	γ_3	−0.800	Other crops	η_3	0.500
Cross-price elasticity wheat			*Cross-price elasticity wheat*		
Rice	δ_{12}	−0.098	Rice	σ_{12}	0.173
Cotton	δ_{13}	−0.02	Cotton	σ_{13}	−0.151
Other crops	δ_{14}	−0.01	Other crops	σ_{14}	−0.100
Cross-price elasticity rice			Urea	φ_{11}	−0.0525
Wheat	δ_{21}	0.098	DAP	φ_{12}	−0.0175
Cotton	δ_{23}	0	*Cross-price elasticity rice*		

Demand elasticity			Supply elasticity		
Descriptor	Symbol	Elasticity	Descriptor	Symbol	Elasticity
Other crops	δ_{24}	−0.02	Wheat	σ_{21}	0.136
Cross-price elasticity cotton			Cotton	σ_{23}	−0.098
Wheat	δ_{31}	0	Other crops	σ_{24}	−0.150
Rice	δ_{32}	0	Urea	φ_{21}	−0.0225
Other crops	δ_{34}	0	DAP	φ_{22}	−0.0075
Cross-Price Elasticity other crops			*Cross-price elasticity cotton*		
Wheat	δ_{41}	−0.01	Wheat	σ_{31}	0
Rice	δ_{42}	−0.02	Rice	σ_{32}	−0.329
Cotton	δ_{43}	0	Other crops	σ_{34}	−0.15
Income elasticity			Urea	φ_{31}	−0.0375
Wheat	μ_1	0.376	DAP	φ_{32}	−0.0125
Rice	μ_2	0.85	*Cross-price elasticity other crops*		
Cotton	μ_3	0.1	Wheat	σ_{41}	−0.1
Other crops	μ_4	1.1	Rice	σ_{42}	−0.15
Import elasticity			Cotton	σ_{43}	−0.15
Wheat	a_1	−1	Urea	φ_{41}	−0.0075
Rice	a_2	−1	DAP	φ_{42}	−0.0025
Cotton	a_3	1	*Technology elasticity*		
Other crops	a_4	−1	Rice	ϑ_1	1
Trade elasticity of crops			Cotton	ϑ_2	1
Wheat	β_1	−5	Wheat	ϑ_3	1
Rice	β_2	−5	Other crops	ϑ_4	1
Cotton	β_3	5			
Other crops	β_4	−5			
Fertilizer market					
Own-price elasticity			*Own-price elasticity*		
Urea	τ_1	−0.3	Urea	v_1	0.8
DAP	τ_2	−0.5	DAP	v_2	0.4
Cross elasticity of urea with supply of crops			*Input elasticity in urea*		
Wheat	∂_{11}	0.82	Quantity of natural gas	ρ_1	0.32
Rice	∂_{12}	0.368	Price of natural gas	ξ_1	−0.075
Cotton	∂_{13}	0.486	Quantity of phosphate	λ_1	0
Other crops	∂_{14}	0.65	Price of phosphate	ς_1	0
Cross elasticity of DAP with supply of crops			*Input elasticity in DAP*		
Wheat	∂_{11}	0.41	Quantity of natural gas	ρ_2	0.16
Rice	∂_{12}	0.184	Price of natural gas	ξ_2	−0.03

Demand elasticity			Supply elasticity		
Descriptor	Symbol	Elasticity	Descriptor	Symbol	Elasticity
Cotton	∂_{13}	0.243	Quantity of phosphate	λ_2	0.4
Other Crops	∂_{14}	0.15	Price of phosphate	ς_2	−0.3
Import elasticity					
Urea	b_1	1			
DAP	b_2	1			
Trade elasticity of fertilizer					
Urea	α_1	1 and 5			
DAP	α_2	1 and 5			

Source: Ali 1990; Nazli et al. 2012; and authors' own judgment assumptions.

Note: Elasticities were drawn from previous literature whenever possible. According to our research, elasticities on fertilizer manufacturing are not available, and our estimates are based on feedback from industry professionals. DAP = di-ammonium phosphate.

Annex F: Simulated Changes from 2013/2014 Base Value Using EDM for Various Policy Interventions with High Import Elasticity ($\alpha = 5$)

Variables	Change from 2013/2014 baseline value				
	Scenario 1	Scenario 2	Scenario 3	Scenario 4	Scenario 5
Fertilizer market					
Domestic supply of urea (1,000s MT)	−956(−19.4)	−913(−18.5)	43(0.9)	−913(−18.5)	385(7.8)
Domestic supply of DAP (1,000s MT)	−58(−8.3)	−56(−8.1)	4(0.6)	−53(−7.7)	30(4.2)
Import supply of urea (1,000s MT)	208(18)	271(23.5)	62(5.4)	270(23.4)	−84(−7.2)
Import supply of DAP (1,000s MT)	69(7.4)	92(9.8)	73(7.8)	142(15.3)	−35(−3.8)
Demand of urea (1,000s MT)	−748(−12.3)	−642(−10.6)	105(1.7)	−643(−10.6)	301(5)
Demand of DAP (1,000s MT)	11(0.7)	35(2.2)	77(4.8)	89(5.5)	−6(−0.4)
Farmer price of urea (PKR/MT)	1317(3.6)	1716(4.7)	−5816(−15.9)	−4499(−12.3)	−529(−1.5)
Farmer price of DAP (PKR/MT)	1082(1.5)	1430(2)	−11238(−15.4)	−10156(−14)	−546(−0.8)
Factory price of urea[a] (PKR/MT)	1125(3.6)	1467(4.7)	339(1.1)	1464(4.7)	−452(−1.5)
Factory price of DAP[a] (PKR/MT)	925(1.5)	1222(2)	973(1.6)	1898(3.1)	−466(−0.8)
Import cost for fertilizer (B PKR)	15(15.5)	20(20.4)	7(8.3)	20(24.1)	−6(−6.5)
Output market					
Overall pressure on output prices (PKR/MT)	−0.03(0)	(−0.5)	(−0.1)	(−0.1)	(0)
Overall trade surplus (B PKR)	0(−0.2)	6(5)	1(0.9)	1(0.7)	0(0.1)

Variables	Change from 2013/2014 baseline value				
	Scenario 1	Scenario 2	Scenario 3	Scenario 4	Scenario 5
Total crop production gain (B PKR)	−3(−0.1)	58(2.4)	13(0.5)	11(0.4)	1(0)
Fertilizer expense for farmers (B PKR)	−18(−5.2)	−9(−2.7)	−46(−13.4)	−59(−17.3)	6(1.9)
Production revenue (B PKR)	−3(−0.1)	58(2.3)	13(0.5)	11(0.4)	1(0)
Overall farmer benefit (B PKR)	15(0.7)	67(3)	59(2.6)	70(3.1)	−5(−0.2)
Gas expense (B PKR)	35(222.3)	36(225.6)	0(0.9)	36(225.7)	1(7.6)
Subsidy and others					
Fertilizer revenue (B PKR)	−23(−14.4)	−20(−12.9)	3(2)	−20(−12.6)	9(5.6)
Overall manufacturer benefit (B PKR)	−58(−40.7)	−56(−39.4)	3(2.1)	−55(−39)	8(5.4)
Production subsidy (urea) (B PKR)	−47(−100)	−47(−100)	0(0.9)	−47(−100)	4(7.6)
Retail subsidy (DAP) (B PKR)	0(0)	0(0)	0(0)	0(0)	0(0)
Distribution subsidy (B PKR)	2(20.2)	3(26.5)	0(5.4)	1(23.4)	−1(−7.9)
Tax revenue from fertilizer (B PKR)	−3(−5.2)	−1(−2.7)	−50(−100)	−50(−100)	1(1.9)
All subsidies (B PKR)	−44(24.4)	−44(25.7)	1(101.3)	−46(11.8)	3(104.5)
Investment on R&D (B PKR)	0(0)	12(0)	0(0)	0(0)	0(0)
Total change in govt. revenue (B PKR)	42(0)	30(0)	−50(0)	−4(0)	−2(0)
Consumer crop demand (B PKR)	−2(−0.1)	52(2.1)	12(0.5)	10(0.4)	1(0)
Eventual social benefit (B PKR)	−3(0)	94(0)	24(0)	20(0)	2(0)

Source: Authors' estimates.

Note: Figures in parentheses are percentage changes with respect to the baseline value of 2013/2014. B = billion; DAP = di-ammonium phosphate; MT = metric tons; GST = general sales tax; α = trade elasticity of fertilizer. The overall social benefit does not incorporate trade loss/profit. We assumed this is already reflected in the loss/gain in crop production.

In scenario 1, we remove the subsidy on natural gas; in scenario 2, we increase investment in crop research and development while removing natural gas subsidy; in scenario 3, we remove the GST; in scenario 4, we remove gas subsidy and GST simultaneously; and in scenario 5, we remove the shortage of gas.

[a] Exclusive of GST.

Chapter 7

AGRICULTURAL PRICES AND TRADE POLICIES

Paul Dorosh, Elena Briones Alonso, Shuaib Malik, and Abdul Salam

Introduction

Pakistan has a long history of market interventions that influence agricultural market prices and trade. Beginning in the colonial period under British India, successive governments have consistently intervened in wheat markets, purchasing wheat from farmers at administratively set prices and selling wheat to flour mills or wheat flour to consumers at subsidized prices. These wheat policies were designed to promote food security at the national level by ensuring adequate supplies, and at the household level by providing the country's primary staple food to urban consumers at affordable prices. There were substantial interventions in markets for other major agricultural commodities as well, and from the 1960s until the early 1990s, the Pakistani government set official producer (procurement) prices for basmati and IRRI rice, cotton, and sugarcane.[1]

Major economic policy reforms in the 1990s led to a much reduced role for government in domestic markets as domestic procurement at fixed support prices for nonwheat crops other than sugarcane essentially ceased. Nonetheless, government control of wheat imports, and import tariffs on vegetable oils remain. Fertilizer subsidies and implicit subsidies on irrigated agriculture, through provision of water at prices that do not cover the maintenance costs of the system, affect farmers' profitability and crop choice. Moreover, exchange rate policies, which resulted in a substantial indirect taxation of agriculture in the 1970s and early 1980s, continue to heavily influence prices and profitability of agricultural exports.

This chapter examines exchange rate policy (because distortions in the macroeconomy have a pervasive effect on price signals throughout the

---

1 IRRI rice refers to modern rice varieties developed in the 1960s and 1970s with support from the International Rice Research Institute (IRRI).

economy), as well as commodity-specific trade and domestic price policies.[2] Most of the chapter considers Pakistan's competitiveness relative to international markets in general, though the chapter concludes with a comparison of the prices of Pakistan's leading agricultural products with prices of those products in India.

The chapter begins with a brief description of the analytical framework for measuring the effects of these factors, followed by a description of the evolution of Pakistan's exchange rate policies—a major determinant of agricultural price incentives. Thereafter, it discusses government interventions in domestic markets of key agricultural commodities since the 1960s, along with estimates of the effects of these policies on market prices as reflected in nominal rates of protection (NRP) (the percentage deviations in domestic prices relative to border prices). It also presents measures of effective rates of protection,[3] which include the effects of input subsidies (fertilizer and irrigation water) on agricultural price incentives. The results of these analyses show that most major agricultural crops (wheat, cotton, basmati and IRRI rice, and maize) have been taxed, though the rate of implicit taxation has fallen over the past two decades. Sugarcane, milk, and vegetable oil, however, have been protected through import restrictions and tariffs. Moreover, given that import tariffs and other trade restrictions have boosted domestic prices of industrial products, the overall effect of trade and pricing policies in Pakistan has been to tax agricultural production relative to industry.

Much of this discussion focuses on wheat, given the large share of wheat in cropped area and the continuing major government interventions in wheat markets. We show that wheat imports by Pakistan's government in the 1990s helped to stabilize prices at levels below the import parity border price, thereby taxing wheat farmers and subsidizing consumers of wheat.[4] Since 2000, however, several major shifts in domestic prices relative to import parity border prices have taken place, while large-scale domestic procurement and subsidized sales of wheat to flour mills have continued. The chapter then presents a set of options for reducing the costs of wheat price stabilization,

2   This chapter focuses on agricultural prices and trade policies rather than on market actors or the structure and governance of markets. In general, Pakistan's domestic marketing in both the agricultural and nonagricultural sectors is dominated by small enterprises that are often constrained by lack of access to sufficient credit. Governance issues also hinder growth, particularly problems with contract enforcement, corruption, and law and order (Sayeed 2010).

3   Effective rates of protection are generally equivalent to the direct rates of assistance as used in WTO negotiations (see Anderson et al. 2008).

4   The border price for imports (exports) is the price of imports (exports) in the absence of tariffs, taxes, or other price distortions.

including allowing greater private-sector participation in the import trade and reducing domestic procurement of wheat. The chapter concludes with a comparison of Pakistan's and India's agricultural price policies for wheat and other major commodities, and a discussion of the implications of potential trade liberalization.

Measuring Impacts of Government Policy Interventions in Agriculture: Analytical Framework

Government policies can affect agricultural price incentives and incomes through various channels, including macroeconomic policies that influence the exchange rate and domestic price inflation, trade policy (government imports, import quotas, tariffs, and taxes), domestic pricing policies (on both outputs and inputs), and market restrictions and direct taxes/subsidies on farmers' incomes. Macroeconomic and exchange rate policies that are not sector specific generally are not considered to be within the scope of international agricultural trade policy agreements. Moreover, for purposes of international trade agreements (in particular, the World Trade Organization), a distinction is made between policies that result in a distortion in price incentives for production and policies (such as direct taxes) that do not directly affect prices.

Various indicators can be used to measure distortions in prices and the total value of the government's support (or tax) on production or consumption of a commodity. In the case of an internationally traded commodity, when there are no binding quantitative restrictions (quotas), the measures are relatively straightforward—comparing domestic prices with border prices.[5] In the case of nontraded commodities or commodities with binding quantitative restrictions, some calculations involving price estimates of supply and demand elasticities may be needed to determine the magnitude of the distortions. The discussion below focuses mainly on tradeable commodities with no quantitative restrictions on trade.[6]

A distortion in the output price of a tradeable good can be measured as the NRP, which is the ratio of the domestic market price to the import or export

---

5   In theory border prices (or medium-term average expected border prices) represent the opportunity cost of using resources for domestic production. Thus, for example, if the domestic price of a product is greater than the border price, economic resources would be saved (and could be put to better use) if the product were imported instead of being produced domestically.

6   The role of administratively set government imports in wheat price formation is discussed in the next section.

parity border price (see Annex A for details).[7] Note that the World Bank's multicountry study on agricultural price distortions (Anderson et al. 2008; Dorosh and Salam 2008) measured distortions in terms of nominal rates of assistance.[8]

In the case where there are other distortions in the economy, such as non-agricultural quotas or tariffs or exchange rate policies that prevent full adjustments to market incentives, then a hypothetical exchange rate in the absence of distortions, E', can be used. One approach, developed for a cross-country study of the effects of trade and exchange rate policy on agriculture in developing countries by Krueger, Schiff, and Valdès (1988), estimated equilibrium exchange rates in the absence of import tariffs and foreign exchange restrictions. However, given a lack of consensus on methodologies and uncertainties in measurement, distortions in exchange rates that are not directly linked to agriculture are not included in World Trade Organization (WTO)–related measures of agricultural policy distortions.[9]

The next section summarizes earlier estimates of the direct effects of trade and pricing policies (following the Anderson and Martin approach [2008]),[10] as well as measures that include distortions in exchange rates (as in the Krueger, Schiff, and Valdès [1988] approach),[11] and presents new estimates of distortions for 2005 through 2013.

---

7   Calculations of border prices generally do not include distortions in international markets caused by policies of other countries. This chapter follows that convention.

8   The nominal rate of assistance (NRA) can be decomposed into the sum of the Nominal Rate of Output Assistance (NRAO) and the Nominal Rate of Input Assistance (NRAI). A similar measure, the Producer Subsidy Equivalent (PSE) as calculated by the OECD, is defined with the distorted prices in the denominator, so that, in general, $PSE_i = NRA_i / (1 + NRA_i)$.

9   Numerous studies have been conducted to measure the effects of government trade, exchange rate, and pricing policies on Pakistan's agriculture. The first major study, by Hamid, Nabi, and Nasim (1990), used a framework developed for a multicountry study of the effects of agricultural trade and pricing policies by Krueger, Schiff, and Valdès (1988). This approach includes a measure of the indirect effects of industrial trade policy on real exchange rates and real agricultural prices. Dorosh and Valdès (1990) extended this analysis to include an econometric estimate of real exchange rate distortions arising from industrial trade policy and a multimarket analysis of effects on supply and demand of major agricultural commodities.

10 Though exchange rate distortions were not considered as policy distortions, the Anderson and Martin methodology uses parallel exchange rate premiums but does not include measures of other exchange rate distortions.

11 Another difference in these methodologies is that the Krueger, Schiff, and Valdès methodology measures distortions by direct price comparisons of estimated border prices with domestic market (or official) prices, not just explicit price distortion due to actual tariffs, taxes, or subsidies. For most commodities, these two approaches were identical up to the early 1990s, when procurement/support prices were eliminated or no procurement took place for basmati and IRRI rice, cotton, and most other agricultural commodities. In this chapter, we use only explicit trade, tax, and pricing policies from 2000 onward in the estimates of distortions for these commodities (see Valdès 2013).

Trade and Exchange Rate Policies

From independence until the mid-1980s, Pakistan operated a fixed nominal exchange rate regime, with few changes in the nominal exchange rate relative to the US dollar.[12] In the 1960s, various multiple exchange rate and export bonus schemes were put into place to increase incentives for exports. The official nominal exchange rate remained fixed throughout the 1960s, however, until a major devaluation in April 1972 (following the secession of East Pakistan/Bangladesh in 1971), when the Pakistani rupee (PKR) was devalued from PKR 4.76 per US$ to PKR 11.03 per US$. Thereafter, from 1972 to 1981, domestic inflation was approximately equal to world price inflation (in US dollar terms), and Pakistan's real exchange rate changed little, in spite of a constant nominal exchange rate from 1973 through 1981 (Dorosh and Valdès 1990).

To improve incentives for export growth, the government, led by Zia ul-Haq from 1977 to 1988, undertook a succession of nominal devaluations of the rupee (totaling 73 percent) from PKR 9.90 per US$ to PKR 17.20 per US$ between fiscal years 1981 and 1987. The devaluations, combined with adjustments in fiscal policy, achieved a real exchange rate depreciation of 65 percent (Figure 7.1).[13]

Pakistan's import substitution trade policy, aimed at promoting the industrial sector, was itself a major factor influencing the real exchange rate in the 1970s and 1980s. By raising the domestic price of industrial goods, import tariffs and quotas reduced demand for imports, thereby tending to reduce the demand for foreign exchange and to lead to an appreciation of the equilibrium real exchange rate (Dornbusch 1974). Using parameters estimated from a time-series regression linking monthly real exchange rates with the implicit tariff rate, the terms of trade, and other factors, Dorosh and Valdès (1990)

---

12 Further details on Pakistan's trade and exchange rate policies from the 1960s through the late 1980s can be found in Hamid, Nabi, and Nasim (1990) and Dorosh and Valdès (1990).

13 According to economic theory, nominal devaluations, in themselves, cannot cause real exchange rate changes. However, these nominal devaluations also directly reduced the implicit tariff on imports due to quotas, a policy shift that does affect relative prices. Moreover, since prices do not instantaneously reach their equilibrium levels (in part because of relatively sticky nominal prices for goods such as wheat procured by the government, electricity, and fuel, and for public-sector wages), nominal devaluations may have real exchange rate effects lasting several years.

FIGURE 7.1 Import tariffs and real exchange rates, Pakistan, 1986–2013

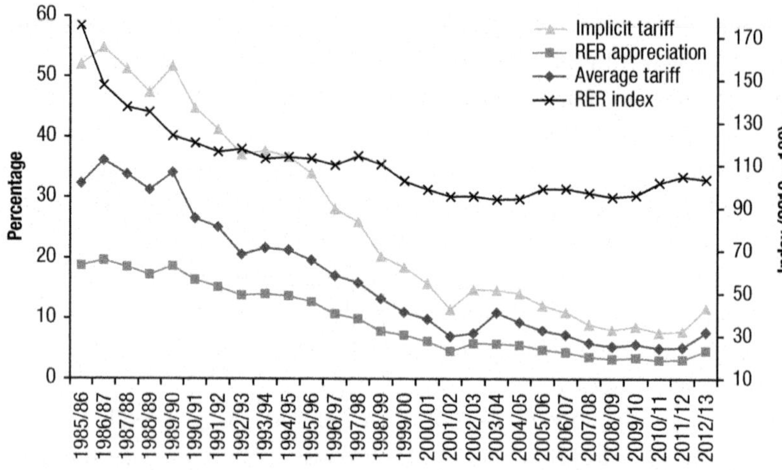

Source: Real exchange rate: IMF (2014); Dorosh and Salam (2009); authors' calculations.
Note: RER = real exchange rate. The percentages in the left-hand y-axis apply to implicit tariff, RER appreciation, and average tariff. The right-hand y-axis applies to RER index.

estimate that an implicit tariff, which averaged 48 percent from 1983 to 1987, resulted in a 17 percent appreciation of the real exchange rate.[14]

To some extent, adverse real exchange rate effects for industrial goods were offset by import tariffs and other import restrictions that raised the domestic price of these imports. For agricultural goods, however, these adverse real exchange rate effects largely offset any protection provided from import tariffs, and for exportable products, substantially decreased incentives for production.

Trade and Exchange Rate Policy Reforms

Beginning in the late 1980s, Pakistan adopted a managed float exchange rate policy that resulted in gradual nominal depreciation of the rupee as fiscal deficits, workers' remittances, and foreign borrowing helped to boost money supply and domestic inflation. Thus, there was relatively little change in real

---

14 The implicit tariff rate, which measures the combined effect of import tariffs and quotas on domestic prices, is defined as the ratio of domestic prices (measured at the border) to import prices. In the absence of detailed data on domestic and import prices, we extend the earlier series of implicit import tariff estimates by Dorosh and Valdès (1990) using the average percentage change in actual average tariff rates. Note that to the extent that domestic goods also pay sales taxes, these sales taxes do not represent a trade policy distortion if they are in lieu of a sales tax on the imported products.

exchange rates from 1987 through 2001. Even during the 1996 and 2001 periods of high domestic inflation, when the nominal exchange rate depreciated by 74 percent from PKR 33.6 per US$ to PKR 58.4 per US$, the real exchange rate depreciated by only 11 percent.

Trade taxes were also sharply reduced. Net customs duties fell from an average of 34 percent of total import value in 1985–1989 to 22 percent in 1990–1996, and to an average of only 12 percent and 9 percent in 1997–2000 and 2001–2003, respectively. Likewise, in a series of reforms, the number of items subject to quantitative restrictions was reduced, from 1,361 in 1988 to only 970 in 1993 (Nabi 1997). Subsequent reforms begun in 1997 led to the elimination of essentially all remaining traditional quantitative restrictions and parastatal import monopolies by 2003, with the important exceptions of a ban on the import of products not included in a positive list of 677 items, and local-content programs in the automobile industry. By 2001 average statutory tariff rates were similar for agricultural and industrial products: 21.8 and 20.2 percent, respectively (World Bank 2004, 22, 44).[15]

Following September 11, 2001, foreign donors greatly increased financial and military support to the Government of Pakistan. These foreign exchange inflows helped Pakistan to increase public spending while avoiding balance of payments problems. There was little change in the nominal exchange rate in US dollar terms between the end of 2000 (PKR 58.0 per US$) and 2007 (PKR 61.2 per US$), but since that time there has again been a steady depreciation of the nominal exchange rate that has contributed to a stable real exchange rate in spite of considerable domestic inflation. By the end of 2013, the nominal exchange rate had reached PKR 105.6 per US$, but the real exchange rate was essentially unchanged from its 2000 level.

Thus, trade liberalization in Pakistan reduced explicit and implicit tariffs sharply over time, from an average of 53 percent in 1985–1989 to an average of only 15 percent in 2001–2003 and an estimated average of 10 percent in 2011/2012–2012/2013. As a result, the effects of trade policy distortions on the real exchange rate also fell sharply, to about 3 percent in the latter period. Nonetheless, fluctuations in nominal and real exchange rates have the potential to dramatically affect profitability of major tradeable crops for which there is little or no current trade policy intervention (cotton, basmati rice, and IRRI rice).

---

15 Trade reforms were partially reversed in 2006 and again after the 2008 global financial crisis, as customs and "regulatory" duties were increased. Statutory Regulatory Orders were often used to provide exemptions from tariffs for specified firms, exemptions not available to other commercial importers (Pursell, Khan, and Gulzar 2011).

Empirical Estimates of Distortions in Pakistan Agriculture

1960s to 1980s: Exchange Rate Effects Dominate Direct Agricultural Market Interventions

Pakistani government interventions in agricultural markets follow the same broad patterns of exchange rates and overall trade policy described above—major interventions in markets in the 1960s, 1970s, and 1980s, followed by liberalization in the 1990s and 2000s. There are, however, major differences across commodities, with far greater liberalization for major agricultural exportables, continued tariffs on vegetable oil and milk powder, and substantial continued interventions in the markets for wheat and sugarcane.

From the 1960s through the early 1980s, the government set procurement prices/support prices for the five major crops: wheat, basmati rice, IRRI rice, cotton, and sugarcane. Government purchases and sales of these commodities were substantial, resulting in major fiscal costs, particularly for wheat and to some extent for rice and cotton.

Although procurement prices were set above border prices (measured at official exchange rates), the substantial overvaluation of the rupee, which was related to industrial trade policy and macroeconomic policy, generally resulted in implicit taxation of these commodities (prices below border prices measured at equilibrium exchange rates) and declining real prices of these commodities over time.

In the 1960–1971 period, procurement prices for all major commodities except basmati rice were on average higher than border prices, estimated using the official exchange rate. At estimated equilibrium exchange rates (that ranged from PKR 9.1 per US$ to PKR 11.6 per US$, compared to the official rate of PKR 4.78 per US$), however, procurement prices were far below border prices. The effect was especially pronounced for major exportable crops (basmati rice, ordinary rice, and cotton[16]), for which domestic prices were on average 54 percent below border prices at equilibrium exchange rates (Table 7.1).

After the major devaluation of the Pakistani rupee in 1972, procurement prices were closer to border prices for most of the 1970s and 1980s, but there was still substantial direct and indirect taxation of exportables, averaging −15 percent (direct effects) and −38 percent (total effects). Likewise, procurement prices of wheat were on average 31 percent below border prices at official exchange rates and 46 percent below border prices at equilibrium exchange

16 Note that during this period, there were no procurement prices for cotton.

TABLE 7.1 Nominal rates of protection for agricultural products (%), 1962–2014

Period	Basmati rice	IRRI rice	Cotton	Wheat	Sugarcane	Milk	Total
1962–1964	−51.0	−42.8	−18.8	−13.2	137.0	—	−1.0
1965–1969	−41.1	−46.0	−17.5	11.4	234.2	70.4	21.7
1970–1974	−37.3	−18.8	−6.3	−16.2	113.4	123.8	9.3
1975–1979	−46.6	−33.8	−5.1	−21.2	33.6	54.6	−11.8
1980–1984	−49.5	−24.6	3.1	−22.3	72.4	47.5	−9.3
1985–1989	−56.2	−20.2	−6.1	−21.7	123.7	54.5	−5.9
1990–1994	−17.9	−0.5	−19.9	−27.1	52.1	25.4	−10.2
1995–1999	0.4	−0.9	−7.9	−20.2	54.3	16.9	−2.6
2000–2004	0.0	0.0	7.0	−13.9	44.6	19.7	−3.9
2005–2009	0.0	0.0	0.0	—	25.8	—	2.0
2010–2014	0.0	0.0	0.0	—	33.2	—	2.6

Source: Dorosh and Salam (2009); authors' calculations.

Note: At import parity, nominal rates of protection (NRPs) for wheat in 2005–2009 and 2010–2013 would be −26.0 percent and −15.5 percent, respectively. Using these figures, the total NRP is −13.3 percent and −6.6 percent for the two periods. However, Pakistan was not an importer of wheat in most of these years. Whether numbers are positive or negative indicates whether domestic prices are above (positive) or below (negative) the border price. — = not available.

rates. Only for sugarcane (and milk) were procurement prices above border prices at both official and equilibrium exchange rates. Although fertilizer and pesticide prices were generally below border prices, these inputs accounted for too small a share of the value of production to offset the taxation on output prices, so effective rates of protection were generally negative as well. Thus, for nearly three decades, most tradeable agricultural products faced substantial price disincentives for production through both direct and indirect taxation.

Since the late 1980s, exchange rate distortions have played a far smaller role in influencing domestic prices of agricultural commodities. Instead, commodity-specific taxes and market interventions have been the dominant determinants of agricultural price distortions in Pakistan, as described below.

Wheat

Over the past several decades, government wheat policy in Pakistan has attempted to balance the competing interests of producers and consumers in an effort to achieve food security in terms of both availability and access to food. On the supply side, policy has aimed at increasing wheat productivity (yields) and output, supporting farmer incomes (though large farmers account for most of the sales to government), and reducing dependence on food imports. On the consumption side, the major policy goals have been ensuring availability of wheat flour at affordable prices and maintaining price stability. In recent years, however, there has been increasing debate regarding the high fiscal cost of wheat subsidies and the substantial amounts of bank credit extended to government agencies for wheat procurement.[17]

The mechanisms for government market interventions in wheat have varied substantially over time. From the 1960s until the early 1980s, large volumes of domestically produced wheat were procured at fixed prices at procurement centers. Net injections of wheat and wheat flour—releases minus domestic procurement—averaged 12 percent of total net availability during the 1970s (Dorosh and Salam 2008). The government also maintained a monopoly on imports. Wheat flour was sold in ration shops at a subsidized price.

During the 1972–1974 period, when world prices of wheat and other grains rose sharply, Pakistan kept its prices relatively stable, effectively insulating its domestic wheat market from the world market through government imports and subsidized sales. Ration shop sales were eliminated in 1987/1988 because of huge leakages and high fiscal costs (Alderman and Garcia 1993). Thereafter, government wheat was sold to flour mills at fixed, subsidized prices. In general, there were no controls on the price of the flour sold by the mills. From 1975/1976 through 1987/1988, net imports were relatively small (averaging 802,000 tons per year—equivalent to just 7.5 percent of net availability),[18] and net domestic distribution (net sales by the government) was only 436,000 tons per year—equivalent to just 4.2 percent of net availability (Table 7.2). Given relatively price-inelastic supply and demand,[19] together with a government monopoly on international wheat trade, these interventions were sufficient to keep the domestic prices far below import parity prices at both the official and equilibrium exchange rates.

In the 1990s (1988/1989–1999/2000), net imports of wheat almost tripled, to 2.37 million tons per year, and net distribution rose to nearly 2.0 million tons per year, equivalent to 15.0 percent and 12.0 percent of net availability, respectively. These interventions kept domestic wheat prices (wholesale price Lahore) below import parity and stable in real terms, as international prices (import parity) trended downward in real terms from the early 1990s to 2000 (except for a price spike in 1995/1996) (Figure 7.2).

---

17 See Salam and Mukhtar (2008) and Dorosh and Salam (2008).

18 Net availability is calculated here using an adjustment of 10 percent for seed, feed, and losses.

19 Own-price elasticities of demand for wheat are estimated to be −0.242 for urban households and −0.360 for rural households (see Chapter 6); own-price elasticities of supply were estimated by Ali (1990) as 0.228 in the short run and 0.327 in the long run.

TABLE 7.2 Overview of wheat policies and the wheat market in Pakistan, 1975/1976–2012/2013

Period	Description	Production (1,000s MT)	Procurement (1,000s MT)	Distribution (1,000s MT)	Net imports (1,000s MT)	Net availability per capita (kg/capita)	Real wholesale price (2013 PKR/kg)	NRP import parity (%)
1975/1976– 1987/1988	Subsidized sales of wheat through ration shops; public imports lower market prices	10,646	2,813	3,249	802	120	19.54	–47
1988/1989– 1999/2000	Liberalized retail sales; large-scale public imports lower market prices	15,845	3,681	5,671	2,369	132	20.85	–40
2000/2001– 2006/2007	Reduced public imports and net availability; domestic prices rise; exports to Afghanistan	19,986	4,572	4,391	–376	114	24.50	–26
2007/2008– 2008/2009	Very high world prices; domestic prices rise; exports banned; large public imports	22,127	4,170	6,052	315	118	29.86	–4[a]
2009/2010	International prices fall; domestic prices at import parity, but little trade	24,033	9,231	5,985	147	106	35.28	1
2010/2011– 2012/2013	Moderate rise in world prices; domestic prices at export parity; net exports	23,999	6,219	6,348	–1,463	116	29.86	10[a]

Source: Authors; GoP (various years) Pakistan Economic Survey; GoP (various years) Agricultural Statistics of Pakistan.

Note: NRP = nominal rate of protection; MT = metric tons; kg = kilograms; PKR = Pakistani rupees.

[a] The export parity price was used for the calculation of the NRP. The NRP measures distortions to the output price and does not take into account assistance to inputs. Border prices and domestic wholesale prices are measured at the wholesale market in Lahore.

FIGURE 7.2 Real wholesale, border, and support prices of wheat, 1991–2013

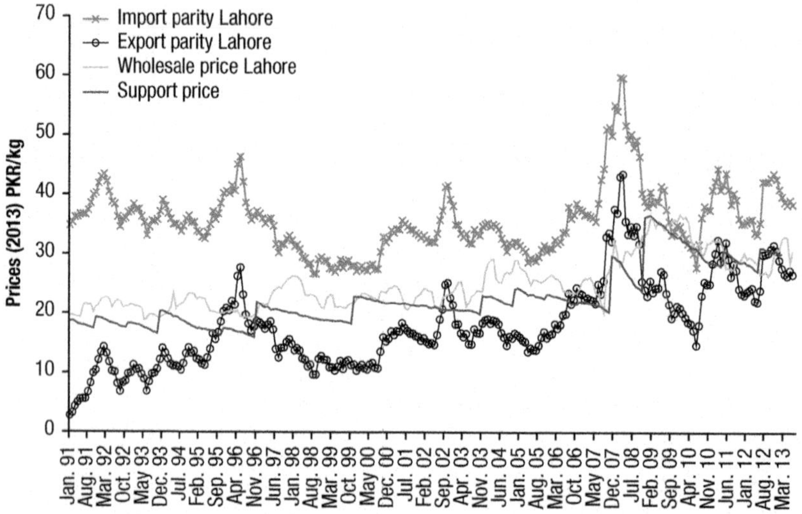

Source: Authors' calculation, based on Anderson and Nelgen (2013); GoP (various years) *Pakistan Statistical Yearbook*; IMF (2014); and FAO (2014).

Note: The support price is the set price at which the government procures wheat. Border prices and domestic prices are measured at the wholesale market in Lahore; PKR = Pakistani rupees; kg = kilograms.

The government cut back on public imports early in the 2000–2009 decade, in part because of a bumper harvest, followed by record procurement of 8.6 million tons, more than double the procurement in the previous year.[20] Moreover, net distribution fell to an average of −181,000 tons per year, reducing net availability per capita to an average of 114 kg per person, 14 percent below the average of 1988/1989–1999/2000. Average real wholesale prices rose to 24.5 (2013) PKR/kg, an increase of 18 percent. With rising world prices, however, the NRP fell in absolute value terms, from −40 percent to −26 percent (Table 7.3 and Table 7.4).

From 2007 to 2011, Pakistan faced a turbulent period involving international and domestic price surges, followed by massive floods in the Indus River basin. In 2006/2007, international wheat prices started to rise while domestic prices fell in response to expectations of a bountiful 2007 harvest. As a result, exports once again became profitable, and in April 2007 the government lifted an export ban on wheat (flour) that had been in place since 2003 and permitted 500,000 tons of private-sector wheat exports (Dorosh

---

20 During this period, Pakistan's exports of wheat flour to Afghanistan surged as domestic production of wheat in Afghanistan fell and commercial wheat mills were damaged in the war (Chabot and Dorosh 2007).

TABLE 7.3 Price decomposition of nominal international and domestic wheat prices, 1975/1976–2012/2013

Period	International wheat price (US$/MT)	Pakistan exchange rate (PKR/US$)	C&F Karachi (US$/MT)	C&F Karachi (PKR/kg)	Import parity (PKR/kg)	Export parity (PKR/kg)	Wholesale price wheat (PKR/kg)	Pakistan CPI 2005 = 100	US CPI 2005 = 100
1975/1976–1987/1988	146.05	12.80	168.26	2.13	3.19	0.89	1.67	20.01	46.39
1988/1989–1999/2000	149.54	32.23	183.80	5.85	7.65	3.48	4.69	50.80	76.61
2000/2001–2006/2007	152.46	59.16	188.33	11.16	13.20	8.18	9.73	91.13	97.58
2007/2008–2008/2009	296.20	68.76	346.62	23.54	26.86	18.81	17.67	134.58	110.05
2009/2010	211.05	83.25	261.05	21.71	25.12	16.74	25.32	165.44	111.66
2010/2011–2012/2013	298.07	89.81	348.07	31.36	34.73	25.42	26.92	208.18	117.34

Source: Authors; GoP (various years) Pakistan Economic Survey; GoP (various years) Agricultural Statistics of Pakistan; IMF (2014).

Note: C&F = cost and freight. Border prices and domestic prices are measured at the wholesale market in Lahore; MT = metric tons; PKR = Pakistani rupees; kg = kilograms; CPI = consumer price index.

TABLE 7.4 Price decomposition of real international and domestic wheat prices, 1975/1976–2012/2013

Period	Real international wheat price (2013 US$/MT)	Pakistan real exchange rate (2013 PKR/US$)	Real C&F Karachi (2013 PKR/kg)	Real FOB Karachi (2013 PKR/kg)	Real import parity (2013 PKR/kg)	Real export parity (2013 PKR/kg)	Real wholesale price wheat (2013 PKR/kg)	NRP import parity	NRP export parity
1975/1976–1987/1988	380.17	58.13	24.46	24.17	37.26	10.79	19.54	-0.47	1.05
1988/1989–1999/2000	232.95	95.36	26.90	25.64	35.87	15.33	20.85	-0.40	0.42
2000/2001–2006/2007	183.38	124.65	28.15	26.80	33.34	20.57	24.50	-0.26	0.21
2007/2008–2008/2009	317.32	109.77	40.73	39.25	46.48	32.60	29.86	-0.35	-0.07
2009/2010	222.88	109.83	30.28	28.83	35.04	23.35	35.28	0.01	0.51
2010/2011–2012/2013	299.25	99.14	34.62	33.38	38.39	28.05	29.86	-0.22	0.07

Source: Authors; GoP (various years) Agricultural Statistics of Pakistan; IMF (2014).

Note: C&F = cost and freight; FOB = free on board; NRP = nominal rate of protection; MT = metric tons; PKR = Pakistani rupees; kg = kilograms. Border prices and wholesale prices are measured at the wholesale market in Lahore. The NRP measures distortions to the output price and does not take into account assistance to inputs.

2008; Persaud 2010). Soon thereafter, however, as international wheat prices continued to rise, the government reinstated the export ban for wheat and wheat flour (except to Afghanistan) in May 2007 and started importing large quantities of wheat in an effort to stabilize domestic supply and avoid large price increases.[21] Despite these interventions, domestic wheat prices started to rise in late 2007, increasing from 11.00 PKR/kg in July 2007 to 19.15 PKR/kg in July 2008, an increase of 74 percent. Yet as Figure 7.3 shows, this domestic price increase was not nearly as great as the surge in international prices in 2007/2008.[22]

Given short supplies in international markets and high domestic wholesale prices of wheat, the government chose, in late 2008, to raise the support price for wheat by 52 percent, from 625 PKR/40kg (15,625 PKR/ton) to 950 PKR/40kg (23,750 PKR/ton). This higher procurement price helped to spur wheat production and contributed to a record harvest of 24 million tons in April–May of 2009. Despite this new record harvest, however, domestic prices increased further, peaking at 26.9 PKR/kg in February 2010 as massive government wheat procurement (9.2 million tons from the 2007/2008 crop), low public imports, and relatively modest wheat releases (5.8 million tons) resulted in a decrease in net availability to 106 kg/capita, from 118 kg/capita on average between fiscal years 2008 and 2009.

Domestic wheat prices started to decline in March 2010 and were at moderate levels when in July 2010 Pakistan was hit by severe floods. Given that the 2010 wheat crop was already harvested and stored, and the planting season for wheat (November–December) was still several months away, the floods had little impact on wheat supply (Dorosh, Malik, and Krausova 2011). In fact, the 2010/2011 harvest in April/May was slightly better than expected and was only 3 percent lower than the record harvest of the previous year. Likewise, the floods in mid-2011 once again left the following wheat harvest unaffected, and wheat production reached a new record level of 25.2 million tons, possibly attributable to nutrient-rich sediments deposited

21 In early 2008, the government extended the export ban to Afghanistan (Persaud 2010). Note, though, that Afghanistan's imports from Pakistan are small relative to Pakistan's wheat supply—only about 500,000 metric tons in 2012/2013, equivalent to about 2 percent of Pakistan's net availability of wheat of 21.4 million tons in 2011/2012. Thus, Afghanistan's wheat imports generally have only minor effects on Pakistan's domestic prices or availability of wheat. See Chabot and Dorosh (2007) and USDA (2013).

22 Nonetheless, the magnitude of the domestic price rise is puzzling given that the 2007 harvest reached a new record of over 23 million tons according to official data. Various explanations have been brought forward, including large-scale informal exports to Afghanistan (World Bank 2010), an overestimate of production (Dorosh 2008), and widespread increases in private stocks due to expectations that domestic prices would eventually increase (World Bank 2010).

FIGURE 7.3 Wholesale, import parity, and support prices of wheat, 2005–2015

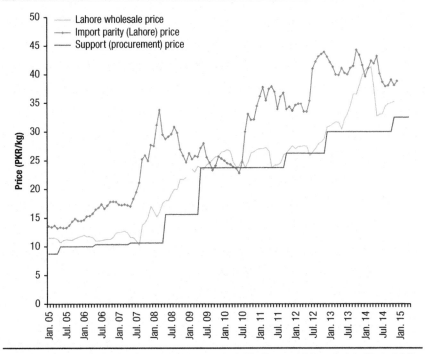

Source: Authors' calculation, based on Anderson and Nelgen (2013); GoP (various years) *Pakistan Statistical Yearbook*; IMF (2014); FAO (2014).

Notes: PKR = Pakistani rupees; kg = kilograms.

from the floodwaters, which may have contributed to increased soil fertility in some areas.

Given the record procurement in April/May 2009 and another above-normal procurement of 6.7 million tons the following year (2009/2010), Pakistan's wheat stocks reached record levels (Figure 7.4), and fiscal costs soared. In most years from 2000 to 2009, domestic procurement had ranged from 3.5 to 4.5 million tons per year. This large-scale procurement at support prices in excess of open-market prices mostly benefitted large farmers, who accounted for almost all the sales to government. Small farmers who sell wheat typically do so at (lower) open-market prices. Significant losses in provincial food departments and Pakistan Agricultural Storage and Services Corporation storage (much of the wheat is stored under tarpaulins in open areas) add to the costs of the system. Moreover, wheat procurement, storage, and distribution requires massive amounts of financing that ties up the banking system's loanable funds. Finally, sales of wheat to flour mills at a fixed

FIGURE 7.4 Initial and estimated peak wheat stocks, 1991/1992–2013/2014

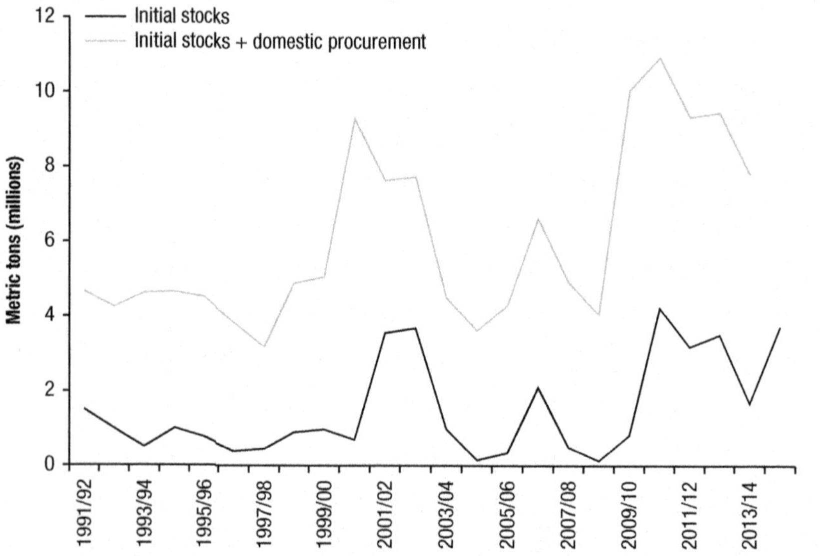

Source: Author's calculations, based on GoP (various years), *Pakistan Economic Survey*.
Note: Years shown are fiscal years (July–June). Initial stocks are stocks as of May 1. Most wheat procurement takes place in May and June, a time when there is little release of stocks. Thus, initial stocks plus domestic procurement is a close approximation to peak stocks (at the end of June) for each fiscal year.

release price below open-market prices (and below full cost-recovery prices) results in enormous financial losses with no benefits to consumers, because flour mills typically sell the flour at open-market prices. In 2009/2010, estimated subsidies reached 4.28 PKR/kg (Table 7.5). If the entire 9.23 million tons of procurement had been sold at the release price, the total loss would have been PKR 39.5 billion.

Since 2009/2010 wheat procurement and subsidies have dropped somewhat, but wheat subsidies are nonetheless still substantially higher than they were in the 2005/2006–2007/2008 period (Figure 7.5): the total value of average wheat subsidies in the 2010/2011–2012/2013 period (measured in billions of 2012/2013 PKR) was 50 percent higher in real terms than in the 2005/2006–2007/2008 period (Table 7.5). This corresponds to a 46 percent increase in the quantity of procurement over this period, from 4.3 to 6.3 million tons per year. Reducing quantities of procurement to these earlier levels could save 6.7 billion PKR per year. Further gradual reductions in quantity of procurement are also possible, allowing the private sector to play a

TABLE 7.5 Estimated possible financial losses on domestic wheat procurement and sales

Year	Procurement quantity (1,000s MT)	Support price (PKR/kg)	Release price (PKR/kg)	Unit subsidy[a] (PKR/kg)	Financial loss[b] (B PKR)	Financial loss[b] (B 2012/13 PKR)
2005/2006	3,939	10.38	10.75	1.40	5.51	12.18
2006/2007	4,514	10.63	11.63	1.13	5.08	10.41
2007/2008	4,422	15.63	15.63	2.15	9.51	17.40
2008/2009	3,917	23.75	18.75	7.76	30.41	46.07
2009/2010	9,231	23.75	24.38	4.28	39.46	53.53
2010/2011	6,715	23.75	26.25	3.50	23.50	28.01
2011/2012	6,150	26.25	33.25	1.08	6.61	7.10
2012/2013	5,948	30.00	33.25	4.18	24.84	24.84
Avg 2006–2008	4,292	12.21	12.67	1.56	6.70	13.33
Avg 2011–2013	6,271	26.67	30.92	2.92	18.32	19.98

Source: Authors; GoP (various years) *Pakistan Economic Survey.*

Note: MT = metric tons; PKR = Pakistani rupees; kg = kilograms; B = billion.

[a] Possible per kg financial loss (unit subsidy) for each year is calculated as the domestic procurement price plus the cost of incidentals minus the release price.

[b] Possible financial loss is unit subsidy times quantity of procurement.

FIGURE 7.5 Wheat procurement quantities, subsidies, and financial loss, 2005/2006–2012/2013

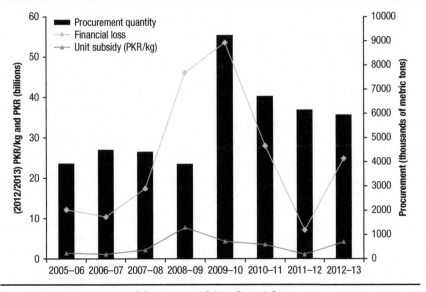

Source: Author's calculations, based on GoP (various years), *Pakistan Economic Survey.*

Note: Unit subsidy for each year is calculated as the domestic procurement price plus the cost of incidentals minus the release price. Financial loss is the unit subsidy times the quantity of procurement. The left-hand axis measures both the financial loss in PKR (billions) and the unit subsidy in PKR/kg. PKR = Pakistani rupees; kg = kilograms.

larger role in marketing.[23] Reforms of the wheat procurement and distribution system could, therefore, bring about major fiscal benefits (Box 7.1).

Cotton[24]

Various combinations of export taxes, export restrictions, and domestic procurement have been used to achieve the multiple objectives of cotton policy: support farmers, provide raw materials to the domestic textile industry, and promote exports of both cotton lint and textiles. Direct purchases of cotton have been minimal since 1995, however.

From 1975 to 1995, the government maintained support prices for cotton lint and seed cotton (*phutti*), and procured cotton lint from ginners. Domestic prices of lint were also affected by the level of exports by the Cotton Export Corporation, which held a monopoly on lint exports from 1974 through 1986. Cotton producers benefitted, however, from import taxes on vegetable oils that boosted the prices of cottonseed and cottonseed oil.

From 1986 through 1993, export taxes on lint cotton were calculated as a fixed percentage of the margin between a benchmark price of lint at the cotton gin (including export costs) and a minimum export price fixed daily by an interagency committee. This system of variable export taxes effectively insulated the domestic market from movements in international prices, but it resulted in significant losses of income for cotton farmers. Collection of export taxes was plagued by underinvoicing of cotton exports through understatement of the quality (grade) of the cotton exports, and the export duty was abolished in 1994.

Since 1994 demand for lint in the textile sector has generally exceeded domestic supply, and Pakistan has become a net importer of cotton lint. Gross imports averaged 259,000 tons per year from 2000 through 2004 when the Multi-Fibre Agreement, which provided special access to markets in developed countries, ended. By 2013 Pakistan was importing about one-third of its cotton requirements (generally higher-quality cotton, in the form of lint). Duties on both exports and imports of cotton were greatly reduced in the mid-1990s,

---

23 In spite of government procurement, the private sector dominates much of the wheat marketing chain. Village traders (*beoparis*) typically purchase wheat directly from farmers at the farm gate. Commission agents (*aarthis*) contract *beoparis* to assemble large quantities of wheat that the *beoparis* sell on the wholesale market to flour millers and stockists. See World Bank (2014b). An earlier detailed description of wheat marketing in Pakistan is found in Cornelisse and Naqvi (1987).

24 The following sections on policies for individual crops (from "Cotton" to "Other Crops: Maize and Oilseeds") are based on Dorosh and Salam (2009).

BOX 7.1 Possible Wheat Sector Reforms

Policy reforms could promote a more-efficient wheat market and reduce the government's fiscal burden from wheat procurement. Below are eight areas for possible reforms: international trade, security stocks, domestic procurement, domestic sales, policy transparency, capacity for policy analysis, safety nets, and use of futures markets.

1. Use international trade and limited national security stocks to promote price stability.
   a. Liberalize food imports by the private sector and announce a government policy of promoting private-sector trade. With this reform, the international market will provide a price ceiling for Pakistan, equal to the import parity price, except in exceptional cases.
   b. Promote exports in years of abundant domestic supplies and moderate international prices.
   c. In exceptional years of high world prices, restrictions on exports and either subsidized open market sales or transfers of government wheat imports may be required to prevent excessive price increases in Pakistan's domestic markets.
2. Maintain a limited security stock of 1.5 to 2.0 million tons (at the end of April) to be used in two ways:
   a. To reduce domestic prices in years of low domestic production and high international prices (case 1c above).
   b. To provide resources for emergency wheat distribution targeted to food-insecure households. Gradually reduce or eliminate domestic procurement of wheat.
3. Limit domestic procurement to a preannounced target quantity of 1–2 million tons per year (for purposes of stock rotation) to be procured at domestic market prices through open tenders or at a preannounced support price that is consistent with about 1–2 million tons of procurement.
4. Eliminate the subsidy on sales of wheat to flour mills by selling wheat (for purposes of stock rotation) through auctions.
5. Establish a wheat policy platform to facilitate information sharing and policy dialogue regarding market conditions and proposed policy changes.
   a. This will enhance transparency of government actions and promote more-efficient markets.
   b. The platform would include representatives of government, private-sector millers and traders, farmers' organizations, and consumers.

(continued)

BOX 7.1 Possible Wheat Sector Reforms *(continued)*

6. Strengthen analytical units within the Ministry of Agriculture or other institutions to enable timely and rigorous analysis of wheat markets and policy options.
7. Strengthen conditional cash transfers and employment safety nets targeted to the poor.
8. Use futures markets that in the medium term could contribute to increased wheat market efficiency.
   a. Use of international futures markets by government agencies could lessen some of the risks involved in reliance on international markets in years of large price increases. This would reduce any subsidy on sales of public-sector imports in the event of a domestic production shortfall and high international prices (see Faruqee and Coleman 1996).
   b. Similarly, in the medium term, if the Pakistan commodity exchange develops, large farmers, private traders, millers, and the government could hedge against price risk through futures market contracts.

---

and domestic procurement and other direct-market interventions have likewise been minimal.[25]

Annual price movements suggest that domestic prices of seed cotton since the mid-1990s have essentially been determined by world prices of cotton lint and the domestic price of cottonseed (Cororaton and Orden 2008).[26] Thus, in the absence of external trade restrictions, the small volumes of domestic procurement in some recent years are unlikely to have had a major effect on domestic prices (and instead simply resulted in a minor decrease in the level of net imports).

Since the mid-1990s, price distortions for cotton have been minimal. After major exchange rate distortions were eliminated in the mid-1980s, export taxes on lint, designed in part to lower lint prices for the domestic textile industry, were the major source of the 20 percent average price distortion from 1990 through 1994 (the taxes were much smaller after 1994). There have

---

25 The Trading Corporation of Pakistan has intervened in years of bumper harvests and low domestic prices, procuring 35,000 tons (2 percent of production) in 2001 and 270,000 tons (11 percent of production) in 2004 in an effort to support prices.

26 Seed cotton consists of the cottonseed as well as the lint. Cottonseed is separated from the lint through the process of ginning.

been essentially no trade policy distortions for lint after 2005, when Pakistan became a net importer of cotton lint. Import tariffs on vegetable oils that help increase the price of cottonseed oil still provided a small measure of protection for seed cotton, however (about 3 percent in the early years of the 2000–2009 decade and 2 percent in 2013).[27]

Basmati and Ordinary (IRRI) Rice

Pakistan has exported substantial quantities of basmati rice since the mid-1970s in response to a surge in rice demand in the Middle East following the large increase in world oil prices of the early 1970s. Initially, under the Bhutto government, these exports were managed by the Rice Export Corporation of Pakistan, a state monopoly.[28] Under the assumption that domestic supply was price inelastic (so that low producer prices would have little effect on quantities produced), the government set a low procurement price. To keep domestic consumption low (and export volumes high), the government also instituted a Monopoly Procurement Scheme for basmati rice, with only limited domestic sales. NRP estimates for basmati paddy suggest that during both the 1960s and 1970s, farmers received only about 50 percent of what they would have received if the government had not intervened.

Following the coup by General Zia in July 1977, rice mills were returned to the private sector, and basmati rice marketing was gradually liberalized. From 1977 to 1987, provincial food departments still retained considerable influence in domestic markets through the annual Monopoly Procurement Scheme for basmati rice. That scheme set licensing rules, restrictions on movement of rice across district boundaries, and quotas to dealers for sales in domestic markets. These dealers were allowed to sell 20 percent of the amount delivered to procurement centers in domestic markets; the remainder was exported. As a result of these restrictions on domestic supply, consumer prices were substantially above procurement prices. Compulsory procurement was abandoned in

---

27 Import duties on refined palm oil in 2013 were PKR 10,040/ton (average of duties on oil from Indonesia and Malaysia, excluding a customs excise duty of 16 percent). Assuming a cost, insurance, and freight price of US$912/ton (the cost, insurance, and freight price of crude palm oil in Europe, December 2013), the import tariff was equivalent to 11.4 percent (FAO 2014). Given that cottonseed accounted for about 30 percent of the value of seed cotton at the gin and cottonseed oil accounts for about 60 percent of the value of cottonseed (2012/2013; seed cotton is two-thirds cottonseed by weight), the import duties raised the price of seed cotton by about .114 × .30 × .60 = 2 percent in 2013.

28 The Bhutto government also nationalized rice milling and other domestic industries. See Hamid, Nabi, and Nasim (1990) for an account of the history of the rice sector in Pakistan from the 1960s through the mid-1980s.

the 1986 harvest season, limited private sector exports were allowed, and voluntary procurement at increased prices was introduced.

The system of voluntary sales of basmati paddy at the announced support price continued through 2009/2010 (there were no support prices for milled basmati rice after 1996/1997 except in 2008/2009), but there have been no government purchases of basmati paddy or milled rice after 1995/1996 and no direct involvement of the government in domestic or export marketing of basmati rice since that time.

Like the policies for basmati rice, government price and trade policies for ordinary (IRRI) rice also included announced support prices and voluntary domestic procurement, although in the 1970s and 1980s the Rice Export Corporation of Pakistan did not procure much IRRI rice in Punjab because the higher transport costs (relative to Sindh, the center of procurement) made exports of ordinary rice produced in Punjab unprofitable.[29] NRP for IRRI rice, calculated on the basis of world rice prices, were about −20 percent, but approached zero rapidly thereafter.

Procurement prices for IRRI paddy and rice were announced in the same period as for basmati rice (that is, most years through 2009/2010), and like with basmati rice, no procurement has taken place since 1995/1996. Price distortions, therefore, are minimal, apart from subsidies to fertilizer and irrigation.

Sugarcane

Pakistan's sugarcane production fluctuates greatly from year to year because of variations in water availability, as well as producer price incentives. To stabilize prices, the Pakistani government has frequently adjusted import tariffs for sugar and related taxes on sugar, and in years of high world prices, even banned exports.

In addition to restrictions and taxes on trade, regulations on the domestic marketing and processing of sugarcane were prevalent until the mid-1980s. Zoning of sugar mills, which required farmers to sell 80 percent of their sugarcane to the mill located in their zone, was abolished in 1987, freeing farmers to sell their sugarcane to whichever mill they preferred. However, the high cost of transporting sugarcane and rapid reductions in the yield of sugar derived from cane (the *rendement*) after the cane is harvested limits the distance that cane can be profitably transported.

---

29 Open-market prices in Punjab during this period were generally above support prices, so little voluntary procurement of paddy or rice took place.

Until 2000 the federal government annually announced the support price of sugarcane, but since then support prices have been decided by provincial governments.[30] Note, however, that there has been no institutional arrangement for public-sector procurement of sugarcane when sugar mills do not pay farmers the full support price, particularly in good harvest years, though sugarcane commissioners of provincial governments put pressure on mills to try to get them to pay farmers the full support price.

Given the wide variations in domestic production that affect domestic prices, as well as large fluctuations in world prices, NRP for sugar in Pakistan are very unstable. In general, though, sugarcane and refined sugar production have been highly protected. NRP averaged over 100 percent in the 1960s and early 1970s, and reached those levels again in the second half of the 1980s when international prices fell again. Even since then, they have continued to be above 50 percent.

These calculations of trade protection are highly sensitive to assumptions used for international shipping costs, milling rates, and costs of processing. Government estimates of border prices typically use high shipping costs for sugar (US$60/ton in 2013/2014), low milling ratios (sugar per ton of sugarcane), and high costs of processing. Assumptions of high world prices raise the import parity price of sugar, and assumptions of low milling ratios and high milling costs for conversion of cane to sugar increase the import parity price of sugarcane even further. The result is that instead of finding that domestic prices are significantly above import parity (and that sugar farmers are protected), alternative calculations show that domestic prices are significantly below import parity (that is, that sugar farmers are facing substantial taxation).

Other Crops: Maize and Oilseeds

Apart from import duties, which have ranged from 10 percent to 25 percent since the mid-1990s, the government has not intervened in maize production and marketing. Nonetheless, production nearly tripled between 2000/2001 and 2013/2014, from 1.64 million tons to 4.53 million tons. Maize has generally been a nontradeable good since the 1980s, with domestic prices below import parity levels (even without the import tariffs), but above export parity levels. Thus, the protection from import competition provided by tariffs has had little effect on domestic prices, and the maize NRP has been close to zero.

---

30 Support prices have varied only slightly across provinces in all years except 2005/2006, when the support price in Sindh was set at 60 PKR/40 kg, 15 PKR/40 kg above the Punjab support price.

Domestic production accounts for less than one-third of edible oil use in Pakistan, and growth in domestic demand has far outpaced growth in production. In terms of quantity, edible oil imports doubled, from 1.1 million tons in 2000 to 2.2 million tons in 2012/2013. In terms of value, imports of edible oils increased more than sixfold, from US$326 million to US$2.03 billion. Traditional sources of domestic edible oil production have been cottonseed, a by-product of cotton farming, and rapeseed and mustard seed, but sunflower seed production has increased rapidly since early in the 2000–2009 decade.[31]

Various forms of palm oil (olein, refined bleached deodorized palm oil, and crude palm oil) accounted for about 90 percent of vegetable oil imports by weight from 2000/2001 to 2010/2011. There was little direct taxation of imported vegetable oils in the 1970s and 1980s, and exchange rate distortions led to an implicit subsidy on imports (and taxation of domestic producers) of just 3 percent in the 1970s and zero in the 1980s. Since the early 1990s, however, vegetable oils have been consistently taxed in Pakistan. For example, from 2000 through 2005, import tariffs were equivalent to about 40 percent of the import value, but they fell to only about 10 percent of the import value by 2013.

Milk

Pakistan has consistently placed tariffs on imported milk powder to protect the domestic dairy industry. NRP because of these tariffs averaged more than 70 percent in the 1960s and 1970s.[32] Tariff rates for milk powder were lowered in the early 1990s and have ranged from 20 percent to 45 percent since the mid-1990s, resulting in an NRP averaging 40 percent in the 1990s, and 20 percent from 2000 through 2005. The contrast between this high level of assistance to the dairy industry, along with that for sugar, and the much lower and usually negative NRPs for the other covered products, can be seen in Figure 7.6.

---

31 Other oilseed crops grown in Pakistan include canola (an improved cultivar of rapeseed), soybean, groundnut, safflower, sesame, and linseed.

32 These calculations are based on the unit import value of dry skim milk, adjusted by a conversion ratio of 1:8 and a quality factor of 90 percent, following Dorosh and Valdès (1990).

FIGURE 7.6 Nominal rates of protection for agricultural products, 1980–2013

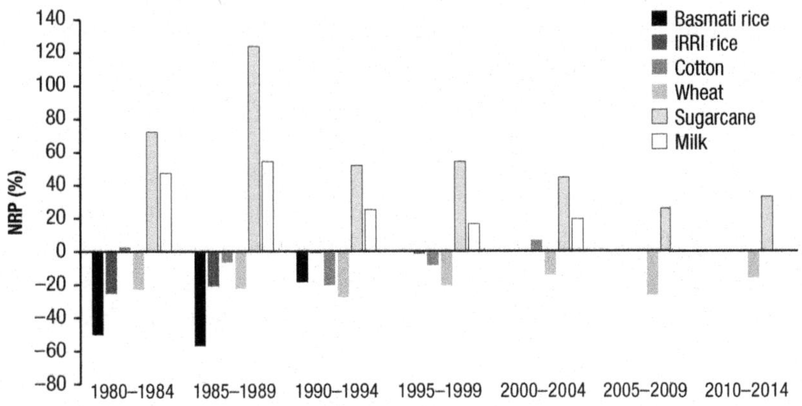

Source: Dorosh and Salam (2009); authors' calculations.
Note: Milk NRP for 2005–2009 and 2010–2014 is not available. NRP = nominal rate of protection.

Distortions to Input Prices

The major distortion to input prices in agriculture in Pakistan has been the subsidy on nitrogenous fertilizer.[33] Domestic producer prices of mainly urea have been kept consistently below import parity border prices. This has been achieved by using domestic natural gas inputs in domestic fertilizer production and passing some of the savings to farmers through a discounted price of natural gas. Since the early 1990s, there has been little or no subsidy on di-ammonium phosphate (DAP) and other major fertilizers, which are mainly imported but not produced domestically (Rashid et al. 2013).

Domestic prices of both urea and DAP averaged from 30 to 45 percent below import parity in the later 1970s and the 1980s. From 1990 to 2005, however, domestic prices of DAP on average were only 4 percent below import parity prices, while prices of urea were 38 percent below border prices. Given that the costs of DAP and urea were 10 percent and 8 percent, respectively, of the value of wheat production (Agricultural Prices Commission estimates for 2002), the implicit subsidy on fertilizer was equivalent to about 3 percent ($0.08 \times 0.38 + 0.10 \times 0.04$) of the value of wheat production from

---

33 Surface irrigation water is also implicitly subsidized, as water charges (*abiana*) are insufficient to cover the cost of maintenance of dams, canals, and other water channels. Measurement of the economic value of these subsidies involves assessment of overall investment and maintenance costs, as well as problems attributing these costs to various crops, so is not attempted in this study.

1990 to 2005. Likewise, for 2007/2008 through 2011/2012, domestic prices of urea were on average 40 percent below import parity prices at the whole-sale (Karachi) level, and the estimated implicit subsidy on urea was about 2 to 3 percent of the value of wheat production.[34]

Thus, the NRPs for wheat should be inflated by about 3 percentage points for most years since 1990. For the late 1970s and the 1980s, when DAP was subsidized as well, the NRPs for wheat should be about 7 percentage points (0.18×0.40) higher. NRPs for paddy, cotton, and sugarcane are also under-stated by similar amounts in these periods. These calculations are rather imprecise and do not include water subsidies, but they are nonetheless added to the NRP time series for the various crops for completeness and because they are nontrivial.

Implications of Trade Liberalization between Pakistan and India

The above calculations and discussion have focused on comparing interna-tional market prices with domestic prices in Pakistan because the interna-tional market prices represent the opportunity cost in terms of alternative sources of supply or demand for Pakistan's products. The huge markets in neighboring India were not considered because historically trade between the two countries has been severely limited through various tariffs, trade bans, or other restrictions, even though both countries joined the WTO when it was formed in 1995. Trade has been increasing since 2000, however, and negoti-ations that began in 2011 may lead to a major trade liberalization that could dramatically increase the level of trade and affect price formation in both countries.[35]

According to the first article of the General Agreement on Trade and Tariffs, all parties to the agreement agree to trade with one another accord-ing to the most-favored-nation (MFN) principle that guarantees that each

---

34 This calculation uses Agricultural Policy Institute's 2010/11 estimates of 6 percent and 11 percent, respectively, for the costs of urea and DAP as shares of the value of wheat production.

35 India maintained substantial trade and pricing controls on agriculture and much of the rest of the economy from independence until July 1991, when the Indian rupee was sharply devalued, a major trade policy reform was introduced, and domestic manufacturing was substantially deregulated. Further reductions in industrial tariffs took place from 1998 to 2001, and again in 2003 and 2007. Tariffs and other trade restrictions (so-called para-tariffs) on agriculture and processed food have remained high, however (averaging over 40 percent in 2006). See Gulati and Pursell (2009).

country will give equal treatment to all other member countries in terms of tariff rates and other trade restrictions (after the establishment of the World Trade Organization, this principle applied to every member of the WTO). Exceptions are permitted, however, for preferential trade agreements and free trade agreements. Member countries are also permitted to discriminate against one another for various political reasons.[36]

India granted MFN to Pakistan soon after joining the WTO, but it retained many nontariff barriers and other trade restrictions. Pakistan did not grant India MFN trading status until January 2013, in part because of India's continuing nontariff barriers inhibiting imports from Pakistan. Initial steps toward liberalization of trade began in 2012, however, as Pakistan reduced trade restrictions by changing from a "positive list" of 1,938 items allowed to be imported from India to a "negative list" of 1,209 items not allowed to be imported from India (bin Najib, Baig, and Ansari 2012). Initial analysis of this reform suggests that there would be little change in domestic output in Pakistan and moderate gains in consumer welfare because of lower consumer prices from this liberalization (Gopalan 2013).[37]

Prospects for trade in major agricultural products may not be very good in the short run because of the political sensitivities in both Pakistan and India about having a significant share of supply come from each neighbor. Nonetheless, negotiating a broad trade agreement could facilitate large-scale trade in the event of a major supply shortfall in one of the countries, similar to the surge in private-sector rice trade flows from India to Bangladesh following a major flood in Bangladesh in 1998 (Dorosh 2001). Currently, however, the price differentials for wheat and sugar are not large, though India's price of rice remains significantly below that of Pakistan (Table 7.6), so neither country has a strong need to import these products from the other.

Note, however, that these price differentials do not reflect the degree of support to agriculture, because they do not take into account the effects of input subsidies, which have generally been substantial in India. As Figure 7.7 shows, NRP to agriculture (a measure that here includes price distortions to

---

36 Article XX and Article XXI of the 1968 General Agreement on Tariffs and Trade provide for general exceptions to the MFN principle. A special exception was included for Pakistan and India in paragraph 11 of Article XXIV, as well. See the discussion in Memon, Rehman, and Rabbi (2014).

37 Using an imperfect substitution trade model with standard parameters, and assuming an implicit tariff of 200 percent for previously banned items, simulations in Gopalan (2013) indicate that the largest declines in domestic production would occur in the tobacco, pharmaceuticals, and cloth sectors, but that the largest percentage declines would be in leather, sporting goods, and footwear.

TABLE 7.6 Wheat, rice, and sugar prices in India and Pakistan, 1990–2013

	1990–1999	2000–2009	2010–2013
Wheat			
Pakistan[a] (US$/MT)	145.9	190.2	293.2
India[b] (US$/MT)	106.6	186.3	267.0
World price[c] (US$/MT)	148.8	184.2	291.3
Pakistan/India ratio	1.38	1.02	1.10
Pakistan/world ratio	1.01	1.06	1.03
Ordinary rice			
Pakistan[d] (US$/MT)	397.4	357.9	488.9
India[e] (US$/MT)	175.1	238.2	327.0
World price[f] (US$/MT)	285.1	312.5	525.2
Pakistan/India ratio	2.29	1.57	1.51
Pakistan/world price ratio	1.41	1.34	0.93
Sugar			
Pakistan[g] (US$/MT)	538.2	474.1	652.9
India[h] (US$/MT)	298.4	357.3	613.7
World Price[i] (US$/MT)	250.2	228.4	476.4
Pakistan/India ratio	1.82	1.38	1.06
Pakistan/world price ratio	2.28	2.24	1.37

Sources:

[a] Wholesale wheat price Lahore: 1962–2004 World Bank (2005); 2005–2013 GoP (various years), *Pakistan Statistical Yearbook.*

[b] Wholesale wheat price Delhi: 1964–2001 World Bank (2005); 2002–2014 National Information Center (GoI 2014).

[c] World wheat price, US hard red winter: 1961–2013 World Bank Pink Sheet (World Bank 2014a).

[d] Wholesale rice price Lahore: 1962–2004 World Bank, IRRI (World Bank 2005); 2005–2013 GoP (various years), *Pakistan Statistical Yearbook.*

[e] Wholesale rice price Delhi: 1964–2000 World Bank (World Bank 2005); 2001–2014 National Information Center (GoI 2014).

[f] World rice price, Thai 5%: 1961–2013 World Bank Pink Sheet (World Bank 2014a).

[g] World sugar price Lahore: 1961–2004 World Bank (World Bank 2005); 2005–2013 GoP (various years), *Pakistan Statistical Yearbook.*

[h] World sugar price Delhi: 1965–2002 World Bank (World Bank 2005); 2003–2014 National Information Center (GoI 2014).

[i] World sugar price: 1962–2014 World Bank Pink sheet (World Bank 2014a).

Note: MT = metric tons.

outputs as well as inputs) have generally been more positive in India than in Pakistan. For the 2006–2010 period, India's NRP averaged 15 percent, compared to −2 percent for Pakistan.

Ultimately, though, private-market trade flows depend on output price differentials, not on the extent of subsidies. Wholesale wheat prices in Pakistan (Lahore) were on average 38 percent higher than wholesale wheat prices in India (Delhi) in the 1990s, but close to international market prices

FIGURE 7.7 Nominal rates of protection to agriculture in Pakistan and India, 1976–2010

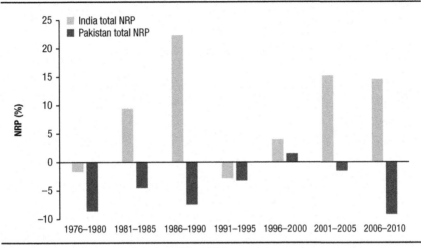

Source: Authors' calculation based on Anderson and Nelgen (2013).
Note: NRP = nominal rate of protection.

(Figure 7.8).[38] This suggests that in this period, if wheat trade had been liberalized, there could have been substantial flows of wheat from India to Pakistan. From 2000 onward, though, the wheat price differentials between Pakistan and India have been small, suggesting little opportunity to trade ordinary wheat, even if restrictions were removed.

Pakistan's prices for rice have been consistently above those of India, though the differential narrowed considerably from 2005 through 2007 (Figure 7.9). Pakistan's price of ordinary (IRRI-6) rice was more than double that of Indian rice in 1990–1999 and averaged about 50 percent higher than Indian rice from 2000 through 2013. However, Pakistan's rice price has been relatively close to the price of rice in international markets since 2000.

Similar to wheat prices, sugar prices in Pakistan were substantially higher than those in India in the 1990s, but the differential has narrowed considerably, so from 2010 to 2013, average Pakistani prices were only 6 percent above those in India.[39] Prices of sugar in both countries have been consistently much

---

38 Note that, unlike the calculations of nominal rates of protection for agriculture for India and Pakistan, no adjustment is made here for transportation or other marketing costs. During this period, the estimated nominal rate of protection in Pakistan was −23 percent.

39 These calculations do not take into account possible quality differences between sugar in India and Pakistan.

FIGURE 7.8 Wheat prices in India, Pakistan, and the world, 1990–2014

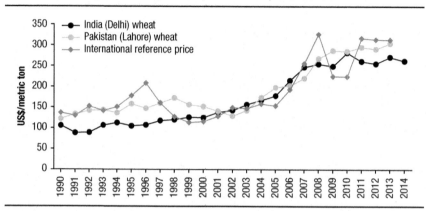

Source: GoI (2014); GoP (various years), *Pakistan Statistical Yearbook*; World Bank (2005); World Bank (2014a).

FIGURE 7.9 Rice prices in India, Pakistan, and the world, 1990–2014

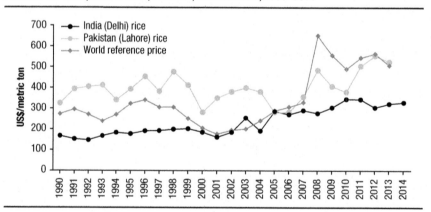

Source: GoI (2014); GoP (various years), *Pakistan Statistical Yearbook*; World Bank (2005); World Bank (2014a).

higher than international prices, as domestic producers in both countries have been subsidized, at a cost to consumers (Figure 7.10).

Trade in other agricultural commodities may be profitable, even if trade in these three major commodities is not. A large volume of pistachios is being exported from Pakistan to India (much of the pistachios originating in Afghanistan), and substantial volumes of fruits and vegetables may be flowing in both directions. Streamlining customs procedures (including sanitary and phytosanitary regulations and inspections) will be important if this trade is to flourish.

FIGURE 7.10 Sugar prices in India, Pakistan, and the world, 1990–2014

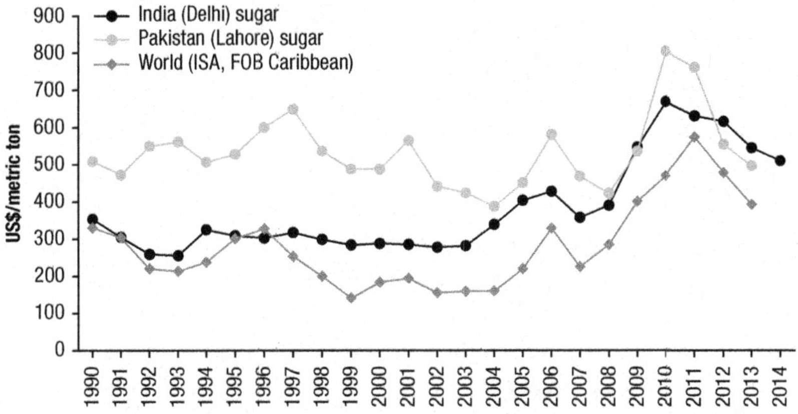

Source: GoI (2014); GoP (various years), *Pakistan Statistical Yearbook*; World Bank (2005); World Bank (2014a).
Note: FOB = free on board.

Summary and Policy Implications

Pakistan's agricultural markets and trade policies have undergone significant changes over the past several decades. State interventions, which dominated agricultural policy in the 1970s and most of the 1980s, were greatly reduced in the late 1980s and the 1990s, and implicit taxation of agriculture through exchange rate distortions, administered agricultural prices, and trade policy have been eliminated for most crops, including cotton, basmati rice, and ordinary (IRRI) rice. The dairy, vegetable oil, and sugarcane sectors still enjoy substantial trade protection through import tariffs and other restrictions, however, and government purchases and sales of wheat entail huge fiscal costs. And subsidies on fertilizer, canal water (irrigation fees less than the maintenance costs of canals), electricity, and fuel for pumps remain a persistent feature of government policy, but they are small, accounting for about 5 percent or less of the value of production.

Reforms in the wheat sector (such as sizable reductions in domestic procurement and elimination of subsidies on wheat supplied to mills) could bring huge benefits in terms of fiscal savings, more efficient wheat markets, more resources for agricultural research or targeted safety nets, and ultimately greater food security for the poor. Liberalization of the wheat market, however, need not mean a total abandonment of Pakistan's wheat producers and consumers to international and domestic market forces. The government would continue to have a role in price stabilization through trade policy interventions (export restrictions or subsidized sales of public imports) to prevent large spikes in world prices from adversely affecting consumers. Moreover, accompanying policies and programs in agricultural research and extension, investments in rural roads and markets, and public-private partnerships in agricultural processing and marketing could enhance economically efficient domestic production and improve farmers' incomes. However, reforms in the wheat sector (and the sugar sector) would need to overcome the resistance of large farmers and mill owners, who capture most of the benefits of subsidies on procurement and government sales.

There are no longer significant real exchange rate distortions such as the ones caused by import tariffs or government interventions in foreign exchange markets to hold fixed the nominal exchange rates, which caused massive indirect taxation of agriculture in the 1960s, 1970s, and much of the 1980s. Nonetheless, a future real appreciation of the Pakistani rupee related to large inflows of foreign capital could seriously harm agricultural growth and incomes. A more likely scenario, though, may be shortages of foreign exchange that could lead the government to place restrictions on imports and prevent a nominal exchange rate depreciation, even in a situation of high domestic inflation, thereby leading to a real exchange rate appreciation and lower real producer incomes.

Perhaps the biggest impacts of trade policy measures on agricultural growth could be from a trade liberalization in agricultural products with India. Expanded trade need not involve only the major agricultural products, however, but could involve fruits, vegetables, dairy, and other livestock products and could benefit producers and consumers on both sides of the border. Greater competition and new markets have the potential to spur increased agricultural productivity and higher incomes in Pakistan if the required public investment, macrostability, and overall security situation enable medium-term private investment in agricultural production, processing, and trade, particularly in high-value products.

References

Alderman, H., and M. Garcia. 1993. *Poverty, Household Food Security, and Nutrition in Rural Pakistan*. International Food Policy Research Institute Research Report 96. Washington, DC: IFPRI.

Ali, M. 1990. "The Price Response of Major Crops in Pakistan: An Application of the Simultaneous Equation Model." *The Pakistan Development Review* 29 (3 & 4) (Autumn–Winter): 305–325.

Anderson, K., M. Kurzweil, W. Martin, D. Sandri, and E. Valenzuela. 2008. *Measuring Distortions to Agricultural Incentives, Revisited.* Policy Research Working Paper 4612. Washington, DC: World Bank.

Anderson, K., and W. Martin, eds. 2008. *Distortions to Agricultural Incentives in Asia.* Washington, DC: World Bank.

Anderson, K., and S. Nelgen. 2013. "Updated National and Global Estimates of Distortions to Agricultural Incentives, 1955 to 2011." Spreadsheet. Washington, DC: World Bank. www.worldbank.org/agdistortions. Accessed June 2015.

bin Najib, W., F. A. Baig, and A. Ansari. 2012. *Implications of Trade Liberalization between Pakistan and India.* Lahore: Punjab Board of Investment and Trade. http://www.pbit.gop.pk/eng/system/files/Working-Paper-PAK-INDIA.pdf.

Chabot, P., and P. A. Dorosh. 2007. "Wheat Markets, Food Aid and Food Security in Afghanistan." *Food Policy* 32 (3): 334–353.

Cornelisse, P. A., and S. Naqvi. 1987. *The Wheat Marketing Activity in Pakistan.* Islamabad: Pakistan Institute of Development Economics; Rotterdam: Centre for Development Planning, Erasmus University.

Cororaton, C. B., and D. Orden. 2008. *Pakistan's Cotton and Textile Economy: Intersectoral Linkages and Effects on Rural and Urban Poverty.* Washington, DC: International Food Policy Research Institute.

Dornbusch, R. 1974. "Tariffs and Non-traded Goods." *Journal of International Economics* 4 (May): 177–185.

Dorosh, P. A. 2001. "Trade Liberalization and National Food Security: Rice Trade between Bangladesh and India." *World Development* 29 (4): 673–689.

———. 2008. "Regional Trade and Food Price Stabilisation in South Asia: Policy Responses to the 2007–08 World Price Shocks." *Pakistan Development Review* 47 (4): 803–813.

Dorosh, P., S. J. Malik, and M. Krausova. 2011. "Rehabilitating Agriculture and Promoting Food Security Following the 2010 Pakistan Floods." *Pakistan Development Review* 49 (3): 167–192.

Dorosh, P. A., and A. Salam. 2008. "Wheat Markets and Price Stabilization in Pakistan: An Analysis of Policy Options." *Pakistan Development Review* 44 (1): 71–88.

———. 2009. "Pakistan." In *Distortions to Agricultural Incentives in Asia*, edited by Kym Anderson and Will Martin, 379–408. Washington, DC: World Bank.

Dorosh, P., and A. Valdès. 1990. *Effects of Exchange Rate and Trade Policies on Agriculture in Pakistan.* International Food Policy Research Institute Research Report 84. Washington, DC: IFPRI.

FAO (Food and Agriculture Organization). 2014. Agricultural Statistics database. http://www.fao
     .org/economic/est/statistical-data/est-cpd/ar/ .

Faruqee, R., and J. R. Coleman. 1996. *Managing Price Risk in Pakistan's Wheat Markets.*
     Discussion Paper 334. Washington, DC: World Bank.

GoI (Government of India). 2014. National Information Center. http://agmarkweb.dacnet.nic.in/
     SA_Pri_MonthD.aspx. Accessed June 2015.

GoP (Government of Pakistan). Various years. *Pakistan Economic Survey.* Islamabad: Finance
     Division, Economic Adviser's Wing of the Ministry of Finance. http://www.finance.gov.pk.

———. Various years. *Pakistan Statistical Yearbook.* Islamabad: Pakistan Bureau of Statistics.

———. Various years. *Agricultural Statistics of Pakistan.* Islamabad: Pakistan Bureau of Statistics.

Gopalan, S. 2013. *The Imperfect Substitutes Model in South Asia: Pakistan-India Trade
     Liberalisation in the Negative List.* London: International Growth Centre.

Gulati, A., and G. Pursell. 2009. "Distortions to Agricultural Incentives in India and Other South
     Asia." In *Distortions to Agricultural Incentives: A Global Perspective, 1955 to 2007,* edited by
     Kym Anderson. London: Palgrave Macmillan; Washington, DC: World Bank.

Hamid, N., I. Nabi, and A. Nasim. 1990. *Trade, Exchange Rate, and Agricultural Pricing Policies in
     Pakistan.* Washington, DC: World Bank.

IMF (International Monetary Fund). 2014. International Financial Statistics. Accessed June 17,
     2014. http://data.imf.org.

Krueger, A. O., M. Schiff, and A. Valdés. 1988. "Agricultural Incentives in Developing Countries:
     Measuring the Effect of Sectoral and Economywide Policies." *World Bank Economic Review* 2
     (3): 255–272.

Memon, N., F. Rehman, and F. Rabbi. 2014. *Pak-India Trade Liberalization: How Will Pakistan's
     Manufacturing Sector Fare? A Comparative Advantage Analysis.* Working Paper. Karachi:
     Manzil Pakistan.

Nabi, I. 1997. "Outward Orientation of the Economy: A Review of Pakistan's Evolving Trade and
     Exchange Rate Policy." *Journal of Asian Studies* 8 (1): 143–163.

Persaud, S. 2010. *Price Volatility in Afghanistan's Wheat Market.* US Department of Agriculture
     Economic Research Service Outlook Report WHS-10d-01. Washington, DC: USDA.

Pursell, G., A. Khan, and S. Gulzar. 2011. *Pakistan's Trade Policies: Future Directions.* IGC
     Working Paper. London: International Growth Centre.

Rashid, S., P. A. Dorosh, M. Malek, and S. Lemma. 2013. "Modern Input Promotion
     in Sub-Saharan Africa: Insights from Asian Green Revolution." *Agricultural Economics* 444
     (6): 705–721. http://onlinelibrary.wiley.com/doi/10.1111/agec.12083/abstract.

Salam, A., and M. M. Mukhtar. 2008. "Public Intervention in Pakistan's Wheat Market: The Story of Two Agencies." In *From Parastatals to Private Trade: Lessons from Asian Agriculture*, edited by Shahidur Rashid, Ashok Gulati, and Ralph Cummings Jr. Baltimore: The Johns Hopkins University Press.

Sayeed, A. 2010. *"Synthesis Report" for the Study on the State of Domestic Commerce in Pakistan for the Ministry of Commerce, Government of Pakistan.* Islamabad: Innovative Development Strategies.

USDA (United States Department of Agriculture). 2013. *Grain and Feed—Afghanistan. April 8, 2013.* Washington, DC: USDA Foreign Agricultural Service, Global Agricultural information Network. http://gain.fas.usda.gov/Recent%20GAIN%20Publications/Grain %20and%20Feed%20-%20Afghanistan_Kabul_Afghanistan_4–8-2013.pdf.

Valdès, A. 2013. *Agriculture Trade and Price Policy in Pakistan.* Policy Paper Series on Pakistan PK 17/12. South Asia Poverty Reduction and Economic Management Unit. Washington, DC: World Bank.

World Bank. 2004. *Trade Policies in South Asia, Volume II: An Overview.* Washington, DC: World Bank.

———. 2005. Agricultural Price Distortions website, "Pakistan." Washington, DC: World Bank. http://go.worldbank.org/U32NJLFN10.

———. 2010. *Food Price Increases in South Asia: National Responses and Regional Dimensions.* Washington, DC: World Bank.

———. 2014a. *Pink Sheet.* Washington, DC: World Bank. http://go.worldbank.org/ 4ROCCIEQ50.

———. 2014b. *Mitigating the Impact of Price Instability on Poverty in Pakistan: The Effectiveness of Public Grain Stocks and Price Stabilization Policy.* Washington, DC: World Bank.

Annex A: Methodological Framework

The nominal rate of protection of commodity i is defined as

$$NRP_i = (P_i / P_i') - 1$$

where P_i is the domestic market price of commodity i and P_i' is the border price of commodity i at the same location (the nominal exchange rate E in PKR/foreign currency units, multiplied by the world price at the border Pw_i).[40]

In the case where the only price distortion is because of a simple ad valorem tariff tm_i, the NRP of commodity i measured at the border is

$$NRP_i = (P_i / P_i') - 1 = [E * Pw_i * (1 + tm_i) / (E * Pw_i)] - 1 = (1 + tm_i) - 1 = tm_i.$$

Similarly, to account for distortions in the costs of inputs, the effective rate of protection of commodity i, ERP_i, is based on the ratio of value added at domestic market and border prices:

$$ERP_i = (VA_i / VA_i') - 1,$$

where VA_i and VA_i' are the value added at private and social (undistorted) prices:

$$VA_i = P_i \, Q_i - \textstyle\sum_j a_{ji} * Q_i * P_j ,$$

$$VA_i' = P_i' * Q_i - \textstyle\sum_j a_{ji} * Q_i * P_j' ,$$

and a_{ji} is the quantity of input j needed to produce a unit of output of commodity i.

---

40 To capture the effects of distortions in the exchange rate, a hypothetical exchange rate in the absence of distortions, E' is used. In the Krueger, Schiff, and Valdès (1988) methodology followed by Dorosh and Valdès (1990), equilibrium exchange rates in the absence of import tariffs and foreign exchange restrictions were calculated using two alternative methodologies—a trade elasticities approach and a real exchange rate regression approach.

Chapter 8

PUBLIC SERVICE DELIVERY FOR RURAL DEVELOPMENT

**Madiha Afzal, Gissele Gajate Garrido, Brian Holtemeyer,
and Katrina Kosec**

Introduction

Despite the recognized, critical role of public services in raising rural welfare, Pakistan has recently struggled with the challenge of providing quality services to its rural population. Efforts to design and implement policies that ensure both access and quality have been hampered by events such as major flooding in 2010, 2011, and 2014, as well as the civil conflict and violence that continually affect the country (UNICEF 2012).[1] In the midst of these exceptional circumstances, Pakistan also experienced a major political transformation in 2010 with the introduction of the 18th Amendment to the constitution, which devolved federal political authority and responsibility for essential services to the provinces (DRI 2010) and made Pakistan the first federation in the world without a national or federal health ministry (Nishtar et al. 2013). Measures to ensure accountability have not kept pace with changes in responsibilities, generating concern about how service delivery can be improved (Arif et al. 2010; Bhutta et al. 2013).[2] This apprehension is well deserved given the state of public services in the country, starting with the health sector but also encompassing education, water, sanitation, and electricity services.

Pakistan's track record of achievements in the provision of public services—especially in rural areas—is recognized as falling below what is necessary to support economic growth and social development, and the country's indicators generally lag behind those of its South Asian neighbors (Table A8.2). Pakistan has the world's third-highest burden of maternal, fetal, and child mortality, owing largely to viral infections, dengue, tuberculosis, malaria, and

---

1   The army campaign against terrorists in North Waziristan since June 2014 has added to the internal instability and the large numbers of internally displaced persons.

2   The 18th Amendment to the constitution and its implications for Pakistan's rural development are discussed further in Chapter 9.

hepatitis B and C (Bhutta et al. 2013; GoP 2014a). In rural areas in particular, one in nine Pakistani children does not survive to his or her fifth birthdays (NIPS 2013).[3] Rural Pakistan similarly lags on education indicators: the net enrollment rate at the primary level (ages five to nine)[4] is 54 percent (far from the Vision 2025 goal of universal primary education with 100 percent net primary enrollment); only 42 percent of children in rural areas complete primary school; and only 51 percent of rural children ages 10 and older are literate (PSLM 2014). The indicators are also worrisome from a gender perspective: the gender parity index in rural Pakistan is 0.84 for the primary level (calculated as the ratio of female to male net enrollment at the primary level), 0.70 for the middle level, 0.82 for the matric or secondary level, and 0.58 for literacy (for 10 years and older), suggesting lingering problems with educating girls (GoP 2014c).[5]

Add to this the problems associated with the provision of water, sanitation, and electricity services: only 50 percent of rural households have access to a piped drainage system, only 45 percent have access to a flush toilet, and only 9 percent have access to a piped water source. Inadequate access to sanitation services alone is estimated to cause Pakistan economic losses totaling US$5.7 billion (PKR 343.7 billion) per year—equivalent to 3.9 percent of gross domestic product (GDP)—and exacerbates many of the already dire health problems mentioned earlier (WSP 2012). Rural households' access to water, sanitation, electricity, and other essentials is further constrained by the power sector crisis. For example, during the summer months of 2012, while urban households experienced up to 8–10 hours per day of power outages because of load shedding, rural areas were subjected to 16–18 hours of outages (USAID 2013). Power sector inefficiencies are estimated to have lowered economic growth by at least 2 percent annually over the past five years (USAID 2013).

Multiple factors likely account for subpar provision of rural public services. On the demand side, illiteracy, gender inequality, social exclusion, and poverty reduce the extent to which people try to access public services. On the supply side, inadequate and unequal public funding limits access for many groups. Further, weak governance and poor accountability have wasted resources and

---

3   Under-five mortality in rural areas is 106 deaths per 1,000 live births.

4   We use the age ranges preferred by the government for primary, middle, and secondary schooling.

5   For the middle level, this is calculated as the ratio of female to male rural net enrollment for grades 6 to 8, ages 10 to 12. For the secondary level, this is calculated as the ratio of female to male rural net enrollment for grades 9 to 10, ages 13 to 14.

prevented the development of coherent and consistent policy frameworks over time.

In the area of health, socioeconomic status poses high barriers to women's ability to access even the most basic maternal care. Moreover, an unregulated, low-quality private sector has filled in for a public sector that is unable to provide adequate delivery care to pregnant women (GoP 2009a). This is a direct consequence of the lack of coherence and stability of the governance environment surrounding health services. Most of the key policy strategies for maternal and child health in the past 20 years have lacked a long-term vision and proper targeting (Bhutta et al. 2013).

In the area of education, Pakistan faces stubborn barriers to school enrollment—especially for poor, rural girls. On the supply side, rural areas have a lack of available schools in each village, especially government middle and high schools, as well as long distances to schools and poor infrastructure within schools. On the demand side, economic and social barriers play a large role, especially in preventing girls from attending school. Limited returns to education are an additional demand-side barrier.

Inadequate access to rural services implies many challenges for Pakistan's policy makers, many of whom are likely cognizant of the demonstrated importance of public services to the rural poor. Several potential pathways exist through which access to high-quality public services might be improved: by directly increasing agricultural labor supply, productivity, and rural incomes; by encouraging investments in physical and human capital; and by more broadly empowering citizens and helping them meet basic needs (World Bank 2007; Mogues 2011). Because of the potential benefits, access to public services belongs at the heart of rural development and poverty reduction strategies. This chapter explores how consistent, coherent policies for five public services in rural Pakistan—healthcare, education, electricity, water, and sanitation—can boost access to services and thereby raise the welfare of people in rural areas.

Public health and education policies have obvious, direct impacts on rural welfare; the unhealthy cannot work productively, and the uneducated are likely to make suboptimal choices on decisions such as crop choice, inputs, insurance, markets in which to sell products, and rural nonfarm work opportunities. Furthermore, education and health have multiple feedback loops: good health improves educational outcomes, and vice versa. Poor health in childhood is associated with poor schooling outcomes (Alderman et al. 2001; Glewwe, Jacoby, and King 2001; Miguel and Kremer 2004; Paxson and Schady 2007), which reduce labor productivity in adulthood. In turn, education provides knowledge and generates income that can improve health and therefore productivity.

Electricity, water, and sanitation policies also directly affect rural welfare. Electrification has been shown to substantially increase labor productivity, leading to significant development gains (Dinkelman 2011; Reinikka and Svensson 2002; Lipscomb, Mobarak, and Barham 2013; Fisher-Vanden, Mansur, and Wang 2012). Giving people access to improved water and sanitation sources greatly improves their health and nutritional status, thereby directly affecting labor productivity (Ewbank and Preston 1990; Cutler and Miller 2005; Zwane and Kremer 2007; Günther and Fink 2010). In addition to having poorer health, those without access to improved water and sanitation are often burdened by high healthcare costs, time spent caring for sick family members, and long treks to fetch water, all of which further lower labor supply and productivity.

In addition to the direct effects of public services on labor supply and productivity, places with high-quality rural services also tend to attract mobile factors of production—both capital and labor. People like to live in places with good public services, and owners of small and medium enterprises prefer to locate in such places. Policies that encourage access to high-quality public services can accordingly attract the kinds of citizens and economic activity that will fuel agricultural productivity and help Pakistan's rural sector contribute to the broader growth and development of the whole country (Stansel 2005; Hatfield and Kosec 2013; Kosec and Mogues 2016).

Clearly, public services in rural areas have been on Pakistan's development agenda for decades: the country's policies on education, health, water, sanitation, and electricity are well intentioned and cognizant of the gaps in these sectors, though policy implementation has consistently fallen short. Multiple causes are commonly identified. First, national and provincial plans have changed frequently over time, reducing policy coherence. Second, central government efforts to empower local community-based organizations to improve access have been underutilized. Where people at the local level have an organic civic interest in improving service delivery, provision of resources by a strong and effective central government can help make them successful (Mansuri and Rao 2013). As examples, Pakistan's National Rural Support Program and the Aga Khan Rural Support Program both combine community development funds with social mobilization, training, capacity building, and other support mechanisms. Third, public resources—both development budgets at the federal and provincial levels and donor funds meant to augment these budgets—have often fallen short. Yet the persistent existence of unused funds in most years suggests that the issue may be one of coordination and implementation as much as one of allocation.

This chapter takes a two-pronged approach to establishing a better understanding of how policies governing these five services in rural Pakistan can improve rural welfare. First, we explore the connection between access to rural public services and agricultural labor supply and input use, as well as nonfarm work and income, using unique data from Rounds 1 and 2 of the Pakistan Rural Household Panel Survey (RHPS) conducted in 2012–2013 (IFPRI/IDS 2012, 2013; see Chapter 1 for details). Second, for each of the five services, we examine how existing policies pose barriers to access, and how these barriers exacerbate disparities. Following this analysis, we examine how a coherent and stable governance environment surrounding service delivery might raise government accountability and citizen welfare. Analyzing these questions, we draw lessons on what reforms might improve services and thereby raise the welfare, labor supply, and productivity of the rural poor.

It is worth noting here the unique value that the Pakistan RHPS adds to this analysis. While there are many other household surveys on Pakistan's rural economy, the Pakistan RHPS provides a panel dataset that expands the opportunities to analyze rural welfare across multiple dimensions. Specifically, the Pakistan RHPS contains a wealth of individual-level information on educational attainment and health shocks, combined with household-level information on access to public services and household characteristics. Further, the Pakistan RHPS contains detailed information on agricultural labor supply by the whole household, the intensity of machinery use for agricultural purposes, nonfarm labor participation, nonfarm earnings, access to public and private services, and gender-related aspects of these elements. Rarely are such expansive panel datasets available to researchers and practitioners. Of course, as discussed in Chapter 1, the Pakistan RHPS is not a nationally representative household survey, so caution is advised in interpreting the analysis presented here as a reflection on all rural public services in Pakistan.

The Importance of Access to Public Services for Rural Development

This section addresses the importance of public services for rural development by testing the hypothesis that there is a strong association between access to services and agricultural and nonfarm activities. It does so by using the Pakistan 2012–2013 RHPS to examine the impact of services on agricultural labor supply, machinery use in agricultural activities, and participation in nonfarm labor by all male and female household members ages 18–65 (IFPRI/ IDS 2012, 2013). We present estimates of these associations where the outcome variables of interest are either (1) agricultural labor (measured in total number of days worked) supplied by the household during the last year, (2) the intensity of machinery use in agricultural activities (measured by the total number of machines used) by the household in the past year, (3) engagement in nonfarm labor (separate indicators are used for men's and women's engagement), or (4) earnings generated from nonfarm labor in the 12 months immediately preceding the survey (again, measured separately for men and women).

This section considers several predictors of agricultural labor supply and inputs: (1) the distance from the household's village to the closest Basic Health Unit (BHU) (an ordinal categorical variable that ranges from 0 to 4);[6] (2) an indicator for whether or not the household incurred medical expenses due to illness or injury in the past year; (3) indicators for different levels of education: primary education (grades 1 to 5), middle education (grades 6 to 8), secondary school (grades 9 and 10), and higher secondary and up (grades 11 onward); (4) the number of hours per day that the household has electricity; (5) the distance (in kilometers [km]) from the household to its water source; (6) an indicator for whether the household has access to a flush latrine; and (7) an indicator for whether the household has access to a piped drainage system. All seven are linked with access to the five services considered in this chapter.

All of the regressions presented in this section are estimated using ordinary least squares (OLS) and include controls for household size, crowding (individuals per room in the household), a household wealth score computed by principal components analysis, and both district and year fixed effects.[7] The estimations include both pooled regressions as well as panel data regressions (which include household fixed effects). The first set of regressions allow us to analyze the impacts of time-invariant variables: the individual's education level and the household's distance to the closest BHU. The second set

---

6   This variable is equal to 0 if the BHU is in the locality, 1 if the distance to the BHU is up to 5 kilometers (km), 2 if the distance is 6–10 km, 3 if the distance is 11–15 km, and 4 if the distance is more than 15 km.

7   The wealth score was constructed using a series of household characteristics (flooring, walls, and ceiling materials, ownership of goods, toilet facilities, type of cooking fuel, and so forth) and conducting a principal component analysis. We take the first principal component from this analysis as our wealth index. We use district fixed effects to flexibly allow the average levels of our outcome variables to vary not only across provinces (an important geographic level given the devolution of substantial service provision authorities to the provinces under the 18th Amendment) but also across districts (which differ in their soil quality, land and labor endowments, and local governance structures).

of regressions exploit the fact that we have data from two different periods; while it does not permit us to analyze the impacts of time-invariant variables, it has the substantial benefit of allowing us to control for all time-invariant household characteristics that may drive access to public services as well as agricultural labor supply, productivity, and inputs. The analysis first examines whether changes in access to public services predict changes in agricultural labor supply and machinery use. All standard errors are clustered at the household level.

Estimation results indicate that education does not affect agricultural labor supply (Table 8.1, column 1). The only exception is that for individuals with a higher secondary education or more (relative to those who have never enrolled), the household allocates 27 fewer days per year to agricultural labor. This decrease is approximately 17 percent of the average number of days worked, and it exists likely because having a higher education allows household members to divert effort away from agriculture to other areas of the rural economy, which are generally more profitable. This is consistent with the findings of Fafchamps and Quisumbing (1999) and Kurosaki (2001) in Pakistan, as well as other research across varied contexts.

In contrast, decreasing the distance to a BHU (and hence increasing the accessibility of health services) substantially increases agricultural labor supply. Specifically, having such a facility 5 km farther away from the household is associated with 18 fewer days per year dedicated to agricultural labor by that household. Reduced distances to these facilities free up time for other activities (such as productive work) and encourage the use of both preventive and curative care. As the use of health services increases, health outcomes improve, leading to a more productive workforce. While we find no evidence that the distance to a BHU is associated with use of machinery (column 2), education is associated with increased machinery use. Specifically, relative to those who have never enrolled in school, individuals who attended middle school, high school, and higher secondary school and up are all predicted to live in households that use a significantly larger number of agricultural machines (approximately 0.4, 0.6, and 0.4, respectively). Because we control for household wealth in these regressions, education does not appear to merely proxy for economic status. This result illustrates how access to education may allow rural dwellers to take advantage of more efficient means of production. The pooled estimates also show that household medical expenses significantly reduce the household's agricultural labor supply.

Next, we turn to the panel data analysis using household fixed effects to better identify the effects of the time-variant predictors of agricultural labor

TABLE 8.1 Determinants of agricultural labor supply and machinery use

Explanatory variables	Pooled estimations		Panel estimations	
	Agricultural labor supply (1)	Machinery use (2)	Agricultural labor supply (3)	Machinery use (4)
Primary education (grades 1–5)	2.337 (6.038)	0.063 (0.112)		
Middle education (grades 6–8)	16.930 (11.510)	0.380 (0.176)**		
Secondary school (grades 9–10)	16.007 (12.377)	0.595 (0.169)***		
Higher secondary school and up (grades 11 onward)	−27.075 (15.454)*	0.399 (0.217)*		
Distance to Basic Health Unit	−18.463 (5.894)***	−0.022 (0.092)		
Medical expenses due to illness or injury	−89.113 (17.429)***	−0.259 (0.243)	−57.995 (26.318)**	0.436 (0.361)
Hours per day of electricity	−4.970 (1.197)***	−0.083 (0.022)***	1.701 (2.091)	0.070 (0.034)**
Distance to water source (km)	−6.219 (12.606)	−0.114 (0.245)	−47.498 (25.281)*	−0.300 (0.342)
Flush latrine	9.840 (12.725)	−0.121 (0.211)	37.600 (23.993)	−0.230 (0.357)
Piped drainage system	23.352 (14.638)	0.066 (0.218)	63.368 (25.157)**	0.020 (0.330)
Household size	16.384 (2.701)***	0.185 (0.042)***	21.312 (12.022)*	0.486 (0.164)***
Crowding	−9.860 (3.023)***	−0.174 (0.051)***	6.606 (5.182)	−0.001 (0.053)
Household wealth score	14.490 (4.042)***	0.531 (0.065)***	−8.486 (10.796)	0.327 (0.121)***
Observations	9,916	9,916	5,033	5,033
Adjusted R²	0.29	0.32	0.38	0.26

Source: Authors, based on 2012–2013 Pakistan RHPS (IFPRI/IDS 2012, 2013).

Note: All estimations include year and district fixed effects. Columns 3 and 4 in addition include household fixed effects. Robust standard errors clustered at the household level appear below coefficients, in parentheses. * = significant at 10%; ** = significant at 5%; *** = significant at 1%. km = kilometers.

supply and inputs from Table 8.1. Agricultural labor supply and machinery use are the dependent variables, respectively, in columns 3 and 4. A negative health shock and increased distance to the water source both significantly decrease the number of days worked by the household in agricultural activities during the year. Also, access to drainage significantly increases the household's time commitment to agricultural labor. In short, the analysis finds that better sanitation and health raise agricultural labor supply. The magnitude of these effects is fairly substantial. The presence of a negative health shock decreases a household's average number of days worked in agriculture by 36 percent, while a 1 km increase in distance to the water source reduces agricultural labor supply by 29 percent. Finally, a household's access to a piped drainage system increases agricultural labor supply by 39 percent. Better access to electricity does not appear to significantly affect agricultural labor supply in the panel specification. Yet as column 4 of Table 8.1 shows, the higher the number of hours per day a household has access to electricity, the more machines that household will use for agricultural activities. For every additional hour of electricity, it will use 0.07 more machines (a modest 2 percent increase in usage). According to the results from column 4, no other public service increases use of machinery in the agricultural sector.

Next, we examine the relationship of our access variables with engagement in nonfarm activities as well as nonfarm income earned within the 12 months preceding the survey. Of most interest is the relationship between education and nonfarm outcomes. For men, the top nonfarm activity is construction labor, followed by factory work, and then work in government and private enterprises. For women, fewer of whom are engaged in nonfarm activities, their major nonfarm activities are teaching, working in government, and working as household or construction labor.

Columns 1 and 2 in Table 8.2 show the impacts of education, healthcare, water, sanitation, and electricity on nonfarm labor participation for men and for women, while columns 3 and 4 look at the impact of these five services on levels of earnings in nonfarm labor for men and women. As anticipated, the analysis finds that individuals with higher levels of education find work in other areas of the rural economy, beyond agriculture. Furthermore, the higher the level of education, the larger the premium for working in nonfarm labor. This relationship is particularly strong in the case of men. For example, men who attended secondary school have a 5 percent higher probability of engaging in nonfarm labor, and on average earn PKR 10,285 more annually, relative to men with no schooling. For women, the corresponding percentage is 2 percent, and the increase in earnings is PKR 2,187 (though this latter number is not significant). Men who attended higher secondary school or beyond have a 6 percent higher probability of engaging in nonfarm labor, and on average earn PKR 36,640 more, relative to men with no schooling. For women, the corresponding percentage is 13 percent, and the increase in earnings is PKR 8,921. It appears that a health shock is associated with higher participation in the nonfarm sector, perhaps because households need additional income to deal with the unexpected expenses related to the shock. Hours of

TABLE 8.2 Determinants of nonfarm labor participation and earnings—pooled estimations

Explanatory variables	Nonfarm labor participation		Nonfarm earnings	
	Men (1)	Women (2)	Men (3)	Women (4)
Primary education (grades 1–5)	0.014	0.003	2,862.22	−173.84
	(0.018)	(0.005)	(1,547.56)*	(196.64)
Middle education (grades 6–8)	0.026	0.025	2,684.07	1,202.26
	(0.022)	(0.012)**	(2,225.19)	(724.16)*
Secondary school (grades 9–10)	0.048	0.024	10,284.57	2,187.47
	(0.022)**	(0.012)*	(2,868.10)***	(1,619.97)
Higher secondary school and up (grade 11 onward)	0.059	0.134	36,640.15	8,920.81
	(0.029)**	(0.023)***	(5,295.32)***	(2,235.00)***
Distance to Basic Health Unit	0.006	0.002	615.82	−66.48
	(0.008)	(0.002)	(893.29)	(176.02)
Medical expenses due to illness or injury	0.047	0.008	2,360.42	−147.17
	(0.017)***	(0.004)*	(1,799.31)	(256.95)
Hours per day of electricity	0.008	0.000	556.82	−71.41
	(0.002)***	(0.000)	(178.36)***	(44.30)
Distance to water source (km)	0.068	0.008	6,201.92	308.92
	(0.016)***	(0.006)	(1,792.80)***	(198.38)
Flush latrine	−0.016	−0.000	−1,822.57	−208.28
	(0.017)	(0.004)	(1,920.94)	(342.56)
Piped drainage system	0.033	0.003	2,288.50	−180.64
	(0.017)*	(0.004)	(1,816.44)	(370.42)
Household size	−0.006	−0.001	−525.33	−42.36
	(0.003)**	(0.001)**	(391.79)	(69.68)
Crowding	0.001	0.001	1.18	85.46
	(0.004)	(0.001)*	(459.10)	(50.73)*
Household Wealth score	−0.023	−0.003	1,838.54	248.26
	(0.005)***	(0.001)**	(640.48)***	(193.61)
Observations	6,513	6,324	6,513	6,324
Adjusted R²	0.07	0.05	0.12	0.03

Source: Authors, based on 2012–2013 Pakistan RHPS (IFPRI/IDS 2012; 2013).

Note: All estimations include year and district fixed effects. Robust standard errors clustered at the household level appear below coefficients, in parentheses. * = significant at 10%; ** = significant at 5%; *** = significant at 1%. km = kilometers.

electricity also appear to be associated with higher participation in nonfarm labor as well as earnings.

These results depict an environment where girls' education yields dividends in the rural economy. Earlier evidence from Fafchamps and Quisumbing (1999, 369), in contrast, found that "female education and nutrition do not affect productivity and labor allocation in any systematic fashion, a finding that is consistent with the marginal role women play in market-oriented activities in Pakistan." This appears to no longer be the case in rural Pakistan, at least for the population represented by the Pakistan RHPS sample; women are participating in the nonfarm sector and contributing to the rural economy, and those with higher education can contribute more. Taken as a whole, the results presented above illustrate the importance of access to public services for improvement in agricultural labor supply, productivity, and rural development. Hence, understanding the policies governing these services as well as the barriers to access is of utmost importance. The following sections turn to our second set of questions: how do existing policies pose barriers to access, and what disparities in access are they creating? And how can a coherent and stable governance environment surrounding service delivery raise government accountability and citizen welfare? We analyze these questions with an exploration of each sector before drawing broader conclusions about rural public services.

Linking Policy to Outcomes

The key roles that health, education, water, sanitation, and electricity services play in agricultural production and rural incomes raise important questions about what policies can best improve access and quality. Pakistan's current public policies governing rural service delivery have evolved substantially over the past several decades. Understanding how policy effectiveness might be improved requires a firm grasp of the existing policy environment, including its basic institutional architecture.

Improving service provision policies requires knowledge of which policies are succeeding and failing, how the institutional architecture enables or impedes policy implementation, which populations are being served and not being served, and which potential new directions for policy are most promising. While we expect that policy environments and institutional architectures surrounding rural service delivery determine service access and quality, the nuances of these relationships are an empirical question. The sections that follow examine these relationships for each of these services in turn.

Health

In Pakistan public healthcare provision is divided into primary, secondary, and tertiary healthcare. Primary healthcare is delivered through BHUs, Rural Health Centers, Maternal and Child Health Centers (MCHCs), and Dispensaries. This level of care mainly provides preventive and promotive health services, though curative services for common illnesses are sometimes

provided.[8] Lady Health Workers (LHWs) are the main public health workers supplying promotive and preventive services in rural areas (Bhutta et al.
2013).[9] They provide family planning advice and some basic curative care, and
they are trained to identify and refer certain serious conditions but do not
assist deliveries (Oxford Policy Management 2009).

The secondary healthcare level includes first- and second-level referral
facilities—such as Tehsil Headquarters Hospitals and District Headquarters
Hospitals—providing three specialized types of care: acute, ambulatory, and
inpatient care. Finally, tertiary healthcare is provided through major hospitals that have personnel and facilities for advanced medical investigation and
treatment (GoP 2009a).

Figure 8.1 shows that the number of public facilities for all levels of healthcare—primary, secondary, and tertiary, supplied through BHUs, Rural
Health Centers, MCHCs, Dispensaries, hospitals located at the tehsil and
district levels,[10] and major hospitals primarily located in urban centers—
increased dramatically between 1960 and 1990, but has since stagnated (GoP
2015; GoP 2009a). In the case of MCHCs, the numbers have even decreased
in recent years. In addition, inadequate public funding for both recurrent
and development-related costs has resulted in health facilities that have a lack
of basic equipment and medicines, insufficient expertise in the management
(Arif et al. 2010), poorly compensated health professionals who engage in dual
(government and private) practices as a norm, and weak quality control and
standardization of care (UNICEF 2012; Callen et al. 2013). Consequently,
the population has turned to an unregulated private sector as the basic provider of health services. Fully 66 percent of total healthcare expenditures
in Pakistan are funded through the private sector, and of these expenditures, 97.5 percent are in the form of out-of-pocket healthcare expenditures
by households (GoP 2009a). In the private sector, healthcare facilities are neither standardized nor classified, resulting in a broad array of facilities that
range from private hospitals and clinics to traditional health providers (such as
homeopaths) to ambulatory healthcare services and nongovernmental organization–run healthcare facilities (GoP 2009a).

---

8   Preventive and promotive health services include maternal and child health services, immuniza-
    tion, diarrheal disease control, malaria control, child spacing, mental health, school health ser-
    vices, prevention and control of locally endemic diseases, and provision of essential drugs.

9   The LHW Program (also known as the National Program for Family Planning and Primary
    Health Care) was launched in 1994 to provide primary care, especially in rural populations.

10 A *tehsil* is a subdistrict administrative unit that consists of a collection of union councils
    and villages.

FIGURE 8.1 Number of national medical and healthcare facilities, 1960–2014

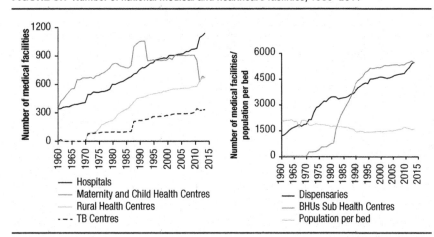

Source: Authors, based on GoP (2015).
Note: 2014 data are provisional data with respect to Punjab province. The decrease in Maternity and Child Health Centres in 2014 is due to the exclusion/separation of family welfare centers from maternity centers in Khyber Pakhtunkhwa Province.

As a result, the healthcare situation in Pakistan is possibly best described as precarious. While the 18th Amendment sought to shift greater responsibility for healthcare provision from the federal to the provincial level, measures to ensure capacity and accountability have not kept pace with changes in responsibilities (Arif et al. 2010; Bhutta et al. 2013). The Federal Ministry of Health was dissolved, and the provincial governments assumed its responsibilities. But while the responsibilities at the provincial government level have increased substantially, the accountability for coverage of specific geographic areas and policies has not. The division of managerial oversight and coordination over several government agencies, as well as the continuation of vertical health programs such as the LHWs and the Expanded Program on Immunization (EPI), pose serious coordination challenges in the sector (Arif et al. 2010; Bhutta et al. 2013).

In addition to the coordination challenges faced after devolution by all provinces, another challenge is the substantial variation in the capacity to provide effective healthcare services in these provinces. As highlighted by Arif et al. (2010), difficult geographical access to BHUs is a much more salient issue in Balochistan than in either KPK or Sindh. In contrast, in Punjab geographical distance is barely mentioned, by 11 percent of people, as a barrier for accessing BHUs. Similarly, when asked about the quality of services received from BHUs, respondents in Punjab and KPK reported that they got good

TABLE 8.3 Indicators of use of maternal care by province and household characteristics (%), 2012

Household characteristic	Received prenatal care	Received tetanus toxoid injection during pregnancy	Took iron tablets/ supplements during pregnancy	Received vitamin A capsule after delivery
Province				
Punjab	0.10	0.37	0.21	0.09
Sindh	0.17	0.34	0.21	0.17
Khyber Pakhtunkhwa	0.05	0.31	0.18	0.22
Mother's education				
Never enrolled	0.09	0.33	0.18	0.08
Primary school or less	0.29	0.49	0.32	0.25
Middle school or higher education	0.25	0.67	0.50	0.34
Monthly household expenditures per adult equivalent				
Bottom quintile	0.11	0.28	0.14	0.09
Top quintile	0.13	0.38	0.32	0.14
Total	0.12	0.35	0.21	0.12

Source: Authors, based on 2012 Pakistan RHPS (IFPRI/IDS 2012).

Note: The table summarizes maternal-care indicators for the most recent pregnancy of married women 14–49 years. All summary statistics use household weights. The sample size is 1,434 women.

care, in contrast to Sindh and Balochistan, where people complained repeatedly about the lack of medical staff and medicines as well as the long waiting times (Arif et al. 2010).

To truly understand the complexity of the country's health problem, we must start with maternal care indicators, because early negative shocks experienced by children (even while in utero) are key determinants of future health (Barker 1995, 2007; Barker, Osmond, and Law 1989; De Boo and Harding 2006). Pakistan RHPS data show extremely low use of pre- and postmaternal services among rural women, strongly suggesting that health issues begin even before a child is born (Table 8.3). Only 12 percent of rural women received prenatal care for their most recent pregnancy. As might be expected, educational attainment is strongly correlated with receiving prenatal care: 25 percent of women who reached middle school or higher education sought prenatal care, while only 9 percent of women with no education did. These differences are not explained by expenditure levels (measured as mean household monthly expenditures per adult equivalent); there is little difference in

TABLE 8.4 Location of delivery by province and household characteristics (%), 2012

Household characteristic	Government hospital, Basic Health Unit, or Rural Health Center	Private hospital or clinic	At home
Province			
Punjab	11.9	18.8	69.2
Sindh	12.3	27.8	59.9
Khyber Pakhtunkhwa	13.7	17.9	68.3
Mother's education			
Never enrolled	9.0	22.4	68.6
Primary school or less	16.8	35.7	47.5
Middle school or higher education	20.4	45.7	33.9
Monthly household expenditures per adult equivalent			
Bottom quintile	9.0	19.9	71.2
Top quintile	10.2	29.5	60.3
Total	12.2	21.2	66.6

Source: Authors, based on 2012 RHPS (IFPRI/IDS 2012).

Note: The table concerns delivery of the most recent pregnancy of married women 14–49 years. All summary statistics use household weights. The sample size is 1,434 women. Because of rounding, percentages might not always add up to exactly 100.

utilization rates between women in the top and bottom quintiles of household expenditure. In contrast, there is provincial variation in prenatal care use, with KPK having the lowest usage level.

According to the 2012 RHPS, 35 percent of women received a tetanus toxoid injection during pregnancy, while only 21 percent took iron tablets at this time, and only 12 percent received a vitamin A capsule after giving birth (Table 8.3). The rural incidence of receiving a tetanus toxoid injection, taking iron supplements during the last pregnancy, and receiving a vitamin A capsule after delivery all vary significantly by educational attainment and expenditure level but not by province.

Similar variations exist in the locations where women deliver children: 69 percent of uneducated women delivered their most recent child at home compared to 34 percent of women with middle school or higher education (Table 8.4). However, the data do not suggest that educated women are replacing home births with births at public facilities: 46 percent delivered at a private healthcare facility, while only 20 percent did so at a public one.

Prior studies explain why government healthcare facilities are underutilized by women. Reasons include a lack of female staff, staff absenteeism,[11] undersupply of medication and equipment, and long distances to such facilities (Arif et al. 2010; Callen et al. 2013). For Pakistan overall, Nishtar et al. (2013) report that the doctor-to-nurse ratio is 2.7:1 instead of the desired 1:4, and the rural ratios are likely far higher. Further, cultural and religious considerations in the rural areas likely deter women from consulting male doctors and encourage reliance on more-traditional in-home health services (Khan 1999), particularly for child deliveries. Low rates of delivery at health facilities and a shortage of professional birth attendants remain of significant concern, because the result is inferior postnatal and newborn care and many newborn deaths at home (UNICEF 2012; GoP 2009a; Siddiqi et al. 2004). Table 8.5 shows that relatives, neighbors, and friends aid in almost half of all deliveries in rural Pakistan, with trained birth attendants accounting for 33 percent of deliveries, and doctors, nurses, or midwives accounting for only 18 percent. Differences across provinces are particularly salient, with almost 64 percent of deliveries in Sindh being aided by relatives, neighbors, and friends compared to only 41 percent in Punjab. Similarly, over 41 percent of deliveries were assisted by a trained birth attendant in Punjab compared to only 18 percent in Sindh.

According to RHPS data, 13 percent of the children to whom women had ever given birth had died. This is an alarming rate of infant mortality. Again, the differences across education groups are salient, with deaths occurring in 1 out of 8 children born to women with no education, but only 1 out of 24 children born to women with middle school or higher education. The major causes of death among children under the age of five are birth asphyxia, sepsis, pneumonia, diarrhea, and premature birth. Respiratory infection and undernutrition also cause many deaths.

Barriers to access to preventive healthcare also exist, parallel to those to maternal care, compounding the risk factors for children in rural Pakistan. As a consequence, just over 56 percent of children between 12 and 23 months of age are fully immunized. Figure 8.2 shows significant differences by socioeconomic status, and a slightly higher vaccination rate for boys than for girls. Yet there are no differences by birth order (which is not shown in the figure).

---

11 "Doctors assigned to rural facilities are sent on 'detailment' to urban centres where they can do private practice, while continuing to draw a salary from the allocation of funds for the under-served area. There is no, or inadequate, incentive for skilled personnel to work in rural areas and without some form of compensatory allowance, and the result is rural facilities without doctors" (UNICEF 2012, 63–64).

TABLE 8.5 Person assisting with delivery by province and household characteristics (%), 2012

Household characteristic	Doctor/ nurse/ midwife	Trained birth attendant	Lady Health Worker	Traditional birth attendant	Relatives/ neighbors/ friends
Province					
Punjab	16.3	41.5	1.0	0.3	40.9
Sindh	17.5	18.1	0.3	0.4	63.6
Khyber Pakhtunkhwa	27.6	19.2	2.9	0.0	50.4
Mother's education					
Never enrolled	16.7	32.4	1.0	0.4	49.5
Primary school or less	21.1	32.2	0.6	0.0	46.1
Middle school or higher education	33.4	23.5	1.2	0.0	42.0
Monthly household expenditures per adult equivalent					
Bottom quintile	12.5	34.9	0.3	0.5	51.8
Top quintile	25.9	26.9	1.5	0.2	45.5
Total	17.6	32.5	0.9	0.3	48.7

Source: Authors, based on 2012 RHPS (IFPRI/IDS 2012).

Note: The table concerns delivery of the most recent pregnancy of married women 14–49 years. All summary statistics use household weights. The sample size is 1,434 women. Because of rounding, percentages might not always add up to exactly 100.

These low immunization results could in part be linked to the lack of integration of the EPI, which continues to be a vertical program,[12] resulting in coordination challenges. However, overriding the limited effectiveness of programs like the EPI are critical security concerns around vaccinations. The Pakistani Taliban have unleashed a sustained armed campaign, which is concentrated in the Federally Administered Tribal Areas and KPK, against healthcare workers and the security personnel who escort them. The goal of this campaign is to block the polio immunization program (Roul 2014). This, along with a misinformation and propaganda campaign by the Taliban and other groups against immunizations, has resulted in high rates of vaccination refusals and is a major factor in the failure of the polio immunization program in Pakistan (Warraich 2009). As a result, Pakistan is one of three remaining countries in the world with residual poliomyelitis, or polio (Bhutta et al. 2013).

---

12 A vertical program is a stand-alone program that is usually disease or service specific. In general it is directed, supervised, and executed, either wholly or to a great extent, by a specialized service using dedicated health workers (Atun, Bennett, and Duran 2008).

FIGURE 8.2 Immunization rates by household characteristics and province, rural Pakistan, 2012/2013

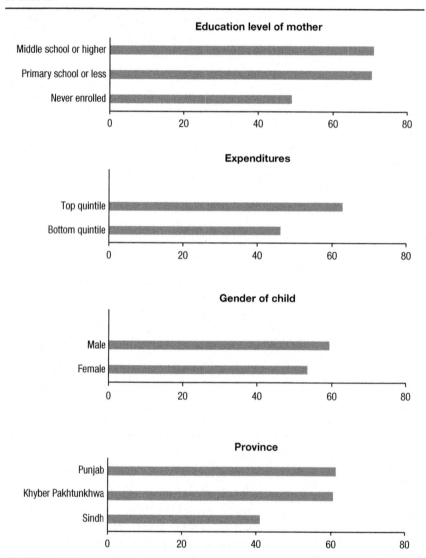

Source: Authors, based on 2012/2013 RHPS (IFPRI/IDS 2012; 2013)
Note: Data from 2012 and 2013 are pooled for the analysis. Children 12–23 months of age are considered fully immunized if they have received the tuberculosis vaccine, three doses of the diptheria, pertusis, and tetanus vaccine, three doses of human papillomavirus vaccine, and one dose of the measles vaccine. All summary statistics use household weights. The sample size is 613 children.

There have been several important health strategies and policy initiatives for maternal and child health in the past 20 years. Yet except for the 2001 National Health Policy, there has been little targeting of poor and vulnerable groups, particularly in rural areas. Most government strategies have lacked a long-term vision and have not been translated into action (Siddiqi et al. 2004). Two programs mentioned earlier deserve note here. The first is the Maternal, Newborn, and Child Health Program (MNCH), launched in 2005. This program aims to coordinate, improve, and promote primary healthcare ser-vice delivery at the district and provincial levels. The program's main outputs (that is, emergency obstetric services and community midwives) have shown marked advances. Nevertheless, this program is a stand-alone, vertical pro-gram, and as such has had issues integrating with existing health programs (Bhutta et al. 2013). Second is the LHW program. Although the LHWs form a relatively isolated vertical health program, their success during the 1990s is worth noting because of the firm political commitment offered to them, the continuation of that commitment across consecutive governments, and allo-cations of resources that have allowed the program to operate (Siddiqi et al. 2004). Programs like the MNCH and LHWs have demonstrated the under-lying capacities in Pakistan's health sector and should be a source of cau-tious optimism.

Education

Parents in both rural and urban Pakistan have a strong stated preference— and a robust, observable demand—for educating their children, but they face constraints, economic and otherwise (Andrabi et al. 2010). Income, shocks to income, and wealth all affect enrollment, especially for girls (Lloyd et al. 2007). Mothers' education is an important determinant of enrollment— again, especially for girls (Lloyd et al. 2005). The number of children in the household matters as well; a larger number of younger children reduces girls' enrollment (Lloyd et al. 2009; Sawada et al. 2009). There is also evidence that migration of a family member positively affects enrollment of rural children, particularly girls (Mansuri 2006). A rationing of resources leads parents to pick winners; they invest in the child they believe is most likely to succeed, at the expense of other children (Andrabi, Das, and Khwaja 2010).

Social barriers also play a significant role in rural Pakistan, for female mobility in particular. Jacoby and Mansuri (2011) find that girls' (but not boys') primary school enrollment is significantly lower if they have to cross hamlet boundaries to attend school. In addition, caste barriers play a role: the authors find that low-caste children, both boys and girls, are deterred from enrolling when the most convenient school is in a hamlet dominated by high-caste households.

While the government is the primary provider of education at the primary, secondary, and tertiary levels in Pakistan, the country also has an active and growing private education sector. According to the Pakistan Social and Living Standards Measurement Survey, 76 percent of primary-level enrollment in rural areas is in government schools (for urban areas, the number is 44 percent) (GoP 2014c). In the Pakistan RHPS data, 25.5 percent of five- to nine-year-olds report attending a private school as their last school. The National Education Census of 2006 shows that virtually every village has a public school and 23 percent of villages have private schools as well (Andrabi, Das, and Khwaja 2012).

While there is a small set of elite private schools and religious madrassas, the vast majority of the private sector is made up of low-cost, low-fee, mom-and-pop-style establishments that follow the government curriculum (Andrabi, Das, and Khwaja 2010). Private schools tend to arise in villages where a supply of educated, low-cost female teachers exists—villages where there is already a government girls' secondary school (Andrabi, Das, and Khwaja 2013).

A gender gap exists in school supply: until the 1990s, the Pakistani government followed a rough rule of thumb of building one girls' school for every two boys' schools (Lloyd, Mete, and Sathar 2005). And in addition to poor access, the education sector also suffers from poor quality. Educational infrastructure is particularly deficient: in 2007/2008, only 64 percent of public sector schools had drinking water, 61 percent had toilets, 60 percent had boundary walls, and 39 percent had electricity (GoP 2009b). This problem is exacerbated in rural areas: according to the *Annual Status of Education in Pakistan Report*, 47 percent of surveyed government primary schools in rural districts had functional toilets, compared to 69 percent of surveyed government primary schools in urban areas (ASER 2014). Learning outcomes, poor across the board, are also disproportionately worse in rural areas: 30 percent of class (grade) 4 students in rural areas surveyed in the *Annual Status of Education in Pakistan Report* can read a story in Urdu, Sindhi, or Pashto, compared to 40 percent of class 4 students in surveyed urban areas (ASER 2014).

Most studies clearly show that overall educational access and gender parity are better in urban areas (ASER 2014; GoP 2014b). Thus, we use RHPS data to shed light specifically on disparities within *rural* Pakistan, focusing on gender and socioeconomic status.

FIGURE 8.3 Percentage of population who have ever attended school by age group and gender, 2012

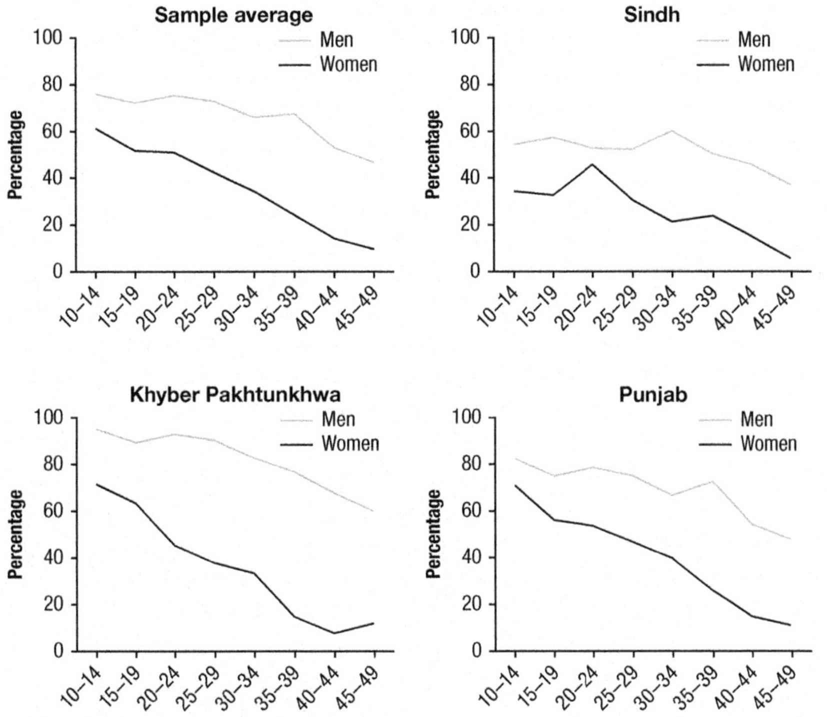

Source: Authors, based on 2012 RHPS (IFPRI/IDS 2012).
Note: All summary statistics use household weights.

Figure 8.3 presents the percentage of respondents for various age groups who reported having ever attended school, by gender. The proportion of the population entering the system decreases as a function of age—enrollment is higher among younger cohorts—and a persistent but narrowing gender gap exists between boys and girls. Sindh lags behind Punjab and the surveyed areas of KPK in overall enrollment and behind Punjab in gender disparity.

Table 8.6 presents descriptive statistics for a complete set of educational outcomes for various age groups by gender.[13] Panel A focuses on enrollment

---

13 The analysis uses the following age categories for children: 5- to 9-year-olds, 10- to 14-year-olds, and 15- to 18-year-olds. These correspond roughly with the ages at which Pakistani children would enroll in primary school (classes 1 through 5), middle school (classes 6 to 8), secondary school (classes 9 to 10) and higher secondary school (classes 11 to 12) and beyond, respectively. Progression past secondary school is determined by a board examination called the *matric* (matriculation) exam.

TABLE 8.6 Enrollment, schooling costs, and dropout rates by province and gender, 2012 and 2013

| | Age | Sample average | Province | | | Gender | |
			Punjab	Sindh	KPK	Male	Female
Panel A: Enrollment							
Enrolled in 2012 (%)	5–9	53.6	62.9	28.8	72.2	59.2	47.7
	10–14	58.4	63.9	39.2	75.8	68.4	47.3
	15–18	30.2	29.9	24.9	46.7	41.6	19.4
Panel B: Schooling cost							
Transportation time (in minutes)	5–18	18.7	18.5	17.5	21.7	20.8	15.6
Transportation cost (PKR)	5–18	769	661	1088	949	850	645
Annual school fees (PKR)	5–18	1951	1821	1903	2816	2167	1624
Panel C: Dropouts							
Dropouts between 2012	5–9	3.3	2.3	5.8	2.0	3.4	3.2
and 2013 (%)	10–14	8.4	7.7	10	8.3	9	7.6
	15–18	8.9	9.9	5.7	10.7	13.8	4.1

Source: Authors, based on 2012/2013 Pakistan RHPS (IFPRI/IDS 2012, 2013).

Note: Panels A and B summarize data using Round 1 of the Pakistan RHPS, carried out during March–April 2012. Panel C looks at dropout rates, based on changes in enrollment for children between Round 1 and Round 2, conducted in 2013. Dropouts are defined as 1 if a child enrolled in Round 1 is no longer enrolled in Round 2, conditional on being part of the household at the time of Round 2; it is 0 otherwise. Thus, a sample average value of 3.3 for children ages 5–9 means that 3.3 percent of students enrolled in Round 1 of the survey (in 2012) in Punjab, Sindh, and KPK are no longer enrolled in Round 2 (in 2013). All summary statistics use household weights, which are the inverse of the probability of being included in the sample. KPK = Khyber Pakhtunkhwa; PKR = Pakistani rupees.

rates for 2012. Enrollment rates roughly halve after age 14, and girls have lower enrollment at each age compared to boys. Sindh lags significantly behind Punjab and KPK, especially for the younger cohorts.

For those children between the ages of 5 and 18 who are currently enrolled in school, Panel B displays summary statistics on transportation time and cost, and school fees. Transportation costs, both in terms of time and money, are higher for boys compared to girls, as are school fees. This signifies a greater distance traveled for boys than for girls, in line with the aforementioned gender mobility norms in rural Pakistan that prevent girls from traveling long distances to reach school, a higher willingness to pay for boys' education, and greater enrollment of boys relative to girls in private schools. Monetary transportation costs are highest in Sindh, while transportation time costs and school fees are highest in the KPK districts surveyed.

Panel C examines dropout rates by age group, based on changes in enrollment for children between RHPS Round 1 and Round 2.[14] Boys 15 to

14 A dropout is defined as 1 if a child enrolled in Round 1 is no longer enrolled in Round 2, conditional on being part of the household at the time of Round 2; it is 0 otherwise.

18 years old have a higher dropout rate (14 percent) compared to girls in that same age group (4 percent). This likely signifies the selective number of girls who make it to high school and is suggestive evidence of families picking winners (that is, investing in the most promising children) when making secondary school education decisions for girls (a phenomenon mentioned by Andrabi, Das, and Khwaja 2010). It could also, however, partly reflect girls being married off between survey rounds. Sindh has the highest dropout rates for the younger age cohorts.

Table 8.7 presents figures on current enrollment for different age groups by gender, tabulated against two indicators of socioeconomic status: household expenditure and the education level of the household head.[15] Panel 1 cross-tabulates current enrollment with the top and bottom quintiles of household expenditure. Unsurprisingly, households with the highest expenditures have higher enrollment rates for each gender-age group compared to low-expenditure households. The group for which expenditure quintile matters the least for enrollment is girls ages 15 to 18—a cohort in which enrollment rates are always low. Barriers to education for girls in high school remain stubborn in the face of income increases. Both supply (lack of access to a nearby government girls' high school and poor infrastructure within available schools such as a lack of adequate toilet facilities) and demand factors (low perceived returns to girls' education, the pressure for marriage, constraints to female mobility, and other social norms) are likely responsible. Panel 2, which examines current enrollment in terms of education of the household head, shows that as the education level of the head of household increases, enrollment in each age-gender category increases. The education of the head of household appears to make an especially large difference for enrollment of 15- to 18-year-old girls.

While Pakistan has no scarcity of education sector policies designed to address both the access and quality issues cited above, policy and regime instability have been a major issue for the sector. Pakistan has had a total of seven national education policies since 1947 (Bengali 1999). In the past 20 years, education policy was highlighted, first under the Social Action Plan (1993–1998), then under the National Education Policy for 1998–2010, and currently under a new National Education Policy (2009). These policy documents generally correspond with political regimes, and although well intentioned, they consistently fail to achieve their goals. The problem is twofold:

---

15 We restrict the sample to only male household heads because female-headed households constitute only 1.5 percent (32 of 2,090) of the households in the sample.

TABLE 8.7 Cross-tabulations for current enrollment by age group and gender, with household expenditure, education of (male) household head, and province (%), 2012

Panel 1: Current enrollment prevalence by monthly household expenditures per adult equivalent

	Age	Bottom quintile	Top quintile
Girls	5–9	37.5	70.2
	10–14	42.8	60.5
	15–18	14.7	18.9
Boys	5–9	47.7	77.2
	10–14	55.8	81.8
	15–18	29.3	71.1

Panel 2: Current enrollment prevalence by household head (male) education

	Age	Never enrolled	Primary or less	Middle school (class 6–8)	Secondary (class 9–10) or higher
Girls	5–9	37.8	47.3	49.3	70.8
	10–14	35.9	46.7	61.5	72.3
	15–18	9.3	13.3	29.3	50.6
Boys	5–9	49.5	59.4	76.2	78.3
	10–14	56.3	62.3	86.2	92.6
	15–18	30.2	42.0	43.1	69.8

Panel 3: Current enrollment prevalence by province

	Age	Punjab	Sindh	KPK
Girls	5–9	56.4	26.9	60.2
	10–14	53.4	26.1	64.3
	15–18	20.8	11.6	27.5
Boys	5–9	68.6	30.7	81.6
	10–14	73.2	50.5	86.4
	15–18	39.3	36.6	64.6

Source: Authors, based on 2012 Pakistan RHPS (IFPRI/IDS 2012).

Note: All summary statistics use household sampling weights, which are the inverse of the probability of being included in the sample. KPK = Khyber Pakhtunkhwa.

not only is accountability poor within the tenure of a regime, but once the regime changes, the wheel is often reinvented so as to disown a political rival's programs and put new interventions in place. As a result, government and education analysts cannot easily identify which educational interventions work and which do not.

The current governing document for the education sector is the National Education Policy of 2009. This is bolstered by the Right to Education Act of 2010, which guarantees the state's obligation to provide free and compulsory education to all children ages 5 to 16 (Pakistan National Report 2011). In the 2009 National Education Policy, the government frames the national educational challenge in terms of two gaps that explain poor educational performance. First is a commitment (or funding) gap, with only 2.7 percent of GDP committed to education in 2009. And despite the Vision 2025 goal of at least 4 percent of GDP committed to education, education spending as a percentage of GDP has declined slightly in recent years. Second is an implementation gap. This gap refers to two particular issues: the (surprising) fact that about 20 percent to 30 percent of funds allocated to education remain unused, and the fact that the system is beset by corruption. The National Education Policy specifically notes that "political influence and favoritism are believed to interfere in the allocation of resources to the districts and schools, in recruitment, training and posting of teachers and school administrators that are not based on merit, in awarding of textbook contracts, and in the conduct of examinations and assessments" (GoP 2009b, 15).

Even so, the provincial governments have undertaken a number of innovative program interventions during the past two decades that deal with both (demand-side) constraints on enrollment as well as supply of schooling. Some of these have been evaluated. Notable examples are the Punjab and Sindh Education Foundations (PEF and SEF, respectively), which are quasi-governmental bodies created by their respective provincial governments. Some of the programs under the SEF are the Adopt-a-School Program, which hands over "sick" public schools to private management; the Support to Private Education Institutes Program, which "provides institutional, technical, and human resource development assistance to low-cost private schools"; and the Promoting Low-Cost Private Schooling in Rural Sindh (PPRS) program, evaluated by Berrera-Osorio et al. (2011).

Under the PPRS, private entrepreneurs are granted a per-student cash subsidy to operate coeducational primary schools that have tuition-free enrollment and are open to all children in the village between the ages of five and nine. Berrera-Osorio et al. (2011) find that the program significantly increases child enrollment (by 51 percent in treated villages) and reduces existing gender disparities (girls' enrollment increases by 4 to 5 percent more than boys').

In Punjab, the PEF operates a New Schools Programme, which invites nongovernmental organizations and private providers to set up new schools where government provision is absent or inadequate across all 36 districts (Barber 2013). In addition, its Foundation Assisted Schools program, initiated in 2005, gives a monthly per-student cash subsidy to low-cost private schools that offer free schooling to all enrolled children who achieve a minimum pass rate on a standardized academic test administered by PEF semiannually. By 2009 the program covered 474,000 students in 1,082 low-cost private schools at the primary, middle, and secondary school levels in 18 of Punjab's 36 districts. Berrera and Raju (2014) evaluate this program in a

regression-discontinuity framework (the discontinuity is around the minimum pass rate needed for program participation), and find large positive
impacts on school enrollment.

In addition, programs that improve school quality have also been
linked to increased enrollment. In Punjab the Programme Monitoring and
Implementation Unit focuses on teacher and student attendance as well as
school infrastructure like electricity, drinking water, toilets, and boundary
walls, and recent successes in increasing enrollment have been attributed to
this program, though there has been no systematic evaluation of the program
(Barber 2013). The evaluation of a pilot teacher performance–pay program in
Punjab showed mixed results: it found a positive impact on school enrollment,
mainly in urban schools, and a positive impact on student exam participation
rates—but not scores—in rural schools (Berrera-Osorio and Raju 2015).

Other interventions are focused on eliminating gender gaps in enrollment.
As an example, a girls' stipend program in Punjab provides cash stipends to
girls in classes 6 to 10 (middle and high school) of government schools as part
of the Punjab Education Sector Reform Programme. Beneficiary girls receive
PKR 2,400 a year, conditional on 80 percent attendance (World Bank 2014a).
During the 2013/2014 year, the program distributed stipends worth PKR
1.5 billion to 411,000 girls in 16 out of 36 districts of Punjab. Sindh has a similar program.

Bilateral and multilateral donors—the World Bank, the UK Department
for International Development, and the US Agency for International
Development, among others—have played a role in the programs described
above as well as others, by providing monetary and technical assistance.
However, coordination within government, between government and donors,
and among donors tends to be poor (Pakistan National Report 2011).

Beyond these government and donor initiatives are the broader questions posed by the 18th Amendment to the constitution for Pakistan's education sector. Prior to the 18th Amendment, education was a subject that
straddled three levels of government, with the federal government responsible for formulating education policy and curriculum, provincial governments
responsible for implementation through their respective education ministries, and individual districts responsible for the provision of educational services, a responsibility further expanded by the 2001 devolution plan (Pakistan
National Report 2011). Following the 18th Amendment, all responsibilities
for education apart from university education were ceded to the provinces.
However, in many cases, the provinces still follow pre-2010 federal decisions
on curricula and policies while struggling to accommodate implementation

plans that followed from the 18th Amendment in the absence of full clarity on the division of responsibility between provincial and district governments (GoP 2009b).

Water, Sanitation, and Electricity

Access to water, sanitation, and electricity services is far from universal in rural Pakistan (Table 8.8). In 2012 less than 10 percent of Pakistan RHPS sample households had access to piped water sources, and only 45 percent had access to flush toilets, with another 20 percent relying on dry-pit latrines and a full 35 percent relying on open defecation. Half of households lacked a piped drainage system. And while 88 percent had access to electricity, the average availability of that electricity was just 10 hours per day. Sindh lags behind Punjab, and even further behind KPK, on most of these service delivery outcomes, revealing important interregional variations in access rates.

Those with the lowest levels of access are the uneducated and poor, as Table 8.9 shows. In the case of electricity, only 85 percent of households whose heads never enrolled in school have electricity at home, while this figure is 96 percent for households whose heads have middle school education (classes 6–8) or higher. Furthermore, among households with access to electricity, those with uneducated heads have it for only 9.6 hours per day on average, while those whose heads have middle school or higher education have it for 11.2 hours per day. Household expenditure also predicts electricity access, though such expenditure is not associated with more hours of electricity per day. This suggests that even those able to pay for more reliable and consistent access to electricity are unable to obtain it.

In the case of piped water, more-educated households again have greater access. While only 7 percent of households with uneducated or primary-educated (classes 1–5) heads use piped water, 13 percent of those with middle school or higher education do. Not surprisingly—because piped water is often available inside the home—households with more-educated heads also live closer to their main water source. While similar disparities in access to piped water are not present across expenditure quintiles, those in the bottom quintile are more than three times as far away from their water source, on average, than are those in the top quintile (0.23 km versus 0.07 km).

Access to improved sanitation is definitively higher among households with more-educated heads and higher expenditures. Among households with uneducated heads, only 40 percent have a piped drainage system, 55 percent use a latrine (whether flush or a dry pit, as opposed to open defecation), and 38 percent have a flush latrine. Conversely, among heads of households with

TABLE 8.8 Households' access to electricity, water, and sanitation services by province, 2012

Service	Sample average	Province		
		Punjab	Sindh	KPK
Household has electricity (%)	88	93	71	98
Hours per day that household with electricity has it available	10.1	9.4	12.8	9.9
Household's main source of water is piped water (%)	9	6	8	28
Distance to household's main water source (km)	0.13	0.13	0.18	0.06
Household has a piped drainage system (%)	50	60	11	87
Household has a latrine (flush or dry pit) (%)	65	66	55	91
Household has a flush latrine (%)	45	51	23	66

Source: Authors, based on 2012 Pakistan RHPS (IFPRI/IDS 2012).
Note: km = kilometers; KPK = Khyber Pakhtunkhwa.

TABLE 8.9 Households' access to electricity, water, and sanitation services by level of education and expenditure, 2012

Service	Education level of household head			Monthly household expenditures per adult equivalent	
	Never enrolled	Primary (class 1–5)	Middle school or higher (class 6+)	Bottom quintile	Top quintile
Household has electricity (%)	85	84	96	84	91
Hours per day that household with electricity has it	9.6	9.7	11.2	10.8	9.7
Household's main source of water is piped (%)	7	7	13	7	6
Distance to household's main water source (km)	0.15	0.15	0.09	0.23	0.07
Household has a piped drainage system (%)	40	48	69	39	55
Household has a latrine (flush or dry pit) (%)	55	63	83	61	71
Household has a flush latrine (%)	38	43	59	38	55

Source: Authors, based on 2012 Pakistan RHPS (IFPRI/IDS 2012).
Note: km = kilometers.

middle school or higher educations, 69 percent have a piped drainage system, 83 percent have a latrine, and 59 percent have a flush latrine. Similar differences are found when comparing across expenditure quintiles.

But beyond these figures is the broader question of what determines differences in rural access to water, sanitation, and electricity services. To explore this question, we test a hypothesis built around the straightforward notion that access to these services depends on citizens (who consume services), technical experts (who furnish the infrastructure or skills required to create the goods being provided), and governments (who deliver services). These factors are key components of a well-functioning rural governance system, which is one where citizens are involved, technical expertise is abundant, and government policy makers are accountable to citizens and work on their behalf. To test these relationships, we estimate how access to electricity, water, and sanitation services are associated with several outcome variables, using OLS. First, we consider citizen involvement, which is measured by whether there are organized village meetings to discuss issues and events, and whether there have been group efforts in the village in the past five years to improve electricity service and water supply facilities. Second, we consider technical expertise, captured by the presence (or absence) of engineering services in the tehsil. Third, we consider government accountability, captured by the share of surveyed village residents who report that they are satisfied with federal government services, provincial government services, and public drinking water facilities.

Findings from estimations using cross-sectional 2012 data from the Pakistan RHPS reveal a number of factors associated with access to these services (Table 8.10).[16] While having organized village meetings does not predict access in the case of access to piped water, households in such villages are about 0.09 km closer to their main water source. One possible explanation for this correlation is that meetings may help communities identify service delivery problems and potential solutions to them—whether that means taking action or pressuring higher levels of government for service improvements. They may also involve citizens more broadly in priority setting. Efforts by community members within the past five years to improve water supply facilities are associated with an approximate 9.6 percentage point increase in access to piped water, suggesting that the degree of involvement of local communities in water governance can affect access outcomes. Of course, these findings should be interpreted in light of evidence from other countries that such efforts are most effective when community members receive community training (Newman et al. 2002), the community has sufficient funds for

---

16 Household controls include agroecological zone, ethnicity, and household size fixed effects and controls for latitude, longitude, latitude multiplied by longitude, elevation, and several characteristics of the household head: his or her gender, marital status, age group (five groups), education level (never enrolled, primary education, and middle school education or higher), logged per capita monthly expenditure per adult equivalent, and logged total household wealth. Village controls include indicators for the village having experienced a flood or typhoon, a drought, and a crop insect or crop disease outbreak in the past five years. We estimate heteroskedasticity robust standard errors.

TABLE 8.10 Correlates of households' access to electricity, water, and sanitation services, 2012

	Electricity	Hours per day of electricity	Piped water	Distance to water source (km)	Piped drainage system	Latrine, flush or dry pit	Flush latrine
Organized village meetings to discuss issues and events	0.029* (0.016)	0.589*** (0.176)	−0.003 (0.011)	−0.088*** (0.026)	0.088*** (0.019)	0.129*** (0.022)	0.036 (0.023)
Group effort to improve electricity service, past 5 years	−0.052 (0.032)	0.520 (0.402)					
Group effort to improve water supply facilities, past 5 years			0.096*** (0.030)	−0.019 (0.038)	0.026 (0.038)	−0.019 (0.041)	−0.055 (0.046)
Engineering services available in tehsil	0.127*** (0.017)	2.630*** (0.258)	0.128*** (0.019)	0.057** (0.024)	−0.000 (0.024)	0.080*** (0.027)	0.044 (0.028)
Share satisfied with federal government services	0.099*** (0.034)	1.068* (0.575)					
Share satisfied with provincial government services			0.104*** (0.026)	−0.164*** (0.056)	−0.200*** (0.057)	−0.008 (0.059)	0.143** (0.059)
Share satisfied with public drinking water facilities			0.046* (0.023)	0.125*** (0.041)	0.045 (0.031)	−0.039 (0.033)	0.012 (0.035)
Observations	2,071	1,787	2,067	1,953	2,067	2,067	2,067

Source: Authors, based on 2012 Pakistan RHPS (IFPRI/IDS 2012).

Note: Robust standard errors appear below coefficients, in parentheses. * = significant at 10%; ** = significant at 5%; *** = significant at 1%. km = kilometers.

upkeep and maintenance (Leino 2007), and when the project is of a sufficiently small size to avoid collective-action problems in upkeep (Kleemeier 2000). Having engineering services in the tehsil—as for electricity—is associated with greater piped-water access. We also find that reported satisfaction with the provincial government is associated with a 10.4 percentage point increase in access to piped water, and with being about 0.16 km closer to the water source—important findings given the provincial governments' strong roles in this sector.

Many of the same factors predict access to sanitation services. In villages with organized meetings, households are 8.8 percentage points more likely to have a piped drainage system and 12.9 percentage points more likely to have access to a latrine. As in the cases of electricity and piped water, having engineering services available is associated with greater access to latrines.

Satisfaction with the provincial government is also associated with greater access to flush latrines.

The governance environment also predicts access to electricity. Households in villages with organized village meetings are 2.9 percentage points more likely to have electricity, and those with electricity have it for an additional 35 minutes per day. In contrast, we find no evidence that group efforts by community members in the past five years to improve electricity service are associated with greater access. Such efforts may be ineffective, or may be made only where electricity access is relatively bad and difficult to improve significantly. Households with engineering services in their tehsil are 12.7 percentage points more likely to have electricity, and those with it have it for an additional 2.6 hours per day—suggesting that technical expertise is an important predictor of access. Policies that remove operational barriers for firms and individuals with such expertise are likely to expand access. Reported satisfaction with the federal government is associated with 9.9 percentage points greater access to electricity, and 1.1 additional hours of electricity per day—an association which makes intuitive sense given the extent of federal government involvement in electricity provision. Where the federal government is seen as accountable, this translates into greater electricity access.

In addition to predicting access to electricity, water, and sanitation services in 2012, these measures of citizen involvement, technical expertise, and government accountability also predict whether vulnerable households *without* access to services in 2012 obtained it a year later (Table 8.11). This provides additional evidence that the governance environment matters for service delivery—including for the poorest of the poor, who are unconnected.

These findings are particularly useful to consider in the context of Pakistan's commitments to improving rural access to water, sanitation, and electricity as set forth in Vision 2025, the development strategy currently guiding public policy and investments. Although large disparities in access exist across both geographic and economic dimensions, Vision 2025 commits to universal access to clean water and 90 percent access to improved sanitation and electricity by 2025. The targets are consistent with priorities set forth by prior policies such as the 2009 National Drinking Water Policy and the 2006 National Sanitation Policy, which together resolve to provide universal access to clean water and improved sanitation by 2025 (GoP 2006, 2009c).

Yet questions remain as to the extent to which these policies and their associated investments stake out sufficient space and complementary roles for public officials, civil society, and the private sector in the governance and provision of water, sanitation, and electricity services. Successful examples exist of

TABLE 8.11 Correlates of households gaining access to electricity, water, and sanitation services, 2012–2013

	Electricity	Piped water	Piped drainage system	Latrine (flush or dry pit)	Flush latrine
Organized village meetings to discuss issues and events	−0.093 (0.080)	0.018 (0.016)	0.116*** (0.033)	0.079* (0.044)	0.101*** (0.029)
Group effort to improve electricity service, past 5 years	0.156 (0.113)				
Group effort to improve water supply facilities, past 5 years		0.201*** (0.043)	0.008 (0.060)	0.194** (0.085)	−0.050 (0.055)
Engineering services available in tehsil	−0.088 (0.133)	0.012 (0.019)	−0.050 (0.044)	−0.003 (0.054)	0.102** (0.040)
Share satisfied with federal government services	0.908*** (0.305)				
Share satisfied with provincial government services		0.070* (0.037)	−0.095 (0.091)	−0.086 (0.116)	−0.094 (0.089)
Share satisfied with public drinking water facilities		0.056** (0.025)	0.073 (0.046)	−0.233*** (0.063)	−0.075* (0.043)
Observations	267	1,760	1,011	745	1,095

Source: Authors, based on 2012–2013 Pakistan RHPS (IFPRI/IDS 2012, 2013).

Note: Robust standard errors appear below coefficients, in parentheses. * = significant at 10%; ** = significant at 5%; *** = significant at 1%.

communities, both rural and urban, that organize the provision of water, sanitation, and electricity with moderate or little assistance from the government. Prime examples are communities organized by the National Rural Support Program and the Aga Khan Rural Support Program (Seattle 2010; Campos, Khan, and Tessendorf 2004). However, the integration of these approaches into national policy remains limited. Similarly, while policies such as the National Sanitation Policy commit government to building the capacities of elected district and local government representatives to ensure their active participation in the governance of public service provision, the extent to which such individuals are involved varies widely across Pakistan. As a result, provincial governments still play a central role in service provision and often exercise administrative control over utilities (Mezzera, Aftab, and Yusuf 2010). And in the power sector, where private investment has been the subject of a long and tortuous history in Pakistan, there is scope for innovating around private (ADB 2013) and community-led provision for rural communities.[17]

---

17 For example, the Karachi Electricity Supply Company—after years of operating at a loss— earned net profits of PKR 2.6 billion and PKR 6.7 billion in fiscal years 2012 and 2013, respectively (ADB 2013), suggesting potential gains from power market privatization.

Overall, this analysis provides several important insights into the effective delivery of water, sanitation, and electricity services in the coming years, especially where these services are likely to continue to be provided through the public sector. First, there is scope to expand existing efforts to involve local governments and community organizations in service provision, accompanied by efforts to more broadly involve citizens in decision making and priority setting. Second, to avoid technical bottlenecks to rural service delivery, there is a clear indication that the presence of technical expertise at the local level is critical. Third, while the government's goals may be easily achieved for some rural subpopulations, there are barriers to getting poorly educated and low-expenditure households connected; tailored solutions designed to target these more vulnerable groups may be of considerable importance to future policy.

Conclusions

The institutional architecture and policy environment governing rural health, education, water, sanitation, and electricity service delivery in Pakistan is both complex and in the process of changing. The architecture stretches across three levels of government—federal, provincial, and local—in the public sector, and engages the private sector and civil society to varying degrees. This chapter makes three observations.

First, access to public services is essential in order to boost agricultural labor supply and machinery use, as well as rural nonfarm labor and incomes. Second, an urgent need exists to improve rural access to public services such as healthcare, education, electricity, water, and sanitation, and many disparities in access remain—both across provinces and by individual and household characteristics like gender and socioeconomic status. Finally, while governance and implementation issues have plagued these services, there is significant scope for change, and ultimately for service improvements.

The results presented in this chapter illustrate the importance of access to public services for achieving improvements in agricultural productivity and rural development. Higher levels of education allow household members to work in areas of the rural economy other than agriculture, which tend to be more profitable. Similarly, higher levels of education are associated with increased use of agricultural machinery by households, suggesting that skills and knowledge can translate into mechanized, more efficient food production. In addition, better sanitation and health are associated with more productive adults who can work longer hours in physically demanding agricultural activities. Negative health shocks as well as increased distance to one's water source are associated with fewer days worked by the household in agricultural activities during the year. In the same way, improved drainage systems are associated with greater time spent on agricultural activities. Finally, better access to electricity increases the number of machines a household uses for agricultural activities. Overall, increased access to rural services results in more productive households with higher levels of mechanization.

This suggests that improved access to rural services can have positive implications for rural welfare and is a worthwhile investment. In particular, considerable attention should be paid to ensuring access for vulnerable populations—such as women and girls, and those households with low educational attainment and incomes—and areas, such as rural Sindh. Without deliberate interventions, these groups and regions will fall further behind in access to these critical services, thus increasing their vulnerability. Critically, Pakistan needs to invest in rigorous evaluations of both previously implemented and future interventions to identify policy and investment options for the future. As noted earlier in this chapter, such evaluations have already begun in the education sector (with evaluations of the PEF and SEF); these efforts should be expanded, and similar evaluations should be put in place in the health sector.

Yet low levels of access to all five services derive, in no small measure, from policy and program instability across changing political regimes. This leads to gaps in implementation and accountability. Responsibilities across the three levels of government are inadequately defined, particularly in the wake of devolution under the 18th Amendment. Further changes and challenges must be surmounted once the local government ordinance is implemented in full. Budgetary commitments are currently insufficiently aligned with long-term development strategies and policies at the provincial and national levels (notably Vision 2025). Donor coordination remains a challenge. And civil society involvement in the governance and provision of rural public services remains important but insufficient. These issues result in both limited access to rural public services and poor quality of those services.

We would be remiss not to note that many in Pakistan—policy makers, analysts, development practitioners, donors, nongovernmental organizations, business leaders, and rural communities themselves—are cognizant of these issues. The government has made significant efforts in these sectors over the years, and it has accordingly seen many recent improvements in access. As discussed in greater detail in Chapter 9, the 18th Amendment provides distinctive opportunities for action and accountability that could lead to substantial improvements in rural service provision. But to succeed, this process will require comprehensive planning, organizational reform, community engagement, and supervision at both the federal and provincial levels.

References

ADB (Asian Development Bank). 2013. Karachi Electric Supply Company LTD. Post-Privatization Rehabilitation, Upgrade & Expansion. Manila. http://www.adb.org/projects/40943-014/details.

Alderman, H., J. R. Behrman, V. Lavy, and R. Menon. 2001. "Child Health and School Enrollment: A Longitudinal Analysis." *Journal of Human Resources* 36 (1): 185–205.

Andrabi, T., J. Das, and A. I. Khwaja. 2010. *Education Policy in Pakistan: A Framework for Reform*. Policy Brief. Lahore: International Growth Center, Pakistan.

———. 2012. "The Madrassa Controversy: The Story Does Not Fit the Facts." In *Under the Drones: Modern Lives in Afghanistan-Pakistan Borderlands*, 162–173. Cambridge, MA: Harvard University Press.

———. 2013. "Students Today, Teachers Tomorrow: Identifying Constraints on the Provision of Education." *Journal of Public Economics* 100: 1–14.

Arif, S., W. Cartier, A. Golda, and R. Nayyar-Stone. 2010. *The Local Government System in Pakistan: Citizens' Perceptions and Preferences*. IDG Working Paper 2010–02.

ASER Pakistan. 2014. *Annual Status of Education Report 2013*. Lahore: South Asian Forum for Education and Development. http://www.aserpakistan.org/document/aser/2013/reports/national/ASER_National_Report_2013.pdf. Accessed September 2014.

Atun, R. A., S. Bennett, and A. Duran. 2008. *When Do Vertical (Stand-Alone) Programmes Have a Place in Health Systems?* WHO Policy Brief. Health Systems and Policy Analysis Series. WHO.

Barber, M. 2013. *The Good News from Pakistan*. London: Reform. http://www.reform.co.uk/content/20419/research/education/the_good_news_from_pakistan.

Barker, D. 1995. "Fetal Origins of Coronary Heart Disease." *British Medical Journal* 311: 171–174.

———. 2007. "The Origins of the Developmental Origins Theory." *Journal of Internal Medicine* 261: 412–417.

Barker, D., C. Osmond, and C. Law. 1989. "The Intrauterine and Early Postnatal Origins of Cardiovascular Disease and Chronic Bronchitis." *Journal of Epidemiology* 43: 237–240.

Barrera-Osorio, F., and D. Raju. 2014. "Evaluating the Impacts of Public Student Subsidies to Low-Cost Private Schools in Pakistan." *Journal of Development Studies* 51 (7): 808–825.

———. 2015. *Teacher Performance Pay: Experimental Evidence from Pakistan*. World Bank Policy Research Working Paper 7307. Washington, DC: World Bank.

Barrera-Osorio, F., D. Blakeslee, M. Hoover, L. Linden, and D. Raju. 2011. *Expanding Educational Opportunities in Remote Parts of the World: Evidence from an RCT of a Public-Private Partnership in Pakistan*. Washington, DC: World Bank.

Bengali, K. 1999. *History of Education Policy Making and Planning in Pakistan*. Working Paper 40. Islamabad: Sustainable Policy Development Institute.

Bhutta, Z. A., A. Hafeez, A. Rizvi, N. Ali, A. Khan, F. Ahmad, S. Bhutta, T. Hazir, A. Zaidi, S. N. Jafarey. 2013. "Reproductive, Maternal, Newborn, and Child Health in Pakistan: Challenges and Opportunities." *Lancet* 381: 2207–2218.

Callen, M., S. Gulzar, A. Hasanain, A. R. Khan, Y. Khan, and M. Zia Mehmood. 2013. "Improving Public Health Delivery in Punjab, Pakistan: Issues and Opportunities." *The Lahore Journal of Economics* 18, SE (September 2013): 249–269.

Campos, N. F., F. U. Khan, and J. E. Tessendorf. 2004. "From Substitution to Complementarity: Some Econometric Evidence on the Evolving NGO-State Relationship in Pakistan." *The Journal of Developing Areas* 37 (2): 49–72.

Cutler, D., and G. Miller. 2005. "The Role of Public Health Improvements in Health Advances: The Twentieth-Century United States." *Demography* 42 (1): 1–22.

De Boo, H. A., and J. E. Harding. 2006. "The Developmental Origins of Adult Disease (Barker) Hypothesis." *Australian and New Zealand Journal of Obstetrics and Gynaecology* 46: 4–14.

Dinkelman, T. 2011. "The Effects of Rural Electrification on Employment: New Evidence from South Africa." *American Economic Review* 101: 3078–3108.

DRI (Democracy Reporting International). 2010. *The 18th Amendment to the Constitution and Electoral Reform in Pakistan*. Briefing Paper 05. Islamabad. http://democracy-reporting.org/files/dri_briefing_paper_5_-_comments_to_the_18th_amendment.pdf. Accessed June 2015.

Ewbank, D., and S. Preston. 1990. "Personal Health Behavior and the Decline in Infant and Child Mortality: The United States, 1900–1930." In *What We Know about Health Transition: The Culture, Social and Behavioral Determinants of Health*, edited by J. Caldwell, S. Findley, and P. Caldwell. Canberra: The Australian National University Printing Service.

Fafchamps, M., and A. R. Quisumbing. 1999. "Human Capital, Productivity, and Labor Allocation in Rural Pakistan." *Journal of Human Resources* 34 (2): 369–406.

Fisher-Vanden, K., E. T. Mansur, and Q. Wang. 2012. *Costly Blackouts? Measuring Productivity and Environmental Effects of Electricity Shortages*. NBER Working Paper 17741. Cambridge, MA: National Bureau of Economic Research.

Glewwe, P., H. G. Jacoby, and E. M. King. 2001. "Early Childhood Nutrition and Academic Achievement: A Longitudinal Analysis." *Journal of Public Economics* 81 (3): 345–368.

GoP (Government of Pakistan). 2006. *National Sanitation Policy.* Islamabad: Government of Pakistan.

———. 2009a. *National Health Accounts Pakistan 2005–06.* Islamabad: Bureau of Statistics, Government of Pakistan.

———. 2009b. *National Education Policy.* Islamabad: Government of Pakistan.

———. 2009c. *National Drinking Water Policy.* Islamabad: Government of Pakistan.

———. 2013. *Pakistan Social and Living Standards Measurement Survey, 2011–12.* Islamabad: Bureau of Statistics. http://www.pbs.gov.pk/sites/default/files/pslm/publications/pslm2011-12/complete_report_pslm11_12.pdf. Accessed July 22, 2016.

———. 2014a. *Pakistan Millennium Development Goals Report 2013.* Islamabad: Ministry of Planning, Development and Reform, Government of Pakistan.

———. 2014b. *Pakistan Economic Survey 2013–2014.* Islamabad: Ministry of Finance, Government of Pakistan.

———. 2014c. *Pakistan Social and Living Standards Measurement Survey, 2012–13.* Islamabad: Bureau of Statistics. http://www.pbs.gov.pk/content/pakistan-social-and-living-standards-measurement-survey-pslm-2012-13-provincial-district.

———. 2015. *Pakistan Economic Survey 2014–2015.* Islamabad: Ministry of Finance, Government of Pakistan.

Günther, I., and G. Fink. 2010. *Water, Sanitation and Children's Health: Evidence from 172 DHS Surveys.* World Bank Policy Research Working Paper 5275. Washington, DC: World Bank.

Hatfield, J. W., and K. Kosec. 2013. "Federal Competition and Economic Growth." *Journal of Public Economics* 97 (1): 144–159.

IFPRI/IDS (International Food Policy Research Institute/Innovative Development Strategies). 2012. Pakistan Rural Household Panel Survey 2012 Round 1 dataset. Washington, DC: IFPRI; Islamabad: IDS.

———. 2013. Pakistan Rural Household Panel Survey 2013 Round 2 dataset. Washington, DC: IFPRI; Islamabad: IDS.

Jacoby, H. G., and G. Mansuri. 2011. *Crossing Boundaries: Gender, Caste and Schooling in Rural Pakistan.* World Bank Policy Research Working Paper 5710. Washington, DC: World Bank.

Khan, A. 1999. "Mobility of Women and Access to Health and Family Planning Services in Pakistan." *Reproductive Health Matters* 7 (14): 39–48.

Kleemeier, E. 2000. "The Impact of Participation on Sustainability: An Analysis of the Malawi Rural Piped Scheme Program." *World Development* 28 (5): 929–944.

Kosec, K., and T. Mogues. 2016. "Decentralization without Representation (or Mobility): Implications for Public Service Delivery." Unpublished paper, International Food Policy Research Institute, Washington, DC.

Kurosaki, T. 2001. "Effects of Human Capital on Farm and Non-farm Productivity in Rural Pakistan." Unpublished paper, World Bank, Washington, DC.

Leino, J. 2007. *Ladies First? Gender and the Community Management of Water Infrastructure in Kenya.* Graduate Student and Research Fellow Working Paper 30. Cambridge, MA: Harvard University, Center for International Development.

Lipscomb, M., A. M. Mobarak, and T. Barham. 2013. "Development Effects of Electrification: Evidence from the Geologic Placement of Hydropower Plants in Brazil." *American Economic Journal: Applied Economics 2013* 5 (2): 200-231. http://dx.doi.org/10.1257/app.5.2.200.

Lloyd, C. B., C. Mete, and M. J. Grant. 2007. "Rural Girls in Pakistan: Constraints of Policy and Culture." In *Exclusion, Gender, and Education: Case Studies from the Developing World,* edited by Maureen Lewis and Marlaine E. Lockheed. Washington, DC: Center for Global Development.

———. 2009. "The Implications of Changing Educational and Family Circumstances for Children's Grade Progression in Rural Pakistan: 1997–2004." *Economics of Education Review* 28: 152–160.

Lloyd, C. B., C. Mete, and Z. A. Sathar. 2005. "The Effect of Gender Differences in Primary School Access, Type, and Quality on the Decision to Enroll in Rural Pakistan." *Economic Development and Cultural Change* 53 (3): 685–710.

Mansuri, G. 2006. *Migration, School Attainment, and Child Labor: Evidence from Rural Pakistan.* World Bank Policy Research Working Paper 3945. Washington, DC: World Bank.

Mansuri, G., and V. Rao. 2013. *Localizing Development: Does Participation Work?* World Bank Policy Research Report. Washington, DC: World Bank.

Mezzera, M., S. Aftab, and S. Yusuf. 2010. "Devolution Row: An Assessment of Pakistan's 2001 Local Government Ordinance." Unpublished, Netherlands Institute of International Relations, Wassenaar.

Miguel, E., and M. Kremer. 2004. "Worms: Identifying Impacts on Education and Health in the Presence of Treatment Externalities." *Econometrica* 72 (1): 159–217.

Mogues, T. 2011. "The Bang for the Birr: Public Expenditures and Rural Welfare in Ethiopia." *Journal of Development Studies* 47 (5): 735–752.

Newman, J., M. Pradhan, L. B. Rawlings, G. Ridder, R. Coa, and J. L. Evia. 2002. "An Impact Evaluation of Education, Health, and Water Supply Investments by the Bolivian Social Investment Fund." *World Bank Econonmic Review* 16 (2): 241–274.

NIPS/ICF (National Institute of Population Studies)/ICF International. 2013. *Pakistan Demographic and Health Survey 2012–13*. Islamabad: NIPS; Calverton, MD: ICF International.

Nishtar, S., T. Boerma, S. Amjad, A. Yawar Alam, F. Khalid, I. Haq, Y. A. Mirza. 2013. "Pakistan's Health System: Performance and Prospects after the 18th Constitutional Amendment." *Lancet* 381: 2193–2206.

Oxford Policy Management. 2009. *Lady Health Worker Program External Evaluation of the National Program for Family Planning and Primary Health Care*. Quantitative Survey Report. Oxford, UK.

Pakistan National Report for United Nations Annual Ministerial Review. 2011. *Pakistan and Commitments to Education: Implementing the Internationally Agreed Goals and Commitments to Education*. http://www.un.org/en/ecosoc/newfunct/pdf/2011_amr_pakistan_june_2011 .pdf. Accessed September 2014.

Paxson, C., and N. Schady. 2007. "Cognitive Development among Young Children in Ecuador." *Journal of Human Resources* 42 (2): 49–84.

Pervez, A. 2011. *Pakistan Power Sector*. Report of Switzerland Global Enterprise. http://www.s-ge .com/en/filefield-private/files/26090/field_blog_public_files/5513. Accessed April 2014.

PPIB (Private Power & Infrastructure Board). 2014. *FAQs*. http://www.ppib.gov.pk/ N_faqs.htm. Accessed April 2014.

Punjab Education Sector Reform Program. *Distribution of Stipend to Girl Students*. http://www .pesrp.edu.pk/pages/Stipend-to-Girl. Accessed July 8, 2015.

Reinikka, R., and J. Svensson. 2002. "Coping with Poor Public Capital." *Journal of Development Economics* 69: 51–69.

Roul, A. 2014. *The Pakistani Taliban's Campaign against Polio Vaccination*. West Point, NY: Combating Terrorism Center. https://www.ctc.usma.edu/posts/the-pakistani-talibans -campaign-against-polio-vaccination. Accessed June 2015.

Sawada, Y., and M. M. Lokshin. 2009. "Obstacles to School Progression in Rural Pakistan: An Analysis of Gender and Sibling Rivalry Using Field Survey Data." *Journal of Development Economics* 88 (2): 335–347.

Seattle, A. 2010. *Contested Aims, Contested Strategies: New Development Paradigm through the Lens of the AKRSP*. Sustainable Development Policy Institute (SDPI) Working Paper 114. Islamabad: SDPI.

Siddiqi, S., I. U. Haq, A. Ghaffar, T. Akhtar, R. Mahaini. 2004. "Pakistan's Maternal and Child Health Policy: Analysis, Lessons and the Way Forward." *Health Policy* 69 (1): 117–130.

Stansel, D. 2005. "Local Decentralization and Local Economic Growth: A Cross-Sectional Examination of US Metropolitan Areas." *Journal of Urban Economics* 57 (1): 55–72.

UNICEF. 2012. *Situation Analysis of Children and Women in Pakistan.* National Report. Islamabad: UNICEF.

USAID (United States Agency for International Development). 2013. *The Causes and Impacts of Power Sector Circular Debt in Pakistan.* Washington, DC: USAID.

Warraich, H. J. 2009. "Religious Opposition to Polio Vaccination." *Emerging Infectious Diseases* 15 (6): 978. Doi:10.3201/eid1506.090087.

WaterAid. 2011. *Off-Track, Off-Target: Why Investment in Water, Sanitation and Hygiene Is Not Reaching Those Who Need It Most.* London.

World Bank. 2007. *Pakistan: Promoting Rural Growth and Poverty Reduction.* Washington, DC: World Bank. https://openknowledge.worldbank.org/handle/10986/7984. Accessed June 2015.

——. 2014a. *Pakistan: Increasing Access and Quality through Education Reforms in Punjab.* Washington, DC: World Bank. http://web.worldbank.org/WBSITE/EXTERNAL/NEWS/0,,print:Y~ isCURL:Y...9868~menuPK:141310~pagePK:34370~piPK:34424~ theSitePK:4607,00.html. Accessed February 2014.

——. 2014b. World Development Indicators. Database. Washington, DC: World Bank Group. http://data.worldbank.org. Accessed June 2015.

WSP (Water and Sanitation Program). 2012. *The Economic Impacts of Poor Sanitation in Pakistan.* Islamabad. https://www.wsp.org/sites/wsp.org/files/publications/WSP-esi-pakistan.pdf. Accessed April 2014.

Zwane, A. P., and M. Kremer. 2007. "What Works in Fighting Diarrheal Diseases in Developing Countries? A Critical Review." *The World Bank Research Observer* 22 (1).

Annex A: Comparisons with South Asia

One way to measure the degree to which governments invest in human capital and labor productivity is to compare the sizes of their expenditures on key services with the sizes of their economies. Table A8.1 presents these expenditures as a share of GDP across the three largest South Asian countries in terms of population: Pakistan, Bangladesh, and India. Overall, health expenditure in Pakistan is equal to 3.1 percent of the country's GDP—less than that of either Bangladesh (3.6 percent) or India (4 percent). Pakistan spends a meager 2.6 percent of its GDP on public education. The number is lower than that of India (3.2 percent) and higher than that in Bangladesh (2.2 percent). Pakistan spends slightly less on water and sanitation as a share of GDP than does Bangladesh (0.22 percent versus 0.26 percent), and less than half of what India spends.

TABLE A8.1 Government expenditure in various categories as a share of gross domestic product in the three largest South Asian countries (%)

Expenditure item	Pakistan	Bangladesh	India
Health (2012)	3.1	3.6	4.0
Public education (2009)	2.6	2.2	3.2
Water and sanitation (2008)	0.22	0.26	0.57
Government operation (2011)	17.6	11.3	14.0
Military (2012)	3.1	1.3	2.4

Source: World Bank Data Catalog (World Bank 2014b); WaterAid (2008).

Note: All data on expenditures except water and sanitation are from World Bank Data Catalog. Water and sanitation expenditures are from WaterAid. For each expenditure item, the data are from the most recent year for which data were available for all three countries. Health expenditure is the sum of public and private health expenditure. It covers the provision of health services (preventive and curative), family planning activities, nutrition activities, and emergency aid designated for health, but it does not include provision of water and sanitation. Expenditure on education is the total public expenditure (current and capital) on education. It includes government spending on educational institutions (both public and private), education administration, and transfers/subsidies for private entities (students/households and other private entities). Government operation is defined as cash payments for operating activities of the government in providing goods and services. It includes compensation of employees (such as wages and salaries), interest and subsidies, grants, social benefits, and other expenses such as rent and dividends. Data on military expenditures use the NATO definition and are from Stockholm International Peace Research Institute. Water and sanitation expenditures include donor funds; because of differences across countries in the levels of government responsible for service delivery, figures for India include both federal and state figures, while for Pakistan, they include only federal figures.

Table A8.2 highlights key indicators of access to public services across these three South Asian countries. The health situation in Pakistan is alarming; in 2012, infant mortality in Pakistan was more than double that of Bangladesh (69 versus 33 deaths per 1,000 births) and far greater than that of India (44 deaths per 1,000 births).

Five indicators on access to education give a sense of where Pakistan stands in comparison to India and Bangladesh. These indicators are gross primary school enrollment, primary school completion rates for girls and for boys, and progression to secondary school for girls and for boys.[18] Pakistan lags behind India on all of these indicators, and behind Bangladesh on all but one (the male primary completion rate, which for Pakistan is 73 percent and for Bangladesh is 70 percent). The gaps are greater for female primary school completion rates (60 percent for Pakistan compared to 80 percent for Bangladesh and 97 percent for India), and for female progression to secondary school

---

18 Note that these ratios measure enrollment and completion, regardless of age group, as a percentage of the official age group for primary school, and may be greater than 100 percent because of children who enter school early or late and who repeat classes. Note also that progression to "secondary school," according to the World Bank definition, really measures progression to class 6 (and therefore middle school) in Pakistan's case.

TABLE A8.2 Indicators of access to health, education, electricity, water, and sanitation services in the three largest South Asian countries

	Pakistan	Bangladesh	India
Infant mortality rate, per 1,000 live births (2012)	69	33	44
Primary school enrollment (%) (2011)	92	114	113
Female primary completion rate (%) (2011)	60	80	97
Male primary completion rate (%) (2011)	73	70	96
Female progression to secondary school (%) (2010)	73	95	89
Male progression to secondary school (%) (2010)	72	84	88
With electricity (%) (2011)	69	60	75
With improved drinking water source (%) (2012)	92	85	93
With improved sanitation facilities (%) (2012)	48	57	36

Source: World Bank Data Catalog (World Bank 2014b).

Note: Bangladesh, India, and Pakistan are the three largest countries in South Asia. In 2012, these three countries constituted over 95 percent of the population of South Asia (World Bank). The data are from the most recent year having data for all of the three countries. If that is not possible, data from earlier years are substituted where necessary. Enrollment and completion rates are expressed as a percentage of the population of official primary education age and therefore can exceed 100 percent due to the inclusion of overage and underage students (because of early or late school entrance and class repetition). Rates of progression to secondary school are defined as the number of new entrants to the first class of secondary education as a percentage of the number of pupils enrolled in the final class of primary education in the previous year. Improved sanitation facilities include flush/pour toilets (to piped sewer system, septic tank, or pit latrine), ventilated improved pit (VIP) latrines, pit latrines with a slab, and composting toilets. Improved drinking water sources include piped water, public taps or standpipes, tube wells or boreholes, protected dug wells, protected springs, and rainwater collection.

(73 percent for Pakistan compared to 95 percent for Bangladesh)—though the gaps for males are also large.

Pakistan ranks second of the three countries on access to electricity, improved drinking water, and improved sanitation. India has the highest rates of access to electricity and improved drinking water, while Bangladesh has the highest rate of access to improved sanitation. While India is the clear leader in access to electricity (75 percent versus 69 percent in Pakistan), Pakistan trails India only slightly on access to an improved water source (93 percent in India versus 92 percent in Pakistan). However, Pakistan trails Bangladesh significantly in access to improved sanitation (48 percent versus 57 percent in Bangladesh).

Chapter 9

DEVOLUTION IN PAKISTAN: IMPLICATIONS FOR AGRICULTURE AND RURAL DEVELOPMENT

Danielle Resnick and Abdul Wajid Rana

Introduction

The 18th Amendment to Pakistan's constitution, which was passed in 2010, holds significant implications for local governance in general and for rural development and food security in particular. Although Pakistan has embarked on various decentralization initiatives in the past, the 18th Amendment represents a fundamental *de jure* restructuring of fiscal, administrative, and political powers between the federal and provincial governments. Most notably, the Ministry of Food and Agriculture, the Ministry of Education, and the Ministry of Health were among the 17 ministries devolved to the four provinces of Balochistan, Khyber Pakhtunkhwa (KPK), Punjab, and Sindh.[1] These ministries play a key part in addressing the welfare of the rural poor. At the same time, a majority of budgetary resources to fund investments under the Public Sector Development Program, which is Pakistan's guiding policy framework for development projects and programs, are now in the hands of the provinces.

Thus, the achievement of any concrete national goals related to agricultural production, food security, or rural development now depends heavily on the ability of subnational governments to maintain momentum for agricultural investments, ensure that provincial agricultural and food security strategies are coherent with national objectives, and provide mechanisms that better integrate rural citizens' priorities into the policy arena. Consequently, understanding the features and implications of the 18th Amendment is critical for analyzing the broader institutional context in which agriculture and rural development take place. Nevertheless, existing research on the interrelationship between devolution and rural development has been relatively scant and focused mostly on health and nutrition (for example, Mazhar and Shaikh

---

1   Khyber Pakhtunkhwa (KPK) was formerly named Northwest Frontier Province. Besides the four provinces, other subnational units include the Islamabad Capital Territory, Federally Administered Tribal Areas (FATA), and the autonomous territories of Azad Jammu and Kashmir as well as Gilgit-Baltistan.

2012; Nishtar et al. 2013; Zaidi et al. 2013), education (Ullah 2013), or population planning (Kugelman and Hathaway 2011), with minimal attention to agriculture.

To fill this gap, this chapter first discusses the ideal prerequisites for effective devolution, emphasizing the need for reforms to enhance authority, autonomy, and accountability. Next it reviews Pakistan's history of decentralization efforts and discusses the *de jure* and de facto results of the 18th Amendment in these three domains. Then it examines the shift in government expenditures for rural development and citizen satisfaction with public services over the period before and after the 18th Amendment was passed to provide an initial evaluation of the reform. The chapter concludes that while the reform signals high-level political commitment to devolution, such a "big bang" approach implies that subnational authorities now have a large number of new responsibilities without the requisite resources to fulfill them or the established mechanisms to ensure accountability to citizens. Therefore, the challenge for Pakistan will be to ensure that achieving pro-poor agricultural growth and broad-based rural development is not jeopardized by halfhearted implementation of this critical governance reform.

The Promise and Premise of Devolution

Pakistan's 2010 reforms are designed to achieve devolution, which is a subtype of decentralization. Theoretically, decentralization is intended to provide greater stability in countries with large and heterogeneous populations (Gurr 2000; Lijphart 1999; Stepan 1999), improve services through subnational competition and better tailoring to citizens' preferences (Musgrave 1959; Oates 1972; Tiebout 1956), and enhance public participation and citizen engagement in policy formulation (Brinkerhoff 2010; Rondinelli, Nellis, and Cheema 1983). Although the evidence remains mixed, recent studies do offer reason for some optimism that decentralization helps governments be more responsive to local needs (Alderman 2002; Faguet and Sánchez 2008), including better targeting of antipoverty programs (Galasso and Ravallion 2005).

Authority, autonomy, and accountability are the three conceptual elements that distinguish among different degrees of decentralization.[2] *Authority* refers to the legal transfer of responsibilities to subnational units that empower local officials to manage the delivery of, and planning for, particular services, and to

---

2 See Dickovick and Riedl (2010) and USAID (2009) for elaboration on these concepts.

collect taxes. In this regard, clear mandates between different levels of government are important.

Autonomy involves the transfer to local officials of not only responsibilities but also certain powers. Such autonomy can be both administrative and fiscal. Administrative autonomy allows local governments to fire and hire employees, while fiscal autonomy includes control over local revenue sources and the power to make decisions about expenditure. Typically, fiscal autonomy is greater when intergovernmental transfers are based on a formula, rather than ad hoc criteria, so local governments can better plan their budgets over a longer period. In addition, autonomy is enhanced if the transfers allow for unconditional expenditures that local governments can determine based on local needs, and if subnational governments are allowed to borrow. Another means of deepening autonomy is the ability to expand tax categories (see Dickovick 2005).

Accountability is the exchange of responsibilities and sanctions between actors, typically involving a principal and an agent (see Schmitter 2004). Decentralization is typically most concerned with enhancing vertical accountability, which refers to the relationships upward from local officials to central government ministries, governors and mayors, or political parties, and downward from local officials to citizens. Accountability is often viewed as a critical component for decentralization's ability to better target services because it requires citizens to give feedback on their priorities and for officials to respond accordingly (see Ahmad et al. 2006; Blair 2000). Upward accountability between local and national government ensures that local officials are adhering to national rules and regulations and providing quality services. Mechanisms of accountability include citizen scorecards, performance-based employee reviews, public meetings, recourse to courts, and media engagement (see Ribot 2002; Dickovick 2005). However, elections represent the sine qua non of downward accountability, allowing citizens to directly sanction or reward officials based on performance (see Schmitter and Karl 1991). Consequently, appointing rather than electing officials undermines accountability. Similarly, a greater number of tiers of government decreases the ability of citizens to discern who exactly is responsible for providing what services (see Treisman 2007).

The three main types of decentralization, which are deconcentration, delegation, and devolution, broadly correspond to differing degrees of authority, autonomy, and accountability. Deconcentration, the most limited form of decentralization, involves the dispersion of authority from central government to local branch offices and involves upward accountability from the branch offices to the central government. In such a situation, the central government still retains authority over decision making, but local government is responsible for implementation. Delegation entails the transfer of substantive managerial authority and often fiscal autonomy to local governments or private corporations. In such a situation, local governments have decision making powers that do not require approval from the central government. Devolution represents the most extensive type of decentralization, and as highlighted in Figure 9.1, should ideally involve the transfer of authority, autonomy, *and* accountability to subnational governments for local decision making, finance, and management (see Cheema and Rondinelli 2007; Kathyola and Job 2011).[3] In particular, for high-quality services to be delivered to citizens, local governments require the necessary fiscal and administrative authority and autonomy from the national government. In addition, mechanisms need to be established for citizens to keep local officials, either at the district or provincial level, accountable. Enhancing participation is believed to alter the incentives faced by public officials who must now compete for votes, encouraging them to be more responsive and less corrupt while improving the effectiveness and efficiency of service delivery (see Faguet 2014).

Importantly, these various domains of authority, autonomy, and accountability can both reinforce one another and demonstrate trade-offs. For instance, citizens rarely participate in local government when subnational authorities have paltry resources and few responsibilities (see Goldfrank 2011). In other words, the ability of citizens to keep local government accountable to them can be undermined when such entities are deemed inconsequential based on circumscribed authority and autonomy. Likewise, many have pointed to the challenge of resource leakage and local capture (see Bardhan and Mookherjee 2000; Prud'homme 1995), which can be magnified when autonomy is increased while accountability is not. On the other hand, increasing the accountability of local officials to citizens may result in service delivery preferences that favor the interests of vocal interest groups to the detriment of marginalized groups. For instance, Keefer, Narayan, and Vishwanath (2006) question whether Pakistan's 2001 devolution exercise resulted in suboptimal delivery of girls' schooling, which was not highly valued in more rural areas of the country.

---

3   Another important distinction relates to federal versus unitary states. In the former, there are at least two tiers of government, the subnational government has representation in the national legislature, the division of power is defined in and protected by the constitution, and each subtier has the same legal autonomy (see Griffiths 2005). Decentralization can, however, occur in unitary states as well.

FIGURE 9.1 Idealized prerequisites for effective devolution

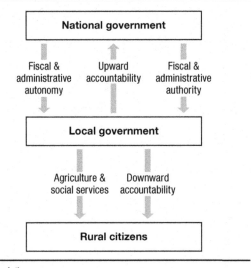

Source: Authors.

The Historical Context of Devolution in Pakistan

Pakistan has officially pursued a federal structure since independence in 1947. Characterized by a bicameral federal parliament and a constitutional division of powers between the central government and the provinces, Pakistan's federalism has in practice been generally weak and hostage to national political dynamics.[4] The degree of actual autonomy accorded to Pakistan's provinces and other subnational units has historically waxed and waned in concert with the country's volatile shifts between military and civilian governments.

General Ayub Khan implemented the Basic Democracies Ordinance in 1959, which established local councils at the district level and below. Half of these councils' members were elected, while the other half were appointed, and intergovernmental transfers favored rural areas because Khan's main support base emanated from the countryside. Local government then became more centralized under the civilian rule of Zulfikar Ali Bhutto to help his regime pursue certain policy priorities, such as the nationalization of industry (Lamb and Hameed 2012). Under General Zia ul-Haq's rule, from 1979 until 1988, the pendulum swung once again as he established the Local Government (LG) system and local officials were elected, though fiscal and

---

4   For details about Pakistan's history as a federation, see Ghaus-Pasha and Bengali (2005).

administrative autonomy were minimal. Local elections were suspended during much of the 1990s under the civilian leadership of both the Pakistan Muslim League (Nawaz) and the Pakistan People's Party.

After staging a coup in 1999, General Pervez Musharraf introduced the Local Governance Ordinance (LGO) in 2001. The LGO stipulated three tiers of government below the provincial level: districts, tehsils, and union councils.[5] Most service delivery was to occur at the district (*zila*) level. The Tehsil Municipal Administration represented the second tier of government and oversaw municipal services such as water supply, sewerage, sanitation, drainage schemes, and street lights, in both urban and rural areas. This was a big change from the prior structure of local governance in which there was a different administrative structure in rural areas than in urban ones.[6] At the lowest tier were union councils that encompassed small villages. Although the union councils had no revenue authority, they engaged in small development projects with federal funding.

One of the key changes under the LGO was allowing elected local authorities. Prior to the LGO, the districts were overseen by a deputy commissioner who was appointed by the provincial government. The LGO stipulated that union mayors (*nazim*) should be elected, albeit on a nonparty basis, and they collectively were members of both the tehsil and the district councils. The district councils then indirectly chose the district mayors (Lamb and Hameed 2012). A district coordinating officer was instituted to coordinate line departments in the district, such as education and health. Another important change under the LGO was the establishment of a Provincial Finance Commission (PFC) that oversaw formula-based resource transfers from the provinces to the districts. In addition, local taxation, budgeting, planning, and development responsibilities were shifted to each tier of the local government.

The effectiveness of the LGO was generally perceived to have been hindered by a number of key issues. First, in both the 2001 and 2005 local elections, political parties were not formally able to compete; candidates had to be unaffiliated (Hasnain 2010).[7] This often favored the election of local

---

5   A *tehsil* is a subdistrict administrative unit, and consists of a collection of union councils and villages.

6   The urban-rural divide dates back to British rule, when urban councils were established to provide municipal services in urban areas while rural councils were used to co-opt the landed elite (Siddiqui 1992). Later on, the divide had been maintained, especially during Zia's tenure, in order to accommodate the interests of the urban middle classes, who did not want to share their growing revenues in municipal areas with the rural masses (Cheema et al. 2006).

7   More specifically, a single nontransferable vote system was used without any party lists (Cheema et al. 2014).

elites entrenched in *biradari,* or patrilineal clan networks, to the *nazim* position, and these were people who could be co-opted by Musharraf's regime (see Cheema and Mohmand 2008). Second, the provincial authorities felt marginalized because there was no concurrent decentralization of powers from the federal to the provincial levels. This tactic was most likely intentional because the country's main political parties have tended to be strongest at the provincial level (Lamb and Hameed 2012). There was a general perception that the center intended to bypass federated units to establish direct administrative and political links with district governments and ultimately weaken the provincial tier.[8] Third, fiscal autonomy remained weak because district governments did not enforce their mandate to levy local taxes out of fear of displeasing their electorates. Consequently, they continued to rely on provincial transfers and were rarely able to raise their own revenue. In addition, the Interim National Finance Commission Award of 2006 did not change the criteria for the horizontal distribution of intergovernmental transfers across provinces and continued to adhere to population size as the only criterion, even though this disproportionately favored Punjab and generated substantial resentment from the other provinces.

The Eighteenth Amendment Bill

The return to civilian rule in 2008 signaled that changes would be forthcoming to Pakistan's decentralization laws.

The genesis for the 18th Amendment was the Charter of Democracy signed in 2006 by the late Benazir Bhutto and Nawaz Sharif. They both agreed that when and if either one of their parties came to power, they would restore the principles of the 1973 constitution, which had been changed under Generals Muhammed Zia ul-Haq and Pervez Musharraf to increase the powers of the presidency (Burki 2015). Indeed, by 2009 a Special Parliamentary Commission on Constitutional Reforms was commissioned by President Asif Zardari to roll back some of the amendments to the 1973 constitution that had been introduced by various military regimes. The 18th Amendment Bill was passed by the National Assembly in April 2010 and an Implementation Committee was set up to help with the transition. In addition, the role of the Council of Common Interests was expanded to help resolve interprovincial disputes (Lamb and Hameed 2012).

---

8   This strategy of weakening provincial authorities by bolstering district level authorities is by no means unique to Pakistan (see Dickovick 2007).

Critically, the 18th Amendment aimed to diminish the central government's power vis-à-vis the provinces, transferring responsibility for local government from the central to the provincial governments, and shifting some privileges away from the historically dominant province of Punjab (Adeney 2012). Achieving these goals involved at least three key changes. The first included the abolition of the Concurrent List of administrative responsibilities to clarify the authority of different subnational levels of government. Based on the 1973 constitution, there was a Federal Legislative List (FLL) as well as a Concurrent List.[9] The latter highlighted sectors in which both the federal and the provincial governments enjoyed equal powers of legislation, which created a great deal of confusion (UNDP 2013). The 18th Amendment retained only the FLL, and any areas that were not included in the FLL became the exclusive mandates of the provinces.[10]

Consequently, 17 federal ministries were devolved to the provinces by June 2011 through three phases. As Table 9.1 shows, and as discussed in previous chapters, this included many of the ministries responsible for agricultural and rural development services such as food and agriculture, local government and rural development, livestock and dairy, the environment, education, and health (Shah 2012). This resulted in the transfer of approximately 116 institutions and organizations, and the relocation of 61,000 government employees to the provinces or across new ministries set up at the federal level (CPDI 2014).

Since the federal Ministry of Local Government was abolished, ministerial oversight for local government rested with the provincial governments. In turn, each of the four main provinces passed their own Local Government Acts (LGAs) between 2010 and 2013. These Acts stipulated the range of responsibilities at the district level and below. Although there is variability across provinces, districts usually have responsibility for primary and secondary education, literacy, primary and secondary healthcare, dispensaries, agriculture, and intradistrict roads (CLGF 2013).

---

9   These lists identify the areas of responsibility for different levels of government. "Concurrent" means that both the federal and provincial governments have legislative authority over a specific responsibility—they are "concurrently" responsible. The FLL means that only the federal parliament can legislate on that responsibility. Part-II of the Concurrent List was the domain of the Council of Common Interests, where both the federal and provincial governments have equal representation.

10 Part-II of the FLL is now regulated by the Council of Common Interests.

TABLE 9.1 Old and new federal ministries under the 18th Amendment

Devolved ministries	New federal ministries/divisions
Food and Agriculture	National Food Security and Research
Local Government and Rural Development	Climate Change
Livestock and Dairy	Capital Administration and Development Division
Environment	Human Resource Development
Education	Inter-Faith Harmony
Health	National Heritage
Social Welfare and Special Education	National Health Services, Regulation and Services
Population Welfare	Education and Professional Training
Youth Affairs	
Sports	
Culture	
Labor and Manpower	
Minorities	
Tourism	
Women's Development	
Special Initiatives	
Zakat and Usher	

Source: GoP (2014a).

Redressing fiscal imbalances in intergovernmental transfers across provinces constituted a second major change. Since the early 1970s, the National Finance Commission (NFC) awards have determined the distribution of pooled tax revenue collected in each province.[11] The 18th Amendment stipulated that the 7th NFC Award from 2011–2016 should allocate 57.5 percent of divisible resources to the provinces, compared with only 45 percent under the 6th NFC award adopted in 2006. This translated into an almost PKR 300 billion increase for provincial budgets (see Adeney 2012).

Historically, population has been the main criterion for the distribution of those transfers across provinces. However, the 7th NFC Award reflected the demands of the provinces and assigned the following weights: 82 percent for population, 10.3 percent for poverty, 5 percent for revenue generation and collection, and 2.7 percent for inverse population density (see Mustafa 2011).

---

11   The taxes consist of income taxes, general sales tax, wealth taxes, capital gains taxes, and customs duties (see Mustafa 2011).

TABLE 9.2 Distribution of pooled tax revenues to provinces under the 7th NFC Award

Province	Share of transfers (%)	Change in share from 6th NFC (%)	Increase in budget from 6th NFC (%)
Balochistan	9.1	1.8	175
Khyber Pakhtunkhwa	14.6	−0.3	79
Punjab	51.7	−1.3	48
Sindh	24.6	−0.4	61

Source: Mustafa (2011); NFC (2009).

Note: NFC = National Finance Commission.

These new criteria and weightings consequently shifted the interprovincial distribution of divisible taxes. Table 9.2 shows that Punjab's share of transfers vis-à-vis the other provinces declined the most, while Balochistan's share increased 1.8 percent compared with the distribution system under the 6th NFC.[12]

The PFCs were retained as a means of distributing resources from the provincial to the district levels and below. As under the LGO, the PFCs give leverage to the provinces to determine their own distribution criteria. All provinces see population as the most important criterion. Yet as Table 9.3 shows, other conditions such as "backwardness," improved efforts to collect taxes, and infrastructure deficits are often taken into consideration as well. In order to maintain in a central place a proper account of revenues and expenditures, a Local Governance Fund was also established at the federal level for each local government in which the revenues collectively obtained from the PFC, local taxes, fees, rates, charges, and other revenue are placed.

Local elections overseen by the Election Commission of Pakistan represent the third main aspect of the devolution reforms. Unlike the LGO, which banned partisan affiliations for candidates, the 18th Amendment stipulates local elections under a closed-list plurality system (see Cheema, Khan, and Myerson 2014). This system involves parties choosing and ordering the candidates who will run on the party ticket, and voters then cast a vote for a party rather than an individual candidate. In theory this provision could have helped sidestep capture of local offices by landed elites and *biradari* networks that occurred during Musharraf's tenure.

---

12 Punjab was willing to shift the distribution criteria away from solely population because it was assured that in absolute terms, all the provinces would receive more transfers from the central government (see Adeney 2012).

TABLE 9.3 Weightings used for distributions of tax revenues to districts under the Provincial Finance Commission Awards (%)

Weightings	Balochistan	KPK	Punjab	Sindh
Population	50	50	75	50
Backwardness[a]	0	25	10	17.5
Tax effort[b]	0	0	5	7.5
Fiscal austerity[c]	0	0	5	0
Area	50	0	0	0
Development incentive[d]	0	25	5	0
Transitional assistance[e]	0	0	0	25

Source: Mustafa (2011); World Bank (2004).

Note: KPK = Khyber Pakhtunkhwa.

[a] "Backwardness" is a technical term in Pakistani public policy. The backwardness measure is based on different indexes for the various provinces. In Punjab it relies on the "development score" index developed by the Punjab Economic Research Institute. For Sindh, it relies on a "deprivation index" compiled by the Social Policy and Development Centre and is a composite of additional indexes capturing education, housing quality, residential services, and employment. For KPK, the "backwardness index" is from the UNICEF-sponsored Multiple Indicators Cluster Survey and is a composite of indicators related to child survival and nutrition, immunization, education and literacy, availability of drinking water, and income.

[b] In Punjab tax effort is based on an index capturing total, own-generated revenues of a district as a share of total revenues generated by all districts in the province. In Sindh an index is calculated based on percentage of provincial tax revenue collected in a particular district.

[c] Fiscal austerity is the inverse proportion of expenditure reduction.

[d] Development incentive is based on a "lag in infrastructure index" consisting of indicators related to urban development, rural sanitation, and transportation and communication.

[e] Transitional assistance is intended to help cushion any type of losses to districts as a consequence of moving to a formula-based distribution of transfers. It helps bridge remaining gaps for expenditures that are required by the district governments but are not covered by the other criteria used to guide the transfers.

Has Pakistan Genuinely Devolved?

How have these *de jure* reforms translated into improved authority, autonomy, and accountability and in turn affected the prospects for pro-poor rural development? The balance sheet is decidedly mixed, with confusion remaining over responsibilities, insufficient fiscal autonomy, and limited downward accountability, especially at the district level.

Confusion over Authority for Agricultural and Rural Services

The removal of the Concurrent List was an important step toward further clarification of the provinces' main mandates and provided protection against federal-level intervention in those areas. In some regards, there were even positive externalities across policy domains. For instance, Flaherty, Sharif, and Spielman (2012, 3) claim that the devolution of agricultural-sector responsibilities to the provinces empowered provincial research systems, which gained "a clearer mandate in science, technology, and innovation" related to agricultural research and development. At the same time, however, Table 9.2 shows that the devolved ministries were replaced by eight new ministries at the federal level. In some cases, only part of a former ministry's functions were devolved to the provinces while the others were either reallocated or reconstituted into a new federal ministry. According to one analysis, this has had the de facto result of only 94 out of a total of 301 functions being devolved to the provinces (see SPDC 2012).

For example, as alluded to in Chapter 1, when the Ministry of Food, Agriculture and Livestock (MINFAL) was dissolved, some of its functions shifted to the provinces while others became the responsibility of the newly federal Ministry of Food Security and Research (MNFSR). The justification for the new federal ministry was that the provision of food is a central function of the national government and that research was listed under the FLL (Dawn 2011). The MNFSR has about 38 areas of responsibility, along with continuing areas of joint responsibility with the provinces. The only exclusive provincial responsibilities are those that include farm management research, collection of agricultural statistics, soil surveys, economic planning that coordinates cooperatives, and research on the introduction of improved germplasm (*Dawn* 2011).

This has added a layer of uncertainty in important policy domains because in some cases the responsibilities of new federal ministries are not clearly distinguished from those that were devolved (see SPDC 2012). For instance, Rana (2014) observes widespread confusion over biosafety laws for seeds as a result of overlapping mandates. He notes that while the Federal Seed Certification and Registration Department (FSC&RD) was established in 1976 to regulate seed safety and provision, these responsibilities were first transferred to the Ministry of Science and Technology and then to the new MNFSR. At the same time, the environment functions shifted to the provincial level, even as a new Ministry of Climate Change was established at the federal level.

This is compounded by the fact that the provinces possess differential capacities to begin with, meaning that, at least initially, devolution of certain ministries could result in widening service delivery inequalities across the country. For instance, Punjab accounts for half of the country's provincial-level investment in agricultural research and development, employing nearly 1,000 full-time agricultural researchers in 2009 compared with Sindh's 380 (see Flaherty, Sharif, and Spielman 2012). Such capacity constraints can become magnified in service delivery arenas that require multisectoral collaboration. In the area of nutrition policy, for example, Punjab is best equipped administratively and in terms of establishing intersectoral links within the provincial Health Ministry, while Balochistan remains the least capable (Zaidi et al. 2013).

Authority below the provincial level has been much more circumscribed than at the provincial level. Because of some resistance by the provinces, the Supreme Court directed the provinces to uphold the 18th Amendment and adopt local government legal frameworks (IFES 2013).[13] Consequently, it was not until 2013 that all four provinces finally adopted LGAs.[14] A wide range of functions, tenure lengths, and procedural principles have been adopted across the different provinces (see Annex A). In addition, all of them have restored the urban/rural distinction that had been eliminated under the LGO.

Low Tax Base Hinders Greater Autonomy

With respect to autonomy, the provinces have again progressed further than district governments, in particular with respect to fiscal autonomy. The formula-based intergovernmental transfer system under the NFC awards provides the provinces with predictability over their resource flows for budgeting purposes. Moreover, an important stipulation of the 7th NFC Award was that it could not be reduced below what was given for the previous NFC award, meaning that the provinces will always know the minimum level of transfers they can expect to receive. Provinces can also now directly raise domestic and international loans; previously, loans to provinces had to be routed through the economic affairs division of the federal government (see SPDC 2012; UNDP 2013). Additional taxing powers for the provinces include value added taxes on services, taxes on immovable property, and zakat and usher (see Shah 2012). In addition, the provinces were allowed to administer general services taxes (GST) on services while the federal government retained the right to administer GST on goods (UNDP 2013). This is particularly a benefit for Punjab and Sindh due to their large service economies.

Some observers claim that at the onset of devolution, central revenue transfers were lower than promised because actual revenues were lower than forecast at the time the NFC was signed (Adeney 2012). In fact, PKR 36 billion less was transferred in the first year of the 7th NFC Award than had been originally predicted (GoP 2012). Because the NFC award was completed

---

13 Judgment in *Sheikh Rashid Ahmed v. Government of Punjab* and others (PLD 2010 SC 573) and reiterated by the Supreme Court of Pakistan in its Judgment dated March 19, 2014, in Civil Appeal No. 297 of 2014.

14 Balochistan passed its LGA in 2010. However, the provincial assembles of KPK, Punjab, and Sindh did not do so until 2013.

TABLE 9.4 Real federal and provincial revenues and expenditures in Pakistan (billions of PKR, 2005/2006 = 100), 2004–2014

Item	FY2004	FY2005	FY2006	FY2007
Total revenues	942.7	998.4	1,080.8	1,150.1
Total expenditures	1,096.3	1,239.0	1,407.3	1,561.8
Federal expenditures	786.2	909.6	1,016.3	1,141.1
Current	*664.8*	*759.5*	*791.4*	*907.1*
Development	*121.4*	*150.1*	*224.9*	*234.1*
Transfers to provinces	238.1	272.1	301.9	372.9
Federal loans and grants to provinces	29.8	26.3	65.5	1.0
Provincial direct tax	8.64	11.1	9.38	7.95
Provincial own revenues (tax and nontax)	59.5	63.2	84.7	67.3
Provincial	328.3	384.9	475.6	545.1
Total expenditures				
Current	*259.3*	*282.3*	*334.0*	*374.9*
Development	*69.1*	*102.6*	*141.6*	*170.2*

Source: Ministry of Finance, PRSP Progress Reports, Economic Survey of Pakistan, Appropriation Accounts, Fiscal Operations (GoP 2014b).

Note: Provincial own revenues refers to locally generated revenue from taxes, property rates, utility fees, and so forth, rather than intergovernmental transfers from the central government. PKR = Pakistani rupees; FY = fiscal year.

[a] Indicates provisional data.

before the 18th Amendment was adopted, the transfer system did not adequately take into account the extra responsibilities that the provincial governments had acquired (UNDP 2013). Table 9.4 suggests, though, that absolute transfers to the provinces increased sizably from 2011, which was when implementation of the amendment effectively began, until 2014. Moreover, provincial direct taxes show a consistent increase since 2011, most likely because of the GST reform noted above.

Although provincial expenditures also demonstrate an upward trend, the increase in these expenditures is less impressive. Specifically, while provincial current expenditures grew by about 30 percent between 2010 and 2014, development expenditures increased by only about 14 percent during the same period. This was partially because the federal government had unilaterally announced a 50 percent increase in the salaries of provincial government employees and the provinces wanted to generate surpluses in order to address their debt problems (SPDC 2012, 99).

Absolute figures, however, are not sufficient for assessing fiscal autonomy. One critical metric of fiscal autonomy relates to possession of adequate

FY2008	FY2009	FY2010	FY2011	FY2012	FY2013	FY2014[a]
1,156.2	1,190.0	1,219.6	1,108.2	1,189.4	1,335.6	1,544.5
1,879.5	1,800.0	1,857.6	1,781.4	1,925.7	2,189.2	2,134.2
1,368.9	1,157.2	1,246.7	1,186.5	1,198.7	1,388.8	1,412.2
1,172.6	*1,023.3*	*1,086.4*	*1,074.9*	*1,057.2*	*1,193.2*	*1,224.9*
196.3	*133.9*	*160.3*	*111.6*	*141.9*	*195.6*	*187.3*
377.6	359.6	391.3	516.4	534.8	552.3	597.2
75.1	65.0	74.1	44.0	43.5	48.9	51.7
8.02	7.33	8.57	8.89	12.65	15.97	33.57
98.0	88.8	75.8	65.6	76.1	100.9	101.7
537.6	511.5	547.1	546.8	659.0	673.5	687.0
360.9	*373.3*	*387.4*	*420.0*	*474.9*	*504.5*	*504.2*
176.8	*138.2*	*159.7*	*126.9*	*184.2*	*168.9*	*182.8*

resources to fulfill administrative responsibilities, captured by the share of provincial (or other subnational) expenditures in total expenditures. Lower shares mean that subnational governments may lack the ability to sufficiently spend in the areas in which they have been granted responsibility. Table 9.5 shows that this share has not drastically changed since the mid-2000s, despite the devolution of greater administrative responsibilities to the provincial level.

Vertical imbalance, or the gap between own spending and own revenue at the subnational level, is another means of assessing fiscal autonomy.[15] There are multiple metrics for assessing this imbalance (see Sharma 2012), including the share of intergovernmental transfers in provincial or other subnational expenditures (Jin and Zou 2001) and the share of intergovernmental transfers in provincial or other subnational revenues (Rodden 2002). Table 9.5 shows that by both measures, the extent of fiscal decentralization is relatively weak and does not appear to have significantly improved despite recent

---

15 Own revenue refers to locally generated revenue from taxes, property rates, utility fees, and so forth rather than intergovernmental transfers from the central government.

TABLE 9.5 Selected measures of fiscal decentralization in Pakistan (%), FY2004–FY2014

Measures of fiscal decentralization	FY2004	FY2005	FY2006
Intergovernmental transfers as share of total provincial revenues	81.8	82.5	81.3
Provincial own revenue as share of total provincial revenues	18.2	17.5	18.7
Provincial tax revenue as share of total provincial revenues	2.6	3.1	2.1
Provincial expenditures as share of total government expenditures	29.9	31.1	33.8
Intergovernmental transfers as share of provincial expenditures	72.5	70.7	63.5

Source: Authors, calculated from data presented in Table 9.4.

Note: Provincial own revenues refers to locally generated revenue from taxes, property rates, utility fees, and so forth, rather than intergovernmental transfers from the central government. FY = fiscal year.

[a] Indicates provisional data.

decentralization reforms. In fact, given that the share of transfers in Pakistan's total provincial revenue averaged 86 percent between 1978 and 1996 (Rodden and Wibbels 2002), arguably little progress has been made even since the introduction of the LGO in 2001. One observable change is the increase in provincial tax revenue as a share of total provincial revenue since 2011, albeit to a still low 4.5 percent as of 2014. In comparison, the same measure for India was 37 percent in 2006 (see Kalirajan and Otsuka 2012).

Local government administrative autonomy is further limited by province-specific regulations. For instance, Punjab and Balochistan require that local governments function under the directives of the provincial government while Sindh and Khyber Pakhtunkhwa enable the provincial governments to supervise and inspect local governments. Punjab now allows members from local government to participate in education and health authorities, which are responsible for establishing, managing, and supervising district educational and health facilities.[16] However, the provincial chief minister will be in charge of appointing and removing members to these authorities.

In addition, as noted earlier, another important measure of autonomy relates to whether subnational authorities can raise their own taxes. The 7th NFC Award stipulated that provincial governments should take more active steps to collect the agricultural income tax (AIT), especially given that the agricultural sector accounts for a significant portion of Pakistan's national income (see SPDC 2012). However, as Table 9.6 shows, only Punjab

---

16 Specifically, the District Education Authority oversees primary education, secondary education, higher education institutions, adult literacy, and nonformal basic education. The District Health Authority is responsible for all primary and secondary healthcare facilities in a district.

	FY2007	FY2008	FY2009	FY2010	FY2011	FY2012	FY2013	FY2014[a]
	84.7	82.2	82.7	86.0	89.5	88.4	85.6	86.5
	15.3	17.8	17.3	14.0	10.5	11.6	14.4	13.5
	1.8	1.5	1.4	1.6	1.4	1.9	2.3	4.5
	34.9	28.6	28.4	29.5	30.7	34.2	30.8	32.2
	68.4	70.2	70.3	71.5	94.4	81.2	82.0	86.9

has been able to significantly and consistently engage in resource mobilization via the AIT over time. Collectively, AIT has declined from composing 8.2 percent of provinces' direct taxes in FY2009 to around 1.8 percent by FY2014. Generally, Pakistan has a relatively low tax-to-GDP ratio, which fell from 14.5 percent in the early 1980s to 10.3 percent in 2002 at the onset of the LGO, rising to 11.1 percent in 2013 (Ahmad 2013; World Bank 2014b). This is a much lower tax-to-GDP ratio than is found in other middle income federations, such as Brazil (15.1 percent) or South Africa (26.7 percent). This has led Ahmad (2013, 13) to be pessimistic about the 18th Amendment, concluding that "under these circumstances, a major structural shift involving a significant decentralization of spending to the provincial governments— unbundling the parallel responsibilities of government—is of little more consequence than shifting deck chairs on the Titanic."

Not surprisingly, the fiscal constraints are even more binding for local governments at the district level and below. Indeed, Table 9.7 shows that the PFC awards have not been fully implemented in practice, because while the total share of transfers from the provinces to local governments has been increasing relatively steadily in Punjab and KPK, they have been falling dramatically in Sindh and Balochistan. In addition, no new taxing powers have been allocated from the provinces to the local governments (Shah 2012).

Vertical Accountability Is Still Weak

In terms of augmenting vertical accountability, the 18th Amendment reforms are thus far judged to be unsatisfactory because of the degree and manner in which they have been implemented. After the 17 ministries were devolved to the provincial level, provincial planning and development departments were

TABLE 9.6 Real agriculture income tax receipts (billions of PKR, 2005/2006 = 100), 2004–2014

Province	FY2004	FY2005	FY2006
Punjab	0.9	0.7	0.7
Sindh	0.3	0.2	0.2
Khyber Pakhtunkhwa	0.1	0.2	0.0
Balochistan	0.0	0.0	0.0
Total AIT receipts	1.3	1.1	0.9
Provincial direct tax	8.6	11.1	9.4
Total federal and provincial revenue	942.6	998.5	1076.6
AIT as share of provincial direct taxes (%)	15.1	9.9	9.6
AIT as share of total revenues (%)	0.14	0.11	0.08

Source: Ministry of Finance Fiscal Operations, Civil Accounts and Economic Surveys of Pakistan (GoP 2014b).

Note: AIT = agricultural income tax. FY = fiscal year.

ᵃ Indicates provisional data.

responsible for facilitating cross-sectoral interventions and representing the newly devolved provincial ministries to the National Planning Commission at the federal level (see Zaidi et al. 2013). However, as noted in Chapter 8, some key pro-poor programs in the areas of health and education—such as the Lady Health Workers and the Expanded Program on Immunization (EPI)—remain at the federal level. Likewise, while approximately 75 percent of the Public Sector Development Program, which is the country's main framework for allocating resources for development projects and programs, was assigned to the provinces in 2011, some agricultural-sector projects are left with unclear responsibility of funding. These include the National Program for the Improvement of Watercourses in Pakistan, the Water Conservation and Productivity Enhancement through High Efficiency Irrigation System, and the National Project for Enhancing Existing Capacity of Grain Storage (FAO 2012; Pasha et al. 2011). These ambiguities raise challenges for policy coordination and implementation while also obscuring both upward and downward accountability.

Public opinion research reveals strong support for greater downward accountability via elections. A survey conducted by Gallup in mid-2013 revealed that a majority of those sampled, 71 percent, supported holding elections.[17] The United Nations Development Programme (UNDP) likewise found that 81 percent of Pakistanis who were sampled for a social audit report

---

17 The survey was nationally representative and included 2,635 men and women in urban and rural areas, across all four provinces (Gallup Pakistan 2013)

FY2007	FY2008	FY2009	FY2010	FY2011	FY2012	FY2013	FY2014[a]
0.7	0.6	0.5	0.5	0.4	0.4	0.4	0.4
0.2	0.2	0.1	0.1	0.1	0.1	0.2	0.2
0.0	0.0	0.0	0.0	0.0	0.0	0.0	0.0
0.0	0.0	0.0	0.0	0.0	0.0	0.0	0.0
0.9	0.8	0.6	0.6	0.5	0.5	0.6	0.6
8.0	8.0	7.3	8.6	8.9	12.7	16.0	33.6
1209.7	1238.2	1266.0	1283.6	1164.3	1255.6	1355.6	1544.5
11.3	10.0	8.2	7.0	5.6	3.9	3.8	1.8
0.07	0.06	0.05	0.05	0.04	0.04	0.04	0.04

TABLE 9.7 Transfers from provincial to local governments (billions of PKR, nominal), 2009/2010–2012/2013

Province	2009/2010	2010/2011	2011/2012	2012/2013[a]
Balochistan	20.9	2.7	0.0	0.0
KPK	38.9	54.8	74.5	93.1
Punjab	124.5	152.7	191.6	213.6
Sindh	104.3	124.4	73.9	37.9

Source: SPDC (2012).

Note: PKR = Pakistani rupees; KPK = Khyber Pakhtunkhwa.

[a] Indicates budgeted rather than actual.

would vote in local elections, though this varied from 84 percent in Punjab to 67 percent in Balochistan (see Khalid et al. 2012).

Ironically then, five years after the 18th Amendment was implemented, local elections under the new reforms were held only in Balochistan. In the other three provinces, the tenure of previously elected local government officials expired in 2009. Instead, the administration of the districts is overseen by appointed administrators (CLGF 2013). According to the Electoral Commission of Pakistan, the other three provinces, as well as Islamabad Capital Territory, were planning local elections in mid to late 2015 (see Butt 2015). These delays bolster Lamb and Hameed's (2012, 49) claim that "real ambiguities therefore exist regarding who has authority at the local level."

In addition, some of the election rules included in the LGAs hinder true downward accountability. All four LGAs allow the provincial authorities to remove or suspend elected heads of local government. Moreover, Cheema, Khan, and Myerson (2014) have lamented the use of closed party lists in some of these provinces because this approach does not actually allow voters to sanction or reward individual politicians. Instead, it reinforces upward accountability between politicians and party leaders. Another concern has been the preference in some of the provinces, such as Punjab and Sindh, for leaders of district councils, *nazims,* to be indirectly elected by members of the tehsil and union tiers. This is problematic for accountability because the *nazim* has significant control over the budget and therefore exerts substantial power and influence (see Keefer, Narayan, and Vishwanath 2006).

The role of informal influences on accountability also remains ever present, especially in rural areas. For instance, a social audit by UNDP found that vulnerable households are more likely to contact a *biradari* elder in their community than a member of their district, tehsil, or union councils when they have concerns over security or service delivery (Khalid et al. 2012).[18] Notably, they were more likely to do this than nonvulnerable households. In other words, informal leaders in poorer rural communities still tend to be viewed as more-legitimate local authorities than public officials.

Devolution's Impact on Service Delivery

Although a detailed evaluation of the impact of the 18th Amendment on service delivery is not possible at this stage, initial expenditure allocations provide one indication of how the reforms affect policy outcomes on the ground. Regarding service delivery, social sector expenditures as a share of total provincial expenditures on health, education, and water and sanitation appear to have increased marginally over 2000–2009—which includes the period after the adoption of the 18th Amendment—increasing from 34.6 percent in 2009/2010 to 38.3 percent by 2011/2012 (SPDC 2012, 101).

Federal expenditures on rural development encompass, among other things, subsidies and expenditures on special initiatives for the (1) lining of canals and water courses, (2) Food Support Program, (3) Benazir Income Support Program (BISP), (4) Village Electrification, and (5) Peoples Works Programme (Table 9.8). These expenditures have proved relatively volatile over time. As of 2014, provisional data suggest that the federal government

---

18 Vulnerability was defined as households (1) whose head of household was either unemployed or an unskilled laborer, (2) whose household roof was constructed with mud or wood or had a tent roof, and (3) lacked latrines inside their home.

allocated PKR 13.2 billion to agricultural development in particular. While the federal transfers to the provinces increased substantially and so did provincial overall expenditures (Table 9.4), the growth in provincial expenditures relating to agricultural development is not markedly changed since the implementation of the 18th Amendment (Table 9.9). In other words, even as many responsibilities related to agricultural development were devolved, the federal government appears to still be outspending the provinces in this domain. If anything, Table 9.9 indicates that provincial disparities in spending on agriculture continue to persist, with Sindh allocating more than three times as much funding for agricultural development in 2014 as the other provinces in the same year.

More seriously, the provincial governments with weak institutions have no capacity to formulate rural development policy, and an integrated planning and implementation framework that enables development policy formulation, capacity building, and implementation remains absent. An evaluation focused on KPK found that even in 2014, the provincial government had prepared only a first draft of its food and agricultural policy, which was shared with neither the provincial assembly nor any key stakeholders (see CPDI 2014). Few stakeholders interviewed for the evaluation were aware of the status of the implementation of the 18th Amendment, which certainly undermines their ability to hold policy makers accountable.

In addition, citizens' perceptions of access to services and satisfaction with the performance of services since the adoption of the 18th Amendment have been relatively negative. For example, 48 percent of households who participated in a UNDP survey in 2004 claimed that they had access to agricultural extension services, but this proportion decreased to 14 percent by 2012 (Khalid et al. 2012). As Table 9.10 shows, access to other services has gradually improved in Pakistan over the past decade.[19] Nevertheless, satisfaction levels still remain low, with performance on education appearing to consistently generate the most satisfaction, at a still mediocre level of 55 percent in 2011/2012.[20]

---

19 See Chapter 8 for more recent data on access for rural Pakistan in particular.

20 Of course, given how recently these reforms were implemented, such findings need to be assessed with caution.

TABLE 9.8 Real distribution of federal spending on agriculture and rural development (billions of PKR, 2005/2006 = 100), 2004–2014

Expenditure	FY2004	FY2005	FY2006	FY2007
Rural development related	97.7	100.6	110.6	56.6
Agriculture current[a]	34.4	37.2	40.2	38.6
Agriculture development[a]	25.4	32.6	45.3	9.2
Rural development current	8.4	4.8	1.0	0.3
Rural development capital	13.7	12.2	14.1	1.0
Food subsidies	10.1	6.0	6.0	4.1
Gross subsidies[b]	n.a.	n.a.	n.a.	n.a.
Food Support Program	3.3	3.0	3.1	0.1
Village electrification	2.4	4.9	1.0	2.3
Peoples Works Program	n.a.	n.a.	n.a.	n.a.
BISP	n.a.	n.a.	n.a.	n.a.
Rural development less subsidies & FSP	84.3	91.6	101.5	51.5

Source: Ministry of Finance, PRSP Progress Reports, Economic Survey of Pakistan, Appropriation Accounts, Fiscal Operations (GoP 2014b).

Note: n.a. = not applicable; BISP = Benazir Income Support Program; FSP = Food Support Program; PKR = Pakistani rupees.

[a] Including irrigation, livestock, fisheries, forestry as well as expenditure on special program Lining of Water Courses/Canals from FY2004.

[b] All subsidies, including power, food, fertilizer, sugar. Since FY2008, food subsidies have been reported at the federal level as part of gross subsidies. The Food Support Program has been discontinued, while the Peoples Works Program and BISP started under the Peoples Party Government. The allocation for village electrification was eventually integrated into the Peoples Works Program.

FY2008	FY2009	FY2010	FY2011	FY2012	FY2013	FY2014
383.4	188.3	206.8	234.5	324.9	224.0	181.1
2.3	1.6	3.7	3.7	1.5	2.0	1.8
43.8	17.6	15.6	10.9	11.6	16.5	13.2
1.7	0.0	0.0	0.0	0.0	0.0	0.0
1.4	0.5	0.6	0.3	0.5	0.3	0.6
n.a.	n.a.	n.a.	n.a.	n.a.	n.a.	n.a.
326.1	145.5	142.3	187.6	272.9	162.7	136.7
3.6	8.5	n.a.	n.a.	n.a.	n.a.	n.a.
2.2	n.a.	n.a.	n.a.	n.a.	n.a.	n.a.
3.9	21.4	26.0	13.6	18.5	20.8	n.a.
n.a.	n.a.	19.8	18.4	19.8	20.0	28.7
8.3	41.2	64.5	46.9	51.9	61.3	44.3

TABLE 9.9 Real provincial expenditures on selected sectors (billions of PKR, 2005/2006 = 100), 2004–2014

Expenditure	FY2004	FY2005	FY2006	FY2007
Punjab expenditure	30.3	30.1	30.3	32.9
Agriculture current[a]	10.4	11.0	10.5	12.3
Agriculture development[a]	2.6	4.4	8.1	10.2
Rural development current	5.6	3.3	0.4	0.1
Rural development capital	7.6	8.1	8.8	8.7
Food subsidies	2.4	1.7	0.7	0.0
Food Support Program	1.7	1.6	1.7	1.7
Sindh expenditure	12.8	12.2	19.2	18.6
Agriculture current[a]	5.0	5.4	7.8	6.0
Agriculture development[a]	2.6	4.5	10.2	10.3
Rural development current	2.4	0.3	0.2	1.2
Rural development capital	1.5	0.7	0.0	0.0
Food subsidies	0.6	0.6	0.4	0.5
Food Support Program	0.7	0.7	0.5	0.7
KPK expenditure	7.1	7.2	10.3	14.5
Agriculture current[a]	2.4	2.5	2.5	3.0
Agriculture development[a]	0.6	1.0	3.3	4.6
Rural development current	0.2	0.3	0.1	1.6
Rural development capital	2.4	1.9	2.9	4.3
Food subsidies	0.8	1.0	0.9	0.5
Food Support Program	0.6	0.6	0.6	0.7
Balochistan expenditure	7.8	10.9	12.3	13.6
Agriculture current[a]	4.6	5.1	6.1	4.8
Agriculture development[a]	1.7	4.2	4.1	4.2
Rural development current	0.2	0.4	0.1	0.5
Rural development capital	1.2	1.0	1.9	4.0
Food subsidies	0.0	0.0	0.0	0.0
Food Support Program	0.1	0.1	0.1	0.1

Source: Ministry of Finance, PRSP Progress Reports, Economic Survey of Pakistan, Appropriation Accounts, Fiscal Operations (GoP 2014b).

Note: n.a. = not applicable; PKR = Pakistani rupees; KPK = Khyber Pakhtunkhwa; FY = fiscal year.

[a] Including irrigation, livestock, fisheries, forestry as well as expenditure on special program Lining of Water Courses/Canals from FY2004.

FY2008	FY2009	FY2010	FY2011	FY2012	FY2013	FY2014
32.4	24.6	24.0	24.1	29.7	96.4	82.4
12.1	13.3	12.4	12.7	13.5	14.6	14.3
10.0	6.2	7.4	3.6	3.8	4.3	3.4
0.2	0.1	0.1	0.2	0.1	0.2	0.2
8.0	3.6	3.8	2.6	5.9	7.6	3.5
0.2	1.3	0.3	5.0	6.3	69.6	60.9
1.9	n.a.	n.a.	n.a.	n.a.	n.a.	n.a.
19.9	11.8	14.8	15.2	20.6	33.1	24.7
5.8	4.2	5.2	9.2	8.7	7.2	7.4
12.1	7.0	7.9	5.1	10.1	7.3	12.6
0.1	0.1	0.1	0.1	0.1	0.2	0.0
0.0	0.0	0.0	0.0	0.2	0.2	0.0
1.2	0.5	1.5	0.9	1.5	18.3	4.5
0.8	n.a.	n.a.	n.a.	n.a.	n.a.	n.a.
13.9	10.8	8.0	9.9	15.9	12.6	17.7
2.7	2.5	2.8	2.5	3.6	3.8	3.4
4.2	2.3	2.5	3.8	4.2	2.6	2.7
0.2	0.3	0.1	0.2	0.2	0.2	0.0
4.5	2.2	1.8	2.4	6.4	4.2	1.0
1.7	3.6	0.9	1.0	1.6	1.8	10.7
0.6	n.a.	n.a.	n.a.	n.a.	n.a.	n.a.
12.8	8.4	9.1	11.1	12.5	11.3	8.9
4.7	4.3	4.6	4.8	5.2	4.1	4.2
3.6	1.6	2.7	3.5	3.9	5.1	3.9
0.3	0.3	0.1	0.2	0.2	0.3	0.2
4.0	2.3	1.8	2.4	2.5	1.5	0.5
0.0	0.0	0.0	0.5	1.5	0.3	0.0
0.2	n.a.	n.a.	n.a.	n.a.	n.a.	n.a.

TABLE 9.10 Households' assessments of access to and satisfaction with select services in Pakistan (%), 2001/2002–2011/2012

	2001/2002	2004/2005	2009/2010	2011/2012
Access to service				
Sewerage and sanitation	49	66	72	78
Water	33	44	68	68
Education	93	96	93	93
Health	68	77	71	76
Agricultural extension	—	48	30	14
Satisfaction with performance				
Sewerage and sanitation	12	20	25	23
Water	18	19	39	37
Education	55	53	58	55
Health	23	27	33	29
Agricultural extension	—	15	4	2

Source: Adapted from Khalid et al. (2012).

Note: These findings were based on a nationally and provincially representative stratified random sample of 10,740 households. — = not available.

Conclusions

Evidence suggests that the implicit rationale underlying the devolution exercise spurred by the 18th Amendment has been broadly welcomed. For instance, as of 2011 a Gallup survey reported that 64 percent of Pakistanis stated that they favored the devolution of ministries to the provinces, with support marginally higher in rural areas than in urban ones.[21] Although UNDP's social audits found important differences across provinces, approximately 60 percent of surveyed individuals also said that they supported the return to elected local government (Khalid et al. 2012). This suggests that opportunities for greater participation and influence of the poor in Pakistan's development policies, and for powers to be more balanced across all the levels of government, are being embraced in theory.

In order for the desired expectations from devolution to translate into real improvements on the ground, research shows that improved authority, autonomy, and accountability of subnational authorities are needed. The 18th Amendment changes have demonstrated mixed achievements in all three domains at the provincial level. Ministerial functions have been devolved, the

---

21 This survey was carried out with a sample of 2,753 men and women, across urban and rural areas of all four provinces. See Gallup Pakistan (2011).

Concurrent Lists have been eliminated, and intergovernmental transfers have been increased absolutely and based on a new formula that takes each province's concerns into account. However, the creation of new federal ministries that have some overlapping mandates with the devolved ones represents at least one contradictory feature of these reforms. In addition, Pakistan's vertical fiscal imbalance remains high, long hampered by low tax revenue collection, and creates the risk of unfunded mandates. Those mandates that are funded appear to rely more heavily on outlays of current rather than development expenditures.

Below the province level, at the district, tehsil, and union council levels, progress seems limited. Despite the formula-based transfers through the PFC, the districts have no new taxing powers. Moreover, accountability is stymied, both by delays in holding local elections in most of the provinces and by the use of electoral institutions that prevent citizens from sanctioning or approving the performance of local authorities. Particularly in more rural, marginalized communities, patron-client relationships within the *biradari* system continue to prevail.

The pace of reform and inappropriate sequencing underlie many of these challenges. "Big bang" approaches to reform, like the 18th Amendment, are useful for allowing political leaders to quickly establish their legacies and sideline potential opponents who could bolster antireform coalitions if the process had been more gradual. Yet devolving a large number of ministries in a context of low and disparate capacities only invites frustration with the pace of promised service delivery and agricultural improvements. Faguet (2008), for instance, notes that Bolivia's "shock treatment" decentralization in 1994 overwhelmed already weak local governments; in contrast, Colombia's more gradual approach was sequenced such that local authorities first confronted fiscal reforms and the task of raising revenue before facing administrative reforms that transferred more responsibilities to them.

Moreover, such a large-scale shift creates predictable misunderstandings over responsibilities and accountability. For instance, one survey in Pakistan revealed a lot of confusion within communities about the new system in terms of the hierarchy and division of responsibilities (see Khalid et al. 2012). A survey by the Pakistan Institute of Legislative Development and Transparency, conducted in mid-2014, captured Pakistanis' impressions of government performance in 30 different domains. Respondents claimed that the devolution process was one of the worst areas of performance for the federal government. When the results are disaggregated by province, Balochistan was viewed as performing the best at implementing the 18th Amendment, especially because it was the first province to hold local elections, while Sindh was rated as the worst (see PILDAT 2014). Even donors have struggled to understand the implications of devolution for their partnerships and funding to Pakistan (see FAO 2012; World Bank 2014a).

In the effort to ensure that devolution actually results in a fundamental restructuring of intergovernmental relations to improve government performance and better target poor citizens' needs, a number of ongoing and potential efforts are promising. To better equip local government with the tools for assessing the economic status of communities, particularly in rural areas, and developing adequate interventions, some donors are currently providing district governments with budget training and collecting data through the use of smartphones and geomapping. The government has initiated the development of a multidimensional poverty index at the provincial and district levels, which will integrate income, health, and education outcomes at the subnational level (UNDP 2014). This information can provide a baseline to assess performance over time and inform local authorities about key constraints.

Moreover, performance grants for districts that pursue innovative ways of delivering services are being piloted by the Department for International Development (DfID) and the World Bank in selected areas of Punjab and KPK, but they could be scaled up across the country.[22] The approach would reward efforts to improve services outside the normal mechanisms of intergovernmental transfers, thereby creating performance incentives for local governments that are not captured in the existing transfer criteria and fostering a degree of subnational competition in the manner originally envisioned by Tiebout (1956). Transparency through the media and other outlets could promote citizen awareness of district grant winners across the country, encouraging knowledge diffusion among local officials of innovative solutions to development challenges.

Besides capacity constraints, another challenge relates to organizational structure and incentives across ministries and levels of government. Certain policy arenas, such as rural development, nutrition, or climate change, require intersectoral coordination across ministries that have now been devolved. Consequently, Nishtar et al. (2013) suggest the creation of a federal institutional mechanism to coordinate across provinces in particular domains. This would increase the likelihood that each province is adhering to important regulations and receiving required technical assistance while also

---

22 See, for instance, the World Bank's Punjab Public Management Reform Program and DfID's Subnational Governance Program (http://www.punjab-prmp.gov.pk/).

mitigating further interprovincial inequalities in service delivery and agricultural investments.

Insufficient political will can prove more difficult to overcome than capacity constraints, but shifts in electoral rules may help augment accountability. As alluded to earlier, one of the challenges with promoting accountability under the 2013 reforms has been the use of a party closed-list plurality voting system. The closed-list approach means that voters do not get to voice their opinions on the performance of individual candidates. Instead, the parties determine the rankings of candidates on the lists. The closed nature of such a system diminishes the incentives of local officials to perform well for their constituencies because accountability is mainly upward to the party that determines their order on the list. Furthermore, the plurality system means that a party does not need a majority of votes to win; it just needs to obtain more votes than any other party.

Consequently, Cheema et al. (2014) have suggested that Pakistan shift to using an open-list, proportional representation system for local elections whereby any party that has representation in the provincial or national assembly can nominate a list of candidates to compete in local elections within that province. Voters would know the order of the candidates in advance, and local council seats would be allocated in proportion to the share of the votes obtained by each party. Party leaders, including at the provincial and national levels, would then realize that there is a symbiotic relationship between the performance of individual candidates at the local level and the reputation of the party. At the same time, instead of seeing local leaders as a threat, this change would increase the likelihood that provincial parties would recognize an opportunity to further institutionalize their parties at the grassroots level, thereby diminishing the incentive to thwart local elections. The vertical accountability link would also be stronger if citizens could directly elect the district *nazim* rather than this important figure being selected indirectly by tehsil and union tier members in some of the provinces (Keefer, Narayan, and Vishwanath 2006).

As experience has shown elsewhere, subnational actors see postdecentralization problems as evidence that they need more resources. Yet national actors can view these same challenges as a justification for recentralization (Eaton, Kaiser, and Smoke 2010). While research findings remain ambiguous about whether decentralization is categorically more effective at delivering services than more centralized approaches, simultaneous processes of decentralization and recentralization are clearly detrimental to giving a voice to the poor and efficiently providing much-needed services (Resnick

2014). Given Pakistan's volatile policy shifts, long-term commitment to the 18th Amendment reforms will therefore be essential to address many of the weaknesses in the current devolution landscape and ensure that it works to strengthen agricultural investment and broader rural development.

References

Adeney, K. 2012. "A Step Towards Inclusive Federalism in Pakistan? The Politics of the 18th Amendment." *Publius: The Journal of Federalism* 42 (4): 536–565.

Ahmad, E. 2013. *Can the New Intergovernmental Structure Work in Pakistan in the Presence of Governance Challenges? Learning from China.* Asia Research Centre Working Paper 58, London: London School of Economics.

Ahmad, J., S. Devarajan, S. Khemani, and S. Shah. 2006. "Decentralization and Service Delivery." In *Handbook of Fiscal Federalism,* edited by E. Ahmad and G. Brosio, 240–270. Northampton, MA: Edward Elgar Publishing.

Alderman, H. 2002. "Do Local Officials Know Something We Don't? Decentralization of Targeted Transfers in Albania." *Journal of Public Economics* 83: 375–404.

Bardhan, P., and D. Mookherjee. 2000. "Capture and Governance at Local and National Levels." *American Economic Review* 90 (2): 135–139.

Blair, H. 2000. "Participation and Accountability at the Periphery: Democratic Local Governance in Six Countries." *World Development* 28 (1): 21–39.

Brinkerhoff, D., with O. Azfar. 2010. "Decentralization and Community Empowerment." In *Making Decentralization Work,* edited by E. Connerley, K. Eaton, and P. Smoke. Boulder, CO: Lynne Rienner Publishers.

Burki, S. J. 2015. *Historical Dictionary of Pakistan.* Lanham, MD: Rowman and Littlefield.

Butt, A. 2015. "ECP Announces Schedule for Local Body Elections." *Dawn.* February 6. http://www.dawn.com/news/1161890/ecp-announces-schedule-for-local-body-elections.

Cheema, A., A. Khan, and R. Myerson. 2014. *Breaking the Countercyclical Pattern of Local Democracy in Pakistan.* Working paper. http://home.uchicago.edu/~rmyerson/research/pakdemoc.pdf.

Cheema, A., A. I. Khwaja, and A. Qadir. 2006. "Local Government Reforms in Pakistan: Context, Content, and Causes." In *Decentralization and Local Governance in Developing Countries,* edited by P. Bardhan and D. Mookherjee, 257–284. Cambridge, MA: MIT Press.

Cheema, A., and S. K. Mohmand. 2008. "Decentralization and Inequality in Pakistan: Bridging the Gap That Divides." In *Devolution and Governance Reforms in Pakistan,* edited by S. M. Ali and M. A. Saqib. Karachi: Oxford University Press.

Cheema, G. S., and D. Rondinelli. 2007. "From Government Decentralization to Decentralized Governance." In *Decentralizing Governance: Emerging Concepts and Practices*, edited by G. S. Cheema and D. Rondinelli. Cambridge, MA: Harvard University; Washington, DC: Brookings Institution Press.

CLGF (Commonwealth Local Government Forum). 2013. *Country Profile: The Local Government System in Pakistan*. London: CLGF. http://www.clgf.org.uk/userfiles/1/file/Pakistan_Local _Government_Profile_2013_CLGF.pdf.

CPDI (Centre for Peace and Development Initiatives). 2014. *Citizens' Oversight of 18th Amendment in Khyber Pakhtunkhwa*. Islamabad: CPDI.

Dawn. 2011. *MINFAL's Devolution: Food Security & Research Department at Centre Proposed*. http://www.dawn.com/news/623856/minfals-devolution-food-security-research-dept-at -centre-proposed. Accessed April 1, 2015.

Dickovick, T. 2005. "The Measure and Mismeasure of Decentralization: Subnational Autonomy in Senegal and South Africa." *The Journal of Modern African Studies* 43 (2): 183–210.

———. 2007. "Municipalization as Central Government Strategy: Central-Regional-Local Politics in Peru, Brazil, and South Africa." *Publius: The Journal of Federalism* 37 (1): 1–25.

Dickovick, T., and R. Riedl. 2010. *Comparative Assessment of Decentralization in Africa: Final Report and Summary of Findings*. Washington, DC: USAID.

Eaton, K., K. Kaiser, and P. Smoke. 2010. *The Political Economy of Decentralization Reforms: Implications for Aid Effectiveness*. Washington, DC: World Bank.

Faguet, J. P. 2008. "Decentralization's Effect on Public Investment: Evidence and Policy Lessons from Bolivia and Colombia." *Journal of Development Studies* 44 (8): 1100–1121.

———. 2014. "Decentralization and Governance." *World Development* 53: 2–13.

Faguet, J. P., and F. Sánchez. 2008. "Decentralization's Effects on Educational Outcomes in Bolivia and Colombia." *World Development* 36: 1294–1316.

Falleti, T. 2005. "A Sequential Theory of Decentralization: Latin American Cases in Comparative Perspective." *American Political Science Review* 99 (3): 327–346.

FAO (Food and Agricultural Organization). 2012. *Prosperity through Sustainable Agriculture: FAO Pakistan Country Programming Framework 1*. Rome: FAO.

Flaherty, K., M. Sharif, and D. J. Spielman. 2012. *Pakistan: Recent Developments in Agricultural Research*. ASTI Indicators Initiative. Washington, DC: IFPRI.

Galasso, E., and M. Ravallion. 2005. "Decentralized Targeting of an Antipoverty Program." *Journal of Public Economics* 89: 705–727.

Gallup Pakistan. 2011. *64% Favour the Devolution of Ministries to Provinces as Opposed to 13% Who Do Not*. http://gallup.com.pk/64-favour-the-devolution-of-ministries-to-provinces-as -opposed-to-13-who-do-not/. Accessed June 5, 2016.

——. 2013. *Opinion Poll: Elections: Local Government*. http://gallup.com.pk/wp-content/ uploads/2016/02/Aug-02-2013-PR1.pdf. Accessed May 31, 2016.

Ghaus-Pasha, A., and K. Bengali. 2005. "Pakistan." In *Handbook of Federal Countries*, edited by Ann Griffiths. Canada: McGill University Press.

Goldfrank, B. 2011. *Deepening Local Democracy in Latin America: Participation, Decentralization, and the Left*. University Park: Pennsylvania State University Press.

GoP (Government of Pakistan). 2012. *Federal Budget: Budget in Brief 2011–12*. Islamabad: Finance Division.

——. 2014a. *Pakistan Cabinet Yearbook, 2012–2013*. Islamabad, Pakistan.

——. 2014b. *Pakistan Economic Survey, 2013–2014*. Islamabad: Ministry of Finance.

Griffiths, A., ed. 2005. *Handbook of Federal Countries*. Canada: McGill University Press.

Gurr, T. R. 2000. *Peoples versus States: Minorities at Risk in the New Century*. Washington, DC: United States Institute of Peace Press.

Hasnain, Z. 2010. "Devolution, Accountability, and Service Delivery in Pakistan." *The Pakistan Development Review* 49 (2): 129–152.

IFES (International Foundation for Electoral Systems). 2013. "Local Government: Balochistan." Washington, DC: IFES.

Jin, J., and H.-F. Zou. 2001. "How Does Fiscal Decentralization Affect Aggregate, National, and Subnational Government Size?" *Journal of Urban Economics* 52: 270–293.

Kalirajan, K., and K. Otsuka. 2012. "Fiscal Decentralization and Development Outcomes in India: An Exploratory Analysis." *World Development* 40 (8): 1511–1521.

Kathyola, J., and O. Job, eds. 2011. *Decentralisation in Commonwealth Africa: Experiences from Botswana, Cameroon, Ghana, Mozambique, and Tanzania*. London: Commonwealth Secretariat.

Keefer, P., A. Narayan, and T. Vishwanath. 2006. "Decentralization in Pakistan: Are Local Governments Likely to Be More Accountable than Central Government?" In *Decentralization and Local Governance in Developing Countries*, edited by P. Bardhan and D. Mookherjee, chap. 9, 285–304. Cambridge, MA: MIT Press.

Khalid, M. Y., S. Kamal, M. T. Noor, S. H. Akbar, B. Hassan, and K. Mahmud. 2012. *Social Audit of Local Governance and Delivery of Public Services*. New York: UNDP.

Kugelman, M., and R. Hathaway, eds. *Reaping the Dividend: Overcoming Pakistan's Demographic Challenges*. Washington, DC: Woodrow Wilson International Center for Scholars.

Lamb, R., and S. Hameed. 2012. *Subnational Governance, Service Delivery, and Militancy in Pakistan*. Washington, DC: Center for Strategic and International Studies.

Lijphart, A. 1999. *Patterns of Democracy: Government Forms and Performance in Thirty-Six Countries*. New Haven, CT: Yale University Press.

Mazhar, A., and B. T. Shaikh. 2012. "Reforms in Pakistan: Decisive Times for Improving Maternal and Child Health." *Healthcare Policy* 8 (1): 24–32.

Musgrave, R. A. 1959. *The Theory of Public Finance: A Study in Public Economics*. New York: McGraw-Hill.

Mustafa, U. 2011. *Fiscal Federalism in Pakistan: The 7th National Finance Commission Award and Its Implications*. PIDE Working Paper 2011: 73. Islamabad: Pakistan Institute of Development Economics.

NFC (National Finance Commission). 2009. *Report of the National Finance Commission*. Islamabad: Government of Pakistan.

Nishtar, S., Z. Bhutta, T. Jafar, A. Ghaffar, T. Akhtar, K. Bengali, Q. Isa, and E. Rahim. 2013. "Health Reform in Pakistan: A Call to Action." *The Lancet* 381: 2291–2297.

Oates, W. 1972. *Fiscal Federalism*. New York: Harcourt Brace Jovanovich.

Pasha, H., M. Imran, M. A. Iqbal, Z. Ismail, R. Sheikh, and S. Sherani. 2011. *Review and Analysis of Pakistan's Public Investment Program: Phase-I Report on Macro-Fiscal and Development Framework*. Working Paper. London: International Growth Centre.

PILDAT (Pakistan Institute of Legislative Development and Transparency). 2014. *Assessment of Quality of Governance in Pakistan*. Islamabad.

Prud'homme, R. 1995. "The Dangers of Decentralization." *The World Bank Research Observer* 10 (2): 201–220.

Rana, M. A. 2014. *The Seed Industry in Pakistan: Regulation, Politics, and Entrepreneurship*. PSSP Working Paper 19. Washington, DC: IFPRI.

Resnick, D. 2014. "Strategies of Subversion in Vertically-Divided Contexts: Decentralisation and Urban Service Delivery in Senegal." *Development Policy Review* 32 (s1): s61-s80.

Ribot, J. 2002. *African Decentralization: Local Actors, Powers, and Accountability*. Programme on Democracy, Governance, and Human Rights, Paper 8. Geneva: UNRISD.

Riedl, R., and T. Dickovick. 2014. "Party Systems and Decentralization in Africa." *Studies in Comparative and International Development* September: 1–22.

Rodden, J. 2002. "The Dilemma of Fiscal Federalism: Intergovernmental Grants and Fiscal Performance around the World." *American Journal of Political Science* 46 (3): 670–687.

Rodden, J., and E. Wibbels. 2002. "Beyond the Fiction of Federalism: Macroeconomic Management in Multitiered Systems." *World Politics* 54 (4): 494–531.

Rondinelli, D., J. R. Nellis, and G. S. Cheema, eds. 1983. *Decentralization in Developing Countries: A Review of Recent Experience*. Washington, DC: World Bank.

Schmitter, P. 2004. "The Ambiguous Virtues of Accountability." *Journal of Democracy* 15 (4): 47–60.

Schmitter, P., and T. Karl. 1991. "What Democracy Is . . . and Is Not." *Journal of Democracy* 2 (3): 75–88.

Shah, A. 2012. "The 18th Constitutional Amendment: Glue or Solvent for Nation Building and Citizenship in Pakistan?" *The Lahore Journal of Economics* 17: 387–424.

Sharma, C. K. 2012. "Beyond Gaps and Imbalances: Restructuring the Debate on Intergovernmental Fiscal Relations." *Public Administration: An International Quarterly* 90 (1): 99–128.

Siddiqui, K. 1992. *Local Government in South Asia*. Dhaka, Bangladesh: University Press Limited.

SPDC (Social Policy and Development Centre). 2012. *Social Development in Pakistan: Annual Review 2011–2012*. Karachi: SPDC.

Stepan, A. 1999. "Federalism and Democracy: Beyond the US Model." *Journal of Democracy* 10 (4): 19–34.

Tiebout, C. 1956. "A Pure Theory of Local Expenditures." *Journal of Political Economy* 64: 416–424.

Treisman, D. 2007. *The Architecture of Government: Rethinking Political Decentralization*. New York: Cambridge University Press.

Ullah, A. 2013. "Right to Free and Compulsory Education in Pakistan after 18th Constitutional Amendment." *South Asian Studies* 28 (2): 329–340.

UNDP (United Nations Development Program). 2013. *Pakistan Strategy Document: Strengthening Participatory Federalism and Decentralization*. New York: UNDP.

———. 2014. "Pakistan's First Multi-dimensional Poverty Index Initiated by the Government, UNDP, and Oxford University." Press release, April 17, 2014. http://www.pk.undp.org/content/pakistan/en/home/presscenter/pressreleases/2014/4/17/pakistan_s-first-multi-dimensional-poverty-index-initiated-by-th/.

USAID (US Agency for International Development). 2009. *Democratic Decentralization Programming Handbook*. Washington, DC: USAID.

World Bank. 2004. *Devolution in Pakistan: Annex 2—Technical Considerations*. Washington, DC: World Bank.

———. 2014a. *Country Partnership Strategy, FY2015–2019*. Washington, DC: World Bank.

———. 2014b. World Development Indicators. Database. Washington, DC: World Bank Group. http://data.worldbank.org.

Zaidi, S., S. K. Mohmand, N. Hayat, A. Mejia Acosta, and Z. Bhutta. 2013. "Nutrition Policy in the Post-devolution Context of Pakistan: An Analysis of Provincial Opportunities and Barriers." *IDS Bulletin* 44 (3): 86–93.

Annex A: Key Elements of the Local Government Acts

TABLE A9.1 Powers given to local governments under provincial Local Government Acts

Powers	Category	Punjab Local Government Act 2013	Sindh Local Government Act 2013
Administrative	Local Government Tiers	Metropolitan Corporations in provincial capital District Councils in rural areas Municipal Corporations and Municipal Committees Union Councils for both urban and rural areas (except for Lahore) All councils to be led by chairman and vice chairman	Metropolitan Corporations in urban areas District Councils in rural areas Municipal Corporations and Municipal Committees Union Councils for both urban and rural areas All councils to be led by chairman and vice chairman
	Reserved Seats	Women: 2 at UC and maximum of 15 at district levels Peasant/laborer: 1 seat at UC and maximum 3 at district levels Minorities: 1 seat at UC, 10 at Metropolitan Corporation, maximum 5 each at District Council and Municipal Corporation, maximum 3 at Municipal Committee Youth: 1 seat at UC, 1 at District Council, 2 at Metropolitan Corporation, 1 at Municipal Corporation, and 1 at Municipal Committee	Women: 1 seat at UC and 22% at remaining tiers Peasant/laborer: 1 seat at UC and 5% at district level Minorities: 1 seat at UC and 5% at district level Youth: no reserved seats
	Key Functions	Municipal functions of health and education under indirectly elected members and technocrats	LGs Council municipal mandate includes functions of water, health, education, and town planning
	Public Safety/ Policing Function	Allows for urban local councils to maintain such police force as directed by the government or create a municipal police Rural councils may report to the police the commission of offenses and assist local police in investigating and preventing crimes and arresting criminals Public safety measures related only to fire, flood, hailstorm, earthquake, famine, and other natural calamities and disasters No mention of Police Order 2002 in Act	Public safety measures limited to firefighting, civil defense, floods, famine, and dangerous and offensive objects and lines of work No mention of the role of local elected officials or citizens in matters related to police or community policing No mention of Police Act 1861

Khyber Pakhtunkhwa Local Government Act 2013	Balochistan Local Government Act 2014
City District Councils District Councils Tehsils/Town Councils Village Councils for rural areas Neighborhood Councils for urban areas The tier of Unions has been omitted in the Act All councils to be led by union mayors (*nazim*) and Naib Nazim	Metropolitan Corporations in urban areas District Councils in rural areas Municipal Corporations and Municipal Committees Union Councils for both urban and rural areas All councils to be led by chairman and vice chairman
Women: 2 at Village and Neighborhood Council level and 33% at the district level Peasant/laborer: 1 seat at VNC and 5% at district level Minorities: 1 seat at VNC and 5% at district level Youth: 1 seat at VNC and 5% at district	New category of professional/social worker has been created for all local councils Women: 33% of the number of general seats at all levels Peasant/worker: 5% at UC and district levels (peasant and worker categories have been merged) Minorities: 5% at UC and district levels Youth: no reserved seats
LGs Council municipal mandate includes functions of health, education, social welfare, revenue and estate, rural development, and so forth Local government may requisition a police contingent in accordance with Police Order 2002 Village Council may supervise performance of police and undertake accountability by making inquiries and sending quarterly performance reports to the concerned authorities	LGs Council municipal mandate includes functions of health, education, town planning, public safety, and so forth Public safety is limited to providing relief during natural disasters No mention of the role of local elected officials or citizens in matters related to police or community policing No mention of the Balochistan Police Act 2011

(continued)

TABLE A9.1 Powers given to local governments under provincial Local Government Acts *(continued)*

Powers	Category	Punjab Local Government Act 2013	Sindh Local Government Act 2013
Political	Elections	Party-based elections at all tiers Direct election at union level	Party-based elections at all tiers Indirect election at all tiers
	Tenure	5-year term of office	4-year term of office
	Provincial Authority over LG	Punjab chief minister can suspend elected LG heads for 90 days	Sindh LG minister may suspend elected LG heads for 6 months, as well as LG departments and institutions
	Political Independence	Local Councils administer local affairs as prescribed by provincial government	Provincial government is empowered to supervise and inspect local councils
Financial	Finance & Revenue	LG councils dependent on Provincial Finance Commission Award Revenue departments work under control of provincial governments	LG councils dependent on Provincial Finance Commission Award Revenue departments work under control of provincial governments

Source: Authors.

Note: UC = Union Council; VNC = Village and Neighborhood Council; LG = local government; KPK = Khyber Pakhtunkhwa.

Khyber Pakhtunkhwa Local Government Act 2013	**Balochistan Local Government Act 2014**
Nonparty-based elections for Village and Neighborhood Councils Party-based elections for Tehsil and District Councils Direct election at VNC levels Indirect election at district and tehsil tiers	Party-based elections at all tiers, according to procedure to be prescribed by the provincial government
4-year term of office	4-year term of office
KPK chief minister may suspend elected LG heads for maximum of 30 days	Balochistan Provincial Government is empowered to remove elected LG heads or council members
LG Councils empowered to appoint inspecting officers	Provincial government empowered to supervise and inspect local councils Local Councils administer local affairs as prescribed by provincial government
LG councils dependent on Provincial Finance Commission Award Revenue departments work under control of provincial governments	LG councils dependent on Provincial Finance Commission Award Revenue departments work under control of provincial governments

Chapter 10

GENDER EQUALITY AND WOMEN'S EMPOWERMENT IN RURAL PAKISTAN

Nuzhat Ahmad, Madeeha Hameed, Huma Khan, and Sara Rafi

Introduction

Social and economic welfare in rural Pakistan is keenly shaped by issues that relate directly to the role and status of women. While gender relations in rural Pakistan are influenced by a wide range of cultural, individual, and household characteristics that are often viewed as immovable barriers to change, there is increasing awareness that underinvestment in women restricts economic growth and poverty reduction (Ghuman, Lee, and Smith 2004; Ankerbo and Hoyda 2003; Mason and Smith 2003; Jejeebhoy 2002; Jejeebhoy and Sathar 2001; World Bank 2010; UN 2009).

This relationship between gender equality, poverty, and development is evident in industrialized and developing countries alike. Countries with higher levels of gender equality tend to have a lower incidence of poverty and rank higher on the United Nations' (UN's) Human Development Index (World Bank 2007). Through several clear pathways, improvements in the status of women and improvements in gender equality can contribute dramatically to better social and economic outcomes. First, changes in gender relations and norms that encourage a greater number of women to earn income can contribute to increasing household expenditures and consumption, thereby providing greater ability to withstand negative shocks. Second, increases in gender equality can foster changes in the allocation of household expenditures, potentially leading to a larger share of resources devoted to children's education and health in situations where women have greater decision making power over the use of individual or household incomes. Finally, improvements in gender equality can influence the distribution of household labor, assignment of tasks and chores, and decisions on reproductive choices, which can in turn improve the efficiency of time and resources allocations within the household. Outside the household, greater gender equality can improve women's access to other productive resources such as land, credit, inputs, and labor markets, as well as technologies that contribute to increases in income in household, agriculture, and nonfarm rural activities.

The body of evidence describing these various pathways is extensive. Studies from developing countries show that when women have greater control over resources, more resources are allocated to food, children's health, and nutrition (Hoddinott and Haddad 1995; Duflo and Udry 2004). In particular, when mothers are the main caregivers in the household, improvements in their control over resources can influence child nutrition directly through better care practices and through improvement in the mothers' own nutrition (Bhagowalia et al. 2012; Thomas and Strauss 1992; Galloway and Anderson 1994). The quality of care that women receive is also associated with children's birth weights and the quality of care the children receive in the household (Haddad et al. 1997; Engle et al. 1999; Kishor 2000). Programs that are designed to increase resources in the hands of women have a positive effect on women's earnings and decision-making ability and children's nutritional and educational outcomes (Quisumbing 2003).

Empirical evidence from multiple countries further attests to the fact that improvements in household food security are often attributable to improvements in the status of women. For example, Smith et al. (2003) find that the malnutrition costs of inequality in the status of women and men in South Asia are high:[1] if women's and men's status were equal, the percentage of underweight children under three years of age would decrease by approximately 13 percent. Similarly, Smith and Haddad (2000) find that the educational advancement of women alone can explain 43 percent of the reduction of child malnutrition in developing countries during the period 1970–1995, with an additional 12 percent of the reduction being attributable to improvements in the status of women relative to men.

Despite this evidence, investment in women in many developing countries is low. Even though studies show that the returns on investments in women's education are in general higher than those in men's education (Psacharopoulos 1994), women have lower rates of completion of secondary and higher levels of education (UN 2009). The UN estimated that 60 percent of the malnourished people in the world were women in 2007 (UN Economic and Social Council 2007). Research also shows that women are far less likely to own income-generating assets such as land, housing, agricultural

---

1   Smith et al. (2003) specifically define women's status as "women's status relative to men in the households, communities and nations in which they live." The definition incorporates both gender equality and the concept of power (the ability to make choices) where power is exercised through decision making.

equipment, large livestock, and formal savings (Deere and Doss 2006). Similarly, men are nearly twice as likely as women to have full-time jobs, and in South Asia they are more than three times as likely (World Bank 2014). The trend in the context of South Asia is particularly grave, because not only is the labor force participation of women exceptionally low, but almost 84 percent of female employment is considered to be "vulnerable employment," that is, unpaid employment, family workers, and self-employed workers.

Comparable figures to Pakistan's are even more revealing. Pakistan's female labor force participation rate of 24 percent is the lowest in South Asia, far lower than the regional average of 32 percent (Figure 10.1). The wage gap between men and women is 39 percent, and it is over 50 percent in agriculture, forestry, and fishing (GoP 2013). Because women make up a large share of the rural labor force, the number of women who are caught in this wage gap is significant. Women make up almost 39 percent of the total labor force in agricultural employment, compared to just 10 percent in nonagricultural employment. Approximately 75 percent of total female employment in the country depends on agriculture, and 84 percent of women employed in Pakistan are in rural areas (Table 10.1) (GoP 2013).

It is thus not surprising that the health and nutrition indicators for women in Pakistan are dismal. The National Nutrition Survey reveals that over 40 percent of women in Pakistan are deficient in one or more main micronutrients, such as iodine, vitamin A, vitamin D, zinc, and calcium. In rural areas, nutritional deficiencies are even higher than in urban areas, especially among pregnant women. In rural areas, 28 percent of women were considered clinically anemic in 2011. That same year, 51 percent of pregnant women in rural areas were deficient in hemoglobin, 52 percent of women were deficient in vitamin A, 57 percent were deficient in calcium, and 66 percent were deficient in vitamin D (Pakistan, Planning Commission 2011). According to the Pakistan Demographic and Health Survey in 2012/2013, only around 35 percent of currently married women are using some method of contraception (NIPS 2013).

Statistics comparing men and women also reveal a gender gap in Pakistan. Compared to men, women have lower wages and health status and lower rates of labor force participation, literacy, political participation, and household headship (Table 10.2). In rural areas, the gender gap is even wider. For instance, the female to male ratio in literacy rates (10 years old and over) in rural areas is as low at 0.57. Recognizing the pronounced gender gap in Pakistan, the World Economic Forum ranked Pakistan as 135th among 136 countries in its 2013 Gender Gap Index (WEF 2013). Some of these

FIGURE 10.1 Estimates of female labor force participation rates in selected countries, 2012

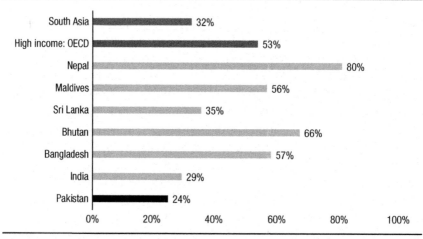

Source: World Development Indicators (World Bank 2012).

Note: Rates are percentages of female participation, based on modeled International Labor Organization estimates. OECD = Organization for Economic Co-operation and Development.

TABLE 10.1 Levels of employment by sector, by gender, and by rural and urban areas (%), 2012/2013

Sector of employment	All areas			Rural			Urban		
	Total	Male	Female	Total	Male	Female	Total	Male	Female
Agriculture	43.7	26.8	16.9	41.9	25.7	16.1	1.8	1.0	0.8
Nonagriculture	56.3	50.9	5.4	28.0	25.3	2.7	28.3	25.6	2.7
Overall employment	100.0	77.7	22.4	69.9	51.0	18.9	30.1	26.6	3.5

Source: GoP (2013).

Note: Percentages do not always add up to given totals because of rounding.

figures have been presented in Chapter 8, but they are worth repeating to put a finer point on the challenges facing women in rural Pakistan and to broadly frame this chapter's exploration of gender equality, women's empowerment, and women's well-being in rural Pakistan.

This chapter explores issues of gender equality and women's empowerment in Pakistan, with an emphasis on the country's rural population. In particular, the chapter examines multiple indicators of empowerment and analyzes the relative influence of men and women over key decisions such as those regarding production activities, household expenditures, reproductive choices, and the education of children, especially daughters.

TABLE 10.2 Gender gaps in Pakistan, selected years

Indicator	Female	Male	Female to male ratio
National labor force participation rate (2012/2013)[a]	22%	69%	0.32
Rural labor force participation rate (2012/2013)[a]	27%	70%	0.39
National average monthly wage, PKR (2012/2013)[a]	7,869	12,805	0.62
Rural average monthly wage, PKR (2012/2013)[a]	5,789	11,074	0.52
National literacy rate (10 years and above) (2013/2014)[b]	47%	70%	0.67
Rural literacy rate (10 years and above) (2013/2014)[b]	36%	63%	0.57
National rate of sickness/injury (2013/2014)[b]	8%	7%	1.23
Rural rate of sickness/injury[b]	8%	6%	1.23
Life expectancy at birth (2013)[c]	68	66	1.03
Seats held in the parliament (2014)[c]	21%	79%	0.27
Household headship (2012)[c]	11%	89%	0.12

Source:

[a] Labor force participation rate and average monthly wages, GoP 2013a.

[b] GoP 2013c.

[c] World Development Indicators (World Bank 2012, 2013, 2014).

Note: PKR = Pakistani rupees. Rate of sickness/injury is the percentage population that reported falling sick or being injured during the past two weeks in the Pakistan Social and Living Measurement Survey 2012–2013 (GoP 2013c).

The chapter proceeds as follows. The second section defines the basic terminology on gender equality and women's empowerment that is used throughout this chapter and examines prior work on women's empowerment in Pakistan. The third section maps out elements of the policy landscape associated with women's empowerment initiatives in the country. The fourth section presents a measure of women's empowerment in Pakistan and analyzes its correlates, followed by a section on analysis of empowerment parity and gaps between men and women within the same household. The last section concludes with a discussion of policy implications.

Defining Women's Empowerment

This section clarifies both the gender-related terminology used throughout the chapter and indicators used to define and measure aspects of these terms and terminology, with particular reference to prior work conducted in Pakistan. We begin with several basic definitions.

The World Health Organization describes *gender* as "a dynamic concept, which looks at the interrelationship between men and women in the context of their society and roles in that society" (WHO 2001). Throughout this chapter, the word *gender* is used to describe the roles, responsibilities, and relationships between men and women within a household, a community, or in society more generally. This usage is distinct from the word *sex* which merely refers to biological characteristics that define humans as females or males (WHO 2001). Therefore, gender equality in this chapter refers to equality of rights, responsibilities, and opportunities for both men and women. The term *women's status* is used more broadly throughout the chapter as a multidimensional term that describes conditions such as a woman's well-being, autonomy, power, authority, valuation, or position in society. Women's status may be self-perceived or may be characterized by others, and may be considered in an absolute sense and relative to men's status (Mason 1986, 1993; Sen and Batliwala 2000; Pasternak, Ember, and Ember 1997; Smith et al. 2003).

The word *empowerment* is more challenging to define in the current context. Sen (1999) broadly defines *empowerment* as "an expansion in an individual's agency that is, expansion in one's ability to act and bring about change." Alsop, Bertelsen, and Holland (2006) describe *empowerment* as "a group's or individual's capacity to make purposive choices, and to transform those choices into desired actions and outcomes." Narayan (2002, 2005) defines *empowerment* as "the expansion of assets and capabilities of poor people to participate in, negotiate with, influence, control, and hold accountable institutions that affect their lives."

But narrowing these definitions down to specifically describe women's empowerment requires further consideration. Ibrahim and Alkire (2007) offer a comprehensive review of the literature on the question, but some definitions of women's empowerment can be considered here. Kabeer (1999), for example, does so with a three-dimensional conceptual framework highlighting "resources as part of the preconditions of empowerment; agency as an aspect of process; and achievements as a measure of outcomes." Kishor (2000) defines it in terms of how much women control key aspects of their lives in relation to resources, self-reliance, decision making, and choice. Kabeer (1999) also sees empowerment in terms of its opposite, that is, disempowerment, and refers to *empowerment* as "the process by which those who have been denied ability to make choices acquire such an ability." Malhotra et al. (2002) also define *empowerment* as a "dynamic process separating the process into components such as enabling factors, agency and outcomes." Drawing upon these various definitions for the purposes of this chapter, we define *empowerment* in its most general terms as "access to and control over both resources and agency." The word *resources* includes assets, income, savings, and time, and in the context of rural households, it can be expanded to include productive factors such as agricultural inputs.

We further define the notion of access and control in terms of an individual's ability to make decisions or have influence on decision making, which in the context of women's empowerment may refer to individual decisions relating to marriage, fertility and contraceptive use, income generation and employment, the allocation of household or individual incomes, or mobility. Mobility in agency refers to the ability of an individual to be free or autonomous within a personal sphere (for example, socializing with neighbors, visiting a hospital, or attending weddings) as well as in the public domain and outside the boundaries of a community (for example, attending public meetings, visiting markets to sell produce, or conducting transactions in a bank or government office).

With these definitions in mind, we turn our attention to the challenge of defining indicators and measuring key aspects of these terms. While there is evidence that women's empowerment in Pakistan, as in many other developing countries, is severely limited, it is often difficult to measure the nature and extent of these limitations and their correlations with alternative measures of well-being, much less the underlying causal relationships.

Empowerment Indicators and Evidence from Pakistan

Past research has explored a wide variety of indicators that are used to measure empowerment, and recent studies on women's empowerment have extended this to develop a multidimensional concept of empowerment (Mason and Smith 2003; Kishor and Gupta 2004; Ibrahim and Alkire 2007). For example, Kabeer (1999) highlights the indicators used by a number of studies to measure women's empowerment and shows that the most useful indicators of empowerment are family structure, marital status, financial autonomy, freedom of movement, and lifetime experience of employment in the modern sector. Malhotra et al. (2002) highlight that the most commonly used indicators of empowerment in empirical research include domestic decision making, finance and resource allocation, social and domestic matters (for example, cooking), access to and control over resources (household income, assets, unearned income, participation in paid employment, welfare receipts) and mobility/freedom of movement.

Decision making with respect to different aspects of life is probably one of the most common indicators used to capture power relations, particularly as reflected in the allocation or division of gender roles within the household. Different indicators include, for example, participation in domestic decision making on education of children; reproduction; and control over income, assets, and other resources (Alsop, Bertelsen, and Holland 2006; Malhotra and Schuler 2005; Kishor 2000; Mayoux 2000; Jejeebhoy 1995; Schuler and Hashemi 1994). In their study of five countries, including Pakistan, Mason and Smith (2003) use women's control over income as their indicator of empowerment. However, in households where women do not earn income or face limits on accessing information about income earned by other household members, there are obvious limits to the utility of this measure. More analytical insight can therefore be gained when several income indicators are combined.

Another useful indicator is control over decision making on land, a particularly relevant measure for households and communities engaged in agricultural production. For example, Mason (1998) shows that land ownership in Pakistan is associated with greater economic empowerment, a finding that is consistent with theoretical and empirical work done in other countries by Allendorf (2007) and Mutangadura (2004), among others. Control over or access to other assets, such as finance and credit, is also a useful indicator of women's empowerment, as demonstrated by numerous studies on microfinance programs in developing countries (see, for example, Mitra and Kundu 2012).

Reproductive choice is another key indicator of women's empowerment, particularly women's autonomy in decision making regarding contraceptive use (Khan and Awan 2011; Jejeebhoy and Sathar 2001; Sathar and Kazi 2000; Winkvist and Akhtar 2000). Several studies of women's autonomy with respect to contraceptive use highlight the importance of a woman's educational status (Jejeebhoy 1995; Saleem and Bobak 2005), while others suggest that mothers-in-law often have considerable influence over such decisions when they are made by young couples in the family (Sultana, Nazli, and Malik 1994).

Freedom of movement is yet another useful indicator. Mobility can provide women with increased access to a variety of opportunities and resources, but access to social and economic development—education, labor market participation, and entrepreneurship—is often constrained by social and cultural limits on women's mobility (Malhotra, Schuler, and Boender 2002). Strong social norms and patriarchal structures that exclude women from participating in the public sphere also limit participation in the economy and override any legal protections that the law may offer. In their study of five Asian countries, Mason and Smith (2003) include women's freedom of movement (that is, their ability to visit local markets, health centers, or fields outside their village without obtaining permission from other family members) in their analysis. They demonstrate that women's empowerment is strongly influenced by social context and institutions rather than women's personal characteristics. Sathar and Kazi (2000) also use mobility as an indicator in their analysis. They find regional differences in mobility across rural Pakistan, with women in northern Punjab having greater mobility than those in southern Punjab.

Time burden also signifies women's lack of empowerment. Double time burden is used to describe the workload of men and women who have to work to earn money and also have the responsibilities of unpaid household tasks (cooking, cleaning, caring for others, fetching water and fuelwood). Domestic work and care responsibilities fall predominantly on women, especially in the rural areas of developing countries, reducing their ability to engage in other, remunerated, activities. Further, a woman's time burden in performing domestic and other activities is therefore often examined as an indicator of women's empowerment. This includes both agricultural activities that are specifically allocated to women such as seed cleaning, planting, weeding, and livestock-related activities in addition to childcare, meal preparation, cleaning, and other household tasks (Prakash 2003; Tibbo et al. 2009; Khan 2008; Jamali 2009).

Finally, a woman's position in the household is closely related to her level of empowerment. These intrahousehold relationships can be measured by a woman's age in absolute terms or in relation to her spouse or other primary household members, whether she has borne sons, and whether she is part of a large, extended household—what is known as a joint family structure. For example, Alkire et al. (2012) in their study of Bangladesh find a larger percentage of women ages 26–55 being empowered compared to younger and older women. Khan and Awan (2011) find similar results for Pakistan, where women ages 40–44 have greater economic decision-making power than younger women. Arguing that significant age and education differentials between husband and wife are likely to indicate less empowerment. Kishor and Gupta (2004) measure the age difference between the male head of household and his wife in their study of female empowerment in India; their analysis shows that large differentials in age and education continue to persist in India. Quisumbing and Maluccio (2003) use a collective household model to examine allocation of resources and bargaining power between a husband and wife, as measured by assets at the time of marriage, and find that in Bangladesh and South Africa increases in a wife's bargaining power are closely associated with higher expenditure on education but not on food.

Behind these indicators and measurements is a growing—but still nascent—body of evidence that draws a link between the status of women in Pakistan and their education, health, and nutritional outcomes. For example, a study conducted in rural Pakistan by Alderman and Garcia (1996) shows that where mothers receive even a primary school education, the incidence of undernourishment in children is reduced by almost one-half. Furthermore, programs designed to improve the status of mothers in Pakistan are associated with improvements in nutrition among children, suggesting important causal relationships in some studies. Guha-Khasnobi and Hazarika (2006) find that less difference in level of education between the wife and the head of household, and less difference in the age of the wife and head of household, are significantly and negatively related to household expenditure on tobacco, adult clothing, and adult footwear. Hou (2011) finds that when women have greater decision-making power at home, budget shares shift toward their preferred goods such as children's clothing and children's education, while children, particularly girls, are more likely to be enrolled in schools. Furthermore, Hou (2011) finds evidence that when women have greater decision-making power, their families eat more nongrain food items and derive calories from more nutritious foods such as fruits and vegetables.

Policy Landscape

Clearly, the studies discussed above demonstrate the importance of enhancing gender equality and women's empowerment in social and economic development. The Government of Pakistan has pursued a range of policy initiatives to improve the status of women and address the issue of gender inequality. These initiatives, although often well intentioned, have met with limited success to date. This section reviews the policy landscape.

Internationally, Pakistan has signed on to the 1979 Convention on Elimination of all Forms of Discrimination against Women and the Beijing Declaration and Platform for Action. The Beijing Declaration highlights 12 critical areas of concern for gender equality and empowerment: women and the environment, women in power and decision making, the girl child, women and the economy, women and poverty, violence against women, human rights of women, education and training of women, institutional mechanisms for advancement of women, women and health, women and the media, and women and armed conflict. While in international agreements Pakistan has committed to providing protection to women in these areas, the domestic legal framework remains far from promulgating these commitments in their full spirit.

The government has pursued four major intervention areas to date: (1) reducing the feminization of poverty, (2) promoting gender equality, (3) ending violence against women, and (4) introducing legislation and changing legislative structures for women's empowerment. Here, we briefly highlight the policies focusing on empowerment of women.

The first major policy initiative was the National Plan of Action for Women in 1998, which mainly focused on education, health, economic empowerment, and other areas set forth in the Beijing Declaration. In 2000 the National Commission on the Status of Women was established as a watchdog to examine policies for improving women's status and rights and to report cases of discrimination against women. Two major initiatives followed: a National Policy for Development and Empowerment of Women in 2002, and mainstreaming of gender in the Pakistan Poverty Reduction Strategy in 2003. These policies focused on social, economic, and political empowerment and attempted to increase access to microcredit and livelihood improvement opportunities, particularly in the agricultural and livestock sectors. Another important initiative was quotas for women in government services and reserved seats in the parliament. Next, the Gender Reform Action Plan of 2004/2005 concentrated on enhancing public-sector employment for women. More recently, there has also been a focus on targeting women through safety nets by introducing programs such as the Benazir Income Support Program (see Aurat Foundation 2011). Vision 2025 (as described in earlier chapters) focuses on ending discrimination faced by women in Pakistan as part of its development strategy.

Despite these efforts to improve the socioeconomic status of women, one of the most regressive laws that directly affects the social status of women remains in effect in Pakistan: the Hudood Ordinances. The Hudood Ordinances, enacted in 1979, have historically provided the most controversial legal challenges for women's rights and gender equality in Pakistan. The laws were established shortly after General Zia ul-Haq's ascent to power in 1979, in an attempt to Islamize Pakistan's legal system and introduce a strict interpretation of Sharia law. The ordinances criminalized all forms of adultery and fornication and in doing so inadvertently codified inherent injustices against women.[2] The gender-discriminatory nature of these laws has served as a powerful weapon to subjugate women in an already patriarchal society.

In an effort to address some of the problems of the Hudood laws, the parliament passed a series of progressive laws during 2006–2015. Along the way,

---

2 For instance, the ordinances require four pious male Muslim witnesses to prove an allegation of rape, failing which the victim herself is punishable for adultery.

this legislation has encouraged a larger discussion within Pakistan on the importance of laws in supporting women's empowerment. For instance, in 2006 the parliament passed the Protection of Women Act to repeal some of the clauses of the highly criticized Hudood Ordinance. This Act served as a major milestone in establishing some protections for women in an otherwise oppressive legal landscape. The passage of the Protection of Women Act in 2006 paved the way for the introduction of new amendments to improve the social environment for women. In 2010, the Criminal Law (Amendment) Act was introduced, and for the first time sexual harassment was declared a crime, punishable by a sentence of up to three years along with a fine of PKR 5,000 (Pakistan, NCSW 2010a). In addition to this, Pakistan took an initial step toward creating a safe professional environment for women by introducing the Protection against Harassment of Women at Workplace Act in 2010, which detailed the code of conduct at work, including complaint mechanisms and penalties for harassment in the workplace (Pakistan, NCSW 2010b). Furthermore, in 2011 the Prevention of Anti-Women Practices Act was passed as an amendment to the Pakistan Penal Code to prohibit social practices such as forced marriages, marriage with the Quran, deprivation of a female of her inheritance, and the giving away of females in *vani* or *swara* (Pakistan, NCSW 2011a).[3] In addition to this, the Criminal Law (Amendment) Act of 2011 addressed the issue of assault against women using corrosive substances such as acid, and introduced a penalty of life imprisonment and PKR 1 million for acid crimes (Pakistan, NCSW 2011b; USAID 2013).

These legal gains for women in Pakistan are encouraging. However, despite successive governments' efforts to address issues of empowerment, Pakistan is still a long way from eradicating gender-based discrimination. Pakistan is unlikely to meet four of the Millennium Development Goals on gender equality and empowerment by 2015: gender parity in primary education, gender parity in secondary education, youth literacy, and an increase in the share of women in wage employment (GoP 2013b). The country has done only slightly better in terms of the political empowerment of women by increased seats in legislative assemblies that are set aside for women only. And while policy changes have advanced in some areas, on-the-ground implementation

---

3   Marriage with the Quran usually prevails in cases where the family fears losing control of ancestral property by a daughter's or sister's inheritance. The woman memorizes the Holy Quran and takes an oath of marriage to it till death, ending any chances of marriage to any man for life. *Vani* and *swara* are practices of marrying young children, usually girls, to members of another clan/tribe to settle disputes.

record has often fallen short of any substantive transformation (Zia 2010; USAID 2013).

It is worth exploring some of the factors behind this poor implementation record. Evidence suggests that the institutions that are entrusted with implementing these policies have limited technical capacity and are constrained by a lack of gender-disaggregated data—that is, data specifically on women. As a result, most of the evidence produced on what works with respect to improving women's status, gender equality, and women's empowerment has depended on proxy measures that capture only limited dimensions of women's empowerment. A keener understanding of the challenges facing efforts to improve women's empowerment in Pakistan is still needed, particularly with respect to the context-specific impediments that women face within the household and community, and the complex gender-related dimensions of these impediments. The next section examines a more comprehensive approach to the analysis of women's empowerment.

Status of Women and Gender Equality in Pakistan

To build a better understanding of women's status, gender equality, and women's empowerment in rural Pakistan, we begin with some basic descriptive statistics. The data for these descriptives have been taken from Rounds 1, 2, and 3 of the Pakistan Rural Household Panel Survey (RHPS) conducted during 2012–2014 (IFPRI/IDS 2012, 2013, 2014; see Chapter 1 for details). This chapter used responses from the main household survey module covering 1,674 households and a separate gender module covering a total of 3,254 women, drawn from a sample of up to three women from each household, including the female head of household or spouse of the head, the oldest female, and the youngest female over 15 years of age. Together, these modules provide a rich sample of respondents and a large and diverse body of data that allows us to explore many domains of empowerment and its correlates in a meaningful way. However, as noted earlier, the RHPS sample is not nationally representative, and results should be viewed in context only. Drawing on data from the 2012–2013 RHPS, we find significant gender differences in labor force participation rates in production activities (Table 10.3). Women are predominantly engaged in unpaid livestock maintenance and paid farmwork while men are engaged in a wider variety of activities such as livestock maintenance, work on their own farms, and paid off-farm work. The participation rate for men engaged in own-farm work is noticeably higher than that of women, while a higher proportion of women are engaged in paid farm work.

TABLE 10.3 Participation in production activities by gender (%), 2012/2013

Category	All females	Principal female respondent	Principal male respondent
Engaged in own-farm work	20.0	22.9	47.7
Engaged in paid farmwork	23.8	27.8	19.7
Engaged in paid off-farm work	3.0	3.1	24.6
Engaged in own livestock maintenance	47.3	55.1	57.3
Engaged in paid livestock maintenance	1.8	2.2	1.7
Engaged in business	2.1	2.8	9.6

Source: Authors' calculations, based on RHPS (IFPRI/IDS 2012, 2013).

Note: The RHPS allows for respondents to report engagement in more than one activity category; column 1 percentages are based on a sample of 3,254 females, and column 2 and 3 percentages are based on a sample of 1,674 households (one male and one female per household).

Similarly, there is a significant gender difference in the proportion of males and females engaged in paid off-farm work. While almost 25 percent of the principal male respondents reported to be engaged in some form of off-farm paid work, only about 3 percent of the women were so engaged. Only about 2 percent of women owned a business.

We can calculate an agricultural gender wage gap from the 2012/2013 RHPS data (IFPRI/IDS 2012, 2013). A comparison of male and female wages in the various agricultural activities (Table 10.4) indicates that on average women receive substantially lower wages than men for the same agricultural activity. This gap is particularly large in wages for livestock-related activities, where women's daily wages are almost 50 percent of the wages earned by men.

Despite their substantial contribution to agriculture in Pakistan, few women own land. Only 4 percent of women in the sample reported owning land separately from their husbands, while almost 80 percent who reported owning land said their husbands, fathers, or other family members make key decisions regarding their land and that they have no control over it. Only 11 percent of women who own land reported making independent decisions regarding the land (Table 10.5).

Next, we examine the RHPS data on a woman's participation in her own reproductive decisions. RHPS data show that of all the married women interviewed, only 18 percent make independent family-planning decisions, while 38 percent make joint decisions with their husbands. But in over 40 percent of the households, the husbands make the decisions without consulting their partners. Over 3 percent of women report that the decision is made by family members other than the couple concerned. This includes family members

TABLE 10.4 Average daily wage for agricultural activities by agricultural season and gender (PKR), 2012/2013

Activity	Male			Female		
	N	Mean	SD	N	Mean	SD
Livestock (all activities)	48	124***	78	95	65***	54
Sowing, kharif	254	250***	86	315	167***	80
Weeding, kharif	201	242***	72	270	166***	60
Harvesting, kharif	282	258***	85	755	193***	79
Sowing, rabi	229	240***	81	237	176***	84
Weeding, rabi	154	233***	75	242	163***	62
Harvesting, rabi	490	311***	150	845	212***	102

Source: Authors' calculations, based on RHPS (IFPRI/IDS 2012, 2013).

Note: Asterisks denote statistical significance at the * 10 percent, ** 5 percent, and *** 1 percent levels, from a two-tailed t-test of difference in means. N = sample size; SD = standard deviation; PKR = Pakistani rupees.

TABLE 10.5 Decision making in the household, 2012/2013

Decision-making categories	Percentage					Number of respondents
	Woman	Husband	Woman jointly with husband	Woman jointly with other family members	Other family members only	
Land	11	40	8	2	38	125
Daughter's education	15	42	36	2	4	2,351
Daughter's marriage	1	1	1	3	94	710
Family planning	18	41	38	1	2	2,342
Everyday purchases	36	27	8	5	24	3,254
Small durable purchases	25	31	14	6	24	3,254
Large purchases	7	38	22	6	27	3,254

Source: Author's calculations based on RHPS (IFPRI/IDS 2012, 2013).

Note: Percentages do not always add up to given totals because of rounding.

such as father, father-in-law, mother, mother-in-law, and other male and female family members of the household (Table 10.5).

We also examine two decisions that are common indicators of household bargaining power and intrahousehold gender relations: daughter's education and daughter's marriage. Approximately 15 percent of the married women interviewed report that they make independent decisions regarding their daughter's education, but only 1 percent make autonomous decisions relating to the daughter's marriage. Decisions pertaining to the daughter's marriage are still within the domain of elders in the family in the rural areas of Pakistan.

The data also illustrate decision-making power with respect to household purchases among females in the sample. Results indicate that a significant proportion of women are the primary decision makers in matters regarding everyday expenses and purchases of small durable items. Decisions regarding large purchases are outside their domain and are mostly made by husbands and other family members.

With respect to access to information, the RHPS data show that women's access to media sources such as television, radio, and newspapers in the rural areas is low. Television is the main source of information among survey respondents, but only 38 percent of women report watching it regularly. Only 20 percent of women reported reading newspapers, and only 7 percent reported listening to the radio regularly.

The RHPS provides insight into three types of mobility patterns based on locations women can visit (IFPRI/IDS 2012, 2013). Women were asked whether they could or could not go to different locations outside the home and if they could go alone or had to be accompanied by someone. If they could go, they were also asked if they needed permission from their husbands or other family members. Those who could go alone and without permission were considered to be the most empowered.

Figure 10.2 illustrates women's mobility patterns with respect to different locations they might travel to. In general, rural women can freely visit nearby homes for socializing with family and friends, visit hospitals and doctors both within and outside the village, and attend weddings and other ceremonies within the village. However, mobility related to other locations such as banks and markets, and for other purposes, such as attending political and social meetings, is more restricted. More than 35 percent of women in the sample reported that their families do not allow them to visit these places even with a companion. Over 60 percent of these women report that they cannot go to most of these places unless they are accompanied by someone, usually a male member of the household. Moreover, 90 percent of these women state that they required permission from someone within the household, usually men in the family, to visit various places outside the home. These figures provide a more nuanced indication of the nature and extent to which women's autonomy is restricted by mobility, which generally is severely restricted for rural women in Pakistan.

The final dimension of female autonomy and empowerment is the extent to which a woman is time burdened. Allocation of time between productive

FIGURE 10.2 Patterns of mobility for women, rural Pakistan, 2012/2013

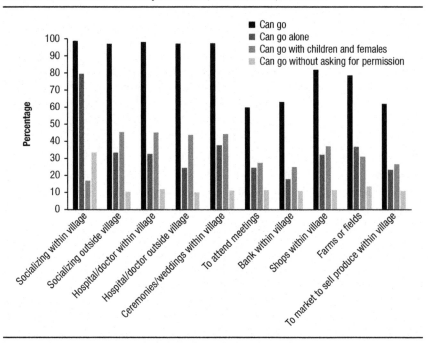

Source: Authors' calculations, based on RHPS (IFPRI/IDS 2012; 2013).

and domestic activities is derived from a detailed time-use module in RHPS where respondents were asked to recall time spent on different activities during the previous 24 hours.[4] Data from the RHPS survey show that women spend 80 percent of their time on domestic activities and only 20 percent on productive tasks.[5] Further data on participation of women in agriculture show that they support men in the fields and are involved in sowing, weeding, and harvesting during peak rabi and kharif seasons. Table 10.6 shows that women in the sample are more often engaged in domestic work than productive (both agricultural and nonagricultural) work. Those who work in productive areas spend more hours, on average, on hired farm and nonfarm work. A relatively small proportion of women's time is spent working on their own farms ("household agriculture"). Domestic responsibilities, including cooking, cleaning the house, and caring for children and adults, take up more of

---

4   The term *domestic* is used in the conventional literature; however, it should not be construed to mean that domestic activities are not productive activities.

5   These percentages are based on the total hours worked on productive and domestic activities and exclude time spent sleeping and resting.

TABLE 10.6 Time spent by women and men on domestic and productive activities, 2012/2013

Activity	All females		Principal female respondents		Principal male respondents	
	Average number of hours spent (per day)	Numbers engaged in activity	Average number of hours spent (per day)	Numbers engaged in activity	Average number of hours spent (per day)	Numbers engaged in activity
Household agriculture	2.09	1,331	2.18	943	3.52	1,005
Hired agriculture	5.18	428	5.29	303	5.02	235
Nonagriculture	4.58	67	4.43	51	5.37	245
Hired nonagriculture	4.08	82	3.70	53	6.23	419
Collecting water	0.91	609	0.92	436	1.00	205
Collecting firewood	1.26	685	1.31	504	2.08	330
Domestic (includes care of others, cooking, etc.)	5.72	2,467	6.24	1,574	2.09	1,201

Source: Authors' calculations based on RHPS (IFPRI/IDS 2012, 2013).

Note: Household agriculture includes time spent in preparing dung cakes.

women's time. A higher proportion of the women in the sample are engaged in these activities.

Measuring Women's Empowerment

Next, this section measures women's empowerment and presents an analysis of correlates between empowerment and individual and household variables. We define empowerment at the individual level only and measure it in absolute terms for all women. We broaden the definition of empowerment to include decision making not just on the allocation of resources within the household (for example, allocations on food, education, and health), but also on allocation of resources to agricultural production inputs.

The women's empowerment calculations rely on a diverse set of indicators drawn from the RHPS data, including measures of participation in productive activities; access to resources; income; decision making on reproduction, employment, children's education, and household purchases; mobility; and time spent on productive activities. We use factor analysis to identify systematic patterns in the data and to group variables in the following factors: mobility, decision making, autonomy, and economic independence (see Annex B). We then calculate a composite weighted Index for Women's Empowerment (IWE) as:

$$IWE = \sum(W_{1j} * \alpha_1) + (W_{2j} * \alpha_2) + (W_{3j} * \alpha_3) + (W_{4j} * \alpha_4) \qquad (1)$$

where, for the jth respondent, W_1 denotes economic independence, W_2 denotes autonomy, W_3 denotes decision making, W_4 denotes mobility, and where α_s denotes the weights assigned to each of the Ws (see Annex C). Our calculations are informed by prior empowerment index exercises but adapted to the Pakistani context and the available data.[6] Data for calculating the index come from a total of 3,254 female respondents surveyed in the RHPS (see Annex Tables A10.1 and A10.2), which unlike prior work on women's empowerment indexes, has the added advantage of capturing data and information not only from the female head of household or female spouse of the male head of household but also from other women in the household who may have different opportunities and resources, or may be subject to different constraints.

Correlates of Women's Empowerment in Rural Pakistan

Next, this section explores the individual and household correlates of our overall composite index and its subindexes on women's mobility, decision making, autonomy, and economic empowerment. The empirical model includes individual attributes: a woman's age, education, and marital status. The model also includes attributes that characterize the household and intra-household relationships: household wealth, household size, family structure, and whether the woman has a son. We estimate these relationships using ordinary least squares regressions, controlling for province fixed effects. Table 10.7 shows results for overall and disaggregated measures of empowerment.

Results indicate the following. First, marital status matters. Two separate variables on marital status—married and divorced/separated from husband—are included in the estimation model. Results indicate that being married or divorced/separated is associated with a greater level of empowerment compared to being unmarried, possibly because of age and experience. This relationship is positive and statistically significant with the overall index, and the relationship is significant in the decision-making and autonomy models.

Second, age demonstrates a strong association with empowerment. While age is often included in estimations of women's empowerment correlates, the

---

6   Our selection of variables/indicators draws from the methodology used for calculating the Women's Empowerment in Agriculture Index (WEAI) by Alkire et al. (2012). However, our measure uses different domains and indicators, and thus is significantly different from the WEAI in design.

direction of this relationship is often ambiguous. The analysis shows a positive and significant relationship between age and level of overall empowerment, suggesting the importance of seniority among women in the household. Age also exhibits a positive and statistically significant relationship with mobility, decision making, economic empowerment, and autonomy. However, the returns to age diminish over time, denoted by a negative and statistically significant squared term for the age variable in these estimates. This may capture the marginal role played by elderly or nonproductive women in the household, or it may reflect other social norms and traditions.

Third, wealth is not necessarily related to women's empowerment. We introduce several indicators of individual and household wealth in the analysis: a factor-analytic asset index, total household expenditure, per capita household expenditure, and a poverty dummy. In general, the analysis finds little to suggest a positive relationship between wealth and women's empowerment in rural Pakistan. Total expenditure, a proxy for household wealth, exhibits an insignificant or inverse relationship with empowerment in most of the estimated models except for the autonomy estimation. This suggests that women in wealthier households in rural Pakistan are not necessarily more empowered than women in poorer households. Wealth also exhibits a negative and significant relationship to overall empowerment. This may be explained by women in wealthier households facing less pressure to work and contribute to family income generation or stronger social norms favoring seclusion, thus making them less empowered in the household. These results are consistent with findings from Sraboni, Quisumbing, and Ahmed (2013), who develop a women's empowerment in agriculture index for Bangladesh.

Fourth, education is negatively and significantly related to overall empowerment (Table 10.7, column 1). These results are robust for a variety of education measurements, whether included in the estimation model as education of the woman, education of the head of household, or education of the eldest male member of the family. Several correlations emerge from the estimation of subindexes against individual and household characteristics. Higher levels of female education are associated with less mobility (Table 10.7, column 2) but greater decision-making power (Table 10.7, column 3). Higher levels of female education are also associated with lower levels of economic empowerment and autonomy (Table 10.7, column 4, 5). In short, higher educational attainment for women is not necessarily associated with greater empowerment for women in all domains.

Fifth, household characteristics and intrahousehold relationships seem to matter significantly. The analysis examines several variables that characterize

TABLE 10.7 Correlates of female empowerment

Variable/index	(1) Overall	(2) Mobility	(3) Decision	(4) Economic	(5) Autonomy
Married	0.010	0.139	0.285	−0.146	0.025
	(0.324)	(2.555) **	(5.515)***	(−2.708)***	(1.36)
Divorced/	0.231	0.130	1.234	−0.131	0.20
separated	(4.579)***	(1.411)	(14.043)***	(−1.430)	(7.78)***
Age	0.020	0.041	0.037	0.013	0.001
	(5.944)***	(6.624)***	(6.338)***	(2.070)**	(7.04)***
Age²	−0.000	−0.000	−0.000	−0.000	−0.00009
	(−6.398)***	(−5.094)***	(−4.844)***	(−3.942)***	(−6.096)***
Total expenditure	−0.000	−0.000	−0.000	−0.000	0.000001
	(−3.912)***	(−0.449)	(−0.590)	(−6.709)***	(3.01)***
Household size	−0.001	−0.009	−0.014	0.013	−0.006
	(−0.420)	(−1.508)	(−2.486)**	(2.246)**	(−3.85)***
Education	−0.013	−0.015	0.026	−0.040	−0.012
	(−4.752)***	(−3.083)***	(5.595)***	(−8.360)***	(9.24)***
Son	0.126	0.124	0.056	0.231	0.011
	(4.795)***	(2.593)***	(1.222)	(4.869)***	(0.05)
Joint family	−0.036	−0.016	−0.022	−0.011	−0.008
	(−1.730)*	(−0.436)	(−0.617)	(−0.291)	(−0.93)
Sindh	0.074	−0.545	−0.298	0.420	−0.08
	(2.333)**	(−9.337)***	(−5.379)***	(7.285)***	(−6.09)***
Punjab	0.274	−0.095	−0.074	0.458	0.017
	(10.064)***	(−1.900)*	(−1.557)	(9.285)***	(1.41)
Constant	−0.521	−0.816	−0.990	−0.249	0.168
	(−7.966)	(−6.813)	(−8.696)	(−2.104)	(5.67)
R²	0.142	0.166	0.214	0.112	0.20
F	45.31	54.28	74.55	34.61	53.93
N	3,017	3,017	3,017	3,017	3,017

Source: Authors' estimates, based on RHPS (IFPRI/IDS 2012, 2013).

Note: Standard errors are reported in parentheses. Asterisks denote statistical significance at the * 10 percent, ** 5 percent, and *** 1 percent levels. N = sample size

the household and intrahousehold relationships: family size, family structure, and presence of a son. Results indicate that a larger household size is significantly associated with a lower level of women's decision-making power and autonomy, probably reflecting greater male control over family income. A positive and significant relationship between economic empowerment and family size (Table 10.7 column 4) may reflect the presence of multiple earners in the family.

Sixth, the results show a negative and statistically significant relation between joint family structure and the overall level of women's empowerment (Table 10.7, column 1). This suggests that nuclear family structures may contribute more than the joint family to women's empowerment and autonomy. However, the effect of a joint family is statistically insignificant in all other estimations (Table 10.7, columns 2, 3, 4, and 5). A dummy variable that captures the presence of a son is significantly related to the overall level of women's empowerment. This suggests that women in Pakistan often gain status from or receive (or depend on) support from sons in the household. The variable exhibits a positive and a significant relationship in the overall empowerment, mobility, and economic empowerment estimations (Table 10.7 column 1, 2, and 4), and shows the largest relationship in the economic empowerment estimation (Table 10.7 column 4).

Finally the results suggest that provincial differences are significant: women residing in rural Punjab and Sindh may enjoy higher levels of overall empowerment and economic empowerment than women residing in Khyber Pakhtunkhwa (KPK). However, women in rural areas in Sindh have less autonomy and less freedom to go to banks, attend political meetings, and go to the market to sell their produce compared to those living in the rural areas of KPK Province. These differences in empowerment levels across provinces may also be a reflection of different levels of provincial infrastructure development. These results are consistent with results from Khan and Awan (2011) that show regional and geographical differences in family planning and economic decision making in the household and find that women in rural areas of Punjab are more economically empowered than are women in the other provinces of Pakistan.

Intrahousehold Empowerment Gaps and Parity between Women and Men

Calculating Empowerment Scores

Next, this section examines the gap in empowerment levels between women and men and the relative empowerment parity within households. The analysis in this section is based on a sample of 1,674 households, with one male and one female respondent from each of the households (Annex Table A10.3). In 82 percent of households, the respondents were the husband and wife, but primary male and female respondents are included irrespective of their relationship to each other. Households without a male respondent or without a female respondent were not included in the analysis, so the results reported are only for dual adult households. To determine gender parity in empowerment within the household, we first calculate empowerment scores for men and women using responses from questions focusing on decision-making aspects of the production, resources, income, autonomy, and time domains of empowerment. Comparing the men's and women's empowerment scores allows us to compare the relative agency of men and women within the household. The empowerment score is calculated through five domains and ten indicators (Table 10.8). The different domains and indicators are described below.

Production: This domain concerns participation in agricultural decision making and captures the agency an individual has in production decisions. Two indicators are used in this domain. The first indicator relates to decisions on production inputs and outputs: an individual is considered empowered if he or she participates in these decisions, that is, makes such decisions independently or jointly. The second indicator relates to the extent that an individual feels he or she can make his or her own decisions regarding production inputs. An individual is considered empowered when he or she feels that he or she can influence such decisions to at least a small extent. The following production decisions are included for the two indicators: (1) food crops to be grown for household consumption, (2) cash crops to be grown for sale in the market, (3) livestock to be raised, (4) nonfarm activities to be undertaken, (5) inputs to buy for agricultural production, and (6) crops to be taken to the market. An individual is considered to be empowered in the production domain if he or she is empowered in both the indicators.

Resources: In this domain, we use land as the main indicator of ownership and control over resources. There are two indicators in this domain. The first indicator relates to ownership of land. The second indicator captures decision-making power over the purchase, sale, or transfer of land.[7] Indicator two in this domain is particularly important in the case of Pakistan, where ownership of assets, especially by women, does not necessarily translate into control over the assets. An individual is considered empowered in this domain if he or she owns land and has control over its purchase, sale, or transfer.

Income: Income domain covers income earned by the respondent and decisions regarding expenditure allocations out of household income. The first indicator in the domain is control over income earned, in cash or in kind, from both farm and nonfarm activities.[8] An individual is empowered if he

---

7   Only land is used here, because information on ownership of other assets by men was not collected in the survey.

8   The individual's income instead of the household's income is considered here.

TABLE 10.8 Domains, indicators, and weights for empowerment score calculations

Domain	Indicator	Indicator weights	Domain weights
Production	Input into production decision (food crop, cash crop, livestock raising, nonfarm activities, buying agricultural inputs, taking crops to market)	1/10	1/5
	Extent of autonomy in production decision making (food crop, cash crop, livestock raising, nonfarm activities, buying agricultural inputs, taking crops to market)	1/10	
Resources	Ownership of land	1/10	1/5
	Control over purchase, sale, or transfer of land	1/10	
Income	Control over income earned	1/20	1/5
	Power to keep part of income	1/20	
	Decision making in income allocation (healthcare/ medicine for household, education of children, large expenditures such as marriage, *bisi*, purchase of land/ property, house renovation)	1/10	
Autonomy	Autonomy in household decisions (method of contraception, daughter's marriage, education of daughter, education of son)	1/10	1/5
	Freedom of movement (doctor/hospital, bank, social/ political gathering, ceremonies, market to sell produce, farm/fields for work)	1/10	
Workload/time burden	Time spent on productive and domestic tasks	1/5	1/5

Source: Authors.

Note: *Bisi* = a form of group saving where individuals contribute collectively and receive lump-sum amounts in turns.

or she has the power to make independent decisions regarding his or her own income. The second indicator consists of the proportion of income kept for oneself. If the individual keeps any proportion of income for himself or herself, the individual is considered to be empowered. The third income indicator concerns control over decisions to allocate money for expenditures out of total household income. The following allocation decisions are considered: (1) food for household, (2) clothing for household, (3) healthcare and medicines for household, (4) education of children, (5) occasional small expenditures, (6) occasional large expenditures (such as marriages), (7) *bisi*, (8) purchase of land/ property, and (9) renovation and maintenance of the house.[9] An individual is considered empowered in the indicator if at least one decision is made

---

9   *Bisi* is a form of group saving where individuals contribute collectively and receive lump-sum amounts in turns.

independently or jointly, excluding decisions on food, clothing, and small occasional expenditures. In Pakistan, income allocation is usually divided along gender lines. A woman may make small income decisions but have no control of overall household income. Therefore, to account for cultural norms in Pakistan, only major income allocation decisions are considered for measuring empowerment. Each indicator in this domain by itself indicates empowerment. For instance, if a person does not earn any income but controls its allocation (indicator number 3), he or she will be considered as empowered as a person who earns income and keeps a proportion of it for himself or herself. Hence, an individual is considered empowered in the income domain if he or she is empowered in any one of the indicators.

Autonomy: Autonomy consists of two separate indicators. The first indicator concerns autonomy in household decisions, and the second captures personal autonomy by measuring freedom of movement. To be empowered in the first indicator, a respondent participates in at least two of the following decisions: (1) what method of contraception should be used, (2) when daughters should be married, (3) how much education female children should receive, and (4) how much education male children should receive. Because these are decisions pertaining to the household, independent as well as joint decision making is considered empowered. The second indicator relates to mobility and is captured by the freedom to visit places alone. Visits to the following places are considered: (1) hospital/doctor within village, (2) hospital/doctor outside village, (3) ceremonies and weddings within village, (4) bank, (5) political/social meetings, (6) market to sell produce, and (7) farms/fields for work. The individual is considered to be empowered if he or she has the freedom to visit at least one place alone. In the context of Pakistan, freedom of movement denotes personal autonomy, especially for women. Each indicator denotes a separate aspect of autonomy; therefore, a person empowered in both indicators will be considered empowered in the domain.

Workload/time burden: The final domain is that of workload/time burden. This domain has one indicator, which is based on allocation of time to productive (both farm and nonfarm) and domestic tasks. Time spent on productive tasks includes all agricultural work and livestock activities. Domestic tasks include cooking, cleaning, caring for children and the elderly, and collecting firewood and water. Respondents were asked to recall the time spent on each activity during the past 24 hours. An individual is considered to be empowered if he or she does not have an excessive workload of more than

10.5 hours in the previous 24 hours.[10] Empowerment in the indicator and the domain is the same because there is only one indicator in this domain.

The final empowerment score is calculated separately for men and women as the weighted average of the scores on the indicators and domains as presented in Table 10.8.[11] We use a cutoff of 0.60 in our calculation of empowerment levels. Individuals with an overall empowerment score across the five domains of above 0.60 are considered to be empowered.[12]

To analyze the differences in empowerment between men and women, we present the headcounts of empowerment in Table 10.9. Empowerment headcount ratios indicate the proportion of individuals empowered. The empowerment headcount ratios show huge differences in levels of empowerment between women and men in rural areas of Pakistan, where overall only 19 percent of the women are empowered compared to 91 percent of the men. Empowerment levels decomposed by domain identify areas in which men and women have lower empowerment and how they compare with each other. The empowerment headcount ratios for women and for men are the lowest (4 percent for women, 40 percent for men) in the resources domain, which consists of access to land and control over its sale and purchase.[13] The largest differences in the empowerment headcount ratios between men and women are in the production and the autonomy domains, and the smallest is in the time domain.

Intrahousehold Empowerment Gaps and Parity in Rural Pakistan

Next, this section presents results for gender empowerment parity and the average empowerment gap in the household using the individual empowerment scores of the principal male and female in the same household.

---

10   The workload burden is calculated using Alkire et al.'s (2012) definition of time burden. This indicator is also used in a number of studies of empowerment in the literature (Malapit et al. 2014; Sraboni, Quisumbing, and Ahmed 2013). These studies also use the satisfaction with the time available for leisure as an additional indicator in this domain, but because data was not collected on this variable in the survey, it is not included in the analysis for Pakistan. The time use does not include time for sleeping or resting.

11   The methodology for calculating empowerment scores, headcount ratios, and parity in this section and the next draws from Alkire et al. (2012). However, our choice of indicators and domains is more context specific to Pakistan and differs from Alkire et al. (2012).

12   Various cutoff levels were tried. At a cutoff of 0.80 (used by Alkire et al. 2012), the empowerment levels were very low, and more than 99 percent of women were disempowered. We use a cutoff of 0.60 on the basis that an individual is empowered in at least three out of the five domains.

13   We use the ownership of land by an individual rather than the household, because using household ownership of land as an indicator of empowerment tends to overstate individual empowerment. An individual may live in a household that owns many assets, but he or she may not always have control over them.

TABLE 10.9 Empowerment headcount ratios by domain for women and men in rural Pakistan, 2012/2013

Domain	Empowerment headcount ratio (%)	
	Women	Men
Production	24	74
Resources	4	41
Income	60	95
Autonomy	33	92
Time	64	72
Overall	19	91

Source: Authors' calculations based on RHPS (IFPRI/IDS 2012, 2013, 2014).

TABLE 10.10 Intrahousehold empowerment parity and gaps by province, rural Pakistan, 2012/2013

Indicator	Percentage			
	Overall	Punjab	Sindh	KPK
Households with gender parity	19	24	10	35
Average empowerment gap	46	43	55	33
Household—both man and woman are empowered	17	19	6	29
Household—both man and woman are disempowered	8	8	8	7
Household—man empowered and woman disempowered	73	71	86	60
Household—woman empowered and man disempowered	2	2	1	4

Source: Authors' calculations based on RHPS (IFPRI/IDS 2012, 2013, 2014).
Note: KPK = Khyber Pakhtunkhwa.

Households have parity if the principal female is empowered, or if the female is disempowered but her empowerment score is higher than or equal to that of the principal male in the household. The empowerment gap is the average percentage shortfall or difference in scores of the principal female and male in households that do not have empowerment parity.

Table 10.10 shows that only 19 percent of the households have parity in empowerment between the principal male and female. In the majority of the households (73 percent), the male is empowered but the female is disempowered. In a small proportion of the households (17 percent), both the man and the woman are empowered. Both the man and the woman are disempowered in 8 percent of the households. In only 2 percent of the households, a woman is empowered and her male counterpart is not. Gender parity by province shows higher empowerment parity in KPK and Punjab than in Sindh

Province. The average empowerment gap is high overall (46 percent); it is the highest in Sindh and lowest in KPK. The results show very low empowerment gender parity and a huge average empowerment gap between men and women in rural households in Pakistan.

Conclusions and Policy Implications

While the poor record on improving gender equality, women's status, and the empowerment of women is well documented, this chapter adds further insight to the severity of the problem in rural Pakistan. Results indicate both substantial wage gaps between women and men and significant levels of disempowerment among women in both absolute and relative terms. These findings confirm and extend evidence set forth in many past studies and draw further attention to the fact that women in Pakistan are constrained in terms of their ability to participate in decisions on their own reproductive rights, on their daughters' education and marriage, on certain types of household purchases, and on moving freely outside the home. In short, women face considerable challenges across multiple dimensions of empowerment, equality, and opportunity.

The findings also shed light on the correlates of empowerment and indicate areas where public policies and investments might have the highest returns to human, social, and economic development in Pakistan. For instance, findings suggest that improvements in education or wealth are not necessarily correlated with women's empowerment, which in turn suggests that social protection programs and rural education may not be sufficient interventions to turn the tide in Pakistan. Further investment in rural business and enterprise development services for women may be a good use of funds earmarked for private-sector development in Pakistan, because off-farm income-generating activities are closely correlated with empowerment. Of particular note is business and enterprise development in the area of livestock, where women play a key role.

Additional attention needs to be given to exploring alternative interventions that affect parity and power structures within the household to bring about change. This will require investing in efforts to change laws and regulations that discriminate against women and campaigning to change social and cultural norms that affect a woman's position in the household. It will also involve introducing gender-sensitive labor market regulations that encourage greater male participation in the care and support of young and elderly dependents in the household. While many of these issues have been investigated in previous studies—Mason and Smith (2003), World Bank (2001), and UN (2009), among others—they continue to receive marginal attention in policy making. Yet the cumulative evidence suggests that in addition to social and economic interventions in the areas of education, microfinance, and enterprise development, the empowerment of rural women in Pakistan depends acutely on changes in the social and economic institutions that govern their day-to-day lives.

References

Alderman, H., and M. Garcia. 1996. *Poverty, Household Food Security, and Nutrition in Rural Pakistan.* Washington, DC: International Food Policy Research Institute.

Alkire, S., and J. Foster. 2011. "Counting and Multidimensional Poverty Measurement." *Journal of Public Economics* 95 (7/8): 476–487.

Alkire, S., R. Meinzen-Dick, A. Peterman, A. R. Quisumbing, G. Seymour, and A. Vaz. 2012. *The Women's Empowerment in Agriculture Index.* Washington, DC: International Food Policy Research Institute.

Allendorf, K. 2007. "Do Women's Land Rights Promote Empowerment and Child Health in Nepal?" *World Development* 35 (11): 1975–1988.

Alsop, R., M. Bertelsen, and J. Holland. 2006. *Empowerment in Practice from Analysis to Implementation.* Washington, DC: World Bank.

Ankerbo, S., and K. Hoyda. 2003. *Education as a Means to Women's Empowerment.* Aarhus, Denmark: Aarhus University.

Aurat Foundation. 2011. *Women's Empowerment in Pakistan: A Scoping Study.* Islamabad.

Bhagowalia, P., P. Menon, A. Quisumbing, and V. Soundararajan. 2012. *What Dimensions of Women's Empowerment Matter Most for Child Nutrition? Evidence Using Nationally Representative Data from Bangladesh.* IFPRI Discussion Paper 01192. Washington, DC: International Food Policy Research Institute.

Deere, C. D., and C. R. Doss. 2006. "The Gender Asset Gap: What Do We Know and Why Does It Matter?" *Feminist Economics* 12 (1): 1–50.

Duflo, E., and C. Udry. 2004. *Intrahousehold Resource Allocation in Côte d'Ivoire: Social Norms, Separate Accounts and Consumption Choices.* NBER Working Paper 10498. Cambridge, MA: National Bureau of Economic Research.

Engle, P. L., P. Menon, and L. Haddad. 1999. "Care and Nutrition: Concepts and Measurement." *World Development* 27 (8): 1309–1337.

Galloway, R., and M. Anderson. 1994. "Pregnancy Nutritional Status and Its Impact on Birth Weight." *SCN News* 11 (6): 6–10.

Ghuman, S. J., K. J. Lee, and H. L. Smith. 2004. *Measurement of Women's Autonomy according to Women and Their Husbands: Results from Five Asian Countries.* Population Studies Center Research Report 04–556. Ann Arbor: University of Michigan.

GoP (Government of Pakistan). 2013a. *2012–2013 Pakistan Labor Force Survey.* Pakistan Bureau of Statistics. http://www.pbs.gov.pk.

———. 2013b. *Pakistan Millennium Development Goals Report 2013.* Planning Commission, Government of Pakistan.

———. 2013c. *2012–2013 Pakistan Social and Living Measurement Survey.* Islamabad: Pakistan Bureau of Statistics. http://www.pbs.gov.pk.

———. 2014. *2013–2014 Pakistan Social and Living Measurement Survey.* Pakistan Bureau of Statistics. http://www.pbs.gov.pk.

Guha-Khasnobis, B., and G. Hazarika. 2006. "Women's Status and Children's Food Security in Pakistan." In *Food Security: Indicators, Measurement, and the Impact of Trade Openness,* edited by B. Guha-Khasnobis, S. S. Acharya, and B. Davis. London: Oxford University Press.

Haddad, L., J. Hoddinott, and H. Alderman, eds. 1997. *Intrahousehold Resource Allocation in Developing Countries: Methods, Models, and Policy.* Baltimore: Johns Hopkins University Press for the International Food Policy Research Institute.

Hoddinott, J., and L. Haddad. 1995. "Does Female Income Share Influence House-hold Expenditures? Evidence from the Côte d'Ivoire." *Oxford Bulletin of Economics and Statistics* 57 (1): 77–96.

Hou, X. 2011. *Women's Decision Making Power and Human Development—Evidence from Pakistan.* Washington, DC: The World Bank.

Ibrahim, S., and S. Alkire. 2007. "Agency and Empowerment: A Proposal for Internationally Comparable Indicators." *Oxford Development Studies* 35 (4): 379–403.

IFPRI/IDS (International Food Policy Research Institute/Innovative Development Strategies). 2012. Pakistan Rural Household Panel Survey 2012 Rounds 1 and 1.5 dataset. Washington, DC: IFPRI/Islamabad IDS.

———. 2013. Pakistan Rural Household Panel Survey 2013 Round 2 dataset. Washington, DC: IFPRI/Islamabad IDS.

———. 2014. Pakistan Rural Household Panel Survey 2014 Round 3 dataset. Washington, DC: IFPRI/Islamabad IDS.

Jamali, K. 2009. "The Role of Rural Women in Agriculture and Its Allied Fields: A Case Study of Pakistan." *European Journal of Social Science* 7 (3): 74–75.

Jejeebhoy, S. J. 1995. *Women's Education, Autonomy, and Reproductive Behaviour: Experience from Four Developing Countries*. Oxford, UK: Clarendon Press.

———. 2002. "Convergence and Divergence in Spouses' Perspectives on Women's Autonomy in Rural India." *Studies in Family Planning* 33 (4): 299–308.

Jejeebhoy, S., and Z. A. Sathar. 2001. "Women's Autonomy in India and Pakistan: A Question of Region or Religion." *Population and Development Review* 27 (4): 687–712.

Kabeer, N. 1999. *The Conditions and Consequences of Choice: Reflections on the Measurement of Women's Empowerment*. Brighton, UK: Institute of Development Studies.

Khan, A. 2008. *Agriculture and Agri-food Sector—Pakistan*. Ontario, Canada: Agriculture & Agri-Food Canada.

Khan, S., and R. Awan. 2011. "Contextual Assessment of Women Empowerment and Its Determinants: Evidence from Pakistan." Munich Personal RePEc Archive. Paper 30820. Australia, Bond University.

Kishor, S. 2000. "Empowerment of Women in Egypt and Links to the Survival and Health of Their Infants." In *Women's Empowerment and Demographic Processes: Moving beyond Cairo*, edited by H. Presser and G. Sen. New York: Oxford University Press.

Kishor, S., and K. Gupta. 2004. "Women's Empowerment in India and Its States: Evidence from the NFHS." *Economic & Political Weekly* 39 (7): 694–712.

Malapit, H. J., K. Sproule, C. Kovarik, R. Meinzen-Dick, A. Quisumbing, F. Ramzan, E. Hogue, and S. Alkire. 2014. *Measuring Progress toward Empowerment: Women's Empowerment in Agriculture Index—Baseline Report*. Washington, DC: International Food Policy Research Institute.

Malhotra, A., and S. R. Schuler. 2005. "Women's Empowerment as a Variable in International Development." In *Measuring Empowerment: Cross-Disciplinary Perspectives*, edited by D. Narayan, 219–246. Washington, DC: World Bank.

Malhotra, A., S. Schuler, and C. Boender. 2002. *Measuring Women's Empowerment as a Variable in International Development*. Background Paper Prepared for the World Bank Workshop on Poverty and Gender: New Perspectives, Washington, DC.

Mason, K. 1986. The Status of Women: Conceptual and Methodological Issues in Demographic Studies. *The Eastern Sociological Society* 1 (2): 284–300.

———. 1993. "The Impact of Women's Position on Demographic Change during the Course of Development." In *Women's Position and Demographic Change*, edited by N. Federici, K. Mason, and S. Sogner. Oxford: Clarendon Press.

———. 1998. "Wives' Economic Decisionmaking Power in the Family: Five Asian Countries." In *The Changing Family in Comparative Perspective: Asia and the United States*, edited by K. O. Mason, 105–133. Honolulu: East–West Centre.

Mason, K. O., and H. L. Smith. 2003. *Women's Empowerment and Social Context: Results from Five Asian Countries*. Gender and Development Group. Washington, DC: World Bank.

Mayoux, L. 2000. *From Access to Empowerment: Gender Issues in Micro-Finance*. NGO Women's Caucus Position Paper for CSD-8, October 1999.

Mitra, S., and A. Kundu. 2012. "Assessing Empowerment through Generation of Social Capital." *International Journal of Business and Social Research* 2 (6): 72–84.

Mutangadura, G. 2004. *Women and Land Tenure in Southern Africa: A Human Rights–Based Approach*. Paper presented at Session Two: Gender, Land Rights and Inheritance, London, November 8.

Narayan, D. 2002. *Empowerment and Poverty Reduction: A Sourcebook*. Washington, DC: World Bank.

———. 2005. *Measuring Empowerment: Cross Disciplinary Perspectives*. Washington, DC: World Bank.

NIPS (National Institute of Population Studies). 2013. *Pakistan Demographic and Health Survey 2012–13*. Islamabad: ICF International.

Pakistan, Bureau of Statistics. 2014. *Pakistan Social and Living Standards Measurement Survey 2012–13*. Islamabad.

Pakistan, Ministry of Planning, Development and Reform. 2014. *Pakistan 2025: One Nation–One Vision*. Islamabad: Ministry of Planning, Development and Reform.

Pakistan, Ministry of Women Development. 2002. *National Policy for Development and Empowerment of Women 2002*. Islamabad: Ministry of Women Development.

———. 2004. *Gender Reform Action Plan*. Islamabad: Ministry of Women Development.

Pakistan, NCSW (National Commission on the Status of Women). 2010a. Criminal Law (Amendment) Act, 2010. Islamabad: National Commission on the Status of Women. http://www.ncsw.gov.pk/prod_images/Section-509-amendments.pdf. Accessed July 2015.

———. 2010b. The Protection against Harassment of Women at the Workplace Act 2010. Islamabad: National Commission on the Status of Women. http://www.ncsw.gov.pk/prod_images/The-protection-against-harassment-of-women-at-the-workplace-act-2010.pdf. Accessed July 2015.

———. 2011a. Criminal Law (Third Amendment) Act, 2011. Islamabad: National Commission on the Status of Women. http://www.ncsw.gov.pk/prod_images/Anti-Women-Practices.pdf. Accessed July 2015.

———. 2011b. Criminal Law (Second Amendment) Act, 2011. Islamabad: National Commission on the Status of Women. http://www.ncsw.gov.pk/prod_images/Acid-criminal-amendment.pdf. Accessed July 2015.

Pakistan, Planning Commission. *National Nutrition Survey.* 2011. Islamabad: Government of Pakistan.

Pasternak, B., C. Ember, and M. Ember. 1997. *Sex, Gender, and Kinship: A Cross-Cultural Perspective.* Upper Saddle River, NJ: Prentice-Hall.

Prakash, D. 2003. *Rural Women, Food Security and Agricultural Cooperatives.* New Delhi: Rural Development & Management Centre.

Psacharopoulos , G. 1994. "Returns to Investment in Education: A Global Update." *World Development* 22: 1325–1343

Quisumbing, A. R., ed. 2003. *Household Decisions, Gender, and Development: A Synthesis of Recent Research.* Washington, DC: International Food Policy Research Institute.

Quisumbing, A. R., and J. A. Maluccio. 2003. "Resources at Marriage and Intrahousehold Allocation: Evidence from Bangladesh, Ethiopia, Indonesia, and South Africa." *Oxford Bulletin of Economics and Statistics* 65 (3): 283–328.

Saleem, S., and M. Bobak. 2005. "Women's Autonomy, Education and Contraception Use in Pakistan: A National Study." *Reproductive Health* 2 (8): 1–8.

Sathar, Z., and S. Kazi. 2000. "Women's Autonomy in the Context of Rural Pakistan." *Pakistan Institute of Development Economics* 39 (2): 89–110.

Schuler, S., and S. Hashemi. 1994. "Credit Programs, Women's Empowerment and Contraceptive Use in Rural Bangladesh." *Studies in Family Planning* 25 (2): 65–76.

Sen, A. 1999. *Development as Freedom.* Oxford: Oxford University Press.

Sen, G., and S. Batliwala. 2000. "Empowering Women for Reproductive Rights." In *Women's Empowerment and Demographic Processes,* edited by H. Presser and G. Sen. Oxford, UK: Oxford University Press.

Smith, L. C., and L. Haddad. 2000. *Explaining Child Malnutrition in Developing Countries.* Washington, DC: International Food Policy Research Institute.

Smith, L. C., U. Ramakrishnan, A. Ndiaye, L. Haddad, and R. Mortorell. 2003. *The Importance of Women's Status for Child Nutrition in Developing Countries.* Washington, DC: International Food Policy Research Institute.

Sraboni, E., A. R Quisumbing, and A. U. Ahmed. 2013. *The Women's Empowerment in Agriculture Index: Results from the 2011–2012 Bangladesh Integrated Household Survey.* Washington, DC: International Food Policy Research Institute.

Sultana, N., H. Nazli, and S. Malik. 1994. "Determinants of Female Time Allocation in Selected Districts of Rural Pakistan." *The Pakistan Development Review* 4: 1141–1153.

Thomas, D., and J. Strauss. 1992. "Prices, Infrastructure, Household Characteristics and Child Height." *Journal of Development Economics* 39 (2): 301–331.

Tibbo, M., A. M. Martini, B. Tariq, P. Salehy, M. A. Khan, M. Z. Anwar, A. R. Manan, B. Rischkowsky, and A. Aw-Hassan. 2009. *Gender Sensitive Research Enhances Agricultural Employment in Conservative Societies: The Case of Women Livelihoods and Dairy Goat Programme in Afghanistan and Pakistan.* Paper presented at the FAO-IFAD-ILO Workshop, Rome.

UN (United Nations). 2009. *World Survey on the Role of Women in Development: Women's Control over Economic Resources and Access to Financial Resources, including Microfinance.* New York: Department of Economic and Social Affairs, United Nations.

UN Economic and Social Council. 2007. *Strengthening Efforts to Eradicate Poverty and Hunger, Including through the Global Partnership for Development.* Report of the Secretary-General. New York: ECOSOC.

USAID (United States Agency for International Development). 2013. *Pakistan: Gender Overview.* Washington, DC: USAID Knowledge Services Center.

WEF (World Economic Forum). 2013. *The Global Gender Gap Report.* New York: World Economic Forum.

WHO (World Health Organization). 2001. *Gender.* Geneva. http://www.who.int/trade/glossary/story032/en/.

Winkvist, A., and Z. A. Akhtar. 2000. "God Should Give Daughters to Rich Families Only: Attitudes toward Childbearing among Low-Income Women in Punjab, Pakistan." *Social Science & Medicine* 51: 73–81.

World Bank. 2001. *World Development Report 2001: Attacking Poverty.* New York: Oxford University Press.

———. 2007. *Global Monitoring Report.* Washington, DC.

———. 2010. "Gender in Crop Agriculture." In *Gender in Agriculture Sourcebook*, 523–524. Washington, DC.

———. 2012, 2013, 2014. World Development Indicators database. http://databank.worldbank.org/data/views/variableSelection/selectvariables.aspx?source=world-development-indicators. Accessed March 30, 2013.

Zia, A. S. 2010. *A Policy Framework for Women's Equal Rights—Issues, Concerns, and Recommendations for Gendered Policy.* Study for the National Commission on the Status of Women, Pakistan. Islamabad: NCSW.

Annex A: Variable Description and Summary Statistics

TABLE A10.1 Variables/indicators used in calculating the Index for Women's Empowerment

Variable	Variable description	Mean	SD	N
Work for remuneration	Ownership of business or engagement in farm work or nonfarm work for remuneration (*1 = yes, 0 = no*)	0.26	0.44	3,254
Land ownership	Ownership of land separately from husband (*1 = yes, 0 = no*)	0.04	0.19	3,254
Own savings	Female in the household has own savings (*1 = yes, 0 = no*)	.072	0.26	3,254
Everyday purchases	Participation in decisions regarding purchase of everyday items (e.g., toiletries, stationery, etc.) (*1 = herself, 0.5 = jointly, 0 = does not participate*)	0.42	0.46	3,254
Small purchases	Participation in decisions regarding purchase of small durables (*1 = herself, 0.5 = jointly, 0 = does not participate*)	0.35	0.42	3,254
Large purchases	Participation in decisions regarding purchase of large and expensive items (e.g., furniture, car, etc.) (*1 = herself, 0.5 = jointly, 0 = does not participate*)	0.21	0.31	3,254
Control of own income	Control over use of own income (*1 = herself, 0.5 = jointly, 0 = does not participate*)	0.13	0.31	3,254
Proportion of income retained	Proportion of own income kept for oneself (*1 = greater than 50%, 0.5 = less than 50%, 0 = none*)	0.07	0.19	3,254
Children's education	Participation in decisions regarding children's education (*Who makes decision: 1 = herself, 0.5 = jointly, 0 = does not participate*)	0.19	0.38	3,254
Contraceptives use	Participation in decisions regarding method of contraception used (*Who makes decision: 1 = herself, 0.5 = jointly, 0 = does not participate*)	0.27	0.36	3,254
Job independence	Participation in decisions regarding taking a job (*Who makes decision: 1 = herself, 0.5 = jointly, 0 = does not participate*)	0.18	0.36	3,254
Socializing	Freedom to socialize outside the village (*Can go: 1 = alone, 0.5 = with others, 0 = cannot go at all*)	0.65	0.26	3,254
Hospital	Freedom to visit hospital/doctor within the village (*Can go: 1 = alone, 0.5 = with others, 0 = cannot go at all*)	0.66	0.25	3,254
Hospital outside village	Freedom to visit hospital/doctor outside the village (*Can go: 1 = alone, 0.5 = with others, 0 = cannot go at all*)	0.61	0.24	3,254
Weddings	Freedom to attend ceremonies/weddings within the village (*Can go: 1 = alone, 0.5 = with others, 0 = cannot go at all*)	0.68	0.26	3,254

(continued)

TABLE A10.1 Variables/indicators used in calculating the Index for Women's Empowerment *(continued)*

Variable	Variable description	Mean	SD	N
Political meetings	Freedom to attend community/social group political meetings within village (*Can go: 1 = alone, 0.5 = with others, 0 = cannot go at all*)	0.42	0.39	3,254
Bank	Freedom to go to a bank (*Can go: 1 = alone, 0.5 = with others, 0 = cannot go at all*)	0.41	0.36	3,254
Shop	Freedom to visit shop within the village (*Can go: 1 = alone, 0.5 = with others, 0 = cannot go at all*)	0.57	0.35	3,254
Farms/fields	Freedom to visit farms/field (*Can go: 1 = alone, 0.5 = with others, 0 = cannot go at all*)	0.58	0.37	3,254
Market	Freedom to visit markets to sell produce (*Can go: 1 = alone, 0.5 = with others, 0 = cannot go at all*)	0.43	0.38	3,254
Time (production)	Time burden from productive activities (*number of hours spent on productive activities per day*)	1.98	2.98	3,254

Source: Authors' calculation, based on RHPS (IFPRI/IDS 2012, 2013).

Note: N = sample size; SD = standard deviation.

TABLE A10.2 Variable description and summary statistics for correlates of women's empowerment

Variable	Variable description	Mean	SD	N
Married	Dummy for married women (*1 = married, 0 = unmarried*)	0.71	0.45	3,254
Divorced/separated	Dummy for divorced or separated women (*1 = woman is divorced or separated, 0 = not divorced or separated*)	0.01	0.09	3,254
Age	Age (*in years*)	36.43	15.87	3,254
Education	Education level of the respondent (*number of years*)	1.92	3.53	3,244
Total expenditure[a]	Total monthly household expenditure (*PKR*)	20,241	11,953	3,128
Household size[a]	Household size	7.66	3.58	3,128
Son	Dummy for presence of a son (*1 = woman has one or more son, 0 = woman does not have a son*)	0.57	0.50	3,146
Joint family[a]	Dummy for joint family household (*1 = woman lives in a joint family household, 0 = woman does not live in a joint family household*)	0.51	0.50	3,008
Sindh[a]	Dummy for province Sindh (*1 = woman lives in Sindh, 0 = woman does not live in Sindh*)	0.23	0.42	3,254
Punjab[a]	Dummy for province Punjab (*1 = woman lives in Punjab, 0 = woman does not live in Punjab*)	0.66	0.48	3,254

Source: Authors' calculations, based on RHPS (*IFPRI/IDS 2012, 2013*).

Note: N = sample size; SD = standard deviation; PKR = Pakistani rupees.

[a] Household variables.

TABLE A10.3 Indicator description and summary statistics for intrahousehold empowerment gap and parity

Indicator	Indicator description	Men			Women		
		Mean	SD	N	Mean	SD	N
Inputs in production decisions	Input into production decision *(1 = participates in at least one major production decision, 0 = participates in no production decisions)*	0.81	0.40	1,674	0.35	0.48	1,674
Autonomy in production decisions	Extent of autonomy in production decision making *(1 = moderate extent or high extent in at least one major production decision, 0 = low or no autonomy in production decisions)*	0.89	0.32	1,674	0.41	0.49	1,674
Land ownership	Own land *(1 = yes, 0 = no)*	0.41	0.49	1,674	0.05	0.21	1,674
Land decisions	Participation in decision regarding purchase, sale, or transfer of land *(1 = yes, 0 = no)*	0.41	0.49	1,674	0.04	0.20	1,674
Use of income	Control over own income *(1 = controls independently, 0 = controls jointly or not at all, or no income earned)*	0.54	0.50	1,674	0.06	0.24	1,674
Proportion of income retained	Proportion of income kept for self *(1 = keeps some or all income earned, 0 = does not keep any income for self)*	0.54	0.50	1,674	0.14	0.34	1,674
Income allocation	Decision making in income allocation *(1 = participates in at least one major income allocation decision, 0 = does not participate in any major income allocation decisions)*	0.91	0.29	1,674	0.54	0.50	1,674
Autonomy	Autonomy in household decisions *(1 = participates in at least half of the major household decisions, 0 = participates in less than half of the household decisions)*	0.92	0.27	1,674	0.52	0.50	1,674
Mobility	Freedom of movement *(1 = can go alone to at least one place outside the immediate vicinity: doctor/ hospital, bank, social/political gatherings, ceremonies, market to sell produce, farm/fields for work, 0 = if cannot go alone to even one of the places listed)*	1	0	1,674	0.59	0.49	1,674
Time burden	Time burden *(number of hours worked per day on domestic and productive activities based on those that participate)*	7.20	4.19	1,674	8.71	5.05	1,674

Source: Authors' calculations, based on RHPS (IFPRI/IDS 2012, 2013, 2014).

Note: N = sample size; SD = standard deviation.

Annex B: Factor Analysis

Factor analysis was used to construct an empowerment index from a set of unknown common factors by relying on the pattern correlation between known indicator variables. The index is a weighted linear combination of the scores from the indicators. Factor analysis is used here to group the variables in a way that suggests a pattern. Rotated factors are used to get a clearer pattern. The Kaiser test method is used to retain factors. Four factors are retained where the eigenvalues were more than 1. The rotated factor loadings show that mobility defines factor 1, decision-making factor 2, autonomy factor 3, and economic independence factor 4 (see shaded factor loadings in the rotated factor analysis). Results for the factor analysis including the unrotated and rotated factor loadings, eigenvalues, and uniqueness for each of the disaggregated factors are presented below.

TABLE B10.1A Factor analysis results

Factor analysis/correlation	Number of observations = 3,254			
Method: principal factors	Retained factors = 4			
Rotation: unrotated	Number of parameters = 78			

Factor	Eigenvalue	Difference	Proportion	Cumulative
Factor1	6.04565	3.81087	0.5746	0.5746
Factor2	2.23478	0.35508	0.2124	0.7871
Factor3	1.8797	1.1319	0.1787	0.9657
Factor4	0.7478	0.305	0.0711	1.0368
Factor5	0.4428	0.18654	0.0421	1.0789
Factor6	0.25626	0.15753	0.0244	1.1033
Factor7	0.09873	0.01539	0.0094	1.1126
Factor8	0.08334	0.05281	0.0079	1.1206
Factor9	0.03053	0.03878	0.0029	1.1235
Factor10	−0.00825	0.01607	−0.0008	1.1227
Factor11	−0.02432	0.0177	−0.0023	1.1204
Factor12	−0.04202	0.02341	−0.004	1.1164
Factor13	−0.06543	0.01252	−0.0062	1.1102
Factor14	−0.07795	0.0228	−0.0074	1.1027
Factor15	−0.10075	0.028	−0.0096	1.0932
Factor16	−0.12875	0.0114	−0.0122	1.0809
Factor17	−0.14015	0.00357	−0.0133	1.0676
Factor18	−0.14372	0.01753	−0.0137	1.0539

Factor	Eigenvalue	Difference	Proportion	Cumulative
Factor19	−0.16125	0.02056	−0.0153	1.0386
Factor20	−0.18181	0.04271	−0.0173	1.0213
Factor21	−0.22452	.	−0.0213	1

Source: Authors' calculations, based on IFPRI/IDS (2012, 2013).

Note: LR test: independent versus saturated: chi2(210) = 3.5e + 04 Prob > chi2 = 0.0000.

TABLE B10.1B Unrotated factor loadings (pattern matrix) and unique variances

Variable	Factor1	Factor2	Factor3	Factor4	Uniqueness
Production for remuneration	0.0855	−0.3816	0.6187	0.0285	0.4635
Land ownership	0.0507	0.1109	−0.0433	0.0809	0.9767
Savings	0.0994	0.0834	0.1367	0.0696	0.9596
Everyday purchases	0.5028	0.5579	0.2404	−0.1076	0.3665
Small purchases	0.4983	0.6187	0.2243	−0.1518	0.2955
Large purchases	0.4111	0.5783	0.2259	−0.0825	0.4388
Use of income	0.1149	−0.307	0.7198	−0.0458	0.3724
Proportion of income retained	0.0541	−0.2902	0.6383	−0.0376	0.504
Children's education	0.1763	0.3577	0.1474	0.0663	0.8148
Contraceptives	0.4001	0.4115	0.0841	0.0196	0.6631
Job independence	0.3655	0.4202	0.2395	0.0369	0.6311
Socializing	0.7606	−0.0647	−0.0838	0.2809	0.3313
Hospital	0.8152	−0.1033	−0.1283	0.3028	0.2166
Hospital outside village	0.795	−0.1188	−0.1406	0.2508	0.2712
Weddings	0.7734	−0.0944	−0.0794	0.2805	0.3081
Political meeting	0.7103	−0.2536	−0.1397	−0.3595	0.2823
Bank	0.6756	−0.235	−0.206	−0.3858	0.297
Shop	0.7893	−0.1239	−0.0892	−0.0426	0.3518
Farms/fields	0.6434	−0.3065	0.0591	−0.0125	0.4884
Market	0.7249	−0.2321	−0.133	−0.2868	0.3207
Time on productive activities	0.1342	−0.2618	0.4061	0.1001	0.7385

TABLE B10.1C Rotated

Factor analysis/correlation	Number of observations = 3,254	Method: principal factors	
Retained factors = 4	Rotation: orthogonal varimax	Number of params = 78	

Factor	Variance	Difference	Proportion	Cumulative
Factor1	4.01755	1.27811	0.3819	0.3819
Factor2	2.73944	0.56277	0.2604	0.6423
Factor3	2.17667	0.20242	0.2069	0.8492
Factor4	1.97425	.	0.1877	1.0368

Note: LR test: independent versus saturated: chi2(210) = 3.5e + 04 Prob > chi2 = 0.0000.

TABLE B10.1D Rotated factor loadings (pattern matrix) and unique variances

Variable	Mobility	Decision making	Autonomy	Economic	Uniqueness
Production for remuneration	0.0563	−0.0689	0.0147	0.7269	0.4635
Land ownership	0.0731	0.0828	−0.0655	−0.0824	0.9767
Own savings	0.0813	0.1449	−0.06	0.0956	0.9596
Everyday purchases	0.1887	0.7652	0.1087	0.0224	0.3665
Small purchases	0.1507	0.8158	0.1259	−0.0181	0.2955
Large purchases	0.1306	0.7365	0.0409	−0.0072	0.4388
Use of income	0.0065	0.0532	0.0448	0.7892	0.3724
Proportion of income retained	−0.0263	0.0128	0.0198	0.7034	0.504
Children's education	0.0875	0.4074	−0.1072	−0.0049	0.8148
Contraceptives	0.234	0.526	0.0341	−0.0656	0.6631
Job independence	0.1915	0.5716	−0.0297	0.0677	0.6311
Socializing	0.7791	0.1684	0.1818	0.0151	0.3313
Hospital	0.8482	0.1384	0.2117	−0.0041	0.2166
Hospital outside village	0.8069	0.1222	0.2503	−0.0099	0.2712
Weddings	0.7934	0.1505	0.1967	0.0328	0.3081
Political meeting	0.4097	0.0818	0.7356	0.0449	0.2823
Bank	0.3744	0.0645	0.747	−0.0256	0.297
Shop	0.6244	0.1842	0.472	0.0398	0.3518
Farms/fields	0.5389	0.0223	0.4047	0.2386	0.4884
Market	0.4585	0.0952	0.6769	0.0426	0.3207
Time on productive activities	0.1471	−0.0378	−0.0137	0.4881	0.7385

TABLE B10.1E Factor rotation matrix

	Mobility	Decision making	Autonomy	Economic
Mobility	0.7763	0.3944	0.4842	0.0851
Decision making	−0.1821	0.8304	−0.3096	−0.4259
Autonomy	−0.1555	0.3542	−0.1976	0.9007
Economic	0.5831	−0.1714	−0.7941	−0.0062

Cronbach's Alpha Statistic

Cronbach's alpha (a) is used for checking the internal consistency of an index. It helps in determining with certainty that the items included in the index calculations relate to a single latent factor that they are associated with. As a rule of thumb, the "scale reliability coefficient" should be at least 0.5; however, higher coefficients suggest greater certainty that the variables tested are correlated with a single latent factor. In our analysis, the scale reliability coefficient for all four factors ranges from 0.74 to 0.89, exceeding the minimum threshold and confirming that each group of variables tested correlates with a single latent factor. Table B10.2 below shows the result of the test for each of the factors used in the index, that is, mobility, decision making, autonomy, and economic independence.

TABLE B10.2 Cronbach's alpha statistic

	Factor 1 mobility	Factor 2 decision making	Factor 3 autonomy	Factor 4 economic independence
Scale reliability coefficient	0.8977	0.8162	0.8840	0.7483

Annex C: Weights for Calculating Index for Women's Empowerment

Index	Weight
Mobility	0.10
Decision making	0.20
Autonomy	0.30
Economic Independence	0.40

Source: Authors.

Chapter 11

UNDERSTANDING THE ASPIRATIONS OF THE RURAL POOR

Katrina Kosec and Huma Khan

Introduction

Aspirations are goals that people set and intend to achieve. The aspirations of Pakistan's rural poor will no doubt play a major role in shaping their activities and investments. But what do aspiration levels in rural Pakistan look like? Do they vary between individuals—and if so, how? What shapes them? Can policy makers influence them? And how does having higher aspirations affect the poor? In the case of farmers, can aspirations influence the agricultural inputs and investments they choose, thereby influencing agricultural productivity? Can they influence the likelihood of someone taking up nonfarm income-earning opportunities? Answering these questions can help us understand the psychological aspects of poverty and prosperity in rural Pakistan.

Pakistan has an extremely young population that is just forming its aspirations; therefore, an understanding of what can raise aspirations is particularly important. With the world's fifth-largest population of 15–25 year olds, Pakistan in the future will rely heavily on whether or not these youth make forward-looking decisions. In rural areas, rapid population growth and the splitting of farms at the point of inheritance will leave many rural-dwelling youths with limited access to land. This problem is especially acute among the poor; in rural areas, the poorest quintile in per capita expenditure terms has 4.0 children under the age of 15, whereas the richest quintile has 1.2 children (IFPRI/IDS 2012). Given that agriculture in Pakistan has not generated many employment opportunities in the past few decades, economic prospects for this surge of rural youth are accordingly grim. As Pakistan's working-age population grows, it is vitally important to understand what drives individuals to aspire to improve their outcomes and to invest in their futures.

Aspirations predict economic behavior (Camerer et al. 1997; Maertens 2012; and Mo 2012) as well as political and community engagement (Kosec and Mo 2015) and may therefore dramatically affect agricultural productivity and rural welfare. Individuals with low aspirations hold beliefs and preferences that magnify restrictive features of their environments. They have few incentives to explore pathways to better well-being if they believe no action on their part can improve their lives. While credit, insurance, education, and other future-oriented opportunities may be available (albeit with some cost), individuals with low aspirations may fail to take them up.

Given the country's deteriorating security situation, two major floods since 2010, and a growing likelihood of extreme weather events resulting from climate change, the aspirations of rural Pakistanis are under threat.[1] Poor access to basic public services such as healthcare, education, electricity, clean water, and improved sanitation—especially for the uneducated and poor, as discussed in Chapter 8—may also threaten aspirations. Chapter 8 shows that better access to rural public services can increase agricultural labor supply, the intensity of machinery use for agricultural purposes, nonfarm labor participation, and nonfarm earnings. In this chapter, we consider whether these positive impacts because of community amenities and infrastructure are actually encouraging rural Pakistanis to aspire to more in the areas of income, assets, education, and social status.

This chapter begins by presenting aspirations as a concept and describing how we measure it. Next, we identify individual and household correlates of aspirations. We then talk about what factors can shape aspirations—and importantly how policy makers might raise aspirations. In doing so, we exploit both cross-sectional and panel data to examine how community institutions and infrastructure predict aspiration levels, changes in them over time, and gender gaps in aspirations. Finally, armed with an understanding of how policy can shape aspirations, we consider what higher aspirations can do for agricultural productivity and rural welfare. We carry out cross-sectional and panel data analysis to examine how well aspirations predict agricultural input choice, crop yields, and individuals' propensity to make forward-looking decisions. Together, these findings reveal why aspirations are an important outcome for Pakistani policy makers to consider—and one that they are capable of changing for the better.

Conceptualizing and Measuring Aspirations

Aspirations is a broad and subjective concept, and capturing the aspirations of different individuals with a comparable measure is challenging. While

---

1   For example, Kosec and Mo (2015) present evidence of a substantial decrease in rural aspirations following Pakistan's 2010 floods, with the greatest decreases occurring among the poor and agriculture dependent.

there are potentially infinite dimensions in which an individual could aspire, income, wealth, education, and social status comprise the central dimensions considered in this chapter. We use these to construct an aspirations index. The index uses respondents' reported *desired* levels of achievement in each dimension, normalized against district average responses for each dimension. When individuals' aspirations are high (low) relative to the average level in their district, we consider their aspiration level to be high (low).

The theoretical literature suggests that people's aspirations are determined by their social circle, life experiences, personality, awareness, perceptions, reasoning, and judgment, all of which affect how they perceive their futures (Appadurai 2004; Ray 2006). A growing empirical literature tests the relationships between these factors. Kosec and Mo (2015) show that aspirations are reduced by negative weather shocks but that social protection programs can significantly offset these reductions. Beaman et al. (2012) show that leadership positions reserved for women in village councils in India have led to a narrowing of gender gaps in aspirations. Knight and Gunatilaka (2012) find that aspirations in China are higher for those with more income, and for those whose peers have more income, but are lower for those who already have a relatively high self-assessment of their own well-being. Bernard, Taffesse, and Dercon (2011) find that fatalism lowers the demand for long-term loans and the use of these loans for productive purposes. Macours and Vakis (2009) find that communication with motivated and successful local leaders in Nicaragua leads to higher aspirations and investment in human capital. And Coleman and DeLeire (2003) find that a greater sense of control over one's life leads to higher high school graduation and college attendance rates.

Failures to set ambitious aspirations and seek to achieve them—what has been termed *aspiration failure*—occur when individuals do not proactively invest to improve their situation (Bernard, Taffesse, and Dercon 2008). Such failures may manifest themselves in fatalism—a deep belief that one's destiny is preordained and beyond one's control—or in frustration that can generate social tensions and violence (Ray 2006). Believing that one's actions *can* affect outcomes is referred to as having an internal locus of control (Coleman and DeLeire 2003). Aspiration failures can thus be linked to having an external locus of control, or a feeling that success in life is determined by external, uncontrollable forces. Policy makers in Pakistan and elsewhere have a vested interest in avoiding aspiration failures.

We measure aspirations using data from an aspirations module included in IFPRI's Pakistan Rural Household Panel Survey (RHPS Rounds 1 and 2) (IFPRI/IDS 2012, 2013; see Chapter 1 for details). The module successfully collected data on aspirations for 3,526 individuals in 2,090 households; it targeted (without replacement) the head of household, the spouse of the head, and the youngest household member (other than the head or spouse) between ages 18 and 35, where such an individual existed.

We measure aspirations using an index similar to that used by Beaman et al. (2012) and Bernard and Taffesse (2012). It incorporates respondents' answers to questions about their aspirations in four dimensions: income, wealth, education, and social status. Respondents were asked to report the level of personal income they would like to achieve, the level (value) of assets they would like to achieve, the level of education they would like a child of their same gender to achieve (recorded as desired years of education), and the level of social status they would like to achieve (on a 10-step ladder of possibilities).[2] We argue that these dimensions capture a large share of what the rural poor aspire to achieve.

We combined the four dimensions into an aspirations index as follows. First, we normalized each respondent's aspiration on each dimension by subtracting the district average from the individual's response and dividing the difference by the district standard deviation. These normalized variables are the number of standard deviations between an individual's aspiration and the district average. Respondents with above-average aspirations have variables with a positive value, while those with below-average aspirations have variables with a negative value.

Second, we took a weighted average of the four normalized outcomes. The resulting measure is the individual's aspiration level. We obtained the weights by asking each individual to allocate 20 tokens across our four dimensions, according to their relative importance; the weights are the share of tokens placed on each dimension. Formally, the index is

$$aspiration\ level = \sum_{n=1}^{4} \left(\frac{a_n^i - \mu_n^d}{\sigma_n^d}\right) w_n^i$$

where a_n^i is the aspiration of individual i on dimension n (income, assets, education, or social status). μ_n^d is the average aspiration in district d on dimension n. σ_n^d is the standard deviation (SD) of aspirations in district d on dimension n. w_n^i is the weight individual i places on dimension n.

---

2   Individuals were shown a ladder with 10 rungs and told that the highest level of social status means that people from the village get advice from them on important matters and decisions and generally respect them.

FIGURE 11.1 Relative importance of four dimensions of aspirations

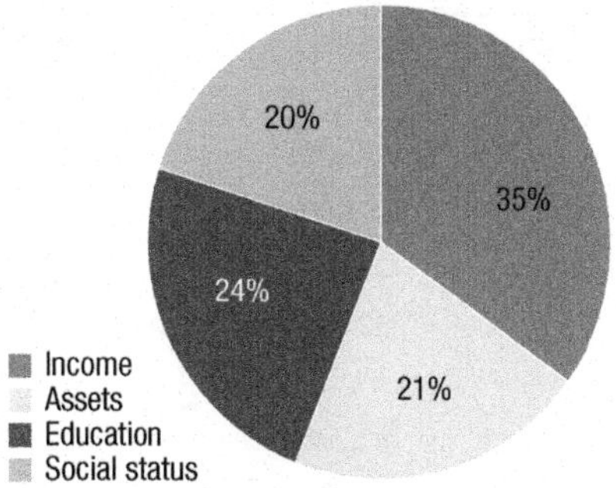

Source: Authors' calculation based on RHPS 2012 (IFPRI/IDS 2012).

Individuals placed the most importance—on average about 35 percent of tokens—on income. The other three categories received less emphasis: on average, 24 percent of tokens were placed on education, 21 percent on assets, and 20 percent on social status (Figure 11.1).

The aspirations index, defined above, measures individuals' aspirations relative to those in their districts. Economic opportunities vary widely across districts. If the district average aspiration level represents what is possible to achieve there, then our measure of aspirations captures the distance between what is possible and what an individual aspires to achieve.

Aspirations vary across sample provinces and by gender, as shown in Table 11.1. The median aspired to income of women (PKR 30,000) is one-fifth that of men (PKR 150,000), possibly reflecting a lack of income-generating opportunities for women. In contrast, women have asset aspirations similar to those of men. This may reflect that assets belong to the family, and thus women may acquire them through marriage and not only work.

The median level of education to which people aspired is 10 years. Men aspired to higher levels of education than did women (10 years versus 5)—with gender differences being most stark in Sindh and Khyber Pakhtunkhwa (KPK), where women aspired to 7 fewer years of education than did men. Aspirations regarding social status are relatively uniform across gender and provinces—suggesting that women aspire to a social status as high as that to which men aspire, even if there are gender-specific notions of what a high

TABLE 11.1 Median aspirations in the areas of income, assets, years of education, and social status, by province and gender

Province	Income (PKR/year)	Assets (PKR)	Years of education	Social status (1–10)
Full sample				
Pakistan	100,000	100,000	10.0	8.0
Punjab	100,000	100,000	10.0	8.0
Sindh	100,000	70,000	10.0	8.0
KPK	200,000	200,000	10.0	8.0
Male				
Pakistan	150,000	100,000	10.0	8.0
Punjab	150,000	100,000	10.0	8.0
Sindh	150,000	100,000	12.0	8.0
KPK	200,000	200,000	12.0	8.0
Female				
Pakistan	30,000	100,000	5.0	8.0
Punjab	40,000	100,000	8.0	8.0
Sindh	20,000	50,000	5.0	7.0
KPK	36,000	200,000	5.0	7.0

Source: Authors' calculation based on the RHPS 2012 (IFPRI/IDS 2012), using household weights.

Note: Pakistan includes only Punjab, Sindh, and 11 districts in KPK. KPK = Khyber Pakhtunkhwa; PKR = Pakistani rupees.

status means. Annex A shows that aspiration levels vary even more substantially across the 19 sample districts.

Correlates of Aspirations

A number of basic individual and household characteristics shape aspirations. Kernel density plots illustrate the impacts of some of these factors. The median aspiration level is −0.01, the average is 0.06, and the standard deviation is 0.64.[3] However, the average woman has an aspiration level that is 0.7 standard deviations lower than that of men. Figure 11.2 shows the distribution of aspiration levels by gender. The existence of a gender gap in aspirations may indicate lower economic opportunities for women, which limit potential achievements. Women also have less variance in their aspirations than do men (their aspirations are more uniformly low).

---

3   The index is a weighted average of four normally distributed variables with mean 0 and standard deviation 1. As such, it is not distributed normally with mean 0 and standard deviation 1.

FIGURE 11.2 Kernel density plot of aspiration levels by gender, rural Pakistan

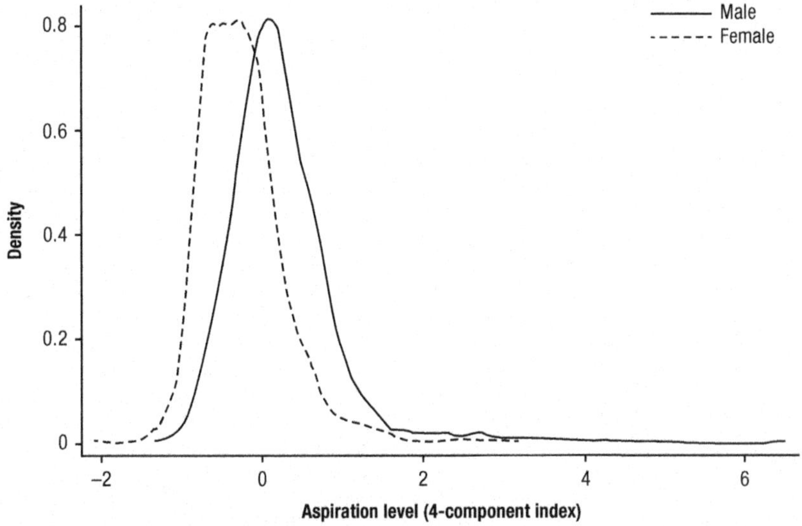

Source: Authors' calculation, based on the RHPS 2012 (IFPRI/IDS 2012).

Looking at each of the four dimensions of aspirations, we find that women lag most profoundly behind men in the education dimension. The average woman has an education aspiration level that is 0.8 standard deviation lower than that of men. For income, the difference is a slightly smaller, 0.7 standard deviation difference. The aspirations of men and women are more nearly equal in the dimensions of social status and assets, where women's aspirations lag a smaller 0.2 standard deviation and 0.04 standard deviation, respectively, behind those of men. This latter finding is especially interesting because both of these dimensions are tied to family rather than individuals in Pakistan. Conversely, education and income relate more to individual achievement. It suggests that gender differences in aspirations in Pakistan are largely driven by differences in perceptions of what one *individually* can achieve. This suggests that creating educational and income-generating opportunities for women will be especially important if women's aspirations are to be raised relative to those of men.

The average individual with no education has an aspiration level that is 0.8 standard deviation lower than that of individuals with some education. Figure 11.3 shows the distribution of aspirations by education level. Lower aspirations among the less educated could be due to cognitive biases that reduce aspirations, or it could indicate fewer opportunities for the uneducated.

FIGURE 11.3 Kernel density plot of aspiration levels by education level, rural Pakistan

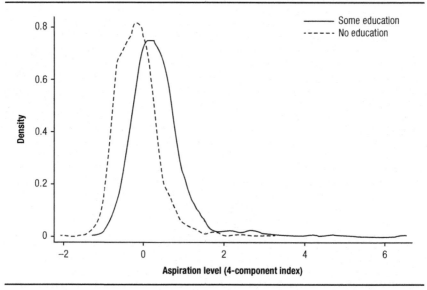

Source: Authors' calculation, based on the 2012 RHPS (IFPRI/IDS 2012).

FIGURE 11.4 Kernel density plot of aspiration levels by quintile of total household wealth, rural Pakistan

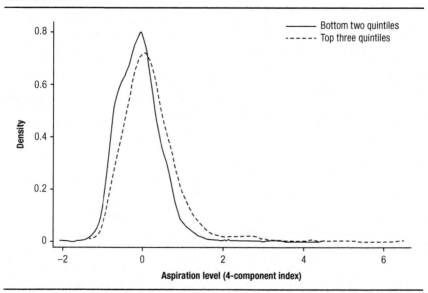

Source: Authors' calculation, based on the RHPS 2012 (IFPRI/IDS 2012).

Aspirations also vary with total household wealth, as shown in Figure 11.4. An individual from a household in the bottom two wealth quintiles has an aspiration level that is 0.4 standard deviation lower than that of individuals in the top three quintiles. This may indicate an intergenerational transmission of poverty; households with less wealth than others in their district may know that it will be difficult to emerge from poverty because they lack productive resources or credit, lowering aspirations. Aspiration differences by wealth may also indicate a perception of strong barriers to upward economic mobility in Pakistani society.

To examine the partial effects of numerous potentially correlated factors in predicting aspiration levels, we estimate an ordinary least squares (OLS) regression model with district fixed effects. Table 11.2 sequentially controls for a number of individual and household characteristics in columns 1–4.[4] Column 4, which includes the full set of controls, forms our baseline speci-fication. Individuals with the highest aspirations tend to be males ages 45 to 54 with postsecondary education and high per capita household expenditures. Neither marital status nor mother's or father's education level predicts aspira-tions. We can explain 32 percent of variation in aspiration levels by some lin-ear combination of our controls variables ($R^2 = 0.32$), suggesting that a large component of aspirations is inherently difficult to predict.

Even controlling for educational opportunities, men aspire to more than women do in rural Pakistan. Aspirations are highest for those ages 45–54 and lowest for those ages 55 plus. Individuals ages 18–45 (the vast majority of the working-age population) have lower aspirations than do those ages 45–54. Education strongly predicts higher aspirations, even when controlling for per capita expenditure and wealth. Aspirations always increase monotonically with the level of education. Individuals with primary (classes 1–5), middle (classes 6–8), high/intermediate (classes 9–12), and postsecondary educa-tions have aspiration levels that are 0.4, 0.6, 0.8, and 1.4 standard deviations, respectively, higher than those of individuals with no education. Higher per capita expenditure and household wealth are also both positively correlated with higher aspirations. From a policy perspective, this is encouraging; effec-tive policy making and social protection can directly influence income and wealth levels.

---

4   These characteristics include gender, age group, marital status, education group, mother's and father's years of education, household size, per-capita household income, household wealth, eth-nicity, district of residence, latitude, longitude, latitude × longitude, and elevation.

TABLE 11.2 Individual and household characteristics correlated with aspiration level

Explanatory variable	(1)	(2)	(3)	(4)
Male	0.506***	0.512***	0.359***	0.373***
	(0.098)	(0.097)	(0.101)	(0.102)
Age 18–24	0.221***	0.234***	0.051	0.076
	(0.047)	(0.045)	(0.047)	(0.044)
Age 25–34	0.150***	0.174***	0.037	0.061*
	(0.036)	(0.038)	(0.034)	(0.032)
Age 35–44	0.112***	0.125***	0.043	0.069**
	(0.030)	(0.032)	(0.030)	(0.025)
Age 45–54	0.103**	0.113**	0.080*	0.087**
	(0.038)	(0.040)	(0.042)	(0.038)
Married			0.004	0.010
			(0.030)	(0.032)
Primary education (classes 1–5)			0.261***	0.250***
			(0.031)	(0.029)
Middle education (classes 6–8)			0.402***	0.354***
			(0.046)	(0.042)
High/intermediate education (classes 9–12)			0.609***	0.530***
			(0.051)	(0.046)
Postsecondary education			0.955***	0.878***
			(0.079)	(0.074)
Mother–years of education			−0.001	−0.004
			(0.008)	(0.007)
Father–years of education			0.009*	0.004
			(0.005)	(0.005)
Per capita expenditure (PKR10,000s/month)				0.739***
				(0.185)
Total household wealth (PKR 100,000s)				0.003**
				(0.001)
Observations	3,509	3,503	3,460	3,460
R-squared	0.146	0.169	0.286	0.323
Ethnicity fixed effects?	No	Yes	Yes	Yes

Source: Authors' calculations, based on the RHPS 2012 (IFPRI/IDS 2012).

Note: All specifications include district and household size fixed effects, and controls for latitude, longitude, latitude x longitude, and elevation. Standard errors corrected for heteroskedasticity and clustered at the district level are shown below the coefficients, in parentheses. PKR = Pakistani rupees.

* = significant at 10 percent; ** = significant at 5 percent; *** = significant at 1 percent.

There is interesting variation in aspirations across households of different types: landowners, tenants, agricultural wage laborers, and rural nonfarm households (Table 11.3).[5] Aspiration levels are highest among landowners (0.22, on average), second highest among rural nonfarm households (0.07), third highest for tenants (0.02), and lowest for agricultural wage laborers (−0.17). Additionally, individual and household characteristics do not have the same effects for all household types. First, being male raises aspirations significantly in land-cultivating households—whether the farmers are tenants or owners. In contrast, being male has no statistically significant impact on aspirations in agricultural wage labor households, and a more modest impact in rural nonfarm households. This may indicate that land cultivation creates fewer economic opportunities for women than do more diversified activities such as wage labor and rural nonfarm employment—raising a need for policies that create such opportunities.

Second, household member's age does not predict aspirations for individuals from land-cultivating households. However, for agricultural wage laborers and rural nonfarm households, youth ages 18–24 have the highest aspirations. Youth appear to have higher aspirations than do older people in households without access to land. This is possibly because they have the most flexible family circumstances (such as fewer children and still-healthy parents), are most able-bodied (opening up local employment opportunities), and are most able to migrate (even if temporarily) to pursue more distant employment opportunities (Chen, Kosec, and Mueller 2015). This raises the need for policy to address potential aspiration failures among older individuals without access to land.

Third, aspirations are increasing in education for every household type. This suggests that public investment in education is uniformly a good way to raise aspirations, which is a nice complement to the finding in Chapter 8 that public investment in education increases agricultural labor supply, the mechanization of agriculture, and pursuit of nonfarm labor opportunities. Finally, aspirations are increasing in both per capita expenditure and wealth for landowning households and households engaged in rural nonfarm

---

5   The four household types are defined as follows: Landowners are individuals from households that own land. Tenants are individuals from households that do not own land but are engaged in cultivation (through renting or leasing land). Agricultural wage laborers are individuals from households that do not own land or cultivate rented or leased land but have income from agricultural or livestock sources. Rural nonfarm households is a residual category comprised of individuals from households that do not own or cultivate land or obtain any income from agriculture or livestock.

TABLE 11.3 Individual and household characteristics correlated with aspiration level by household type

Dep. variable: Aspiration level (score on 4-component index)					
	All	Landowner	Tenant	Agricultural wage laborer	Rural nonfarm
Explanatory variable	mean = 0.06 SD = 0.64 (1)	mean = 0.22 SD = 0.73 (2)	mean = 0.02 SD = 0.62 (3)	mean = −0.17 SD = 0.48 (4)	mean = 0.07 SD = 0.58 (5)
Male	0.373*** (0.102)	0.459*** (0.117)	0.656*** (0.122)	0.200 (0.121)	0.289*** (0.093)
Age 18–24	0.076 (0.044)	0.059 (0.077)	−0.070 (0.088)	0.114* (0.063)	0.185*** (0.064)
Age 25–34	0.061* (0.032)	0.061 (0.069)	0.045 (0.095)	0.049 (0.051)	0.106* (0.058)
Age 35–44	0.069** (0.025)	0.026 (0.056)	−0.038 (0.088)	0.113** (0.052)	0.135** (0.063)
Age 45–54	0.087** (0.038)	0.079 (0.061)	0.017 (0.115)	0.047 (0.067)	0.139*** (0.047)
Married	0.010 (0.032)	0.036 (0.065)	0.022 (0.099)	0.011 (0.054)	−0.008 (0.049)
Primary education (classes 1–5)	0.250*** (0.029)	0.248*** (0.058)	0.212*** (0.062)	0.220*** (0.053)	0.180*** (0.037)
Middle education (classes 6–8)	0.354*** (0.042)	0.280*** (0.072)	0.056 (0.092)	0.334*** (0.061)	0.404*** (0.062)
High/intermediate education (classes 9–12)	0.530*** (0.046)	0.505*** (0.072)	0.430*** (0.093)	0.571*** (0.115)	0.469*** (0.039)
Postsecondary education	0.878*** (0.074)	0.946*** (0.181)	1.317*** (0.399)		0.594*** (0.081)
Mother—years of education	−0.004 (0.007)	0.003 (0.016)	−0.103* (0.057)	0.020 (0.023)	−0.015 (0.015)
Father—years of education	0.004 (0.005)	−0.002 (0.008)	0.012 (0.015)	0.003 (0.012)	0.007 (0.007)
Per capita expenditure (PKR 10,000s/month)	0.739*** (0.185)	0.722** (0.261)	0.095 (0.206)	0.445 (0.257)	0.789*** (0.256)
Total household wealth (PKR 100,000s)	0.003** (0.001)	0.002** (0.001)	0.005 (0.009)	−0.0001 (0.015)	0.020*** (0.005)
Observations	3,460	1,240	459	863	898
R-squared	0.323	0.336	0.540	0.295	0.327

Source: Authors' calculations, based on the RHPS 2012 (IFPRI/IDS 2012).

Note: All specifications include district fixed effects, ethnicity fixed effects, household size fixed effects, and controls for latitude, longitude, latitude × longitude, and elevation. Standard errors corrected for heteroskedasticity and clustered at the district level are shown below the coefficients, in parentheses. PKR = Pakistani rupees. SD = standard deviation. * = significant at 10%; ** = significant at 5%; *** = significant at 1%.

TABLE 11.4 Summary statistics, indexes of cognitive features

Cognitive feature	Mean	SD
Internal locus of control	0.03	0.42
Self-esteem	0.02	0.48
Religiosity	0.00	0.56
Trust	0.07	0.57
Envy	−0.02	0.85
Poverty seen as due to external factors	0.01	0.39
Openness to change	0.01	0.44
Monthly effective discount rate	0.02	0.96

Source: Authors' calculations, based on the RHPS 2012 (IFPRI/IDS 2012).

activities (though no relationship can be established for tenants and agricultural wage laborers).

Cognitive Features

To better understand aspirations, we next examine the cognitive attributes, or features, of an individual with high aspirations. Possibly important features include the extent to which an individual has an internal locus of control, as well as levels of self-esteem, religiosity, trust, envy, the extent to which an individual sees poverty as being caused by external factors, openness to change, and an individual's discount rate. For each of these features, we considered respondents' answers to a series of questions aimed at eliciting information about that feature (see Annex B). We normalized responses to each question in the series to create a variable with mean 0 and standard deviation 1. Taking the average of these normalized variables across all questions in the series, we constructed an index score for each cognitive feature. Table 11.4 summarizes these indexes.[6]

As Table 11.5 shows, a number of cognitive features predict higher aspirations. This table presents the results from eight separate regressions of the aspiration level on each of the eight indexes. Each regression controls for our full set of individual and household characteristics. Effectively, we aim to compare how aspiration levels vary between two otherwise similar individuals who differ on the given cognitive feature. Neither individuals' degree of openness to change nor their discount rate predict aspiration levels. However, the other six cognitive features do.

---

6   As each index is an average of standard normal variables, their means are unsurprisingly close to 0.

TABLE 11.5 Correlations of aspiration levels with cognitive features

Cognitive feature	Aspiration level	N
(1) Internal locus of control	0.107*** (0.025)	3,440
(2) Self-esteem	0.148*** (0.020)	3,453
(3) Religiosity	0.047** (0.020)	3,452
(4) Trust	0.057*** (0.021)	2,050
(5) Envy	−0.058*** (0.012)	3,411
(6) Poverty seen as caused by external factors	−0.113*** (0.025)	3,455
(7) Openness to change	0.031 (0.025)	2,459
(8) Monthly effective discount rate	0.008 (0.011)	3,049

Source: Authors' calculations, based on the RHPS 2012 (IFPRI/IDS 2012).

Note: The coefficient on each cognitive variable comes from a separate regression of aspirations on the cognitive variable and a set of control variables. These include district, ethnicity, and household size fixed effects, controls for latitude, longitude, latitude × longitude, and elevation, and education group dummies, age group dummies, gender dummies, and marital status dummies. Standard errors corrected for heteroskedasticity and clustered at the household level are shown below the coefficients, in parentheses.
* = significant at 10%; ** = significant at 5%; *** = significant at 1%.

An individual's locus of control is an important predictor of aspirations. A standard deviation increase in locus of control (that is, the degree to which one's locus of control is internal, and the individual therefore feels in control of her or his life outcomes) is associated with an approximate $(0.11 \times 0.42) = 0.05$ point, or $(0.05 / 0.64) = 0.07$ standard deviation, increase in aspirations. This suggests that to aspire, individuals first require clear pathways to achievement that make them confident that they can obtain their goals through hard work. Policy makers might use this information to create training programs aimed at helping individuals identify and reach their goals. In addition, exposure to success stories about achievements through personal efforts might also help inculcate the perception that one can be in control of life outcomes—and accordingly boost aspirations.

High self-esteem is also an important predictor of high aspirations. A standard deviation increase in self-esteem is associated with an approximate $(0.15 \times 0.48) = 0.07$ point increase in the aspirations index. This is about a $(0.07 / 0.64) = 0.11$ standard deviation increase in aspirations. Religiosity is also associated with higher aspirations. A standard deviation increase in religiosity is associated with around a $(0.05 \times 0.56) = 0.03$ point, or $(0.03 / 0.64) = 0.04$ standard deviation, increase in aspirations. It could be that religiosity increases safety nets and social support, or is associated with more productive interactions between neighbors and friends.

Greater trust is associated with higher aspirations, while greater envy is associated with lower aspirations. A standard deviation increase in trust is associated with about a $(0.06 \times 0.57) = 0.03$ point, or $(0.03 / 0.64) = 0.05$ standard deviation, increase in aspirations. Conversely, a standard deviation increase in envy is associated with around a 0.06 point, or 0.08 standard deviation, decrease in aspirations. That these effects go in opposite directions is not surprising; trust suggests the presence of a wealth of individuals on whom respondents feel they can rely in order to improve their livelihood. Envy suggests the presence of few such individuals, as well as a feeling among respondents that others' gains are their losses.

Finally—and in line with our findings on locus of control—individuals who think poverty is caused by external factors have significantly lower aspirations. A standard deviation increase in the degree to which poverty is seen as caused by external factors is associated with a $(0.11 \times 0.39) = 0.04$ point, or $(0.04 / 0.64) = 0.06$ standard deviation, decrease in aspirations. This evidence supports policies that teach individuals how they might control and change their poverty status.

The Effects of Community Institutions and Infrastructure on Aspirations

An important role of policy is to create and cultivate institutional conditions that permit and encourage individuals to aspire to improve their lives. Indeed, the existence of government is often justified by its ability to promote the welfare of its citizens through good policies and investments. But what types of institutional conditions are most likely to raise aspirations? We separately analyze the aspirational impacts of having a functioning justice system that instills confidence and promotes productive investments; high-quality infrastructure that increases opportunities for trade, cooperation, investment, and exchange; and social protection mechanisms (formal or informal) that help ensure resilience to negative shocks.

Table 11.6 summarizes several important community characteristics that may affect aspirations. The average individual in our sample lives in a community with mud internal roads, nonmud external roads, and a main road connecting the village to a nearby city. The nearest post office is about 7

TABLE 11.6 Summary statistics of community characteristics

Community characteristic	Mean	SD	N
Organized village meetings to discuss issues and events	0.60	0.49	3,526
Justice index	0.02	0.53	2,612
Railway station within walking distance	0.17	0.37	3,526
Distance to the nearest post office in 2012 (km)	7.14	7.58	3,526
A main road connects the village to a nearby city	0.81	0.40	3,526
Most common road surface type of external roads is mud	0.21	0.41	3,526
Most common road surface type of internal roads is mud	0.54	0.50	3,526
Fixed-line telephone service available in the village	0.23	0.42	3,526
Access to cylinder gas	0.56	0.50	3,526
Distance to the nearest commercial center (km)	16.88	16.20	3,526
Public transportation to the nearest commercial center available	0.79	0.41	3,526
Number of NGOs active in the tehsil	0.16	0.42	3,526
Number of NGOs providing training	0.03	0.18	3,526
Safety nets index	0.02	0.52	2,953
Relatives in another district?	0.19	0.39	3,515
Relatives in another province?	0.70	0.46	3,519

Source: Authors' calculation, based on the RHPS 2012 (IFPRI/IDS 2012).

Note: km = kilometers; NGOs = nongovernmental organizations.

kilometers (km) away, the nearest commercial center is about 17 km away, and public transportation is available to that center. The typical community has access to cylinder gas but no fixed-line telephone service. There are meetings of village residents to discuss village issues and events, though the village has a less than one in five (16 percent) chance of having a nongovernmental organization operating there. Of course, there is a lot of variation across villages, and this variation may help predict aspiration levels.

A number of community characteristics predict higher aspirations, as shown in Table 11.7. The "Aspiration level" column presents the coefficient on the listed community characteristic for each of 16 separate regressions of an individual's aspiration level on each of the 16 community characteristics in Table 11.6, always including our full set of controls. First, holding organized meetings of village residents to discuss issues and events is associated with an approximate 0.11 point, or $(0.11 / 0.64) = 0.17$ standard deviation, increase in aspirations. This is a substantial effect. In contrast, a standard deviation (PKR 1,500) increase in monthly per capita expenditure is associated with only

TABLE 11.7 Correlations of aspiration levels with community characteristics

Community characteristic	(1) Aspiration level	N	(2) Gender gap in aspiration level	N
Organized village meetings to discuss issues and events	0.111*** (0.027)	3,459	−0.074 (0.068)	1,147
Justice index	0.054** (0.024)	2,576	0.084 (0.060)	801
Railway station within walking distance	0.131*** (0.039)	3,459	0.011 (0.074)	1,147
Distance to the nearest post office in 2012 (km)	−0.004*** (0.002)	3,459	0.006 (0.004)	1,147
A main road connects the village to a nearby city	0.028 (0.028)	3,459	−0.142*** (0.052)	1,147
Most common road surface type of external roads is mud	−0.106*** (0.028)	3,459	0.094* (0.051)	1,147
Most common road surface type of internal roads is mud	−0.060** (0.026)	3,459	−0.015 (0.067)	1,147
Fixed-line telephone service available in the village	0.034 (0.036)	3,459	0.003 (0.070)	1,147
Access to cylinder gas	0.025 (0.023)	3,459	−0.078 (0.048)	1,147
Distance to the nearest commercial center (km)	−0.001 (0.001)	3,459	0.001 (0.001)	1,147
Public transportation to the nearest commercial center available	0.013 (0.025)	3,459	−0.039 (0.053)	1,147
Number of NGOs active in the tehsil	0.033 (0.027)	3,459	0.037 (0.082)	1,147
Number of NGOs providing training	0.064 (0.047)	3,459	0.094 (0.089)	1,147
Safety nets index	0.020 (0.018)	2,912	0.185*** (0.055)	932
Relatives in another district?	0.025 (0.034)	3,449	−0.074 (0.102)	1,143
Relatives in another province?	0.055** (0.022)	3,453	−0.024 (0.049)	1,145

Source: Authors' calculations, based on the 2012 Pakistan RHPS, Round 1 (IFPRI/IDS 2012).

Note: The coefficient on each community variable in column 1 comes from a separate regression of aspiration on the community variable and a full set of control variables. These include district, ethnicity, and household size fixed effects, and controls for latitude, longitude, latitude × longitude, elevation, education group dummies, age group dummies, gender dummies, marital status dummies, household type dummies (landowner, tenant, agricultural wage laborer, or rural nonfarm), per capita expenditure, and wealth. Regression coefficients in column 2 come from regression of the gender gap in aspirations and uses only household control variables. Standard errors, corrected for heteroskedasticity and clustered at the household level, are shown below the coefficients, in parentheses. km = kilometers; NGOs = nongovernmental organizations. * = significant at 10%; ** = significant at 5%; *** = significant at 1%.

about a 0.13 standard deviation increase in aspirations.[7] Having organized village meetings thus has the same impact as providing approximately PKR 2,000 extra expenditure per household member per month.

The results also suggest that instilling confidence in the justice system may be an important institutional investment to raise aspirations. A standard deviation increase in an index of perceived access to justice is associated with an approximate $(0.05 \times 0.53) / 0.64 = 0.05$ standard deviation increase in aspirations. Compared with the coefficient on per capita monthly expenditure in the same regression, it suggests that a standard deviation increase in perceived access to justice has the same association with aspirations as does providing about an additional PKR 430 expenditure per household member per month.

Connectivity within the village and to outside villages also matters for aspirations. Having a railway station that is within walking distance from the village center is associated with about a $(0.13 / 0.64) = 0.20$ standard deviation increase in aspirations. Having mud internal roads is associated with an approximate $(0.06 / 0.64) = 0.09$ standard deviation decrease in aspirations. And having mud external roads is associated with an even larger, about $(0.11 / 0.64) = 0.17$ standard deviation decrease in aspirations. The ease of mobility within a village, and especially between the village and outlying areas, may be an important policy lever to raise aspirations. Similarly, linkages with individuals in other communities are also associated with higher aspirations; having a relative in another province is associated with around a $(0.06 / 0.64) = 0.09$ standard deviation increase in aspirations. This may be because of additional income generation or migration opportunities that such linkages afford, or simply because of the expanded set of ideas and potential role models that they entail.

We find that the higher aspirations predicted by having access to high-quality communities are mostly because of higher education aspirations—and, to a slightly lesser extent, because of higher asset and social status aspirations. This can be seen in Annex C, which analyzes correlations between each of the four components of aspirations and community characteristics. We find limited evidence that high-quality communities raise income aspirations; the only community features that seem to raise income aspirations are having organized village meetings and having relatives in another province.

---

7   The coefficient on household expenditures, like those on other control variables included in the Column 1 regressions of Table 11.7, is not presented due to space limitations.

Given the robust association between community characteristics and aspiration levels, we also examined whether these characteristics influence the gap between men's and women's aspirations. There is less evidence for this hypothesis. Column 2 of Table 11.7 presents the results from 16 separate, household-level regressions of the distance between the average male and the average female aspirations in a household—the gender gap in aspirations— on each of the 16 community characteristics.[8] A larger gender gap indicates a larger disparity between the generally higher aspirations of men and those of women in the household. We find that the presence of a main road connecting the village to a city is correlated with a lower gender gap in aspirations, indicating that greater ease of mobility might reduce the aspirations gap by making opportunities more equally accessible for both genders. Similarly, the gender gap in aspirations is lower when external roads—connecting the village with outlying areas—are made of an improved material other than mud. However, in general, we find that community characteristics matter little for gender gaps in aspirations. The only other statistically significant finding is that greater access to safety nets—provided by family, friends, other community members, NGOs, or the government—is associated with a higher gender gap in aspirations. This is possibly because having ample informal safety nets makes households less dependent on women's income or on cash transfers to women such as those from the Benazir Income Support Program, which specifically targets women.

These findings suggest that high-quality communities are strong predictors of high aspirations among individuals—at least as reflected by 2012 data from Round 1 of the Pakistan RHPS (IFPRI/IDS 2012). However, do such strong communities actually predict that aspirations are increasing over time? To examine this question, we took advantage of a second round of data on aspiration levels, collected a year later (in 2013) during Round 2 of the Pakistan RHPS (IFPRI/IDS 2013). We examined whether the same community characteristics from Table 11.7 are correlated with an individual's aspiration level in 2013, when controlling for the 2012 aspiration level and locational controls (district fixed effects and controls for latitude, longitude, latitude × longitude, and elevation). We thus observe whether individuals in similar locations and with similar 2012 aspirations are predicted to have even higher 2013 aspirations because of community characteristics.

---

8   In some households, the main male and female respondents are not married. When we restrict the analysis to only examine gender gaps in aspirations between husbands and wives, the results (available upon request) are similar.

Current aspiration levels are likely to be heavily determined by past levels, resulting in autocorrelation. Given that we have two rounds of data on aspiration levels, we can address this issue and check the robustness of our main findings on community characteristics by controlling for the 2012 level of the aspirations index when analyzing predictors of the 2013 level. Annex Table D11.1 presents this analysis and reveals that many of the same community characteristics—and a few additional ones—predict higher aspirations. Overall, these findings suggest that creating high-quality communities predicts increases in aspiration levels. The next section turns to the question of why aspirations matter for households in rural Pakistan.

The Importance of Aspirations for Economic Decisions and Outcomes

Until now we have not quantified the relationship between aspirations and individual and household outcomes. Table 11.8 summarizes several economic decisions and outcomes that might be affected by an individual's aspiration level. First, aspiration levels may affect the input choices of land-cultivating households, including expenditures on seeds, pesticide and herbicide, and fertilizer per acre. Second—perhaps through impacts on inputs—aspiration levels may affect crop yields (defined as the amount harvested per acre planted) and losses (defined as the amount lost, pre- or postharvest, as a share of total production) for the two most important crops in rural Pakistan: cotton and wheat. Finally, aspiration levels may affect economic and financial decisions of households, including savings as a share of monthly expenditure (18 percent, on average), cash loans as a share of yearly expenditures (35 percent, on average), migration outside the village in the last year (9 percent sent a migrant, on average), and ownership of a nonagricultural enterprise (16 percent of households, on average).

We take two approaches to estimate whether having higher aspirations predicts different economic decisions and outcomes. First, we undertake a cross-sectional analysis and examine whether in 2012 individuals with higher reported aspirations have different characteristics than those with lower reported aspirations. Of course, these estimates cannot be interpreted as causal, because higher aspirations may be correlated with unobserved attributes of individuals and their households (not among our set of 2012 controls), which themselves affect economic decisions and outcomes. Second, we exploit the fact that we have two different years of data on both aspirations and economic decisions and outcomes: 2012 and 2013, from Rounds 1 and 2 of the

TABLE 11.8 Summary statistics for individual economic decisions and outcomes

	Mean	SD	N
Panel A: Input choice			
Household expenditure on seeds per acre cultivated (PKR)	2,495	3,606	1,655
Household expenditure on pesticide and herbicide per acre cultivated (PKR)	2,300	3,085	1,655
Household expenditure on fertilizer per acre cultivated (PKR)	8,745	8,673	1,655
Panel B: Crop yields			
Cotton harvested per acre of cotton planted (10s of 40 kg bags)	1.78	1.08	509
Wheat harvested per acre of wheat planted (10s of 40 kg bags)	2.88	1.13	1,257
Cotton lost (pre- or postharvest) as a share of cotton production	0.90	2.83	481
Wheat lost (pre- or postharvest) as a share of wheat production	0.10	0.50	1,257
Panel C: Financial and economic decisions			
Total savings as a share of monthly expenditure (%)	18	169	3,526
Total cash loans outstanding as share of yearly total expenditure (%)	35	61	1,156
Households with member who migrated outside the village in the last twelve months (%)	9	29	3,526
Household with member who operates a nonagricultural enterprise (%)	16	37	3,526

Source: Authors' calculations, based on the RHPS 2012 (IFPRI/IDS 2012).

Note: The different sample sizes (N) are due to the fact that not all rural households cultivate crops and not all of those that cultivate crops cultivate cotton and wheat. In some cases, they are due to data missing for certain variables. PKR = Pakistani rupees; SD = standard deviations.

RHPS (IFPRI/IDS 2012, 2013). Using this short panel of data, we estimate a model with individual fixed effects. Individual fixed effects control for all features of a given individual, the individual's household, and his or her surroundings that do not vary over time. In doing so, we control for not only observable but also *unobservable*, time-invariant factors correlated with both aspirations and economic decisions or outcomes. While not causal estimates, individual fixed effects help better address the endogeneity of aspirations to such outcomes and argue for a robust relationship between aspirations and individual economic decisions and outcomes.

Agricultural Input Expenditures

Having higher aspirations in 2012 is significantly associated with higher expenditure on fertilizer per acre in that same year, as shown in Table 11.9. A standard deviation increase in aspirations is associated with a (0.64 × 578) = PKR 370 increase in annual expenditure on fertilizer per acre (column 2). This is roughly a 4 percent increase over the mean fertilizer expenditure (PKR 8,745). Annex Table D11.2 examines whether the same results hold in a

TABLE 11.9 Correlations between agricultural input expenditures and aspiration levels

Explanatory variable	(1)	(2)	(3)	(4)	(5)	(6)
	Household expenditure on fertilizer per acre cultivated		Household expenditure on pesticide and herbicide per acre cultivated		Household expenditure on seeds per acre cultivated	
Aspiration level	625.413** (272.029)	578.032* (331.546)	161.481* (90.652)	127.274 (107.278)	−50.356 (98.762)	63.970 (117.350)
Male		−341.166 (375.626)		−163.112 (119.815)		101.419 (184.493)
Age 18–24		711.351 (803.562)		−48.265 (282.255)		213.731 (651.276)
Age 25–34		−568.968 (575.281)		-97.144 (216.980)		−403.818* (242.381)
Age 35–44		364.094 (662.728)		−167.519 (260.563)		155.063 (317.459)
Age 45–54		153.915 (639.608)		−46.796 (232.420)		−8.700 (288.158)
Married		177.818 (681.977)		91.058 (240.536)		207.665 (336.558)
Primary education (classes 1–5)		763.208 (472.660)		57.059 (178.133)		−77.420 (236.991)
Middle education (classes 6–8)		−519.956 (637.011)		249.718 (253.208)		57.352 (306.301)
High/intermediate (classes 9–12)		742.809 (705.619)		359.027 (223.334)		−578.517** (265.810)
Postsecondary education		2,424.123* (1,313.098)		860.791 (532.252)		−137.338 (350.180)
Mother—years of education		−55.703 (145.139)		−33.124 (52.296)		−22.555 (45.119)
Father—years of education		20.633 (61.764)		17.003 (24.151)		26.820 (24.768)
Observations	1,644	1,619	1,644	1,619	1,644	1,619
R-squared	0.277	0.332	0.331	0.370	0.109	0.132

Source: Authors' calculations, based on the RHPS 2012 (IFPRI/IDS 2012).

Note: All regressions include district, ethnicity, and household size fixed effects, and controls for latitude, longitude, latitude x longitude, elevation, education group dummies, age group dummies, gender dummies, marital status dummies, and household type dummies (landowner, tenant, agricultural wage laborer, or rural nonfarm). Standard errors, corrected for heteroskedasticity and clustered at the household level, are shown below the coefficients, in parentheses. * = significant at 10%; ** = significant at 5%; *** = significant at 1%.

panel data analysis. Here, we see an even larger, about $(832.25 \times 0.64) / 8745 = 6$ percent, increase over the mean (column 1). This suggests that we may underestimate the magnitude of the relationship between aspirations and fertilizer expenditure when failing to control for time-invariant individual characteristics influencing both aspirations and input decision making.

The cross-sectional analysis suggests that when including our array of controls variables, no significant relationship exists between aspirations and expenditure on pesticides and herbicides, or on seeds, per acre. However, a panel data analysis that incorporates individual fixed effects (Annex Table D11.2)—while similarly finding that higher aspirations predict higher expenditure on fertilizer—additionally shows that higher aspirations are significantly associated with greater expenditure on pesticide and herbicide. Column 2 shows that a standard deviation increase in aspirations is associated with about a $(0.64 \times 320) = $ PKR 205 increase in annual expenditure on pesticides and weedicides per acre (roughly a 9 percent increase over the mean). Oddly, in contrast to the cross-sectional analysis, the panel data analysis suggests that higher aspirations are associated with less expenditure on seeds—possibly reflecting different trade-offs between fertilizers, pesticides, herbicides, and seeds among individuals with high aspirations, with a relatively greater emphasis on the first three. Overall, the results suggest that having higher aspirations may motivate farmers to invest more in inputs—especially fertilizers—that raise productivity. Uptake of such inputs may be hindered by aspiration failures and helped by policies boosting aspirations.

Crop Yields and Pre- and Postharvest Losses

Having higher aspirations is also significantly associated with higher crop yields and less pre- and postharvest waste as a share of production, as shown in both the cross-sectional analysis of Table 11.10 and the panel data analysis of Annex Table D11.3. However, the findings are not uniform across crops (cotton versus wheat) or types of farmers (landowners versus tenants).

In the cross-sectional analysis, higher aspirations are significantly associated with higher cotton yields (in kg of output per acre planted) (Table 11.10, Panel A). A standard deviation increase in aspirations is associated with about an additional $(0.114 \times 0.64 \times 400 \text{ kg}) = 29$ kg of cotton harvested per acre of cotton planted. Given average cotton yields, this is a 4 percent average increase over mean cotton yields. The panel data analysis with individual fixed effects yields similar results (Annex Table D11.3, Panel A); a standard deviation increase in aspirations is associated with an additional 39 kg of cotton harvested per acre planted—a 5 percent increase over the mean yield. While the cross-sectional analysis suggests that aspirations predict the largest increases in cotton yields for tenants, the panel data analysis that controls for time-invariant individual characteristics suggests that it is in fact landowners for whom aspirations predict the largest increases in cotton yields.

TABLE 11.10 Correlations between cotton and wheat crop yields and pre- and postharvest losses and aspiration levels

Explanatory variable	All	Landowners	Tenants
Panel A: Cotton harvested per acre planted (10s of 40 kg bags)			
Aspiration level	0.114*	0.111	0.236**
	(0.068)	(0.070)	(0.106)
Observations	495	399	96
R-squared	0.420	0.348	0.862
Panel B: Wheat harvested per acre planted (10s of 40 kg bags)			
Aspiration level	0.035	0.004	0.066
	(0.043)	(0.042)	(0.137)
Observations	1,225	984	241
R-squared	0.356	0.359	0.500
Panel C: Cotton lost (pre- or postharvest) as a share of cotton production			
Aspiration level	0.094	0.140	0.389
	(0.215)	(0.143)	(1.242)
Observations	468	389	79
R-squared	0.434	0.429	0.799
Panel D: Wheat lost (pre- or postharvest) as a share of wheat production			
Aspiration level	−0.048**	−0.018	−0.184
	(0.024)	(0.014)	(0.122)
Observations	1,225	985	240
R-squared	0.168	0.202	0.458

Source: Authors' calculations, based on RHPS 2012 (IFPRI/IDS 2012).

Note: All regressions include district, ethnicity, and household size fixed effects, and controls for latitude, longitude, latitude × longitude, elevation, education group dummies, age group dummies, gender dummies, marital status dummies, and household type dummies (landowner, tenant, agricultural wage laborer, or rural nonfarm). Standard errors, corrected for heteroskedasticity and clustered at the household level, are shown below the coefficients, in parentheses. * = significant at 10%; ** = significant at 5%; *** = significant at 1%.

While the coefficient on aspirations is positive in the cross-sectional analysis of factors predicting wheat yields (Table 11.10, Panel B), it is not statistically significant. However, it is both positive and statistically significant in the panel data analysis (Annex Table D11.3, Panel B). There, we see that a standard deviation increase in aspirations is associated with about an additional $(0.169 \times 0.64 \times 400 \text{ kg}) = 43$ kg of wheat harvested per acre planted—almost a 4 percent increase over mean wheat yields. As in the case of cotton yields, the panel analysis reveals that having higher aspirations predicts larger wheat gains for landowners than it does for tenants.

In neither the cross-sectional nor the panel analysis does having higher aspirations predict the amount of cotton lost (pre- or postharvest) as a share of total cotton production (Table 11.10 and Annex Table D11.3, panel C). However, both analyses reveal a predicted reduction in wheat losses when an individual has higher aspirations (Table 11.10 and Annex Table D11.3, panel D). From the cross-sectional analysis, a standard deviation increase in aspirations is associated with a $(0.048 \times 0.64) = 0.03$ point, or 30 percent reduction (over the mean) in pre- and postharvest wheat losses as a share of wheat kept. Because of small sample sizes, however, the effects are not statistically significant among either the landowner or the tenant subpopulations of farmers—though the magnitude of the coefficient for landowners (column 2) is smaller than that for tenants (column 3)—suggesting that the results are driven mostly by tenants. In the panel data analysis, however, having higher aspirations predicts significantly lower wheat losses both overall *and* for each type of farmer. As in the cross-sectional analysis, a standard deviation increase in aspirations is associated with a $(0.052 \times 0.64) = 0.03$ point, or 30 percent reduction (over the mean) in pre- and postharvest wheat losses. The reduction realized by tenants is larger than that of landowners, suggesting that tenants especially may benefit from lower wheat losses if policy can raise their aspirations.

Financial and Economic Outcomes and Aspiration Levels

Having higher aspirations is also associated with higher savings, use of credit (as a share of expenditures), and likelihood of operating a nonagricultural enterprise, as shown in the cross-sectional analysis of Table 11.11 and the panel analysis of Annex Table D11.4. However, aspirations are not significantly associated with individual migration outside of the village during the last 12 months in either analysis.

In the cross-sectional analysis, a standard deviation increase in aspirations is associated with an increase of about $(0.115 \times 0.64) = 0.07$ in savings as a share of monthly expenditure. This is a 39 percent increase over mean savings. We estimate even larger coefficients in the panel data analysis; a standard deviation increase in aspirations is associated with an increase of around $(0.393 \times 0.64) = 0.25$ in savings as a share of monthly expenditure, or about a 140 percent increase over the mean. Both analyses indicate an important association between aspirations and the propensity to save.

In the case of propensity to take out loans, the cross-sectional analysis suggests that a standard deviation increase in aspirations is associated with an increase of about $(0.147 \times 0.64) = 0.09$ in cash loans outstanding as a share of yearly total expenditure. This is a 26 percent increase over the mean amount of loans. However, our panel data analysis with individual fixed effects suggests a

TABLE 11.11 Correlation of financial and economic outcomes with aspiration levels

Explanatory variable	(1) Total savings as a share of monthly expenditure	(2) Total cash loans outstanding as share of yearly total expenditure	(3) Individual migrated outside the village, last 12 months	(4) Individual's household operates a nonagricultural enterprise
Aspiration level	0.115**	0.147***	−0.001	0.026**
	(0.058)	(0.057)	(0.007)	(0.012)
Male	−0.071**	−0.036	−0.008	−0.057***
	(0.032)	(0.026)	(0.006)	(0.011)
Age 18–24	−0.110	−0.066	−0.009	−0.009
	(0.115)	(0.076)	(0.014)	(0.027)
Age 25–34	0.051	−0.150**	−0.017	−0.008
	(0.082)	(0.063)	(0.013)	(0.023)
Age 35–44	−0.067	−0.152**	−0.019	0.000
	(0.108)	(0.067)	(0.013)	(0.023)
Age 45–54	−0.058	−0.142**	−0.011	0.002
	(0.109)	(0.062)	(0.014)	(0.024)
Married	0.159**	0.053	−0.015	−0.001
	(0.075)	(0.049)	(0.012)	(0.022)
Primary education (classes 1–5)	−0.040	−0.088	0.011	0.056***
	(0.049)	(0.062)	(0.010)	(0.020)
Middle education (classes 6–8)	0.268	0.019	0.000	0.028
	(0.185)	(0.091)	(0.014)	(0.024)
High/intermediate education (classes 9–12)	0.231**	−0.043	0.007	0.043*
	(0.094)	(0.089)	(0.014)	(0.025)
Postsecondary education	0.376*	−0.103	0.023	−0.001
	(0.219)	(0.118)	(0.032)	(0.047)
Mother—years of education	0.033	−0.012	−0.007***	−0.005
	(0.030)	(0.011)	(0.002)	(0.006)
Father—years of education	0.004	0.017**	−0.001	0.002
	−0.012	(0.007)*	−0.002	−0.003
Observations	3,460	1,128	3,460	3,460
R-squared	0.037	0.135	0.566	0.075

Source: Authors' calculations, based on the RHPS 2012 (IFPRI/IDS 2012).

Note: All regressions include district, ethnicity, and household size fixed effects, and controls for latitude, longitude, latitude × longitude, elevation, education group dummies, age group dummies, gender dummies, marital status dummies, and household type dummies (landowner, tenant, agricultural wage laborer, or rural nonfarm). Standard errors, corrected for heteroskedasticity and clustered at the household level, are shown below the coefficients, in parentheses. * = significant at 10%; ** = significant at 5%; *** = significant at 1%.

more muted correlation; a standard deviation increase in aspirations is associated with an increase of around $(0.08 \times 0.64) = 0.05$ in cash loans as a share of expenditure—around a 15 percent increase in loans. While smaller, both effect sizes indicate an important correlation between aspirations and accessing credit.

Finally, the cross-sectional analysis suggests that a standard deviation increase in aspiration levels is associated with an increase of $(0.026 \times 0.64) = 0.02$ in the probability of operating a nonagricultural enterprise. This is about a 13 percent increase over the mean rate of operation of a nonagricultural enterprise. A slightly smaller effect size emerges from the panel data analysis; a standard deviation increase in aspiration levels is associated with about a 6 percent increase. This is an especially relevant finding given the importance for policy makers of expanding opportunities in rural nonfarm employment because of Pakistan's burgeoning youth population. Polices that raise aspirations may boost entrepreneurial behavior, as measured by operating such an enterprise.

Conclusions

Eradicating poverty requires two main conditions: first, availability of opportunities to break the poverty cycle, and, second, the will to take advantage of these opportunities. The poor must be *able* to and *willing* to change their conditions. Understanding aspirations is important for policy makers to determine the pockets in society where this *will* is systemically low.

We show that aspirations vary widely across rural Pakistan. This chapter identifies several characteristics predicting aspiration levels, highlighting the groups that are vulnerable to aspiration-induced poverty traps: women have lower aspirations than men, the uneducated have lower aspirations than those with some education, the middle-aged (25–44) have lower aspirations than the young (ages 18–24), and agricultural wage laborers have lower aspirations than rural nonfarm workers. Further, various cognitive factors—including an internal locus of control (a sense of control of one's own life), high self-esteem, religiosity, trust, a lack of envy, and a sense that poverty is not caused by external factors but rather can be avoided by one's own efforts—predict higher aspiration levels. These findings identify factors that must be encouraged for a progressively aspiring rural Pakistan. Cognitive factors such as having an internal locus of control and high self-esteem, as well as factors such as gender inequality, literacy patterns, and occupational inequalities can be influenced by effective policy.

We also present evidence that having higher aspirations is associated with higher rates of adoption of fertilizer, pesticides, and herbicides, higher crop yields, lower crop losses, higher savings, more use of credit, and higher rates of operation of nonfarm enterprises. These initial findings can have transformative results if causation is established. Understanding what encourages profitable agricultural practices will be crucial for improving the economic outcomes for a large part of the Pakistani population that is still dependent on agriculture. Further research is needed to see if these correlations can be given a causal interpretation.[9]

The initial findings suggest that a number of potential policy levers could be used to increase aspirations in rural Pakistan, including holding organized meetings of village residents to discuss issues and events, improving the quality of and general faith in the justice system, upgrading road surfaces (from mud to other types), expanding communication and transportation linkages with other localities, and providing training through NGOs. This evidence suggests that good policy can create and cultivate the institutional conditions that permit and encourage individuals to aspire to improve their lives.

References

Appadurai, A. 2004. "The Capacity to Aspire: Culture and the Terms of Recognition." In *Culture and Public Action,* edited by Vijayendra Rao and Michael Walton, 59–84. Stanford, CA: Stanford University Press.

Beaman, L., E. Duflo, R. Pande, and P. Topalova. 2012. "Female Leadership Raises Aspirations and Educational Attainment for Girls: A Policy Experiment in India." *Science Magazine* 335 (6068): 582–586.

Bernard, T., and A. Seyoum Taffesse. 2012. *Measuring Aspirations: Discussion and Example from Ethiopia.* International Food Policy Research Institute Discussion Paper 01190. Washington, DC: IFPRI.

Bernard, T., A. S. Taffesse, and S. Dercon. 2008. *Aspirations Failure and Well-Being Outcomes in Ethiopia: Towards an Empirical Exploration.* IFPRI Discussion Paper 01190. Washington, DC: IFPRI.

---

9   There are a number of promising directions for future work on aspirations, which can hopefully circumvent the endogeneity concerns raised in this work. The first involves research on what policy interventions (such as social protection, training, or extension services) are effective in raising aspirations. The second involves research on how raising aspirations affects behavior. Given exogenous variations in each, one could go even further, examining how policy and aspirations interact and complement each other in improving the livelihoods of the poor.

————. 2011. *Beyond Fatalism: An Empirical Exploration of Self-Efficacy and Aspirations Failure in Ethiopia.* International Food Policy Research Institute Discussion Paper 01101. Washington, DC: IFPRI.

Camerer, C., L. Babcock, G. Loewenstein, and R. Thaler. 1997. "Labor Supply of New York City Cab Drivers: One Day at a Time." *Quarterly Journal of Economics* 112: 407–441.

Chen, J., K. Kosec, and V. Mueller. 2015. *Temporary and Permanent Migrant Selection: The Roles of Ability, Wage Expectations, and Familial Networks.* IFPRI Discussion Paper 1496. Washington, DC: International Food Policy Research Institute.

Coleman, M., and T. DeLeire. 2003. "An Economic Model of Locus of Control and the Human Capital Investment Decision." *Journal of Human Resources* 38 (3): 701–721.

IFPRI/IDS (International Food Policy Research Institute/Innovative Development Strategies). 2012. Pakistan Rural Household Panel Survey 2012 dataset. Washington, DC: IFPRI; Islamabad: IDS.

————. 2013. Pakistan Rural Household Panel Survey 2013 dataset. Washington, DC: IFPRI; Islamabad: IDS.

Knight, J., and R. Gunatilaka. 2012. "Income, Aspirations and the Hedonic Treadmill in a Poor Society." *Journal of Economic Behavior and Organization* 82: 67–81.

Kosec, K., and C. Mo. 2015. *Aspirations and the Role of Social Protection: Evidence from a Natural Disaster in Rural Pakistan.* IFPRI Discussion Paper 1467. Washington, DC: International Food Policy Research Institute.

Macours, K., and R. Vakis. 2009. *Changing Households' Investments and Aspirations through Social Interactions: Evidence from a Randomized Transfer Program.* World Bank Policy Research Working Paper 5137. Washington, DC: World Bank.

Maertens, A. 2012. "Does Education Pay Off? Subjective Expectations with Regard to Education in Rural India." *Economic and Political Weekly* 46 (09): 58–63.

Mo, C. H. 2012. "Essays in Behavioral Political Economy: The Effects of Affect, Attitude, and Aspirations." PhD dissertation, Stanford University, Stanford, CA.

Ray, D. 1998. *Development Economics.* Princeton, NJ: Princeton University Press.

————. 2006. "Aspirations, Poverty, and Economic Change." In *Understanding Poverty*, edited by A. V. Banerjee, R. Bénabou, and D. Mookherjee, 409–443. Oxford, UK: Oxford University Press.

Annex A: Median Income, Assets, Years of Education, and Social Status Aspired to, by District

District	Income (PKR/year)	Assets (PKR)	Years of education	Social status (1–10)
Attock	180,000	120,000	10	7
Bahawalnagar	100,000	100,000	10	8
Bhakkar	100,000	100,000	10	8
D. G. Khan	140,000	100,000	10	9
Dadu	50,000	100,000	10	8
Faisalabad	144,000	90,000	10	9
Hyderabad	40,000	15,000	5	7
Jacobabad	200,000	200,000	10	8
Jhang	100,000	150,000	10	8
Kasur	90,000	50,000	10	7
Khanewal	120,000	150,000	10	8
Mansehra	170,000	100,000	10	7
Multan	100,000	90,000	10	10
Nowshera	200,000	300,000	10	8
Rahim Yar Khan	100,000	100,000	8	8
Sanghar	120,000	100,000	10	10
Sargodha	120,000	150,000	10	6
Thatta	60,000	20,000	5	8
Vehari	60,000	85,000	8	8

Source: Authors' calculations, based on the RHPS 2012 (IFPRI/IDS 2012), using household weights.
Note: PKR = Pakistani rupees.

Annex B: Data Assembly Detail

We constructed a number of indexes using answers to a series of questions eliciting information about a particular issue (for example, perceived access to justice, or perceived access to safety nets). In most cases, these questions have four possible responses indicating the degree of agreement with a given statement (though in some cases they have two): strongly disagree (1), disagree (2), agree (3), and strongly agree (4). The survey questions are listed below. See the second section for details on the normalization and index construction procedure.

Community Characteristics Indexes

Justice Index

The justice index quantifies an individual's perceived access to justice using the following questions:

1. The laws and law enforcement in my community generally prevent crime.

2. If someone commits a crime against me, members of my community will be able to help me.

3. If someone commits a crime against me, the police will be able to help me.

4. If someone commits a crime against me, I can get justice through the courts system.

5. In the end, victims of crime usually see justice done.

6. I can get justice through the courts if someone tries to take my land.

7. A land title means that I can get justice through the courts if someone tries to take away my land.

8. Being harassed by the police is a problem for young men in my community.

Safety Nets Index

The safety nets index measures an individual's perceived degree of access to safety nets using the following questions:

1. Members of my family will take actions to help me if I face unexpected economic hardship.

2. Nonfamily members of my community will take actions to help me if I face unexpected economic hardship.

3. The government will take actions to help me if I face unexpected economic hardship.

4. NGOs will take actions to help me if I face unexpected economic hardship.

5. I have spoken with someone in my community about how we can help one another in case of economic hardship.

6. Adults in my community expect that their children will provide for them in old age.

7. If a women loses her husband, his family will financially support her.

8. If a women loses her husband, her family will financially support her.

Cognitive Features Indexes

Locus of Control Index

The locus of control index measures the extent to which an individual feels he or she has control over his or her own life (an "internal locus of control") using the following questions:

1. Please choose one option (different from standard questions with four responses):

   1.1   Each person is primarily responsible for his or her own success or failure in life.
   1.2   One's success or failure is a matter of his or her destiny.

2. Please choose one option (different from standard questions with four responses):

   2.1   To be successful, above all one needs to work very hard.
   2.2   One is successful if this is his or her fate/destiny.

The following are standard questions with the four responses described above:

1. To a great extent my life is controlled by accidental/chance happenings.

2. I feel like what happens in my life is mostly determined by powerful/influential individuals.

3. When I make plans, I am almost certain/guaranteed/sure to make them work.

4. Often there is no chance of protecting my personal interests from bad luck happening.

5. My experience in my life has been that what is going to happen will happen.

6. My life is chiefly controlled by other powerful individuals.

7. Individuals like myself have very little chance of protecting our personal interests when they conflict with those of more powerful individuals.

8. It's not always wise for me to plan too far ahead because many things turn out to be a matter of good or bad fortune.

9. Getting what I want requires making those individuals above me (individuals with higher status) happy with me.

10. I can mostly determine what will happen in my life.

11. I am usually able to protect my personal interests (I can usually look after what is important to me).

12. When I get what I want, it's usually because I worked hard for it.

13. In order to have my plans work, I make sure that they fit in with the desires of individuals who have power over me.

14. My life is determined by my own actions.

Perceptions of Causes of Poverty Index

The perceptions of causes of poverty index measures the extent to which poverty is seen as caused by external factors using the following questions:

1. People are poor because they lack the ability to manage money or other assets.

2. People are poor because they waste their money on inappropriate items (for example, alcohol, cigarettes, gambling).

3. People are poor because they do not actively seek to improve their lives.

4. People are poor because they are exploited by rich individuals (for example, rich individuals pay poor individuals a very low wage).

5. People are poor because society fails to help and protect the most vulnerable (for example, disabled individuals, individuals living with HIV/AIDS).

6. People are poor because the distribution of land between poor and rich individuals is uneven/unequal.

7. People are poor because they lack opportunities because they come from poor families.

8. People are poor because they have bad fate/destiny.

9. People are poor because they have encountered misfortunes.

10. People are poor because they are not motivated because of food aid (for example, direct support programs, food parcels from NGOs not during famine).

11. People are poor because they are born with less talent/they are less gifted.

Attitudes to Change Index

The attitudes to change index quantifies individuals' eagerness to change or hesitancy to change using the following questions:

1. Below are two different reactions when one encounters changes in life. Which one comes closest to your usual outlook when you encounter change?

    1.1   I worry about the difficulties changes may cause.
    1.2   I welcome the fact that something new is beginning.

Please select which of the following options best describes your outlook in life:

2.

    2.1   To be cautious/careful about starting major life changes is reasonable.
    2.2   You will never achieve much unless you act boldly/with courage.

3.

3.1 Ideas that have stood the test of time are definitely best.

3.2 New ideas are generally better than old ones.

4.

4.1 Compared to most of my neighbors, I am more willing to try new farming techniques (such as new crops, irrigation, improved seeds, fertilizers, using a tractor).

4.2 If an agricultural extension worker proposes a new farming technique, I am usually one of the last farmers to adopt it.

5.

5.1 A woman should devote almost all her time to her family.

5.2 A wife and husband should share the load of generating income for the household.

6.

6.1 If a man and woman want to get married and the father is against it, they should get married.

6.2 If a man and woman want to get married and the father is against it, they should not get married.

7.

7.1 I strictly follow the advice of elders of the community.

7.2 I listen to the advice of elders of the community but make my decisions independently.

Self-Esteem Index

The self-esteem index measures the extent to which an individual is proud, self-satisfied, and feels capable and confident in what she or he can do using the following questions:

1. I feel that I have a number of good qualities.

2. All in all, I am inclined to feel that I am a failure.

3. I am able to do things as well as most individuals.

4. I feel I do not have much to be proud of.

5. On the whole, I am satisfied with myself.

6. I wish I could have more respect for myself than I have now.

Envy Index

The envy index measures willingness to have less as long as one is compara-
tively rich using the following questions:

1. Which situation would you prefer? Prices in both situations are
   the same.

   1.1 You get PKR 100,000 a year and others get half of that (PKR
        50,000 a year).
   1.2 You get PKR 250,000 a year and others get more than double that
        (PKR 500,000 a year).

2. Which situation would you prefer?

   2.1 You have a one-room pucca house, and others have a one-room
        kacha house.
   2.2 You have a two-room pucca house, and others have a three-room
        pucca house.

3. Which situation would you prefer?

   3.1 Your child completes inter (grade 12), and others have children
        who complete primary school.
   3.2 Your child completes a one-year diploma, and others have children
        who complete a university (bachelor's) degree.

Trust Index

The trust index measures the extent to which individuals trust the individuals
and institutions around them using the following questions:

1. Most individuals are basically honest.

2. Most individuals can be trusted.

3. I believe the government wants to do what is right for the individuals.

4. I trust my neighbors to look after my house if I am away.

5. I could rely on my neighbor to give someone an important message for me.

6. I believe tehsil officials want to do what is right for the individuals.

7. I trust the staff in the local health center to do their best to keep me healthy.

8. I trust the NGOs working in this village to act in my best interest.

9. I trust banks to be fair to me.

10. I trust that the police will act in the individuals' interest.

11. I trust that judges will make fair and impartial decisions.

12. I trust national government politicians to serve the interests of the individuals.

Religiosity Index

The religiosity index measures the extent to which individuals are religious in their actions and the extent to which religiosity plays a role in their worldview using the following questions:

1. How often do you offer prayers (*namaz*)?

    1.1 Five times a day
    1.2 Between two and four times a day
    1.3 Occasionally
    1.4 Rarely
    1.5 Never

2. How often do you offer prayers (*namaz*) at the mosque?

    2.1 Five times a day
    2.2 Between two and four times a day
    2.3 Occasionally
    2.4 Rarely
    2.5 Never

3. How often do you fast other than Ramadan?

    3.1 Several times per month
    3.2 Once a month
    3.3 Once every few months
    3.4 Very rarely

3.5   Never

The following are standard questions with the four responses described above:

1. A lack of Islamic religiosity is leading to problems in my country.

2. It's my duty to pressure individuals to be more religious.

3. Violence is justified if it is in defense of religious values.

4. A lack of understanding of the Islamic teaching is leading to problems in my country.

Monthly Effective Discount Rate

We measured individuals' discount rates by asking them if they would prefer PKR 500 today or PKR 625 after one month. If individuals indicated that they would prefer PKR 500 today, we asked if they would accept PKR 750 after one month in lieu of PKR 500 today. If they still indicated that they would like PKR 500 today, we asked what amount they would have to receive in one month's time in order to convince them to wait the full month instead of simply receiving PKR 500 today. Using responses to these questions, we mapped out each individual's tendency to trade off the future for the present as follows, computing the individual's "monthly effective discount rate":

$$monthly\ effective\ discount\ rate = \frac{X-500}{X}$$

where $X = 625$ if the individual will accept 625 in one month over 500 today, $X = 750$ if the individual will not accept 625 in one month but will accept 750 in one month, and $X =$ the amount the individual indicated they will accept in one month in exchange for forgoing 500 today (a value we know only for those who would not accept 750 in one month).

The monthly effective discount rate captures how much of the value of the future payment (whether 625, or 750, or some higher amount) is considered lost due to being received in one month instead of today. By design (and thus no matter what the value of X), it is between 0 and 1, and increases with the individual's impatience. As an example, an individual who requires PKR 750 in one month in order to give up PKR 500 today has a monthly effective discount rate of 0.33. Essentially, they must be paid PKR 250—one-third of the value of the total transfer—just to be willing to wait for one month to be paid.

Annex C: Correlations of Components of Aspirations with Community Characteristics, Rural Pakistan

Community characteristic	Aspiration level in			
	income	assets	education	social status
Organized village meetings to discuss issues and events	0.154***	0.115**	0.004	0.133***
	(0.046)	(0.048)	(0.034)	(0.048)
Justice index	−0.034	0.036	0.093***	0.164***
	(0.046)	(0.043)	(0.030)	(0.038)
Railway station within walking distance	0.085	0.112*	0.164***	0.082
	(0.067)	(0.063)	(0.043)	(0.064)
Distance to the nearest post office in 2012 (km)	−0.002	−0.006**	−0.006***	−0.005*
	(0.002)	(0.003)	(0.002)	(0.003)
A main road connects the village to a nearby city	0.028	0.016	0.059	0.006
	(0.045)	(0.043)	(0.037)	(0.052)
Most common road surface type of external roads is mud	−0.043	−0.121**	−0.048	−0.129***
	(0.046)	(0.054)	(0.033)	(0.048)
Most common road surface type of internal roads is mud	−0.016	−0.001	−0.093***	−0.115**
	(0.051)	(0.042)	(0.033)	(0.047)
Fixed-line telephone service available in the village	0.021	−0.013	0.098**	0.057
	(0.060)	(0.057)	(0.048)	(0.069)
Access to cylinder gas	0.013	0.112***	−0.012	0.011
	(0.038)	(0.038)	(0.033)	(0.047)
Distance to the nearest commercial center (km)	−0.000	−0.001	−0.001	−0.001
	(0.001)	(0.002)	(0.001)	(0.001)
Public transport to the nearest commercial center available	0.060	0.037	−0.067*	0.038
	(0.038)	(0.035)	(0.035)	(0.053)
Number of NGOs active in the tehsil	−0.049	0.034	0.079***	0.045
	(0.056)	(0.045)	(0.030)	(0.049)
Number of NGOs providing training	−0.015	0.066	0.140**	0.038
	(0.076)	(0.095)	(0.064)	(0.078)
Safety nets index	−0.020	−0.020	−0.042	0.194***
	(0.030)	(0.034)	(0.026)	(0.038)
Relatives in another district?	0.013	0.060	−0.106***	0.012
	(0.054)	(0.060)	(0.037)	(0.058)
Relatives in another province?	0.076*	0.056*	−0.014	0.006
	(0.041)	(0.033)	(0.029)	(0.045)

Source: Authors' calculations, based on the RHPS 2012 (IFPRI/IDS 2012).

Notes: The coefficient on each community characteristic in each column comes from a separate regression of each component of the aspiration index on the community variable and a full set of control variables. These include district, ethnicity, and household size fixed effects, and controls for latitude, longitude, latitude x longitude, elevation, education group dummies, age group dummies, gender dummies, marital status dummies, household type dummies (landowner, tenant, agricultural wage laborer, or rural non-farm), per capita expenditure, and wealth. The number of observations is the same as in the Table 11.11, column 1 regressions. Standard errors corrected for heteroskedasticity and clustered at the household level are shown below the coefficients, in parentheses. * = significant at 10%; ** = significant at 5%; *** = significant at 1%.

Annex D: Panel Data Analysis of Correlates of Aspirations

TABLE D11.1 Correlations between aspiration levels in 2013 and 2012 community characteristics, controlling for 2012 aspiration levels

Community characteristic	Aspiration level, 2013	N
Organized village meetings to discuss issues and events	0.092** (0.038)	2,531
Justice index	0.038 (0.029)	1,874
Railway station within walking distance	−0.024 (0.047)	2,531
Distance to the nearest post office in 2012 (km)	−0.003 (0.002)	2,531
A main road connects the village to a nearby city	0.067* (0.035)	2,531
Most common road surface type of external roads is mud	−0.046 (0.035)	2,531
Most common road surface type of internal roads is mud	−0.076** (0.035)	2,531
Fixed-line telephone service available in the village	0.083* (0.050)	2,531
Access to cylinder gas	0.081*** (0.031)	2,531
Distance to the nearest commercial center (km)	−0.000 (0.001)	2,531
Public transportation available to the nearest commercial center	0.104*** (0.038)	2,531
Number of NGOs active in the tehsil	0.068* (0.035)	2,531
Number of NGOs providing training	0.061 (0.067)	2,531
Safety nets index	0.110*** (0.026)	2,109
Relatives in another district?	0.038 (0.036)	2,523
Relatives in another province?	0.045 (0.031)	2,525

Source: Authors' calculations, based on the RHPS (2012/2013) (IFPRI/IDS 2012, 2013).

Note: The coefficient on each community characteristic comes from a separate regression of the 2013 aspiration level on the 2012 aspiration level, district fixed effects, and controls for latitude, longitude, latitude × longitude, and elevation. Standard errors, corrected for heteroskedasticity and clustered at the household level, are shown below the coefficients, in parentheses. * = significant at 10%; ** = significant at 5%; *** = significant at 1%.

TABLE D11.2 Correlations between agricultural input expenditures and aspiration levels, using panel data and individual fixed effects

Explanatory variable	(3) Household expenditure on fertilizer per acre cultivated	(2) Household expenditure on pesticide and herbicide per acre cultivated	(1) Household expenditure on seeds per acre cultivated
Aspiration level	832.251***	319.588***	−189.244**
	(212.112)	(95.325)	(80.456)
Observations	3,477	3,477	3,477
R-squared	0.016	0.009	0.006

Source: Authors' calculations, based on the RHPS (2012/2013) (IFPRI/IDS 2012, 2013).

Note: All regressions include individual fixed effects. Standard errors, corrected for heteroskedasticity and clustered at the household level, are shown below the coefficients, in parentheses. * = significant at 10%; ** = significant at 5%; *** = significant at 1%.

TABLE D11.3 Correlations between cotton and wheat crop yields and pre- and postharvest losses and aspiration levels, using panel data and individual fixed effects

Explanatory variable	(1) All	(2) Landowners	(3) Tenants
Panel A: Cotton harvested per acre planted (10s of 40 kg bags)			
Aspiration level	0.154**	0.137*	0.052
	(0.068)	(0.075)	(0.130)
Observations	1,050	817	233
R-squared	0.029	0.025	0.042
Panel B: Wheat harvested per acre planted (10s of 40 kg bags)			
Aspiration level	0.169***	0.152***	0.126
	(0.043)	(0.049)	(0.091)
Observations	2,694	2,084	610
R-squared	0.026	0.020	0.048
Panel C: Cotton lost (pre- or postharvest) as a share of cotton production			
Aspiration level	−0.182	−0.164	0.086
	(0.246)	(0.328)	(0.613)
Observations	1,000	791	209
R-squared	0.002	0.002	0.246
Panel D: Wheat lost (pre- or postharvest) as a share of wheat production			
Aspiration level	−0.052***	−0.027**	−0.116**
	(0.015)	(0.011)	(0.047)
Observations	2,676	2,074	602
R-squared	0.069	0.007	0.104

Source: Authors' calculations, based on the RHPS (2012/2013) (IFPRI/IDS 2012, 2013).

Note: All regressions include individual fixed effects. Standard errors, corrected for heteroskedasticity and clustered at the household level, are shown below the coefficients, in parentheses. * = significant at 10%; ** = significant at 5%; *** = significant at 1%.

TABLE D11.4 Correlation of financial and economic outcomes with aspiration levels, using panel data and individual fixed effects

Explanatory variable	(1) Total savings as a share of monthly expenditure	(2) Total cash loans outstanding as share of yearly total expenditure	(3) Individual migrated outside the village, last 12 months	(4) Individual's household operates a nonagricultural enterprise
Aspiration level	0.393***	0.077***	−0.007	0.016**
	(0.105)	(0.027)	(0.005)	(0.008)
Observations	7,164	2,576	7,164	7,164
R-squared	0.011	0.009	0.011	0.011

Source: Authors' calculations, based on the RHPS (2012/2013) (IFPRI/IDS 2012, 2013).

Note: All regressions include individual fixed effects. Standard errors, corrected for heteroskedasticity and clustered at the household level, are shown below the coefficients, in parentheses. * = significant at 10%; ** = significant at 5%; *** = significant at 1%.

Chapter 12

AGRICULTURAL GROWTH, POVERTY, AND THE RURAL NONFARM ECONOMY: A SPATIAL ECONOMY-WIDE ANALYSIS

Paul Dorosh, Emily Schmidt, and James Thurlow

Introduction

Pakistan's economy did not perform particularly well over the past decade. Per capita gross domestic product (GDP) grew at only 1.3 percent per year between 2005/2006 and 2013/2014 (PBS 2014). New research presented in this book suggests that the welfare of poorer households was virtually unchanged over this period (see Chapter 3). Various domestic factors contributed to these trends. First, agricultural GDP grew at 2.4 percent per year, which was only slightly above Pakistan's annual population growth rate of 2.3 percent. At the same time, energy demand outpaced supply, leading to widespread electricity shortages that hampered growth in the nonfarm economy (HDIP 2012). External factors that were largely beyond the control of the government also played a role. Foreign capital inflows had virtually ceased by the end of the decade, although this was offset by a surge in foreign remittances to households (SBP 2014). The rapid rise and subsequent fall in world food and energy prices late in the 2000–2009 decade also contributed to Pakistan's variable growth performance. Finally, the ongoing conflict in parts of the country has imposed a sizable economic cost (GoP 2014). Thus, numerous drivers were behind Pakistan's poor growth and poverty performance, of which slow agricultural growth was only one.

Agriculture undeniably plays a crucial role in Pakistan's economy. Farming is a major income source for most the country's poor households, so slow agricultural growth over the past decade is one obvious explanation for the persistence of rural poverty. However, numerous studies also emphasize the importance of the rural *nonfarm* economy (RNFE) and its contribution to rural households' livelihoods in Pakistan (see, for example, Arif, Nazli, and Haq 2000; Davis et al. 2010; Chaudhry, Malik, and Ashraf 2006; Dorosh,

Niazi, and Nazli 2003; Kurosaki 2006). Lanjouw and Lanjouw (2001) caution against the traditional view of the RNFE as a low-productivity sector whose contribution to the broader economy inevitably declines as development progresses. Instead, the authors cite evidence from numerous developing countries showing how growth in the RNFE can actively contribute to rural poverty reduction. Haggblade, Hazell, and Reardon (2010) provide a more recent review of the literature and conclude that the RNFE not only supports agricultural modernization during the early stages of development (by providing necessary inputs and services) but can also act as a continuing engine of rural economic growth. In fact many of the benefits from agricultural growth materialize from within the RNFE, which can generate sizable income and production multiplier effects that reach back into the agricultural sector (Haggblade, Hazell, and Dorosh 2007). Of course, the RNFE is not a panacea for rural development, and smallholder farmers must overcome numerous barriers to entry, sometimes with support from governments, before the benefits of the RNFE are fully realized (Reardon et al. 2000). Education, for instance, is found to be necessary for accessing decent rural nonfarm jobs in Pakistan (Kurosaki and Khan 2006). Nevertheless, there is strong evidence suggesting that the RNFE could play an instrumental role in promoting rural development in the country.

Our analysis, presented below, indicates that half of the new nonfarm jobs created in Pakistan between 2005/2006 and 2013/2014 were in the RNFE. However, this mainly reflects the size of the RNFE rather than its current dynamism. In fact, after rapidly expanding in the 1980s and 1990s, the RNFE has recently lagged behind agriculture in creating new jobs, leading to a rising share of farm employment over the past decade. In order to reverse this trend, Malik (2008) calls for a reframing of Pakistan's national development strategy so that it gives greater recognition to the potential contribution of the RNFE. This is supported by Kousar and Abdulai (2013), who find that participation in the rural nonfarm sector significantly increases per capita expenditures and reduces poverty in rural Pakistan. Various studies identify areas where institutional reforms and policy interventions could promote the expansion of the RNFE, including improving access to education and credit and market infrastructure (see Mohammad 1999; SPDC 2012; Sur and Zhang 2006; World Bank 2007). Financing and implementing these interventions would, however, require a shift in Pakistan's national strategy, which has traditionally focused on agricultural growth and urban development, with less attention given to the RNFE.

This chapter has three objectives. The first is to review recent growth patterns in Pakistan and to identify the contribution of the RNFE to structural change processes. This is done in the section "Agriculture and Structural Change in Pakistan" using structural decomposition analysis and recent data from labor force surveys. We find that economic growth over the past decade was *not* associated with positive structural change (that is, there was no reallocation of workers from low- to higher-productivity sectors). Our analysis suggests that the weak expansion of the RNFE may have contributed to this lackluster performance.

The second objective is to empirically examine the structure of the RNFE. The section "Pakistan's Rural Nonfarm Economy" describes a new economy-wide database, or social accounting matrix (SAM), that distinguishes between both producers and households in peri-urban and more remote rural areas. This database, which includes estimates (constructed from national accounts, household surveys, and other information) of various types of households' sources of income, forms the basis for a new economy-wide model of Pakistan described in the section "Measuring Growth and Poverty Linkages." The model provides a simulation laboratory for experimenting with alternative sources of economic growth.

The chapter's final objective is to evaluate the implications of growth in agricultural and rural nonfarm sectors for poverty reduction in Pakistan. The economy-wide model is used to compare the welfare gains for poor households from growth driven by agriculture (that is, crops or livestock) with these households' gains from growth driven by nonagriculture (that is, manufacturing or services). Taking advantage of the spatial dimensions of the new SAM, the scenarios also contrast the welfare effects of growth in peri-urban and rural areas. Finally, we consider how improvements in Pakistan's energy supply and urban economic growth might also benefit the poor.

Overall, our findings suggest that growth in agriculture is still most effective at raising the incomes of Pakistan's poorest rural households. However, the RNFE is only slightly behind agriculture in the "pro-poorness" of its growth. Moreover, rural *manufacturing* growth (that is, agro-processing) is even more effective than agriculture in raising incomes among the poor, especially in more remote rural areas. Our analysis therefore supports efforts to raise the profile of the RNFE in Pakistan's national development strategies and policies.

Agriculture and Structural Change in Pakistan

Agriculture has lagged behind the rest of the economy over the past decade. Agricultural GDP per capita was virtually unchanged between 2005/2006 and

TABLE 12.1 Employment and labor productivity in Pakistan, 2005/2006–2013/2014

Indicator	Value		Annual growth rate or total point change (%)
	2005/2006	2013/2014	
Population (millions)	155.4	185.3	2.23
Rural population share (%)	66.5	65.3	−1.18
National youth (10–24 years) share (%)	33.2	32.9	−0.29
Youth in rural areas (%)	32.1	32.1	0.02
Total employment (millions)	47.0	56.5	2.35
Rural employment share (%)	69.2	69.1	−0.04
Informal sector share (%)	72.9	73.6	0.70
Rural nonfarm employment (millions)	13.0	15.5	2.19
Share of total rural employment (%)	40.1	39.7	−0.47
Employment share (%)	100.0	100.0	0.00
Agriculture	43.4	43.5	0.11
Industry	20.7	22.5	1.75
Services	35.9	34.1	−1.85
Value added per worker (US$)	2,325	2,560	1.21
Agriculture	1,233	1,239	0.06
Industry	17,875	16,110	0.65
Services	11,746	14,508	−1.63
Value added per capita (US$)	702.4	780.7	1.33

Source: Authors' calculations using the 2005/2006 and 2013/2014 Labor Force Surveys (PBS 2012, 2015) and national accounts data (PBS 2013a, 2014).

Note: US dollars are measured in constant 2005/2006 prices.

2013/2014 compared to 1.2 and 1.8 percent growth in industry and services, respectively. The main drivers of nonagricultural growth during this period were small-scale manufacturing and transportation and government services. Together, these sectors accounted for 30 percent of the increase in total GDP, which is much higher than their 20 percent share of GDP in 2005/2006. Accordingly, these sectors saw their GDP shares increase while agriculture's share steadily declined. Within agriculture, livestock grew relatively quickly at 3.3 percent per year—more than twice the growth rate of crop GDP.

Table 12.1 reports changes in employment patterns between 2005/2006 and 2013/2014. The table shows how Pakistan's population has been urbanizing at a fairly slow pace. The share of youth in the working-age population is high at nearly one-third, and this is only gradually declining from the peaks of early in the 2000–2009 decade. It is urban populations who are aging, while the share of youth in the rural population has remained unchanged. This partly explains why the share of employment in rural areas remained constant despite ongoing urbanization. Agriculture continues to create most of the new jobs in rural areas, with the share of employment in the RNFE falling slightly. Nevertheless, employment in nonfarm activities still accounted for two out of every five rural jobs in 2013/2014, thus underscoring the importance of the RNFE for Pakistan. At the national level, the increased share of industrial-sector jobs in national employment was almost offset by a declining share of service-sectors jobs, leaving little change in the share of total jobs in agriculture. Overall, labor productivity increased modestly over the past decade, with value added per worker rising from US$2,325 in 2005/2006 to US$2,560 in 2013/2014.[1] Note that because value added includes both returns to labor (wages and salaries) and returns to land and capital (rents and profits), incomes of laborers are less than value added per worker.

This chapter is primarily concerned with how the benefits of economic growth are distributed throughout the population. One of the main channels through which economic growth affects households, particularly poorer households, is through jobs. Economic growth benefits households if it leads to higher wages within workers' existing sectors of employment or if it creates new job opportunities in sectors that command higher returns. The migration of workers from low- to higher-productivity sectors is called "positive structural change" and is a process typically associated with sustained economic development (McMillan, Rodrik, and Verduzco-Gallo 2014).

Using the data behind Table 12.1, we examine whether economic growth in Pakistan over the past decade was associated with positive structural change. We decompose changes in labor productivity (that is, GDP per worker) into two components. The first component—termed the "within sectors" component—is the sum of sectoral productivity gains weighted by initial employment shares (that is, assuming no change in sectoral employment shares over the past decade). The second "structural change" component is the additional productivity gains from reallocating workers between sectors with different levels of productivity (after accounting for productivity changes within each sector). When workers move from low to high productivity sectors or when job creation is faster in higher-productivity sectors, then structural change is said to have contributed positively to national labor productivity growth.

---

1   All $ in this chapter denote US dollars measured in constant prices.

TABLE 12.2 Decomposition of gains in labor productivity, 2005/2006–2013/2014

Sector	Change in value added per worker (US$)		
	Within-sectors	Between-sectors	Total change
Total for all sectors	326.6	−91.8	234.8
Agriculture	2.5	1.3	3.8
Industry	−1.4	47.3	45.9
Services	325.5	−140.4	185.1

Source: Authors' calculations using the 2005/2006 and 2013/2014 Labor Force Surveys (PBS 2012, 2015) and national accounts data (PBS 2013a, 2014).

Table 12.2 reports the results from the productivity growth decomposition for the period 2005/2006–2013/2014.[2] As mentioned earlier, the total increase in value added per worker over eight years was about US$235 (final column in table). The decomposition reveals that most of this gain (US$185.1) originated from within the services sector, with a smaller contribution from industry (US$45.9) and a negligible contribution from agriculture (US$3.8). Moreover, while worker productivity rose over the past decade, this was entirely due to labor productivity gains occurring *within* sectors (US$326.6). In fact this growth period in Pakistan was associated with *negative* structural change (−US$91.8), with workers moving out of higher-productivity service sectors into lower-productivity industrial sectors. Put another way, a disproportionate share of the new jobs created over the past eight years were in industry rather than services.

Figure 12.1 provides more detailed results. The vertical axis shows initial value added per worker. A positive value means that a sector generated above-average value added per worker in 2005/2006. The horizontal axis shows the percentage point change in employment shares between 2005/2006 and 2013/2014. A negative value means that a sector's share of total employment has fallen, even if it has grown in absolute terms. Finally, the size of the circles represents a sector's initial contribution to total employment. Agriculture has the largest circle because two out of every five Pakistanis are farmers.

As indicated by their position along the vertical axis, agriculture (AGR) and construction (CON) have the lowest average value added per worker in Pakistan. The highest labor productivity is in mining, electricity, and natural

2   The data used for the decomposition comes from the 2001/2002 and 2013/2014 Labor Force Surveys (PBS 2012, 2015) and official national accounts data (PBS 2013a, 2014). The Labor Force Surveys covered all urban and rural areas in the four provinces but excluded Federally Administered Tribal Areas and military restricted areas (that is, about 2 percent of the total population).

FIGURE 12.1 Structural change in Pakistan's employment patterns, 2005/2006–2013/2014

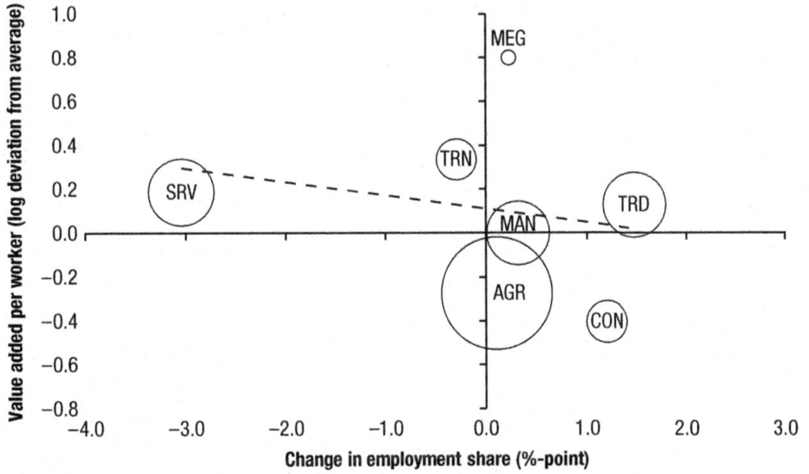

Source: Authors' calculations using the 2005/2006 and 2013/2014 Labor Force Surveys (PBS 2012, 2015) and national accounts data (PBS 2013a, 2014).
Note: Size of circles equals sector's initial employment share. AGR = agriculture; MAN = manufacturing; MEG = mining, electricity, and gas; CON = construction; TRD = trade and hotel services; TRN = transportation and communication; SRV = public administration, health, education, and other private services.

gas (MEG). The MEG sectors are some of the most capital-intensive sectors in the economy, so the capital value added generated per worker is high.[3] The figure shows that there was a sizable reduction in the share of labor working in transportation and communications services (TRN) and the "other services" sector (SRV). The latter includes business and community services (for example, education, health, and social work). This reduction was only partly offset by an increase in employment within trade services (TRD), although this has lower value added per worker than other services. This explains the negative structural change occurring within services. In contrast, there was an increase in employment shares for all industrial sectors, including manufacturing (MAN). On average, the industrial sectors have lower labor productivity than services, so industry's rising share of employment led to negative overall structural change in the economy.

---

3 Note that a high value added per worker does not imply that workers' wages or salaries are high. In other words, labor productivity may be high because workers are coupled with machines with high returns or use value.

Agriculture has played a modest role in growth processes over the past decade. Its share of national employment and its average value added per worker remained virtually unchanged, suggesting that the sector's main contribution was in helping the economy absorb the growing number of young job seekers in rural areas. Data from the labor force surveys indicate that 46 percent of the increase in nonfarm jobs in Pakistan between 2005/2006 and 2013/2014 was in rural areas. Of the 6.6 million new jobs in rural areas, 2.5 million were in the RNFE.

Unfortunately, it is not possible to accurately estimate the RNFE's contribution to negative structural change in Pakistan because national accounts do not disaggregate sectoral value added across rural and urban areas. However, the labor force surveys report a disproportionate increase in rural manufacturing and construction jobs and a large decline in rural employment within "other services" (mainly within the education sector). This suggests that much of the shift in employment patterns that led to negative structural change in Pakistan occurred within the RNFE. If we assume that value added per worker in rural areas is half that of urban workers, then the RNFE accounted for about half of the negative structural change that occurred between 2005/2006 and 2013/2014. If labor productivity is the same in rural and urban areas, then the RNFE economy accounted for as much as two-thirds of the negative structural change.

In summary, not only did Pakistan's economy grow fairly slowly over the past decade, but the growth that did occur was associated with negative structural change. Most of this negative structural change is likely to have occurred within the RNFE, especially because agricultural productivity and its rate of labor absorption remained virtually unchanged. This suggests that the performance of the RNFE significantly influences national development outcomes, so the sector should not be overlooked when designing pro-poor growth strategies. In the next section, we examine the structure of the RNFE in greater detail, including its linkages to the broader economy and to the incomes of poor households.

Pakistan's Rural Nonfarm Economy

National Economic Structure

Table 12.3 describes the structure of Pakistan's economy in 2010/2011, derived from the new SAM that was purpose-built for this chapter (see below). Agriculture generated about one-quarter of national GDP, and this was fairly

TABLE 12.3 National economic structure, 2010/2011

Sectors	Share of total (%)			Exports/ output (%)	Imports/ demand (%)
	GDP	Exports	Imports		
Total GDP/exports/imports	100.0	100.0	100.0	5.3	9.2
Agriculture	25.9	2.4	2.7	0.8	1.5
Crops	12.0	1.5	2.7	1.0	3.1
Livestock	13.2	0.0	0.0	0.0	0.0
Other agriculture	0.8	0.9	0.0	8.5	0.0
Industry	22.1	86.9	80.9	9.7	15.5
Mining	2.9	1.9	0.0	5.8	0.0
Manufacturing	14.8	85.0	80.9	13.3	20.3
Food processing	4.6	9.5	10.4	3.8	7.9
Textiles and clothing	4.1	60.1	2.4	31.6	2.7
Other manufacturing	6.0	15.4	68.1	6.5	36.7
Other industry	4.4	0.0	0.0	0.0	0.0
Services	51.9	10.7	16.3	1.8	3.4

Source: Authors' calculations using the 2010/2011 Pakistan Social Accounting Matrix (IFPRI 2016).

Note: The table reports exports as a share of total output for each sector, and imports as a share of total domestic demand for each product group. Higher values mean that more of a sector's output is exported to foreign markets, or that imports satisfy a larger share of product demand in domestic markets.

evenly divided between crops and livestock. In contrast, while agriculture was responsible for almost half of all employment in 2007, four out of five of these jobs were from growing crops rather than from livestock. Finally, forestry and fishing, that is, "other agriculture," are relatively minor subsectors.

The manufacturing sector is as important as agriculture in its contribution to national GDP. That being said, one-third of manufacturing GDP comes from food processing, including foods and sugar refining. Worker productivity is fairly high in manufacturing; for example, GDP per worker is twice as high as agriculture's. As such, manufacturing's share of employment is lower than its share of GDP. The one exception is textiles, which is the most labor-intensive manufacturing subsector, although it is still only half as labor-intensive as agriculture. Manufacturing is the country's main source of exports (for example, textiles and clothing), and import demand (for example, machinery and vehicles; see "other manufacturing" in the table). Finally, while energy and construction (denoted "other industry" in the table) are crucial industrial sectors, together they account for less than 5 percent of total GDP. Nevertheless, these sectors play a broader role in the economy, that is, in supplying electricity and new capital to other sectors.

Services generate more than one-half of national GDP and one-third of employment. Trade and transportation services alone account for one-third of GDP and one-quarter of employment. Services therefore include some of the more labor-intensive economic activities in Pakistan. They also include some of the least labor-intensive subsectors, such as finance and public administration. These two subsectors are particularly skills intensive, so most of the returns to labor accrue to a relatively small number of higher-paid workers. These characteristics of production and trade are important in our analysis when measuring the effects of sector-level growth on household incomes.

Identifying Rural, Peri-urban, and Urban Areas

Rural and urban areas operate along a continuum that stretches from remote rural areas with little infrastructure and few public services to densely populated major cities with diverse economies and public and private resources. Most studies and statistics in Pakistan separate rural and urban areas. Given that there is still considerable heterogeneity within rural areas, we distinguish between peri-urban areas situated closer to urban centers and more remote rural areas.

In defining *peri-urban areas*, we follow the approach described in Kedir, Schmidt, and Waqas (2014). The authors develop an agglomeration index for 2010 using a range of GIS data, including travel time, population densities, and other nationally collected biophysical and infrastructure variables (for example, roads, railroads, and water bodies). The agglomeration index identifies urban areas by taking into account three indicators: population size of a major city, population density, and travel time to a major city. Urban, peri-urban, and rural areas are identified using a set of threshold criteria. An area is classified as *urban* if the population density is greater than 150 people per square kilometer and the area is located within one hours' travel time from a city of at least 500,000 people. *Peri-urban areas* are locations between one and three hours' travel time from a city of at least 500,000 people regardless of population density (and under one hour's travel time from a city of at least 500,000 if population density is less than 150 people per square kilometer). Finally, *rural areas* are designated as being more than three hours' travel time from a city of at least 500,000 people, regardless of population density.

Kedir, Schmidt, and Waqas (2014) estimated that 32 percent and 38 percent of Pakistan's total population in 2010 lived in urban and peri-urban areas, respectively. The former is close to the roughly 35 percent urban population share reported in the 2013/2014 Labor Force Survey (see Table 12.1). Unfortunately, the 2011/2012 *Household Integrated Expenditure*

Survey (HIES) (PBS 2013b), which is the main survey used to construct the SAM, has a tehsil as its smallest spatial unit.[4] We use the agglomeration index to estimate the share of households within each tehsil residing in rural, peri-urban, and urban areas. We then adopt the HIES definition of urban areas in order to remain consistent with other studies. For the remaining non-urban areas that official statistics call "rural," we set an 80 percent peri-urban population threshold, at which point we classify all households within a tehsil as living in a "peri-urban tehsil." So, for example, if 85 percent of a tehsil's population live in peri-urban conditions (according to the agglomeration index) then we assume that the remaining 15 percent of rural households are also peri-urban. This is clearly a rough approximation of the higher-resolution approach found in Kedir, Schmidt, and Waqas (2014). Nonetheless, we generate by this method a peri-urban population share of 40 percent, which is, by design, close to the authors' 38 percent.

Having identified peri-urban areas in HIES, we then used the survey to disaggregate the national SAM across rural, peri-urban, and urban areas. The SAM reconciles a wide range of data sources, including national accounts, trade and tax information, and agricultural and industrial census and survey data.[5] The HIES is used to disaggregate households and workers into different groups. The incomes and expenditures reported by households in the survey rarely match each other, so it is necessary to reconcile these flows. Moreover, the household survey does not capture as much of Pakistan's economy as national accounts, and this inadequate coverage explains some of the imbalances contained in the initial SAM. We use cross-entropy estimation techniques to remove these imbalances (see Robinson, Cattaneo, and El-Said 2001). This approach equates household income and expenditure flows while making as few adjustments as possible to the original survey data. The final SAM represents a "best estimate" of the structural characteristics of Pakistan's rural and urban economies.

Characteristics of the Rural Nonfarm Economy

Table 12.4 shows how the national economic structure described in Table 12.3 is now divided across rural, peri-urban, and urban areas. Note that "rural" in this table (and all subsequent tables) refers to officially defined rural areas

---

4   A *tehsil* is a subdistrict administrative unit, which consists of a collection of union councils and villages.

5   Dorosh, Niazi, and Nazli (2003) describe an earlier 2001/2002 SAM for Pakistan and use the model for multiplier analysis.

TABLE 12.4 Regional economic structure characteristics, 2010/2011

Indicator	National	Rural	Peri-urban	Urban
GDP (US$ billions)	202.0	42.4	64.9	94.7
Regional GDP share (%)	100.0	21.0	32.1	46.9
Total population (millions)	130.4	35.5	51.5	43.3
Regional share (%)	100.0	27.3	39.5	33.2
Population in the lowest consumption quartile (millions)	32.6	12.4	14.3	5.9
Regional share (%)	100.0	37.9	44.0	18.2
Share of region's total population (%)	25.0	34.7	27.8	13.7
GDP per capita (US$)	1,550	1,194	1,260	2,185
Share of total GDP (%)	100.0	100.0	100.0	100.0
Agriculture (%)	25.2	50.5	43.8	2.7
Crops (%)	12.0	23.7	19.6	1.5
Livestock (%)	13.2	25.7	22.8	0.9
Other agriculture (%)	0.8	1.0	1.3	0.3
Industry (%)	22.1	16.3	18.1	27.5
Manufacturing (%)	14.8	6.5	9.8	21.9
Services (%)	51.9	33.2	38.1	69.8

Source: Authors' calculations using the 2010/2011 Pakistan Social Accounting Matrix (IFPRI 2016) and Pakistan CGE model.

less those areas that we have classified as being "peri-urban." In other words, combining rural and peri-urban areas in Table 12.4 gives officially defined rural areas.

Urban areas account for almost half of national GDP in Pakistan, but only about one-third of the population. As such, average GDP per capita in urban areas is higher than the national average. In contrast, rural and peri-urban areas account for a lower share of national GDP than they do of the national population. GDP per capita is only slightly higher in peri-urban areas than in rural areas. Nevertheless, a much larger share of the *rural* population (34.7 percent) falls into the country's lowest per capita consumption quartile (that is, our definition of poor households). By comparison, only about 14 percent of the urban population are in the lowest quartile.

Despite having similar GDP per capita, the rural and peri-urban economies differ in their structural characteristics. Agriculture in the rural economy, for example, generates approximately 51 percent of total GDP compared to approximately 44 percent in peri-urban areas. The peri-urban economy, on the other hand, has a larger manufacturing sector, although even here manufacturing is much smaller than in urban areas, where it makes up a little over

TABLE 12.5 Household income and expenditure characteristics, 2010/2011

Indicators	National	Lowest quartile	Other quartiles	Rural	Peri-urban	Urban
Population (millions)	130.4	32.6	97.8	35.5	51.5	43.3
Share (%)	100.0	25.0	75.0	27.3	39.5	33.2
Income per capita (US$)	1,615	526	1,978	1,044	1,275	2,487
Consumption per capita (US$)	1,300	503	1,565	917	1,074	1,882
Total expenditure share (%)	100	100	100	100	100	100
Food (%)	38.5	56.0	37.0	48.2	43.2	32.4
Nonfood (%)	42.0	39.5	42.2	39.6	41.1	43.3
Direct taxes (%)	2.1	0.0	2.3	0.7	1.3	3.1
Savings (%)	17.4	4.4	18.5	11.5	14.5	21.2
Total income share (%)	100.0	100.0	100.0	100.0	100.0	100.0
Labor (%)	33.9	51.1	32.4	36.8	31.5	34.5
Farm (%)	5.3	9.3	4.9	12.5	8.5	0.8
Low education (%)	13.2	36.1	11.2	16.0	14.3	11.6
High education (%)	15.5	5.7	16.3	8.2	8.8	22.1
Cropland (%)	8.8	12.3	8.5	21.2	14.8	0.9
Livestock capital (%)	10.7	15.6	10.2	23.8	19.8	0.6
Informal nonfarm capital (%)	17.9	17.1	18.0	10.3	19.3	19.8
Formal nonfarm capital (%)	22.7	0.0	24.8	2.6	7.1	39.2
Government transfers (%)	0.7	1.8	0.6	1.3	0.7	0.5
Foreign remittances (%)	5.2	2.1	5.5	4.1	6.8	4.6

Source: Authors' calculations using the 2010/2011 Pakistan Social Accounting Matrix (IFPRI 2016).

Note: National per capita consumption spending is used to derive household expenditure quartiles. Percentages may not sum to 100 due to rounding errors.

one-fifth of total urban GDP. Most rural manufacturing is in food processing, whereas even peri-urban areas have some textiles and clothing as well as metals and machinery production. This indicates that the RNFE becomes more diverse as one moves to peri-urban and urban areas. That being said, at the regional level, the rural and peri-urban economies have much more in common with each other than they do with the urban economy. While there is some urban agriculture in Pakistan, this is a relatively small sector.

Table 12.5 describes household income and expenditure patterns at the national and regional levels. Two things should be noted from the table. First, like in Table 12.4, the total population is 130 million, which is below the 185 million reported in Table 12.1. This is because the HIES excludes certain more remote rural areas. Second, average per capita income is higher than average per capita GDP because households are net beneficiaries of government transfers that are partially paid for by net foreign capital inflows, such as foreign aid and foreign borrowing.

Households in the lowest quartile earned and spent about US$500 per person in 2010/2011 (at market exchange rates). Almost all of this income was used for consumption spending, primarily on food products. Households in the other quartiles (that is, the second, third, and fourth) allocated a smaller share of their incomes to food and had higher average savings rates than poor households. Higher quartile households also paid direct taxes and made social contributions to the government. The differences in expenditure patterns between rural, peri-urban, and urban households largely reflect the fact that a greater share of urban households are in higher-consumption quartiles.

Income patterns show greater variation across regional household groups. Poorer and rural households are more dependent on labor incomes, particularly farm labor and less educated labor. They are more reliant on agriculture for their livelihoods, including incomes from crops and livestock. Peri-urban and urban households, on the other hand, are more likely to engage in nonfarm self-employment, as reflected in their larger income shares from informal capital returns. At the national level, incomes from nonfarm enterprises (as reflected in informal capital returns) are similar for households in the lowest and higher quartiles. Finally, even though rural and poorer households pay less in taxes to the government, a larger share of their incomes comes from government transfers (for example, state pensions and social grants). Higher-income households are more likely to receive remittance incomes from family members living and working abroad. Overall, while GDP per capita is similar for rural and peri-urban households, on average, the sources of income vary significantly across these two regions. This justifies disaggregating the SAM across rural and peri-urban areas.

Table 12.6 examines rural households' economic characteristics in greater detail. We separate households into small-scale and medium/large-scale farmers (that is, small-scale farmers cultivate less than 12.5 acres of cropland). Per capita incomes for small-scale farmers are less than half those of medium/large-scale farmers. Small-scale farmers derive a larger share of their incomes from livestock, as opposed to crops, than medium/large-scale farmers do, and they earn more of their incomes from nonfarm enterprises (that is, informal capital). We also separate out farmers who do not own their own land but instead rent cropland or are sharecroppers. These non-landowning farmers may cultivate small, medium, or large-scale farms, but as a group, they derive a larger share of their incomes from nonfarm enterprises than do landowning

TABLE 12.6 Rural and peri-urban household income and expenditure characteristics

Indicator	Farm households				Nonfarm households	
	Small-scale	Medium/ large-scale	Non-landowning	Farm wage laborer	Rural	Peri-urban
Population (millions)	19.8	3.1	10.6	14.6	14.5	24.4
Share of national population (%)	15.2	2.4	8.2	11.2	11.1	18.7
Income per capita (US$)	1,475	3,228	1,248	763	802	1,127
Consumption per capita (US$)	1,253	2,449	1,120	731	710	927
Total expenditure share (%)	100.0	100.0	100.0	100.0	100.0	100.0
Food (%)	46.4	37.6	50.4	54.8	47.4	38.6
Nonfood (%)	38.5	38.3	39.4	41.0	41.2	43.6
Direct taxes (%)	0.5	0.5	2.0	0.7	1.2	1.5
Savings (%)	14.6	23.7	8.2	3.5	10.2	16.3
Total income share (%)	100.0	100.0	100.0	100.0	100.0	100.0
Labor (%)	22.1	25.6	28.7	42.1	56.6	37.2
Farm (%)	15.5	21.6	15.1	13.7	0.0	0.0
Low education (%)	3.8	0.8	9.0	20.7	36.8	23.0
High education (%)	2.7	3.2	4.7	7.7	19.8	14.2
Cropland (%)	27.6	45.7	37.4	0.0	0.0	0.0
Livestock capital (%)	38.8	25.4	21.3	45.7	0.0	0.0
Informal nonfarm capital (%)	5.7	0.9	8.6	9.0	24.7	35.3
Formal nonfarm capital (%)	0.0	0.0	0.0	0.0	8.3	16.9
Government transfers (%)	0.6	0.3	0.8	1.3	2.2	0.9
Foreign remittances (%)	5.2	2.1	3.2	1.9	8.2	9.7

Source: Authors' calculations using the 2010/2011 Pakistan Social Accounting Matrix (IFPRI 2016).

Note: Share of national population derived from national population estimate of 130.4 million. National per capita consumption spending is used to derive household expenditure quartiles.

farmers. Finally, about 11 percent of Pakistan's population are in rural households that do not cultivate land but instead work as wage laborers on other households' farmland. Wage laborer households do not earn cropland returns, but they do earn farm labor incomes. They are, however, most dependent on livestock earnings and on low-educated nonfarm labor wages. Overall, per capita incomes decline for farmers with greater dependence on rented lands or farm wages.

Finally, we compare nonfarm households in rural and peri-urban areas. Rural nonfarm households have lower average per capita incomes than farm households have, which is consistent with findings from other studies (see, for example, Kousar and Abdulai 2013). Rural nonfarm households are more dependent on labor incomes than peri-urban nonfarm households are. Peri-urban households, on the other hand, generate more of their incomes from nonfarm enterprises, which is consistent with there being fewer barriers to entry in the nonfarm sector within peri-urban areas, possibly due to improved access to input, output, and financial markets (see SPDC 2012). Nonfarm households in both areas earn a greater share of their incomes from foreign remittances than do farm households. Evidence suggests that these remittances may help overcome certain barriers to entry into the RNFE, such as by helping households acquire productive assets (see Adams 1998).

The new spatial SAM reveals considerable heterogeneity within rural areas. While our treatment of the rural-urban continuum is still somewhat coarse, the distinction between "rural" and "peri-urban" reveals notable differences between farm and nonfarm households in these areas. In the previous section, we found that the RNFE has been a major source of recent employment patterns and structural change in Pakistan. Two-thirds of the expansion of industrial employment over the past decade, for example, occurred within the RNFE. In this section, we found that this industrial expansion is more likely to have occurred in peri-urban areas, where industry is a more important economic activity. What is not clear is to what extent slow nonfarm growth and negative structural change explains the persistence of rural poverty over the past decade. Conversely, it is difficult to determine what the implications of a renewed expansion of the RNFE would be for future poverty reduction and agricultural development, and hence whether greater attention should be paid to the RNFE in Pakistan's national strategies and policies. The sections that follow develop an economy-wide model of Pakistan and use this to answer these questions.

Measuring Growth and Poverty Linkages

Economic growth is measured by GDP, whereas poverty is determined by the level and distribution of household consumption. The well-known national accounting identity below provides a useful framework for explaining GDP and consumption linkages. The key point to note is that GDP not only consists of private consumption C but also investment demand I, government consumption G, and the foreign trade balance (that is, exports X less imports M). It is clear from the identity that an increase in GDP need not lead to a proportional increase in private consumption. The extent to which GDP growth affects private consumption is determined top-down by the mechanisms that govern macroeconomic balances (that is, changes in aggregate consumption, investment, and trade). Of course, the macroeconomic aggregates are themselves determined bottom-up by a country's unique economic structures and the behavior of its economic agents (for example, individual producers and consumers and the government). One of the main features of the Pakistani model is that it tracks changes in economic outcomes at both the micro- and macroeconomic levels.

$$GDP = (C + I + G) + (X - M)$$

We first describe how GDP is determined in the model.[6] Using information from the 2010/2011 SAM, the model separates Pakistan's economy into 64 sectors and three regions (that is, rural, peri-urban, or urban). Producers in each sector and region use a unique combination of land, labor, capital, and intermediate inputs.[7] Resources are assumed to be in limited supply, so in order to increase production, producers must compete with one another by, for example, offering higher wages to workers. We assume that regional labor markets are segmented by education levels, that is, workers who have completed secondary schooling are in the "high skilled" labor market, and those without secondary schooling are in the "low skilled" market. Workers within regional markets can migrate across sectors within, but not between, the farm and nonfarm economies. This reflects seasonal labor constraints for farm households but allows farmers to allocate their time to nonfarm activities outside of the growing season. Agricultural land is separated into lands operated by small-scale farmers (less than 12.5 acres), medium-scale farmers (between 12.5 and 50 acres), and large-scale farmers (more than 50 acres). Note that the model distinguishes between farmers who operate their own lands and those who rent others' lands or who are sharecroppers. Farmers can reallocate their lands between crops. Finally, the model distinguishes between formal and informal sector capital because these have different implications for distributional outcomes (Tables 12.5 and 12.6). The level of aggregate GDP is therefore the result of complex interactions between sectoral and regional resource constraints and producer technologies and behavior.

We next consider how private consumption C is determined in the model. Households or consumers are the main recipients of land, labor, and capital

---

6 For a detailed specification and discussion of the core model, see Diao and Thurlow (2012). Table A12.1 in Annex A describes in detail the model's sectors, factors, and households.

7 Producers substitute between factors based on relative prices. This behavior is governed by a constant elasticity of substitution (CES) function, with intermediate demand derived from fixed shares within a Leontief function.

incomes. Households also have other sources of income, such as foreign remittances or social transfers from the government. Households use their incomes to pay taxes, consume goods and services, and save. The model separates all households in the country into groups using information from the 2010/2011 HIES. Households are separated into rural, peri-urban, and urban areas and according to whether they are crop farmers or not. Farmers are further divided into small and medium/large-scale farms, landless (non-landowning) farmers, and those who work on other people's farms. Finally, households are grouped according to per capita consumption quartiles. Each of the 28 representative household groups in the model has unique income and expenditure patterns, reflecting differences in their factor endowments, income levels, and consumer preferences.[8]

So far we have explained the derivation of GDP and private consumption. Next we consider how the model tracks the other components in the national accounting identity. Government consumption G depends on tax revenue collections. The government in the model collects indirect taxes imposed on the sale of goods and services and direct taxes imposed on household incomes and formal corporate profits. These revenues are used to finance the public consumption of goods and services, including administration, health, and education services. Any remaining revenues are used to finance public investments. The government may also borrow from domestic banks and other sources in order to finance public investments.

The model captures changes in imports M and exports X by allowing producers and consumers to shift between domestic and foreign goods depending on changes in relative prices. If the world price of a good falls relative to its domestic equivalent, then consumers increase their demand for the foreign good. Conversely, falling world prices prompts producers to supply more to domestic markets.[9] Pakistan is a small economy, so we assume that domestic decisions do not affect world prices.

The "current account" tracks the supply and demand of foreign exchange. For the current account to be balanced, total import payments M must equal the sum of total export earnings X plus any foreign remittance incomes or capital inflows. The current account is measured in foreign rather than local currency. In order to capture the scarcity of foreign exchange in Pakistan, we

---

8 Households' consumption behavior is governed by a linear expenditure system of demand with nonunitary income elasticities estimated from household survey data.

9 Import demand is governed by a CES Armington function and exports by a constant elasticity of transformation (CET) function. Elasticities of substitution between domestic and foreign goods are taken from Dimaranan (2006).

assume that foreign capital inflows are fixed and the real exchange rate adjusts to equate the supply and demand of foreign exchange.

The final component in the national accounting identity is investment demand I. Standard accounting rules dictate that total investment must equal total savings in equilibrium. The latter includes private, public, and foreign savings (that is, capital inflows). We want to minimize any biases resulting from assumptions about the behavior of the macroeconomic aggregates in the accounting identity. For example, we do not want GDP growth to benefit only private consumers because this is likely to overestimate household welfare gains. We therefore assume that any changes in the nominal value of absorption (that is, $C + I + G$) is evenly distributed across absorption's three components. This is a distribution-neutral assumption governing the model's macroeconomic adjustment mechanisms or "closures."

The Pakistani model is recursive dynamic and is run annually over a five-year period. Between years, the model is updated to reflect growth in the population, land and labor supply, and productivity. More importantly, the previous period's investment determines the availability of new capital, after accounting for depreciation. New capital stocks are allocated to sectors based on their relative profitability. Sectors with above-average profits receive a larger share of new capital than their existing share of capital stocks (see Diao and Thurlow 2012). Once invested, new capital becomes locked in place and cannot be repurposed for use in other sectors.

In summary, the Pakistani model provides a comprehensive and consistent framework that links sector-level economic growth to household-level incomes and consumption spending. The model provides a simulation laboratory for experimenting with alternative sources of growth and allows researchers to trace the effects of national growth on household incomes and welfare.

Growth and Poverty Scenarios

Baseline and Alternative Scenarios

We first establish a baseline growth scenario. Following the growth patterns described in "Agriculture and Structural Change in Pakistan," we assume that population and labor supply grow at just over 2 percent per year. *Pakistan Economic Surveys* (see GoP 2014) suggest that the total cultivated land area remained virtually unchanged after 2005/2006, so we impose a zero land expansion rate on the model. We also control the amount of capital in the energy sector so that it tracks the observed supply of electricity, which grew

TABLE 12.7 Required GDP growth-rate acceleration, for each sector/regional growth scenario, in order to achieve national GDP target (percentage-point increase over baseline scenario outcomes)

Sectors leading the growth acceleration	Regions leading the growth acceleration			
	All Pakistan	Rural areas	Peri-urban areas	Urban areas
All	0.20	0.98	0.65	0.43
Farm sectors	0.73	1.82	1.37	n.a.
Crops	n.a.	4.68	4.14	n.a.
Livestock	n.a.	4.01	2.67	n.a.
Nonfarm sectors	0.26	2.00	1.15	n.a.
Manufacturing	n.a.	16.96	8.44	n.a.
Services	n.a.	4.28	2.43	n.a.
Electricity sector	1.94	n.a.	n.a.	n.a.

Source: Pakistan CGE model results.

Note: GDP = gross domestic product; n.a. = not applicable.

more slowly than the population. In the absence of supporting data, we assume that national capital stocks grow at a 3 percent per year rate after applying a 5 percent annual depreciation rate. Finally, total factor productivity (TFP) grows faster in the nonagricultural sectors, that is, at 1 and 2 percent per year in industry and services, respectively, compared to only 0.5 percent per year in agriculture.

The baseline scenario produces total GDP growth of 4 percent per year, which is similar to observed economic patterns during 2005/2006–2013/2014. It is worth noting that the baseline is only of marginal interest for our analysis, because it merely provides a common reference point for analysis of subsequent scenarios. Nevertheless, our baseline broadly conforms to Pakistan's recent economic trends, including slower-than-average agricultural growth.

We accelerate economic growth from the baseline trajectory by increasing TFP in different sectors (for example, agriculture or manufacturing) and regions (for example, rural or peri-urban areas). This does not imply that growth is restricted to these sectors, because there are spillover effects resulting from production and consumption linkages (Haggblade, Hazell, and Dorosh 2007). We therefore refer to these simulations as being "led" by a specific sector, for example, manufacturing-led growth. In order to control for the different size of each sector, we target the same percentage increase in total GDP per capita in all growth scenarios, that is, a 0.2 percentage point increase in the average annual growth rate of total GDP over the five-year simulation period.

Table 12.7 reports the required increases in the GDP growth rates *of the targeted sectors and regions*, that is, the sectors and regions that are leading the growth acceleration. Each entry in the table corresponds to a separate growth scenario. The rows identify the targeted sectors, and the columns are the targeted regions. For example, when the target is all sectors and regions, the total increase in the combined GDP growth rate of these targeted sectors/regions is 0.2 percentage points (over and above baseline growth). When the target is only farm sectors (in all regions), these sectors must grow at a faster rate of more than 0.7 percentage points in order to achieve the same 0.2 percentage point increase in the *national* GDP growth rate. This is because farming accounts for only one-quarter of total GDP in Pakistan (see Table 12.4). The required growth acceleration increases as we move from targeting national- to regional-level sectors and as we move from agriculture to smaller sectors. Again, all scenarios generate the same absolute increase in national GDP over the simulation period, which is important for making comparisons across growth scenarios.

Comparing Farm and Nonfarm Growth

Table 12.8 reports detailed results for the four national-level growth scenarios. The first scenario uniformly increases TFP growth in all sectors in order to achieve the targeted 0.2 percentage point acceleration in the total GDP growth rate (relative to the baseline). As expected, balanced sectoral growth implies similar 0.2 percentage point increases for most economic indicators. This becomes the reference scenario for comparing subsequent uneven sectoral and regional growth scenarios.

In the second and third scenarios in Table 12.8, we increase TFP growth in the farm and the nonfarm sectors. In the farm-led growth scenario, there is a 0.73 percentage point increase in agricultural growth rate with some small spillover or linkage effects to nonagricultural sectors. In the nonfarm-led growth scenario, there is a 0.26 percentage point increase in the industrial and services GDP growth rate, with only small spillover effects for agriculture. The nonfarm sector generates most of Pakistan's exports, so faster nonfarm productivity growth increases exports and causes the real exchange rate to appreciate (fewer foreign currency units are required per rupee). This makes imports more attractive for domestic consumers, particularly for non-poor households whose consumption baskets tend to be more import intensive. In contrast, faster farm productivity growth faces marketing constraints, which cause agricultural prices to fall, thus reducing returns to cropland and livestock assets. Falling food prices benefit both poor and non-poor

TABLE 12.8 Results from national-level scenarios

Indicators	Baseline growth rate (%)	Deviation from baseline growth rate (%-point)			
		All sectors	Farm sectors	Nonfarm sectors	Electricity sector
GDP at market prices	3.95	0.20	0.20	0.20	0.17
Private consumption	3.58	0.20	0.24	0.18	0.18
Public consumption	5.01	0.20	−0.19	0.33	0.15
Investment demand	3.53	0.19	0.19	0.18	0.13
Exports	5.84	0.22	0.04	0.29	0.51
Imports	4.17	0.20	0.03	0.25	0.45
GDP at factor cost	3.95	0.20	0.20	0.20	0.20
Agriculture	2.35	0.19	0.73	0.01	0.02
Industry	4.43	0.21	0.05	0.26	0.47
Services	4.50	0.20	0.02	0.26	0.17
Real exchange rate	−0.02	0.00	0.19	−0.07	0.09
Labor wages	3.13	0.19	0.39	0.12	0.13
Cropland returns	4.66	0.19	−0.45	0.38	0.30
Livestock returns	5.49	0.22	−0.30	0.38	0.23
Capital returns	3.49	0.20	0.47	0.11	−0.06
Household consumption	3.58	0.20	0.24	0.18	0.18
Lowest quartile	3.63	0.20	0.22	0.19	0.27
Other quartiles	3.58	0.20	0.24	0.18	0.17

Source: Pakistan CGE model results.

Note: GDP = gross domestic product.

households. Overall, we find that farm-led growth is more effective than nonfarm-led growth at raising household consumption spending, including for poorer households.

Finally, given the crucial role of the electricity sector in economic growth, we simulate the effects of increasing electricity generation in Pakistan. According to the *Pakistan Economic Survey* (GoP 2014), a total of 16,600 megawatts (MW) of new system capacity is planned for the period 2013/2014–2018/2019. This is a large expansion given that total capacity in 2012/2013 was 22,800 MW. Our simulated increase in electricity generation is modest by comparison. Nonetheless, the results indicate that improved electricity production is strongly pro-poor, even though more energy-intensive industry and services benefit more than agriculture. Faster overall economic growth under the electricity generation scenario raises demand for

FIGURE 12.2 The poverty-reducing effects of growth led by different sectors or regions

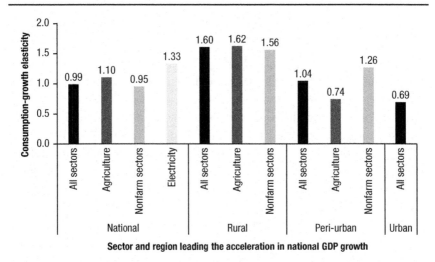

Source: Pakistan CGE model results.
Note: Consumption-growth elasticity is the ratio of average poor household consumption growth to national GDP growth. GDP = gross domestic product.

agricultural products, leading to higher cropland and livestock returns and hence higher incomes for poorer farm households. Overall, however, it is the impact on nonfarm wages and the lower price of electricity that causes poor household incomes to increase by more than what would be expected given the relatively small increase in private consumption. On average, electricity accounts for just over 7 percent of total consumption spending—a share that is fairly constant throughout the income distribution (PBS 2013b). When electricity supply grows more rapidly, it causes energy prices to fall and labor wages in industry and services to rise. This increases real incomes and consumption, particularly for poorer households. Electricity investments are therefore one means of stimulating growth in the RNFE and reducing poverty.

Comparing Rural and Peri-urban Growth

Finally, we examine the implications of productivity growth by region, that is, urban, peri-urban, and rural. Figure 12.2 reports consumption-growth elasticities for households in the lowest per capita consumption quartile. For example, the 0.99 elasticity for the national all sectors scenario means that a 1 percent increase in total GDP driven by all sectors and regions leads to a

0.99 percent increase in the consumption levels of all households within the lowest consumption quartile. This elasticity is higher for national farm (agriculture)-led growth than for national nonfarm-led growth (that is, 1.10 = 0.22 / 0.20 is greater than 0.95 = 0.19 / 0.20), which is consistent with the finding in Table 12.8 that farm-led growth generates larger consumption gains for poorer households. Overall, however, the elasticity for electricity-led growth is higher than for either farm-led or nonfarm-led growth. This suggests that while agricultural growth is important for reducing poverty in Pakistan, it is not likely to be the most effective means of reducing national poverty. Note, however, that this calculation does not include the costs of achieving accelerated productivity growth, which is likely to vary across sectors and by region.

Table 12.9 reports results for more detailed subsector-led growth scenarios and for specific household groups. Growth driven from within rural areas is far more effective than growth driven from urban or peri-urban areas at raising incomes of poorer households. Crop-led growth in rural areas, for example, has an elasticity of 1.91, which is twice the elasticity of national nonfarm-led growth. Livestock-led growth in rural areas is found to be more effective than crop-led growth in raising the incomes of poorer rural farm households. Not surprisingly, rural farm-led growth in general mainly benefits rural households, particularly rural farm households. However, higher rural farm productivity reduces farm goods prices in national markets, and this reduces incomes for peri-urban farmers. The reverse is true for peri-urban agriculture-led growth, which causes a decline in rural farmers' consumption levels.

Importantly, our results suggest that while agriculture-led growth is more effective at the national level at reducing poverty than comparable nonfarm-led growth, this is not the case within peri-urban areas. In these areas, a 1 percent increase in nonfarm GDP raises poor households' incomes by 1.26 percent, which is well above the 0.74 percent from similar growth led by agriculture. If we consider specific subsectors, we find that in peri-urban areas both manufacturing- and services-led growth is more pro-poor for farm households than either crop- or livestock-led growth. Within rural areas, however, services-led growth has similar and even greater poverty-reducing effects compared to agriculture-led growth. Only faster productivity growth in manufacturing is far more beneficial for rural farm households than is agricultural-led growth, including crop-led growth. This is because farm households benefit from rising nonfarm wages and from increased nonfarm households' demand for farm goods. A similar result is obtained from urban-led growth, albeit with smaller gains for farm households and even losses for nonfarm households in rural and peri-urban areas. Finally, growth

TABLE 12.9 Elasticity between national GDP growth and poor household consumption growth

Sector or region leading the growth acceleration	Households in the lowest per capita consumption quartile					
	All households	Rural households		Peri-urban households		Urban households
		Farm	Nonfarm	Farm	Nonfarm	
All Pakistan	0.99	1.03	0.93	1.02	0.94	0.98
Farm sectors	1.10	−0.82	2.89	−0.18	2.96	2.41
Nonfarm sectors	0.95	1.61	0.29	1.40	0.28	0.51
Electricity sector	1.33	1.34	0.81	1.53	1.25	1.48
Rural areas	1.60	3.11	4.54	−0.89	1.14	0.89
Farm sectors	1.62	3.47	2.90	−2.93	2.97	2.12
Crops	1.91	3.03	3.78	−2.70	3.83	2.58
Livestock	1.25	3.25	2.04	−2.77	2.13	1.74
Nonfarm sectors	1.56	2.58	5.97	1.10	−0.59	−0.26
Manufacturing	2.43	4.84	1.16	3.78	−0.07	0.47
Services	1.64	3.02	6.60	1.25	−0.95	−0.76
Peri-urban areas	1.04	−0.83	0.77	2.14	2.81	0.71
Farm sectors	0.74	−3.88	2.86	2.09	2.94	2.10
Crops	1.16	−3.75	3.60	2.38	3.68	2.53
Livestock	0.41	−3.71	2.19	1.62	2.29	1.79
Nonfarm sectors	1.26	1.39	−0.73	2.09	2.69	−0.26
Manufacturing	2.47	4.68	0.18	4.00	0.68	0.51
Services	1.29	1.65	−0.78	2.29	2.63	−0.65
Urban areas	0.69	1.35	−0.52	1.09	−0.39	1.18

Source: Pakistan CGE model results.

Note: GDP = gross domestic product.

in rural services is more effective at improving consumption levels for poorer nonfarm rural households than for farm rural households. This suggests that there are trade-offs between policies targeting sectors within the RNFE, just as there are trade-offs between targeting rural or peri-urban areas. Overall, our results suggest that policies should prioritize rural areas and that growth in rural manufacturing (agro-processing) is the most effective means of reducing poverty.

Conclusions

In spite of continued urbanization and a rising share of nonagriculture in overall GDP, agricultural growth remains crucial for reducing rural poverty in Pakistan, particularly for the one-quarter of the population living relatively far from major urban centers. Increased crop and (especially) livestock productivity have strong poverty-reducing effects in more remote rural areas. Moreover, productivity growth in the RNFE (for example, agro-processing) is also highly pro-poor, suggesting that greater attention should be given to spurring growth in this subsector. Agricultural productivity growth also reduces poverty in peri-urban areas, but here, the rural nonfarm economy is larger, and poor households in these areas gain more from productivity growth in RNFE sectors than from productivity gains in agriculture.

Greater emphasis on the RNFE in Pakistan's national development strategy can help reverse the negative structural change that Pakistan experienced between 2005/2006 and 2013/2014, where employment grew faster in sectors with low average labor productivity (for example, agriculture and services) than in sectors with higher average labor productivity. Without efforts to stimulate job creation and income opportunities in the RNFE, Pakistan will find it difficult to achieve more rapid economic growth, positive structural change, and overall poverty reduction.

References

Adams, R. H. 1998. "Remittances, Investment, and Rural Asset Accumulation in Pakistan." *Economic Development and Cultural Change* 47 (1): 155–173.

Arif, G. M., H. Nazli, and R. Haq. 2000. "Rural Non-agriculture Employment and Poverty in Pakistan." *The Pakistan Development Review* 39 (4): 1089–1110.

Chaudhry, I. S., S. Malik, and M. Ashraf. 2006. "Rural Poverty in Pakistan: Some Related Concepts, Issues and Empirical Analysis." *Pakistan Economic and Social Review* 44 (2): 259–276.

Davis, B., P. Winters, G. Carletto, Katia Covarrubias, E. J. Quinones, A. Zezza, K. Stamoulis, C. Azzarri, and S. Digiuseppe. 2010. "A Cross-country Comparison of Rural Income Generating Activities." *World Development* 38 (1): 48–63.

Diao, X., and J. Thurlow. 2012. "A Recursive Dynamic Computable General Equilibrium Model." In *Strategies and Priorities for African Agriculture: Economywide Perspectives from Country Studies*, edited by X. Diao, J. Thurlow, S. Benin, and S. Fan. Washington, DC: International Food Policy Research Institute.

Dimaranan, B. V. 2006. *Global Trade, Assistance, and Production: The GTAP 6 Database.* Center for Global Trade Analysis, Purdue University.

Dorosh, P., M. K. Niazi, and H. Nazli. 2003. "Distributional Impacts of Agricultural Growth in Pakistan: A Multiplier Analysis." *The Pakistan Development Review* 42 (3): 249–275.

GoP (Government of Pakistan). 2014. *Pakistan Economic Survey 2013/14: Annexure 3.* Islamabad: Ministry of Finance.

Haggblade, S., P. B. R. Hazell, and P. A. Dorosh. 2007. "Sectoral Growth Linkages between Agriculture and the Rural Non-farm Economy." In *Transforming the Rural Nonfarm Economy: Opportunities and Threats in the Developing World,* edited by S. Haggblade, P. B. R. Hazell, and T. Reardon. Baltimore: Johns Hopkins University Press.

Haggblade, S., P. Hazell, and T. Reardon. 2010. "The Rural Non-Farm Economy: Prospects for Growth and Poverty Reduction." *World Development* 38 (10): 1429–1441.

HDIP (Hydrocarbon Development Institute of Pakistan). 2012. *Pakistan Energy Yearbook.* Islamabad: Hydrocarbon Development Institute of Pakistan.

IFPRI (International Food Policy Research Institute). 2016. *2010/11 Social Accounting Matrix for Pakistan.* Washington, DC: International Food Policy Research Institute.

Kedir, M., E. Schmidt, and A. Waqas. 2014. "Pakistan's Changing Demography: Urbanization and Peri-Urban Transformation over Time." Unpublished manuscript. Washington, DC: International Food Policy Research Institute.

Kousar, R., and A. Abdulai. 2013. *Impacts of Rural Non-Farm Employment on Household Welfare in Pakistan.* Paper prepared for the Second Italian Association of Agricultural and Applied Economics (AIEAA) Conference, Parma, Italy, June 6–7.

Kurosaki, T. 2006. "Consumption Vulnerability to Risk in Rural Pakistan." *Journal of Development Studies* 42 (1): 70–89.

Kurosaki, T., and H. Khan. 2006. "Human Capital, Productivity, and Stratification in Rural Pakistan." *Review of Development Economics* 10 (1): 116–134.

Lanjouw, J. O., and P. Lanjouw. 2001. "The Rural Non-farm Sector: Issues and Evidence from Development Countries." *Agricultural Economics* 26: 1–23.

Malik, S. 2008. "Rethinking Development Strategy: The Importance of the Rural Non Farm Economy in Growth and Poverty Reduction in Pakistan." *The Lahore Journal of Economics* 13 (SE): 189–204.

McMillan, M., D. Rodrik, and I. Verduzco-Gallo. 2014. "Globalization, Structural Change, and Productivity Growth, with an Update on Africa." *World Development* 63 (1): 11–32.

Mohammad, I. 1999. *Rural Non-farm Sector in Pakistan.* MPRA Paper 38152. http://mpra.ub.uni-muenchen.de/38152. Accessed July 14, 2015.

PBS (Pakistan Bureau of Statistics). 2012. *Pakistan Employment Trends 2011*. Islamabad: Pakistan
    Bureau of Statistics.

———. 2013a. *National Accounts of Pakistan: Change of Base from 1999–2000 to 2005–2006*.
    Islamabad: Pakistan Bureau of Statistics.

———. 2013b. *Household Integrated Economic Survey (HIES) 2011–12*. Islamabad: Pakistan
    Bureau of Statistics.

———. 2014. *National Accounts Tables*. Islamabad: Pakistan Bureau of Statistics. http://www.pbs
    .gov.pk/national-accounts-tables. Accessed July 2015.

———. 2015. *Labor Force Survey 2013–14*. Islamabad: Pakistan Bureau of Statistics.

Reardon, T., J. E. Taylor, K. Stamoulis, P. Lanjouw, and A. Balisacan. 2000. "Effects
    of Non-farm Employment on Rural Income Inequality in Developing Countries: An
    Investment Perspective." *Journal of Agricultural Economics* 51 (2): 266–288.

Robinson, S., A. Cattaneo, and M. El-Said. 2001. "Updating and Estimating a Social Accounting
    Matrix Using Cross Entropy Methods." *Economic Systems Research* 13 (1): 47–64.

SBP (State Bank of Pakistan). 2014. *Balance of Payments (BPM5)*. Islamabad. http://www.sbp.org
    .pk/ecodata/Balancepayment_BPM5.pdf. Accessed June 2014.

SPDC (Social Policy and Development Center). 2012. *Gender Dimensions of
    Rural Non-Farm Employment in Pakistan*. Gender Research Program, Research Report
    7. Karachi: Social Policy and Development Center.

Sur, M., and J. Zhang. 2006. *Investment Climate and Enterprise Performance in Rural Pakistan:
    Implications for Rural Non-farm Employment Generation and Poverty Reduction*. Paper
    prepared for the American Agricultural Economics Association Annual Meeting, Long
    Beach, California, July 23–26.

World Bank. 2007. *Pakistan: Promoting Rural Growth and Poverty Reduction*. Report 39303-PK.
    Washington, DC: Sustainable and Development Unit, The World Bank.

Annex A

TABLE A12.1 Model structure

Regions	Rural areas; Peri-urban areas; Urban areas
Sectors (by region) and national products	*Agriculture:* Wheat (irrigated); Wheat (nonirrigated); Paddy rice (IRRI); Paddy rice (basmati); Cotton; Sugarcane; Maize; Oilseeds; Other crops; Potatoes; Vegetables; Fruits and nuts; Cattle, sheep, and goats; Raw milk; Poultry; Forestry; Fishing
	Industry: Crude oil; Natural gas; Coal; Other mining; Meat processing; Dairy processing; Vegetables and oils; Wheat milling; Rice husking and milling (IRRI); Rice husking and milling (basmati); Sugar refining; Other foods, beverages, and tobacco; Cotton ginning; Spinning of fibers; Cotton weaving; Knitted textiles; Clothing; Other textiles; Leather and footwear; Wood products; Petroleum products; Fertilizers and pesticides; Other chemicals; Cement; Nonmetal products; Basic metals; Metal products; Appliances; Machinery; Vehicles; Other manufacturing; Electricity generation; Electricity distribution; Construction
	Services: Wholesale and retail trade; Hotels and restaurants; Transport and storage; Communications; Financial services; Business services; Real estate; Own dwellings; Public administration; Education; Health; Domestic services; Other services
Factors	*Labor (all by region):* Small-scale workers on own or rented farms; Medium and large-scale workers on own or rented farmers; Farm wage workers; Low-skilled nonfarm workers; Skilled nonfarm workers
	Cropland (all by region): Small-scale farm land (<12.5 acres); Medium-scale farmland (12.5–50.0 acres); Large-scale farmland (>50.0 acres)
	Capital: Livestock (by region); Agricultural capital (by region); Nonagricultural capital (formal sector); Nonagricultural capital (informal sector)
Households	*Farm households (by rural and peri-urban areas):* Small-scale farmers (quartile 1); Small-scale farmers (quartiles 2–4); Medium- and large-scale farmers (quartile 1); Medium- and large-scale farmers (quartiles 2–4); Non-landowning farmers (quartile 1); Non-landowning farmers (quartiles 2–4); Farm wage laborers (quartile 1); Farm wage laborers (quartiles 2–4)
	Nonfarm households (by rural and peri-urban areas): Rural nonfarm (quartile 1); Rural nonfarm (quartile 2); Rural nonfarm (quartile 3); Rural nonfarm (quartile 4)
	Combined farm and nonfarm households: Urban (quartile 1); Urban (quartile 2); Urban (quartile 3); Urban (quartile 4)

Source: 2010/2011 Pakistan Social Accounting Matrix (IFPRI 2016).

Note: Economic sectors in the model are disaggregated across regions, but they supply national product markets. As such, there are three regional activities that produce the same product.

Chapter 13

SUMMING UP: POLICY AND INVESTMENT PRIORITIES FOR AGRICULTURE AND THE RURAL ECONOMY IN PAKISTAN

David J. Spielman and Sohail J. Malik

For Pakistan a vibrant agricultural sector and rural economy are essential to improving the welfare of its people and for overall economic growth and development. The country's history attests to this. From independence in 1947 through the 1980s, Pakistan's agricultural sector played a central role in the economy, in terms of overall output, employment, and external trade, and helped put Pakistan on a solid growth trajectory beginning as early as the 1950s. Much of the country's initial economic success was due to the historical Indus River basin accord with India in 1960, which opened the way for the construction of the Tarbela Dam and other major irrigation investments that subsequently enabled Pakistan to take advantage of fertilizer-responsive, high-yielding varieties of wheat and rice during the Green Revolution of the late 1960s and early 1970s. Yields and output grew remarkably during this period, increasing both the availability of major food staples, particularly wheat, as well as cotton that in turn drove substantial expansion in Pakistan's textile industry, providing the country with a critical source of foreign exchange earnings.

Although agriculture is no longer the largest sector of Pakistan's economy today, it remains a major source of income for Pakistan's rural poor and an important driver of the rural nonfarm economy where there is untapped potential for pro-poor growth (Chapter 12). Unfortunately, the agricultural sector's underperformance in recent decades attracts precisely the wrong kind of attention to its problems. Once central to Pakistan's economic policy and development plans, the agricultural sector has a role in policy debates, particularly at the federal level, that has dwindled. Declining public investment over time, especially in infrastructure, irrigation, and agricultural research, combined with changes in demographics, markets, and international trade, has contributed to stagnation in the agricultural sector. Without sufficient policy attention, needed new investments in rural infrastructure (roads, irrigation, electricity, markets, communications) or rural public services (nutrition, health, education, and sanitation) have little chance of being made.

Symbolic of this downward progression of the policy attention given to agriculture and the rural economy was the national Planning Commission's 2011 Framework for Economic Growth, in which agriculture was virtually ignored in favor of urban growth, connectivity, competitive markets, trade openness, and better government. While the framework addressed some of Pakistan's needs, the clear omission of agriculture suggested that agriculture—and therefore food insecurity, malnutrition, and rural poverty—were merely *local* issues that had been devolved to the provinces under the 18th Amendment.

Importantly, the Framework for Economic Growth came up against many of the same shortcomings that limited the impact of many past strategies and policies for agricultural development and the rural economy, from the land reforms introduced in the late 1950s to the detailed recommendations of the National Commission on Agriculture in 1987. Successive governments simply have been unable to operationalize national strategies and policies because they have used highly aggregated targets without giving due attention to how Pakistan's socioeconomic and agroclimatic diversity affects investments made under these strategies and policies. Had Pakistan's federal and provincial governments developed more detailed subsector priorities, allocated more resources commensurate with these priorities, monitored program implementation more closely, and revised programs when performance fell short of plans and expectations, the account set forth in this book might have been far more positive. And, more importantly, the welfare status of rural Pakistan might have been far better than it is today.

Today, there is an opportunity for a new approach to improving the agricultural sector and the rural economy. The government's latest strategy, Vision 2025, released by the Planning Commission in 2014, goes some distance in reintroducing agriculture and food security into the national policy dialogue. Meanwhile, provincial governments now have a stronger mandate to chart their own courses and secure resources for agricultural development processes that may be more transparent, accountable, and responsive to the needs of rural constituents (Chapter 9). Of course, the question remains as to whether good intentions will translate into actionable policies, greater allocation of resources, and coherent plans for implementation, monitoring, and evaluation.

It is possible to return Pakistan to a state with high levels of agricultural growth and where real progress is made in reducing poverty (Chapter 3).

However, growth and development can no longer rely on the intensive exploitation of Pakistan's natural resource endowment (Chapters 2 and 4) and market interventions that are difficult to roll back once they have out-lived their usefulness (Chapter 7). And while continued efforts to improve and expand the application of modern science and technology to agriculture remain necessary, they will not be sufficient (Chapters 5 and 6). Much has changed in Pakistan: the landscape of domestic politics, the international environment, and the understanding of the causes of poverty and sources of growth. Increasingly, growth and development in Pakistan hinges not only on the aggregate numbers of crop production and per capita gross domestic product (GDP), or on the reach of the country's public services and social safety nets but also on investments in human and social capital, in social and economic institutions, and in governance structures and systems that empower people to make their own choices and pursue their needs and aspirations. These issues have been severely overlooked in the discourse on agricultural and economic policy in Pakistan to date.

Achieving higher growth rates, accelerating poverty reduction, and empowering Pakistan's rural population will require—as a basic first step—in-depth analyses to ensure that policies and investments address current con-straints. At its most basic level, this requires good data, and transformation of sound analysis based on such data, into implementable policy steps. It also requires better monitoring and evaluation for the purposes of fine-tuning, replicating, and scaling up public policies, investments, and programs to encourage agricultural-sector growth, productivity improvement, and poverty reduction in Pakistan.

This also means moving beyond aggregate production statistics to more in-depth studies of higher-quality data on the causes, impacts, and constraints associated with technological change, better rural governance, public-service provision, and improvements in the health and nutrition of the population, especially women and children (Chapters 8 and 10). Such work would also inform policy to proactively address and anticipate continuing changes in the forces that will drive agriculture and rural poverty outcomes. Bringing rigor-ous analyses to bear on policy design and decision making would help to cre-ate an enabling environment that allows both competitive markets and the provision of public goods and services to revitalize agricultural growth and improve the prospects for food security and poverty reduction. Similar anal-yses could also help ensure that new and existing policies and regulations do not distort economic incentives or open the door for elite capture—two prob-lems that continue to plague Pakistan's fragile economy (Chapters 2 and 9).

New Drivers of Agricultural-Sector Growth and Rural Development

There is great value in thinking more specifically about these priorities. The future of Pakistan's agricultural sector and welfare of the country's poor over the next two to three decades likely will be shaped by major drivers of change and the policy response to them. These drivers include (1) climate change and the management of a diminishing natural resource base; (2) agricultural productivity growth; (3) rapid urbanization and the development of value chains that link value-added production with urban markets; (4) developments in international markets, trade, and macroeconomic policy; (5) progress in improving the current poor health, nutrition, and educational outcomes in the rural population; and (6) the response to governance challenges posed by political instability and conflict. Designing appropriate policies to address these issues is not a simple task, as these policies must take into account factors such as the time horizon along which the effects of policy changes accrue, the urgency with which policy makers and society at large are affected, and the extent to which the effects of policy changes are specific to small or large populations, markets, or agroecologies. Most importantly, efforts to address these issues require a sustained commitment to policy reforms, coupled with the resources and capacity needed to operationalize and implement policy reforms. With levels of commitment, resources, and capacity varying so widely across the country and between different levels of government, concerted attention to these issues is critical to Pakistan's agricultural sector and the poor.

Long-term climate change and short-term weather shocks loom large in Pakistan, particularly because of the semiarid climate in much of the country and the heavy reliance of the agricultural sector on irrigation. The Indus River basin system is in need of major investments in water storage and distribution, including canal rehabilitation and maintenance. Proposed investments, such as the Diamer-Bhasha Dam, appear to have high economic returns (Chapter 4). Substantially greater investments in water storage, surface irrigation, drainage, and improvements in the efficiency of water use will be required over the next few decades to maintain the availability of water, minimize the devastation of major flood events, and increase the returns to water use. Without these investments, output from Pakistan's agricultural sector is likely to become increasingly erratic over time, and may experience an overall deceleration of growth, particularly if average temperatures gradually rise, the snow pack in the Himalayas diminishes, and rainfall variability increases, as is forecast in many climate change models. Funding these investments, implementing construction projects while ensuring the rights of displaced people, and effectively maintaining the system should be among the highest priorities of the federal and provincial governments.

Over the next several decades, Pakistan will also need to build up the resilience of its agricultural sector. The worst-hit areas may be the arid and semiarid agroecologies of Federally Administered Tribal Areas, Khyber Pakhtunkhwa, Punjab, Sindh, and Balochistan Provinces; the flat and poorly drained flood-prone areas of lower Punjab and Sindh; and the coastal areas, where overexploitation of underground water sources and intrusion of seawater are creating salinity problems for aquifers along irrigated coastal areas. With these threats looming over Pakistan's agricultural sector, science and technology will need to play an even more significant role than they have to date. This means setting priorities and ensuring that the scientific community has the right tools with which to design policies and allocate resources to solutions that have high probabilities of success and can affect technological change among large numbers of farmers and rural communities. Greater investment in agricultural research and extension is needed, not only to maintain and increase yields but also to build tolerance to abiotic stresses such as droughts, floods, heat, and cold, and to strengthen resistance against pests and diseases—both new and emerging. Improved organizational structures and incentives for researchers and extension agents could help reinvigorate Pakistan's agricultural science and technology system. Better regulation of seed markets and stronger incentives to encourage private investment in research and development could also speed dissemination of improved cultivars, hybrids, transgenics, and other products that could increase yields or the value of crops to consumers or could reduce yield variability, losses to biotic and abiotic stress, or costs of production (Chapter 5). Improvements in delivery of veterinary services for smallholders can have particularly large payoffs given the importance of livestock in the incomes of the rural poor.

Funding for these public expenditures could be found by significantly reducing expenditures on domestic procurement, storage, and distribution of wheat, which accounted for PKR 24.84 billion in 2012/2013 (Chapter 7). Substantial savings could be achieved by reducing the level of annual domestic procurement, eliminating the subsidy on sales of government wheat to flour mills, reducing the level of government stocks, and planning for subsidies on wheat imports in the event of domestic shortfalls in years of high international prices. Similar funds could be found by significantly reducing the subsidies received by the fertilizer industry and reallocating those resources into research and extension efforts designed to improve soil fertility management (Chapter 6).

Given that Pakistan is also urbanizing rapidly, agricultural policy makers need to capitalize on the diverse dietary preferences that accompany city life. Demand patterns are likely to change not only in areas traditionally classified as urban centers (which account for about one-third of Pakistan's population) but also in peri-urban areas near large cities (which account for another one-third of the population). These growing urban centers are already providing market opportunities for agriculture, particularly for high-value, perishable products such as fruits, vegetables, dairy, and meat. But significant public and private investments are needed to ensure that farmers and rural entrepreneurs can benefit from this demand. This means investing in more stable electricity services, reliable transportation networks, and other hard infrastructure needed to build modern supply chains that include cold storage facilities, quality assurance systems, and other services. These investments promote productivity growth in the rural nonfarm economy (for example, agro-processing) and are also highly pro-poor, especially in rural areas outside the peri-urban areas closer to major urban centers (Chapter 12).

Public investment in soft infrastructure is also needed. This means reforming the regulations that govern how commodities are brought to market and who brings them, with the aim of reducing the direct costs of marketing agricultural products and the transaction costs for both farmers and consumers associated with participating in markets (Chapter 7). There are success stories of partnerships between farmers, traders, and local government in local economic clusters that have focused on a small set of commodities (for example, citrus fruits, vegetables, and dairy in Punjab) and overcome many of these constraints. More successes on this scale would go a long way to improving the efficiency and profitability of agricultural value chains in Pakistan.

Moving forward, the competitiveness of Pakistan's agricultural products in domestic and international markets will depend on a strategic combination of technology and infrastructure, on the one hand, and appropriate price incentives for investment and production, on the other hand. This was partly demonstrated in the late 1980s with policy changes—exchange rate adjustments, changes in wheat and sugarcane procurement prices, and the gradual withdrawal of the government from direct interventions in cotton and rice markets—that greatly reduced the taxation on agricultural products. Today, the possibility of real exchange rate appreciation, linked to inappropriate policy responses to inflation and balance of payments problems, remains a major threat to the profitability of Pakistan's tradeable agriculture. Although the implications of real exchange rate appreciation go far beyond the agricultural sector, adverse effects for the agricultural sector, including adverse effects on efforts to promote exports of citrus and livestock products, could be especially damaging.

Looking beyond Economic Policy

The economic policies and investments recommended above are essential to increasing productivity and reducing poverty in Pakistan (Chapters 3 and 12). But future progress will depend on more than just good economic policy and strategic investments in science, technology, infrastructure, and markets. Solutions to Pakistan's challenges demand a far more complex and nuanced approach to poverty reduction and welfare improvement. The persistence of poverty—particularly rural poverty—in Pakistan remains the single most complex challenge facing the country. Today, a lot more is known about not only the contribution of social safety nets to development but also the contributions to development of social equity, gender equality, individual empowerment, community participation, and good governance. All of these elements must be central elements of Pakistan's growth and development agenda if progress is to be made.

High rates of agricultural growth may have only modest effects on rural employment and the welfare of the poor in Pakistan if growth is concentrated mainly on larger farms (Chapter 2). Without a broad-based growth strategy, downstream growth linkages arising from higher farm incomes and consumption expenditures may accrue mainly to enterprises and better-off households producing nonagricultural goods and services in urban centers. Further, in addition to broad-based economic growth, rapid improvements in the welfare of the poor will require direct interventions: expanded, well-targeted social safety nets; improved health and education service delivery; and an expansion of hygiene and sanitation infrastructure in rural areas (Chapters 8 and 10). These direct interventions should be accompanied by efforts to encourage dietary changes away from the consumption of fats and sugars and toward the consumption of more micronutrient-rich and diverse diets (Chapter 3).

In this context, concerns about gender equality need to be reiterated (Chapter 10). In today's policy discourse, too little attention is being given to the role of women in Pakistan's rural society and economy, their entrapment in low-productivity rural activities, and their disempowerment in economic and social aspects of day-to-day life. There are many well-documented factors that explain their deprivation: for example, low levels of skills; educational, health, and nutritional attainment; and male out-migration that adds to the burden of women who remain on the farm. Major investments in healthcare and education can also significantly improve the welfare of the rural poor. Improving access to basic health services could potentially have a major effect on nutrition, health, and infant mortality with massive implications for the productivity of the labor force. There is currently wide variation in access and outcomes across regions and ethnic groups, suggesting a need for adequate funding to subnational governments as well as programs and interventions that are well suited to local conditions and cultures.

But across this social policy landscape, insufficient attention is being paid to the impact of the gender norms, governance systems, and judicial processes that should provide women with the means to make decisions that improve their welfare and that of their households and communities. In particular, greater attention must be given to improving access to social, economic, and legal services for women, to involve women in the design and implementation of development programs, and to gear the political and administrative systems to be more responsive to gender issues. Only with greater emphasis on the human dimensions of Pakistan's economic woes, particularly in the country's vast rural areas, will progress be made.

Some of these issues are being addressed in various social protection and rural development programs in Pakistan. The Zero Hunger Program launched in 2012, the Pakistan Integrated Nutrition Strategy of 2013, and initiatives such as the Water, Sanitation, and Hygiene program and the Scaling-Up Nutrition program are important efforts to address poverty, health, and nutrition. Similarly, the Benazir Income Support Program and the Pakistan Poverty Alleviation Fund provide social protection services to the poor—both with an explicit mandate to focus on the welfare of poor women— and strive to ensure that those who are excluded from the wider growth process are given access to resources and opportunities. Community-driven development initiatives such as the National Rural Support Program and its counterparts in each province are helping to integrate rural communities into national development activities and empowering them to pursue their own development objectives. An array of microfinance programs aim to extend credit and savings services to rural households, many of them specifically targeted toward female entrepreneurs, who would otherwise be overlooked by the formal financial system. The community organizations that these initiatives foster and nurture contribute to building greater resilience among the rural households that are so vulnerable to the recurring shocks that affect their lives and livelihoods.

With a stronger focus on better targeting, participation, and graduation, these social protection programs and community-driven development programs can be central to Pakistan's poverty reduction strategy. And with more—and more rigorous—evaluation of their contribution, program designs can be refined to concentrate on what types of interventions work, for whom, and at what cost, opening the door for scaling up to ever larger numbers of communities, households, and individuals throughout Pakistan. But even with these improvements, more needs to be done beyond the limited scope of social protection programming. Greater improvement is needed in the overarching governance systems and socioeconomic institutions that influence every dimension of rural livelihoods in Pakistan.

Finally, it is important to reflect on the difficult security situation in Pakistan. Insecurity and the threat of violence affect the day-to-day life and livelihoods of people in many parts of the country, taking an enormous toll in terms of human lives and suffering. Security concerns inhibit basic economic activities in both agricultural and nonagricultural sectors. Fighting and civil unrest destroy human lives and physical capital. They also discourage productive investments, both domestic and foreign, that can increase incomes and welfare in the medium-term. This includes discouraging or even preventing investments in education either though threats of violence, destruction of schools, or denigration of aspirations of individuals, thereby lessening their efforts to invest in their own educations (or in productive businesses).

How best to remedy these problems is a complicated question. Social and economic development cannot occur in conflict-ridden areas throughout Pakistan without a major reduction in violence, a significant increase in political stability, and efforts to address the psychological and social trauma associated with instability and violence. Only when these basic functions are fulfilled can efforts to reduce poverty, create employment opportunities, and provide essential public services make a contribution. And only then will people reestablish their confidence and trust in the state and abide by rules and norms that are required for a productive and progressive society to flourish.

Conclusions

Pakistan's agricultural sector has enormous potential. Tapping this potential, however, will require higher levels of investment and some major reforms to public policy. This includes policies designed to address long-standing issues relating to land ownership, irrigation infrastructure, fertilizer markets, and the science required to provide farmers with improved cultivars and other technologies. It also calls for close scrutiny of policies on domestic input and commodity markets, international trade and macroeconomic policy, and the consequences of policy reforms for Pakistan's agricultural sector. Finally, more attention must be given to policies and programs that can directly influence both the provision of public services for health, education, and social protection and the intrahousehold decision-making process that affects gender relations and how scarce household resources are allocated to ensure welfare. Provided that there is political stability and security, these policies and investments can enable Pakistan not only to boost overall economic growth but also to enhance food security at the national and household levels and significantly improve the welfare of the poor.

Authors

Madiha Afzal (mafzal@umd.edu) is an assistant professor at the University of Maryland's School of Public Policy, College Park, US.

Nuzhat Ahmad (drnuzhatahmad@hotmail.com) is a senior research fellow in the Development Strategy and Governance Division of the International Food Policy Research Institute (IFPRI), Washington, DC.

Faryal Ahmed (faryal06@gmail.com) is a research analyst in the Pakistan Strategy Support Program of IFPRI, Islamabad.

Mubarik Ali (mubarik520@yahoo.com) is a senior research fellow in the Pakistan Strategy Support Program of IFPRI, Islamabad.

Shujat Ali (shujatpk@yahoo.com) is an additional finance secretary in the Finance Division of the Government of Pakistan, Islamabad.

Elena Briones Alonso (elena.brionesalonso@kuleuven.be) is a PhD candidate at the LICOS Centre for Institutions and Economic Performance in the Faculty of Economics and Business at the University of Leuven (KU Leuven), Belgium.

Hira Channa (hirachanna@gmail.com) is a research analyst in the Pakistan Strategy Support Program of IFPRI, Islamabad.

The authors' titles and affiliations reflect the period when they contributed to this book. In a few cases, current titles and affiliations are provided.

Stephen Davies (s.davies@cgiar.org) is a senior research fellow in the Development Strategy and Governance Division of IFPRI, Islamabad, Pakistan.

Paul Dorosh (p.dorosh@cgiar.org) is the director of the Development Strategy and Governance Division of IFPRI, Washington, DC.

Gisselle Gajate Garrido (gissele_g@yahoo.com) is a research fellow in the Development Strategy and Governance Division of IFPRI, Washington, DC.

Arthur Gueneau (arthur.gueneau@gmail.com) is a research analyst in the Development Strategy and Governance Division of IFPRI, Washington, DC.

Madeeha Hameed (mxhameed@gmail.com) is a research assistant in the Development Strategy and Governance Division of IFPRI, Washington, DC.

Brian Holtemeyer (b.holtemeyer@cgiar.org) is a research assistant in the Development Strategy and Governance Division of IFPRI, Washington, DC.

Huma Khan (h.khan@cgiar.org) is a senior research assistant in the Development Strategy and Governance Division of IFPRI, Washington, DC.

Katrina Kosec (k.kosec@cgiar.org) is a senior research fellow in the Development Strategy and Governance Division of IFPRI, Washington, DC.

Mehrab Malek (mehrab.malek@gmail.com) is a research analyst in the Development Strategy and Governance Division of IFPRI, Washington, DC.

Shuaib Malik (shuaib006@gmail.com) is an assistant economic adviser in the Economic Advisor's Wing in the Ministry of Finance in the Government of Pakistan, Islamabad.

Sohail J. Malik (sjmalik@idspak.com) is a visiting senior research fellow in the Development Strategy and Governance Division of IFPRI, Washington, DC.

Amina Mehmood (amina1804@gmail.com) is a research assistant in the Pakistan Strategy Support Program of IFPRI, Islamabad.

Dawit Mekonnen (d.mekonnen@cgiar.org) is an associate research fellow in the Environment and Production Technology Division of IFPRI, Washington, DC.

Hina Nazli (hinanazli@gmail.com) is a research fellow in the Pakistan Strategy Support Program of IFPRI, Islamabad.

Sara Rafi (sararafi@gmail.com) is a research analyst in the Pakistan Strategy Support Program of IFPRI, Islamabad.

Muhammad Ahsan Rana (ahsanrana11@gmail.com) is an associate professor at the Lahore University of Management Sciences, Pakistan.

Abdul Wajid Rana (awrana.rana@gmail.com) is a member of the Federal Public Service Commission of Pakistan, Islamabad.

Danielle Resnick (d.resnick@cgiar.org) is a senior research fellow in the Development Strategy and Governance Division of IFPRI, Washington, DC.

Khalid Riaz (kriaz100@gmail.com) is a professor at the COMSATS Institute of Information Technology in Islamabad, Pakistan.

Abdul Salam (drsalam46@gmail.com) is a professor at the Federal Urdu University of Arts, Science and Technology in Islamabad, Pakistan.

Emily Schmidt (e.schmidt@cgiar.org) is an associate research fellow in the Development Strategy and Governance Division of IFPRI, Washington, DC.

Asma Shahzad (alhuda120@gmail.com) is a research assistant in the Pakistan Strategy Support Program of IFPRI, Islamabad.

David J. Spielman (d.spielman@cgiar.org) is a senior research fellow in the Environment and Production Technology Division of IFPRI, Washington, DC.

James Thurlow (j.thurlow@cgiar.org) is a senior research fellow in the Development Strategy and Governance Division of IFPRI, Washington, DC.

Ahmad Waqas (w2571@yahoo.com) is an assistant professor at the COMSATS Institute of Information Technology in Islamabad, Pakistan.

Edward Whitney (edwardmw@gmail.com) is a senior research assistant in the Development Strategy and Governance Division of IFPRI, Washington, DC.

Fatima Zaidi (f.zaidi@cgiar.org) is a program manager in the Environment and Production Technology Division of IFPRI, Washington, DC.

Index

Page numbers for entries occurring in boxes are followed by a *b*; those for entries in figures, by an *f*; those for entries in notes, by an *n*; and those for entries in tables, by a *t*.

Lightning Source UK Ltd.
Milton Keynes UK
UKOW01n0602070318
319028UK00006B/216/P